REVISED AND UPDATED
LEAVING CERTIFICATE

Biology

MICHAEL O'CALLAGHAN

SPECIAL ADVISOR: ANGELA BURY

Edco

First published 2009
The Educational Company of Ireland
Ballymount Road
Walkinstown
Dublin 12

A trading unit of the Smurfit Kappa Group

© 2009 Michael O'Callaghan

9 8 7 6 5 4 3 2

Editing, layout and typesetting: Bookworks
Illustration: Daghda
Book and cover design: Brosna Press

Photographs: Science Photo Library, Alamy, Corbis,
Getty Images, Oxford Scientific Films, Natural Visions,
Nature Picture Library, Still Pictures, Shutterstock,
Visuals Unlimited

Reproduction: Impress Digital

Printed in the Republic of Ireland
by ColourBooks Ltd.

QUALITY
I.S. EN ISO 9001:2008
NSAI Certified

The paper used in this book comes from Managed Forests in Northern Europe For every tree felled, at least one new tree is planted

Acknowledgements

Writing a textbook is a partnership between many people. I wish to acknowledge the great assistance provided to me by all the staff at Edco, especially Ms. Michele Staunton for her liaison work behind the scenes. Their encouragement and support are greatly appreciated.

In particular I wish to thank the editor, Mr. Warren Yeates. His support, patience and guidance were, as always, exemplary.

Great credit is also due to Mr. Michael Phillips of Daghda for his artwork on the diagrams and to the design team at Brosna Press.

In preparing the text I was greatly and courteously assisted by a wide range of experts. These included the librarian and staff in the library of DCU; Prof. Matthew Harmey (UCD), Dr. John Breen (UL), Dr. Ciarán Ó Fagáin (DCU), Dr. Gabrielle McKee (TCD), Dr. Ken Whelan (Marine Institute), Richard Flynn (IFA), John McLoughlin (Coillte), Eanna Ní Lamhna, and the staff at the Institute of Biology in London for their advice in special areas of the book.

I am also grateful to the many students, teachers and mentors (in both UCD and TCD) who provided very valuable ideas and suggestions for the book.

In particular I wish to thank Mr. Paul de hÓra, Ms. Margaret Hourigan and Ms. Mary O'Connor, who provided extensive written submissions that enabled me to redraft some sections of the book.

In conclusion I especially wish to thank my wife Mary and my children Sinéad and Shane for being so patient and understanding during my work on this revision. Your silence, patience and fortitude are greatly appreciated. I trust it will prove to be a symbiotic production!

Contents

STUDIED   REVISED

UNIT 1 **THE STUDY OF LIFE**

UNIT 2 **THE CELL**

UNIT 3 **THE ORGANISM**

Activities

*   Note that Activity 11 is Higher Level.

**   The syllabus offers a choice between completing either Activity 19a or Activity 19b.

Introduction

This book is written for the Leaving Certificate Biology course. It has been revised to allow it to comply more precisely with the requirements of the course as outlined in the Syllabus and Guidelines. The revisions were necessary for the following reasons:

- clarifications provided at the In-Service courses
- guidelines provided by the Department of Education and Science in *Syllabus and Guidelines for Teachers*
- feedback from a wide range of teachers and pupils
- the contents of the Leaving Certificate examinations and marking schemes, 2004 to 2008
- changes in scientific knowledge and understanding

The book is written for both Higher level and Ordinary level students. Higher level material is placed at the end of the chapters (where possible) and is marked with a grey bar in the margin.

Each chapter is followed by a concise summary that is intended to be of assistance to students in preparing for examinations.

A greatly increased number of definitions has been included, both in the text and in the glossary.

Many questions are included at the end of each chapter. These questions are graded for Higher or Ordinary level. In general the questions follow the sequence of the material presented in the chapter.

Each chapter includes samples of questions asked at recent Leaving Certificate examinations. These questions are followed by a checklist of questions on each chapter that have been asked in previous years at both Ordinary and Higher levels.

There are 22 mandatory activities specified on the syllabus. These are all included in yellow panels in the relevant chapter. In order to relate the activities to the theory they are placed in the chapter in association with the theory. Diagrams are included with each activity so that the student can visualise how the apparatus is to be used. Guidelines are provided for writing up each activity as well as for presenting a notebook or portfolio containing all the activities.

A particular feature of the book is the large range of diagrams and photographs used throughout. Where possible each photograph is selected to be relevant to some aspect of the material being covered. In addition most of the photographs are light or electron microscope images that help to enhance the understanding and enjoyment of the material being explained.

Material related to various topics is included in 'Did you know' panels. This material enhances the understanding of the topic but is not required to be learned for examination purposes.

Where possible everyday examples are used to explain and deepen the understanding of the topics covered.

A comprehensive index is included, along with a glossary of definitions mentioned in the syllabus. A student checklist for chapters studied and revised is included with the table of contents.

With some minor alterations, the sequence of chapters (and the presentation of material in each chapter) follow the sequence used in the syllabus. This does not mean that the course must be taught in the sequence presented.

An online student test facility is available to support the book at **www.edcoexamcentre.ie**

Michael O'Callaghan
March 2009

Laboratory safety

Safety rules

The following rules are enforced to keep yourself and your classmates safe while in a school laboratory.

1. Do not enter the laboratory without permission.
2. Do not use any equipment unless permitted to do so by your teacher.
3. Make sure you know exactly what you are supposed to do. If in doubt, ask your teacher.
4. Make sure you know the position of all safety equipment in the laboratory, e.g. fire extinguishers, first-aid equipment etc.
5. Always wear eye protection or gloves when instructed to do so.
6. Long hair must be tied back during practical classes.
7. Place your bag and other personal items safely out of the way.
8. Never handle any chemicals with bare hands.
9. Nothing must be eaten, tasted or drunk in the laboratory.
10. Any cut, burn or other accident must be reported at once to your teacher.
11. Always check that the label on the bottle is exactly the same as the material you require. If in doubt, ask the teacher.
12. Any chemical spilled on the skin or clothing must be washed at once with plenty of water and reported to your teacher.
13. Test-tubes should never be overfilled. When heating a test-tube ensure that the mouth of the test-tube is pointed away from yourself and everyone else.
14. All equipment should be cleaned and put back in its correct place after use.
15. Always wash your hands after practical work.
16. Students should behave in a responsible manner at all times in the laboratory.

Safety symbols

The following labels appear on bottles in the laboratory. They also appear on many everyday chemicals such as cleaning products and solvents. These labels indicate chemicals that could be dangerous if not used or handled properly.

TOXIC

Substances that can cause death if they are swallowed, breathed in or absorbed through the skin. Example: weedkiller.

HARMFUL OR IRRITANT

Substances that should not be eaten, breathed in or handled without gloves. Though not as dangerous as toxic substances, they may cause a rash, sickness or an allergic reaction.

OXIDISING

Substances that provide oxygen, allowing other materials to burn more intensely. Example: hair bleach.

HIGHLY FLAMMABLE

Substances that easily catch fire. Example: petrol.

CORROSIVE

Substances that attack and destroy living tissue, including skin and eyes. Example: oven cleaner.

WARNING

This sign is often used to draw attention to a warning of danger, hazards and the unexpected.

Recording and reporting practical activities

General guidelines

- A folder or notebook should be used to record details of all the practical activities required by the syllabus.

- These records should be neatly and properly written so that they are clearly presented.

- Diagrams should be included whenever possible (and drawn in HB pencil).

- The main steps in any calculations (not including roughwork) should be included where appropriate.

- Where relevant, the results should be used.

- The scale used in any graph should be suitable, the graph should be labelled, and the points on the graph should be clearly circled and joined.

- A table of contents of all the activities should be placed at the beginning of the notebook or folder.

Activity reports

The following headings should be included (where relevant) when writing up the report on each of the 22 mandatory activities specified in the syllabus.

- **Title and date**. A title and the date(s) on which the activity was carried out should be given.

- **Description of procedure**. A brief report should be written by each student to include (where possible):

  - a labelled diagram of the assembled apparatus;

  - reference to any adjustments to the apparatus that were required;

  - details of any measurements taken (including the units used);

  - details of any safety procedures followed.

- Refer to the use of a **control**, if one was carried out.

- **Results and observations**. The results or observations of each activity should be stated clearly. Reference should be made (where relevant) to any errors that may have arisen, and to any precautions that might be taken to reduce such errors.

- **Conclusions**. By interacting with other students, or groups of students (where possible) a conclusion or conclusions should be stated.

UNIT 1
THE STUDY OF LIFE

This transgenic mouse glows green under blue light because it contains a green fluorescent protein from a glowing jellyfish. The egg from which this mouse developed was infected with a virus carrying the jellyfish gene, causing the gene to be incorporated into the mouse's DNA. This genetic engineering technique could be used to mark cancer cells in human patients and follow their movement around the body.

Chapter 1 **The scientific method**

Science

Science is the organised and objective study of the physical, material and living world. The word *science* comes from the Latin word *scienta*, meaning knowledge.

The range of topics that can be studied in science is vast. Science is classified into three main subject areas: physics, chemistry and biology.

Biology

> **Biology** is the study of living things.

The word biology comes from the Greek words *bios*, which means life, and *logos*, which means knowledge.

> An **organism** is a living thing.

The study of biology now covers such a huge area that biology itself is subdivided into many branches.

AREAS OF STUDY IN BIOLOGY

Originally biology consisted of botany (the study of plants), zoology (the study of animals) and microbiology (the study of small, living things).

Biology later expanded to include a wide range of studies such as taxonomy (classification), anatomy (overall structure), physiology (overall function), cytology (cells), biochemistry (chemical reactions), ecology (relationships between organisms and their environments) and genetics (inheritance).

As biology progresses, the areas of study become greater in number and more specific in content. For example, microbiology can be divided into three disciplines. These are bacteriology (bacteria), mycology (fungi) and virology (viruses).

The scientific method

The essence of science is a knowledge of the physical world. This knowledge is obtained by asking relevant questions and then searching for the answers to these questions.

The scientific method is an attempt at using an organised approach to solving problems. The core of the scientific method involves asking questions and searching for answers.

> The **scientific method** is a process of investigation in which problems are identified and their suggested explanations are tested by carrying out experiments.

Although the scientific method may vary from situation to situation, the seven steps outlined on the next page are taken whenever possible.

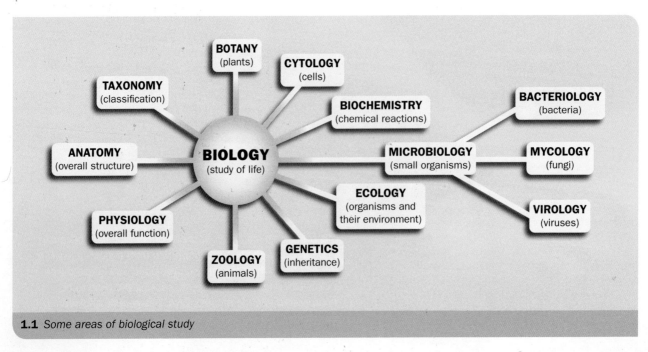

1.1 *Some areas of biological study*

1. Observation

Observation is the most important part of the scientific method. Observations may be obtained directly by our senses (seeing, hearing, etc.) or indirectly by the use of equipment such as microscopes and thermometers.

Observations that are properly taken and recorded provide the basis for all the facts relating to a problem.

2. Hypothesis

> A **hypothesis** is an educated guess based on observations.

A hypothesis should (a) account for all the facts that have been observed and (b) lead to the prediction of new information.

3. Experimentation

An experiment is designed to test a hypothesis. The results of the experiment (or more often a series of experiments) will either support or contradict the hypothesis. The methods used for experimentation are outlined later in this chapter.

4. Collection and interpretation of data

The information that arises in the course of an experiment is collected, recorded and analysed.

> **Data** consists of the measurements, observations or information gathered from experiments.

5. Conclusion

As in the saying 'it is the bottom line that counts', so in an experiment it is the conclusion that is often of greatest value. The data from an experiment is interpreted to reach a conclusion or result.

6. Relating the conclusion to existing knowledge

The conclusion of an experiment should tie in with the existing knowledge of the topic being examined. On the basis of the conclusion(s) reached, the hypothesis is:

- supported if the results agree fully
- changed if the results agree only partly, or
- rejected if the results contradict it

Very often the conclusion reached in one experiment will lead to the need to design further experiments.

7. Reporting and publishing the results

The results of experiments should be written down and reported so that they can be examined and analysed by others. In this way new ideas are made available to all scientists. This adds to the growth of scientific understanding.

Experimental procedures and results are often published in journals, magazines, newspapers, on the world wide web and on television.

One of the key concepts of the scientific method is that an experiment should be repeatable. If someone else follows the same procedures and gets the same results, then the conclusions are more likely to be valid. Experiments are published in order to allow them to be repeated.

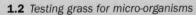

1.2 *Testing grass for micro-organisms*

THE STUDY OF LIFE

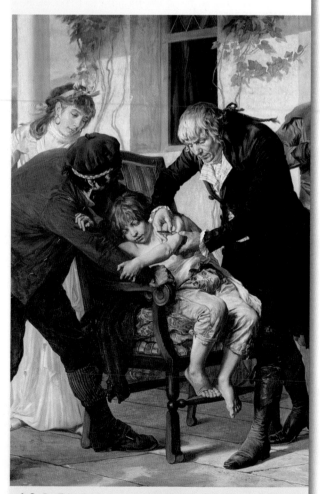

1.3 *Dr Edward Jenner inoculating an eight-year-old boy with cowpox virus, the first operation of its kind.*

Theories and principles

> A **theory** is a hypothesis that has been supported by many different experiments.

The formation of a theory requires many years and involves many experimental results. The word *theory* means an idea that is uncertain but is widely accepted as a correct explanation. Theories may be altered but are rarely discarded.

> A **principle** or **law** arises from a theory that has been shown to be valid when fully tested over a long period of time.

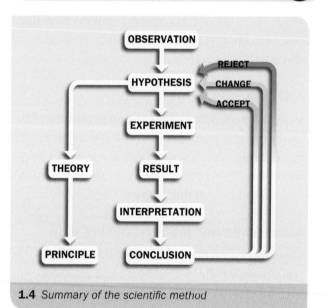

1.4 *Summary of the scientific method*

Principles of experimentation

To ensure that experiments are conducted fairly the following four concepts should be considered.

1. Careful planning and design

> A **variable** is a factor that may change in an experiment.

For example, it is observed that seedlings bend as they grow. The hypothesis is that they are growing towards light coming from one side. However, other variables, including temperature and wind (such as a draught), may be responsible for the bending response.

An experiment might be designed to grow the seedlings in a black box with a hole in one side. In this case, the seedlings are seen to grow towards the light source, regardless of which way the box is turned.

In most experiments, only a single factor (or variable) is tested. All other variables should be kept **constant**. In the example of the seedlings, this would involve ensuring that temperature and wind do not influence the results (i.e. the experiment should be conducted in a draught-free room at a constant temperature).

2. Ensure that the experiment is safe

It is important that safety is borne in mind when designing experiments. The following safety features should be observed for classroom experiments.

- Tie back long hair.
- Wear a laboratory coat if handling biological material.
- Wear safety goggles when necessary.
- Never place your fingers in your eyes or mouth unless you have washed your hands.
- Avoid contact between electrical equipment and water.
- Be aware of the safety information when using chemicals.
- Report all accidents to a teacher.

3. Design a control experiment

> A **control** is used to provide a standard against which the actual experiment can be judged.

There should be only one variable (or difference) between the actual experiment and the control.

Did you know?

Consider the hypothesis that a new drug reduces the effects of arthritis. A number of arthritic patients are x-rayed and their deformities noted. The drug is administered for 6 months. The patients are then x-rayed again and are found to have improved.

However, these results may not have been caused by the drug. They may have been caused by the attention paid to the patients.

Patients in a control group (who should be similar in age, gender, lifestyle, severity of disease and many other features) are given a harmless, tasteless pill at the same times as the patients in the experimental group. This pill is called a **placebo**. *Neither the patients nor the medical staff know who is getting the placebo and who is getting the real drug.*

If the patients in the placebo (or control) group do not improve, and those taking the real pill do improve, then it may be the case that the drug improves arthritis.

For instance, in the experiment to test whether seedlings are growing towards the light, the control could be to grow the same type of seedlings in a similar box, which does not have a hole to let in light. In other words, grow the seedlings in the dark and observe the results for the control seedlings.

4. Experiments must be fair

SAMPLE SIZE

When carrying out an experiment it is important that more than one person or object is tested. Normally as large a sample as possible is tested.

A large sample reduces the risk that the results are due to individual differences, rather than being caused by the factor being investigated.

Accordingly, when testing whether seedlings grow towards the light, a large number of seedlings are grown in each case.

In the same way, when testing a new drug to treat arthritis, if only one person was treated and recovered, it may have been due to the person recovering of his/her own accord. However, if several hundred people are tested and all (or most) of them improve, then the result is more likely to be due to the medication given.

1.5 *Biotechnology researcher holding a seedling*

1.6 *DNA analysis under ultraviolet light*

RANDOM SELECTION

When selecting a sample to be tested, the selection should be random. For instance, it would not be fair to grow and test seeds of only one type, or only large seeds, or only seeds that looked fully rounded. By testing a random selection of seeds (and seedlings) of different types, it is seen that the results apply to all seeds or seedlings.

In the same way, when testing the drug for arthritis, it would not be fair to select only males or only people over 50 years of age. If a certain type of sample is selected, the results may be influenced by the factor selected (e.g. the results may apply differently to females or those under 50 years of age).

OTHERS MUST BE ABLE TO REPLICATE EXPERIMENTS

Experimental work is reported so that the information discovered is widely available to all. Once the work is properly reported it can be repeated by others. In this way the results can be shown to be always true and not caused by some unknown influence.

A **replicate** is a repeat of an experiment.

We often hear in the media of new 'wonder' cures. However, very often the work on which such cures is based is not published. Consequently the experiment(s) cannot be repeated or replicated by others.

For this reason, all experimental work is rigorously reported in scientific journals, so that other scientists can repeat the test and confirm or deny the results.

Guidelines for students on the recording and reporting of the twenty-two Activities on this course are given on page vii.

DOUBLE BLIND TESTING

In a properly designed experiment neither the person being tested nor the tester should know who is receiving the real treatment or who is receiving the placebo.

This means that the tester cannot influence the results of the experiment by consciously or unconsciously giving clues to the person being tested. When both parties are unaware of the arrangements the test is said to be 'double blind'.

Limitations of the value of the scientific method

1. The extent of our knowledge

The ability to form a hypothesis and design an experiment is dependent on the amount we know relating to our observations. It has often been said that more information would be discovered if we could only ask the correct questions. However, a basic amount of knowledge is required before the correct questions and hypotheses can be framed.

As time goes by, more knowledge is accumulated and more questions can be asked and, hopefully, answered. This is how science progresses.

2. The basis of investigation

If an investigation is badly designed or improperly carried out it will not yield results that are as valid as they should be.

The source of all scientific fact is careful observation and properly designed experiments. Experiments provide the information on which the conclusions are based.

Very often, control experiments are difficult to set up. This can lead to invalid experiments with dubious results. Sometimes hypotheses are based on such experiments.

For example, it is suggested that human activity (namely increased fossil fuel burning and deforestation) has increased carbon dioxide levels and this, in turn, has caused global temperatures to increase.

The obvious control in this case would be a planet Earth on which there was no human activity. Obviously, such a control is not possible. The lack of a suitable control may mean that factors apart from those proposed are causing the changes.

3. Interpreting results

If the results of an experiment are interpreted wrongly, then faulty conclusions and hypotheses will be drawn. It is important that the results of any experiment are analysed and considered in a proper manner.

Did you know?

Faulty interpretation of results occurred during the development of the drug **thalidomide** *in the 1950s. This drug was used to treat morning sickness in human pregnancy.*

Thalidomide was safely tested on many animals (including mammals such as rats and rabbits). The results of these tests were wrongly interpreted as suggesting that the drug was safe for humans.

The problem was that the drug was not tested for its effects on the embryo in the womb.

In fact, it caused major limb deformities in many babies born to women who took thalidomide during pregnancy. The drug was withdrawn in 1961.

4. Changes in the natural world

Sometimes the scientific method can lead to results that apply only to living things at one particular time. As living things are constantly changing (evolving), hypotheses must be constantly altered.

An example of this is the way in which antibiotics were thought to kill all bacteria. As a result, there was very little research into new antibiotics. In recent times bacteria have emerged that are resistant to some, or more seriously, all antibiotics.

5. Accidental discoveries

Despite the most rigorous observations and thought, new insights are often provided by accidental discoveries. Such findings have contributed enormously to the development of scientific thinking.

1.7 *A thalidomide child at home playing the xylophone*

Did you know?

The discovery of the antibiotic **penicillin** *in 1928 by Sir Alexander Fleming is a good example of an accidental discovery. Fleming carelessly left a petri dish of bacteria uncovered and it became contaminated by patches of a fungus. He noticed that the bacteria were killed in areas around the patches of fungus. He later confirmed that the chemical penicillin, produced by the fungus, had the ability to kill bacteria.*

This accidental discovery had a huge effect on the treatment of bacterial infections. Notice that, although it was accidental, Fleming's discovery had much to do with his careful **observation** *of the 'accident' and his accurate* **interpretation** *of the results. In addition, his discovery arose from his prior knowledge and work in the area of bacteria.*

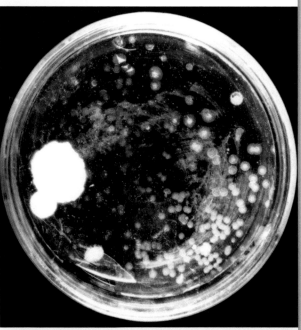

1.8 *Fleming's petri dish of bacteria with patches of penicillin fungus – an accidental discovery*

Ethical issues

Ethics relates to whether conduct is right or wrong. Sometimes there are arguments over whether the application of the scientific method is good or bad. The main areas of disagreement tend to be based on issues such as:

- the use of captive animals in experiments
- the origin of life
- whether or not evolution took place
- the way in which evolution may have taken place
- medical issues such as contraception, abortion and assisted fertilisation
- the development and use of genetically altered plants and animals in agriculture
- cloning animals
- freezing human sperm and embryos
- the use of stem cells from embryos to form new tissues or organs
- organ transplants, especially from animals to humans

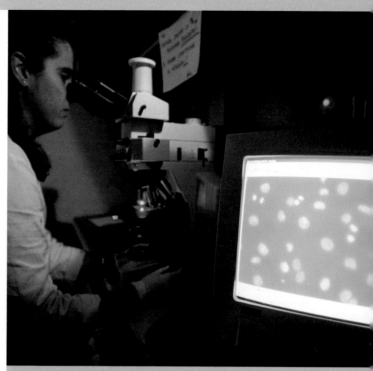

1.9 *Researcher studying stem cell nuclei (white on screen) under a light microscope. Stem cell research is controversial and subject to ethical debate.*

Summary

Science is the study of the physical, material and living world.

Biology is the study of living things.

The scientific method is based on:

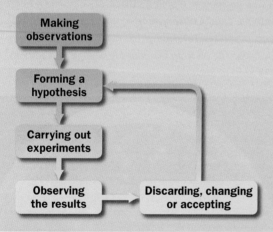

A **hypothesis** is an educated guess based on observations.

Data is the information gathered in experiments.

A **theory** is an explanation based on repeated hypotheses and experimentation.

A principle or law arises from a theory when it is seen always to be true under all conditions over a long period of time.

Experiments are based on:
- careful planning and design
- safe procedures
- establishing a control (or comparison) which differs in only one variable from the real experiment
- fair procedures such as
  - large sample size
  - random selection
  - reporting experiments publicly so they can be replicated
  - double blind testing

A **replicate** is when an experiment is repeated.

The value of the scientific method is limited by problems such as:
- lack of basic knowledge
- the design of the experiment
- difficulty in interpreting results
- changes in nature
- accidental discoveries

Ethics refers to whether issues are right or wrong.

Revision questions

1 Define:
   (a) science, **(b)** biology.

2 Name the area of biology studied by each of the following:
   (a) botanist, **(b)** ecologist, **(c)** biochemist,
   (d) mycologist, **(e)** zoologist, **(f)** geneticist.

3 Jenner's work can be criticised on the grounds of **(a)** bad experimental design and **(b)** lack of safety. Explain these criticisms of his work.

4 Different humans have different heartbeat rates. List four variables (factors) that might cause such variations.

5 A test is given to a class of twenty pupils. The average result is 42%. Half the class is given homework for two weeks and the other half is not given homework. When re-tested, those given homework scored 58%.
   (a) What hypothesis is being tested?
   (b) Suggest a major flaw in this experiment.
   (c) How could this flaw be corrected?
   (d) Do the results, as given here, support the hypothesis that homework improves test results? Explain your answer.

6 List the three ways in which the results of an experiment may affect the hypothesis.

7 If the results of an experiment do not fully support the hypothesis, what should be done next?

8 Explain what is meant by:
   (a) an observation
   (b) a hypothesis
   (c) data   *(continued)*

   (d) a theory
   (e) a principle
   (f) a replicate
   (g) a variable.

9 List four safety procedures that should be followed in a classroom experiment.

10 In terms of experimentation:
   (a) What is a control?
   (b) How should the control compare to the actual experiment?

11 State the need for each of the following experimental procedures:
   (a) large sample sizes
   (b) random selection
   (c) reporting the experiment
   (d) repeating the experiment.

12 **(a)** What do you understand by double blind testing?
   (b) State the importance of this procedure.

13 **(a)** What is meant by ethical issues?
   (b) Name three ethical issues associated with biology.
   (c) Give a full account of the arguments surrounding any one of the issues you have named.

14 **(a)** Why was the drug thalidomide developed?
   (b) Why is it no longer used for this purpose?
   (c) What flaw in the scientific method resulted in the drug originally being put on the market?

15 **(a)** Who discovered penicillin?
   (b) How was it discovered?
   (c) State two ways in which this discovery was based on elements of the scientific method.

Sample examination questions

Section A

16 Answer the following, which relate to the scientific method, by completing the blank spaces.
   (a) As a result of her observations a scientist may formulate a _____. She will then progress her investigation by devising a series of _____ and then carefully analysing the resulting _____.
   (b) Why is a control especially important in biological investigations?
   (c) If a scientist wished to determine the effect of a certain herbicide on weed growth she would

include a control in the investigation. Suggest a suitable control in this case.
   (d) The use of replicates is an important aspect of scientific research. What, in this context, are replicates?
   (e) Suggest where a scientist may publish the results of her investigations.

                               (2008 HL Q 3)

17 Explain each of the following terms in relation to the scientific method.
   (a) hypothesis, **(b)** control, **(c)** data,
   (d) replicate, **(e)** theory

                               (2005 HL Q 2)

Previous examination questions

Ordinary level	Higher level
n/a	2003 (sample) Q 4
	2005 Q 2
	2008 Q 3

*For latest questions go to **www.edco.ie/biology***

Chapter 2 The characteristics of life

The diversity of life

We are surrounded by a wide variety of living things as we go about our daily existence.

Some of these living things are microscopic organisms such as the bacteria found on our skin and in decaying material, plankton in ponds and seawater, and single-celled organisms such as *Amoeba*, which are found in freshwater ponds and pools.

Larger organisms include fungi such as moulds and mushrooms; ferns and mosses; flowering plants such as grasses, flowers, shrubs and trees; along with animals such as earthworms, insects, snails, fish, frogs, snakes, birds and humans.

The features and behaviours shared by these organisms that allow us to identify them as living things include the following:

- They are comprised of cells. These cells can form new cells, allowing the organism to grow in size. Very often, their cells are arranged into structures such as leaves, flowers, seeds, skin, hearts, and structures for gas exchange, feeding and reproduction.
- They all require a supply of food. Plants make food in their green parts; animals feed on other organisms to get food.
- They all produce some sort of waste products, including gases, liquid and solid wastes.
- They all respond to stimuli such as light, gravity, sound, temperature and touch. For example, most plants grow faster at higher temperatures, plant stems grow towards light, a dog responds to its owner's voice.

- They are all capable of producing new versions of themselves. Fungi produce invisible spores that blow away to form new fungal growth, some plants produce seeds and animals produce baby versions of the adult.

Metabolism

> **Metabolism** is the sum of all the chemical reactions in an organism.

Metabolism includes reactions and processes such as growth, movement, response, respiration and excretion. Metabolic reactions are controlled by chemicals called enzymes.

Organisms with a high metabolic rate are fast-acting, e.g. mice and rabbits. Those with low metabolic rates are slow-acting, e.g. koalas.

Continuity of life

About 350 BC, the famous Greek thinker Aristotle concluded that living things could arise from non-living matter. This notion is called spontaneous generation. He saw that maggots formed on rotting meat and frogs emerged from dried mud. The presumption was that the meat made the maggots and the mud formed the frogs.

It was not until the 1800s that the idea of spontaneous generation was finally disproved. Since then it has been accepted that life originates only from living things of the same type.

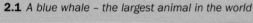

2.1 *A blue whale – the largest animal in the world*

Aristotle's maggots developed from eggs laid in the meat by flies (with the maggots themselves developing into flies) and the frogs emerged from the mud because they had hibernated there.

> **Continuity of life** means that living things arise from other living things of the same type. This is also called **biogenesis**.

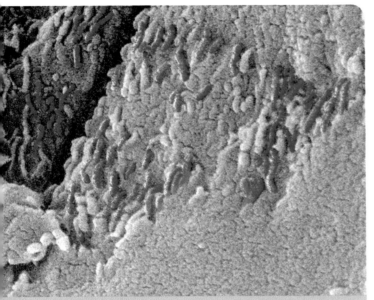

2.2 *Possible evidence for life on Mars. Coloured scanning electron microscope (SEM) image of tube-like structures (coloured pink) on a meteorite that originated from Mars.*

Life

It is relatively easy to determine that a human, a dandelion and a ladybird are alive and that a rock is not. However, the distinction between living and non-living cannot be reduced to one single factor.

Life consists of the possession of **all** of a series of five characteristics. The possession of any one, or a number, of these characteristics does not constitute life. They must all be present.

> **Life** is defined as the possession of all the following characteristics: organised, requiring nutrition and excretion, capable of responding and reproducing.

The characteristics of life

The following characteristics are necessary for living things to maintain their need for metabolism and continuity of life. In particular, these characteristics allow organisms to carry out all the reactions necessary to survive and reproduce.

1. ORGANISATION

> **Organisation** means that living things are composed of cells, tissues, organs and organ systems.

Life requires that living things be highly organised. The basic organisational feature of life is that living things are composed of cells.

Some organisms, such as bacteria and *Amoeba*, are single-celled (unicellular) whereas organisms such as trees and humans are composed of billions of cells. Cells contain all the chemicals that are necessary for life. The structure of cells is outlined in Chapter 7.

As Chapter 8 explains, cells are arranged into groups, called tissues, that perform similar functions. In turn, a number of tissues may be arranged into structures called organs.

A series of organs forms an organ system. Each individual organism may be composed of a number of organ systems. Finally, a group of similar organisms forms a population.

Levels of organisation in life	
Structure	**Example in humans**
Cell	Cheek cell
Tissue	Lining of cheek
Organ	Stomach
Organ system	Digestive system
Organism	Individual human
Population	All the people living in one area

It is often said that structure relates to function. If any of the structures shown in the table above is damaged in any way, there is a loss of some basic function.

2. NUTRITION

> **Nutrition** is the way organisms obtain and use food.

Food is needed for energy and to supply the materials needed for normal life.

- Plants, algae, some bacteria and plankton absorb chemicals from their surroundings and use sunlight energy to make food in a process called photosynthesis.
- Animals, fungi, *Amoeba* and most bacteria take in food from other organisms.

The sun is the basic source of energy for all nutrition. Plants use sunlight directly to make food. The energy in plants is passed on to animals when they eat plants. In this way, energy is said to **flow** from the sun to plants and then to animals.

Sun — energy → Plants — energy → Animals

3. EXCRETION

In order to survive, organisms must maintain a fairly constant balance between their inside and outside environments. Excretion helps to provide this balance.

> **Excretion** is the removal of waste products of metabolism from the body.

Many processes produce poisonous waste that could damage the organism if allowed to accumulate. It is important to remove (excrete) these toxic materials.

- Plants have less need for excretion than animals because they make their own food and do not produce or take in as much waste. Plants excrete waste gases through openings called stomata on the underside of their leaves.
- Advanced animals transfer waste internally from their cells to the blood. The liver is especially important in this process because it breaks down toxic material. The blood carries the waste to the structures that take it out of the organism. In humans these excretory structures are the skin, lungs and urinary system (i.e. kidneys and bladder). The main products excreted are carbon dioxide, salts and surplus water.

4. RESPONSE (OR BEHAVIOUR)

Living things have to respond in certain ways in order to react to changes in their internal and external environments.

> **Response** is the way in which all living things react to changes (called **stimuli**) in their environment or surroundings.

- Animals show rapid responses to stimuli such as light, temperature, pressure and sound. Animals have organised structures such as eyes, ears, nose, tongue and skin that allow them to respond to stimuli. Animals often respond by movement.

2.3 *Baby elephant suckling: an example of nutrition and reproduction*

- Plant responses tend to be slower and less obvious. Plants grow and move in response to factors such as water, light, gravity, touch and chemicals.

Most animals move very obviously from place to place (this is called locomotion). Plants move more slowly, e.g. stems bend towards light, brambles grow out of hedges, leaves turn to face the sun, the daisy opens and closes its petals in response to light (hence the name *daisy,* from *day's eye*).

5. REPRODUCTION

The ability to produce offspring could be said to be the essence of life. All life develops from only living things and it is essential that organisms can produce offspring of their own type.

> **Reproduction** is the production of new individuals.

- Asexual reproduction involves simple organisms splitting into two or more identical offspring.
- Sexual reproduction occurs in most animals and plants. It involves the union of sex cells (called gametes) formed by two parents. The offspring will carry genetic information from both parents and will show features that are a combination of maternal (mother's) and paternal (father's) features.

Living versus non-living

The space probe that landed on Mars some years ago contained apparatus to determine if life existed on that planet. The problem the scientists faced was to define life.

As we saw earlier, there is no simple, clear-cut definition of life. Instead we say that living things must display a number of characteristics. Some of these are shared by non-living things, but only living things show **all** of them.

The following table lists the characteristics present in some living and non-living things.

Living vs. non-living

Characteristic	Living		Non-living	
	Dog	Oak	Car	Flame
1 Made of cells etc.	✓	✓	✗	✗
2 Nutrition	✓	✓	✓	✓
3 Excretion	✓	✓	✓	✓
4 Response (Behaviour)	✓	✓	✓	✓
5 Reproduce	✓	✓	✗	✓

Summary

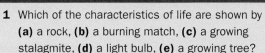

Life and living things show all of the following characteristics:
- organised into cells, tissues, organs, organ systems
- nutrition
- excretion
- behaviour
- reproduction

Metabolism is the sum of all the chemical reactions in an organism.

The continuity of life means that life can arise only from living things of the same type.

Revision questions

1 Which of the characteristics of life are shown by **(a)** a rock, **(b)** a burning match, **(c)** a growing stalagmite, **(d)** a light bulb, **(e)** a growing tree?

2 You receive a sample of Moon dust. In observing it you notice a small particle moving in it. Can you conclude that there is life on the moon? Explain your answer.

3 How does plant movement differ from animal movement?

4 What characteristic of life distinguishes a dead log from a rock?

5 One candle is used to light a second candle.
   (a) Is this reproduction?
   (b) How does it differ from reproduction in an organism?

6 There must have been one exception to the statement that life comes from life. What is the exception?

7 **(a)** List three stimuli in each case to which **(i)** plants and **(ii)** animals respond.
   (b) Name a stimulus that affects only animals.

8 Give a reason why animals tend to have complex excretory systems when compared to plants.

9 **(a)** What is metabolism?   *(continued)*

   (b) Name three processes that form part of an organism's metabolism.
   (c) What kind of metabolic rate has a hyperactive child?
   (d) How does the metabolic rate of a frog differ between summer and winter?

10 It was once thought that swallows appearing in spring and mould appearing on bread were examples of spontaneous generation.
   (a) Explain the term spontaneous generation.
   (b) Where do **(i)** the swallows and **(ii)** the mould, come from?

11 **(a)** Life involves the interaction of five processes. Name these processes.
   (b) Give a brief description of each process.

12 Say whether the following statements are true or false. In the case of a false statement, give a reason why it is false.
   (a) Metabolism includes both digestion and respiration.
   (b) Energy is recycled between plants and animals.
   (c) The growth of bacteria on rotten meat is an example of the continuity of life.
   (d) Excretion does not occur in all forms of life.

Previous examination questions

Ordinary level	Higher level
n/a	n/a

*For latest questions go to **www.edco.ie/biology***

Chapter 3 **Food**

The need for food

Nutrition is the way in which an organism obtains and uses food. Nutrients are the chemical substances, present in food, that are used by organisms. Nutrients are essential to maintain metabolism and continuity of life for all living organisms. In particular, nutrients are used for the following reasons:

- as a source of energy
- to make chemicals needed for cell or metabolic reactions
- as the raw materials for the growth and repair of structures in the organism

The elements present in food

The six common elements found in food are:

- carbon (C)
- hydrogen (H)
- oxygen (O)
- nitrogen (N)
- phosphorus (P)
- sulfur (S)

The first four of these elements make up over 99% of the mass and atoms present in living organisms.

Most of the chemical compounds found in living things are made from carbon atoms bonded together. Compounds made from carbon are said to be **organic** compounds.

Five elements that are present as dissolved salts are:

- sodium (Na)
- magnesium (Mg)
- chlorine (Cl)
- potassium (K)
- calcium (Ca)

The three trace elements (found only in tiny amounts in organisms) are:

- iron (Fe)
- copper (Cu)
- zinc (Zn)

Apart from carbon, hydrogen and oxygen, the rest of these elements are often called minerals.

3.1 *A selection of healthy foods*

Biomolecules

Biomolecules are chemicals that are made inside a living thing.

Biomolecules contain carbon and are also called biochemicals.

The four major types of biomolecules found in food are:

- carbohydrates
- lipids (fats, oils)
- proteins
- vitamins

Carbohydrates

Elements in carbohydrates

The elements present in carbohydrates are suggested by the name itself: carbon (C), hydrogen (H) and oxygen (O).

These elements are usually present in the ratio $C_x(H_2O)_y$ where x and y are the same number (i.e. $x = y$). This means there is always twice as much hydrogen as oxygen in a carbohydrate.

Glucose is a simple carbohydrate in which x and y are both equal to 6. The formula for glucose is $C_6H_{12}O_6$.

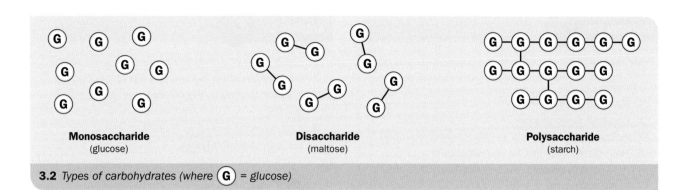

3.2 *Types of carbohydrates (where* **G** *= glucose)*

Structure of carbohydrates

There are three categories of carbohydrates: monosaccharides, disaccharides and polysaccharides.

1. MONOSACCHARIDES

Monosaccharides are the smallest units of carbohydrates. They are sweet to taste and soluble in water. They consist of a single sugar unit. A sugar unit is essentially a ring of carbon atoms.

- **Glucose** is a very common carbohydrate in living things. It is the main molecule from which organisms get their energy and is found in fruit, sweets, chocolate and soft drinks. Plants make glucose in photosynthesis.
- **Fructose** is also a monosaccharide and has the same formula as glucose. However, its atoms are arranged differently. It is sweeter than glucose and commonly found in fruits.

2. DISACCHARIDES

Disaccharides are also sweet to taste and soluble in water. They consist of two monosaccharides joined together. Common examples are:

- **sucrose** (table sugar) = glucose + fructose
- **maltose** (found in germinating seeds) = glucose + glucose
- **lactose** (found in milk) = glucose + galactose

3. POLYSACCHARIDES

Polysaccharides are insoluble or only slightly soluble in water. They contain many monosaccharides linked together. Most have thousands of repeating units. Examples of polysaccharides include the following:

- **Starch** (also called amylose) is the carbohydrate stored by plants. It is composed of long chains (branched and unbranched) of glucose molecules. It is stored by plants. Rice, potatoes, flour, bread and pasta all contain starch.

  Starch is easily digested because the glucose molecules are arranged in a line.

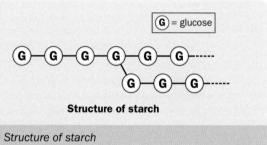

Structure of starch

3.3 *Structure of starch*

- **Cellulose** is a structural carbohydrate in plants. It is also composed of long chains of glucose molecules bonded together. Cellulose has more cross bonding between the chains than starch. Common forms of cellulose are paper and cotton. Because of its structure cellulose is:
  - More difficult to break down (or digest) than starch. This is why it is used as fibre (or roughage) in the diet. The fibre stimulates the intestines to contract – a process called peristalsis.
  - Very strong. For this reason it is used in the cell walls of plants.

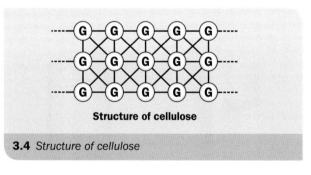

Structure of cellulose

3.4 *Structure of cellulose*

- **Glycogen** is a carbohydrate stored by animals. It is made of many glucose molecules and is more branched than starch. It is mostly stored in the liver and muscles.

Sources of carbohydrates

Sources of carbohydrate are breads, potatoes, rice, sugars, fruits, sweets and cakes.

THE STUDY OF LIFE

Activity 1a To test for reducing sugar

Note that all monosaccharides and some disaccharides (e.g. maltose but not sucrose) are reducing sugars.

A Benedict's test

1 Dissolve some glucose in water in a test tube.
2 Add an equal volume of Benedict's solution (blue).
3 Heat the mixture in a boiling water bath.
4 If glucose is present, the solution turns red (often called brick red).
5 As a control, Benedict's solution is added to distilled water and heated. The colour remains blue.

B Fehling's solution

Fehling's solution can be used instead of Benedict's solution. However, Fehling's I and II solutions have to be kept separate until just before the test.

When mixed they give a blue colour, which turns red when heated in the presence of reducing sugars.

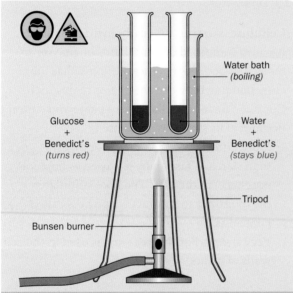

Water bath *(boiling)*
Glucose + Benedict's *(turns red)*
Water + Benedict's *(stays blue)*
Tripod
Bunsen burner

3.5 *Testing for reducing sugar*

3.6 *Benedict's test: reducing sugar is present in the right-hand test tube but not in the one on the left*

Activity 1b To test for starch

1 Add a few drops of iodine solution to some starch dissolved in water. (Iodine is a red-yellow colour.)
2 If starch is present the colour turns blue-black or purple.
3 If starch is absent (e.g. in distilled water), the solution stays red-yellow.

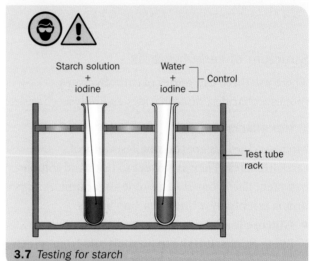

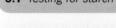

Starch solution + iodine
Water + iodine — Control
Test tube rack

3.7 *Testing for starch*

IODINE

3.8 *Starch test: iodine solution turns blue-black in the presence of starch*

Lipids (fats and oils)

Elements in lipids

Lipids contain the elements carbon, hydrogen and oxygen. Unlike carbohydrates, lipids have no simple ratio. However, lipids have very little oxygen.

- Fats are lipids that are solid at room temperature (20°C).
- Oils are lipids that are liquid at room temperature.

Structure of lipids

The smallest lipids are made of one molecule of glycerol linked to three fatty acid molecules. This structure is called a triglyceride. Different fats and oils have different types of fatty acids.

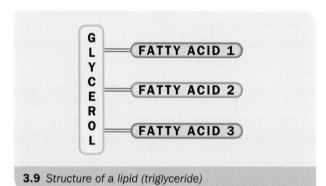

3.9 *Structure of a lipid (triglyceride)*

Phospholipids are fat-like substances where one of the fatty acids is replaced by a phosphate group or has a phosphate group added to it.

Phospholipids are important in the structure of cell membranes (see Chapter 7).

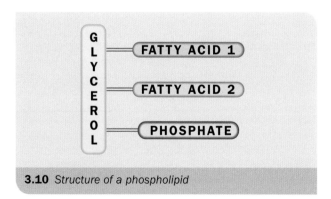

3.10 *Structure of a phospholipid*

Sources of lipids

Sources of lipids are butter, oils, margarine, cream, lard, fat on meat, olives. (Lipids stain clothing.)

Activity 1c To test for fat

1 Label a piece of brown paper (or filter paper) as fat.
2 Place a small piece of butter or cooking oil on the paper.
3 Rub the paper.
4 Repeat the process using a few drops of water on a piece of paper labelled 'water'. *(This acts as a control.)*
5 Leave the two pieces of paper over a radiator to dry.
6 The butter (fat) produces a permanent stain; the water does not.

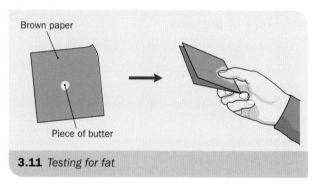

Brown paper

Piece of butter

3.11 *Testing for fat*

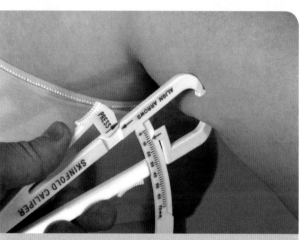

3.12 *Measuring body fat*

Proteins

Elements in proteins

Proteins contain carbon, hydrogen, oxygen and nitrogen. They sometimes contain smaller amounts of sulfur and some may contain phosphorus and other elements.

There is no ratio for the atoms, but proteins are very complex, often containing tens of thousands of atoms. Therefore proteins are very large, bulky substances.

Structure of proteins

Proteins are composed of amino acids. There are twenty common and several rare amino acids found in proteins.

The bond between amino acids is called a peptide bond.

- A peptide is made of a small number of amino acids (less than 20).
- A polypeptide has more than 20 amino acids.
- A protein is a long polypeptide (at least 200 amino acids).

The amino acids that make up a protein can be thought of as the letters in an alphabet. By combining them in different sequences, nature can make an infinite range of proteins.

However, protein function does not depend on the amino acid sequence alone. The way in which the proteins are folded to take up three-dimensional (3-D) shapes is equally important.

- **Fibrous proteins** show little or no folding. They form long fibres and are strong and tough, e.g. keratin in hair, nails and feathers.
- **Globular proteins** show lots of folding. They form rounded shapes, e.g. in egg white (albumen) and enzymes (see Chapter 9).

Sources of proteins

Sources of protein include meat, fish, eggs, nuts, milk, peas and beans.

It is important to note that amino acids are not stored in the body. Surplus amino acids are taken to the liver and converted into urea, which is a toxic waste product. This process is called deamination.

Urea is carried by the blood from the liver to the kidneys. In the kidneys, urea becomes part of urine and is excreted.

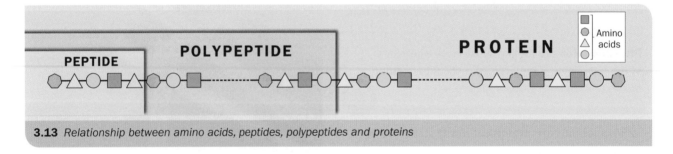
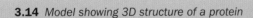

3.13 *Relationship between amino acids, peptides, polypeptides and proteins*

3.14 *Model showing 3D structure of a protein*

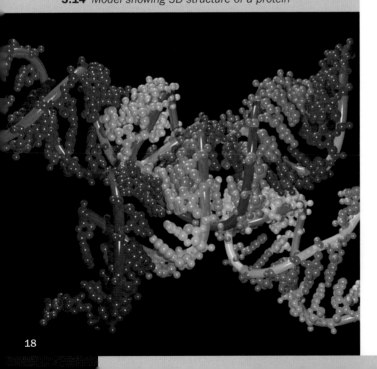

3.15 *Keratin: a protein found in hair and nails*

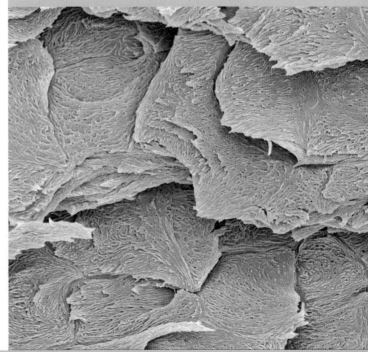

Activity 1d To test for protein (biuret test)

1 Dissolve a sample of soluble protein (e.g. egg white) in water.
2 Add sodium hydroxide (colourless) until the solution clears.
3 Then add a few drops of dilute copper sulfate (blue). Alternatively add an equal volume of biuret solution. This contains sodium hydroxide and copper sulfate and is blue.
4 The appearance of a purple-violet colour shows that proteins are present.
5 As a control, add sodium hydroxide and copper sulfate (or biuret solution) to water. The colour remains blue.

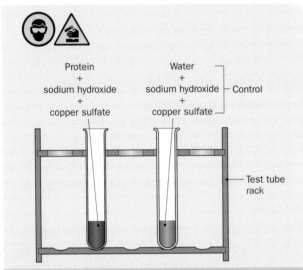

3.16 Biuret test: The control (with no protein) is blue; protein gives a purple-violet colour

3.17 Biuret test: protein is absent from the left test tube but present in the one on the right

Did you know?

The importance of proteins folding in the correct way is seen when they fold incorrectly.

Prions are proteins that do not fold correctly. They cause similar proteins to fold incorrectly and are responsible for brain and nervous system diseases such as BSE (in cattle), nvCJD (in humans) and scrapie (in sheep).

Summary of food tests

Food	Reagent	Negative result	Positive result
Reducing sugar	Benedict's solution	Blue	Red
Starch	Iodine	Red-yellow	Blue-black
Fat	Paper	No stain	Stain
Protein	Biuret reagent (sodium hydroxide and copper sulfate)	Blue	Purple-violet

Vitamins

Syllabus

Although a wide range of vitamins are known, you are required by the syllabus to know only **one water-soluble vitamin** and **one fat-soluble vitamin**.

Vitamins are complex carbon-based substances that the body cannot make. They are needed only in tiny amounts. Vitamins can be referred to by letters or by names based on their chemical structure.

Water-soluble vitamin

Vitamin C is called ascorbic acid. It is soluble in water. Common sources of vitamin C include vegetables and fresh fruits, especially citrus fruits such as oranges and lemons.

Fat-soluble vitamin

A range of different chemicals is referred to as vitamin D. The most common form is vitamin D_2, called calciferol. Vitamin D is soluble in fat.

Good sources of vitamin D include liver, fish oils such as cod liver oil, milk and egg yolk. Vitamin D can be made by the action of ultraviolet rays on chemicals in the skin.

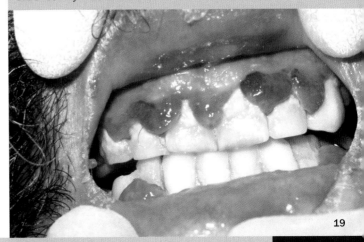

3.18 Scurvy: one of the effects of a lack of Vitamin C

Energy transfer reactions

All the reactions taking place in an organism are referred to as its metabolism. Metabolic reactions can be divided into **anabolic reactions** and **catabolic reactions**.

Anabolic reactions

Anabolic reactions convert smaller molecules into larger ones.

Anabolic reactions require enzymes and use energy. Examples of anabolic reactions are the formation of muscle from amino acids and the formation of cellulose from glucose.

Did you know?

Anabolic steroids are drugs used (illegally in sports) to build up muscle and other tissues.

Photosynthesis is also an example of an anabolic reaction. In photosynthesis, plants absorb energy from sunlight and use it to convert the simple molecules, carbon dioxide and water, into the much more complex molecule, glucose. Oxygen is also produced in this process.

Catabolic reactions

In a **catabolic reaction**, a complex molecule is broken down to simpler ones.

Catabolic reactions release energy and also require enzymes. The enzymes used in anabolic and catabolic reactions are different, i.e. anabolism and catabolism are not opposite processes.

Catabolic reactions include the digestion of food and the decay of dead plants and animals.

Respiration is also an example of a catabolic reaction. In respiration, a complex molecule such as glucose is broken down to simpler molecules, releasing energy in the process.

Structural role of biomolecules

CARBOHYDRATES

■ The carbohydrate cellulose is used to form plant cell walls.

PROTEIN

■ Fibrous protein such as keratin is found in skin and hair; myosin is found in muscle.

LIPIDS

■ Lipids are important food (or energy) stores in plants and animals. One gram of lipid contains twice as much energy as a gram of carbohydrate. This means that twice as much energy can be stored as lipid, compared with an equivalent amount of carbohydrate. This is especially important for animals who have to carry their stored energy around with them.

■ In animals, the stored lipids can have secondary functions such as heat insulation (fat under the skin) and protection of organs (fat around the heart and kidneys).

■ Lipids combine with phosphorous to form phospholipids and with proteins to form lipoproteins. Both of these are important in the structure of cell membranes.

Metabolic role of biomolecules

CARBOHYDRATES AND LIPIDS

■ Carbohydrates and lipids are broken down in respiration to release energy. This energy is used to carry out many other metabolic reactions. Note that proteins are not used to supply energy.

PROTEINS

■ Proteins are used as enzymes to control reactions and as antibodies to fight infection. In addition, some hormones are protein-based and are used to regulate body reactions.

VITAMIN C

■ Vitamin C is necessary for the formation of connective tissue (tissue that surrounds body structures and holds them together) such as skin, gums, cartilage, ligaments and the cells that line the inside of blood vessels. It is also necessary for the growth and maintainance of bones and teeth. Vitamin C helps wounds to heal and is necessary for the immune system to function properly.

Deficiency (or lack) of vitamin C causes a disease called **scurvy**. Symptoms of scurvy include poor healing of skin, bleeding that is often seen under the skin as bruising and bleeding gums with loose teeth.

VITAMIN D

■ Vitamin D helps to absorb calcium from the intestine. Therefore it is needed for healthy bone and tooth formation.

A deficiency of vitamin D in children results in **rickets**. The adult equivalent of rickets is called **osteomalacia**. The symptoms of both diseases are weak, deformed bones that tend to break easily.

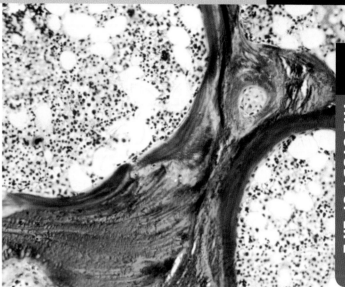

3.20 *Bone showing osteomalacia: normal bone is green; bone with no calcium appears brown*

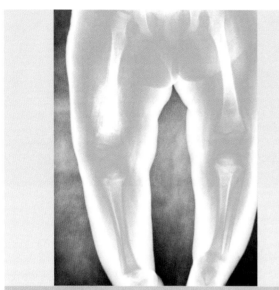

3.19 *Rickets results from a vitamin D deficiency*

Minerals

Minerals are needed by plants and animals in small amounts for four main reasons:

■ to form rigid body structures such as bone and the cement between plant cell walls (both contain calcium)

■ to make soft body parts such as muscle (which requires nitrogen and sulfur)

■ they play a role in forming cell and body fluids (tears, saliva and the liquid part of blood all contain sodium)

■ to form biomolecules (such as haemoglobin, which is based on iron, and chlorophyll, which is based on magnesium)

Some of the minerals needed by plants and animals are summarised in the table below.

Water

Water is the most abundant chemical in living things. It accounts for 99% of all the molecules in the human body. It comprises 60% of human body mass and 90% of the mass of most plants.

Life originated in water and living things are still dependent on water for their survival. Water is essential to life for three main reasons:

1 It is the liquid in which all metabolic reactions take place.
2 It provides the basis for transport systems in organisms.
3 It is the environment in which many organisms live.

Importance of water for living things

1. COMPONENT OF CYTOPLASM AND BODY FLUIDS

Water is the most common chemical in cells. It makes up 75–90% of the mass of most cells. Water is mainly found in the cytoplasm, which is the liquid that surrounds the nucleus in a cell.

In humans, about one-third of the body's water is found outside the cells. Some of this is in the form of tissue fluid, which surrounds all body cells, and the rest forms plasma, the liquid part of blood.

Minerals required by plants and animals				
Plants	**Mineral**	**Symbol**	**Source**	**Use**
	Calcium	Ca	Salts absorbed from soil	Helps bind cell walls together
	Magnesium	Mg	Salts absorbed from soil	Part of the structure of chlorophyll
Animals	**Mineral**	**Symbol**	**Source**	**Use**
	Calcium	Ca	Milk, cheese, hard drinking water	Forms bones and teeth
	Iron	Fe	Liver, meat, green vegetables	Part of the structure of haemoglobin

2. GOOD SOLVENT

Water is a good solvent, i.e. it is able to dissolve a wide range of molecules. This allows chemical reactions to take place in water, in the cytoplasm and in cell organelles. It also allows many molecules to be dissolved in water for transport in plants and animals.

3. PARTICIPATES IN CHEMICAL REACTIONS

Water is directly involved in a number of biochemical reactions. These include:

■ **Condensation reactions:** where smaller molecules join to form a larger molecule, with the loss of a water molecule. An example of this is the formation of maltose from two glucose molecules.

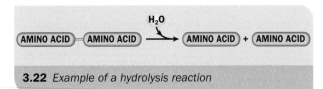

3.21 *Example of a condensation reaction*

■ **Hydrolysis reactions:** where a molecule gains water and is broken down to form smaller molecules. Many forms of digestion are examples of hydrolysis, as shown in Figure 3.22.

3.22 *Example of a hydrolysis reaction*

■ **Photosynthesis:** where water is broken down to supply hydrogens and electrons.
■ **Respiration:** where water is formed as an end product.

4. MOVEMENT THROUGH MEMBRANES

Water can easily pass in or out through biological membranes (as will be described more fully in Chapter 13). When cells absorb large amounts of water they become swollen. If cells lose water they shrivel and lose their shape.

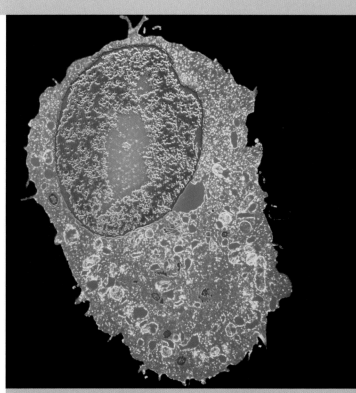

3.23 *Mammalian cell: nucleus red, cytoplasm blue (transmission electron microscope (TEM) image)*

The loss of shape of cells can have serious results for the function of the cell. For example, if red blood cells lose shape, they absorb and carry less oxygen. If plant cells lose shape, the overall plant may lose shape (a process called wilting).

The requirement of cells to have sufficient water often results in other larger molecules having to be moved in or out of cells.

5. GOOD ABSORBER OF HEAT

Water is a good absorber of heat energy. It is slow to heat up and slow to cool down. This means that:

■ The oceans and other large bodies of water (and the organisms in them) have relatively stable temperatures.
■ The high water content of organisms helps to keep their temperature stable. This allows biological reactions to take place over a narrow temperature range (the speed at which biological reactions take place is very dependent on temperature).

Summary

Food:
■ provides the nutrients needed for organisms to get their energy and the materials they require to live.

Living things need 14 elements:
■ the most common six elements are carbon (C), hydrogen (H), oxygen (O), nitrogen (N), phosphorus (P) and sulfur (S)

■ the five elements in dissolved salts are sodium (Na), magnesium (Mg), chlorine (Cl), potassium (K) and calcium (Ca)
■ the trace elements are iron (Fe), copper (Cu), zinc (Zn)

Biomolecules are chemicals made inside living things.

The biomolecules in food are carbohydrates, lipids, proteins and vitamins.

Carbohydrates:

- made of C, H and O in the ratio $C_x(H_2O)_y$, where x = y
- types:
  - (i) monosaccharides (1 unit), e.g. glucose, fructose
  - (ii) disaccharides (2 units), e.g. sucrose, maltose
  - (iii) polysaccharides (many units), e.g. starch, cellulose, glycogen
- sources: bread, potato, rice, flour, sweets
- structural role: cellulose forms cell walls
- metabolic role:
  - (i) glucose is made in photosynthesis
  - (ii) glucose releases energy in respiration
- uses:
  - (i) to supply energy
  - (ii) to store energy
- test:
  - (i) reducing sugars – Benedict's or Fehling's solution
  - (ii) starch – iodine

Lipids:

- made of C, H and O
- fats are solid and oils are liquid at room temperature
- structure: glycerol and 3 fatty acids = triglyceride
- sources:
  - (i) butter, cream, lard
  - (ii) cod liver oil, sunflower oil
- structural role:
  - (i) store energy
  - (ii) insulate
  - (iii) form membranes
- metabolic role: release energy in respiration
- test: brown paper

Proteins:

- made of C, H, O, N, (S, P)
- structure: amino acids, peptides, polypeptides, protein
- sources: meat, fish, eggs, milk
- structural role: form structures such as skin, hair, nails, muscle
- metabolic role:
  - (i) enzymes
  - (ii) some hormones
  - (iii) antibodies
- test: sodium hydroxide, then copper sulfate (the biuret test)

Vitamin C (ascorbic acid):

- water soluble
- sources: vegetables and fresh fruit
- metabolic role: forms connective tissue, bones and teeth, helps healing and immune system
- deficiency: scurvy (poor skin, bleeding, bad teeth and gums)

Vitamin D (calciferol):

- fat soluble
- sources: liver, fish oils, milk, made in skin (UV rays)
- metabolic role: helps absorb calcium for bones and teeth
- deficiency: rickets in children, osteomalacia in adults (weak, deformed, brittle bones)

Metabolism is all the reactions in an organism.
- In anabolic reactions, energy is taken in and used to convert small molecules to larger ones, e.g. photosynthesis.
- In catabolic reactions, larger molecules are broken down to smaller ones and energy is released, e.g. respiration.

Minerals:

- plants need calcium (absorbed from the soil) to hold cell walls together, and magnesium for chlorophyll
- animals need calcium (in milk and cheese) for bones and teeth, and iron (in liver and green vegetables) for haemoglobin

Water is important to living things because it:
- makes up the bulk of the cytoplasm and is also found in tissue fluid and blood
- is a good solvent which allows (i) cell reactions and (ii) transport
- participates in chemical reactions
- moves in and out of cells, giving them the correct shape
- is a good absorber of heat (i.e. maintains its temperature despite temperature changes around it) which provides stable temperatures for living things and their reactions

Revision questions

1 Give the name and chemical symbol for **(a)** the six most important elements in organisms, **(b)** the five elements found in dissolved salts, **(c)** three trace elements.
2 **(a)** Explain what is meant by biomolecules.
   (b) Name four types of biomolecules found in food.
3 What elements are present in **(a)** table sugar (sucrose), **(b)** meat, **(c)** butter?

4 Ribose is a 5-carbon sugar. How many hydrogens and oxygens does it have?
5 **(a)** Distinguish between monosaccharides, disaccharides and polysaccharides.
   (b) Name one biomolecule from each of these three categories.

(continued overleaf)

6 Name three polysaccharides and give one use for each of them.

7 A sample of urine when boiled with Benedict's solution turned red. What does this result tell you: **(a)** about the urine and **(b)** about the person from whom it was taken?

8 **(a)** Distinguish between fats and oils.
   (b) Name one food that is rich in **(i)** fat and **(ii)** oil.

9 **(a)** Name the four elements in phospholipids.
   (b) Give one use for phospholipids.

10 Why is fat used for long-term energy storage, especially in animals?

11 **(a)** Describe how you would test milk for the presence of fat.
   (b) What observation indicates a positive result?

12 State one structural role and one metabolic role for **(a)** carbohydrates, **(b)** lipids, **(c)** proteins.

13 Sailors often chewed on lime skins, hence the nickname 'limeys'.
   (a) What substance did they get from the fruit?
   (b) What are the symptoms of a lack of this substance?
   (c) Name the defiency disease associated with this substance.
   (d) Is this vitamin water- or fat-soluble?

14 **(a)** Name a vitamin that is formed in the skin in sunlight?
   (b) What mineral does it help to absorb?
   (c) State the symptoms of a lack of this vitamin.

15 **(a)** What is meant by **(i)** metabolism, **(ii)** anabolism, **(iii)** catabolism?
   (b) State two examples of each process.

16 **(a)** Name two minerals required by plants.
   (b) State where plants get the named minerals.
   (c) Give one use for each mineral named.

17 **(a)** Name two minerals required by animals.
   (b) State where animals get the named minerals.
   (c) Give one use for each mineral named.

18 A picnic basket consists of brown bread, butter, apples, oranges, milk, ham, salmon, salt, cakes.
   (a) Name one good source from this list for:
      (i) carbohydrate, **(ii)** protein, **(iii)** fat, **(iv)** vitamin C, **(v)** vitamin D, **(vi)** roughage, **(vii)** calcium, **(viii)** phosphorus.
   (b) Name three different carbohydrates and their sources from the above list.
   (c) Name a water-soluble and water-insoluble **(i)** carbohydrate, **(ii)** vitamin, found in these foods.

19 **(a)** What is meant by **(i)** cytoplasm, **(ii)** tissue fluid, **(iii)** plasma?
   (b) Name the most common molecule in each substance named at (a).

20 **(a)** What is a solvent?
   (b) Give two biological benefits of water being a good solvent.

21 Name three reactions in which water plays a role.

22 'Water is a <u>good absorber of energy</u>, which helps it to maintain a <u>stable temperature</u>. This affects entire <u>organisms</u> and <u>metabolic reactions</u>.'
   (a) Explain each of the <u>underlined</u> terms.
   (b) In what way are **(i)** entire organisms and **(ii)** metabolic reactions, affected by water being a good absorber of energy?

23 Say whether the following statements are true or false. In the case of a false statement, give a reason why it is false.
   (a) Carbohydrates contain hydrogen and oxygen in the same ratio as water (H_2O).
   (b) Amino acids do not contain nitrogen.
   (c) Fish is a good source of protein and lipid, but not carbohydrate.
   (d) Amino acids are required to make fatty acids.
   (e) Keratin is a protein found in egg white.
   (f) The biuret test indicates the presence of proteins.
   (g) Chewing food is an example of anabolism.

Sample examination questions

Section A

24 **(a)** **(i)** Name a fat-soluble vitamin.
      (ii) State a good source of this vitamin in the human diet.
      (iii) What disease can you get if this vitamin is absent from your diet?
   (b) **(i)** Name two minerals required by the human body.
      (ii) In the case of one of these minerals, state its function in the body.
                              (2003 OL Sample Q 5)

25 Answer five of the following by writing a word in the space provided.

   (a) Cellulose is an example of a structural _____.
   (b) Vitamins are either water-soluble or _____-soluble.
   (c) Fats are composed of oxygen, hydrogen and _____.
   (d) When an iodine solution is added to a food sample and remains red-brown in colour, _____ is absent.
   (e) When two monosaccharides unite they form a _____.
   (f) Removal from the body of the waste products of metabolism is called _____.
                              (2005 HL Q 1)

26 Answer **five** of the following.
  (a) Biomolecules of the general formula $C_x(H_2O)_y$ are examples of _____.
  (b) Give **two** functions of water in a living organism.
  (c) Is energy release a feature of anabolic or catabolic reactions?
  (d) How do fats differ from oils at room temperature?
  (e) Name the test or give the chemicals used to detect the presence of protein in a food sample.
  (f) Name a structural polysaccharide.

(2008 HL Q 2)

Section B

27 (a) (i) State **one** reason that your body needs protein.
  (ii) Name the element, other than carbon, hydrogen and oxygen, which is always found in protein.
  (b) Answer the following questions in relation to tests that you carried out for protein.
  (i) Name **two** foods in which you found protein.
  (ii) What reagent or chemicals did you use to test for protein?
  (iii) Was heat necessary in the test that you carried out?
  (iv) What was the initial colour of the reagent or chemicals?
  (v) What colour change occurred if protein was present?
  (vi) Was there a colour change in the control?

(2007 OL Q 8)

Section C

28 (a) Water has many functions in the human body. State **three** of these functions.
  (b) (i) Name the chemical elements present in carbohydrates.
  (ii) Give an example of a carbohydrate that has a structural role. Where would you expect to find this carbohydrate in a living organism?
  (iii) State a role of carbohydrates other than a structural one.

  (iv) Name a test that you would carry out to show the presence of a reducing sugar (e.g. glucose).
  (v) Describe how you would carry out the test that you have named in **(iv)**.
  (c) (i) Name a chemical element found in proteins that is not found in carbohydrates.
  (ii) State two good sources of protein in the human diet.
  (iii) Proteins are digested to simpler substances. What are these simpler substances called?
  (iv) State one function of protein in the human body.
  (v) Name a test for protein.
  (vi) Describe how you would carry out the test that you have named in **(v)**.

(2004 OL Q 10)

29 (a) (i) The same elements are found in carbohydrates and fats. Name these elements.
  (ii) State one way in which carbohydrates differ from fats.
  (iii) How do phospholipids differ from other lipids?
  (b) Carbohydrates are classified as monosaccharides, disaccharides and polysaccharides.
  (i) Name a monosaccharide and state a role for it in living organisms.
  (ii) What is a disaccharide?
  (iii) Cellulose is a polysaccharide. What is it formed from? State a role for cellulose in living organisms.
  (iv) Name a polysaccharide that has a different role to cellulose. What is the role of the polysaccharide that you have named?
  (v) Describe a test for a named polysaccharide.
  (c) Answer the following in relation to a test for 1. A reducing sugar 2. A protein.
  (i) Name the reagent(s) used.
  (ii) State the initial colour of the reagent.
  (iii) State whether the test requires heat.
  (iv) What colour indicates a positive result?

(2003 HL Sample Q 10)

Previous examination questions

Ordinary level	Higher level
2003 Sample Q 5	2003 Sample Q 10
2004 Q 5, 10	2005 Q 1
2005 Q 5	2006 Q 7
2006 Q 3	2007 Q 1
2007 Q 1, 8	2008 Q 2
2008 Q 2	

*For latest questions go to **www.edco.ie/biology***

THE STUDY OF LIFE

Chapter 4 **Ecology**

Ecology

> **Ecology** is the study of the interactions between living things (organisms) and between organisms and their environment.

All the external factors that influence an organism are referred to as its **environment**.

Biosphere

> The **biosphere** is that part of the planet containing living organisms.

The biosphere extends from about 8 km deep in the oceans to 8 km high in the sky. It includes the air (atmosphere), the seas (hydrosphere) and the soil and rock (lithosphere).

Ecosystem

> An **ecosystem** is a group of clearly distinguished organisms that interact with their environment as a unit.

The climate, soil, plants and animals in specific ecosystems are similar, even though they may be located in different regions.

The entire earth is itself an ecosystem because no part of it is completely isolated from the rest. This global ecosystem forms the biosphere.

The biosphere consists of many large ecosystems. The table below outlines some common ecosystems.

4.1 *A grassland*

4.2 *A rocky seashore*

Ecosystems can be very large indeed. For example, deciduous forests once covered much of Europe. Nowadays, because of pressure on land for agriculture and housing, large areas of forest have been cleared. As a result, forests have been divided up into smaller units called woodlands.

Woodlands are clearly distinguished ecosystems, as are grasslands, bogs, lakes, sand dune systems, salt-marshes, rocky seashores and hedgerows.

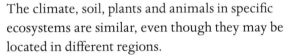

Sample ecosystems		
Ecosystem	**Features**	**Sample location**
Temperate deciduous forest	Warm summer, rain plentiful	Western Europe (includes Ireland), Eastern USA
Desert	Low rainfall	Sahara Desert, Gobi Desert
Tropical rain forest	High temperatures and high rainfall	Brazil, West Africa, parts of South-East Asia
Grassland	Mild temperatures, low rainfall	Steppes of Asia, pampas in South America, prairies in North America
Freshwater	Non-salty water	Rivers, lakes, wetlands
Marine	Salt water	Seashores and oceans

Habitat

A **habitat** is the place where a plant or animal lives.

A habitat is also the place that we study to learn more about an ecosystem.

As ecosystems can be very large, it is common to select a number of small, local areas or habitats to study. The study of the local habitat gives a representation of how an ecosystem functions.

A **population** is all the members of the same species living in an area.

We speak of a population of frogs in a pond or a population of primroses in a wood.

A **community** is all the different populations in an area.

For instance, all the plants, animals, fungi and micro-organisms living in a field or bog is a community.

Environmental factors affecting organisms

The four categories of factors that influence the life and distribution of organisms are: abiotic, biotic, climatic and edaphic factors.

Abiotic factors are non-living factors.

Biotic factors are living factors.

Climatic factors refer to weather over a long period of time.

Edaphic factors relate to soil: factors such as the soil pH, soil type and the moisture, air and mineral content of soil.

The tables below and overleaf summarise some effects of these factors on organisms.

Note that the four factors listed above can affect living things by their variations (a) in levels and (b) from season to season. For example, the daily variation in temperature may affect the types of plants growing in an area. Plants are also affected by the changes in temperature from season to season.

Note also that the climatic factors and most of the edaphic factors are also abiotic factors.

Some effects of abiotic factors on organisms		
Factor	Effect	Example
Altitude	Higher altitudes are cooler, wetter, windier than lower altitudes.	Trees cannot live at very high altitudes.
Aspect (direction a surface faces)	North-facing slopes are cooler and darker than south-facing slopes.	More plants grow on south-facing slopes.
Steepness	Steep slopes lose water quickly and soils are washed away.	Conifers can grow on steep slopes (because their leaves lose very little water).
Currents	Plants and animals are washed away.	Need for attachment (e.g. limpets and many seaweeds attach to rocks).
Exposure	Shore plants lose water when tide is out.	Organisms on shores have shells or mucilage to retain water.

Some effects of biotic factors on organisms

Factor	Effect	Example
Food	The more food that is available, the greater the number of organisms that will survive.	The number of berries affects the number of blackbirds. The amount of plankton affects the number of mussels.
Competition	Plants and animals fight for scarce resources such as food, space, mates, shelter.	Barnacles and limpets compete for space on rocks. Rabbits compete with each other for food.
Predation (the catching and eating of organisms)	Predators reduce the numbers of their prey.	Foxes reduce the numbers of rabbits. Hawks keep down the numbers of mice.
Parasitism (organism taking food from a living host)	Parasites weaken the host and may reduce their numbers.	Fleas infect foxes and rats. Sea lice infect fish.
Pollination and seed dispersal	Many plants require animals to carry pollen and seeds.	Insects pollinate many plants. Birds disperse seeds when they eat fruits and egest the seeds.
Humans	Humans can have a huge positive or negative effect on other organisms.	Pollution destroys the environment. New parks form new environments for life.

Some effects of climatic factors on organisms

Factor	Effect	Example
Temperature	Affects the rate of reactions in living things.	Higher temperatures cause rapid plant growth in summer. Lower temperatures cause hibernation in hedgehogs and frogs in winter.
Rainfall	Water is essential for life.	Plants such as cacti live in areas of low rainfall (deserts). Tropical rain forests require high and regular rainfall (along with high temperatures).
Humidity (amount of water vapour in the air)	High humidity reduces evaporation.	Woodlice are restricted to the humid conditions under decaying leaves.
Day length	Affects plant flowering and germination along with migration, hibernation and reproduction in animals.	Many plants produce flowers due to the longer days in spring. Swallows migrate due to shorter autumn days.
Light intensity	Affects the rate of photosynthesis.	Plankton grow best in the upper layers of water due to the higher light intensity. Trees grow tall to get more light.
Wind	Causes physical damage. Increases evaporation.	Trees exposed to wind grow better on the sheltered side and appear to be leaning away from the wind. Helps spread spores and some pollen and seeds.
Salinity (salt content)	Causes problems with water moving in or out of organisms and their cells.	Limpets live in seawater, not freshwater. Organisms in seashore ponds must be able to withstand changes in salinity (due to rainfall and evaporation).

Effects of some edaphic factors on organisms

Factor	Effect	Example
Soil pH	Plants and animals are adapted to specific pH values	Acid soils (e.g. bogs) have a pH less than 7, and support bog moss and heather. Neutral soils have pH values close to 7, and are preferred by most plants. Alkaline soils have pH values greater than 7, and are preferred by lime-loving plants, e.g birdsfoot trefoil and bee orchid.
Soil type (determined by particle size)		
(a) Sand (large particles)	Good drainage and air content. Low mineral and water content	Few earthworms in sand (no humus to eat). Marram grass growing in sandhills has long, deep roots to absorb moisture.
(b) Clay (small particles)	Impermeable to water and air. Easily waterlogged	Plants do not grow well, as the soil is too wet and difficult for roots to penetrate.
Organic matter (humus)	Decaying organic matter (humus) provides food, helps bind soil particles, retains water and minerals	Vital to plant life. Provides food for organisms such as earthworms.
Water content	Absorbed by roots	Plants need to absorb water for transpiration, photosynthesis, and general metabolism. Minerals dissolve in water and are absorbed by roots.
Air content	Provides oxygen for roots, micro-organisms, and animals	Lack of oxygen in soil prevents plant and animal growth.
Mineral content	Needed by plants	A lack of any mineral causes stunted growth and yellowing of plants.

4.3 *Anemones (red), top shells (around anemones), limpets (large shells on left and right) on a pale coloured alga*

Aquatic environments

Syllabus

Even if you are studying a land-based habitat you must be aware of the following factors that relate to aquatic habitats.

Aquatic environments (e.g. ponds, lakes, oceans, rivers, streams) have special factors of influence. In land-based (terrestrial) ecosystems, the most important environmental factors are often temperature and rainfall, with light being relatively abundant.

In aquatic environments, temperature is less important because it doesn't vary so rapidly, and although water is plentiful, lack of light may be a problem.

Special factors in aquatic environments

LIGHT

Water interferes with the penetration of light. This means plants are limited to the upper layers of water and those that attach to the bottom can grow only in shallow waters.

Animals can be found at great depths. They feed off organisms that fall down from the upper layers.

CURRENTS

Flowing water will cause plants to be carried away if they are not attached. Animals are better able to resist currents because they can move.

WAVE ACTION

Waves create currents. They also cause physical damage to organisms. Seaweeds avoid this by being flexible. Animals are often protected by shells (e.g. limpets and barnacles).

SALT CONTENT

Most aquatic organisms are adapted to either freshwater or saltwater environments. If the external solution is unsuitable, they have problems with gaining or losing water (osmoregulation).

Some organisms (especially those in rock pools), can survive changes in salt content (salinity) due to rain or freshwater.

OXYGEN CONCENTRATION

The oxygen concentration in water is much lower than that of air. This affects the plant and animal life in water. They must be able to extract oxygen from the water (e.g. they may have gills or large surface area to volume ratios).

4.4 *A hawk (kestrel) catching a mouse: hawks are usually top consumers.*

Energy flow

Every ecosystem requires a constant input of energy from an external source in order to function properly. **The sun is the primary source of energy for our planet.** Feeding allows energy to **flow** from one organism to another in an ecosystem.

Producers

> **Producers** are organisms that carry out photosynthesis.

All plants and seaweeds are producers. About 1% of sunlight is trapped by green plants and used to make food. The sun's energy is stored by plants in the chemical bonds of molecules such as glucose and starch.

Plants break down most of these molecules to release the energy. This process is called respiration. They use the energy to do work such as making new cells or repairing old ones. Most of their energy is lost in the form of heat and only a small proportion (about 10%) is passed on to other organisms.

When an animal eats a plant or another animal, the food that is consumed contains energy. Feeding represents a flow of energy. This means that energy moves in one direction, i.e.

- *sun → plant → animal 1 → animal 2 → etc.*
- *sun → primary → primary → secondary → etc.*
  *   producer   consumer   consumer*

Consumers

> **Consumers** are organisms that take in food from another organism.

All animals are consumers.

Primary consumers feed on producers. They include herbivores (animals that feed on vegetation). They also include organisms that feed on dead plants, e.g. decomposers (mostly bacteria and fungi) and detritus feeders (such as mussels and earthworms, which feed on small parts of dead and decomposing plants and animals).

Secondary consumers are animals that feed on primary consumers. They include carnivores (meat eaters) and scavengers (who feed on animals killed by other sources).

Tertiary consumers feed on secondary consumers. They are not always present. If no other organism feeds on them, they are called **top consumers**.

Organisms that feed on both plants and animals are called omnivores. Examples include gulls, blackbirds, badgers and humans.

Food chain

> A **grazing food chain** is a sequence of organisms in which each one is eaten by the next member in the chain.

In a grazing food chain the first organism is a producer or a green plant. An example of a grazing food chain is:

- *dandelion → butterfly → thrush → hawk*

Sample food chains and their trophic levels				
Trophic level	**1st**	**2nd**	**3rd**	**4th**
Stage	**Producer**	**Primary consumer** (herbivore)	**Secondary consumer** (carnivore)	**Tertiary consumer**
Grassland examples	buttercup	caterpillar	blackbird	fox
Seashore examples	plankton	barnacle	whelk	crab

Trophic level

> A **trophic level** is a feeding stage in a food chain.

Producers form the first trophic level. Primary consumers are the second trophic level and secondary consumers form the third trophic level. (See table at top of page.)

Other examples of grazing food chains are:

GRASSLAND HABITAT
- grass → rabbit → fox
- buttercup → caterpillar → thrush → fox

SEASHORE HABITAT
- algae → limpet → starfish → gull
- plankton → barnacle → whelk → crab

Scavengers, decomposers or detritus feeders (which feed on small pieces of dead or decomposing plants and animals) can take food from each trophic level.

Length of food chain

About 10% of the energy in each trophic level is passed on to the next level. The remaining 90% is used by the organisms or is lost as heat, waste or detritus.

For this reason the amount of energy (food) passing along a food chain decreases from one trophic level to the next. This limits the length of a food chain.

In the food chain shown in Figure 4.5, the rabbit does not have to travel too far to get food. The fox must range over a much larger area in order to get its food.

If any consumer was to feed off foxes, it would have to use far too much energy hunting for its prey. This is why this food chain finishes with foxes.

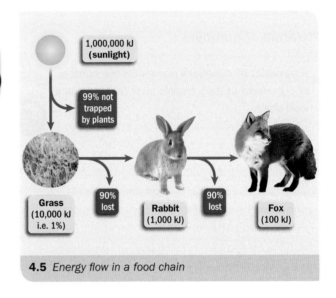

4.5 *Energy flow in a food chain*

Food web

> A **food web** consists of two or more interlinked food chains.

Food chains and food webs are attempts to show the feeding inter-relationships in an ecosystem. They show the flow of energy through the ecosystem.

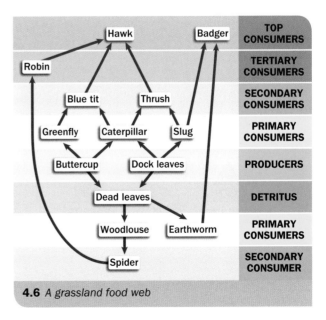

4.6 *A grassland food web*

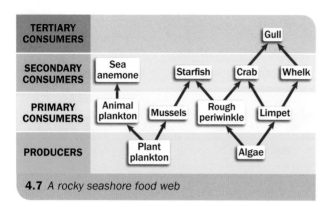

4.7 *A rocky seashore food web*

Pyramid of numbers

A pyramid of numbers represents the number of organisms at each trophic level (or stage) in a food chain.

The number of organisms at each trophic level in a food chain normally decreases as you move up the food chain. This is due to high energy loss at each trophic level and the fact that the organisms usually increase in size the further they are along the food chain (i.e. organisms tend to feed on organisms smaller than themselves).

A pyramid of numbers is prepared by counting the number of organisms at each trophic level as follows:

1 Count the primary producers and place them at the base of the pyramid.
2 Count the primary, secondary etc. consumers and place each of them above each other in the pyramid.
3 The top of the pyramid contains the top consumers (secondary or tertiary consumers).

In the food chain *grass → rabbits → fox* there are many grass plants feeding a smaller number of rabbits which support very few foxes. The relative number of organisms at each trophic level is shown by Figure 4.8.

4.8 *A pyramid of numbers*

Niche

The **ecological niche** of an organism is the functional role it plays in the community.

The organism's niche (or way of life) includes what it eats, what it is eaten by and how it interacts with other organisms and with its abiotic environment.

Two species that have identical niches cannot survive for long in the same habitat. This is because they would both compete in some way (e.g. for food, space, nesting sites). This results in organisms occupying different niches.

For example, swallows, thrushes and blackbirds prevent competition by occupying different niches in the same habitat. The swallow feeds on aerial insects, the thrush feeds on ground insects and snails, while the blackbird takes insects on trees, but mostly eats fruit and worms.

Edible and flat periwinkles have different niches. Edible periwinkles feed on algae scraped from rocks; flat periwinkles feed on larger seaweeds.

Nutrient recycling

Nutrient recycling is the way in which elements (such as carbon and nitrogen) are exchanged between the living and non-living components of an ecosystem.

Whereas **energy flows** in from the sun and through the ecosytem, the nutrients that make up the bodies of living things are recycled and used time and time again. Such cycles are called biogeochemical cycles. Although many **nutrients are recycled**, we will focus on two, carbon and nitrogen.

The carbon cycle

The carbon cycle is the process by which carbon from the environment is converted to carbon in living things. The carbon in living things is later released back into the environment.
Carbon is an essential element for living things. It is normally exchanged between living things and their environment in the form of the gas, carbon dioxide.

Plants have been removing carbon dioxide from the atmosphere for millions of years. It is important that this gas is replaced in order to allow photosynthesis to continue.

Role of organisms in the carbon cycle

Three groups of organisms have roles to play in the carbon cycle:

- Plants remove carbon from the environment in photosynthesis and return it in respiration.
- Animals obtain their carbon by eating plants; they release carbon in respiration.
- Micro-organisms (such as fungi and bacteria) return carbon to the environment when they decompose dead plants and animals.

Global warming

In recent years there has been concern that the concentration of carbon dioxide in the atmosphere is rising. For example, the concentration of carbon dioxide 200 years ago was 0.028%. Now it has risen to 0.038%.

The main causes of the rise in carbon dioxide concentration are thought to be increased combustion of fossil fuels and deforestation.

Carbon dioxide is a 'greenhouse gas'. This means it allows heat radiation from the sun to pass into the earth's atmosphere, but does not allow reflected heat rays back out. (It is not the only gas that does this.)

Increased levels of carbon dioxide may contribute to global warming, i.e. a rise in the average temperature of the planet. Global warming may cause the following effects:

- Sea levels may rise due to ice melting and the expansion of hot water. This may cause increased flooding.
- Weather patterns may alter (e.g. more stormy weather), which in turn will affect wildlife and agriculture.
- Another major concern is that global warming may cause the Gulf Stream to reverse its direction of flow. This would cause very cold water to flow past Ireland and would have a huge impact on our climate.

The nitrogen cycle

The function of the nitrogen cycle is to take nitrogen from the air and make it available for use by living things. The nitrogen in living things is later converted to nitrogen in the air.

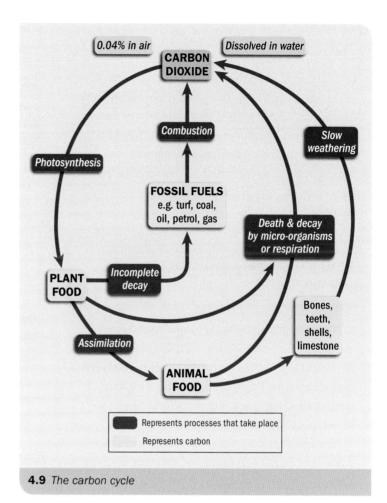

4.9 *The carbon cycle*

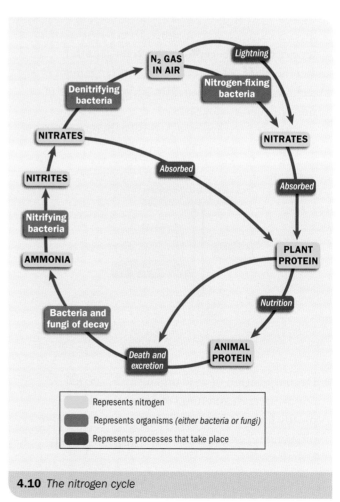

4.10 *The nitrogen cycle*

Refer to Figure 4.10 (previous page) while reading the following.

1 Living things need the element nitrogen (to make proteins, DNA, RNA and other molecules). Nitrogen gas (N_2) makes up about 79% of the air. However, this form of nitrogen is inert and cannot be used by plants and animals.

2 Nitrogen fixation is carried out by volcanic action, lightning, industrial processes and by some bacteria.

Nitrogen fixation is the conversion of nitrogen gas into ammonia (NH_3), ammonium (NH_4^+) or nitrate (NO_3^-).

Nitrogen-fixing bacteria can be found free in the soil or they may be associated with the roots of certain plants. The latter group of bacteria live in nodules (swellings) on the roots of a group of plants called legumes. These include clover, soya beans, peas and beans.

Nitrogen fixation is an anaerobic process (i.e. it does not require oxygen) and the root nodules allow the bacteria to escape from oxygen.

The relationship between the bacteria and the legume is a form of symbiosis, i.e. two different species living closely together. In this case both species benefit, because the bacteria get food and the plant gets nitrates, so the arrangement is technically called mutualism (although it is often simply called symbiosis).

Nitrates are converted (assimilated) into plant and animal protein, DNA and RNA.

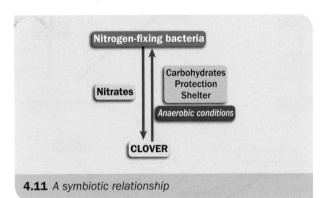

4.11 A symbiotic relationship

3 **Decomposition** of dead organisms is carried out by bacteria and fungi of decay, which are mostly found in the soil. These organisms release nitogenous compounds such as ammonia (NH_3) into the soil.

4 Nitrification is carried out by bacteria in the soil called nitrifying bacteria.

Nitrification is the conversion of ammonia and ammonium (NH_4^+) compounds to nitrite and then to nitrate.

These bacteria are chemosynthetic, i.e. they make their own food using energy from chemical reactions.

5 Some of the nitrate formed in the soil is absorbed and assimilated by plants.

6 Denitrification is carried out by denitrifying bacteria in the soil.

Denitrification is the conversion of nitrates to nitrogen gas.

Denitrifying bacteria are anaerobic and live in swampy soil or deep down in the soil (where water collects to produce anaerobic conditions).

Role of organisms in the nitrogen cycle

- **Bacteria** play a central role in the nitrogen cycle. The four types of bacteria and their functions are:
  1 nitrogen-fixing bacteria, which convert atmospheric nitrogen to nitrates
  2 bacteria of decay, which convert decaying nitrogen waste to ammonia
  3 nitrifying bacteria, which convert ammonia to nitrates
  4 denitrifying bacteria, which convert nitrates to nitrogen gas

- **Fungi**, like bacteria, help to convert dead plants and animals and their wastes into ammonia in the soil.
- **Plants** absorb nitrates from the soil and use the nitrogen to form proteins.
- **Animals** consume plants and use their nitrogen to form animal protein.

4.12 Nitrogen-fixing nodules on the roots of a pea plant

Human impact on ecosystems

Humans have been on earth for about one hundred and fifty thousand years. This is a short period of time in relation to the age of the planet, four and a half billion years (4 500 000 000 years). In this short time humans have had a huge effect on the earth's resources and organisms in many ways.

We will consider three ways that humans affect ecosystems: pollution, conservation and waste management.

Pollution

Pollution is any harmful addition to the environment.

Most pollution arises from human activities such as dumping, littering, sewage disposal, electricity generation, transport, radioactive processes and noisy activities.

Natural pollutants include volcanic emissions and smoke from natural forest fires.

Pollution can affect air, fresh water, sea and soil or land.

Pollutants are substances that cause pollution.

There are many types of pollution.
- **Domestic pollution** includes household wastes.
- **Agricultural pollution** includes the use of sprays to control pests and weeds, the overuse of fertilisers and disposal of farmyard wastes such as slurry and sileage effluent.
- **Industrial pollution** includes smoke that causes acid rain and wastes that may damage streams, rivers and lakes.

Syllabus

*You are required to study the effects and control of **any one pollutant**.*

Ozone depletion – an example of air pollution

Ozone (O_3) is a gas that forms a protective layer in the upper atmosphere, between 10 and 45 km above the surface of the earth. It helps to absorb and shield the Earth from incoming ultraviolet radiation.

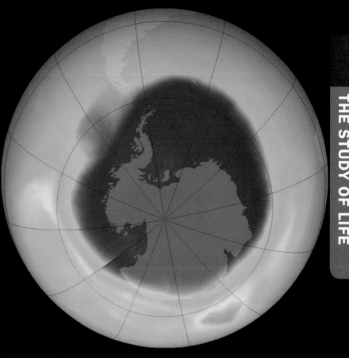

4.13 *The ozone hole (purple) over the Antarctic in 2007*

Ozone depletion (or thinning) was first noted in 1984 as a 'hole' in the ozone layer over Antarctica. Since then a similar, but smaller, 'hole' has developed over the Arctic.

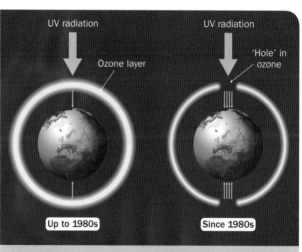

4.14 *Effects of ozone depletion*

Ozone depletion is caused by a range of manufactured chemical pollutants. These include chlorofluorocarbons (CFCs) used in aerosols, refrigerators (Freon gas), insulating foams (styrofoam) and industrial detergents.

Some fire extinguishers (halons) and agricultural sprays (fumigants) also destroy ozone, as do emissions from high-flying aircraft.

EFFECTS OF OZONE DEPLETION

Ozone absorbs ultraviolet rays. Less ozone in the outer layers of the atmosphere allows more ultra-violet radiation to penetrate to the Earth's surface.

Increased ultraviolet levels have a number of effects, such as the following:

- Increased numbers of skin cancers, cataracts (the lens in the eye loses transparency) and weakened immunity.
- Serious damage to crops and plant life.
- There is great concern that plankton will be depleted. This would have huge effects on aquatic food chains and therefore on fish, penguins, birds, seals and whales. It might even result in less oxygen being produced for organisms to breathe.

CONTROL OF OZONE DEPLETION

- A reduction in the use of CFCs will eventually allow the ozone layer to be replenished. Ozone is formed naturally by the reaction of ultraviolet light with oxygen.

    CFCs are now being replaced with other chemicals such as hydrofluorocarbons (HFCs). These chemicals break down much faster than CFCs. This means they do not reach the upper atmosphere and therefore do not cause ozone to break down.
- Do not use sprays or foam products that contain CFCs.
- Fridges should not be dumped in landfill sites. They should be returned to organisations that will dispose of their CFCs in an environmentally friendly way.

In recent years the hole in the ozone layer has stabilised. It looks like the control methods are allowing ozone to be replenished.

4.15 *A weather balloon being launched from the Arctic to study the levels of ozone gas in the stratosphere.*

Conservation

> **Conservation** is the wise management of our existing natural resources, in order to maintain a wide range of habitats and prevent the death and extinction of organisms.

Modern humans exploit nature in order to live in the way they do. For example, they obtain fish from the sea, grow plant species such as grass and cereals in areas where they would not normally be found, remove timber for building and fuel, resulting in deforestation, and alter the environment for roads, homes, industry and recreation.

In all these cases an element of control must be exercised. This responsibility rests on the individual and on larger organisations. It is important that we slow down and prevent damage to habitats. Such damage is causing a huge loss of biological diversity.

The present rate of extinction is greater than at any time in the Earth's history. We have a duty to future generations to pass on the natural environment that we inherited.

The benefits of conservation

- It prevents organisms from becoming extinct.
- It maintains the balance of nature.
- It maintains a wide range of living things (biodiversity).
- Organisms may be found to be useful in the future.
- Organisms and habitats are enjoyable to see and visit.
- We have no right to wipe out other life forms.

> **Syllabus**
>
> *You are required to outline any **one conservation practice** from the areas of agriculture, fisheries or forestry. As an example of good conservation practices, we will examine the area of fisheries.*

Fisheries

Some of the main problems associated with the fishing industry are as follows:

- Pollution of the rivers, lakes and the sea reduces the amount of fish in these waters. Once depleted, fish stocks may take many years to regenerate.

- Overfishing has reduced (and in some cases wiped out) fish stocks at sea. For this reason, fish quotas have been assigned to different countries to try and ensure that enough fish are left in the sea to replenish the stocks.
- The use of small-mesh nets can result in too many young (small) fish being caught. The ideal is to allow fish to reproduce for a number of years before being caught.

It is important to continuously monitor the environment in order to prevent problems such as these from developing and becoming too serious. In relation to fisheries this involves measures such as:
- taking and analysing water samples
- checking fish catches and fishing equipment
- sampling fish stocks to calculate their numbers

EXAMPLE OF CONSERVATION IN FISHING

The size of the mesh in fishing nets is crucially important. If the mesh size is too small then young, small fish are trapped as well as older, larger fish.

Removing too many young fish may reduce the ability of the fish to maintain a viable population number. Fishing with large-mesh nets does not remove the young, small fish. This allows the fish numbers to be maintained.

Waste management

Modern life produces large amounts of waste material. It is important to manage these wastes wisely in order to conserve the environment and prevent excessive pollution.

Examples of waste management procedures in three different industries are outlined below. Note that in each case the basic principle is that the waste is recycled in a safe manner.

Agriculture

Many of our inland lakes have been (and are) depleted of fish. This has happened because of the lack of oxygen caused mainly by the release of slurry.

Slurry is liquified waste material produced by animals. It contains high levels of minerals such as nitrogen and phosphorus. When slurry enters rivers or lakes the minerals it contains cause increased algal growth. This often results in algal blooms.

When the algae die they are decomposed by bacteria. This results in the absorption of oxygen and the water becomes depleted in oxygen. Aquatic animals and plants die when they cannot get sufficient oxygen.

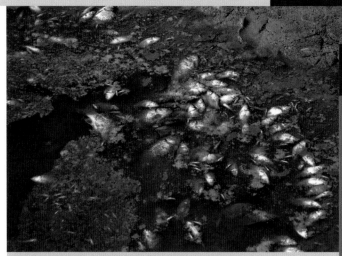

4.16 *Fish kill due to eutrophication*

The addition of nutrients to fresh water in this way is called **eutrophication**.

By controlling the release of nutrients into rivers and lakes the water quality can be improved. Examples of this control involve storing slurry in leakproof pits. The stored slurry is spread on dry land in summer. In this way it is not washed away into streams and rivers and the nutrients can be absorbed by plant roots and recycled by the plants. In time, lakes can be (and are) restocked with fish to return them to their original state.

4.17 *Almost all the organisms in Lough Sheelin in Co. Cavan were killed by pig slurry in the 1970s. Good conservation practices have allowed fish (and many other organisms) to return to the lake.*

Fisheries

When fish are processed the waste materials consist of heads, tails, fins, intestines, dead (and decaying) fish and blood diluted by large amounts of water.

The solid wastes are highly alkaline and are first neutralised by the addition of formic acid. The product is pulped, dried and recycled as fertiliser or pig feed.

Forestry

Potential waste products in forestry include the tops of trees, small branches, tree stumps, roots and sawdust. These products are treated as follows.

Small branches spread on the forest floor form a surface that can help machinery to move (especially in very wet land). These branches, along with the stumps and roots are allowed to rot naturally. The nutrients released into the soil by this rotting process 'feed' the next generation of trees, which grow much faster.

Tops of trees and large branches are converted to sawdust, which is used to form processed wood products such as medium-density fibreboard (MDF).

Problems associated with waste disposal

- Wastes may contain many micro-organisms that could cause disease. If the waste is not properly treated, disease-causing micro-organisms may be spread by wind or enter drinking water supplies.
- Toxic chemicals released from wastes can easily be washed out and enter drinking water supplies. They may also have serious effects on plant and animal life in the environment.
- Nutrients released from waste can cause enrichment (eutrophication) of water supplies, which may lead to the death of plants and animals.
- Waste that is disposed of in landfill sites (dumps) can be unsightly, attract undesirable scavengers such as rats and gulls, and produce odours.
- Dumping waste at sea may lead to pollution of the sea, especially with the large amounts of waste now being generated by industrial societies.
- Incinerators burn waste at high temperatures. However, there is a fear that poisonous gases may be released in the process.

An overall problem with waste disposal is the 'NIMBY' syndrome. This stands for *Not In My Back Yard* and refers to the fact that most people do not want waste disposal sites near their locality.

Role of micro-organisms in waste management and pollution control

Landfill sites

Most of our waste is disposed of in landfill sites. In these sites (dumps) the waste is covered with soil. Bacteria and fungi in the soil break down the organic (biodegradeable) materials.

Sewage

Sewage is waste from toilets, bathrooms and industry, and rainwater from drains.

- Primary sewage treatment involves physically screening waste and allowing it to settle. This removes large objects and solids.
- Secondary sewage treatment occurs when the waste is acted on by bacteria and fungi of decay. The liquid waste is aerated to allow this to happen. This **biological treatment** breaks down most of the organic matter.

  The remaining sludge is disposed of and the cleaned water is treated with chlorine to destroy any remaining organisms.
- Tertiary sewage treatment is sometimes used to remove mineral nutrients (such as phosphates and nitrates).

Control of waste production

Control of waste production can be achieved by implementing the three Rs: reduce, reuse, recycle.

4.18 *Biological treatment of sewage*

Reduce

Individuals (and societies) can reduce their waste output by reducing their consumption of goods that they do not really need.

In addition, they could reduce the amount of packaging used unnecessarily (as happened in Ireland when a charge was placed on plastic bags). If consumers request less packaging then governments and industry may act to reduce these wastes.

Reuse

Some objects can be reused. For instance, glass bottles can be reused up to forty times, after which they can then be broken down and recycled. Another example is the reuse of unwanted clothing by charities.

Recycle

Many modern materials can now be collected, treated and re-formed into new products. Examples include the recycling of paper, glass, different metals, plastics and organic waste.

Up to 40% of household rubbish is organic matter. This waste can be broken down by oxygen-requiring bacteria to form a dark-coloured material called compost or humus. This compost can be added to soil to improve the growth of plants.

Summary

Ecology is the study of the interactions between living things and their environment.

The biosphere:
- is the part of the planet (air, water, soil) in which life is found
- contains many ecosystems, e.g. desert, grassland, freshwater

A population is all the members of the same species in an area.

A community contains many different populations.

A habitat is the place in which an organism lives. It is also the area studied on field trips.

The distribution of organisms is affected by four sets of factors:
- abiotic (non-living) factors, which include altitude, aspect (i.e. north- or south-facing), steepness, currents, exposure
- biotic (living) factors, which include food, competition, predation, parasitism, pollination, seed dispersal, human activity
- climatic (long-term weather) factors, which include temperature, rainfall, humidity, day length, light intensity, moisture, wind, salinity (salt content)
- edaphic (soil) factors, which include pH, particle size, organic matter, water/air/mineral content

Aquatic (water) habitats have special problems compared to terrestrial (land-based) habitats. These problems include:
- light may not penetrate
- currents move organisms
- wave action moves and damages organisms
- salt content means organisms adapt to freshwater or saltwater
- oxygen is in lower concentration

The sun is the main source of energy for the planet. Energy flows in one direction, from the sun through the producers and into the consumers.
- Producers are autotrophic, i.e. make their own food.
- Primary consumers feed on producers. They are herbivores (plant eaters).
- Secondary and tertiary consumers feed on animals. They are carnivores (meat eaters).

A food chain is a one-to-one series of organisms, with each organism feeding on the previous member.
- A grazing food chain starts with a producer.
- A food chain is limited in length by the loss of 90% of the energy at each trophic level.
- Each feeding stage is a trophic level, e.g. producers, primary consumers, etc.
- In most food chains the number of organisms decreases along the chain.

A food web is a series of interlinked food chains.

A pyramid of numbers is a representation of the number of organisms at each trophic level.

A niche is the role an organism plays in the community.
- Organisms with identical niches will compete with each other.

Energy flows through an ecosystem, whereas nutrients (minerals) are recycled.

In the carbon cycle:
- carbon (dioxide) is removed from the environment by photosynthesis in plants
- carbon (dioxide) is returned to the environment by
  - respiration in plants, animals and micro-organisms
  - decay caused by micro-organisms
  - combustion
  - weathering

The role of micro-organisms in the nitrogen cycle is summarised below:

Role of micro-organisms in the nitrogen cycle

Type of bacterium	Location	Acts on	Product
Nitrogen fixing	Free in soil or in nodules in legumes	N_2 gas	Nitrates (NO_3)
Bacteria and fungi of decay	Soil	Dead organic matter	Nitrogenous waste (e.g. ammonia)
Nitrifying	Soil	Nitrogenous waste (e.g. ammonia)	Nitrates
Denitrifying	Soil	Nitrates	N_2 gas

Three ways in which humans affect ecosystems are pollution, conservation and waste management.
- Pollution is any harmful addition to the environment. It is caused by pollutants.

Ozone depletion is an example of air pollution.
- Ozone is a gas that absorbs ultraviolet radiation in the upper atmosphere.
- Ozone is broken down by manufactured chemicals such as CFCs.
- Ozone depletion results in increased skin cancers and cataracts, damage to plants and the immune systems of animals.
- Ozone depletion is being reduced by replacing CFCs with other chemicals (HFCs) which decompose before they reach the upper atmosphere and by not using sprays that contain CFCs.

Conservation is the wise management of existing resources, in order to maintain habitats and species. Conservation problems in fishing include:
- water pollution
- the use of nets with small mesh sizes
- depletion of fish stocks due to overfishing.

Eutrophication is the addition of nutrients to fresh water. This leads to a lack of oxygen in the water.
- Storing slurry (liquid animal wastes) and spreading it on land in dry summer weather helps to prevent fish kills in rivers and lakes. This is an example of good conservation practice.

Waste management involves preventing pollution and conserving the environment. Where possible it involves recycling. Examples of waste management are:
- in agriculture, slurry is stored and spread on dry land
- in the fishing industry, the waste parts of the fish are neutralised, pulped, dried and recycled as fertiliser or pig feed
- in forestry, any parts of trees not removed from the forest are allowed to decay and return nutrients to the soil

Important problems in waste disposal are:
- wastes may cause disease
- poisonous chemicals from wastes can enter drinking water supplies or plants
- waste nutrients can result in eutrophication and the death of aquatic plants and animals
- landfill sites may be unsightly, smelly and attract undesirable wildlife
- dumping at sea may lead to pollution of the sea
- incinerators may release toxic fumes

Micro-organisms break down organic waste in landfill sites.

Sewage treatment involves:
- primary (physical) treatment, which removes particles from the waste by screening and sedimentation
- secondary (biological) treatment, in which bacteria and fungi break down organic waste
- tertiary treatment, if used, removes minerals from the waste

The amount of waste we produce can be controlled by the three Rs.
- **R**educe the consumption of unnecessary materials.
- **R**euse as many materials as possible.
- **R**ecycle as much as possible.

Revision questions

1 Define: **(a)** ecology, **(b)** biosphere, **(c)** ecosystem, **(d)** abiotic factors, **(e)** edaphic factors, **(f)** a habitat.

2 **(a)** Name three parts of the biosphere.
  (b) Name a plant and an animal found in each part of the biosphere.

3 **(a)** Give three examples of ecosystems.
  (b) For each example, **(i)** state the main factors that define it, **(ii)** give a geographical location where it is found.

4 **(a)** Name the ecosystem or habitat you have studied.
  (b) Name a producer and a consumer from your habitat.
  (c) The number of producers and consumers is determined by four categories of factors. Name these categories.
  (d) Give one example from each category that affects the number of **(i)** producers, **(ii)** consumers, in your selected habitat.

5 Distinguish between each of the following, giving one example in each case: **(a)** climatic, and **(b)** edaphic, factors affecting living things in a habitat.

6 **(a)** Distinguish between sand and clay.
  (b) Give one advantage and one disadvantage for each soil type.

7 **(a)** What is humus?
  (b) Suggest three ways in which humus is of benefit to a producer.

8 Suggest a biological explanation for the following:
  (a) Waterlogged soils often cause plants to die.
  (b) Conifers survive on steep slopes better than broadleaved trees.
  (c) Plants grow better in summer in Ireland.
  (d) Mosses may grow better on one side of a tree.
  (e) Lawn grass does not survive in sandhills.
  (f) Limpets do not survive in freshwater.
  (g) Many plants produce flowers in spring or summer.

9 Give a reason, based on feeding, why plants can survive only in the upper layers of water, but animals can be found at great depths.

10 What problem does rainfall cause to animals in seawater pools?

11 Define each of the following and give one example from the ecosystem you have studied: **(a)** producer, **(b)** heterotroph, **(c)** primary consumer, **(d)** detritus feeders, **(e)** carnivore, **(f)** top consumer.

12 In the food chain:
  dandelion → *butterfly* → *robin* → *falcon*
  (a) What is the initial source of energy for the dandelion?
  (b) How many trophic levels are indicated?
  (c) Which way does energy flow?
  (d) What happens to the energy that does not pass to the next level?
  (e) Draw a pyramid of numbers to represent this food chain.

  (continued)

(f) If a herbicide is sprayed to kill the dandelion, suggest two negative effects this might have on the top consumers.

13 Most food chains are limited to about four (or fewer) trophic levels. Explain why this is the case.

14 Suggest the effects on a food chain of:
  (a) increasing the number of producers
  (b) disease killing off the primary consumers
  (c) an immigration of more top consumers

15 **(a)** Refer to the diagram of the carbon cycle (Figure 4.19) and name the processes represented by the letters A to H.
  (b) Why are the levels of CO_2 thought to be rising worldwide?
  (c) What are the possible results of a rise in CO_2 concentrations?

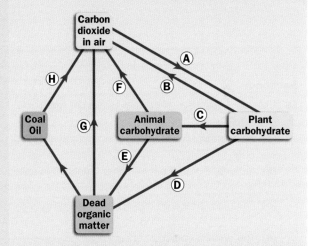

4.19

16 **(a)** Name three types of organism that have a role in the carbon cycle.
  (b) Outline the role of each type of organism in the carbon cycle.

17 **(a)** Why do plants and animals require nitrogen?
  (b) Why do plants not use atmospheric nitrogen?
  (c) In what form(s) do plants require nitrogen?
  (d) Name two processes that convert nitrogen gas into compounds that plants can use.

18 **(a)** Name four types of bacteria that play a role in the nitrogen cycle.
  (b) In the case of each bacterium, state:
    (i) where it is found, **(ii)** what it acts on, **(iii)** what it produces.
  (c) Three of these bacteria are beneficial and the other one is harmful. Explain why.

19 **(a)** What is meant by **(i)** pollution, **(ii)** pollutant?
  (b) Name any pollutant and state:
    (i) its effect on the environment
    (ii) any problem caused by this effect
    (iii) how the named pollutant can be controlled.

20 (a) What is meant by conservation?

(b) Outline one practice that helps to conserve fish stocks.

21 (a) Define eutrophication.

(b) State one cause of eutrophication.

(c) Explain why this process kills aquatic life.

22 State one waste product and explain how it is dealt with in each case for **(a)** agriculture, **(b)** fisheries, **(c)** forestry.

23 (a) Distinguish between primary and secondary waste treatment.

(b) Name four problems associated with waste disposal.

(c) Distinguish between physical and biological stages in waste management.

24 Name three practices that would result in the production of less waste.

25 Say whether the following statements are true or false. In the case of a false statement, give a reason why it is false.

(a) Animals are producers.

(b) Heavy rainfall can affect the salinity of the water in rock pools.

(c) Marram grass can grow only on a damp site.

(d) A trophic level denotes the height of an organism.

(e) A pyramid of numbers represents the relative numbers of organisms at each trophic level.

(f) Nitrifying bacteria produce ammonia gas (NH_3).

(g) The ozone layer causes global warming.

(h) Freon gas helps to produce ozone.

(i) Eutrophication is the reduction of minerals and nutrients in lakes.

(j) Methane gas is produced in biogas generators.

(k) Chlorine is used at the end of the sewage treatment process.

Sample examination questions

Section A

26 Use your knowledge of ecology to answer **four** parts of the following.

(a) An organism which makes its own food is called a(n) _____.

(b) An organism that eats another organism is called a _____.

(c) The place where an organism lives is called its _____.

(d) The primary source of energy in an ecosystem is the _____.

(e) The parts of the earth and atmosphere in which life is found is called the _____.

(2006 OL Q 1)

27 Answer the following questions in relation to the food web shown below.

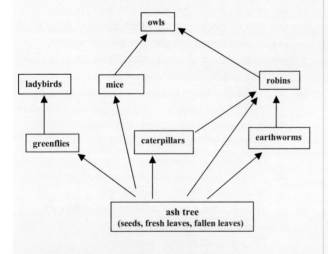

Write out a food chain with **four** organisms in it.
Name the primary producer in the web.
Name **two** secondary consumers in the web.

Name **two** herbivores in the web.
Name **one** omnivore in the web.
Name **one** carnivore in the web.

(2004 OL Q6)

28 Answer the following questions in relation to your study of ecology.

(a) What is the biosphere?

(b) What is meant by a qualitative survey? *(see Chapter 6)*

(c) Construct a grazing food chain containing at least four trophic levels.

(d) In your food chain in **(c)** identify each of the following.

1. A predator

2. A producer

3. A secondary (second order) consumer

4. A primary (first order) consumer

(2006 HL Q 2)

29 The following food chain is from a hedgerow.
hawthorn leaves → caterpillar → blue tit → sparrowhawk
Complete any four of the following by reference to this food chain.

(a) The primary consumer in this food chain is _____.

(b) If the number of sparrowhawks increases, the number of blue tits may _____.

(c) In this food chain the hawthorn leaves represent the _____.

(d) Name a carnivore from this food chain _____.

(e) The number of trophic (feeding) levels in this food chain is limited by the small transfer of _____ from one level to the next.

(2008 OL Q 1)

Section B

30 (i) What is meant by nitrogen fixation?

(ii) Name a group of organisms involved in nitrogen fixation.

(2008 OL Q 10)

Section C

31 (a) Answer the following questions in relation to the flow of energy through an ecosystem.

(i) What is the source of energy for the earth's ecosystems?

(ii) Name the process that takes place in plants in which this energy is converted to a usable form.

(iii) What substance do plants possess that allows them to carry out this conversion?

(iv) Energy flows along food chains. In the food chain A → B → C give an example of each from the organisms that you found in a **named** ecosystem.

(v) Is there more energy available for organism B or C? Explain your answer.

(vi) A food web can be thought of as a number of interlinked food chains. Using the named organisms A, B, C from **(iv)** above and **three** other named organisms, construct a food web that is found in the ecosystem you have studied.

(b) (i) Explain what is meant by pollution.

(ii) Give an example of pollution and describe how this form of pollution can be controlled.

(iii) Human populations are producing waste materials in ever-increasing amounts. Many of these wastes are serious threats to the environment.

1. Describe some of the problems associated with waste disposal.

2. Give an outline account of one example of waste management.

(iv) Explain what is meant by conservation.

(v) Give a brief account of a conservation practice with which you are familiar.

(2003 OL Sample Q 14)

32 (i) Explain what is meant by pollution.

(ii) Give an account of the effects of a **named** pollutant of domestic, agricultural or industrial origin.

(iii) Describe one way in which the pollution that you have indicated in **(ii)** might be controlled.

(iv) Outline the problems associated with the disposal of waste. Suggest two ways of minimising waste.

(2006 HL Q 10)

33 (a) Explain the following terms that are used in ecology: niche, edaphic factor, symbiosis.

(b) (i) What is the function of the nitrogen cycle?

(ii) What is meant by nitrogen fixation?

(iii) What is meant by nitrification?

(iv) Describe, using words and/or labelled diagrams, the events of the nitrogen cycle.

(2007 HL Q 12)

34 (i) Waste management is a matter of growing concern in Ireland as the population expands. Outline **three** problems associated with waste disposal.

(ii) Give an example of waste produced in agriculture or fisheries or forestry and describe how it is managed.

(iii) Suggest **two** methods of waste minimisation.

(iv) Give one example of the use of micro-organisms in waste management.

(2008 HL Q 10)

*For latest questions go to **www.edco.ie/biology***

Chapter 5 **Higher level ecology**

Pyramids of numbers

A pyramid of numbers represents the number of organisms at each trophic level in a food chain.

Normally a pyramid of numbers is shown as a modified bar chart. In general the numbers decrease as you proceed up the chart, as shown in Fig. 5.1.

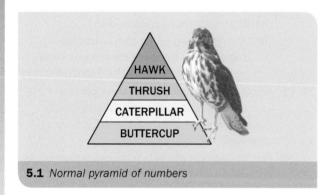

5.1 *Normal pyramid of numbers*

Inference of pyramid shape

Two inferences can be drawn from the normal shape of a pyramid of numbers.

■ The number of organisms declines as you go up a pyramid of numbers. This happens due to the large energy losses (about 90%) between each trophic level. This means there is less energy available to the organisms higher up the pyramid.

■ The body size of the organisms usually increases as you go up a pyramid of numbers. This is mainly because bigger animals tend to eat smaller animals, e.g. hawks are bigger than thrushes.

Limitations of pyramids of numbers

■ Pyramids of numbers do not take into account the size of the organisms. One million microscopic plankton will be represented by a wide rectangle. A huge oak tree will be represented by a narrow rectangle.

Therefore, two main shapes of pyramid are possible, a normal pyramid and an inverted pyramid.

Parasitic food chains can give rise to an inverted pyramid of numbers, e.g. many tiny mites can live on a single greenfly (as shown in Fig. 5.2).

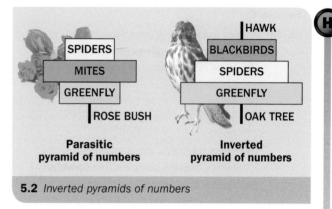

5.2 *Inverted pyramids of numbers*

■ The numbers can be so great that the pyramid cannot be drawn to scale. For example, millions of greenfly might live on a single oak or hundreds of millions of bacteria could live on a decomposing whale.

Population control

A **population** comprises all the members of a species living in an area. We speak of a population of oak trees in a woodland, a population of rabbits in a locality or the population of humans on earth.

A number of factors tend to reduce the population when numbers are high and increase the population when numbers are low. These factors mainly act on birth rates (causing more or less offspring to be produced) and death rates (causing more or less offspring to die).

In affecting birth and death rates, these factors help to maintain a balance in population numbers called the balance of nature. This allows the population to remain close to the number of organisms that the habitat can support.

Factors that control populations

The factors that control the size of a population include:

■ competition
■ predation
■ parasitism
■ symbiosis

The ways in which these factors work to control the numbers of organisms will be dealt with in the following sections.

Competition

> **Competition** occurs when organisms actively struggle for a resource that is in short supply.

The consequence of competition is that the number of organisms is reduced. Plants compete for resources such as space, light, water and minerals. Animals compete for food, water, shelter, territory and reproductive rights (mates).

> **Intra-specific competition** takes place between members of the same species.

For example, bladder wracks compete with each other for space on rocks.

> **Inter-specific competition** occurs between members of different species.

For example, blackbirds and thrushes compete for insects and snails.

It is vital that species should avoid competition if they are to survive. They do this by adapting to their environments. These adaptations may involve changes in feeding habits, camouflage, protective coats, alterations to mouth parts and reproductive strategies.

Types of competition

There are two main types of competition: contest competition and scramble competition.

CONTEST COMPETITION

> In **contest competition**, there is an active physical contest between two individual organisms.

Contest competition results in one individual getting the resource, while the second is left without it.

A good example of contest competition is the way in which animals such as birds or deer select and defend an area or territory. This territory is used for feeding, nesting, reproduction and raising young. It is usually selected and defended by the male animal.

By displaying territorial behaviour, only the fittest animals can reproduce. This helps to improve the species. It also reduces population growth and helps conserve food supplies.

5.3 *Contest competition: European starlings fighting*

SCRAMBLE COMPETITION

> In **scramble competition**, all of the competing individuals get some of the resource.

Scramble competition may mean that none of the individuals get as much of the resource as they need and they may not be able to grow and reproduce efficiently.

An example of scramble competition is the overcrowding of seedlings in flower beds. Unless some of the seedlings are removed, none of them will get sufficient light, water, minerals or space and they all will grow poorly and fail to flower.

Scramble competition causes large changes in population sizes and in general it reduces the numbers in a population.

5.4 *Scramble competition: a purple orchid flowering in a meadow, surrounded by buttercups*

Did you know?

An adaptive technique to survive competition...
The caterpillar of the cabbage white butterfly chews on cabbage leaves, while the adult butterfly drinks nectar from flowers. In this way they avoid competition for food.

THE STUDY OF LIFE

Predation

Predation is the catching, killing and eating of another organism.

A **predator** is an organism that catches, kills and eats another organisim.

The **prey** is the organism that is eaten by the predator.

Examples of predators and their prey include ladybirds and aphids, blackbirds and earthworms, hawks and mice, whelks and mussels.

The predator–prey relationship is used in the area of biological control of pests. This involves the use of one organism to control the numbers of another. For example, ladybirds are used to control aphids, and certain types of bacteria are used to control the larvae of butterflies and prevent them from destroying crops (e.g. cabbage).

5.5 *Predator and prey: a ladybird eating a greenfly*

Adaptations of predators and prey

PREDATORS

Features that improve the efficiency of predators include the following:

- Hawks and other birds of prey have excellent sight so that they can locate their prey.
- Ladybirds have strong mouth parts to enable them to chew aphids.
- Whelks produce an acid that dissolves through the shell of mussels, limpets or barnacles.

PREY

Features that assist prey species to avoid being eaten include the following:

- Mice flee and hide to avoid being eaten.
- Frogs are well camouflaged so that they are hard to see and attack.
- Ladybirds contain large amounts of formic acid, which is unpalatable to predators. Predators learn to avoid eating the brightly coloured ladybirds.

Parasitism

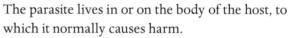

Parasitism occurs when two organisms of different species live in close association and one organism (the **parasite**) obtains its food from, and to the disadvantage of, the second organism (the **host**).

The parasite lives in or on the body of the host, to which it normally causes harm.

Exoparasites (also called ectoparasites) live on the outside of the host. Examples include fleas on a dog, mosquitoes or blood-sucking leeches on human skin and aphids such as greenfly on a rose bush.

Endoparasites live inside the host. Examples include liver flukes in sheep and cattle, potato blight fungus in potato plants, bacteria of disease in the human body and tapeworms in human intestines.

Parasites are often thought of as predators. They differ from predators by:

- being smaller than the host
- often attacking from within
- being dependent on one particular host
- doing only a small amount of damage to the host so that they do not harm their food source or their home

Therefore, parasites often do not significantly reduce the numbers of their host. However, in some cases (e.g. potato blight infection or disease-causing bacteria) they can reduce the numbers in a population.

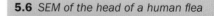

5.6 *SEM of the head of a human flea*

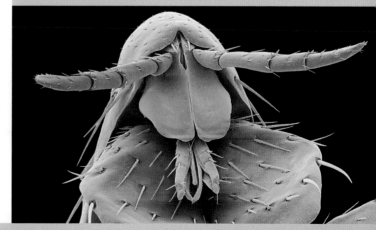

Symbiosis

Symbiosis occurs when two organisms of different species live (and have to live) in close association and at least one of them benefits.

There are a number of different types of symbiosis. For example, parasitism is a form of symbiosis (the parasite gets the benefit of food but the host is harmed).

Another form of symbiosis is **mutualism**. In this case *both* organisms benefit from the association. Symbiosis is often taken to refer to mutualism.

Examples of symbiosis (or mutualism) include:
- cellulose-digesting bacteria in mammal intestines, where the mammal gets digested food and the bacteria get shelter, warmth, moisture and food
- bacteria in the large intestines of humans, which produce vitamins B and K and get food and shelter
- lichens (which are composed of an alga and a fungus). The algae get protection, minerals and support, while the fungus gets food
- nitrogen-fixing bacteria in the nodules of plants such as clover. The bacteria gain food, shelter, anaerobic conditions and the clover gets nitrates.

Symbiosis increases the numbers of both organisms involved in the relationship.

5.7 *Lichens growing on a rock*

Population dynamics

Population dynamics refers to the factors that cause population numbers to change.

Predator–prey relationships

The numbers of predator and prey are inter-related. As the number of prey builds up, the number of predators will rise. This will result in more of the prey being killed and so their numbers will fall. This in turn will result in fewer predators and so their numbers will fall.

Eventually the numbers of prey will begin to rise again, starting the cycle once more. This repeated pattern is shown in Figure 5.8.

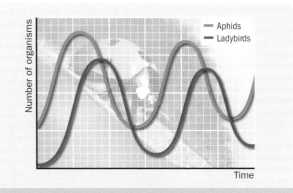

5.8 *The predator–prey relationship*

The variables or factors that contribute to predator–prey interactions include:
- **Availability of food.** A large number of prey can cause an increase in the numbers of predators. As the prey are killed off there is less food for the predators and their numbers decline. This in turn allows the numbers of prey to rise again.
- **Concealment.** The prey are prevented from being totally wiped out because, when their numbers are low, they may successfully conceal or camouflage themselves so that the predators can no longer locate them easily. This allows a small population of prey to survive and eventually to re-establish itself.
- **Movement of predators.** If the number of prey is so small that the predator cannot easily catch sufficient numbers to survive, the predators normally move to areas where the prey are more numerous. This allows the prey in the old location to increase in number.

The balance between factors such as these results in a repeated cyclical change in the numbers of predators and prey.

Human population growth

Since the origin of modern humans (some time in the last 150 000 years) our numbers initially increased slowly. By 400 AD, Chinese and ancient Roman records kept for tax purposes indicate that the world's population was about 100 million. By 1650 it was still below 500 million.

Human numbers passed 2000 million (2 billion) in the early 1930s, 4000 million in the mid-1970s and had passed 6000 million in the year 2000. By 2008 there were over 6.8 billion people on earth.

World population is now increasing by about 85 million people each year (this is equivalent to about 230 000 additional people each day or 160 every minute).

The rapid increase in human numbers in recent years is often referred as the 'population explosion'. The growth in human population is shown on the graph in Figure 5.9.

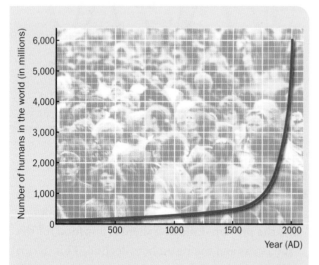

5.9 *The human population explosion*

5.10 *World population is increasing by about 85 million people every year*

It is important to realise that although the world's population is rising continuously, the rate at which it is rising may be slowing down (see table below).

Human population growth rates		
Year	Number of years taken to produce 1 billion extra humans	Number of humans (billions)
1832	~ 100,000	1
1932	100	2
1962	30	3
1977	15	4
1989	12	5
2000	11	6
2010	12	7
2024	14	8

Future predictions are extremely difficult to make. Some experts predict that the world's population will stabilise at around 10.5 billion sometime later this century. Others predict that it will continue to increase to above 12 billion by the year 2050.

The increasing number of humans is not due to an increase in birth rates. In fact, birth rates are declining in many countries, especially in developed countries. In this context it should be noted that about 66% of the world's population lives in Asia. The increase in population has been caused by reduced death rates.

Factors affecting human population numbers

Some of the factors that influence human population numbers are war, famine, contraception and disease.

WAR

In general, war reduces human population numbers due to death. However, these effects can be temporary because an increase in birth rates (baby boom) often follows a war.

FAMINE

A lack of food leads to malnutrition and death due to disease or starvation. This was seen in the Great Irish Famine of 1845–47, when about one million people died of starvation and disease.

Although some countries still suffer from famine, the cause is generally related to food distribution problems rather than absolute food shortages. Advances in agricultural techniques have so far allowed food supplies to match population growth.

CONTRACEPTION

Increased availability of contraceptives has reduced birth rates since the 1960s. This is particularly evident in developed countries. For example, in much of western Europe and the USA the average number of children born to a woman (the fertility rate) is about 2.1. This is close to the level needed to ensure that the population remains constant.

The fertility rate in developing countries has fallen from 6.1 in 1970 to about 3.1 today. Much of this decline can be attributed to increased use of contraceptives.

THE STUDY OF LIFE

DISEASE

The ability to control and cure disease was mainly developed in the 20th century. The use of vaccines has reduced the incidence of diseases such as typhoid, cholera, diphtheria, TB, polio and many others. Smallpox was declared to have been eradicated worldwide in 1980 – the first disease ever wiped out by humans.

Improved sanitation and the use of insecticides have helped to control diseases such as malaria, yellow fever and sleeping sickness.

Safe anaesthetics, improved surgical methods and new drugs have combined to save many lives. The use of antibiotics (since 1940) has prevented many deaths caused by bacterial infections.

All of these disease-control methods have helped to reduce the death rate and increase human numbers. This is especially so in developed countries.

5.11 *Cervical cancer vaccination*

Summary

A normal pyramid of numbers indicates that:
- the number of organisms falls as you ascend each pyramid
- the body size of the organisms increases as you ascend each pyramid

Some pyramids of numbers are not standard because:
- the size of the organisms can change the standard shape
- it may not be possible to represent large numbers of organisms correctly

A population is made up of all the members of a species living in an area.
- The factors that control the numbers in a population act mainly on the birth and death rates.
- Factors controlling population size include competition, predation, parasitism and symbiosis.

Competition occurs when two or more organisms seek a scarce resource.
- Intra-specific competition takes place between members of the same species.
- Inter-specific competition involves different species.

Competition reduces population numbers. The two main types of competition are:
- contest competition, where one organism gets the resource, while the second is left without
- scramble competition, which means that all of those competing get some (but often not enough), of the resource

Predation is the catching, killing and eating of another organism. A **predator** catches, kills and eats other organisms. **Prey** are the organisms that are eaten.
- Predation initially increases the number of predators and decreases the number of prey.
- The numbers of predators and prey often show repeated cycles of rising and falling numbers.

A parasite is an organism that feeds from and harms another organism.
- Exo- or ectoparasites live on the outside of the host.
- Endoparasites live inside the host.
- Parasites sometimes reduce the numbers in a population, but often have little effect on host numbers.

Symbiosis occurs when two organisms from different species live (and are are usually obliged to live) in close association for the benefit of at least one of the organisms. Symbiosis (often called mutualism) increases the numbers of both species. Symbiosis includes:
- parasitism (where one organism benefits but the other is harmed)
- mutualism (where both organisms benefit)

Population dynamics refers to factors that cause changes in population numbers. Predator–prey numbers interact due to:
- availability of food, which increases predator numbers when high but reduces them when low
- concealment, which means that some prey survive by hiding from the predators
- movement of predators, which means that predators move to new areas when prey numbers are low

Human population growth has continued to rise rapidly since the 1900s because of falling death rates.
- Factors affecting human population numbers include war, famine, contraception and disease control.
- War normally reduces population numbers temporarily.
- Famine reduces population numbers.
- The increased use of contraceptives has reduced the birth rate and the rate of population growth, especially in developed countries.
- Improved disease-control methods have reduced the death rate and caused an increase in human numbers.

THE STUDY OF LIFE

Revision questions

1 (a) Draw the pyramid of numbers you would expect for each of the following food chains.
   (i) *grass → grasshopper → pheasant → fox*
   (ii) *oak tree → caterpillar → blackbird → hawk*
   (iii) *rose bush → caterpillars → mites*
(b) Name the type of pyramid in each case.
(c) Account for the difference in shape between the pyramids in (i) and (iii) above.
2 (a) Draw a pyramid of numbers to show a dead whale, worms feeding off the dead flesh, parasitic lice feeding off the worms.
(b) What factor(s) affect the shape of this pyramid?
(c) Why is this pyramid difficult to draw to scale?
3 In the pyramid of numbers shown in Figure 5.12:
(a) Name the producer.
(b) Name the secondary consumer.
(c) Name the organism at the third trophic level.
(d) Why is the rectangle for rabbits larger than that for foxes?
(e) Give a reason for the fox flea rectangle being so large.

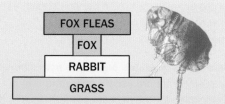

5.12

4 (a) Distinguish between contest and scramble competition.
(b) Give one example of each of these types of competition.
(c) State one way in which each type of competition can affect the numbers in the competing populations.
5 Naming one example in each case, describe what is meant by **(a)** predation, **(b)** predator, **(c)** prey.
6 In a predator–prey relationship give one reason in each case for the following:
(a) The number of prey controls the number of predators.
(b) The number of predators controls the number of prey.
(c) The predators rarely kill all the prey.
(d) The predators survive even when the number of prey is small.
7 Name one adaptation in each case used by **(a)** predators and **(b)** prey, to improve their survival rates. Explain the benefit of each adaptation.
8 (a) What is meant by symbiosis?
(b) Give two examples of symbiosis, and in each case, state how the organisms benefit from the process.

9 Referring to Figure 5.13, answer the following.
(a) Estimate human numbers in **(i)** 1000 AD, **(ii)** 1500 AD.
(b) In what year did human numbers reach 1000 million?

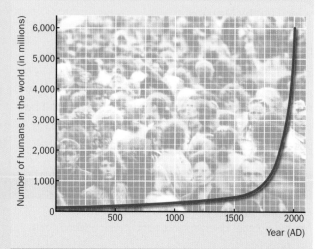

5.13

10 (a) Name and explain the effects of two factors that tend to reduce human numbers.
(b) Account for the present increase in human numbers.
11 Human numbers are rising faster in developing countries than in developed countries. Give two reasons why this is the case.
12 Name three disease-control techniques that have affected human population numbers in the last 100 years.
13 Say whether the following statements are true or false. In the case of a false statement, give a reason why it is false.
(a) A parasite is an organism that provides food for a host.
(b) There are always more predators than prey in a habitat.
(c) Animals compete for mates, territory, shelter, light and food.
(d) Bacteria living on human teeth is an example of symbiosis.
(e) Between 1989 and 2000, the world's human population increased by 1 billion.
(f) In a pyramid of numbers, the number of carnivores is always greater than the number of herbivores.
(g) Population numbers are controlled by competition, predation, parasitism and symbiosis.

Sample examination questions

Section B

14 (a) In ecology what is meant by a trophic level?

(b) Complete the pyramid of numbers by naming an organism in each case of A, B, C and D. (*Note: the examiners gave no marks for naming D.*)

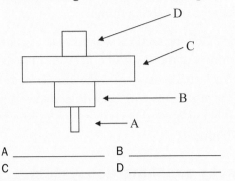

A _____   B _____
C _____   D _____

(c) Which letter represents the producer in the pyramid?

(d) Comment on the relative sizes of an individual producer and an individual primary consumer in the pyramid.

(2007 HL Q 2)

Section C

15 (i) What term do ecologists use to describe an animal which kills and eats other animals?

(ii) What term is used to describe the animal that is killed and eaten?

(iii) If the population of the animals in **(ii)** declines suggest **two** possible consequences for the animals in **(i)**.

(iv) Give **four** factors that influence the size of the human population.

(2007 HL Q 12c)

16 (a) (i) What does an ecologist mean by competition?

(ii) Distinguish clearly between <u>contest competition</u> and <u>scramble competition</u>.

(b) Read the following extract, study the graph below and answer the questions that follow.

'The application of pesticides to strawberry plants in an attempt to destroy cyclamen mites that were damaging the strawberries killed both the cyclamen mites and the carnivorous mites that preyed on them. But the cyclamen mites quickly re-invaded the strawberry fields while the mites that preyed on them returned much more slowly. The result was that the cyclamen mites rapidly increased in density and did more damage to the strawberries than if the pesticide had never been applied.'

(Adapted from W.T. Keeton and J. L. Gould. 1993. *Biological Science.* New York: W.W. Norton & Co.)

(i) Which graph, A or B, represents the carnivorous mites? Explain your answer.

(ii) What term is used to describe the relationship between the cyclamen mites and the carnivorous mites?

(iii) Suggest **two** reasons why the cyclamen mite managed to quickly re-invade the strawberry fields.

(iv) Suggest an alternative to the use of pesticides for controlling the cyclamen mite population.

(v) Draw a pyramid of numbers to include each of the organisms mentioned in the extract above.

(vi) Apart from competition and the factor illustrated in the above example, state another factor that limits population growth.

(2008 HL Q 10)

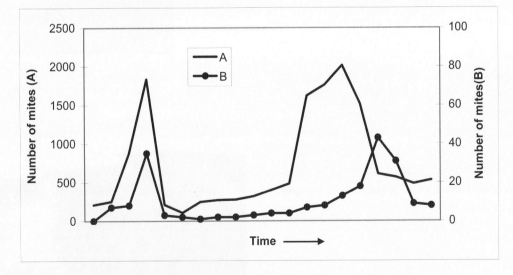

Previous examination questions

Ordinary level	Higher level
n/a	2004 Q 10, 2007 Q 2, Q 12, 2008 Q 10

For latest questions go to www.edco.ie/biology

Chapter 6 **Study of an ecosystem**

Syllabus

*You are required to carry out a practical investigation of **any one ecosystem**. The results of this special investigation should be presented in the form of a portfolio of work carried out.*

Working through Activities 2 to 5 as outlined later in this chapter is the correct procedure for preparing your portfolio.

Within your chosen ecosystem you are required to study ten organisms. These must include five animals (fauna) and five plants or algae (flora). A detailed knowledge is required of any one animal or plant.

Diversity of ecosystems

Ireland offers a wide range of ecosystems. Depending on your location, it is possible to study ecosystems such as a rocky seashore, rock pool, grassland, hedgerow, stream, freshwater pond, old wall, small woodland, waste land, overgrown garden or peatland.

Syllabus

*You are required to study **one ecosystem**. The type of ecosystem you choose will depend on your local circumstances. This chapter will focus on two representative ecosystems: a rocky seashore and a grassland.*

Rocky seashore

A **rocky seashore** is a mixed ecosystem, i.e. it is both aquatic (water) and terrestrial (land). It is a harsh environment in that there is no soil, wave action occurs, there are periodic tidal changes and general exposure to sun and wind. It is a particularly easy ecosystem to study because many of the organisms are stationary and cannot easily hide below ground. It shows clear changes (called zonation) in organisms from the water's edge to the high rocks.

Grassland

A **grassland** is an ecosystem that is maintained by cutting or grazing. For these reasons it is not a fully natural environment. Due to cutting, grazing or the application of fertilisers and weedkillers the grassland may not have a full range of natural plants.

By comparison, an unnused meadow may have a wider range of living things.

The following sections will provide a general overview of the range of organisms in each of the two selected ecosystems. The inter-relationships of the organisms with each other and with the non-living (abiotic) parts of each ecosystem will also be outlined.

Rocky seashore ecosystem

A rocky seashore is normally divided into four zones, based on tidal movements:

- The **splash zone** is that area on the higher ground which is rarely (if ever) covered by the tide.
- The **upper shore** is the area covered by high tides, but not by normal tides.
- The **mid shore** (intertidal zone) is covered by the incoming tide and exposed at normal low tide.
- The **lower shore** is exposed only at very low tides. Very often the organisms here are similar to those found in rock pools.

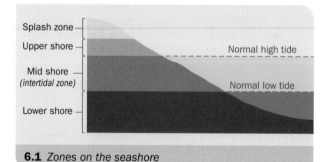

6.1 *Zones on the seashore*

6.2 *A rocky seashore habitat*

Organisms found on a rocky seashore

In the following examples some adaptations of the organism to its habitat are given in brackets.

Splash zone

Flora in the splash zone must be able to withstand high salt levels.

FLORA

- Sea pink, a flowering plant (often found in crevices, has narrow leaves with many hairs to reduce water loss).
- Lichens, which may be black, orange, grey or green. These grow on the rocks above the water level.

6.3 *Sea pink and lichens*

ANIMALS

- Black periwinkles (herbivores on lichens and algae, motile (i.e. able to move), have lungs).
- Shore crab (carnivore or scavenger, strong pincers for opening shells, flat body to shelter under rocks).

6.4 *Common or edible crab*

Upper shore

FLORA

- Green algae such as sea lettuce (contain lots of chlorophyll, which allows them to carry out photosynthesis at high light levels).
- Channel wrack (brown seaweed covered in mucilage to retain moisture, attached to rock by a holdfast, fronds are folded to hold water, can survive if out of the water 90% of the time).

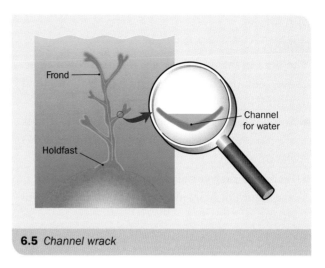

6.5 *Channel wrack*

ANIMALS

- Sand hoppers (detritus feeders on dead seaweed, nocturnal, i.e. active at night, hop rapidly to avoid being eaten).
- Barnacles (tiny animals attached to rocks, covered in shell plates, feet are feathery and project from the shells to filter plankton when covered by tide, a lid closes over to protect when tide is out).

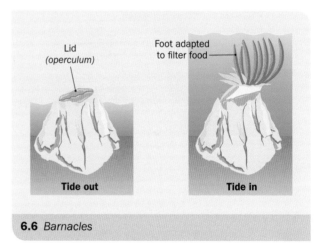

6.6 *Barnacles*

6.7 *Whelks (larger shells) and barnacles*

Mid shore

FLORA

The flora in the mid shore are mainly brown algae. These contain a brown pigment which allows them to absorb light in dimly lit waters.

- Spiral wrack (upper reaches of mid shore, fronds are twisted, can survive if out of the water 60% of the time).
- Bladder wrack (air bladders allow it to float for maximum light, can survive out of water 50% of time).

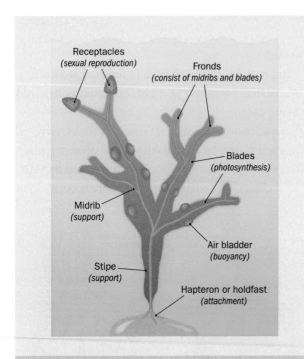

6.8 Bladder wrack

6.9 Bladder wrack

ANIMALS

- Dog whelk (carnivore that bores through shells of barnacles, mussels and limpets using a sharp tongue and acid).

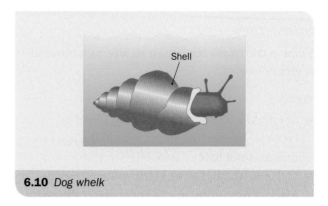

6.10 Dog whelk

- Limpet (herbivore, feeds on algae growing on rocks when the tide is out, returns and attaches to the same place on the rocks when tide comes in).

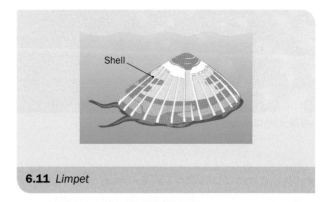

6.11 Limpet

6.12 Limpets

- Mussels (attach to rocks by threads, filter feeders on plankton when tide is in).
- Edible periwinkle (scrapes algae off rocks, heavy protective shell, can breathe out of water for a short time).

6.13 A mussel

Lower shore

The flora in the lower shore are mainly brown and red algae. Red algae contain high levels of the pigment carotene, which absorbs light in dim conditions.

FLORA

- Serrated wrack or *Fucus serratus* (edges of fronds are zig-zag shaped, does not tolerate lack of water).

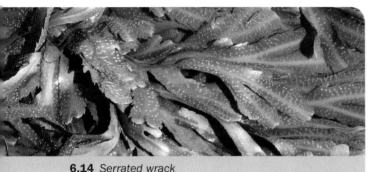

6.14 *Serrated wrack*

- Corallina (pink alga growing on rocks, red pigments allow it to absorb light in very dim conditions, must be covered by water).

ANIMALS

- Sponges (attach to rocks, filter feeders on plankton and detritus).

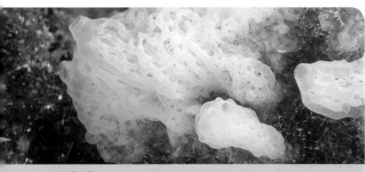

6.15 *Yellow sponge*

- Flat periwinkle (feeds on wrack, does not tolerate lack of water, breathes through gills, dislikes high temperatures).

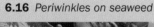

6.16 *Periwinkles on seaweed*

Grassland ecosystem

A grassland is usually an artificial ecosystem. It is maintained by human (and livestock) activities. These activities may include fertilising, cutting, draining, spraying, trampling and grazing. For these reasons the grassland may not contain a wide variety of plant, and therefore, animal life.

Grasslands are often maintained as a monoculture (i.e. only one species of plant or grass is encouraged to grow).

6.17 *A grassland habitat*

Organisms found in grasslands

PLANTS

The defining species in a grassland are grasses. Sometimes only one species of grass is found, but often a number of grass species are growing. Clover is often sown in grasslands because it contains nitrogen-fixing bacteria. These form nitrates and reduce the need for the artificial addition of expensive fertiliser.

6.18 *Root nodules on the roots of white clover*

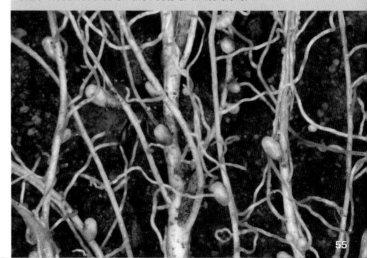

Other plants that are often found in grasslands include buttercups, dandelions, daisies and nettles. If the ground has been disturbed you may find poppies, thistles and dock (leaves). Near a hedge you may find hedgerow plants such as primrose or bluebells.

6.19 *Poppies (red) and daisies*

6.20 *Dandelion (before flower opens, in flower and in seed)*

ANIMALS

In the grass and soil you will find earthworms, snails, slugs, spiders and beetles.

On the leaves of some of the plants you may find aphids (mostly small greenflies which drink sugar-water from the leaf), ladybirds (which eat aphids) and caterpillars (which chew the leaves). On the flowers you may find bees, wasps, butterflies and moths.

Larger animals may include rabbits, badgers, foxes, hedgehogs, thrushes, blackbirds and hawks.

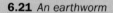
6.21 *An earthworm*

6.22 *Aphids on a leaf*

6.23 *Blackbird with a worm*

6.24 *A hedgehog*

6.25 *Fox cub feeding on a rabbit*

Scientific study of an ecosystem

Due to the large size of ecosystems it is not possible to study all of an ecosystem. Instead, local areas of study are selected from within the ecosystem. These areas of study are called habitats. If the habitats are well chosen and if a number are studied for the ecosystem, they provide a fair reflection of the ecology of the overall ecosystem.

Identification of habitats

At a **rocky seashore** the habitats would comprise a number of strips. Each strip could be 1 metre wide, running from the high rocks down to the water's edge.

In a **grassland** a number of sample areas (normally ten) are studied using a square frame called a quadrat.

The quadrats may be chosen at random in the grassland. Alternatively the quadrats may be placed one after another in a line. This second method can be used to show how living things differ along a line or strip of land (e.g. from the base of a hedge out into the field or from a hill down to a wet piece of land near a stream).

A habitat study

A **habitat study** involves the five main steps summarised below:

1 Map the habitat(s).
2 Identify the plants and animals present.
3 Estimate the numbers of plants and animals.
4 Measure the environmental (abiotic) factors.
5 Present the information gathered.

The habitat should be studied on a number of occasions, e.g. autumn, winter and spring/summer if possible.

Mapping the habitat

Although it is not essential to do so, a simple hand-drawn map (or photograph) of the ecosystem can be quickly made. This helps to give an overall impression of the area being studied.

Figures 6.26 and 6.27 show sample results.

Identify plants and animals

The easiest way to identify organisms is to have an expert name them for you in the habitat. Alternatively, there are excellent pocket guidebooks available for most habitat types.

Where these methods are not successful, use an identification key in the field (habitat) as described below (Activity 2). Collect organisms and identify them back in the laboratory only when identification on the site is impossible.

When collecting plants and animals it is important to be sensitive to the ecology of the ecosystem. This involves the following rules:

- Follow the Countryside Code (i.e. ask permission to enter private land, close gates, cause no damage to fences etc., leave no litter).
- Only collect an organism if it is absolutely necessary and you cannot identify it in the field.
- Return organisms to the habitat if possible.
- Leave the habitat as you found it.
- Beware of dangers such as deep water, waves, thorns, stinging insects, bulls and aggressive dogs.

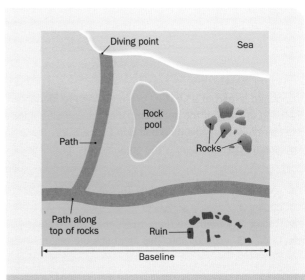

6.26 *Map of a rocky seashore habitat*

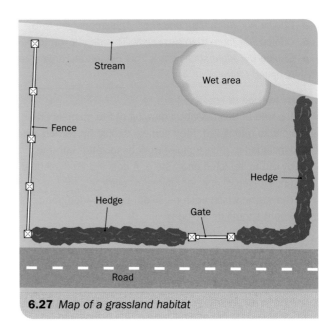

6.27 *Map of a grassland habitat*

Activity 2 *To use simple keys to identify any five fauna and any five flora*

Identification

Plants and animals are identified using keys. A wide range of keys is available. Some deal with seaweeds alone, others with flowering plants, trees, insects, etc. In addition charts, guidebooks and photographs can be used to identify organisms.

The simplest type of key is a so-called 'spider' key. These are so named because of their shape. They are often used to place an organism into a major category. The spider key presented opposite can be used to identify the four animals in Figure 6.28.

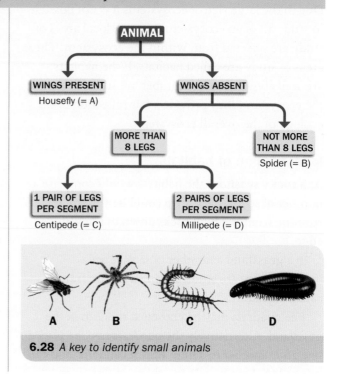

6.28 *A key to identify small animals*

Opposite is part of a key that could be used to identify shelled animals at the seashore. This key could be used to identify the organisms A and B in Figure 6.29. The procedure used to identify the organisms is as follows:

For organism A:

- Choice number 1 = *attached*. This means you go to choice 2.
- Choice 2 = *worm-like tube*. This sends you to choice 3.
- Choice 3 = *coiled tube*. This identifies the organism as *Spirorbis*.

For organism B:

- Choice number 1 = *attached*. This means you go to 2.
- Choice 2 = *not worm-like*. This sends you to 4.
- Choice 4 = *more than one shell*. This sends you to 5.
- Choice 5 = *more than two shells*. This sends you to 6.
- Choice 6 = *eight shell plates*. This means the organism is called *Chiton*.

Presentation of results

By the end of this activity, a drawing of five animals and five plants (along with their names) should be carried out and included in a portfolio of work associated with the study of the selected ecosystem. A detailed study should be undertaken of any one animal or plant.

The way in which each organism gets its food (mode of nutrition) should be included.

In addition, the reproductive parts of any flowering plants should be drawn and their method of pollination (e.g. wind or insect) should be stated. A magnifying lens may be helpful for these drawings.

Finally, the habitat of each of the ten organisms should be identified on the original map of the ecosystem.

Identification key

Choice		Go to
1	Attached to rocks or similar	2
	Free moving	8
2	Worm-like (tubular)	3
	Not worm-like	4
3	Triangular shape	*Pomatoceras*
	Coiled tube	*Spirorbis*
4	Cone shaped, single shell	Limpet
	More than one shell	5
5	Two dark blue shells	Mussel
	More than two shells	6
6	Six shell plates in pyramid	Barnacle
	Eight shell plates	*Chiton*

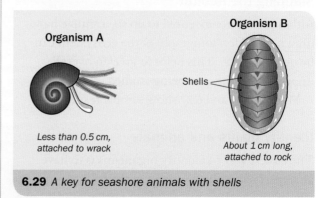

6.29 *A key for seashore animals with shells*

Activity 3 *To use various pieces of apparatus to collect plants and animals in an ecosystem*

Collecting plants

Plants are collected by breaking off a piece of the plant (preferably with flowers and leaves). Store them in labelled plastic bags.

Collecting animals

Animals that do not move, or move slowly, can be collected directly by hand. For other animals, a variety of devices are used, as shown in the following table.

Mammals can be collected using special live mammal traps. Earthworms can be collected by pouring water, to which potassium permanganate (or formaldehyde or washing up liquid) is added, on to the soil. The worms crawl to the surface and are collected, washed and stored.

Devices for collecting animals *(Note: You do not have to use all of these devices.)*		
Device	**Use**	**Collects**
Pooter Flexible tube Suck in here Gauze Jar Insect	Suck the organism into the jar.	Insects, spiders, sand hoppers
Beating tray Centipede Spider Handle Beetle	Place under bush. Shake or beat the plants to knock the organisms down.	Insects, caterpillars, spiders
Pitfall trap Rock Stone Jar Periwinkle	Place tin or jar in soil or sand. Cover to prevent rain entering.	Crawling insects, snails, periwinkles
Sweep net Strong handle Net Butterfly	Swept through long grass or at the edge of a hedge.	Insects
Plankton net Fine mesh Plankton Collecting jar	Drawn through water from a rock or a boat. Plankton collect in the jar.	Plankton
		(continued overleaf)

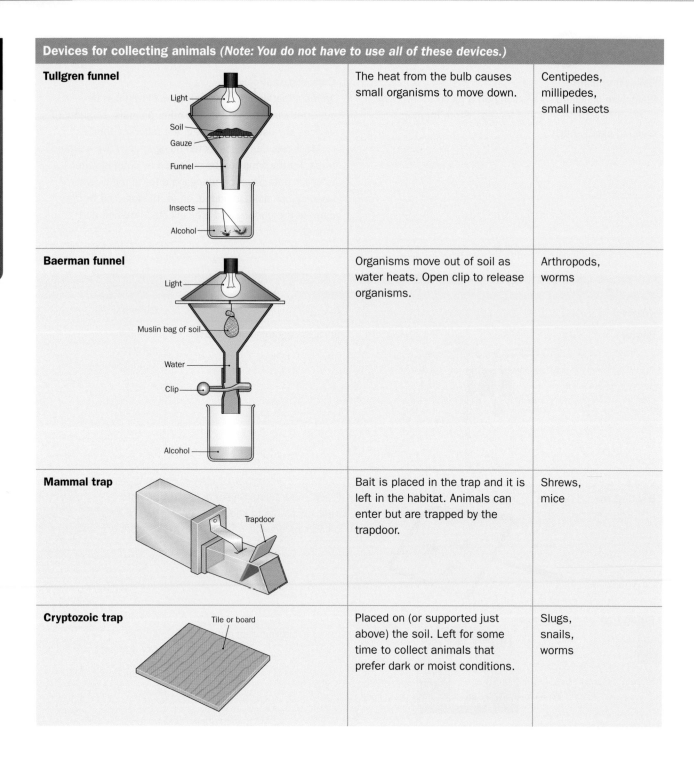

Devices for collecting animals *(Note: You do not have to use all of these devices.)*

Tullgren funnel Light, Soil, Gauze, Funnel, Insects, Alcohol	The heat from the bulb causes small organisms to move down.	Centipedes, millipedes, small insects
Baerman funnel Light, Muslin bag of soil, Water, Clip, Alcohol	Organisms move out of soil as water heats. Open clip to release organisms.	Arthropods, worms
Mammal trap Trapdoor	Bait is placed in the trap and it is left in the habitat. Animals can enter but are trapped by the trapdoor.	Shrews, mice
Cryptozoic trap Tile or board	Placed on (or supported just above) the soil. Left for some time to collect animals that prefer dark or moist conditions.	Slugs, snails, worms

Qualitative vs. quantitative study

A **qualitative study** records the presence or absence of something.

A **quantitative study** records the numbers or amounts that are present.

A **qualitative study** is carried out by identifying and naming the species directly in the habitat or by collecting and later naming the species.

A **quantitative study** of a habitat gives the numbers of each species that are in the habitat.

A quantitative study provides a great deal more information than a qualitative study.

THE STUDY OF LIFE

Activity 4 *To carry out a quantitative study of a habitat*

Select a suitable sample area of the ecosystem to study. This local area of study is called a habitat. Within any habitat there are two methods of calculating the numbers of each species.

Subjective estimates involve an individual judgement as to how numerous an organism is in the habitat. This method is flawed because individuals may have different estimates for the same species in a habitat.

Objective estimates are better because they do not rely on individual judgements. A grid quadrat is often used to provide an objective estimate.

Quantitative survey of plants (and stationary animals)

Quadrats

A quadrat is a square made of metal, wood or plastic. Quadrats can vary in size, but typically have sides of 1 m, 0.5 m or 0.25 m. A quadrat is thrown randomly (over the shoulder is best) into the habitat. Alternatively they can be laid out in a line across part of the habitat. The species within each quadrat are examined as a guideline to what is present within the overall habitat.

The use of quadrats is limited by the fact that fast-moving animals will not remain in a quadrat. Also they are limited by the size of the species, e.g. if used in a woodland they would indicate that there are no trees present (as no tree would be inside a quadrat).

Within each quadrat two sets of measurements are taken: percentage cover and frequency.

PERCENTAGE COVER

The percentage cover is an estimate of the amount of ground in a quadrat covered by any species. Within each quadrat the percentage cover of each species is estimated by using one of two methods.

■ **Subjective estimate.** The area of a quadrat covered by each species is calculated as a percentage of the total area of the quadrat.

For example, a pencil was thrown at random over the shoulder ten times in a grassland habitat. A 0.5 m² quadrat was placed (centred) at each of the ten locations.

Within each quadrat the percentage of the area covered by each type of plant (i.e. the % cover) was estimated. Sample results are shown in the table at the bottom of the page (remember you must study at least five plants).

These results show that grass covered 70% of quadrat 1, 90% of quadrat 2, etc. Dandelions covered 15% of quadrat 1, but were not present in quadrat 3 etc.

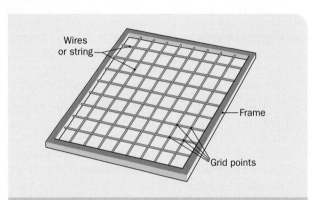

6.30 *A graduated or grid quadrat*

6.31 *A student using a grid quadrat*

Percentage cover of plants (subjective estimate)

| Name of plant | % cover in each quadrat ||||||||||| Total % cover | Average % cover |
	1	2	3	4	5	6	7	8	9	10		
Grass	70	90	100	80	70	100	40	70	60	80	760	76
Dandelion	15	10	0	0	0	0	0	5	0	0	30	3
Buttercup	5	0	0	0	20	0	0	15	40	0	80	8
Daisy	10	0	0	0	10	0	0	5	0	20	45	4.5
Thistle	0	0	0	20	0	0	10	5	0	0	35	3.5

Percentage cover of plants (objective estimate)

| Name of plant | Number of grid points covered in each quadrat | | | | | | | | | | Total no. grid points covered | Total no. grid points | Average % cover |
	1	2	3	4	5	6	7	8	9	10			
Grass	74	92	100	84	67	100	37	70	55	77	756	1000	75.6
Dandelion	13	8	0	0	0	0	0	4	0	0	25	1000	2.5
Buttercup	4	0	0	0	23	0	0	16	40	0	83	1000	8.3
Daisy	9	0	0	0	10	0	0	5	0	21	45	1000	4.5
Thistle	0	0	0	16	0	0	9	5	0	0	30	1000	3

■ **Objective estimate.** A grid quadrat is a square frame subdivided by wires or string. The quadrat is placed over the pencil as before. Instead of calculating (estimating) the percentage of each quadrat covered by each type of plant, a more objective method is used.

Count the number of times each plant touches a point of intersection (grid point) of each small square. Then express this figure as a percentage of the number of squares.

For example, if dandelions touched the top right of 26 squares in the quadrat shown, then the % cover of dandelions in the quadrat would be calculated as:

$$\frac{\text{Number of points covered}}{\text{Total number of grid points}} \times \frac{100}{1} = \frac{26}{100} \times \frac{100}{1} = 26\%$$

A table prepared in this way will appear similar to the one at the top of this page, but the percentages are more accurate than those found by the subjective method on the previous page.

FREQUENCY

The frequency is the chance of finding a named species with any one throw of the quadrat.

To calculate the frequency of bladder wrack or serrated wrack it is sufficient to record whether they are present or absent in each quadrat, as shown in the table below.

$$\frac{\text{Number of quadrats containing the plant}}{\text{Total number of quadrats}} \times \frac{100}{1}$$

The frequency for bladder wrack is: $\frac{4}{10} \times \frac{100}{1} = 40\%$

The frequency for serrated wrack is: $\frac{3}{10} \times \frac{100}{1} = 30\%$

This method is fast and easy to use. It has the disadvantage of being dependent on the organism and quadrat size and presumes that organisms are evenly distributed throughout the habitat.

Transects

Transects are used where changes along a gradient are suspected, e.g. across a rocky seashore or from one side of a field to another. They are non-random, because you decide where they should be placed. There are two types of transects.

LINE TRANSECT

A line transect is a string or rope marked off at regular intervals, e.g. 25 cm or 1 m. The names of the plants or animals that touch the line are recorded. Line transects are of limited use, as they sample only a narrow strip of the habitat.

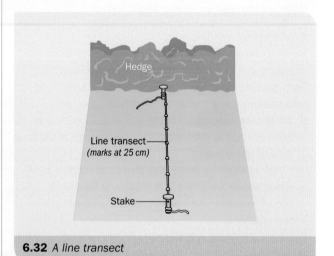

6.32 *A line transect*

Frequency of plants in each quadrat

| Name of plant | Quadrat number | | | | | | | | | | Total | Frequency |
	1	2	3	4	5	6	7	8	9	10		
Bladder wrack	✓	✓	✓	✓	–	–	–	–	–	–	4	40%
Serrated wrack	–	–	–	✓	✓	✓	–	–	–	–	3	30%

The frequency is calculated as:

BELT TRANSECT

Belt transects consist of two ropes parallel to each other with (usually) 1 m^2 squares made out by tying lengths of string between the two ropes. They are laid down across the habitat to form a series of quadrats in a line (as shown in Figure 6.33).

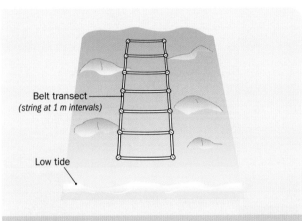

Belt transect
(string at 1 m intervals)

Low tide

6.33 *A belt transect*

Alternatively, the same effect can be achieved by placing one edge of a quadrat along a line transect. The contents of each square can be sampled in the same way as normal quadrats or graduated quadrats (i.e. percentage cover and frequency).

The environmental conditions should be measured at each mark or quadrat of a transect.

Quantitative survey of animals

Quadrats and transects are suited to estimating the numbers of plants and animals that do not move too fast (such as barnacles, limpets and mussels).

The capture–recapture method is used to calculate the number of moving animals in a habitat.

Capture–recapture method

This method involves capturing a number of animals of the same species, marking them and releasing them unharmed. The animals should be marked in such a way as not to endanger them.

On a second visit (some day(s) later), a similar number of animals is collected. Some of these will be marked. The total number of animals can be calculated from the formula:

$$\text{Number} = \frac{\text{C 1st} \times \text{C 2nd}}{\text{M 2nd}}$$

(where **C 1st** = number of animals caught and marked on 1st visit

C 2nd = number of animals caught on 2nd visit

M 2nd = number of animals marked on 2nd visit)

EXAMPLE 1

Sixty snails were caught and marked with paint on the lower edge of their shells. They were released into the habitat. Two days later sixty more snails were collected. Fifteen of these were marked. Calculate the number of snails in the habitat.

ANSWER 1

$$\text{Number of snails} = \frac{\text{C 1st} \times \text{C 2nd}}{\text{M 2nd}}$$

$$= \frac{60 \times 60}{15}$$

$$= 240$$

EXAMPLE 2

In attempting to estimate the number of wild deer in a woodland, 40 deer were trapped. A tag was placed in the ear of each deer and they were released. A week later 40 more deer were trapped, of which 16 had ear tags. A week later 40 more deer were trapped, of which 20 had ear tags.

(a) Calculate the population range of deer in this woodland.

(b) Calculate the mean (average) population size of deer in this woodland.

ANSWER 2

(a) Compare the 1st and 2nd visits.

$$\text{Number of deer} = \frac{\text{C 1st} \times \text{C 2nd}}{\text{M 2nd}}$$

$$= \frac{40 \times 40}{16}$$

$$= 100$$

Compare the 1st and 3rd visits (for the calculations the 3rd visit is now called the 2nd visit).

$$\text{Number of deer} = \frac{\text{C 1st} \times \text{C 2nd}}{\text{M 2nd}}$$

$$= \frac{40 \times 40}{20}$$

$$= 80$$

Therefore, population range = 80 to 100 deer

(b) Mean population size $= \dfrac{80 + 100}{2}$

$$= 90 \text{ deer}$$

The capture–recapture method can be used for animals such as snails, crabs, periwinkles, woodlice (all marked with paint), fish, whales, seals, deer (tagged) and birds (legs are ringed).

The capture–recapture technique makes the following assumptions.

1 Marking must not harm the animals (e.g. make it more visible to predators).
2 Animals mix evenly in the habitat (i.e. they are not bunched as in colonies of ants or shoals of fish).
3 Animals are restricted to a local area.
4 Marked animals must be given time to mix with the unmarked population.

Results of habitat study

The information gathered in habitat (and therefore ecosystem) studies can be displayed in a number of ways for inclusion in a portfolio.

As an example, consider the results of a belt transect at the seashore as shown in the following tables. These charts could be extended to include all the flora and, later, all the animals found in the belt transect.

Number of animals

Quadrat number	Black periwinkle	Barnacle	Limpet
1	4	0	0
2	2	20	0
3	0	36	0
4	0	15	4
5	0	0	6

% cover of flora

Quadrat number	Sea pink	Yellow lichen	Channel wrack
1	30	0	0
2	10	30	20
3	0	10	30
4	0	0	30
5	0	0	10

6.34 Using a pooter to catch ants

PRESENTING THE RESULTS OF A HABITAT STUDY

These results can then be presented in association with a profile map as in Figure 6.35. This helps to explain the trends as you move down the seashore.

Alternatively, the numbers of plants and animals can be shown on histograms as indicated by Figure 6.36.

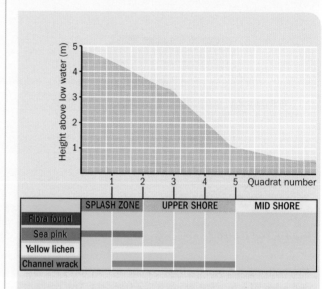

6.35 Relating the results of a habitat study to a profile map of the habitat

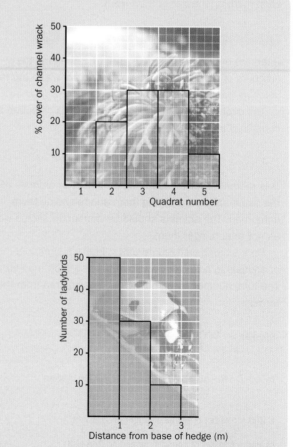

6.36 Results of a habitat study

Sources of error in an ecosystem study

The possible sources of error in studying an ecosystem can be considered under four headings.

Human error

When studying an ecosystem it is possible to make mistakes in measuring or recording information. This possibility is increased by the work being outdoors, perhaps in poor weather. For example, there is an element of judgement to be made in deciding if a plant covers 20% or 30% of a quadrat. Equally, a transect may be located in an area that is easy to survey, but this area may not be typical of the ecosystem.

Changing conditions

Nature is never static or constant. Ecosystems are subject to changes, both natural (e.g. seasonal) or artificial (e.g. the effects of pollution). As a result, the findings of an ecosystem study may not apply all of the time to that ecosystem.

To allow for the influence of changing conditions it is best to study an ecosystem a number of times, e.g. in autumn, winter and spring.

Accidental discovery

Accidental discoveries have played a significant role in many areas of science. In the study of an ecosystem it is often possible that accidental discoveries will play an important role.

For example, if an animal is very shy it will be scared off by a class visit but may be discovered by an individual walking quietly in the ecosystem. Alternatively, a rare animal (such as a bird of prey) may be present in the area only on rare occasions or at night (e.g. owls).

Sample size

A single habitat may not be a fair representation of the entire ecosystem. For this reason, a number of habitats are studied within each ecosystem. The larger the number of habitats examined, the more accurately the results will reflect the overall ecosystem.

Equally, the size of each habitat studied is important. If the habitat is too small, many plants and animals will be left out of the study.

Influence of abiotic factors

The influences of three abiotic factors on animal and plant life are given below.

Rocky seashore

EXPOSURE

The length of time that a plant can survive when exposed out of the water has a huge influence on where it can grow. There is usually a clear relationship between exposure to the air and the growth of the three species of wrack.

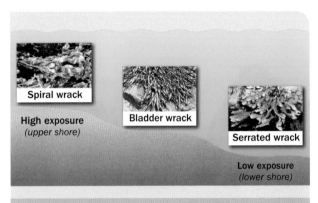

6.37 *Zonation of wracks on the seashore*

Limpets feed safely when out of water. As there are not enough algae on the upper shore, this restricts limpets to the mid shore (i.e. there are sufficient algae and they can feed when the tide is out).

Mussels on the lower shore are usually bigger than those on the mid shore (due to being covered by the tide more often). This allows them to feed more often.

AIR TEMPERATURE

There can be up to four species of periwinkle found on a rocky seashore. Each of them has a tolerance for a different maximum temperature. This causes them to be limited to certain regions of the seashore.

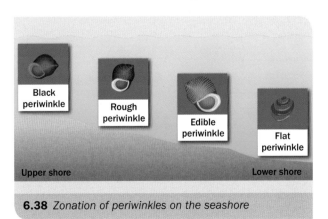

6.38 *Zonation of periwinkles on the seashore*

WAVE ACTION

If you compare a sheltered shore with a shore exposed to greater wave action, you will note two main features:

- Different plants can be found higher up on the exposed site. This is due to increased cover by waves or by spray.
- Plants with large fronds (e.g. wracks) suffer more damage and are replaced on exposed shores by species with narrow fronds, such as thong weed and corallina.

6.39 *Rocks on a wave-exposed shore*

Grassland

LIGHT INTENSITY

Light intensity is lower near a hedge. This normally means that there is less grass growing at the base of a hedge compared with the middle of a field.

SOIL TYPE

Soils can be sandy, clay or loam based. Sandy soils contain large soil particles and allow easy root penetration and good drainage. Clay soils have small particles, which results in difficult root penetration and poor drainage. Loam soils are a mixture of sand and clay and provide ideal conditions for grassland plants.

PH OF SOIL

Most grassland plants prefer a neutral or slightly basic soil pH. Acid soils are mainly associated with boglands and support a totally different community of plants.

6.40 *Grassland with different light intensities*

6.41 *Clay soil (top left), sandy soil (bottom left) and loam-based soil (centre right).*

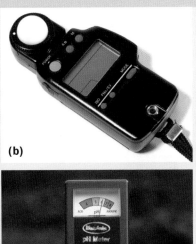

6.42 (a) *A pitfall trap sunk in soil (flat-topped cover lifted to one side)* **(b)** *Light meter* **(c)** *pH meter* **(d)** *Catching a butterfly with a sweep net*

Activity 5 *To investigate three abiotic factors in a selected ecosystem*

Abiotic factors are non-living factors that affect an organism's ability to live in a habitat. There is a wide range of abiotic factors, some of which are relevant only to particular habitats.

Samples of abiotic factors are given for the rocky seashore and a grassland ecosystem. Other possible abiotic factors might include the percentages of air, water and humus in the soil.

Syllabus

Depending on the ecosystem being studied, only three abiotic factors are required. In general these readings should be taken at each habitat or quadrat studied.

Rocky seashore

1 The degree of exposure to the air (i.e. when the tide is out) can be judged by comparing the location of each organism on the upper, middle or lower shore.
2 Air temperature should be taken in the shade, using a thermometer. The temperature of rock pools should be taken at different depths.
3 The effects of exposure to wave action can be investigated by examining habitats on exposed shores and comparing them with those on more sheltered locations.
4 The aspect (i.e. the direction it is facing) of the seashore can be determined with a compass. This may relate to prevailing currents and, in turn, the size of the waves.

Grassland

1 Air temperatures in different parts of the grassland are taken using a thermometer.

2 The soil pH is recorded using a pH meter or universal indicator. The indicator, along with some distilled water, is added to a small soil sample in a test tube. A little barium sulfate is added to cause soil particles to clump (flocculate). This means the water is less cloudy. The colour is compared with the colour on the chart provided to find the exact pH.
3 Light intensity is measured with a photographic light meter. These readings are taken in different locations, varying from near a hedge to farther out. Care should be taken to avoid mixing bright sunshine readings with cloud cover readings.
4 If the grassland is sloping then its aspect (i.e. direction it is facing) can be discovered using a compass. Aspect will affect light intensity and temperature (i.e. both are higher on south facing sides of grasslands). It also has a bearing on exposure to prevailing winds.
5 Wind speed and direction can be measured using an anemometer and wind gauge. The rate of rotation of the marker cup is measured.

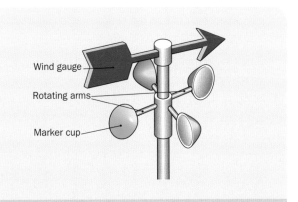

6.43 *An anemometer and wind gauge*

Adaptations

Evolution ensures that only those organisms that are suited (adapted) to their environment will survive.

An **adaptation** is any alteration that improves an organism's chances of survival and reproduction.

Examples of adaptations in the two selected habitats are given in the following table.

6.44 *Dandelion seeds dispersing in the wind*

Sample adaptations			
Ecosystem	**Organism**	**Adaptation**	**Benefit**
Rocky seashore	Bladder wrack	Covered with mucilage	Retains moisture when tide is out
	Limpets	Shell	Protection and water retention
Grassland	Dandelions	Seeds have parachutes	Easily dispersed and not overcrowded
	Ladybirds	Brightly coloured	Easily seen and recognised (and avoided – ladybirds are full of acid)

Reporting the results of the study of a selected ecosystem

1 A report outlining the main details and especially the results obtained in Activities 2, 3, 4 and 5 should be drawn up. This report should form part of a portfolio of work relating to these activities.

2 Include a title and the date or dates when each aspect of the work was carried out in this report.

3 Write a brief report to include:
   - a map of the ecosystem and habitats selected
   - the procedures used to collect organisms
   - details of how the organisms were identified
   - an account of how the numbers of organisms were estimated

Suitable diagrams should be included in the report where possible.

4 Present the results for five fauna and five flora in the form of tables, histograms, pie-charts or other suitable methods.

   Present sample food chains, food webs and pyramids of numbers, based on your results. Sample food chains, food webs and pyramids of numbers are given in Chapter 4.

5 Comment on any possible errors or difficulties that may have arisen and on any local ecological issues that may relate to the chosen ecosystem.

6 Local factors relevant to a particular habitat should be noted and investigated. These factors might include the effects of a local sewage works, factory, dump, town or village, harbour, road or path, crops in the field and spraying patterns.

THE STUDY OF LIFE

Summary

Two sample ecosystems are featured in this chapter: the rocky seashore and the grassland.
- You are required only to study any one ecosystem, and to know five animals and five plants from your ecosystem.

Rocky seashore

Zone	Flora	Animals
Splash	Sea pink, lichens	Black periwinkles, shore crabs
Upper shore	Channel wrack	Sand hoppers, barnacles
Mid shore	Spiral wrack, bladder wrack	Dog whelk, limpet
Lower shore	Serrated wrack, corallina	Mussels, edible periwinkle, sponges, flat periwinkle

Grassland

Plants			Animals H = herbivore, C = carnivore, O = omnivore, D = detritus feeder (detritus is dead and decomposing organisms)		
Grasses	Daisies	Dock	Earthworms (D)	Caterpillars (H)	Rabbits (H)
Clover	Nettles	Primrose	Snails (H)	Ladybirds (C)	Badgers (O)
Buttercups	Poppies	Bluebell	Slugs (H)	Bees (H)	Foxes (C)
Dandelions	Thistles		Spiders (C)	Wasps (H, C)	Hedgehogs (O)
			Beetles (C, H, O)	Butterflies (H)	Thrushes (C)
			Aphids (H)	Moths (H)	Blackbirds (O)

The study of an ecosystem involves studying a number of sample habitats, as follows:
- mapping
- identifying plants and animals
- estimating the numbers of plants and animals
- measuring the environmental (abiotic) factors
- presenting the information

Collecting plants and animals involves some of the methods shown in the table below.

A habitat is the place where an organism lives or the local area of study within an ecosystem.

Collection methods

Device	Procedure	Collected	Device	Procedure	Collected
Knife	Cut	Plants, limpets	**Plankton net**	Sweep through water	Plankton
Trowel	Dig	Plants, animals in soil	**Tullgren funnel**	Heat soil (using a lamp)	Small organisms from soil
Pooter	Suck	Insects	**Baerman funnel**	Heat soil in water	Small organisms from mud
Beating tray	Shake bushes	Insects	**Mammal traps**	Set the trap	Mammals
Pitfall trap	Sink into soil or sand	Crawling animals	**Potassium permanganate solution**	Pour onto soil	Earthworms
Sweep net	Sweep through grass	Insects	**Cryptozoic trap**	Place on ground	Slugs, snails, worms, woodlice

A suitable key is used to identify and name organisms.

A qualitative study records the presence or absence of species.

A quantitative study records the number of each species. Quantitative studies can be:

- subjective (i.e. a personal judgement is made as to the number)
- objective (i.e. an independent method of calculating numbers is used)

Subjective methods are not recommended, because they depend on individual judgements, which may vary from person to person.

Errors may arise in the study of an ecosystem in the following ways:

- mistakes may be made in judgement and recording
- conditions change in the ecosystem over time
- accidental discoveries may be made
- the habitats studied may not accurately reflect the overall ecosystem

A quantative study of plants in a habitat involves using:

- quadrats, which are examined for:
  - (a) Percentage cover of plants or stationary animals.
  - (b) Frequency
- transects:
  - (a) Line transect (rope marked at intervals – record what touches the line).
  - (b) Belt transect (equivalent to quadrats taken in a line – methods used are the same as for quadrats).

A quantitative study of animals in a habitat involves using:

- the capture–recapture method, i.e.

$$\text{Number} = \frac{\text{C 1st} \times \text{C 2nd}}{\text{M 2nd}}$$

Three abiotic factors are measured and their effects are related to the organisms that are present in one selected ecosystem as shown in the following table:

Three sample abiotic factors		
Ecosystem	**Sample factors**	**Measured by**
Rocky seashore	Exposure to air	Position on shore
	Air temperature	Thermometer
	Wave action	Compare sheltered and exposed habitats
Grassland	Air temperature	Thermometer
	Soil pH	pH meter or universal indicator
	Light intensity	Light meter

The influence of the abiotic factors measured is examined for one ecosystem, as in the table below.

Effects of abiotic factors		
Ecosystem	**Abiotic factor**	**Influence**
Rocky seashore	Exposure	Different species of wrack and animals are found on different zones of the shore
	Temperature	Periwinkles are arranged along a temperature gradient
	Wave action	High wave action forces plants higher on the shore, and favours species with narrow fronds
Grassland	Air temperature	Temperature differences in different parts of the grassland will affect how well the plants (and animals) grow
	Soil pH	Soil pH will favour some plants and therefore some animals
	Light intensity	Grasses grow better at higher light intensities

Organisms show many adaptations that allow them to survive in their habitat.

The results of a study can be presented in tables, lists, charts, graphs, diagrams, etc.

- The results of a study should include food chains, food webs, and pyramids of numbers.
- The work carried out in Activities 2–5 should be presented in a portfolio.

Revision questions

1 (a) Name five ecosystems that can be studied.
   (b) Name the ecosystem you have studied.
   (c) From this ecosystem, name five flora and five fauna.

2 For any one animal or plant in your study state:
   (i) its range in height, weight, size, colour or any other measurable factor
   (ii) any adaptation it displays to the named ecosystem.

3 Give two different food chains from your chosen ecosystem.

4 From your ecosystem (or habitat) give one example of each of the following:
   (a) producer
   (b) herbivore
   (c) carnivore
   (d) scavenger
   (e) detritus feeder
   (f) top consumer.

5 (a) Name five plants from the habitat you have studied.
   (b) Give two distinguishing features, (e.g. colour, shape, size, adaptation, location) for each one.
   (c) For each plant, name a different animal that feeds on it.

6 (a) Distinguish between an ecosystem and a habitat.
   (b) Name the five main procedures carried out when studying a habitat.

7 (a) Give a food chain from your habitat.
   (b) Indicate each of the following on the food chain:
      (i) producer
      (ii) consumer
      (iii) herbivore
      (iv) carnivore
      (v) third trophic level.

8 Draw a food web for the habitat you have studied.

9 (a) Name two methods in each case used to collect:
      (i) plants
      (ii) animals.
   (b) Draw labelled diagrams of three pieces of apparatus used for collecting animals.
   (c) Explain how each piece of apparatus is used and give examples of what may be collected using the named apparatus.

10 Use this key to answer the questions that follow.

1	Segmented legs	2
	No legs	6
2	Three pairs of legs	Insect
	More than three pairs of legs	3
3	First and second pairs of legs equal	Harvest spider
	Legs not equal	4
4	Rounded body	Mite
	Elongated body	5
5	One pair of legs per segment	Centipede
	Two pairs of legs on most segments	Millipede

Organism A   Organism B

6.45

(a) Name the organisms shown in Figure 6.45.
(b) Using the information in the key above, state five features of centipedes.
(c) Name the following animal: it has four pairs of segmented legs, with the first two pairs being equal in length.

11 The following is part of a key used to identify animals from a freshwater pond.

1	Soft bodied	2
	Hard covering or shell on body	6
2	Tentacles at end of body	Hydra
	No tentacles on worm-like body	3
3	Body not divided into segments	4
	Body divided into segments	5
4	Body rounded, like a thread	Roundworm
	Body flat, like a ribbon	Flatworm
5	Suckers absent	16
	Suckers present	Leech
6	Limbs not present	7
	Limbs present	9
7	Two shells present	Freshwater mussel
	One shell present	8
8	Shell not spiralled	Freshwater limpet
	Shell spiralled	Pond snail

(a) Use the information in the key to draw a diagram of **(i)** a leech, **(ii)** a roundworm.
(b) Name the animal that fits the following description: it has no limbs, but has a single shell which is not spiralled.
(c) State two differences between a roundworm and a leech.

12 A woodland was 20 m wide and 30 m long. Ten quadrats (each 0.5 m × 0.5m) were thrown and the number of bluebells in each was counted. The results are shown below.

Quadrat number	Number of bluebells
1	4
2	2
3	0
4	0
5	2
6	6
7	4
8	2
9	0
10	0

Calculate: **(a)** the frequency of bluebells, **(b)** the total number of bluebells growing in the wood.

13 In estimating the number of periwinkles in a habitat 80 periwinkles were collected, marked and released. Some time later 80 more periwinkles were collected in the same habitat. Only 64 of these were marked.

(a) Suggest one way to collect periwinkles for this study.

(b) Suggest one way to mark the periwinkles.

(c) What name is given to this method of calculating animal numbers?

(d) Calculate the number of periwinkles in the habitat.

14 A woodland measured 5 km × 2 km. In attempting to find the number of blue tits in the woodland a habitat 100 m × 100 m was used. Thirty blue tits were trapped in this area and marked. They were then released. The next day 30 more blue tits were trapped, of which 25 were marked. The next day 30 more were trapped, all of which were marked. Calculate:

(a) the population range of blue tits in **(i)** the habitat, **(ii)** the woodland

(b) the average number of blue tits in **(i)** the habitat, **(ii)** the woodland

15 Suggest any two reasons why your survey may not produce an absolutely accurate description of life in the selected ecosystem.

16 (a) List three abiotic factors measured in a named ecosystem.

(b) Suggest how each factor might influence the distribution of two named plants and two named animals.

Sample examination questions

Section A

17 (a) A 2.5 hectare field was surveyed for clover plants using the quadrat method. A quadrat of side 0.5 m was used. The results of the survey are shown in the table below.

Quadrat number	1	2	3	4	5	6	7	8	9	10
Number of plants	6	2	2	2	4	0	2	5	5	2

Estimate the number of clover plants in the field. (1 hectare = 10 000 m²)

(b) A survey of field mice was carried out in the field mentioned in **(a)** using the capture/recapture method. The field mice were caught using small mammal traps which were set at random points in the field. Forty field mice were captured, tagged and released at their capture points. One month later the traps were again set at the same locations and forty field mice were caught. Five of these were found to be tagged. Estimate the population density of the field mice in numbers per hectare.

(2003 HL Sample Q 5)

Section B

18 (a) (i) What is meant in ecology by a **quantitative** survey?

(ii) What is a quadrat frame?

(b) (i) In the case of a **named** plant describe how you would carry out a quantitative survey in the ecosystem that you have studied.

(ii) Describe how you recorded the results of your survey.

(iii) Suggest a possible source of error in your study.

(2006 OL Q 8)

19 (a) (i) What is meant in ecology by a **quantitative** survey?

(ii) What is a quadrat frame?

(b) Answer the following questions in relation to a quantitative survey of plants that you carried out.

(i) How did you use the quadrat frame to carry out the survey?

(ii) Why did you use a number of quadrats or use the quadrat frame a number of times?

(iii) How did you identify the plants?

(iv) How did you present your results?

(v) Is the quadrat method suitable for animal populations? Explain your answer.

(2007 OL Q 9)

20 (a) (i) What is a habitat?

(ii) What is an ecosystem?

(b) Answer the following questions by reference to a named ecosystem that you have investigated. Name the ecosystem.

(i) List **three** abiotic factors that you investigated.

(ii) For each of the three abiotic factors that you have listed describe how you carried out the investigation.

(iii) In the case of a **named** organism give an adaptation feature that you noted.

(iv) Briefly explain how the adaptation feature that you have given in **(iii)** is of benefit to the organism.

(2008 HL Q 7)

Section C

21 Answer the following questions <u>in relation to a named ecosystem you have investigated</u>.

(i) Name the ecosystem.

(ii) Describe how you collected a **named** animal.

(iii) State one way in which a **named** organism was adapted to the ecosystem.

(iv) What is meant by an abiotic factor?

(v) Give **two** abiotic factors that you investigated.

(vi) In relation to the abiotic factors you have named, describe how you measured each one.

(2007 OL Q 10)

22 Describe how you carried out a quantitative survey of a **named** animal in the ecosystem that you have studied.

(2006 HL Q 10)

23 (i) Give an account of how you carried out a quantitative survey of a named plant species in an ecosystem that you have studied. In your answer describe how you recorded the results of your survey.

(ii) As a result of a disease, a species of plant disappeared from an ecosystem. Suggest **three** possible effects of the disappearance of this plant on the populations of other plants and animals in the ecosystem.

(2005 HL Q 12)

24 Answer the following questions by reference to an ecosystem that you have studied.

(i) Name the ecosystem.

(ii) Name **two** habitats from the ecosystem.

(iii) Name an animal that is present in one of these habitats and describe **one** way in which it is adapted to that habitat.

(iv) Describe briefly how you carried out a quantitative survey of a **named** plant found in the ecosystem.

(2008 OL Q 10)

Previous examination questions	
Ordinary level	**Higher level**
2003 Q 8	2003 Q 5
2004 Q 8	2005 Q 12c
2005 Q 10b	2006 Q 9, 10b
2006 Q 8	2008 Q 7
2007 Q 9, 10c	
2008 Q 10b	

*For latest questions go to **www.edco.ie/biology***

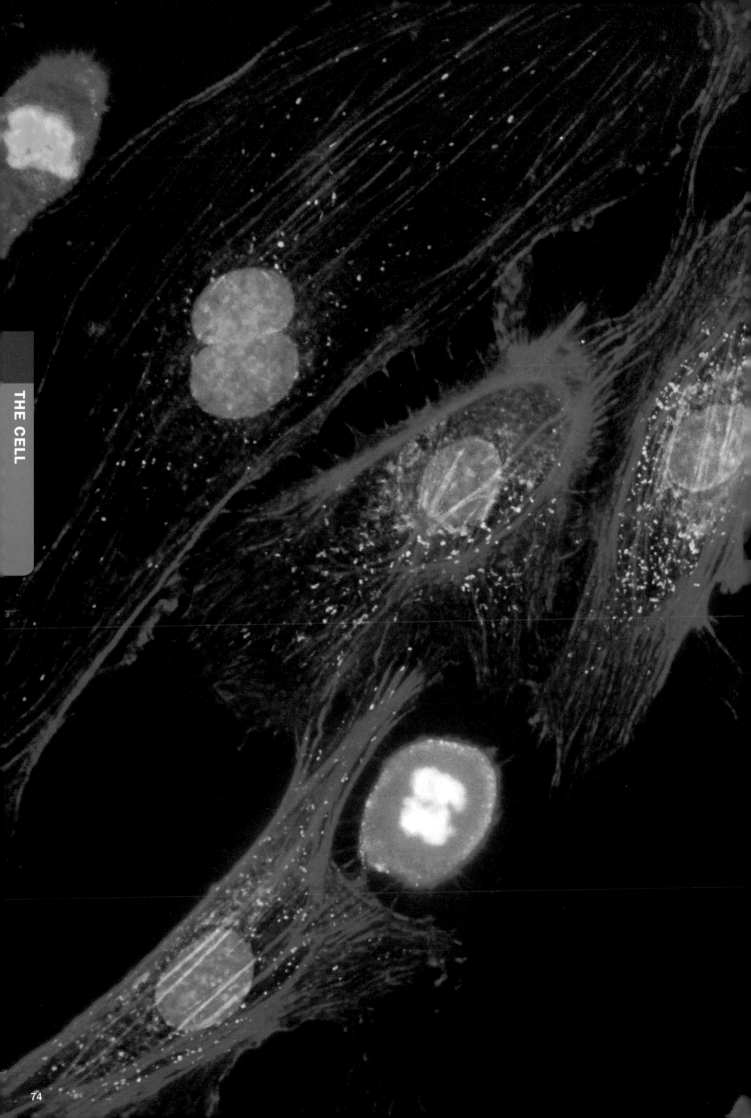

UNIT 2
THE CELL

THE CELL

Cells in the lining of human blood vessels. Cell nuclei are blue, and some are in the process of dividing. At lower left is a later stage of cell division, where the chromosomes (white) are being pulled apart (light microscope image).

Chapter 7 **Cell structure**

THE CELL

Microscopes

The word microscope comes from the Greek *micro* (small) and *skopein* (to look at). Microscopes were first used in the 1600s. At that time a single lens was used, somewhat like we would use a magnifying glass. Such a microscope is called a **simple microscope**.

The **compound microscope** uses two lenses, an objective lens and an eyepiece lens, as shown in Figure 7.1. The total magnification of the image is calculated by multiplying the power of the two lenses (see table below).

Magnification		
Eyepiece	**Objective**	**Total**
× 5	× 10	× 50
× 10	× 40	× 400

Both simple and compound microscopes use light to show the image. The maximum magnification that can clearly be achieved is about × 400 for the simple and × 1000 for the compound microscope.

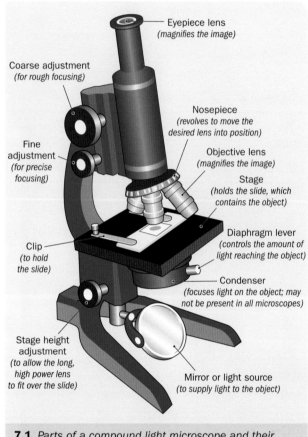

7.1 *Parts of a compound light microscope and their functions*

Labels in figure:
- Eyepiece lens (magnifies the image)
- Coarse adjustment (for rough focusing)
- Fine adjustment (for precise focusing)
- Nosepiece (revolves to move the desired lens into position)
- Objective lens (magnifies the image)
- Stage (holds the slide, which contains the object)
- Clip (to hold the slide)
- Diaphragm lever (controls the amount of light reaching the object)
- Condenser (focuses light on the object; may not be present in all microscopes)
- Stage height adjustment (to allow the long, high power lens to fit over the slide)
- Mirror or light source (to supply light to the object)

Activity 6 *To be familiar with and to use a light microscope*

Examine a range of prepared slides as follows:

1. Make sure that the lenses are clean.
2. Use the coarse adjustment knob to place the low-power objective lens about 2 cm above the stage.
3. Place a microscope slide on the stage. Ensure that the object to be viewed is in the centre of the opening in the stage.
4. Clip the slide in position.
5. View the stage from the side and use the coarse adjustment knob to move the low-power objective lens down so that it is 5 mm above the slide.
6. View the object through the microscope and turn the coarse adjustment knob to move the lens upwards until the object is in focus. (*Steps 5 and 6 prevent the slide from being damaged by the objective lens.*)
7. Adjust the amount of light so that the object can be seen most clearly (*this often involves reducing the amount of light*). Depending on the type of microscope being used this may involve one or more of the following procedures:
   - adjusting the condenser to focus light on the object
   - adjusting the diaphragm to control the amount of light reaching the object
   - adjusting the angle of the mirror
   - using the concave side of the mirror
   - placing a sheet of paper between the bulb and the microscope to cause the light to be diffused
8. When the object is focused under low power, move the slide so that the part of the object you wish to view is in the centre of what you can see (called your **field of view**).
9. Click the high-power objective lens into place.
10. The object should be in focus. If it is not, use the fine adjustment knob to focus it correctly. Be careful not to move the objective lens down too far (*which would crack the slide*).

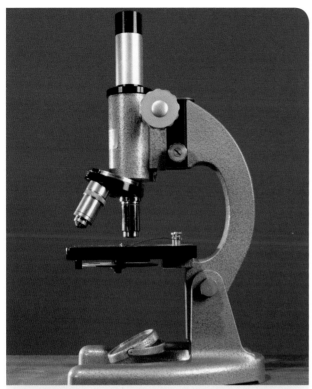

7.2 *A typical light microscope. In 1665 Robert Hooke used a simple microscope to look at thin slices of cork. He described many small boxes or compartments present in the cork sample. He used the word* **cell** *to describe them because they reminded him of prison cells.*

Cell structure as seen using a light microscope

It is now accepted that all organisms are composed of cells. Most cells are very small (often about 0.025 mm in length. A normal human thumbnail is about 1 mm in thickness, so about 40 cells can fit across the thumbnail). The largest known cell is an ostrich egg.

Cells are measured in units called micrometres (μm). There are one thousand micrometres in a millimetre, i.e. 1 μm = 0.001 mm. This means most plant and animal cells are about 25 μm long.

Animal cells

Animal cells are surrounded by an outer membrane, called the cell or plasma membrane. This membrane surrounds the protoplasm.

The **protoplasm** is all the living parts of a cell.

The protoplasm of a cell is made up of the nucleus and the surrounding cytoplasm. An animal cell is comparable to a balloon full of water (i.e. it is flexible, just like human skin cells).

The cytoplasm is the living material outside the nucleus. Most of the reactions in a cell take place in the cytoplasm.

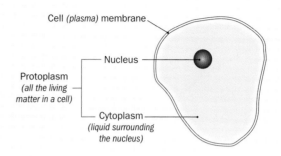

7.3 *Animal cell as seen under a light microscope*

Plant cells

Plant cells are enclosed by a rigid cell wall made of cellulose. Cellulose is a strong structural carbohydrate and is the main component in paper and cotton wool.

The function of the cell wall is support.

The cell wall gives the cell strength and makes it less flexible. The cell membrane is usually found just inside the cell wall. The wall and membrane are often so close that the membrane is not seen clearly.

Vacuoles contain a fluid called cell sap. This is a solution of salts, sugars and pigments.

The vacuole helps to give the cell strength and shape and may also store materials.

Plant cells also have a nucleus and cytoplasm. Plant cells that are green contain structures called chloroplasts. These are the structures in which photosynthesis takes place.

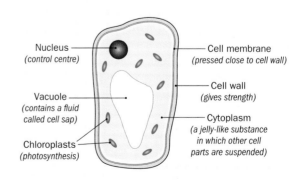

7.4 *Plant cell as seen under a light microscope*

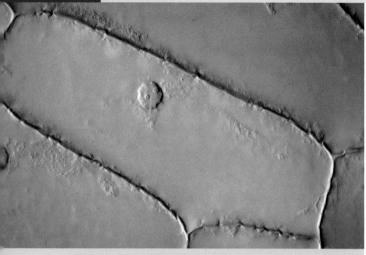

7.5 *Plant (onion) cells as seen under a light microscope*

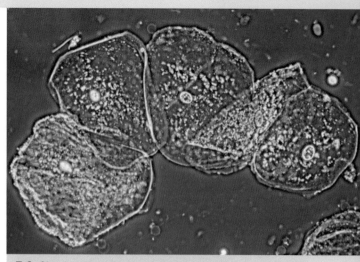

7.6 *Cheek cells: as seen under high power*

Activity 7a *To prepare and examine plant (onion) cells, stained and unstained, using a light microscope*

A Prepare the slide

1 Remove the outer, dry scaly leaves of an onion.
2 Use a forceps to pull a strip of thin, transparent epidermis from a fleshy, inner leaf.
3 Place a small piece of the epidermal strip on a glass slide.
4 ⚠ Add iodine solution. *(This is a red-yellow stain. It shows up the membranes and starch very clearly. A mixture of potassium iodide and iodine gives a better result.)*
5 Blot off any surplus iodine.
6 Add a few drops of water and then add a cover slip *(this prevents the cells from drying out and prevents the lens from getting wet)*. Lower the cover slip at an angle *(this eliminates air bubbles)*.
7 The cells can be viewed unstained by leaving out steps 4 and 5 above. Note that the use of a stain can highlight and clarify certain parts of the cell.

B Examine under the microscope

1 This can be carried out in the same way as described in Activity 6.
2 The results will appear similar to those shown in Figure 7.5 (top left).
3 Draw diagrams of what you can see at magnifications of × 100 and × 400.
4 Note that if the plant cell examined is green then chloroplasts may be visible.

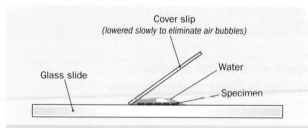

7.7 *Preparation of a slide for use under a microscope*

Activity 7b *To prepare and examine animal (cheek) cells, using a light microscope*

A Prepare the slide

1 Rinse your mouth out with water.
2 Scrape the inside of your mouth with a lollipop stick or a cotton wool bud *(this will collect many cheek cells)*.
3 Spread the smear of cells thinly on to a glass slide.
4 Add a few drops of methylene blue *(this stains the nuclei a deep blue)* and leave for a few minutes.
5 Rinse or blot off excess stain.
6 Add a few drops of water.
7 Add a cover slip at an angle *(to eliminate air bubbles)*.
8 The cells can be viewed unstained by leaving out steps 4 and 5.

B Examine under the microscope

1 Using the coarse adjustment knob, move the eyepiece away from the stage.
2 Place the slide on the stage, with the specimen over the hole. Secure it with the clips.

3 Click the lowest-power lens on the nosepiece into place.
4 Looking at the stage from the side, lower the lens until it is just above the slide.
5 Looking through the eyepiece, turn the coarse adjustment knob to move the objective lens up *(to prevent cracking the slide)* until the image is in focus.
6 Move the slide so that the area you wish to observe is in the middle of the field of view.
7 Click the high-power objective lens into place and use the fine adjustment knob to get the exact focus.
8 Alter the light using the condenser, diaphragm, mirror or paper, as appropriate *(to achieve the sharpest image)*.
9 The result will appear as shown in Fig. 7.6 (top right).
10 Draw diagrams of the cells at magnifications of × 100 and × 400.

Cell ultrastructure

The best light microscopes will magnify an image only about 1000 times. At this magnification on a light microscope, many small objects appear blurred.

Electron microscopes use a beam of electrons instead of light. The electrons are focused, using magnets, onto the specimen. As electrons are invisible, the image is shown on a TV screen or as a photograph.

There are two main types of electron microscope.

- A **transmission electron microscope** (TEM) sends a beam of electrons through a thin section of the specimen. This shows the internal structure of the specimen in great detail.
- A **scanning electron microscope** (SEM) uses a beam of electrons to provide a surface view of the specimen.

Electron microscopes can give magnifications of 250 000 and higher. In addition, they can produce very clear images. This makes electron microscopes ideal for observing very small details.

Ultrastructure is the fine detail of a cell as seen with an electron microscope.

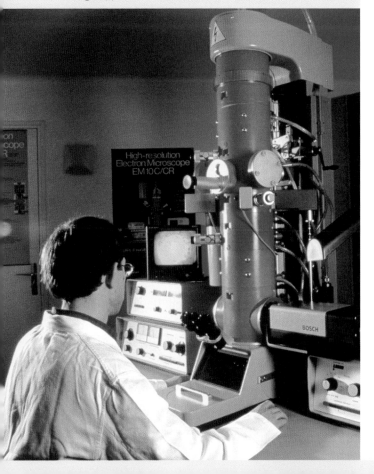

7.8 *A transmission electron microscope (TEM): the image appears on the screen in the lower centre*

Ultrastructure of a generalised cell

Cell (or plasma) membrane

All membranes in biology are thought to have the same structure. They are composed of phospholipids and proteins.

The phospholipids, which have a water-loving phosphate group and a water-hating lipid group, are arranged into double layers (bilayers). The phosphates are on the exposed outer surfaces with the lipids in the middle.

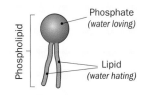
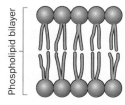

7.9 *Phospholipid bilayer*

Protein molecules are completely or partially embedded in the phospholipid bilayer. Some of these proteins are attached to the bilayer, others are detachable and can move throughout the bilayer.

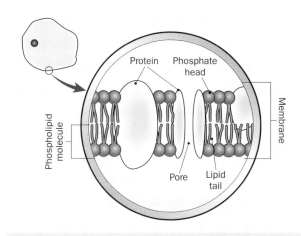

7.10 *Structure of a membrane*

FUNCTIONS OF MEMBRANES

- Membranes retain the cell contents.
- Membranes control what enters and leaves the cell. Membranes can allow the free passage of some molecules and prevent the passage of others. In this way they are said to be selectively (or semi) permeable.

  For example, water and oxygen can pass freely across a membrane, but sodium ions and large proteins have to be moved across using energy.
- Membranes give some support to the cell.
- Membranes recognise molecules that touch them.

Nucleus

The nucleus is the control centre of the cell.

The nucleus is surrounded by a double membrane with numerous nuclear pores. These allow the controlled entry and exit of molecules in and out of the nucleus.

The nucleus contains strands of DNA (deoxyribonucleic acid). DNA is arranged into structures called chromosomes (*chroma* colour, *soma* body; so-called because DNA readily absorbs many stains and becomes darkly coloured under the microscope).

Every organism has a definite number of chromosomes in each nucleus (e.g. humans have 46, some roundworms have only 2, while some ferns have more than 1000).

Genes are located randomly along chromosomes. Humans are thought to have between 20 000 and 30 000 genes in each cell. Genes are the structures that inform the cell how to make certain proteins. Genes control the number of fingers, colour of eyes, production of enzymes and thousands more tasks. They are the units of inheritance.

When a cell is not dividing (i.e. most of the time), the chromosomes are very elongated and interwoven. In this form they are called chromatin.

Chromatin is the name given to chromosomes when they are not dividing.

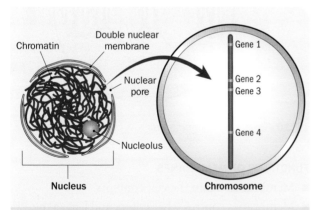

7.11 *Nucleus and chromosome*

NUCLEAR PORES

Nuclear pores allow a type of RNA (ribonucleic acid) called mRNA (messenger RNA) to pass in and out of the nucleus.

We will look at RNA in detail in Chapter 16.

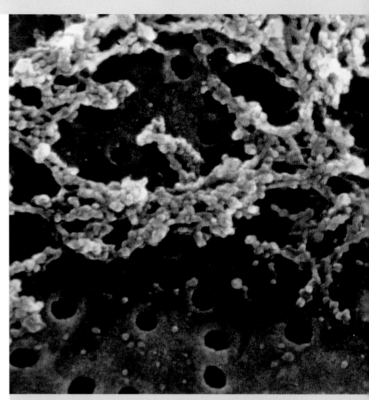

7.12 *Nuclear pores (black circles) and chromatin (yellow)*

Nucleolus

The nucleolus (plural nucleoli) is an area in the nucleus which stains very darkly. It is where ribosomes are made.

As ribosomes are composed of RNA, the nucleolus makes and contains a lot of rRNA (ribosomal RNA).

Cytoplasm

The cytoplasm is the jelly-like liquid in a cell that surrounds the nucleus.

A number of small bodies called organelles (such as mitochondria, chloroplasts and ribosomes) are suspended in the cytoplasm.

Mitochondria

Mitochondria (singular *mitochondrion*) supply energy to the cell. They are the sites of respiration.

Cells with many mitochondria (e.g. muscle and liver in animals, meristems in plants) produce lots of energy. Cells with few mitochondria (e.g. fat in humans, ground tissue in plants) produce less energy.

It is on the inner membrane, especially the infoldings, that energy is released. If more infoldings are present they will cause the mitochondria to produce more energy.

Each mitochondrion has its own loop of DNA.

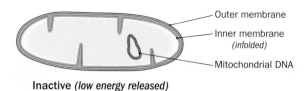

Inactive *(low energy released)*

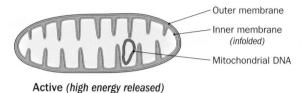

Active *(high energy released)*

7.13 *Ultrastructure of inactive and active mitochondria*

Did you know?

Active mitochondria convert to the inactive form if the cell rests for too long. This is why prolonged bed rest can cause tiredness when we try to resume normal life. Exercise causes the number of infoldings to increase again.

7.14 *Mitochondrion (pink) as seen under a transmission electron microscope: membranes in the cytoplasm are covered with ribosomes*

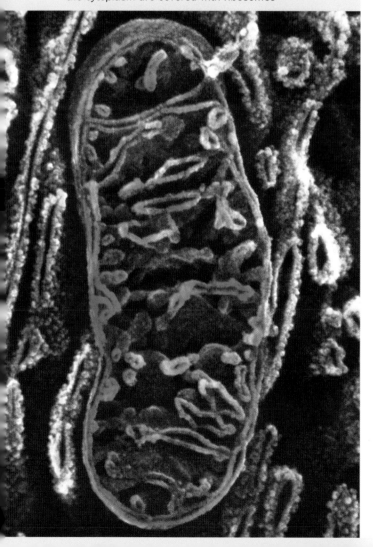

Chloroplasts (plants only)

Chloroplasts are green structures in plants in which photosynthesis takes place.

Chloroplasts contain the green pigment chlorophyll. We will examine the role of chloroplasts in detail in Chapter 11.

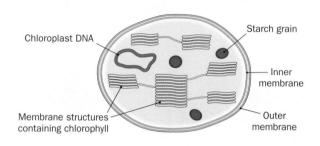

7.15 *Ultrastructure of chloroplast*

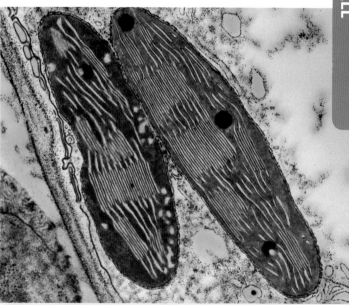

7.16 *Chloroplasts (TEM)*

Cell wall (plants only)

Plant cell walls are made of cellulose. Their function is to support and strengthen the cell.

Cell walls are fully permeable. This means that all molecules can pass in or out through cell walls.

Ribosomes

Ribosomes are very tiny, bead-like structures. They are made of RNA and protein.

The function of ribosomes is to make proteins. They do this by combining a sequence of amino acids to form the protein.

THE CELL

Generalised cells

The ultrastructure of a general animal and plant cell is shown in Figures 7.17 and 7.18.

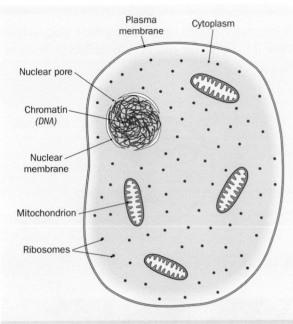

7.17 *Ultrastructure of animal cell*

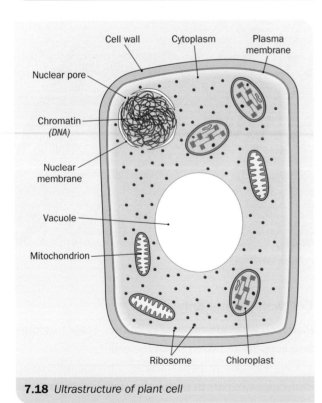

7.18 *Ultrastructure of plant cell*

Differences between plant and animal cells	
Plant cells	**Animal cells**
Have cell walls	No cell walls
Contain chloroplasts	Do not contain chloroplasts
Contain chlorophyll	Do not contain chlorophyll
Have large vacuoles	Have small (if any) vacuoles

Prokaryotic and eukaryotic cells

Living things (also called organisms) can be placed into two categories depending on the structure and complexity of their cells.

> **Prokaryotic cells** do not have a nucleus or membrane-enclosed organelles.

Prokaryotes are single-celled organisms such as bacteria and belong to the kingdom *Monera*, also called *Prokaryotes* (see Chapter 20).

The DNA of prokaryotic cells is found as circular loops located in the cytoplasm. Prokaryotic cells are generally small and do not have structures such as mitochondria and chloroplasts. Reactions such as respiration and photosynthesis (if it occurs) are carried out on infoldings of the plasma membrane.

> **Eukaryotic cells** have a nucleus and cell organelles, all of which are enclosed by membranes.

Eukaryotes are more advanced than prokaryotes and include the organisms in the four other kingdoms. They have a nucleus and membrane-enclosed organelles such as mitochondria and chloroplasts.

Eukaryotic cells are larger than prokaryotic cells. The plant and animal cells studied earlier in this chapter are eukaryotic cells.

Eukaryotic cells evolved from prokaryotic cells about 3000 million years ago.

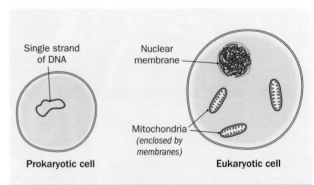

7.19 *Prokaryotic and eukaryotic cells*

Summary

Microscopes:
- simple = one lens
- compound = two lenses
- electron microscopes show ultrastructure
  - transmission electron microscope shows internal structures
  - scanning electron microscope shows surfaces

Observing cells:
- Prepare and stain cells on a slide.
- Examine under low power, then high power.

Plasma (cell) membrane:
- surrounds the cell
- function is to control the entry and exit of molecules to the cell

Nucleus:
- function is to control the cell
- contains chromosomes which are made of DNA
- elongated, non-dividing chromosomes are called chromatin

DNA:
- deoxyribonucleic acid
- found in chromosomes or chromatin in the nucleus

Nucleolus, located in nucleus:
- makes ribosomes

Cell wall (plants only):
- made of cellulose
- function is support

Vacuoles (plants mostly):
- functions are to strengthen the cell and storage

Mitochondrion:
- function is to provide energy (respiration)
- numerous in active cells
- many infoldings imply large energy output

Ribosomes:
- make protein

Chloroplasts (only in plants):
- are green and carry out photosynthesis

Prokaryotic cells:
- do not have a nucleus or membrane-enclosed organelles
- are small and more primitive
- are found as bacteria

Eukaryotic cells:
- have a membrane-enclosed nucleus and cell organelles
- are larger and more advanced
- are found as plant and animal cells, fungi and amoeba

THE CELL

Revision questions

1 (a) Name the parts labelled A, B, C, D, E and F on the diagram of the microscope below.

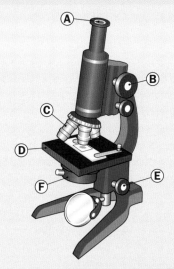

7.20

(b) Give the reason why this is an example of a compound microscope.
(c) What are the functions of the parts labelled B and C?

2 A microscope has an eyepiece marked × 10 and an objective lens marked × 10.
What is the total magnification of the image?

3 When using microscopes explain why:
(a) thin specimens are used
(b) the specimen is placed in water
(c) stains are sometimes used
(d) you should focus the objective lens upwards (away from the slide) first
(e) you use low power first, followed by high power
(f) a cover slip is used
(g) the cover slip is placed on the slide at an angle.

4 (a) Name any stain you have used for microscopic examination.
(b) What was the stain used to highlight?
(c) What colour did the stain appear under the microscope?

5 Suggest any advantage of an electron microscope compared with a light microscope.

6 What is meant by cell ultrastructure?

7 (a) In what cell organelle are amino acids joined together?
(b) Name the food type formed in these organelles.

8 Name the material(s) that form the **(a)** cell wall, **(b)** nucleus, **(c)** cell membrane.

9   What structure in animals carries out the function of the cell wall in plants?

10 (a) Give the functions of (i) plasma membrane, (ii) cell wall, (iii) nucleus, (iv) vacuoles, (v) mitochondria, (vi) chloroplasts, (vii ribosomes.

    (b) Which of the structures named in part (a) are found only in plants?

11 (a) Draw a labelled diagram of an animal cell as seen using the light microscope.

    (b) What extra structures might be seen if a plant cell were drawn?

12 (a) Draw a diagram to show the ultrastructure of an animal cell. Label at least six parts.

    (b) Repeat part (a) for a plant cell.

13 (a) Why do sperm cells have many mitochondria?

    (b) Name a type of animal cell that has few mitochondria.

14 Distinguish between:

    (a) protoplasm and cytoplasm

    (b) mitochondrion and chloroplast

    (c) microscope slide and cover slip

    (d) iodine and methylene blue.

15 Distinguish between prokaryotic and eukaryotic cells on the basis of (a) nucleus, (b) cell organelles, (c) size, (d) evolutionary origins and (e) examples in modern organisms.

16 Copy out the table below and fill in the spaces in relation to the structure of a cell.

Structure of a cell

Cell part	Number in cell (one or more)	Location in cell	Found in animal cell, plant cell or both	Function
Cell wall				
Cell (plasma) membrane				
Cytoplasm				
Nucleus				
Nuclear pores				
Ribosome				
Mitochondrion				
Chloroplast				
Vacuole				

Sample examination questions

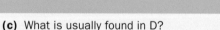

Section A

17 Use ticks (✓) to show if the named structure is present in an animal cell, in a plant cell or in both. The first has been completed as an example.

Structure	Cytoplasm	Cell wall	Chloroplast	Nucleus	Vacuole
Animal cell	✓				
Plant cell	✓				

(2005 OL Q 2)

18 The diagram shows a plant cell.

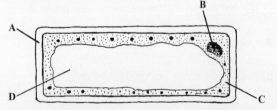

    (a) Label A, B, C and D.

    (b) Name **two** features shown in the diagram which are not normally associated with an animal cell.

    (c) What is usually found in D?

    (d) Name a carbohydrate found in A.

(2006 OL Q 2)

Section B

19 (a) State a function of each of the following components of a cell.

         (i)   Ribosome

         (ii) Cell membrane

    (b) Answer the following questions in relation to the preparation, staining and microscopic observation of a slide of an animal cell.

         (i)   What type of animal cell did you use?

         (iii) After staining, a cover slip is placed on the slide. Give a reason for this.

         (iv) How did you apply the cover slip? Why did you apply it in this way?

         (v)   Describe the difference in colour or depth of colour, if any, between the nucleus and cytoplasm when the stained cell was viewed under the microscope.

(2006 HL Q 8)

20 (a) (i) Name the parts of the light microscope labelled A and B.

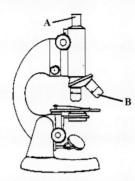

(ii) If the magnification of A is × 10 and the magnification of B is × 40, what magnification results when a slide is viewed using B?

(b) Answer the following in relation to preparing a slide of stained plant cells and viewing them under the microscope.

(i) From what plant did you obtain the cells?

(ii) Describe how you obtained a thin piece of a sample of the cells.

(iii) What stain did you use for the cells on the slide?

(iv) Describe how you applied this stain.

(v) What did you do before placing the slide with the stained cells on the microscope platform?

(vi) State **two** features of these cells that indicate that they are typical plant cells.

(2004 OL Q 7)

Previous examination questions	
Ordinary level	**Higher level**
2004 Q 7	2006 Q 8
2005 Q 2	
2006 Q 2	
2007 Q 3	

*For latest questions go to **www.edco.ie/biology***

Chapter 8 **Cell diversity**

Tissues

> A **tissue** is a group of similar cells that are modified (or adapted) to carry out the same function(s).

Different types of tissues have different structures, but in all cases the structure of a tissue is designed to allow the tissue to perform its special task or function.

A simple tissue has only one cell type. Complex tissue has more than one cell type.

Syllabus

You are required to know examples of two plant tissues.

Plant tissues

There are four main types of plant tissues: dermal, vascular, ground and meristematic tissue. These tissues will be discussed in detail in Chapter 24. In this chapter we will look briefly at dermal and vascular tissue.

Dermal tissue

Dermal tissue is normally a single layer of cells that surrounds the different parts of a plant. Epidermis is one type of dermal tissue.

- *Location:* Dermal tissue (or epidermis) is like the skin on a plant. Epidermis is found as a covering on leaves, stems and roots.
- *Description:* Epidermis cells are living, rectangular cells. They often have a slightly thickened cell wall. Sometimes the epidermis has a waterproof layer, called a cuticle, on its outer surface.
- *Function:* The main function of dermal tissue is to protect the plant. If a cuticle is present, the dermal tissue has the secondary function of preventing water loss from the plant.

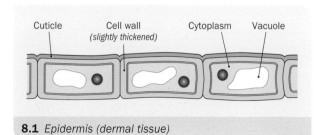

8.1 *Epidermis (dermal tissue)*

Vascular tissue

Vascular tissue transports materials around a plant. It is a complex tissue because it consists of two types of cells: xylem and phloem.

XYLEM
- *Description:* Xylem consists of hollow tubes that run continuously from the roots, up through the stem and into the leaves.
- *Function:* The main function of xylem is to transport water (and dissolved minerals) throughout the plant. A second function of xylem is to provide support in woody plants (xylem forms the wood in trees).

PHLOEM
- *Description:* Phloem also consists of a series of tube-like structures. Phloem is found in the leaves, stems and roots of a plant.
- *Function:* The function of phloem is to transport food from the leaves to the other parts of the plant.

Xylem and phloem are covered in more detail in Chapter 24.

8.2 *A vascular bundle: xylem is orange and phloem is pink*

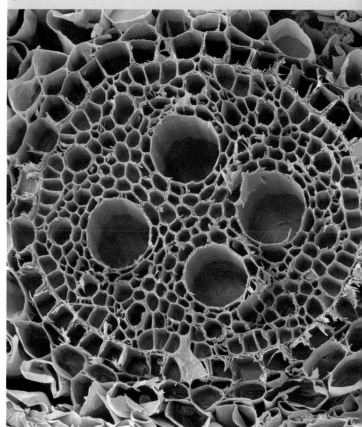

Syllabus

You are required to know examples of two animal tissues.

Animal tissues

There are four main types of animal tissues: epithelial, connective, muscular and nervous tissue. Epithelial tissue covers the internal and external surfaces of the body. Muscular tissue can contract and is found in muscles and many internal organs

In this chapter, connective and nervous tissue are described in more detail.

Connective tissue

- *Description:* Connective tissue consists of a number of cells spread out in a matrix (or material) that is produced by the connective cells. Connective tissue joins and supports other body structures.

   Examples of connective tissues are adipose tissue (which stores fat, e.g. under the skin), cartilage, bone and blood.
- *Example:* Blood is a connective tissue because it consists of red cells, white cells and platelets suspended in a matrix called plasma (see Chapter 26). Red cells carry oxygen, white cells defend the body and platelets clot the blood.

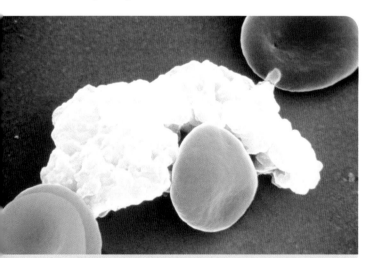

8.3 *Red and white blood cells*

Nervous tissue

- *Description:* Nervous tissue is composed of nerve cells called neurons.
- *Function:* Neurons are adapted to carry electrical impulses to and from the brain and spinal cord.

The detailed structure and functions of neurons are explained in Chapter 34.

Tissue culture

Tissue culture is the growth of cells in or on a sterile nutrient medium outside an organism.

The process of tissue culture is very similar to cell culture. In tissue culture, *groups* of cells (tissues) are grown. In cell culture, *isolated* cells are grown outside the organism.

The growth of cells (or tissues) outside the body in an artificial environment is called *in vitro* growth (from the Latin *vitreus*, meaning glass). *In vivo* refers to something happening inside the body of an organism (from the Latin *vivus*, meaning living).

Tissue culture generally works on the basis that a sample of a tissue is removed from a plant or animal. The tissue sample is grown in glassware, or in a bath or bioreactor, under carefully controlled conditions.

Very often cells are grown in a bath of sterile fluid containing a source of nutrition. It is common to also include hormones and other substances to enhance growth.

A major consideration in tissue culture is the need to prevent micro-organisms from growing in the bioreactor. Bacteria and yeasts, in particular, grow much faster than other cells and produce many waste products. These wastes contaminate the container and often kill the desired cells.

Successful tissue culture also requires the correct nutrients. These include an energy source such as glucose, chemicals to stimulate growth (such as growth regulators or hormones), along with vitamins and minerals.

8.4 *Plants growing from tissue culture in a petri dish*

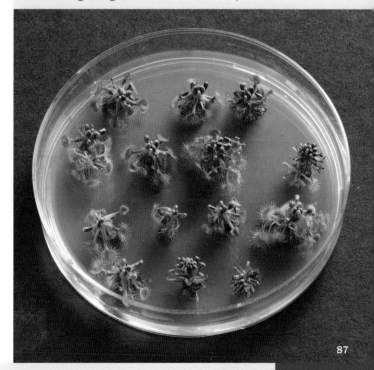

You are required to know two applications of tissue culture.

Applications of tissue culture

Plant breeding

Micropropagation is the growth of large numbers of plants from very small plant pieces, often simply from plant tissues or cells.

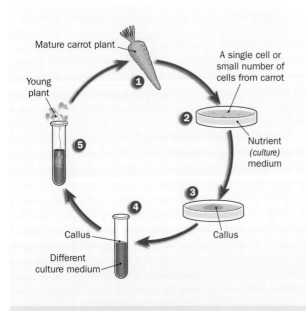

8.5 *Micropropagation in carrot plants*

In micropropagation, a desirable plant is cut into many small pieces (containing from one to a few thousand cells). The cells are grown or cultured in a laboratory on a suitable medium. In time they form a clump of similar cells called a callus.

The growing conditions are then changed so that the callus continues to grow. After some time it forms a young plant embryo and then a young plant. When the young plants are sufficiently large they may be planted out as normal small plants.

The formation of a new plant from a single cell or a small number of cells in this way shows that each nucleus has all the genes or instructions necessary to form an entire adult organism.

BENEFITS OF MICROPROPAGATION

- A large number of plants are produced in a short time.
- The plants grown in this way are genetically identical.
- It is an inexpensive way to produce large numbers of similar plants.

8.6 *Micropropagation*

Cancer research

Antibodies are special proteins that react with (or join onto) one particular chemical (called an antigen). Antibodies are produced by white blood cells.

Cancer cells produce special antigens that are not produced by any other normal body cells. Using tissue culture, it is now possible to produce special antibodies (called monoclonal antibodies or MABs) that will react with the antigens on cancer cells or a vast range of other types of antigens.

BENEFITS OF MONOCLONAL ANTIBODIES

- Monoclonal antibodies may change colour when they react with cancer antigens. In this way they are used to tell if a sample of cells is cancerous.
- If toxic drugs are attached to the monoclonal antibodies the drug is delivered only to cancer cells (i.e. the MABs will not join to normal cells).

8.7 *Herceptin – a monoclonal antibody for the treatment of breast cancer*

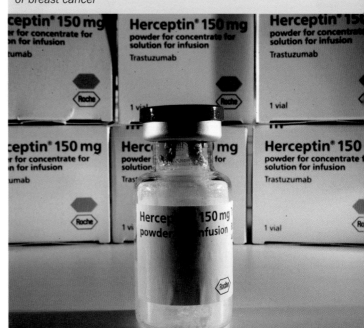

8.8 *Skin grown for transplant back to the donor*

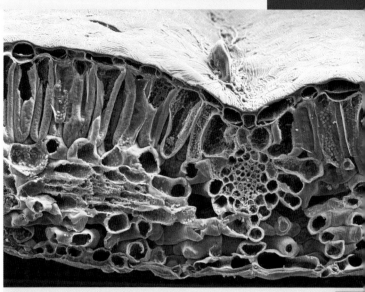

8.10 *The structure of a leaf (SEM)*

THE CELL

Skin grafts

Tissue culture can be used to grow new skin for patients who have been badly burned. Previously skin had to be taken from a healthy part of the body and transplanted on to the burned areas.

Very often the cells used to grow the new skin are stem cells. These are the cells that can develop into any body tissue. Originally stem cells were taken from embryos but now they can be found in places such as bone marrow and umbilical cords.

Organs

> An **organ** is a structure composed of a number of tissues that work together to carry out one or more functions.

Plant organs include structures such as the root, stem and leaf, along with reproductive organs such as flowers, seeds and fruits.

Animal organs include the stomach, brain, liver, kidney and heart.

An example of a plant organ

A leaf contains three types of plant tissue:

1 Dermal tissue is found in the epidermis.
2 Vascular tissue is found as xylem and phloem in the vascular bundle(s).
3 Ground tissue is found as the palisade and mesophyll cells.

All of these tissues combine so that the leaf can carry out the function of photosynthesis. A more detailed account of the leaf is given in Chapter 25.

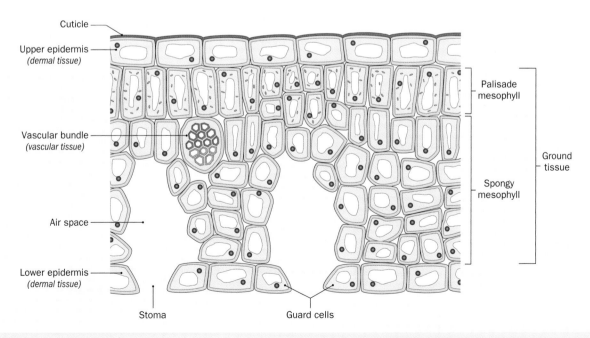

Cuticle

Upper epidermis
(dermal tissue)

Vascular bundle
(vascular tissue)

Air space

Lower epidermis
(dermal tissue)

Stoma

Guard cells

Palisade mesophyll

Spongy mesophyll

Ground tissue

8.9 *The leaf as an organ*

An example of an animal organ

The heart is an organ designed to pump blood. It contains all four types of animal tissue.

1 The walls of the heart are made of cardiac muscle (muscular tissue).
2 The heart is enclosed in a membrane called the pericardium (epithelial tissue).
3 Blood and numerous blood vessels are present (connective tissue).
4 The heart is controlled by nervous tissue.

(The structure of the heart is described in Chapter 27.)

Organ systems

An **organ system** consists of a number of organs working together to carry out one or more functions.

Animals such as humans consist of ten organ systems. These are the epithelial, skeletal, muscular, digestive, circulatory, respiratory, urinary, nervous, endocrine and reproductive systems. All of these organ systems, except the reproductive system, are essential for the survival of the individual.

While each organ system has its own functions, all the systems combine to allow the animal to survive and reproduce. All the organ systems combine to form the organism.

Two examples of animal organ systems

The **circulatory system** consists of the heart, blood vessels and blood. It also includes lymph vessels and lymph. Its functions are to transport materials around the body and to fight infection.

The **digestive system** consists of the mouth, oesophagus, stomach, small intestine, large intestine and anus (in association with the liver and pancreas). Its functions are to take in food, break it down and transfer the digested food into the circulatory system so that it can be carried to all the cells in the body.

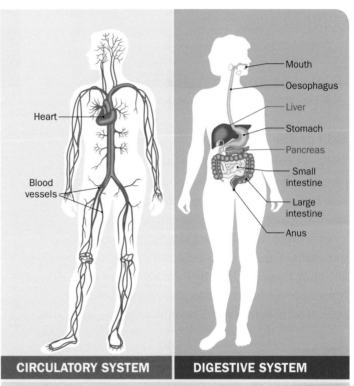

8.11 *Human circulatory and digestive systems*

Biological organisation

The way in which living things are organised as outlined in this chapter is represented by Figure 8.12 below.

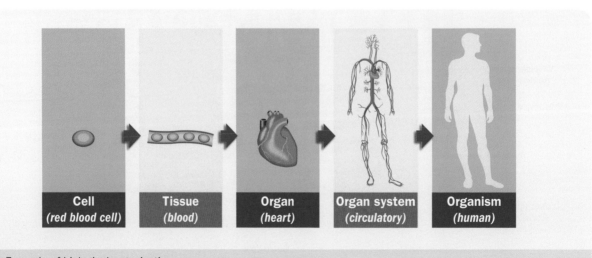

8.12 *Example of biological organisation*

Summary

A tissue is a group of similar cells modified to carry out the same function(s).

The four basic plant tissue types are: dermal, vascular, ground and meristematic tissues.
- Dermal tissue surrounds and protects the plant, e.g. epidermis.
- Vascular tissue transports materials throughout the plant.
  - Xylem transports water and dissolved minerals.
  - Phloem transports food.

The four basic animal tissue types are: epithelial, connective, muscular and nervous tissues.
- Connective tissue consists of cells dispersed in a matrix, and it surrounds and supports body parts.
  - Blood has red cells, white cells and platelets carried in plasma.
- Nervous tissue is adapted to carrying electrical impulses throughout the body.
  - Neurons are nerve cells.

Tissue (or cell) culture is the growth of cells in or on a sterile nutrient artificial medium outside the body.

In vitro means outside the body, **in vivo** means inside the body.

The main conditions necessary for tissue culture are:
- the absence of other contaminating micro-organisms
- food, vitamins and minerals
- substances (such as hormones) to stimulate growth

Micropropagation and the production of monoclonal antibodies are forms of tissue culture.

Micropropagation:
- is the growth of large numbers of plants from cells, tissues or small parts of a plant
- rapidly produces new genetically identical plants

Monoclonal antibodies:
- combine with a specific, single type of antigen
- may be used to attach to and show the presence of antigens on cancer cells

An organ is made of a number of tissues working together to carry out one or more functions.
- Plant organs include the root, stem and leaf.
- Animal organs include the brain, liver and heart.

An organ system contains a number of organs working together to carry out one or more functions.
- Animal organ systems include the circulatory and the digestive systems.

Multicellular living things are organised in the following manner:
- Cells → Tissues → Organs → Organ systems → Organism

Revision questions

1. (a) Define a tissue.
   (b) Distinguish between simple and compound tissues.
2. (a) Name two types of plant tissue.
   (b) State a function for each tissue named.
   (c) Name one type of cell from each of the tissue types named.
3. Distinguish between the two types of plant vascular tissue under the headings **(a)** names of tissue and **(b)** functions.
4. (a) Name two types of animal tissue.
   (b) State a function for each of the two tissues named.
   (c) Name an actual animal cell from each type of tissue.
5. (a) What is meant by tissue culture?
   (b) Why is tissue culture sometimes called *in vitro* culture?
   (c) State two conditions necessary for successful tissue culture and suggest a reason for each condition.
6. (a) Name two applications of tissue culture.
   (b) Name a product formed in each case.
   (c) Suggest one benefit for the production of the products named.
7. Explain one way in which tissue culture is of benefit in cancer research.
8. (a) Define an organ.
   (b) Name a plant organ.
   (c) Give the main function of this organ.
   (d) Name two types of tissues found in the named plant organ.
9. (a) Name an animal organ.
   (b) State the function of this organ.
   (c) Name two types of tissue present in the named organ.
10. (a) Define an organ system.
    (b) Name two animal organ systems.
    (c) Name one organ from each of the named organ systems.
11. State which of the following options, (i), (ii), (iii) or (iv), is the correct answer.
    (a) Which of the following is a tissue?
        (i) blood vessel   (ii) leaf
        (iii) epidermis   (iv) oesophagus
    (b) Which of the following is an organ?
        (i) mesophyll   (ii) epidermis
        (iii) pancreas   (iv) blood
    (c) Which of the following is an organ system?
        (i) blood vessels   (ii) brain cells
        (iii) leaf   (iv) nervous system
    (d) Micropropagation is an example of:
        (i) leaf culture   (ii) cancer culture
        (iii) spleen culture   (iv) tissue culture

THE CELL

Sample examination questions

Section C

12 (a) (i) What is a tissue?

  (ii) Name two tissues found in animals.

(b) Tissue culture is used to make a skin graft for patients who have been severely burned.

  (i) What is meant by tissue culture?

  (ii) Name the gas needed to release energy to make a skin graft.

(iii) Suggest the most suitable temperature to make skin cells grow.

(iv) Suggest a reason why sterile conditions are needed in tissue culture.

(v) What type of cell division, mitosis or meiosis, is involved in tissue culture?

(vi) Give one other application of tissue culture apart from skin grafting.

(2007 OL Q 11)

Previous examination questions

Ordinary level	Higher level
2007 Q 11	n/a

For latest questions go to www.edco.ie/biology

Chapter 9   **Enzymes**

Metabolism

Metabolism is the sum of all the chemical reactions that take place within an organism. These reactions involve growth, movement, maintainance of a constant internal state, repair, response to stimuli and reproduction. Each of these changes requires energy to be released or absorbed. This means that metabolism is closely associated with energy conversions.

Cells need energy to maintain themselves in an orderly manner. Without supplies of energy, things tend to become chaotic. Metabolism is the way in which this energy is obtained and utilised within the cell.

Metabolism is necessary to control the chemical and energy requirements of a cell. By doing this, metabolism maintains a balanced internal state (called homeostasis) within an organism.

Some metabolic reactions break down complex molecules to simpler forms and so release energy. These reactions are said to be catabolic, e.g. respiration or digestion.

Reactions in which energy is consumed to convert simpler molecules to more complex ones are said to be anabolic, e.g. photosynthesis or the conversion of amino acids into muscle (a process that is stimulated by anabolic steroids).

Most cell reactions proceed by a series of steps (often as many as 30 for each reaction). These steps must be carefully controlled if the cell is to function properly. The most important controllers of cellular reactions are enzymes.

9.1 *Energy drinks such as Red Bull stimulate the metabolism.*

Sources of energy

Solar energy

The primary source of energy for life on earth is sunlight. Some of the energy in sunlight (solar energy) is trapped by organisms that contain pigments which can absorb light. Chlorophyll is one of these pigments.

Producers such as green plants use solar energy to form the chemical bonds of carbohydrates and other biomolecules. This form of energy conversion is carried out in the process of photosynthesis.

Cellular energy

Cellular energy refers to sources of energy that are capable of being released by reactions within a cell, i.e. the energy stored in the bonds of biomolecules. Some of the chemical energy stored in the bonds of biomolecules is transferred to consumers when they eat producers. The energy can then pass along the entire food chain.

Each organism breaks down energy-rich biomolecules in the process of respiration. This releases energy, some of which is used by the cells, while the rest is released into the environment as heat.

9.2 *Like plants, solar panels trap the sun's energy.*

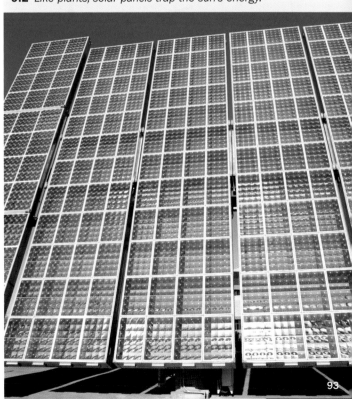

Enzymes

A **catalyst** is a substance that speeds up a reaction, without itself being used up in the reaction.

Enzymes are catalysts made of protein. Because of this, enzymes are called biological (or organic) catalysts, i.e. they are made in living cells and speed up reactions without being used up themselves. Note that while all enzymes are proteins, not all proteins are enzymes.

Enzymes are proteins that speed up a reaction without being used up in the reaction.

We saw in Chapter 3 that proteins are formed by joining a sequence of amino acids together to form a long chain. The functions of most proteins are determined not only by the sequence of amino acids, but also by the three-dimensional shape of the protein. Enzymes, in particular, are **folded** into globular shapes.

The three-dimensional shape of an enzyme means that it will fit neatly and react only with a substance of a shape that matches the enzyme. This is similar to the way in which a glove fits neatly on a person's hand, but not on his/her foot.

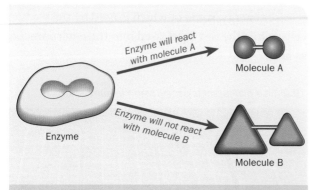

9.3 *The shape of an enzyme determines the type of molecule it can react with.*

Anything that changes the shape of an enzyme will reduce the efficiency of the enzyme to speed up a reaction. Changing the pH or temperature of a reaction will change the shape of enzymes, which in turn will affect the speed of the reaction.

In any cell, there are thousands of reactions taking place all the time. At normal cell temperatures, in the absence of enzymes, these reactions would occur too slowly for the cell to stay alive. Enzymes are used to speed up chemical reactions and allow them to proceed at normal cell temperatures.

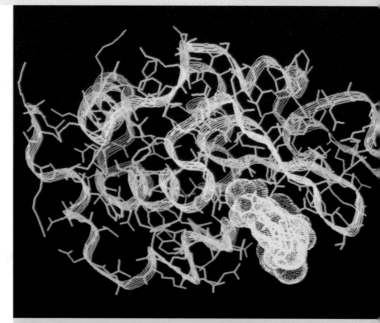

9.4 *Enzyme (purple and blue) and its substrate (yellow)*

Features of enzymes

The **substrate** is the substance with which an enzyme reacts.

The **product** is the substance(s) the enzyme form(s).

- Enzymes are made of protein.
- Enzymes work because they have the correct **shape** to fit the substrate. This means the enzyme must have a complex, three-dimensional shape in order for it to fit with the substrate.
- Enzyme reactions are **reversible**. Just as a key can either open or close a lock, an enzyme can cause a reaction to proceed in either direction. This means any enzyme can be anabolic (forms more complex compounds) or catabolic (breaks down larger compounds).

  For example, in Figure 9.5, the enzyme can digest molecule X into molecules Y and Z. However, the same enzyme can also combine Y and Z to form molecule X.

$$X \underset{}{\overset{\text{ENZYME}}{\rightleftharpoons}} Y + Z$$

9.5 *Enzyme reactions are reversible.*

- Enzymes are named by adding the ending *ase* to the name of their substrate. For example, the enzyme lipase acts on lipids, amylase acts on amylose (usually called starch).

The role of enzymes

Enzymes are necessary in plants and animals to control metabolic reactions. Of the vast range of enzymes controlling metabolic reactions we will consider the following examples.

Catabolic enzymes

Amylase (sometimes called diastase) is an enzyme that converts starch into maltose. It is a catabolic enzyme, because it breaks down a substance into simpler parts.

- Amylase is produced by the salivary glands in the mouth and by the pancreas. It converts starch to maltose.
- Seeds contain starch. When seeds germinate, the enzyme amylase converts starch into maltose.

Starch ──Amylase──▶ Maltose

Anabolic enzymes

DNA polymerase is an enzyme that forms and repairs DNA. It is an anabolic enzyme, because it converts simpler molecules into a more complex form. DNA polymerase is found in both plants and animals.

The enzymes that control photosynthesis are also examples of anabolic enzymes. They convert water and carbon dioxide into glucose.

The enzyme **DNA ligase** is used in genetic engineering to join two pieces of DNA together (see Chapter 19).

Factors affecting enzyme activity

Enzymes work best under certain ideal conditions. Any change in these conditions will slow down the rate of the reaction. These conditions include temperature and pH values.

Temperature

At very low temperatures (0°C for pure water), ice forms. This means that cell contents become solid and enzymes cannot work.

As the temperature increases from 0°C, the rate of molecular movement increases. This causes substrate molecules and enzymes to 'bump' into each other more often. As a result the rate of reaction increases. (See Figure 9.6.)

Human enzymes are designed to work best at 37°C (body temperature) while most plant enzymes prefer 20–30°C.

Above a certain temperature, enzymes begin to lose their three-dimensional shape. Consequently, the rate of reaction falls.

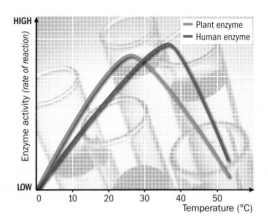

9.6 *Temperature and rate of reaction*

When the shape of an enzyme is fully lost (usually above 50°C), the enzyme is said to be **denatured**. In this condition it has lost its ability to function. This is often a permanent condition.

Enzymes may also be denatured by other factors such as unsuitable pH, inhibitors and radiation.

A **denatured enzyme** has lost its shape and can no longer carry out its function.

pH

The pH scale runs from 0 to 14. Values between 0 and 7 are acidic, pH 7 is neutral and 7 to 14 is basic (or alkaline).

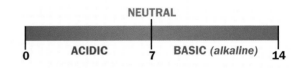

9.7 *The pH scale*

Enzymes work over a very narrow pH range. For most enzymes this is pH 6–8. Outside this range the activity of the enzyme falls quite rapidly. This is because the enzyme loses its shape, i.e. it becomes denatured (see Figure 9.8 overleaf). The optimum (or ideal) pH for most enzymes is pH 7.

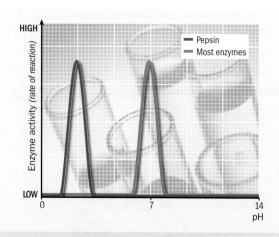

9.8 *pH and rate of reaction*

Note: Pepsin, an enzyme in the stomach, has a pH optimum of 2. This allows it to work efficiently in the acid conditions of the stomach.

Enzyme activity is also affected by the enzyme and substrate concentration, but these factors are beyond the scope of this course.

In experiments measuring the rate of enzyme action (such as Activities 8 and 9) there are four factors to be considered: temperature, pH, enzyme concentration and substrate concentration.

In each of these experiments one factor is varied, while the other three must be kept constant. This is achieved by adopting the following procedures.

Variables for Activities 8 and 9

Factor	Method used to keep factor constant	Method used to vary factor
Temperature	Water baths at the same temperature	Water baths at different temperatures
pH	Use the same pH buffer	Use different pH buffers
Enzyme concentration	Add the same volumes of enzyme	*Not on Leaving Cert. Biology course*
Substrate concentration	Add equal volumes of the same substrate solution	*Not on Leaving Cert. Biology course*

Activity 8 *To investigate the effect of pH on the rate of catalase activity (i.e. rate of enzyme activity)*

Note that catalase is an enzyme that is found in a wide range of living things, e.g. liver, radishes, celery and potatoes. It converts the toxic substance hydrogen peroxide (H_2O_2) into water and oxygen. In this investigation the oxygen forms a bubbly froth. The volume of the froth indicates the activity of the enzyme.

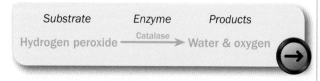

Substrate	Enzyme	Products
Hydrogen peroxide	$\xrightarrow{\text{Catalase}}$	Water & oxygen

1 Place 10 cm³ of pH buffer 4 in a graduated cylinder. *(pH buffer 4 ensures that the pH will remain at 4.)*
2 Using a dropper, add one drop of washing-up liquid to the graduated cylinder. *(The washing-up liquid traps the oxygen that is released, forming froth.)*
3 Blend three stalks of celery in a blender and add 100 cm³ of water. Filter this solution using coffee filter paper into a large beaker. Add 10 cm³ of this solution to the graduated cylinder. Alternatively, finely chop 5 g of celery and add it to the graduated cylinder. *(The celery contains the enzyme catalase.)*
4 Use a syringe to add 5 cm³ of 20% hydrogen peroxide to a test tube. *(Hydrogen peroxide is the substrate.)*
5 Stand the graduated cylinder and the test tube in a large beaker of water at 25°C for a few minutes. *(This ensures a constant temperature.)*

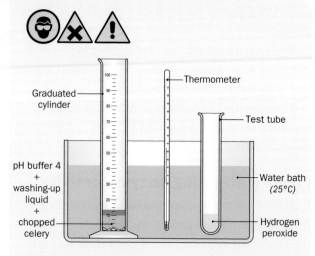

9.9 *Investigate the effects of pH on catalase activity*

6 Pour the hydrogen peroxide into the graduated cylinder.
7 Immediately note and record the volume in the graduated cylinder.
8 Note and record the volume at the top of the froth after 2 minutes.
9 Calculate the volume of froth produced by subtracting the original volume from the volume after 2 minutes, i.e. subtract the reading at point 7 from the reading at point 8.
10 Repeat steps 1–9 using pH buffers 7, 10 and 13.

11 Record the results as shown; the first set of figures are filled in as an example.

Activity 8 results

pH buffer	4	7	10	13
Original volume (cm^3)	25			
Volume after 2 minutes (cm^3)	28			
Volume of froth (cm^3)	3			

12 Draw a graph of the results. Put pH on the horizontal axis and the volume of froth produced on the vertical axis. The graph should have a similar shape to those in Figure 9.8 (page 96).

13 As controls, repeat each procedure but do not add blended or chopped celery (*i.e. no catalase is present*). In each case no froth is formed.

9.10 *Hydrogen peroxide being broken down by catalase in liver (seen at bottom of flask)*

Activity 9   *To investigate the effect of temperature on the rate of catalase activity (i.e. rate of enzyme action)*

1 Place 10 cm^3 of pH buffer 9 solution in a graduated cylinder. (*Catalase works best at pH 9, i.e. pH 9 is the optimum pH for catalase. pH buffer 9 ensures the pH remains constant at 9.*)

2 Using a dropper, add one drop of washing-up liquid to the graduated cylinder. (*The washing-up liquid traps the oxygen that is released, forming froth.*)

3 Blend three stalks of celery in a blender and add 100 cm^3 of water. Filter this solution using coffee filter paper into a large beaker. Add 10 cm^3 of this solution to the graduated cylinder. Alternatively, finely chop 5 g of celery and add it to the graduated cylinder. (*The celery contains the enzyme catalase.*)

4 Use a syringe to add 5 cm^3 of 20% hydrogen peroxide to a test tube. (*Hydrogen peroxide is the substrate.*)

5 Stand the graduated cylinder and the test tube in a large beaker of ice-cold water until they are at 0°C.

6 Pour the hydrogen peroxide into the graduated cylinder.

7 Immediately note and record the volume in the graduated cylinder.

8 Note and record the volume at the top of the froth after 2 minutes.

9 Calculate the volume of froth produced by subtracting the original volume from the volume after 2 minutes.

10 Repeat steps 1–9 at 10°C, 20°C, 30°C, 40°C, 50°C and 60°C.

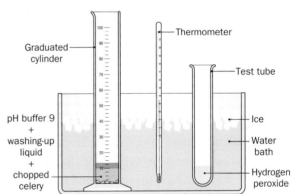

9.11 *Investigating the effect of temperature on catalase activity*

11 Record the results as shown; the first set of figures are shown as an example.

12 Draw a graph of the results. Put temperature on the horizontal axis and the volume of froth produced on the vertical axis. The graph should have a similar shape to those in Figure 9.6 (page 95).

13 As a control each apparatus should be set up but do not add blended or chopped celery (*i.e. no catalase is present*). In each case no froth is formed.

Activity 9 results

Temperature (°C)	0	10	20	30	40	50	60
Original volume (cm^3)	25						
Volume after 2 minutes (cm^3)	27						
Volume of froth produced (cm^3)	2						

Immobilised enzymes

> **Bioprocessing** is the use of enzyme-controlled reactions to produce a product.

> A **bioreactor** is a vessel or container in which living cells or their products are used to make a product.

Traditionally, bioprocessing involved the use of micro-organisms, such as yeast and bacteria, to produce foodstuffs such as cheeses, yoghurts, breads, beers and wines.

In recent times bioprocessing has been developed to produce a vast range of products, including antibiotics, drugs, vaccines, methane gas (biogas), food colourings and flavours, vitamins, amino acids, sugar syrups, enzymes and perfumes.

From the early 1900s, but especially since the mid-1950s, the cells (micro-organisms) used in many of these bioprocesses have been replaced by purified enzymes.

The use of enzymes freely dissolved in a vessel to carry out a biological reaction (a bioreactor) is very wasteful. This is because the enzymes are removed from the vessel at the end of the process and it is not normally possible to isolate the enzymes for reuse.

To prevent this problem, enzymes are often immobilised or fixed. In this way they become insoluble and are easier to recover and reuse. The immobilisation process forms enzymes in a similar state to the way in which they are found in nature, i.e. immobilised within cells rather than being free outside a cell.

> **Immobilised enzymes** are enzymes that are attached, or fixed, to each other, or to an inert material.

9.12 Bioreactors producing artificial sweeteners

Methods of immobilising enzymes

Immobilised enzymes may be attached to each other, to insoluble supports or enclosed within a membrane or gel. A range of different immobilisation techniques is used, as shown in Figure 9.13.

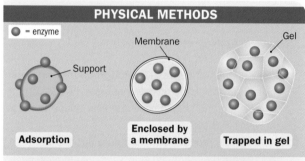
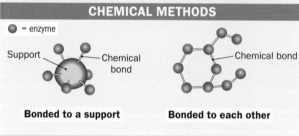
9.13 Enzyme immobilisation techniques

Adsorption means that the enzymes are physically attached to inactive supports such as glass beads, ceramics, cellulose particles or artificial polymers.

In the case of trapping the enzyme in a gel, it is common to use sodium alginate as the gel. This material is prepared from algae and is permeable to the entry of the substrate and to the exit of the products. However, the enzyme is prevented from leaving the gel.

Advantages of immobilised enzymes

- Immobilised enzymes can be reused. This is an important consideration, because the cost of replacing enzymes can be quite high.
- Immobilised enzymes can be recovered from the reaction vessel at the end of the process. This allows the product to be purified easily.
- Very often the process of immobilising an enzyme increases its stability. This reduces the amount of enzyme needed in the reaction.
- The production process is cheaper than if free enzymes are used.
- The efficiency of the enzyme is not affected by the immobilisation process. Therefore, an immobilised enzyme can catalyse a reaction as quickly as if the enzyme were free in the solution.

THE CELL

Uses of immobilised enzymes

- Soft drinks are often sweetened with a sugar called fructose. Fructose is sweeter than glucose. An immobilised enzyme called glucose isomerase is used to convert glucose to the sweeter-tasting fructose.

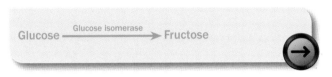

- Penicillin acylase is a very expensive enzyme used to alter the structure of the antibiotic penicillin. This allows the development of new antibiotics that may kill a wider range of bacteria. Penicillin acylase is used in an immobilised form in large bioreactors, so that it can be recovered and reused to reduce costs.

- Lactase is another expensive enzyme. It is immobilised in porous beads and used to convert lactose (a sugar found in a byproduct of cheese-making called whey) into two sweeter-tasting sugars (glucose and galactose). These products are used to replace condensed milk in the manufacture of soft toffee and caramel.

Activity 10 *To prepare an enzyme immobilisation and examine its application*

Preparing the immobilised enzyme
Note that, as the formation of alginate beads is a delicate process, all equipment must be clean before use. If possible all the water used in this activity should be distilled water.

Refer to bioprocessing with immobilised cells on page 123 for further details.

1 Add 0.4 g of sodium alginate to 10 cm³ of water in a large beaker.
2 Stir the mixture with a glass rod until it is equally smooth throughout and leave it to soak for 5 minutes.
3 Add 2 g of dried brewers' yeast to 10 cm³ of water. *(The yeast contains the enzyme to be immobilised – sucrase.)*
4 Stir the yeast solution and leave it for 5 minutes.
5 Dissolve 1.5 g of calcium chloride in 100 cm³ of water.

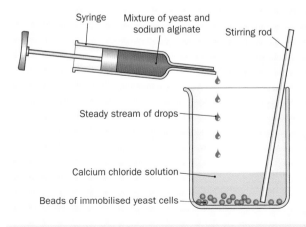

9.14 *Preparing immobilised cells*

6 Mix the alginate and yeast solutions thoroughly in a large beaker.
7 Draw some of the resulting mixture into a 10 ml syringe with no needle attached.
8 Slowly and steadily add a stream of alginate and yeast drops from the syringe to the calcium chloride solution. Hold the syringe at the same height (10 cm) above the solution and gently stir the solution as you add the drops. *(This prevents them from clumping.)*
  A gel of calcium alginate forms, enclosing and immobilising some of the yeast cells.
9 Leave the beads to harden for 15 minutes in the calcium chloride solution.
10 Filter the hardened beads of immobilised yeast cells and rinse them with water. *(This removes any yeast cells from outside the hardened beads.)* If necessary the beads can be stored in water or dried in filter paper and stored in a refrigerator.

Examining the application of the immobilised enzyme
Yeast contains the enzyme sucrase, which converts sucrose into glucose. We will compare the ability of free yeast and immobilised yeast to convert sucrose into glucose.

1 Add 2 g of dried brewer's yeast to 10 cm³ of water.
2 Pour this mixture into a separating funnel, as shown in the top diagram of Figure 9.15 (overleaf).
3 Pour the beads of immobilised yeast into a second separating funnel. A twisted-up paper clip may be used to prevent the beads from blocking the outlet of the funnel.
4 Dissolve 1 g of sucrose in 100 cm³ of warm water.
5 Pour 50 cm³ of the sucrose solution into each separating funnel. *(continued overleaf)*

6   Test the products using glucose test strips such as *Clinistix* or *Diastrix*.

7   Continue to test every minute until glucose is found coming from each separating funnel.

8   Note and record the time taken for glucose to first form.

Note that in most cases glucose is formed more quickly in the separating funnel containing the free yeast. The immobilised yeast is slower to start forming glucose. This is because it takes longer for the sucrose to penetrate the alginate beads and for the glucose to emerge from the alginate beads. However, once they start producing glucose the immobilised enzymes can be reused very easily.

9   Observe the products in each beaker. Compare the cloudiness of each solution. *(The free yeast solution contains many yeast cells and is very cloudy. The product of the immobilised yeast is much clearer because there are no yeast cells present.)*

10   Present the results as shown below.

Activity 10 results		
	Free yeast	Immobilised yeast
Time taken (mins) for glucose to appear		
Cloudiness of product (cloudy or clear)		

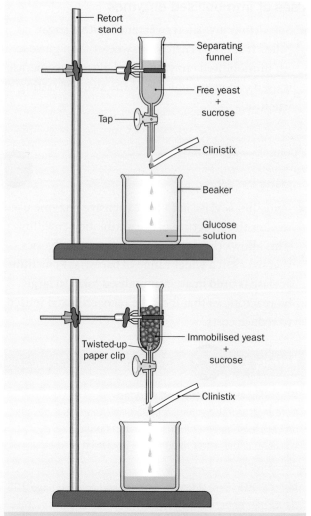

9.15 *Comparing free and immobilised enzymes*

Summary

Metabolism is all the chemical reactions that take place in an organism.

Sunlight (solar) energy is the primary source of energy for life on Earth.

Cellular energy is contained in bonds found in molecules within cells.

A catalyst speeds up a reaction without being used up in the reaction.

An enzyme is a protein (or organic) catalyst.

Enzymes work because they have the three-dimensional shape to fit a particular molecule. Enzymes:
- act on a substrate
- form products
- are made of protein
- are named by adding '-ase' to the name of their substrate

Enzymes control metabolic reactions in plants and animals.

- Amylase is a catabolic enzyme that breaks starch down to maltose.
- DNA polymerase is an anabolic enzyme that repairs damaged DNA.

Enzyme activity is affected by:
- temperature
- pH

To investigate the effect of pH on catalase activity
- mix blended or chopped celery (catalase), hydrogen peroxide, pH buffer 4 and washing-up liquid
- note the volume of froth formed after 2 minutes at different pH values

To investigate the effect of temperature on the rate of catalase activity
- mix blended or chopped celery (catalase), hydrogen peroxide, pH buffer 9 and washing-up liquid
- note the volume of froth formed after 2 minutes at different temperatures

Immobilised enzymes are attached to each other or to an inert material.

THE CELL

The benefits of immobilised enzymes are:
- they may be reused
- they are easy to separate from the product (therefore it is easy to purify the product)
- they are often more stable than the natural enzyme
- the process is cheaper
- their efficiency is not reduced

Immobilised enzymes are used to:
- produce fructose (sweetener) from glucose
- convert penicillin to different forms
- produce sweet-tasting sugars from whey

Yeast contains the enzyme sucrase. This enzyme is immobilised by:
- mixing yeast with sodium alginate
- adding beads of the mixture to calcium chloride
- filtering and rinsing the hardened beads

The application of an immobilised enzyme is shown by:
- adding sucrose solution to immobilised yeast (containing sucrase) in a separating funnel
- testing for the production of glucose

Revision questions

1 **(a)** What is metabolism?
  (b) Distinguish between anabolism and catabolism.
  (c) Why is metabolism necessary?
2 **(a)** Distinguish between solar and cellular energy.
  (b) Name the biological process that converts **(i)** solar energy to cellular energy, **(ii)** cellular energy to energy that can be used in a cell.
3 Distinguish between:
  (a) an enzyme and a catalyst
  (b) a substrate and a product.
4 **(a)** Explain why the shape of an enzyme is important.
  (b) Explain why high temperatures may prevent an enzyme from working.
5 Name and give the function of one **(a)** anabolic and **(b)** catabolic, enzyme.
6 Name two factors that affect the rate of enzyme action.
7 Give a reason for each of the following:
  (a) Amylase is active in the mouth.
  (b) Amylase works in the mouth but not in the stomach.
  (c) Pepsin works in the stomach, but amylase does not.
  (d) Putting food in a refrigerator slows bacterial action.
  (e) Putting food in a freezer stops bacterial action.
8 Answer the following questions with reference to investigating the effect of temperature on enzyme action.
  (a) Name the enzyme and substrate used.
  (b) Why is washing-up liquid used?
  (c) Why are the ingredients placed in a water bath before mixing them?
  (d) What factor was kept constant during this experiment?
  (e) Describe how the named factor is kept constant.
  (f) What control is used in the experiment?
  (g) How is the activity of the enzyme judged?
  (h) Explain why less froth forms at 10°C compared to 20°C.

(continued)

  (i) How did you know when the enzyme had completed its activity?
9 The graph shown in Figure 9.16 refers to an enzyme-controlled reaction carried out at two temperatures.

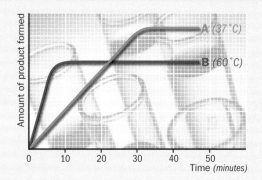

9.16

  (a) At what time does the amount of product formed level off in graph A?
  (b) Suggest a reason why graph A levels off at this time.
  (c) At which temperature is most product formed after 10 minutes?
  (d) At which temperature is the greatest amount of product formed after 50 minutes?
  (e) Suggest a reason why graph B levels off sooner than graph A.
  (f) After 20 minutes, at which temperature has most substrate been broken down?
10 In testing for the effects of pH on enzyme activity:
  (a) Name a suitable enzyme.
  (b) What substrate would you use with this enzyme?
  (c) How do you ensure a constant temperature?
  (d) How do you vary the pH?
  (e) Name the end products of the reaction.
  (f) How is the activity of the enzyme estimated?
  (g) Describe a suitable control.
  (h) What result would you expect for the control?
  (i) If the enzyme was pepsin, at what pH would you expect it to be most effective?

(continued overleaf)

THE CELL

11 (a) Explain what is meant by **(i)** bioprocessing, **(ii)** immobilised enzymes, **(iii)** a bioreactor.

(b) Give two traditional and two modern examples of bioprocessing.

(c) Suggest one problem with the use of freely dissolved enzymes in bioprocessing.

12 Explain, with the aid of a diagram, any three methods by which enzymes can be immobilised.

13 Give three benefits for using immobilised (compared to free) enzymes.

14 Give two uses for immobilised enzymes. In each case name the substrate, enzymc and product of the reaction.

15 In preparing an enzyme immobilisation:

(a) Name the enzyme that was immobilised.

(b) Name the material that immobilises the enzyme.

(c) Why is the immobilised enzyme **(i)** left in calcium chloride for some time, **(ii)** filtered and rinsed?

(d) Describe the appearance of the immobilised enzymes.

16 In examining the application of an immobilised enzyme:

(a) Name the enzyme, substrate and product.

(b) How did you test for the presence of the product?

(c) State one advantage of using immobilised enzymes for this reaction.

Sample examination questions

Section A

17 The graph shows how the rate of reaction of a carbohydrate-digesting enzyme in the human alimentary canal varies with pH.

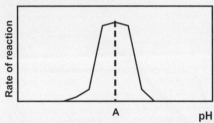

(a) Name a carbohydrate-digesting enzyme in the human alimentary canal.

(b) Where in the alimentary canal does this enzyme act?

(c) State the enzyme's product(s).

(d) What is the pH at A?

(e) A is said to be the enzyme's _____ pH.

(f) Suggest a temperature at which human enzymes work best.

(g) What term best describes the shape of an enzyme?

(2006 HL Q 3)

Section B

18 (a) (i) Is an enzyme a lipid, a protein or a carbohydrate?

(ii) Where in a cell are enzymes produced?

(b) As part of your practical activities you investigated the effect of temperature on the rate of activity of an enzyme.

(i) Name the enzyme that you used.

(ii) Name the substrate with which the enzyme reacts.

(iii) How did you vary the temperature?

(iv) How did you keep a constant pH during the investigation?

(v) How did you measure the rate of activity of the enzyme?

(vi) What was the result of your investigation?

(2007 OL Q 7)

19 (a) Immobilised enzymes are sometimes used in bioreactors.

(i) What is a bioreactor?

(ii) State one advantage of using an immobilised enzyme in a bioreactor.

(b) Answer the following questions in relation to an experiment that you carried out to immobilise an enzyme and use that immobilised enzyme.

(i) Name the enzyme that you used.

(ii) Draw a labelled diagram of the apparatus that you used to immobilise the enzyme.

(iii) Describe how you used this apparatus to immobilise the enzyme. In your answer name the solutions that you used and explain their purpose.

(iv) Describe briefly how you used the immobilised enzyme.   *(2005 HL Q 7)*

Section C

20 What is metabolism? Describe briefly the part played by enzymes in metabolism.

(2004 OL Q 13a)

21 Enzymes can be immobilised and then used in bioprocessing.

(i) What is meant by immobilisation?

(ii) Name a substance that is used to immobilise enzymes.

(iii) Give **two** advantages of using immobilised enzymes.

(iv) Give **one** application of a named immobilised enzyme. In your answer, refer to substrate, enzyme and product.   *(2007 HL Q 11c)*

Previous examination questions

Ordinary level	Higher level
2003 Sample Q 7	2003 Sample Q 7
2004 Q 13a	2005 Q 7
2005 Q 8	2006 Q 3
2007 Q 7	2007 Q 7, Q 11c

*For latest questions go to **www.edco.ie/biology***

Chapter 10 Enzymes (advanced) and energy carriers

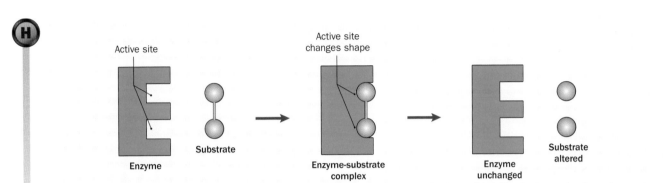

10.1 *The induced fit model of enzyme action*

Active site

The **active site** is the part of an enzyme that combines with the substrate.

It was thought that active sites were rigid areas that had an opposite or complementary shape to the substrate. This idea was similar to the complementary shape of a lock and a key (and was called the lock and key model of enzyme action).

It is now known that the active site is not a rigid shape. Instead the active site is a depression or pocket on the surface of the enzyme. The enzyme itself is a protein that has a complex three-dimensional shape, as has the active site. Many enzymes are composed of two or more globular sections, called domains, joined together.

When the substrate enters the active site it causes (or induces) it to change shape slightly. The active site then fits more precisely around the substrate. This process is called the **induced fit model** of enzyme action (see Figure 10.1). Very often the active site is larger than the substrate to which it combines.

The induced fit model of enzyme action can be compared to the way a bean bag, with a large hollow in it, will change shape to fit snugly around our body shape when we sit in it.

Mechanism of enzyme action – the induced fit model

1 The substrate combines with the active site of the enzyme.
2 The active site is induced or caused to change shape slightly.
3 The substrate and enzyme form an enzyme-substrate complex. The bonds in the substrate are altered so that the substrate changes into the product(s).
4 The products leave the active site. This means the active site returns to its original shape and can now accept a new substrate molecule.

These four steps happen very quickly. In some enzymes they take place more than 1000 times every second. For this reason, and because the enzyme is unchanged in the process, a small amount of enzyme can process a large number of substrate molecules in a short space of time.

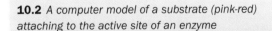

10.2 *A computer model of a substrate (pink-red) attaching to the active site of an enzyme*

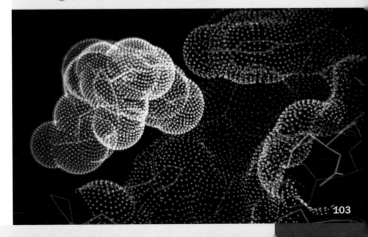

THE CELL

THE CELL

Enzyme specificity

Most enzymes are said to be specific to a single substrate. This means that an enzyme will only react with one particular substrate. The reason for this is that each active site will only fit or react with a single substrate.

Anything that alters the shape of the active site will reduce the ability of the enzyme to work effectively.

The shape of the active site is particularly sensitive to pH. Each enzyme is adapted to have the correct shape at a particular pH value (e.g. pH 2 for pepsin and pH 6 to 8 for most enzymes).

If the pH is unsuitable, then the protein changes shape and the active site will no longer accept a substrate molecule. Enzymes are said to have their optimum activity at specific pH values. The optimum activity means that the enzyme works best and most rapidly at a particular pH value. The graph in Figure 9.8 on page 96 illustrates this.

Enzymes are also sensitive to temperature changes. An increase in temperature causes increased molecular movement. As a result, substrate molecules collide more frequently with enzymes. This means that reaction rates rise as temperatures rise.

However, each enzyme and active site starts to change its shape and lose its efficiency above a certain temperature. This temperature is between 20°C and 30°C for most plant enzymes and 37°C for human enzymes. (Refer to the graph shown in Figure 9.6 on page 95.)

Denaturation

When most proteins are heated above 40°C (or treated with certain chemicals or radiation) they gradually lose their three-dimensional shape. In the case of an enzyme, this means that it will lose its ability to react with its substrate. Such a change in shape and loss of biological activity is called **denaturation**. It is normally a permanent process.

> A **denatured enzyme** has lost its shape and can no longer carry out its function.

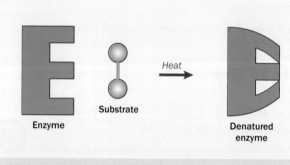

10.3 *Denaturing an enzyme*

Activity 11 *To investigate the effect of heat denaturation on catalase activity*

1 Blend three stalks of celery using a blender and add 100 cm³ of water. *(Celery contains the enzyme amylase.)*
2 Filter this solution into a large beaker using coffee filter paper.
3 Pour half of this solution into another beaker and boil for 10 minutes. *(This denatures the enzyme catalase.)*
4 Place 10 cm³ of this boiled catalase solution into a graduated cylinder and place in a water bath at 25°C.

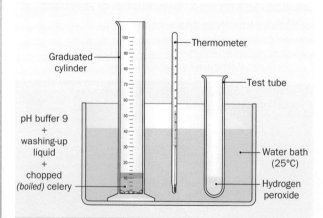

10.4 *Investigating the effect of denaturation on catalase*

5 Add 10 cm³ of pH 9 buffer solution to the graduated cylinder. *(This ensures a constant pH.)*
6 Using a dropper, add one drop of washing-up liquid. *(The washing-up liquid traps bubbles of oxygen, causing the formation of froth.)*
7 Add 5 cm³ of hydrogen peroxide to a test tube. Place this test tube in the water bath. *(Hydrogen peroxide is the substrate.)*
8 Leave both solutions until they have reached 25°C.
9 Add the hydrogen peroxide to the cylinder.
10 Swirl the cylinder carefully.
11 Note the volume of foam produced after 2 minutes.
12 Repeat the above steps using the unboiled catalase solution *(as a control).*
13 Results may be presented as:

Activity 11 results		
	Boiled enzyme	Unboiled enzyme
Froth forms (yes or no)		

14 The conclusion is that boiling catalase prevents it from working.

Energy carriers

In photosynthesis, some of the energy in sunlight is used to make food. In respiration, food is broken down to release energy. Energy is involved in both processes.

A molecule called ATP has a vital role in trapping and transferring energy in these processes (and in many other cell activities). Molecules called NAD^+ and $NADP^+$ also have a vital role in trapping and transferring energy in the form of high-energy electrons in these (and other) processes.

ADP and ATP

ADP is the abbreviation for **A**denosine **Di**Phosphate. This molecule is found in the cells of all organisms.

ADP is made of the base adenine (this base is also found in DNA and RNA), a 5-carbon sugar called ribose and two phosphate groups. Sometimes each phosphate group is shown as Pi. This indicates it is inorganic phosphate.

The bond between the two phosphate groups is an unstable bond. These unstable bonds are represented by the symbol '~'. While these bonds are sometimes referred to as high-energy bonds, this term is misleading. They are in fact lower in energy than many bonds in organic material.

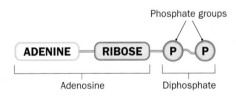

10.5 *Structure of ADP*

ADP can be thought of as a low-energy molecule. In this respect it is similar to an empty delivery van.

10.6 *ADP as a low-energy molecule*

If another phosphate group is added to ADP then it will form ATP (**A**denosine **Tri**Phosphate). Extra energy is also added, in the form of the unstable bond between the last two phosphate groups.

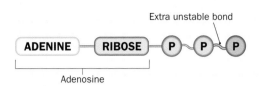

10.7 *Structure of ATP*

The process of adding a phosphate group is called **phosphorylation**. This process can be shown as:

ATP is an energy-rich compound. It is equivalent to a delivery van full of cargo (or energy).

10.8 *ATP as a high-energy molecule*

ATP stores energy. It can be moved around inside a cell, i.e. it is an energy carrier (just like a delivery van). However, it cannot be stored for very long. The energy in ATP must be used immediately.

When ATP breaks down it releases energy and a phosphate, and forms ADP. The energy released is used to carry out most of the reactions in cells. The breakdown of ATP can be shown as:

In photosynthesis, ATP is used to make glucose.

In respiration, glucose breaks down to form ATP. This ATP is used for functions such as muscle movement, protein (and enzyme) production, urine formation and brain activity.

 **Did you know?**

It is estimated that most cells release the energy from ATP about 10 million times every second.

THE CELL

NADP⁺ and NADPH

NADP⁺ (**N**icotinamide **A**denine **D**inucleotide **P**hosphate) is a low-energy molecule, involved in photosynthesis.

A hydrogen atom (H) consists of a proton, symbolised as H⁺, and an electron.

NADP⁺ can accept a pair of high-energy electrons (combined with a hydrogen ion or proton) to form NADPH, as shown below.

NADP⁺ + 2 electrons + H⁺ ⟶ NADPH
(low-energy)   (high-energy)   (high-energy)

The addition of electrons to a molecule is called reduction. NADP⁺ is said to be reduced to NADPH.

NADPH is a very high-energy molecule. It can be thought of as a juggernaut full of energy (compared with ATP, which is merely a vanload of energy).

NADPH is an electron carrier. It also carries hydrogen. The energy it contains is used in photosynthesis to form glucose.

When NADPH breaks down it releases energy in the form of two high-energy electrons and a hydrogen ion or proton. The breakdown of NADPH can be shown as:

NADPH ⟶ NADP⁺ + 2 electrons + H⁺
(high-energy)   (low-energy)   (high-energy)

NAD⁺ and NADH

NAD⁺ is used in respiration as an equivalent low-energy molecule to NADP⁺. In the same way, respiration uses NADH as an equivalent high-energy molecule to NADPH.

Remember that photosynthesis (starting with the letter P) uses the molecules with the letter P, i.e. NADP⁺ and NADPH.

These details are summarised below.

Energy carriers

Process	Low-energy	High-energy
Photosynthesis	ADP, NADP⁺	ATP, NADPH
Respiration	ADP, NAD⁺	ATP, NADH

Summary

The active site is the part of the enzyme that combines with the substrate.

In the induced fit model of enzyme action:
- the substrate causes the active site to change shape slightly
- the enzyme and substrate form a temporary enzyme-substrate complex
- the substrate is altered
- the enzyme remains unchanged and the active site returns to its original shape

Most enzymes are specific to a single substrate, due to the matching shapes of the substrate and active site.

The shape of the active site is sensitive to pH and temperature.

Enzymes (and other proteins) are denatured (lose their shape and activity) by temperatures above 40°C (and also by unsuitable pH and radiation).

The effect of heat denaturation on catalase can be investigated by:
- boiling catalase
- testing if it will then form froth when it reacts with hydrogen peroxide

ADP (adenosine diphosphate) is a low-energy molecule; **ATP** (adenosine triphosphate) is an energy-rich molecule.

ATP is the source of energy used for most cell reactions.

ADP and ATP are interconvertible, i.e.
- ADP + energy + P → ATP + water
- ATP + water → ADP + energy + P

Phosphorylation is the addition of phosphate to a molecule.

NADP⁺ is a low-energy molecule; **NADPH** is a high-energy molecule. Both molecules are involved in photosynthesis.

NADP⁺ and NADPH are interconvertible i.e.
- NADP⁺ + energy *(high-energy electrons)* + H⁺ → NADPH
- NADPH → NADP⁺ + energy *(high-energy electrons)* + H⁺

Respiration uses NAD⁺ (instead of NADP⁺) and NADH (instead of NADPH).

Revision questions

1 (a) Explain what is meant by:
   (i) the active site
   (ii) the enzyme-substrate complex
   (iii) enzymes are specific
   (b) How does the active site explain the specificity of enzymes?

2 (a) Explain, with the aid of diagrams, the induced fit model of enzyme action.
   (b) In this model explain how the active site relates to the substrate **(i)** before the reaction starts, **(ii)** when the enzyme-substrate complex is formed, **(iii)** after the reaction is complete.

3 Suggest two reasons why a small concentration of enzyme can speed up a reaction dramatically.

4 Draw simple graphs to show the effect on the activity of catalase of **(a)** pH, **(b)** temperature. Label the axes on each graph.

5 Why do changes in **(a)** pH, and **(b)** temperature, affect the activity of an enzyme?

6 (a) What is meant by denaturation?
   (b) Use a diagram to illustrate the effect of denaturation on an enzyme.
   (c) Name two factors that cause enzymes to be denatured.
   (d) Suggest one reason why plant enzymes are often denatured at lower temperatures than human enzymes.

7 In investigating the effect of heat denaturation on an enzyme:
   (a) Name the enzyme used.
   (b) Name the substrate for this enzyme.
   (c) State precisely how the enzyme was denatured.
   (d) What control was used?
   (e) What test was applied to determine the activity of the enzyme?
   (f) State the result of the test on **(i)** the control, **(ii)** the denatured enzyme.

8 (a) Give the full name for each of the following:
   (i) ADP **(ii)** ATP.
   (b) Which of the following are high-energy molecules?
   NAD^+, ATP, NADPH, $NADP^+$, ADP, NADH

9 (a) Draw a diagram to show where the available energy is located in a molecule of ATP.
   (b) What does ATP convert to when it releases its energy?
   (c) What is meant by phosphorylation?
   (d) Give an equation to show the phosphorylation of ADP.

10 Distinguish between $NADP^+$ and NADPH in terms of:
   (a) energy content, **(b)** electrons, **(c)** hydrogens.

11 In the case of each of the following, suggest whether it is a protein only or a protein that is also an enzyme:
   keratin, amylase, sucrase, insulin, maltase, ATPase, albumen, pepsin.

Sample examination questions

Section B

12 (i) To which group of molecules do enzymes belong?
   (ii) What is a denatured enzyme?
                                    (2003 Sample HL Q 7a)

13 (a) (i) What is meant by an enzyme's optimum pH?
      (ii) What is a denatured enzyme?
   (b) In the course of your studies you investigated the effect of denaturation by heat application on the activity of an enzyme.
      (i) Name the enzyme that you used.
      (ii) What substrate did you use?
      (iii) Describe how you carried out the investigation. In your answer you must refer to the way that you measured the enzyme's activity.
      (iv) State the results that you obtained.
                                    (2008 HL Q 9)

Section C

14 (i) For what is ATP an abbreviation?
   (ii) What is the role of ATP in cells?
                                    (2007 HL Q 11a)

Previous examination questions

Ordinary level	Higher level
n/a	2003 Sample Q 7a
	2004 Q 11a
	2007 Q 11a
	2008 Q 9

*For latest questions go to **www.edco.ie/biology***

THE CELL

Chapter 11 **Photosynthesis**

Introduction

The Sun is the ultimate source of energy for our planet. There are many forms of solar radiation. The most important types of solar radiation in biology are infrared rays (which help to heat the Earth), ultraviolet rays (which cause sunburn and cancer) and light rays.

Autotrophs are organisms that can make their own food. Autotrophs are also called producers. The vast majority of autotrophs are green plants. Green plants make their food by photosynthesis.

Photosynthesis is the process by which glucose and oxygen are made from carbon dioxide and water. Light is needed as a source of energy for this process. The green pigment (or dye) called chlorophyll is necessary as a catalyst for the process. Photosynthesis takes place in plants, especially in the green parts, such as leaves, because they contain chlorophyll.

Photosynthesis is represented and defined by the balanced equation:

$$6CO_2 + 6H_2O + light \xrightarrow{chlorophyll} C_6H_{12}O_6 + 6O_2$$
(carbon dioxide) (water)   (glucose)   (oxygen)

Cells need energy to carry out their reactions. This energy is needed in small, usable amounts and is best supplied by the breakdown of a molecule called Adenosine TriPhosphate (ATP). In photosynthesis, light energy is initially used to make ATP. ATP is then used to supply energy to make glucose.

Plants can use glucose at a later stage to re-form ATP in order to provide themselves with cellular energy. Animals consume glucose made by plants and convert it to ATP for their own use. This means that solar energy is the basic source of energy for all organisms on Earth.

Role of photosynthesis

Life on Earth depends on photosynthesis for the following reasons:

- Plants use it to make food.
- Animals get their food from plants. Thus, both plants and animals get food from photosynthesis.
- Photosynthesis produces the oxygen that most living things need in order to obtain energy in respiration.
- Photosynthesis was responsible for forming fossil fuels (e.g. turf, coal and oil). These fuels were formed over millions of years by the death and decay of plants and animals.

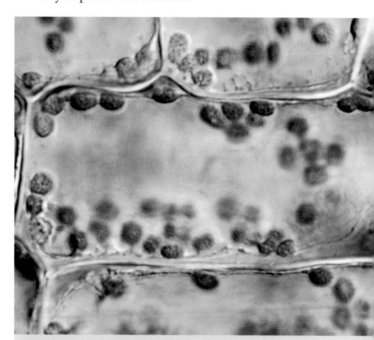

11.1 *Photosynthetic cells in an* Elodea *leaf: chloroplasts are the round, dark-green structures inside each cell*

The main events in photosynthesis

1. Light is absorbed

Some of the sunlight that strikes a plant is trapped by chlorophyll. Chlorophyll is normally found in cell organelles called chloroplasts. Therefore it is in chloroplasts that photosynthesis takes place.

The trapped sunlight provides the energy that a plant needs to make glucose (see Figure 11.2, opposite).

2. Water is split

Some of the trapped sunlight energy is used in the chloroplast to split water molecules.

Every hydrogen atom is made of a hydrogen ion or proton (H^+) and an electron (e^-). Water has the formula H_2O.

When two water molecules are split they form four protons, four electrons and a molecule of oxygen gas (O$_2$), as shown by the following equation:

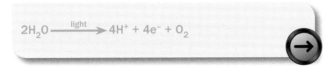

$$2H_2O \xrightarrow{\text{light}} 4H^+ + 4e^- + O_2$$

3. The products of the splitting of water

The three products formed when water is split (i.e. protons (H$^+$), electrons and oxygen) behave as follows:

a. The electrons are passed to chlorophyll.
b. The protons are released into a storage pool of protons in the chloroplast for later use.
c. The oxygen may pass from the chloroplast out into the cytoplasm and eventually out of the leaf into the atmosphere. (The oxygen released by plants is the oxygen that humans and other organisms take in for respiration; photosynthesis maintains Earth's oxygen levels.)

Alternatively, the oxygen may be used within the cells or the leaf, in the process of respiration.

4. Light energises electrons

Some of the sunlight energy trapped by chlorophyll is passed on to electrons in chlorophyll to form high-energy electrons.

5. Glucose is formed

The high-energy electrons from chlorophyll, along with protons from the pool of stored protons, are combined with carbon dioxide to form a carbohydrate (glucose C$_6$H$_{12}$O$_6$). See Figure 11.2.

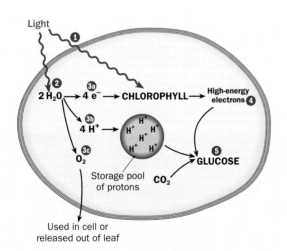

11.2 *Summary of the main events in photosynthesis (note that the numbered points refer to the numbered points explained in the text)*

Sources of light, carbon dioxide and water for photosynthesis

Light

Sunlight is the normal source of light for photosynthesis. However, artificial light sources such as electric light bulbs can also be used.

Artificial light is often used in greenhouses to stimulate crop growth. This is especially the case in countries that lie near the Earth's poles, because they receive very little sunlight in winter.

Carbon dioxide

Plants have two sources of carbon dioxide: one is external, the other is internal.

EXTERNAL

Most of the carbon dioxide that a plant uses in photosynthesis enters the leaf from the atmosphere. With the destruction of the Earth's forests there are decreasing numbers of plants to absorb carbon dioxide. This is one of the reasons why worldwide carbon dioxide levels are rising (see *The carbon cycle* on page 32).

INTERNAL

Some of the carbon dioxide used in photosynthesis is produced by the leaf cells in the process of respiration.

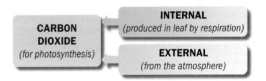

11.3 *Sources of CO$_2$ for photosynthesis*

The amount of carbon dioxide available to a plant is relatively low. This is due to the low levels of carbon dioxide in the atmosphere (only 0.04%). The lower the level of carbon dioxide, the slower the rate of photosynthesis.

Sometimes artificial sources of carbon dioxide (e.g. burning gas) are used in greenhouses to increase crop growth.

Water

Water is absorbed from the soil by the roots of plants. This water then passes up through the plant stem and into the leaves, where it is used in photosynthesis.

THE CELL

There is a choice of activity here. This account refers only to the influence of light intensity on the rate of photosynthesis.

Activity 12   *To investigate the influence of light intensity or carbon dioxide on the rate of photosynthesis*

1   Add sodium bicarbonate (also called sodium hydrogen carbonate) to some water in a test tube until it will no longer dissolve. This means that excess bicarbonate has been added and the water is saturated with carbon dioxide. *(As a result there will be a constant concentration of carbon dioxide during the experiment.)*

2   Cut a section of *Elodea* and place it (cut end upwards) in the test tube. Set up the apparatus as shown in Figure 11.4 in a darkened room. *(The water bath ensures that the temperature stays constant.)* The lamp should be 1 metre from the apparatus.

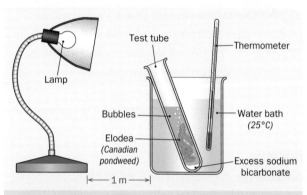

11.4 *Apparatus to show the effect of light intensity on rate of photosynthesis*

3   Allow the *Elodea* to stabilise for 5 minutes.

4   Count the number of bubbles of oxygen coming from the cut end of the stem per minute. *(This gives an indication of the rate of photosynthesis.)*

5   Repeat step 4 twice more.

6   Calculate the average number of bubbles per minute. *(This is a measure of the rate of photosynthesis.)*

7   Increase the light intensity by moving the lamp closer to the apparatus.

8   Repeat steps 3, 4, 5 and 6 each time the lamp is moved (i.e. at 80 cm, 60 cm, 40 cm and 20 cm).

9   Record your results as shown in the following table.

Activity 12 results

Distance between lamp and apparatus (cm)	Number of bubbles per minute	Average number of bubbles per minute
100	8 10 9	9
80	12 14 13	13

(other values should be recorded in this way)

10 You will see that as the lamp is moved closer to the apparatus the rate of bubble production increases. However, at some point, the rate of bubble production ceases to increase. The plant is then said to be saturated with light.

11 Draw a graph of the rate of bubble production vs. light intensity (putting light intensity on the horizontal axis). The graph should appear as:

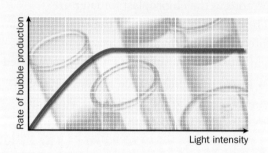

11.5

Note 1: *To convert from distance (in cm) to light intensity use the formula:*

$$\text{light intensity} \propto \frac{10\,000}{(\text{distance})^2}$$

where the symbol $\propto$ means 'is proportional to'.

The final table of results (based on the figures in step 9) will appear as:

Distance between lamp and apparatus (cm)	Light intensity	Average number of bubbles per minute
100	1	9
80	1.56	13
60	2.78	...
40	6.25	...
20	25	...

11.6 *Elodea (pondweed)*

Note 2: *This experiment can also be carried out using the apparatus in Figure 11.7. In this case the rate of photosynthesis can be calculated by:*
(a) counting the number of bubbles, as before, or
(b) measuring the volume of oxygen gas collected in the top of the test tube after a suitable length of time (e.g. 15 minutes).

In addition, the gas collected in the test tube can be shown to be oxygen as it rekindles a glowing splint.

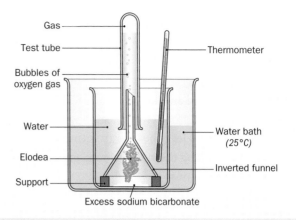

11.7 *Alternative apparatus to show the effect of light intensity on rate of photosynthesis*

Detailed study of photosynthesis

The stages of photosynthesis

Photosynthesis is a process that takes place in two stages or phases: the light stage and the dark stage.

The reactions in the light stage are dependent on the energy provided by light (they cannot take place in darkness). This stage is also called the light-dependent stage.

The dark stage reactions do not require light; they are said to be light-independent. However, the dark stage reactions depend on some of the products of the light stage.

Light stage

The events of the light stage take place in the chloroplast. The light stage reactions involve electrons flowing. As this happens very rapidly, the light stage reactions are so fast that they are not controlled by enzymes.

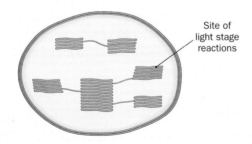

11.8 *Site of the light stage reactions in a chloroplast*

Events in the light stage

The events of the light stage can be explained under the headings of light absorption, light energy transferred to electrons and the flow of electrons along pathways 1 and 2.

1. Light is absorbed

White light is composed of different wavelengths (colours) of light, which can be remembered by:

Richard	Of	York	Gave	Battle	In	Vain
RED	ORANGE	YELLOW	GREEN	BLUE	INDIGO	VIOLET

Chloroplasts contain a range of pigments, including chlorophyll. Each of the chloroplast pigments absorbs a different colour of light. By having a range of pigments, plants ensure that they can absorb a range of colours of light.

In general, plants absorb all the colours of white light except green. Green light is normally reflected by plants. This is why most plants are green.

2. Light energy is transferred to electrons

Pigments are arranged in clusters in the chloroplast. Each cluster consists of a variety of pigments, a strategically placed chlorophyll molecule and an electron acceptor. This special chlorophyll molecule is called the reaction centre chlorophyll.

Note that there may be many chlorophyll molecules in a cluster, but only one is located beside the electron acceptor.

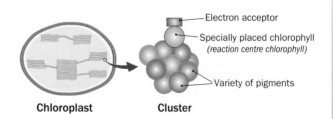

11.9 *Structure and location of a cluster*

THE CELL

In each cluster, the different pigments absorb light energy of different wavelengths (or colours). The function of the cluster is to absorb as much light as possible.

The different pigments transfer the absorbed energy from one to another until it reaches the reaction centre chlorophyll associated with the electron acceptor. Here the energy is transferred to electrons, causing them to become energised, or high-energy, electrons.

The energised electrons are passed from the chlorophyll to the electron acceptor. From here the energised electrons flow from the electron acceptor along one of two different pathways.

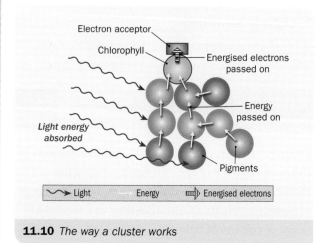

11.10 *The way a cluster works*

11.11 *A chloroplast*

3. Electron flow: Pathway 1

In pathway 1, the high-energy electrons pass from chlorophyll to the electron acceptor. They then pass from the electron acceptor to a series of other electron acceptors and back again to the chlorophyll molecule. All these molecules are located in the chloroplast.

In this pathway, the electrons are said to recycle (to chlorophyll). When the electrons return in this way they lose energy. The energy they release is trapped by ADP and a phosphate, and used to form ATP and water as shown below.

ADP + energy + P ⟶ ATP + water

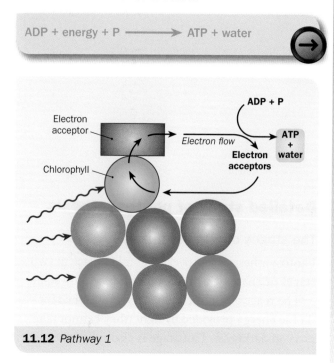

11.12 *Pathway 1*

This pathway is said to be cyclic, because the electrons flow from chlorophyll to the electron acceptor and back again to chlorophyll. The method of making ATP used in *pathway 1* is called **cyclic electron flow**.

4. Electron flow: Pathway 2

Two high-energy electrons at a time are passed from chlorophyll to the electron acceptor and along another series of electron acceptors. Again, all of these are in the chloroplast (Figure 11.13, next page).

This time, the energised electrons do not return to chlorophyll. Instead, they lose some energy as they pass from acceptor to acceptor.

The energy they release is used to make more ATP as shown below.

ADP + energy + P ⟶ ATP + water

Eventually the two electrons combine with $NADP^+$ to temporarily form $NADP^-$.

$NADP^+$ + 2 electrons ($2e^-$) ⟶ $NADP^-$

The chlorophyll molecule is now short of electrons. It gains new electrons from the splitting of water.

H Recall that when two water molecules are split they form four protons (4H⁺), four electrons (4e⁻) and oxygen (O₂). Two of these electrons replace the electrons lost by chlorophyll.

The protons formed by the splitting of water are stored in a pool of protons in the chloroplast. These protons are now attracted to NADP⁻ and combine with it to reduce it to NADPH as shown below.

NADP⁻ + **proton** *(or hydrogen ion, H⁺)* ⟶ NADPH →

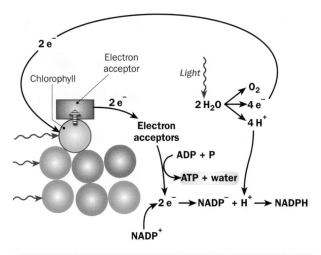

11.13 *Pathway 2*

As a result of the events in *pathway 2*, electrons pass (two at a time) from a water molecule to chlorophyll.

Here they are energised by light and flow to the electron acceptor. From here they move away, along a series of electron acceptors, and are eventually used to form NADPH. As they flow, some of their energy is used to convert ADP into ATP.

In this pathway, the electrons start with water and end up in NADPH. The electrons do not recycle. For this reason, *pathway 2* is also called **non-cyclic electron flow**.

End products of the light stage

By the end of the light stage, three end-products have formed.

1 ATP is made. This will supply energy for the dark stage reactions.
2 NADPH is made. This will supply protons and energised electrons for the dark stage reactions.
3 Oxygen is made when water is split. The oxygen can be used for respiration or it can be released into the atmosphere.

11.14 *Geothermally powered greenhouses in Iceland*

Dark stage

The dark stage reactions take place in a different part of the chloroplast to the light stage reactions. The events of the dark stage were discovered by Melvin Calvin, who received a Nobel prize for his work in 1961. The dark stage is sometimes called the Calvin cycle.

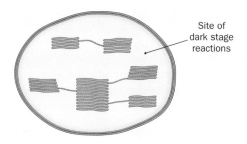

11.15 *Site of the dark stage reactions in a chloroplast*

The reactions of the dark stage are controlled by enzymes. This means that the dark stage is affected by temperature.

Events in the dark stage

Carbon dioxide from the air or from respiration enters the chloroplast. In the chloroplast, carbon dioxide molecules combine with hydrogen ions (H⁺) and electrons to form glucose.

The hydrogen ions (H⁺) and electrons come from the conversion of NADPH (made in the light stage) to NADP⁺, as shown below.

Recall that the addition of electrons is called reduction. For this reason it is said that carbon dioxide is reduced to glucose.

NADPH ⟶ NADP⁺ + 2 electrons + H⁺

The energy to form glucose comes from the conversion of ATP (made in the light stage) to ADP and phosphate.

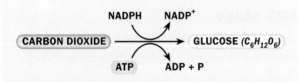

$$ATP + water \longrightarrow ADP + P + energy$$

All the NADP⁺ and ADP molecules that are produced in the dark stage are reused in the light stage. The formation of glucose is outlined in Figure 11.16.

$$\text{CARBON DIOXIDE} \xrightarrow{\substack{NADPH \quad NADP^+ \\ ATP \quad\quad ADP + P}} \text{GLUCOSE } (C_6H_{12}O_6)$$

11.16 *The formation of glucose*

Figure 11.17 shows an overall representation of the light and dark stages of photosynthesis. In particular, it shows how the two stages are interconnected.

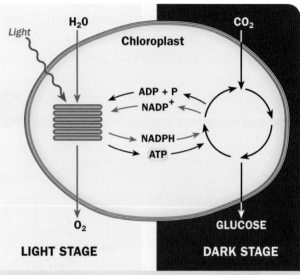

11.17 *The light and dark stages of photosynthesis*

Summary

Autotrophs make their own food.

Photosynthesis:
- is vital because it produces food and oxygen
- mostly takes place in leaves
- can be represented by the balanced equation

$$6CO_2 + 6H_2O + light \xrightarrow{\text{chlorophyll}} C_6H_{12}O_6 + 6O_2$$

The main events in photosynthesis are:
- Light energy is absorbed by chlorophyll.
- Water is split using absorbed sunlight energy.
- The products of the splitting of water are electrons (passed to chlorophyll), protons (stored in the chloroplast) and oxygen gas (released or used for respiration).
- Sunlight energy is used to form high-energy electrons in chlorophyll.
- The high-energy electrons, stored protons (hydrogen ions) and carbon dioxide are used to make glucose.

Sources of light, carbon dioxide and water for photosynthesis:
- Sunlight is the normal source of light for photosynthesis.
- Carbon dioxide is obtained from the atmosphere or from the process of respiration in the leaf.
- Water is obtained from the soil.

To investigate the influence of light intensity on the rate of photosynthesis:
- The number of bubbles of gas released per minute from *Elodea* is counted to calculate the rate of photosynthesis.

- Excess sodium hydrogen carbonate ensures constant CO_2 concentrations.
- A water bath ensures a constant temperature.
- Light intensity is varied by altering the distance between the lamp and the apparatus.
- The results indicate that increasing light intensity increases photosynthesis, up to a point.

The light stage requires light and takes place in the chloroplast. The events in the light stage are:
1. Light energy is absorbed by a range of pigments in the chloroplast.
2. The absorbed energy is transferred to a special chlorophyll, where it energises electrons.
3. The energised electrons may return to chlorophyll, using their energy to make ATP *(pathway 1)*, or
4. The energised electrons may be taken away from chlorophyll and combined with NADP⁺ and H⁺ to form NADPH *(pathway 2)*.
5. Water is split to produce:
   - electrons, which replace those lost by the chlorophyll molecule
   - protons (H⁺), which help to form NADPH
   - oxygen, which is used in respiration or released

Electron flow:
- In cyclic electron flow, ATP is made using light energy, by a process that involves electrons from chlorophyll returning to chlorophyll *(pathway 1)*.
- In non-cyclic electron flow, light energy is converted to ATP and NADPH by a process that involves electrons flowing from chlorophyll but not returning to it *(pathway 2)*.

THE CELL

The end products of the light stage are ATP, NADPH and oxygen. Both ATP and NADPH are used in the dark stage.

The dark stage does not require light and takes place in the chloroplast. The events of the dark stage are:
1 NADPH releases H$^+$ and two electrons.
2 CO$_2$ combines with the H$^+$ and electrons.
3 Energy is provided by ATP converting to ADP.
4 Glucose is made.
5 ADP and NADP$^+$ return to the light stage.

THE CELL

Revision questions

1 Explain what is meant by **(a)** autotroph and **(b)** photosynthesis.
2 **(a)** In what part of a plant does photosynthesis normally take place?
   (b) Give a balanced equation for photosynthesis.
   (c) Name four substances necessary for photosynthesis.
   (d) Name the two main products of photosynthesis.
3 State two benefits of photosynthesis for **(a)** plants, **(b)** animals.
4 Give two reasons in support of the statement that 'photosynthesis is the most important reaction on Earth'.
5 **(a)** Name the organelle in plant cells in which photosynthesis takes place.
   (b) Name the most important pigment in this organelle.
   (c) What is the main function of this pigment?
6 In photosynthesis water is split.
   (a) What supplies the energy to split water?
   (b) Name the three products formed when water is split.
   (c) State what happens to each of these products.
   (d) Which of the three products may be used directly by humans?
7 How do plants get **(a)** light, **(b)** carbon dioxide and **(c)** water for photosynthesis?
8 Name any two methods that growers can use to increase their yield of greenhouse plants.
9 The following apparatus was used to investigate the effect of light intensity on photosynthesis.

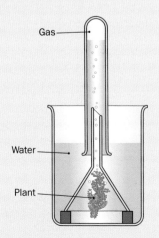

11.18

   (a) Name a suitable plant for this experiment.
   (b) Name the gas produced.
   (c) State the normal test for this gas.
   (d) How can the CO$_2$ concentration in the water be kept constant?
   (e) What adaptation could be made to ensure that the temperature remained constant?
   (f) How could the light intensity be varied?
   (g) State one way in which the rate of photosynthesis could be measured.
   (h) Why should the experiment be carried out in a darkened room?
10 In carrying out the experiment outlined in the previous question, the following results were obtained.

The effect of light intensity on photosynthesis	
Light intensity	**Bubbles per minute**
0	0
1	6
2	14
3	26
4	38
5	40
6	40

   (a) Use graph paper to draw a graph of these results.
   (b) Explain, referring to specific numerical values, the results of the graph.
   (c) Estimate from your graph **(i)** the number of bubbles per minute produced at a light intensity of 2.5 and **(ii)** the light intensity at which 30 bubbles per minute would be produced.
11 Distinguish between the light and dark phases of photosynthesis on the basis of **(a)** the need for light, **(b)** the need for enzymes, **(c)** end products.
12 **(a)** In what cell organelle is water split?
   (b) Name two products of the splitting of water that are necessary for the light stage.
   (c) What gas is produced when water is split?
   (d) State two possible fates of this gas.
13 **(a)** What is the function of pigments in a chloroplast?
   (b) Why do chloroplasts have a range of such pigments?
   (c) In what cell organelle are these pigments located?

14 The light stage reactions involve a flow of energised electrons.
(a) What molecule is necessary to allow these electrons to be energised?
(b) What is the source of the energy used to energise them?
(c) The energised electrons can follow pathway 1 or pathway 2. Distinguish between these pathways in terms of **(i)** the paths taken by the electrons, **(ii)** the end products of each route.

15 Give a brief, outline account of **(a)** the light stage and **(b)** the dark stage of photosynthesis.

16 Relate the following events to either the light or dark stage of photosynthesis:
(a) formation of ATP
(b) use of CO_2
(c) breakdown of NADPH
(d) O_2 production
(e) absorption of light
(f) phosphorylation
(g) production of ADP
(h) the splitting of water
(i) formation of glucose.

Sample examination questions

Section A

17 The following graph shows how the rate of photosynthesis varied when a plant was subjected to varying levels of light intensity or carbon dioxide concentration.

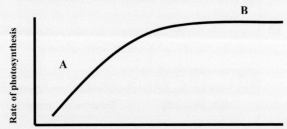

Light intensity or carbon dioxide concentration

(a) What is happening at A?
(b) What is happening at B?
(c) Suggest a reason for your answer in **(b)**.
(d) Where in a cell does photosynthesis take place?
(e) Give **two** sources of the carbon dioxide that is found in the atmosphere.
(f) Suggest **one** way in which the rate of photosynthesis of plants in a greenhouse could be increased.

(2005 HL Q 4)

Section B

18 (a) State a precise role for each of the following in photosynthesis:
(i) Carbon dioxide
(ii) Water
(b) Answer the following questions in relation to an activity that you carried out to investigate the influence of light intensity **or** carbon dioxide concentration on the rate of photosynthesis.
(i) Name the plant that you used.
(ii) How did you vary light intensity **or** carbon dioxide concentration?
(iii) State a factor that you kept constant during the investigation.
(iv) How did you ensure that the factor that you mentioned in **(iii)** remained constant?

(v) How did you measure the rate of photosynthesis?
(vi) Using labelled axes, sketch a graph to show how the rate of photosynthesis varied with the factor mentioned in **(ii)** above.

(2007 HL Q 9)

Section C

19 (a) What is metabolism? Describe briefly the part played by enzymes in metabolism.
(b) The following equation summarises the process of photosynthesis.

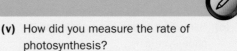

$$\text{Gas A} + \text{Water} \xrightarrow[\text{Chlorophyll}]{\text{Energy}} \text{Glucose} + \text{Gas B}$$

(i) Name Gas A.
(ii) Name Gas B.
(iii) Name the energy source.
(iv) Plants obtain Gas A from the air. Name **two** processes that release this gas into the air.
(v) Suggest **two** possible fates for Gas B, following its production in the plant.
(vi) Where in a leaf would you expect to find cells with most chlorophyll?
(vii) What term is used to describe the nutrition of plants?
(c) The apparatus shown below may be used to investigate the effect of an environmental factor on the rate of photosynthesis.

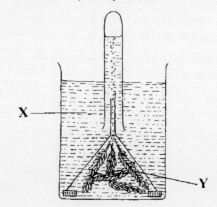

(continued)

(i) Name X and Y.

(ii) How would you measure the rate of photosynthesis?

(iii) Name an environmental factor that you would vary in this experiment.

(iv) Explain how you would vary the factor that you have named in **(iii)**.

(v) Other environmental factors should be kept constant during the experiment. Name **one** of these factors.

(2004 OL Q 13b, c)

20 (a) ATP is an abbreviation. What does it stand for? Explain briefly the role of ATP in the energy exchanges of a cell.

(b) (i) The first stage of photosynthesis is commonly known as the light-dependent stage. It involves the energising of electrons and their subsequent passage along two possible pathways. Give an account of what happens on each of these pathways.

(ii) What is the fate of each of the products of the light-dependent stage?

(c) The effect of changing light intensity or carbon dioxide concentration on the rate of photosynthesis may be investigated by using the pondweed *Elodea*. Answer the following in relation to this investigation.

(i) Why is a water plant rather than a land plant used in this experiment?

(ii) How is the temperature kept constant in this experiment?

(iii) If pond water is used in the experiment, it is likely to contain dissolved carbon dioxide. Suggest two possible sources of carbon dioxide in pond water.

(iv) Explain how light intensity or carbon dioxide concentration may be varied.

(v) Each time light intensity or carbon dioxide concentration is varied a precaution is necessary. What is this precaution and why is it necessary?

(2004 HL Q 11)

21 (i) During photosynthesis oxygen is produced.
1. From what substance is oxygen produced?
2. In which stage of photosynthesis is oxygen produced?
3. Give **two** possible fates of oxygen following its production.

(ii) Give an account of the role of each of the following in photosynthesis:
1. ATP, 2. NADP.

(2008 HL Q 14(ii), (iii))

Previous examination questions

Ordinary level	Higher level
2004 Q 13	2003 Sample Q 12
2005 Q 11	2004 Q 11
2006 Q 4	2005 Q 4
2008 Q 12	2006 Q 11
	2007 Q 9
	2008 Q 14a(ii), (iii)

*For latest questions go to **www.edco.ie/biology***

Chapter 12 Respiration

Introduction

External respiration is the process by which organisms exchange gases with their environment.

External respiration takes place in the lungs of mammals, through the gills in fish, through openings in plant stems and on the bottom surface of leaves.

Internal respiration is the controlled release of energy from food. The food involved is usually glucose.

The process of internal respiration is controlled by enzymes. They allow energy to be released in small amounts, which can easily be trapped for later use. The energy is trapped in the form of a molecule called ATP (adenosine triphosphate).

12.1 *Summary of respiration*

Aerobic respiration

Internal respiration can be either aerobic or anaerobic.

Aerobic respiration is the controlled release of energy from food using oxygen.

Most living things get their energy from aerobic respiration and are therefore called aerobes.

In this process, the energy stored in the bonds of a molecule such as glucose is released and used to make ATP.

When ATP breaks down, it supplies energy for all the metabolic reactions in the cell, e.g. muscular movement, production of new cells and growth.

The process of aerobic respiration can be represented by the balanced equation:

$$C_6H_{12}O_6 + 6O_2 \xrightarrow{\text{enzymes}} 6CO_2 + 6H_2O + \text{energy}$$
$$\text{(glucose)} \quad \text{(oxygen)} \qquad \text{(carbon dioxide)} \quad \text{(water)}$$

Aerobic respiration is a relatively efficient method of obtaining energy. About 40% of the energy in glucose is converted to ATP during aerobic respiration.

This high efficiency is due to the substrate (glucose) being completely broken down. The end products (carbon dioxide and water) have very low energies. Most of the energy that is not converted to ATP is lost as heat.

Stages in aerobic respiration

Respiration may occur as either a one-stage or a two-stage process. Aerobic respiration is a two-stage process.

STAGE 1

Stage 1 starts with a process called **glycolysis**. It is an anaerobic process. This means it does not use or require oxygen in order to take place. It only releases a small amount of energy. As a result, it is inefficient as an energy-release system.

Glycolysis (or stage 1) takes place in the cytosol of the cell. The cytoplasm consists of all of the living parts of the cell surrounding the nucleus. The cytosol is the cytoplasm minus the cell organelles.

Glycolysis involves the splitting of glucose (a 6-carbon sugar) into two 3-carbon molecules. In doing this, a small amount of energy is released and used to produce a small number of ATP molecules. Glycolysis can be represented by the word equation:

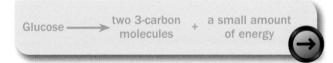

In glycolysis, glucose is incompletely or partially broken down. Much of the energy that was stored in the bonds of the glucose molecule is retained in the bonds of the two 3-carbon molecules. This is why glycolysis produces only a low yield of energy.

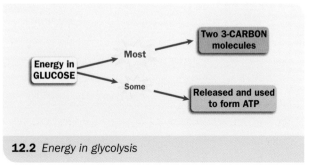

12.2 *Energy in glycolysis*

STAGE 2

Stage 2 requires and uses oxygen. It is aerobic. It releases a large amount of energy. This means it is efficient as an energy-release system.

Stage 2 occurs in the mitochondria.

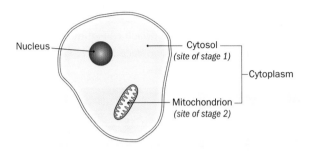

12.3 *Location of the stages of respiration in a cell*

The stage 2 reactions are very complex. They involve the breakdown of the 3-carbon molecules (formed in stage 1) to carbon dioxide and water. One of the steps in this breakdown requires oxygen.

As stage 2 is a complete breakdown of the 3-carbon molecules, it releases a large amount of energy (which is used to form a large number of ATP molecules). Very little energy remains in the carbon dioxide and water molecules.

Carbon dioxide and water are the end-products of both stage 2 and of aerobic respiration.

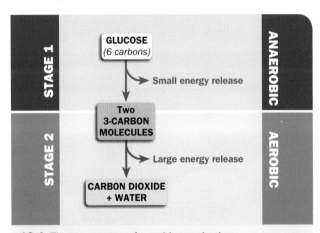

12.4 *The two stages of aerobic respiration*

Anaerobic respiration

Anaerobic respiration is the controlled release of energy from food without the use of oxygen.

Although anaerobic respiration can occur in the presence of oxygen, it does not use oxygen. It is a stage 1 process (because stage 2 requires the use of oxygen).

In anaerobic respiration, glycolysis occurs, i.e. glucose is first broken down to two 3-carbon molecules. A small amount of energy is released in this way.

There are many different forms of anaerobic respiration. In each of them, the 3-carbon molecules are converted to some other end-products, but no extra energy is released.

Anaerobic respiration is a far less efficient process than aerobic respiration, because glucose is only partially broken down.

Anaerobic respiration is also known as fermentation (especially in micro-organisms). Two common types of fermentation are lactic acid fermentation (usually simply called anaerobic respiration) and alcohol fermentation.

Lactic acid fermentation

Lactic acid fermentation occurs in some bacteria and fungi (which are called anaerobes) and in mammal muscle when it is short of oxygen. The end-product of lactic acid fermentation is lactic acid. This type of fermentation can be represented by the word equation:

Glucose ⟶ 2 lactic acid + a small amount of energy

Lactic acid (which can easily form a similar substance called lactate) is formed when bacteria cause milk to go sour, when bacteria respire on cabbage to produce sauerkraut and in silage making. It is also formed when bacteria act on dairy products to make cheese and yoghurt.

When the supply of oxygen to a human muscle is not sufficient to meet the energy needs of the muscle (i.e. when we are out of breath), then anaerobic respiration takes place in the muscle.

Lactic acid build-up causes cramp and muscular stiffness. When the person rests, the lactic acid is taken to the liver by the blood and broken down.

12.5 *A footballer being treated for cramp*

THE CELL

Alcohol fermentation

Alcohol fermentation is another form of anaerobic respiration. It takes place in some bacteria, in fungi (such as yeast) and in plants when they are deprived of oxygen.

It is also a partial breakdown of glucose. The end-products of alcohol fermentation are ethanol (ethyl alcohol) and carbon dioxide.

This process produces a high-energy product (ethanol or ethyl alcohol) and carbon dioxide. It releases very little energy. Alcohol fermentation can be represented by the word equation:

$$\text{Glucose} \longrightarrow \text{2 ethanol} + \text{2 carbon dioxide} + \text{a small amount of energy}$$

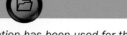
Did you know?

Alcohol fermentation has been used for thousands of years in baking and in beer and wine production.

In baking, special yeasts are mixed with flour and liquid to form a dough. Alcohol fermentation occurs in the dough. The alcohol evaporates, but the carbon dioxide produced causes the dough to rise.

In modern baking, yeast (which cannot withstand high temperatures) is often replaced with baking powder as a source of carbon dioxide.

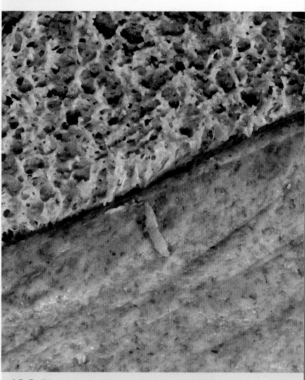

12.8 *Risen, baked bread (top) and unbaked, unrisen dough (bottom)*

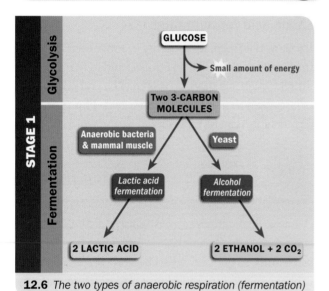

STAGE 1

Glycolysis

Fermentation

GLUCOSE

Small amount of energy

Two 3-CARBON MOLECULES

Anaerobic bacteria & mammal muscle

Yeast

Lactic acid fermentation

Alcohol fermentation

2 LACTIC ACID

2 ETHANOL + 2 CO$_2$

12.6 *The two types of anaerobic respiration (fermentation)*

12.7 *Lactic acid producing bacteria (brown) in yoghurt*

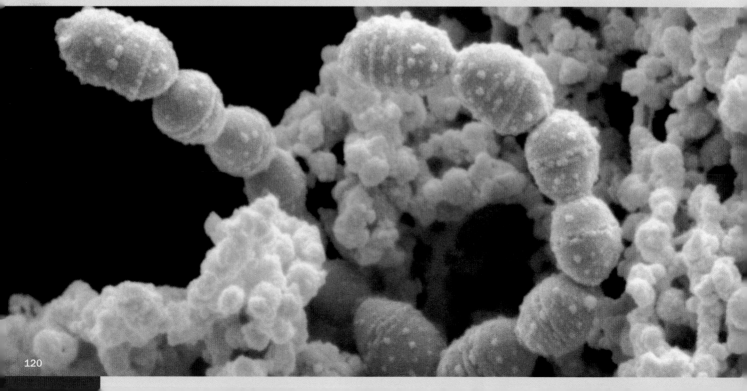

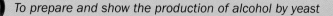

Activity 13   *To prepare and show the production of alcohol by yeast*

Preparation of alcohol

1 Prepare a glucose solution by dissolving 5 g of glucose in 100 cm³ of water.

2 Boil the solution in a conical flask for 5 minutes. *(This eliminates gases from the solution, forming anaerobic conditions.)*

3 When the solution cools, add 5 g or a sachet of dried yeast.

4 Cover the liquid in the flask with oil. *(This prevents oxygen from re-entering the solution.)*

5 Set up either of the two pieces of apparatus as shown in Figure 12.9.

6 Carbon dioxide produced in this fermentation will turn the limewater from a clear colour to a milky or cloudy colour.

7 As a control, the apparatus in Figure 12.9 can be set up without adding any yeast cells. In this case, the limewater remains clear and the potassium dichromate remains orange (or the iodoform test remains brown-orange).

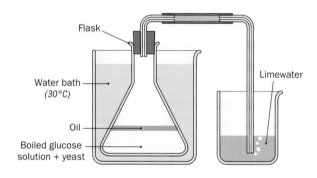

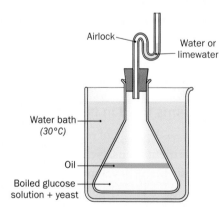

The airlock allows the release of carbon dioxide and prevents the entry of micro-organisms.

12.9 *Preparing alcohol using yeast: use either apparatus*

Syllabus

*In testing for the production of alcohol you can carry out the test for alcohol **or** the test for ethanol.*

To show that alcohol is produced

1 Filter the solution *(to remove yeast cells)*.

2 Put 5 cm³ of potassium dichromate solution in a test tube. *(Note the orange colour of the solution.)*

3 Add 5 drops of the filtered solution from the flask to the test tube.

4 Carefully add 5 drops of concentrated sulfuric acid to the test tube.

5 Warm the test tube gently in a beaker of hot water.

6 Potassium dichromate turns from orange to green in the presence of alcohol (note also the unpleasant smell). This test is the basis of the breathalyser test that was used to test vehicle drivers for alcohol consumption.

12.10 *Test for alcohol: orange–brown colour indicates no alcohol; green indicates alcohol*

To show the production of ethanol
(the iodoform test)

1 Filter the solution *(to remove yeast cells)*.

2 Place 3 cm³ of solution into a test tube.

3 Add 3 cm³ of potassium iodide solution.

4 Add 5 cm³ of sodium hypochlorite solution *(note that the solution turns a brown-orange colour)*.

5 Place the test tube in a hot water bath. *(The appearance of pale yellow crystals indicates that alcohol is present.)*

THE CELL

Micro-organisms in industrial fermentation

> **Biotechnology** refers to the use of living things or their components (especially cells and enzymes) to manufacture useful products or to carry out useful reactions.

Biotechnology can use micro-organisms, plants or animals to manufacture products. However, micro-organisms are the basis of most production techniques.

Fermentation is the foundation of much of the biotechnology industry. The production of substances using fermentation techniques is a form of bioprocessing (see Chapter 9).

Strictly speaking, fermentation means anaerobic respiration. However, in the bioprocessing industry, fermentation is taken to mean the growth of micro-organisms in liquid under any condition (i.e. it can be aerobic or anaerobic).

Production method

The micro-organisms are placed in a container along with a suitable substrate on which they can react. The vessel in which the biological reactions take place is called a **bioreactor**. (See also pages 225–7.)

Many different bioreactors are used, but Figure 12.11 shows a typical example.

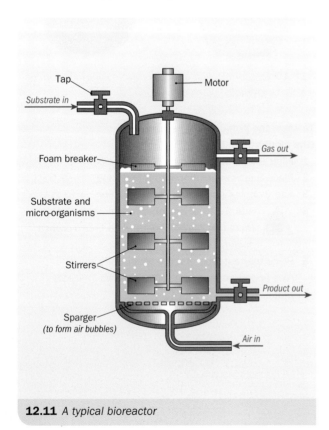

12.11 *A typical bioreactor*

12.12 *Bioreactors: fermentation vats used to make alcohol*

The contents of the bioreactor are mixed so that the micro-organisms are brought into contact with the substrate. Sometimes the mixing (or the reaction itself) produces foam. This is reduced by the use of a foam breaker, as shown in Figure 12.11.

The culture medium is the liquid (including a suitable substrate) in which the micro-organisms grow.

In many bioreactors it is important to get as much oxygen dissolved in the culture medium as possible. For this reason air (or oxygen) is pumped into the vessel. The air passes through a device called a sparger, which forms small air bubbles that dissolve more readily into the culture medium.

Apart from using the correct micro-organism and substrate, the quality and yield of the product depend on a number of other factors. These include the materials and design of the bioreactor, elimination of micro-organisms that would contaminate the process, the correct rate of mixing and control of environmental factors such as temperature and pH.

Micro-organisms used in bioprocessing

There is a very wide range of micro-organisms used in industrial fermentations. New micro-organisms are continuously being developed and used. Many of these are produced using genetic engineering techniques (see Chapter 19).

In general, the main organisms used are bacteria and fungi (especially different yeast strains). Note that very often different organisms may be used to produce the same end-product, e.g. antibiotics are produced by bacteria, fungi and yeast.

The use of yeast in beer and wine production, and of carbon dioxide in baking, are very old examples of bioprocessing. Some modern examples of bioprocessing are given in the following table.

THE CELL

Modern bioprocessing		
Micro-organism	**Product**	**Use**
Bacteria	Ethanol	Beer, wine, solvent for paints, polishes, perfumes
	Acetone	Solvent (e.g. nail varnish remover)
	Amino acids and vitamins	Food (e.g. added to breakfast cereals)
	Yoghurt	Food
	Methane gas	Fuel (often called biogas)
	Antibiotics	Kill (other) bacteria
	Enzymes	Washing powders (e.g. to remove stains)
	Drugs	Maintain good health
	Hormones	Maintain good health (e.g. insulin controls diabetes)
Yeasts	Ethanol	Beer, wine, solvent
	Carbon dioxide	Causes dough to rise
	Single-cell protein (SCP)	Edible protein
Other fungi	Citric acid	Food additive (e.g. soft drinks)
	Antibiotics	Kill bacteria

Bioprocessing with immobilised cells

When micro-organisms are used in a bioreactor they are removed, along with the product, at the end of the process. They then have to be separated from the product and new micro-organisms must be grown to replace those lost. This is wasteful and costly.

To prevent these problems, the micro-organisms are often fixed or immobilised in the bioreactor.

PROCEDURE FOR IMMOBILISING CELLS

Whole cells are immobilised in the same way that enzymes are immobilised. They may be bonded to each other, bonded or attached to an insoluble support or enclosed in a gel or membrane (see Figure 9.13, page 98).

The technique of immobilising cells has been used for hundreds of years to produce vinegar. In this case, wood shavings are coated with a film of bacteria and alcohol is trickled down the shavings. The bacteria convert the alcohol to vinegar.

In a similar manner, immobilised micro-organisms have been used for treating waste sewage since the early 1900s. In this case bacteria, fungi and other micro-organisms are immobilised on sand, gravel and rocks while they decompose the wastes.

Immobilised cells are increasingly being used in industrial fermentations to produce a vast (and growing) range of products. Trapping the cells in a gel is the most common technique used.

For example, in the production of alcohol, yeast cells are mixed with sodium alginate (a chemical derived from brown algae). Beads of this mixture

are soaked in calcium chloride, which causes the alginate to enclose and immobilise the yeast cells. This is the same technique that is used in Activity 10 (page 99).

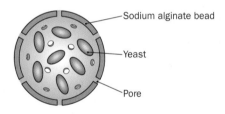

Sodium alginate bead
Yeast
Pore

12.13 *Immobilised yeast cells*

Sucrose can enter the pores of the alginate and glucose can leave through the same pores. The pores are too small, however, to allow the yeast cells to pass through.

12.14 *Bacteria (blue/green) fixed or immobilised on wood: as alcohol trickles down the wood it is converted to vinegar*

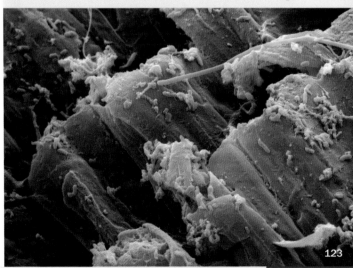

ADVANTAGES OF IMMOBILISED CELLS

- Immobilised cells can be reused. This saves in both time and the cost of growing new cells.
- Immobilisation is a gentle process. It does not damage the cells or affect their ability to carry out the reaction.
- The immobilised cells can easily be recovered from the culture medium at the end of the process. This means that the product contains less unwanted material.
- If the cells are free in the culture medium they have to be separated from the product at the end of the process. This often involves long and difficult filtrations. Immobilised cells substantially reduce the need for filtration.

USES OF IMMOBILISED CELLS

The use of immobilised cells is growing rapidly. In particular, immobilised cells are being used instead of immobilised enzymes. This saves having to prepare and purify enzymes, a slow and expensive process.

Examples of products made using immobilised cells include new artificial antibiotics, fertilisers, steroids and other drugs and, as described previously, vinegar and alcohol.

H Detailed study of respiration

Aerobic respiration

Aerobic respiration is a two-stage process (as outlined earlier in this chapter). We will now look at these stages (especially stage 2) in more detail.

STAGE 1

The stage 1 reactions start with glycolysis. This takes place in the cytosol of the cell. In glycolysis, a 6-carbon carbohydrate (glucose) is converted into two 3-carbon molecules called pyruvic acid. This molecule is electrically neutral (not charged). It may be found as the negatively charged ion called pyruvate.

Glycolysis does not require oxygen (it is anaerobic). Some of the energy released in glycolysis is used to form two ATP molecules. More of the energy is used to form NADH. However, over 75% of the energy that was in a glucose molecule is retained in the bonds of pyruvic acid.

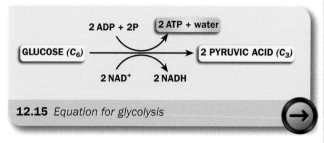

12.15 *Equation for glycolysis*

STAGE 2

In stage 2 a complex series of reactions take place. (see Figure 12.16). Some of these reactions require oxygen.

If oxygen is present, pyruvic acid (or pyruvate) enters a mitochondrion. Here it loses a carbon dioxide molecule to form a 2-carbon (C_2) molecule called acetyl coenzyme A (often shortened to acetyl CoA).

Pyruvic acid also loses two high-energy electrons. These combine with NAD^+ and a proton (H^+) to form NADH, i.e.

$$NAD^+ + 2e^- + H^+ \longrightarrow NADH$$

Each NADH will enter an electron transport system as outlined later.

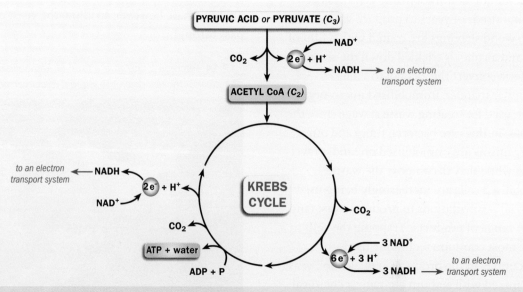

12.16 *The events in stage 2 of respiration*

Krebs cycle

Acetyl CoA now enters into a series of reactions called Krebs cycle.

Did you know?

The reactions in Krebs cycle were first discovered by the German biochemist (Sir) Hans Krebs (1900–81) and others in 1937. For his work in this area he shared the Nobel Prize in 1953.

12.17 *Sir Hans Krebs*

In Krebs cycle, acetyl CoA is broken down to carbon dioxide and protons (H^+) in a number of reactions (see Figure 12.16). The energy that was in acetyl CoA is released in a number of steps in the form of high-energy electrons.

These electrons (along with protons, H^+) are picked up by the electron acceptor NAD^+ to form NADH. The NADH molecules enter an electron transport system.

$$NAD^+ + 2e^- + H^+ \longrightarrow NADH$$

At one point in Krebs cycle a single ADP (and a phosphate) is converted to ATP and water.

Electron transport system

The electron transport systems, or chains, are located on the inner membrane of the mitochondrion. Infoldings of the inner membrane increase the surface area and allow larger numbers of these systems to fit on the membrane.

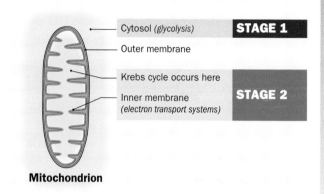

Cytosol *(glycolysis)* **STAGE 1**

Outer membrane

Krebs cycle occurs here

Inner membrane *(electron transport systems)* **STAGE 2**

Mitochondrion

12.18 *Location of the stages of respiration*

Each electron transport system consists of a number of molecules, mostly proteins. High-energy electrons are passed from NADH to the first of these molecules, as shown in Figure 12.19.

As the electrons pass from molecule to molecule within each system they lose some of their energy. This is similar to the way water loses energy as it flows down a waterfall. Some of the energy released by the electrons is used to form ATP. The rest of the energy is lost as heat.

At the end of each system, low-energy electrons are removed by combining them with oxygen and hydrogen to form water.

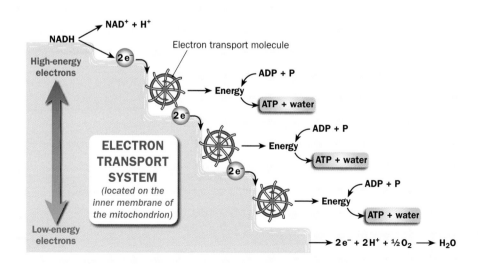

12.19 *The production of ATP by the electron transport system*

The importance or significance of the electron transport system is that it produces the energy-rich carrier ATP.

The electron transport system cannot work in the absence of oxygen. This is because there is no oxygen at the end of the system to remove the low-energy electrons. As a result, electrons cannot flow along the system and so no further ATP is produced. Aerobic organisms die due to a lack of available energy (ATP), in the absence of oxygen.

Did you know?

Certain chemicals, such as cyanide, are fatal because they prevent some of the proteins in the system from receiving or passing on electrons. This means that ATP is not produced.

Summary of aerobic respiration

Aerobic respiration involves stage 1 and stage 2 reactions; see Figure 12.20.

- **Stage 1** (glycolysis) is anaerobic and releases very little energy.
- **Stage 2** includes the Krebs cycle reactions and the electron transport systems. These are aerobic and release a large amount of energy due to the complete breakdown of glucose.

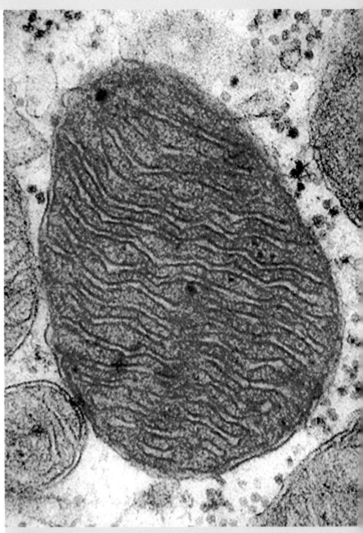

12.21 *A mitochondrion*

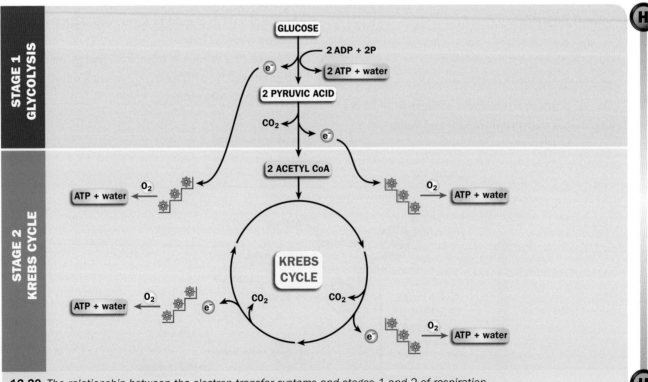

12.20 *The relationship between the electron transfer systems and stages 1 and 2 of respiration*

THE CELL

Anaerobic respiration

In anaerobic respiration, the stage 1 reactions convert glucose into two molecules of pyruvic acid or pyruvate. Two molecules of ATP and two molecules of NADH are produced in this process.

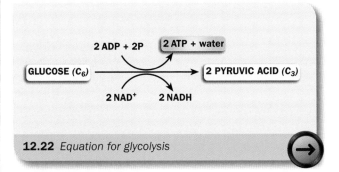

12.22 *Equation for glycolysis*

In the absence of oxygen, pyruvic acid is converted to either lactic acid or ethanol and carbon dioxide. In both these forms of anaerobic respiration (also called fermentation) no further ATP is produced.

In each case, the two NADH molecules break down to release two electrons and a proton.

$$NADH \longrightarrow NAD^+ + 2e^- + H^+$$

The electrons and the proton are added to pyruvic acid, forming either lactic acid or ethanol and carbon dioxide.

Reduction is a process in which a substance gains electrons. In both forms of anaerobic respiration, pyruvic acid gains electrons. Pyruvic acid is said to be reduced to either lactic acid or ethanol and carbon dioxide.

All the reactions in lactic acid fermentation and in alcohol fermentation are stage 1 reactions. These reactions take place in the cytosol and do not involve the electron transport systems.

In conclusion, both types of fermentation only involve stage 1. As you saw earlier in this chapter, stage 1 is anaerobic and releases a small amount of energy.

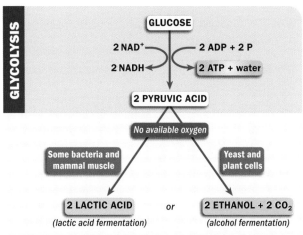

12.23 *Relationship between the two forms of fermentation*

THE CELL

Summary

External respiration is the process of gas exchange or breathing.

Internal respiration is the release of energy (ATP) from food using enzymes.

Aerobic respiration:
- uses oxygen
- is a complete breakdown of glucose
- releases a large amount of energy
- is a two-stage process
- is represented by the balanced equation

$$C_6H_{12}O_6 + 6O_2 \xrightarrow{\text{enzymes}} 6CO_2 + 6H_2O + \text{energy}$$

Stages in aerobic respiration:
Stage 1
- does not use oxygen (it is anaerobic)
- takes place in the cytosol of the cell
- releases very little energy
- splits glucose into two 3-carbon molecules

Stage 2
- uses oxygen (it is aerobic)
- takes place in the mitochondrion

- releases a large amount of energy
- converts the 3-carbon molecules formed in stage 1 to carbon dioxide and water

Anaerobic respiration (or fermentation):
- does not use oxygen
- is a partial breakdown of glucose
- releases a small amount of energy
- is a stage 1 process
- takes place in the cytosol
- is represented by the word equations

Glucose $\longrightarrow$ 2 lactic acid + some energy

Glucose $\longrightarrow$ 2 ethanol + 2 carbon dioxide + some energy

Stage 1 in anaerobic respiration is the same as stage 1 in aerobic respiration, except that the 3-carbon molecules are converted to:
- lactic acid in lactic acid fermentation (takes place in some bacteria and mammal muscle)
- ethanol and carbon dioxide in alcohol fermentation (takes place in some bacteria and yeast)

To prepare alcohol:
■ mix glucose and water
■ boil the solution
■ add yeast
■ cover with oil
■ leave in a warm place

To show the production of alcohol:
■ add acidified potassium dichromate
■ warm in hot water
■ if the colour turns from orange to green then alcohol is present

or

To show the production of ethanol:
■ add potassium iodide
■ add sodium hypochlorite
■ if the colour changes from brown-orange to pale yellow, ethanol is present

Biotechnology is the production of useful products using living cells or their parts.

A large range of micro-organisms, especially bacteria and yeast, are used in industry to carry out different anaerobic or fermentation reactions.

The production of substances by fermentation is an example of bioprocessing.

A bioreactor is a vessel in which bioprocessing takes place.

Immobilised cells are attached to each other or to an inert solid.

The advantages of immobilised cells are:
■ they can be reused, resulting in cheaper production
■ the cells are not damaged by the process
■ the cells are easy to separate from the product

The stage 1 reactions include glycolysis and take place in the cytosol. In glycolysis:
■ glucose is split into two molecules of pyruvic acid (or pyruvate)
■ no oxygen is used
■ 2 ATPs and 2 NADHs are formed

In the presence of oxygen, stage 2 proceeds in the mitochondrion.

Stage 2 involves both the Krebs cycle reactions and the electron transport system.

Pyruvic acid loses carbon dioxide and high-energy electrons (in the form of NADH), forming acetyl CoA.

In Krebs cycle:
■ acetyl CoA goes through a cycle of reactions
■ acetyl CoA is converted to carbon dioxide and hydrogen
■ high-energy electrons and protons (H^+) are released to form several NADHs
■ ADP is converted to ATP

In the electron transport systems (located on the inner membrane of the mitochondrion):
■ NADH releases high-energy electrons
■ the electrons are passed from molecule to molecule along the system
■ the electrons release energy as they pass along
■ the energy is used to form ATP
■ at the end of the system, low-energy electrons combine with oxygen and hydrogen to form water

Aerobic respiration involves both stage 1 (anaerobic, low energy release) and stage 2 (aerobic, high energy release).

Anaerobic respiration only involves stage 1 and is a low-energy release process.

There are two forms of anaerobic respiration:
■ in lactic acid fermentation, glycolysis is followed by the conversion of pyruvic acid to lactic acid
■ in alcohol fermentation, glycolysis is followed by the conversion of pyruvic acid to ethanol and carbon dioxide

Revision questions

1 (a) Distinguish between internal and external respiration.
   (b) State a location for each.
2 (a) Why is respiration essential for all living things?
   (b) Name the normal respiratory substrate.
3 Give two (a) similarities and (b) differences, between aerobic and anaerobic respiration.

4 Name the end-products of:
   (a) aerobic respiration
   (b) alcohol fermentation
   (c) lactic acid fermentation.
5 Name one type of organism in each case that carries out:
   (a) aerobic respiration
   (b) alcohol fermentation
   (c) lactic acid fermentation.

6 (a) Give a balanced equation for aerobic respiration.
   (b) Give word equations to represent:
       (i) anaerobic respiration in yeast
       (ii) anaerobic respiration in mammal muscle.

7 Aerobic respiration is a two-stage process. Say whether each of the following statements relate to stage 1 or stage 2.
   (a) requires oxygen
   (b) takes place in the cytosol
   (c) occurs in the mitochondrion
   (d) releases a large amount of energy
   (e) produces carbon dioxide and water
   (f) is a partial breakdown of glucose
   (g) is anaerobic.

8 The apparatus below may be used to demonstrate aerobic respiration. Air is drawn through the apparatus by attaching it to a vacuum pump at X. Sodium hydroxide is placed in flask 1 to remove carbon dioxide.

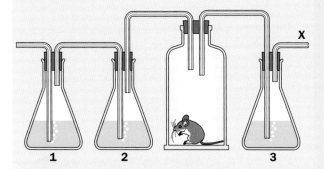

12.24

   (a) What is the purpose of removing carbon dioxide?
   (b) Limewater is put in flasks 2 and 3. Suggest a reason for putting it in each flask.
   (c) What is the purpose of a control in an experiment? Suggest a suitable control for **this** experiment.
   (d) If the animal in the apparatus were replaced by a plant, and the experiment carried out in daylight, would you expect a similar result? Explain your answer.

9 Distinguish between each of the following pairs of terms.
   (a) aerobic and anaerobic
   (b) cytoplasm and cytosol
   (c) aerobic respiration and fermentation.

10 (a) Under what conditions do humans respire anaerobically?
   (b) What is the end-product of this process?
   (c) What is the effect of this product?
   (d) State one possible fate of this product in a person.

11 (a) What is **(i)** biotechnology, **(ii)** bioprocessing, **(iii)** a bioreactor?
   (b) Name any one organism used in industrial fermentation and state the product of this fermentation.

12 Micro-organisms are used to produce each of the following in large quantities: **(a)** methane gas, **(b)** enzymes, **(c)** vitamins, **(d)** single cell proteins, **(e)** citric acid.
   State one commercial application for each of the products named at **(a)** to **(e)** above.

13 Alcohol fermentation is the oldest known form of industrial fermentation.
   (a) Name an organism that carries out this process.
   (b) Name two industries based on this process.
   (c) State the end-product of this process used in each of the industries named.
   (d) Outline one use for each of the products named in part **(c)**.

14 (a) What is meant by immobilised cells?
   (b) State any one way in which a named type of cell can be immobilised.
   (c) State two advantages of bioprocessing using immobilised cells.
   (d) Give any one benefit of using immobilised cells instead of immobilised enzymes.
   (e) Name three products formed using immobilised cells.

15 (a) Give a word equation for glycolysis.
   (b) Name the end-products of glycolysis.
   (c) State the location in a cell for glycolysis.

16 State what happens to the products of glycolysis **(a)** in the presence of oxygen, **(b)** in the absence of oxygen.

17 With regard to Krebs cycle:
   (a) State its location in a cell.
   (b) Name the end-products.
   (c) Name the molecule that continuously enters the cycle.
   (d) Name the energy rich compound that links the cycle with the electron transport system.

18 (a) What is the benefit to a cell of the electron transport system?
   (b) What is the fate of the electrons that pass through the system?
   (c) State the precise location of the electron transport systems in a cell.

19 Respiration may be a one or a two-stage process. Distinguish between these stages in terms of:
   (a) the need for oxygen
   (b) the amount of energy released
   (c) whether one or both occur in **(i)** aerobic, **(ii)** anaerobic respiration.

THE CELL

THE CELL

20 Aerobic respiration can be represented as a two-stage process as shown in Figure 12.25.

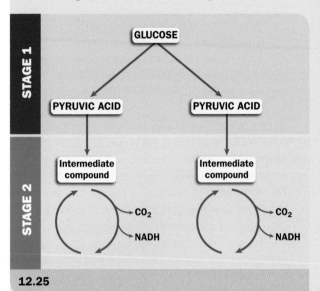

STAGE 1

STAGE 2

12.25

(a) Name the two stages shown as 1 and 2.

(b) Name the intermediate compound shown.

(c) What is the fate of the (i) carbon dioxide and (ii) NADH, produced at stage 2?

(d) Name two places on the diagram where ATP is produced.

21 Choose which of the options **(i)**, **(ii)**, **(iii)** or **(iv)** represents the correct answer in each case below.

(a) Krebs cycle reactions occur in:
  (i)   the chloroplasts
  (ii) the cytosol
  (iii) the mitochondria
  (iv) yeast

(b) The largest ATP (energy) output results from:
  (i)   gylcolysis
  (ii) aerobic respiration
  (iii) anaerobic respiration
  (iv) stage 1 reactions

(c) To immobilise yeast cells, you use:
  (i)   sodium chloride
  (ii) calcium carbonate
  (iii) sodium alginate
  (iv) ethanol

(d) Immobilised cells are:
  (i)   unreactive
  (ii) illegal
  (iii) reusable
  (iv) slow in their reactions

(e) During anaerobic respiration, lactic acid may be directly produced from:
  (i)   glucose
  (ii) ethanol
  (iii) pyruvic acid
  (iv) ATP.

Sample examination questions

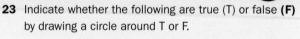

Section A

22 (a) What is the first stage process of respiration called?

(b) In this first stage there is a release of ATP as glucose is converted to another substance. Name this other substance.

(c) To what is the substance you have named in **(b)** converted under anaerobic conditions in:
  1. Yeast?
  2. A human muscle cell?

(d) Under aerobic conditions the substance that you have named in **(b)** is converted to an acetyl group and in the process a small molecule is released. Name this small molecule.

(e) The acetyl group now enters a cycle of reactions. What name is given to this cycle?

(f) Where in the cell does this cycle take place?

(2006 HL Q 4)

23 Indicate whether the following are true (T) or false **(F)** by drawing a circle around T or F.

Example: Carbon dioxide is produced during respiration.	Ⓣ	F

(a) Stage 1 of respiration requires oxygen	T	F
(b) Stage 1 of respiration takes place in the cytoplasm	T	F
(c) Stage 2 of respiration also takes place in the cytoplasm	T	F
(d) Some of the energy released in respiration is lost as heat	T	F
(e) Lactic acid is a product of anaerobic respiration	T	F

(2008 OL Q 3)

24 (a) Write a balanced equation to represent aerobic respiration.

(b) The first stage of respiration takes place in the cytosol. What is the cytosol?

(c) Does the first stage of respiration release a small or large amount of energy?

(d) What is fermentation?

(e) Where in the cell does the second stage of aerobic respiration take place?

(f) Is oxygen required for the second stage of aerobic respiration?

(g) Suggest a situation in which some cells in the human body may not be able to engage in the second stage of aerobic respiration.

(2008 HL Q 5)

Section B

25 (a) Yeast cells produce ethanol (alcohol) in a process called fermentation. Is this process affected by temperature? Explain your answer.

(b) Answer the following in relation to an experiment to prepare and show the presence of ethanol using yeast.

(i) Draw a labelled diagram of the apparatus that you used.

(ii) Name a substance that yeast can use to make ethanol.

(iii) What substance, other than ethanol, is produced during fermentation?

(iv) Describe the control that you used in this experiment.

(v) Explain the purpose of a control in a scientific experiment.

(vi) How did you know when the fermentation was finished?

(vii) Why were solutions of potassium iodide and sodium hypochlorite or potassium dichromate added to the reaction vessels after a certain period of time?

(viii) Name a substance produced during aerobic respiration that is not produced during fermentation.

(2004 HL Q 7)

Section C

26 (i) What name is given to the first stage of respiration?

(ii) Where in a cell does this first stage take place?

(iii) To what substance is glucose normally converted in this first stage of respiration?

(iv) Is oxygen required for this conversion?

(v) Name a compound to which the substance that you have named in **(iii)** may be converted, in the absence of oxygen.

(vi) In aerobic respiration, the product of the first stage moves to the mitochondrion. Outline subsequent events in the total breakdown of this product.

(2007 HL Q 11B)

27 (a) (i) Complete the following equation, which is a summary of **aerobic** respiration.
$$C_6H_{12}O_6 + 6O_2 \rightarrow$$

(ii) Aerobic respiration is a two-stage process. The first stage takes place in the cytoplasm. Where does the second stage take place?

(b) The apparatus below may be used to demonstrate aerobic respiration. Air is drawn through the apparatus by attaching it to a vacuum pump at X. Sodium hydroxide is placed in flask 1 to remove carbon dioxide.

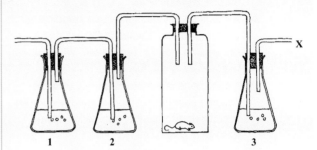

(i) What is the purpose of removing carbon dioxide?

(ii) Limewater is put in flasks 2 and 3. Suggest a reason for putting it in each flask.

(iii) What is the purpose of a control in an experiment? Suggest a suitable control for **this** experiment.

(iv) If the animal in the apparatus were replaced by a plant, and the experiment carried out in daylight, would you expect a similar result? Explain your answer.

(c) The apparatus below may be used to demonstrate **anaerobic** respiration in yeast. The water was boiled and cooled before adding the yeast.

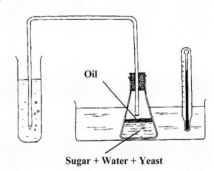

(i) Why was the water boiled before adding the yeast?

(ii) Why do you think a layer of oil has been put on top of the water?

(iii) Would the same apparatus containing water and yeast but without sugar be a suitable control? Explain your answer.

(iv) Give **two** industrial uses of the anaerobic respiration of yeast.

(2003 Sample OL Q 13)

THE CELL

28 (a) (i) Distinguish between aerobic and anaerobic respiration.

(ii) Write a balanced equation to summarise aerobic respiration.

(b) Answer the following questions in relation to the **first stage of respiration**.

(i) Where in the cell does this stage occur?

(ii) During this stage a small amount of energy is released. Explain the role of ADP in relation to this released energy.

(iii) What is the final product of this stage under aerobic conditions?

(iv) If conditions in the cell remain aerobic the product you have named in **(iii)** is used for the second stage of respiration. Where does this second stage take place?

(v) If conditions in a human cell (e.g. muscle) become anaerobic the product named in **(iii)** is converted to another substance. Name this other substance.

(vi) When the substance named in **(v)** builds up in the blood, a person is said to be in oxygen debt. This debt must eventually be paid. Suggest how the debt is paid.

(c) If yeast cells are kept in anaerobic conditions alcohol (ethanol) and another substance are produced.

(i) Describe, with the aid of a diagram, how you would keep yeast under anaerobic conditions in the laboratory.

(ii) Name a carbohydrate that you would supply to the yeast as an energy source.

(iii) Give an account of a chemical test to demonstrate that alcohol (ethanol) has been produced. Include the initial colour and final colour of the test.

(iv) What is the other substance produced under anaerobic conditions?

(v) Alcohol (ethanol) production is an example of fermentation. How would you know when fermentation has ceased?

(vi) Why does fermentation eventually cease?

(2005 HL Q 11)

Previous examination questions	
Ordinary level	**Higher level**
2003 Sample Q 13	2004 Q 7
2005 Q 11c	2005 Q 11
2006 Q 13	2006 Q 4
2007 Q 12	2007 Q 11b
2008 Q 3	2008 Q 5

*For latest questions go to **www.edco.ie/biology***

Chapter 13 **Diffusion and osmosis**

Selective permeability of membranes

All the membranes in a cell (all biological membranes) are similar in structure and in the way they operate. This means that the cell or plasma membrane is the same as the membranes around organelles such as mitochondria or chloroplasts.

A membrane is said to be **permeable** to a substance if the substance can pass through it and **impermeable** if it cannot pass through.

> A **selectively permeable** membrane allows some but not all substances to pass through.

Biological membranes are selectively permeable, as are materials such as cellophane, visking tubing and dialysis tubing. These membranes allow molecules such as water, oxygen and carbon dioxide to pass through freely. They do not, however, allow sugars, proteins and salts to pass through easily.

Although membranes are relatively impermeable to some substances, cells have specialised mechanisms in their membranes to allow these substances to pass through when necessary.

For example, glucose has to pass in through the plasma or cell membrane to allow for respiration. Equally, proteins have to pass out through membranes in the form of hairs, nails and hormones.

Diffusion

> **Diffusion** is the spreading out of molecules from a region of high concentration to a region of low concentration.

Diffusion is said to take place along a concentration gradient. Everyday examples of diffusion include the way the smell of perfume, bread baking or the unpleasant effects of a stink bomb can spread through a house. If sugar is placed in hot tea it initially stays at the bottom. However, in time, the sugar will spread throughout the tea by diffusion.

Diffusion is caused by the kinetic energy of the molecules. These molecules are moving randomly and will tend to spread out if they can. This movement does not need external energy and is said to be passive.

Examples of diffusion in biology are CO_2 diffusing into a leaf, O_2 diffusing out of a leaf, O_2 diffusing from the blood into a cell and CO_2 diffusing out of a cell.

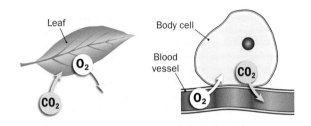

13.1 *Examples of diffusion*

13.2 *An example of diffusion*

Osmosis

Before dealing with osmosis it is important to understand the following terms:

- **Solvent**. A solvent is a liquid that dissolves other substances. Water is the most common biological solvent.
- **Solute**. A solute is a substance that has been dissolved. Salt or sugar dissolved in water are both solutes.
- **Solution**. The mixture of the solvent and solute is a solution (e.g. salty water).

> **Osmosis** is the movement of water molecules across a semi-permeable membrane from a region of high water concentration to a region of low water concentration.

Osmosis is a special type of diffusion. Like diffusion it is also passive (i.e. it requires no external energy).

Another way to define osmosis is to say it is the movement of water (solvent) across a semi-permeable membrane from a region of low solute concentration to a region of high solute concentration.

The fact that both definitions are the same should be clear from Figure 13.3.

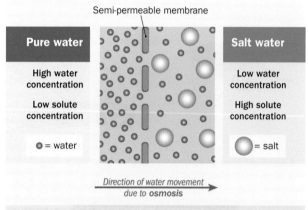

13.3 *Movement of water due to osmosis*

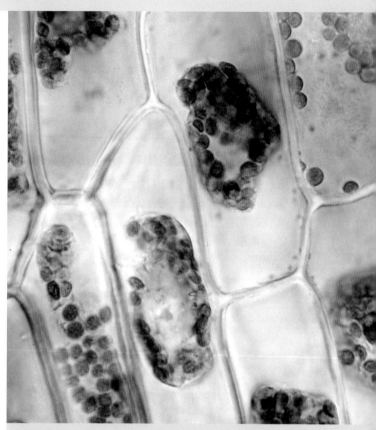

13.4 *Plant cells in a very salty solution lose water due to osmosis.*

 Activity 14 *To demonstrate osmosis*

Note: *Visking tubing is a selectively permeable membrane. Water can pass freely through visking tubing, but sucrose cannot.*

1 Soften two strips of visking tubing by soaking them in water. *(Visking tubing is selectively permeable.)*
2 Tie a knot in one end of each of the strips.
3 Dissolve 80 g of sucrose in 100 ml of water. This forms an 80% sucrose solution.
4 Use a syringe to half-fill one piece of visking tubing with distilled (or tap) water. Tie a knot to seal the contents. *(This bag acts as a control.)*
5 Half-fill the second piece of visking tubing with the 80% sucrose solution. Tie a knot to seal the contents.
6 Rinse any sucrose off each bag, dry them and note and record the mass and 'fullness' of each bag.
7 Place each 'bag' of visking tubing in a container of distilled (or tap) water, as shown in Figure 13.5.
8 Leave the apparatus for about 30 minutes.
9 Remove the bags, dry them and note and record the mass and 'fullness' of each bag.
10 The expected results are:
   ■ The visking tubing containing the distilled water shows no change in mass or 'fullness' *(i.e. it has not gained or lost water).*
   ■ The visking tubing containing the 80% sucrose solution will have filled with water so that it has gained mass and is more full. *(This is due to water entering the tubing as a result of osmosis.)*

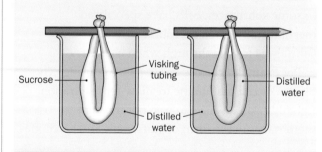

13.5 *To demonstrate osmosis*

11 Record the results as follows.

Tube contents	Sucrose solution	Distilled water
Mass at start (g)		
Mass after activity (g)		
'Fullness' at start (high/low)		
'Fullness' after activity (high/low)		

Osmosis and animal cells

Animal cells are enclosed only by a cell (or plasma) membrane. They do not have cell walls (unlike plant cells).

Animal cells in a solution that is the same concentration as their cytoplasm

If an animal cell is in a solution that is the same concentration as its cytoplasm, water will move in and out through its cell membrane at the same rate. The volume of the cell will remain the same.

Seawater has the same concentration as the cytoplasm of many animals that live in the sea. Also the cells of most land animals are surrounded by tissue fluid that has the same concentration as the cells (see Chapter 28).

In the same way, one of the functions of the kidneys is to ensure that plasma, the liquid portion of our blood, has the same concentration as our blood cells.

Animal cells in less concentrated solution

If an animal cell is in a solution that is less concentrated than the cell, it will gain water due to osmosis. The cell will enlarge and may burst and die.

Amoeba is a single-celled organism (dealt with in more detail in Chapter 23) that lives in freshwater pools and ponds. The fresh water is less concentrated than the cell contents of *Amoeba*. This means that *Amoeba* must have a method of controlling osmosis or it will enlarge and burst. The osmoregulation system in *Amoeba* consists of a contractile vacuole. The contractile vacuole expels water, which prevents the cell from bursting.

Amoeba species that live in seawater do not have contractile vacuoles. This is because the seawater has the same concentration as their cells. Hence excess water does not enter their cells.

13.6 Amoeba *with a contractile vacuole (clear circle at top left)*

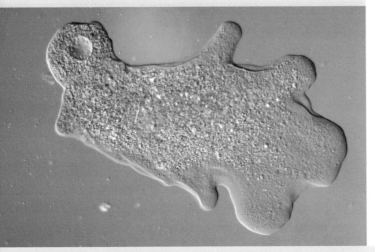

Animal cells in more concentrated solution

If an animal cell is in a solution that is more concentrated than the cell, it will lose water due to osmosis. This will cause the cell to shrivel (a condition known as crenation) and possibly die.

This sometimes happens to aquatic animals if their environment becomes too salty. It also happens to red blood cells if they are in a very salty solution.

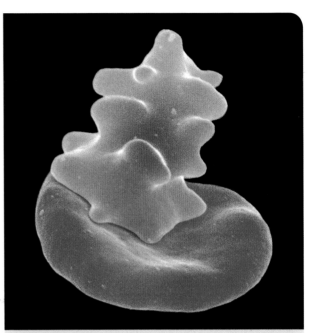

13.7 *A red blood cell that has been exposed to very salty water (top) and a normal cell (bottom)*

Osmosis and plant cells

Plant cells are enclosed by a cell membrane, which in turn is surrounded by a strong cell wall. Cell walls are **fully permeable** to water, gases and many solutes (e.g. salts and sugars). The cell wall gives a certain amount of strength to a plant cell.

Plant cells in less concentrated solution

If a plant cell has a higher concentration of solutes than its surroundings, water moves into the cytoplasm and vacuole of the cell by osmosis. This is how plant roots absorb water from the soil.

The water enters the vacuole and the plant cell swells slightly, but the cell wall is relatively rigid and prevents the cell from swelling too much.

Turgor, or **turgor pressure**, is the pressure of the cytoplasm and vacuole against the cell wall of a plant.

Turgor pressure gives a plant cell great strength. In this state, the cell is said to be turgid.

Plants that do not have wood, such as most house plants or lettuce, get their strength because their cells are fully turgid.

The strength of a plant cell can be compared to a car tyre. The cell wall is like the rubber wall of the tyre. Both these walls provide some (but not enough) strength. If the tyre is inflated (with air) it becomes much stronger. If the cell is inflated (with water) it becomes turgid or firmer.

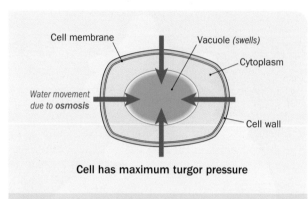

Cell has maximum turgor pressure

13.8 *Plant cell in less concentrated solution*

Plant cells in more concentrated solution

If the cytoplasm of a plant cell has a lower concentration of solutes than the surroundings, then the cell is less concentrated than its surroundings.

Equally, the surroundings are more concentrated than the cell contents. In this case, water moves out of the cell due to osmosis. The vacuole and cytoplasm shrivel and the cell membrane moves away from the cell wall. The more concentrated solution fills the space between the cell membrane and the cell wall.

The cell loses turgor pressure. As a result it is not as strong as it was and is said to be flaccid (limp).

The loss of water from the cytoplasm and the movement of the cell membrane away from the cell wall is called **plasmolysis**.

13.9 *A wilted plant and a normal plant*

When all the cells of a plant are plasmolysed the plant is said to wilt. This can be seen when lettuce becomes limp due to soaking in salty salad dressing. It is also seen when cut flowers lose water due to evaporation.

Plasmolysed cells can be restored to normal by placing them in a less concentrated solution. This is called deplasmolysis.

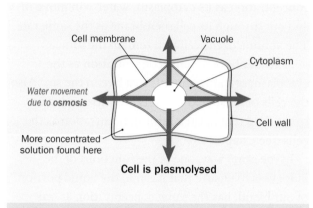

Cell is plasmolysed

13.10 *Plant cell in more concentrated solution*

Osmosis and food preservation

Bacteria and fungi are similar to plants in that they are also enclosed by walls. Osmosis is often used to prevent micro-organisms such as bacteria and fungi from growing on food. This prevents them from producing harmful toxins (poisons) and from decaying the food.

Examples of food preservation techniques based on osmosis are:

- Foods such as fish and meat (bacon) may be soaked in a very salty solution. Any micro-organisms in or on the food will lose water and die due to osmosis.
- In a similar manner, the growth of micro-organisms can be prevented by using a high sugar concentration. Examples of this are jams and marmalades.

13.11 *Salted fish*

Summary

All biological membranes are similar.

Selectively permeable membranes allow some substances to pass through easily, but other substances cannot pass through easily.

Diffusion is:
- the movement of molecules from high to low concentration
- passive (needs no external energy)

Osmosis is:
- the movement of water from a high water concentration to a low water concentration through a semi-permeable membrane
- a special case of diffusion
- passive

To show osmosis:
- Place bags of visking tubing half-filled with **(a)** distilled water, **(b)** 80% sucrose solution, in distilled water.
- Bag **(a)** stays the same mass and size.
- Bag **(b)** increases in mass and swells as water enters due to osmosis.

Animal cells in a:
- solution that is the same concentration as their cytoplasm stay the same size
- less concentrated solution gain water, swell and may burst
- more concentrated solution lose water, shrivel and may die

Amoeba survives in a less concentrated (freshwater) environment due to its contractile vacuole, which eliminates water.

Plant cells in a:
- less concentrated solution than their cytoplasm gain water and become turgid and strong
- more concentrated solution lose water and become plasmolysed and weak

High salt and sugar concentrations:
- can be used to remove water from micro-organisms by osmosis
- are used as food preservation techniques

THE CELL

Revision questions

1 Explain the following terms as they relate to membranes:
   (a) permeable
   (b) impermeable
   (c) selectively permeable
2 Explain why diffusion is:
   (a) said to operate along a concentration gradient
   (b) passive
   (c) faster at high temperatures
3 Give two examples in each case of diffusion in:
   (a) plants, **(b)** animals.
   In each case, name **(i)** the substance that diffuses, **(ii)** where it is moving from and **(iii)** the place to which it moves.
4 Explain the meaning of each of the following, giving a named example in each case:
   (a) solute
   (b) solvent
   (c) solution
5 **(a)** What is osmosis?
   (b) Explain briefly why osmosis is a special case of diffusion.
   (c) How do osmosis and diffusion differ?

6 The experiment in Figure 13.12 demonstrates osmosis.

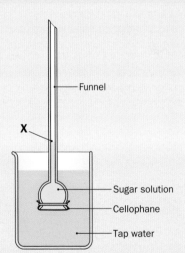

Funnel

X

Sugar solution

Cellophane

Tap water

13.12

(a) Why is cellophane used?
(b) What do you expect will happen to the level of liquid at X?
(c) Which solution is less concentrated?
(d) If extra sugar is added to the solution in the funnel how will the final result change?
(e) What causes the changes in water levels?

7   Three cellophane bags were half filled with a 2% sugar solution. The bags were then placed in three different solutions as shown in Figure 13.13.

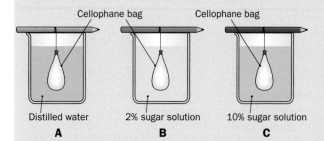

Distilled water   2% sugar solution   10% sugar solution
     A   **B**   **C**

13.13

(a) Which solution is **(i)** more concentrated, **(ii)** less concentrated, **(iii)** the same concentration, with reference to the contents of the bags?

(b) Explain, giving reasons, what will happen to the mass of each bag.

8   (a) Why should blood plasma have the same concentration as the blood cells?

(b) What organ carries out this function?

(c) What is the likely result if blood plasma became less concentrated than the blood cells?

9   (a) What is *Amoeba*?

(b) Where does *Amoeba* normally live?

(c) Name the structure that *Amoeba* uses to carry out osmoregulation.

(d) Why do seawater *Amoebae* not have the structure named in (c)?

10 Figure 13.14 represents a plant cell.

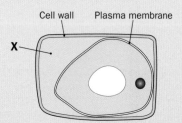

Cell wall   Plasma membrane

X

13.14

(a) What term describes the condition of the cell?

(b) What does this result tell about the solution outside the cell?

(c) The solution at X has the same concentration as the external solution. What does this tell about the cell wall?

11 (a) What is turgor?

(b) Why is turgor pressure not associated with animal cells?

12 If steak is salted before the cooking process it often becomes very dry. Explain why this happens.

13 (a) What happens to red blood cells in distilled water?

(b) Explain why plant cells in distilled water do not behave in exactly the same way.

14 Thirty cubes of equal size were cut from a fresh potato. They were weighed and the average weight was calculated. Ten cubes were placed in distilled water, ten in a 10% salt solution and ten in a 1% salt solution. After 1 hour all the cubes were again weighed. The results were:

Sample	Average weight of each cube
Fresh potato	7.2 g
Distilled water	9.3 g
10% salt	4.1 g
1% salt	7.2 g

(a) What process accounts for the gain or loss in weight?

(b) Why were ten cubes used in each case?

(c) What does this tell you about the salt concentration of the potato cytoplasm?

15 The apparatus shown in Figure 13.15 was set up and left for 15 minutes. Note that iodine molecules can pass through visking tubing.

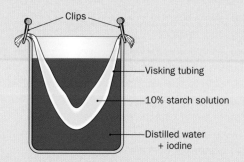

Clips

Visking tubing

10% starch solution

Distilled water + iodine

13.15

Give a reason for each of the following results:

(a) The volume of liquid in the visking tubing increased.

(b) The contents of the visking tubing turned blue-black.

(c) The colour of the distilled water and iodine changed.

(d) The liquid in the beaker did not turn blue-black.

16 (a) Why does salting a fish help to preserve it?

(b) Suggest why fungus does not easily grow on the surface of jams.

Section B

17 (a) (i) What is osmosis?

    (ii) What is a selectively permeable (semi-permeable) membrane?

  (b) (i) Draw a labelled diagram of the apparatus that you used to demonstrate osmosis.

    (ii) Describe how you carried out the experiment to demonstrate osmosis.

    (iii) How were you able to tell that osmosis had taken place?

(2005 OL Q 7)

Section C

18 (i) Water enters the outermost cells of the root by osmosis. What does this tell you about the cell sap of these outermost cells?

  (ii) Osmosis has been described as a special case of diffusion. Explain why.

  (iii) Describe an investigation that you carried out to demonstrate osmosis.

(2008 HL Q 14c(i), (ii), (iii))

Previous examination questions

Ordinary level	Higher level
2005 Q 7	2008 Q 14c

For latest questions go to ***www.edco.ie/biology***

THE CELL

Chapter 14 **Cell division**

Cell continuity

> **Cell continuity** means that all cells develop from pre-existing cells.

Cell continuity gives rise to the continuity of life, which was discussed in Chapter 2.

When a new cell forms (from an existing cell) it goes through three phases before it can divide again:

- firstly, it produces or synthesises all the materials it will need
- then it grows larger
- finally, it reproduces to form new cells

Cell continuity implies that most cells spend a lot of time producing the chemicals and substances they need to survive and grow. They are not actively dividing into new cells during this phase of their life. Cells spend a relatively short time engaged in cell division.

Chromosomes

> **Chromosomes** are coiled threads of DNA (which forms genes) and protein that become visible in the nucleus at cell division.

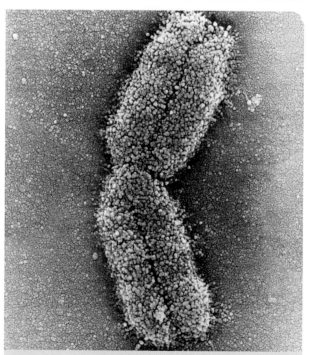

14.1 *Coloured SEM of a human chromosome*

When a cell is not dividing, the chromosomes are in long, thin threads called chromatin. A normal human cell has about 3 metres of chromatin.

At cell division, chromatin contracts to form a number of clearly distinguishable chromosomes. Every species has a definite number of chromosomes in each cell. For example, humans have 46 chromosomes in each body cell.

Each chromosome is composed of hundreds, or even thousands, of genes. These genes are arranged along the chromosome as shown in Figure 14.2.

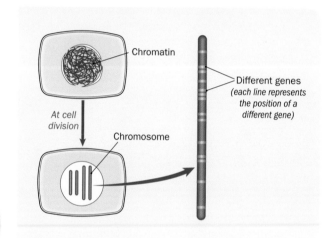

14.2 *Relationship between chromosomes and genes*

Genes

A gene is a short section of DNA which contains the instructions for the formation of a protein. Many of the proteins produced by genes are enzymes. As these enzymes control the activities of the cell, it can be said that genes (or chromosomes) control the cell.

Genes are also said to be units of inheritance. All the genes in an organism make up its **genome**.

In humans, genes control features such as eye colour, production of skin pigment (melanin), number of fingers, the shape of the face and about 25 000 other features. In plants, genes control petal colour, leaf shape, fruit taste and many more features.

Haploid and diploid cells

> A **haploid cell** has one set of chromosomes, i.e. it has only one of each type of chromosome in the nucleus.

Note that in Figure 14.3, all the cells shown are haploid because in each case there is only one of each *type* of chromosome

Haploid is symbolised by the letter 'n' and the number of chromosomes in the cell is given as n = 2 or n = 3 etc.

In humans, eggs and sperm are haploid cells and each contains 23 chromosomes (i.e. n = 23).

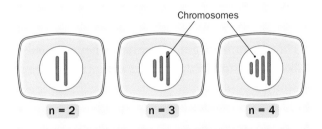

Chromosomes

n = 2   n = 3   n = 4

14.3 *Haploid cells*

A **diploid cell** has two sets of chromosomes, i.e. it has two of each type of chromosome in the nucleus.

This means that the chromosomes are in pairs in a diploid cell. As each pair of chromosomes has similar genes, they are called **homologous pairs**.

A **homologous pair** consists of two chromosomes that each have genes for the same features at the same positions.

Diploid is symbolised as '2n' and the total number of chromosomes in the cell is given as 2n = 4 or 2n = 6 etc.

In diploid cells, one chromosome from each homologous pair is derived from the mother and the other one from the father. This is shown in Figure 14.4 where the maternal and paternal chromosomes are shaded differently.

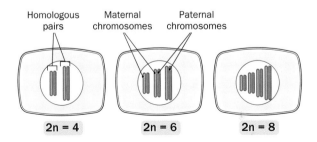

Homologous pairs   Maternal chromosomes   Paternal chromosomes

2n = 4   2n = 6   2n = 8

14.4 *Diploid cells*

The diploid number for humans is 46 (2n = 46). This means that each human cell has 23 chromosomes that were obtained from the person's mother and 23 that were obtained from the father.

The cell cycle

A small number of cells, such as nerve and red blood cells, do not divide when they reach full size. Most cells, however, grow until they reach a certain size and then divide.

The cell cycle describes the life cycle of a cell. The cell cycle includes the changes that take place in a cell during the period between one cell division and the next.

At its simplest, the cell cycle is divided into a period when the cell is not dividing, called interphase, and a period when the cell divides, called mitosis (or meiosis).

14.5 *The cell cycle*

Interphase

Interphase is the phase in the cell cycle when the cell is not dividing.

Interphase is the longest phase in the cell cycle, often accounting for 90% of the cycle.

During interphase, the chromosomes are very elongated. It is not possible to distinguish individual chromosomes in the nucleus during interphase. Instead, they appear as a mass of material called chromatin.

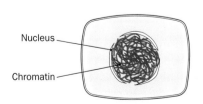

Nucleus

Chromatin

14.6 *The nucleus during interphase*

Although cells are not dividing during interphase, they are very active in other ways during this phase, as outlined below.

■ In the early part of interphase, the cell is very active, producing new organelles such as mitochondria or chloroplasts. It also forms many chemicals that are needed for growth, especially enzymes and other proteins.

■ In the later part of interphase, the chromosomes produce identical copies of themselves. The duplication (or doubling) of a chromosome produces a chromosome with two strands. The two strands have identical genes. The duplication of a chromosome is shown in Figure 14.7.

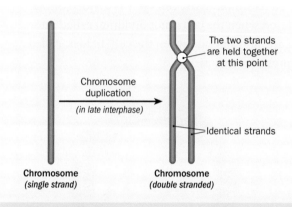

Chromosome duplication
(in late interphase)

The two strands are held together at this point

Identical strands

Chromosome
(single strand)

Chromosome
(double stranded)

14.7 *Chromosome duplication*

Mitosis

Mitosis is a form of nuclear division in which one nucleus divides to form two nuclei, each containing the same number of chromosomes with identical genes.

Each of the new nuclei formed in mitosis becomes enclosed within a cell called a daughter cell, even when the process occurs in male cells.

The two daughter cells each have the same number of chromosomes. Not only do they have the same number of chromosomes, but the genes on the chromosomes in each cell are identical to each other.

This means that mitosis produces two cells that are *identical* to each other in terms of chromosome numbers and the genes present on the chromosomes. For example, if mitosis takes place in a diploid cell, two diploid daughter cells will be formed.

In some respects mitosis is like a photocopier, producing two identical copies of the original cell.

Mitosis takes place in cells that are not associated with the reproductive system. These cells are called somatic cells.

Stages of mitosis

Mitosis is a continuous process that is often described as if it had four definite stages or phases. Each stage runs smoothly into the next and it is often difficult to say exactly when each stage starts and ends.

The account of mitosis that follows refers to an animal cell with four chromosomes, i.e. an animal cell with a diploid number of four (2n = 4).

STAGE 1

■ At the end of interphase, and early in stage 1, chromosomes begin to contract. They gradually become visible in the nucleus as short, thickened strands.

■ Each chromosome appears as a duplicated strand.

■ Fibres begin to appear in the cytoplasm of the cell.

■ The nuclear membrane starts to break down.

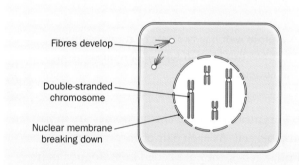

Fibres develop

Double-stranded chromosome

Nuclear membrane breaking down

14.8 *Stage 1*

STAGE 2

■ The nuclear membrane completes its breakdown.

■ The chromosomes contract even more, so they appear more thickened.

■ Fibres attach to each of the chromosomes. The chromosomes move so that they appear to be lined up across the centre of the cell.

■ By the end of this stage each chromosome has two fibres attached, one from each end of the cell.

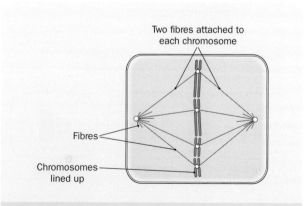

Two fibres attached to each chromosome

Fibres

Chromosomes lined up

14.9 *Stage 2*

STAGE 3

- The fibres now contract. This means that each chromosome is pulled apart.
- The two strands within each chromosome are pulled to opposite ends of the cell.
- Recall that each of the strands in a duplicated chromosome has identical genes. As a result of the chromosomes splitting at this stage, an identical set of genes is pulled to each end of the cell.

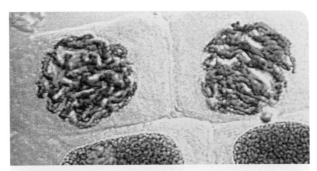

14.12 *Plant cells in interphase*

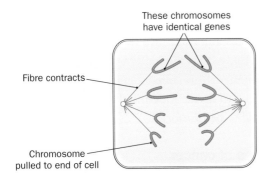

14.10 *Stage 3*

14.13 *Plant cell in stage 1 of mitosis*

STAGE 4

- A nuclear membrane forms around each of the two sets of chromosomes.
- The chromosomes elongate within each nucleus and revert to chromatin. Mitosis is now complete.

14.14 *Plant cell in stage 2 of mitosis*

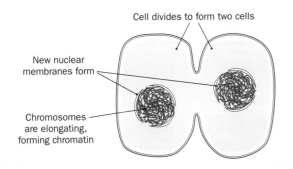

14.11 *Stage 4*

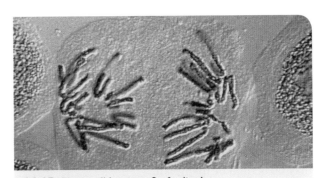

14.15 *Plant cell in stage 3 of mitosis*

Cell division

Once mitosis is complete, the original cell immediately divides to form two cells. These daughter cells will contain the same number of identical chromosomes as each other.

In addition, each daughter cell will have some (approximately half) of the cell organelles and biomolecules that were in the parent cell.

14.16 *Plant cell in stage 4 of mitosis*

THE CELL

Function of mitosis

Unicellular organisms

In single-celled (unicellular) organisms such as *Amoeba*, described in Chapter 23, mitosis increases the number of individuals. In these cases, it is a method of reproduction or multiplication of numbers.

Reproduction that does not involve the joining of two cells is called asexual reproduction. In other words, asexual reproduction only involves a single parent or cell. Mitosis is the basis of asexual reproduction.

Multicellular organisms

In many-celled (multicellular) organisms, mitosis produces new cells, not new individuals. In these organisms mitosis is mainly responsible for growth, but is also involved in renewal and repair of cells.

For example, in humans a sperm and an egg unite to form a single cell called a zygote. The zygote develops into an embryo (and eventually an adult) by repeatedly going through mitosis.

Even when a person is fully grown, mitosis is essential to replace old and damaged cells. This happens when new blood cells are produced, when skin damaged by a cut is repaired or when torn muscles are healed.

Mitosis is also responsible for growth and repair in plants.

Cancer

Normally the rate of mitosis and cell division is carefully controlled. This means that just enough new cells are formed to allow for normal growth and repair.

Sometimes a cell or a group of cells lose the ability to control the rate of mitosis and cell division. They form a mass of cells called a tumour. Tumours may be benign or malignant.

Benign tumours

Benign means 'kind'. In a benign tumour the cells stop dividing after some time. Benign tumours are not life-threatening. They do not invade other tissues.

Examples of benign tumours are warts (caused by a virus) and skin 'tags' (small blobs of raised skin). Most breast tumours are benign. Benign tumours can be surgically removed.

Malignant tumours

> **Cancer** may be defined as a group of disorders in which certain cells lose their ability to control both the rate of mitosis and the number of times mitosis takes place.

Cancer results in an uncontrolled multiplication of abnormal cells. These abnormal cells form a malignant tumour.

Malignant tumours, called 'cancers', may be life-threatening. This is because they can invade other cells and can move from one place to another in the body. This movement (or migration) of malignant cells is called metastasis. Cancer cells continue to divide indefinitely. For this reason they are said to be immortal.

Causes of cancer

Cancer is caused when normal genes are altered to form cancer-causing genes (called **oncogenes**). These alterations are brought about by cancer-causing agents called **carcinogens**. Some common carcinogens are cigarette smoke, asbestos fibres, dioxins, ultraviolet radiation and some viruses.

It is important to realise that most cancers can be cured. This is especially so if they are discovered and treated early. Treatment includes surgery, radiation (to burn out the cancer) and the use of chemicals that slow down mitosis (chemotherapy).

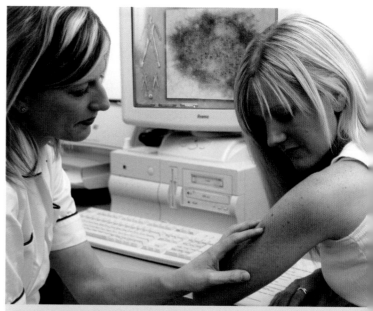

14.17 *Skin cancer screening*

Meiosis

> **Meiosis** is a form of nuclear division in which the four daughter nuclei contain half the chromosome number of the parent nucleus.

Immediately after meiosis, the daughter nuclei are enclosed by cells.

When meiosis takes place in a diploid cell, the daughter cells will be haploid. If these cells are capable of joining with another haploid cell from the opposite sex, they are called sex cells or **gametes**.

Most human cells have 46 chromosomes. Meiosis occurs in the ovaries and testes to produce gametes called eggs and sperm respectively. As a result of meiosis, there are 23 chromosomes in each egg or sperm.

Functions of meiosis

Meiosis has two basic functions in multicellular organisms:

- it allows for sexual reproduction without increasing the number of chromosomes in the offspring
- it allows for new combinations of genes to be formed, which will give rise to variations amongst organisms

MEIOSIS ALLOWS FOR SEXUAL REPRODUCTION

In sexual reproduction, two cells join to form a zygote. These cells are called gametes or sex cells.

In animals, the gametes are the sperm and egg. In flowering plants, the gametes are the male gamete nuclei and the egg and polar nuclei. The zygote will contain the normal number of chromosomes.

Meiosis is essential for sexual reproduction because it halves the chromosome number. This means that the normal chromosome number is restored at fertilisation.

The role of meiosis in humans is outlined in Figure 14.18. The normal human chromosome number per cell is 46. Meiosis halves this number to 23 in the gametes. Fertilisation restores the chromosome number to 46.

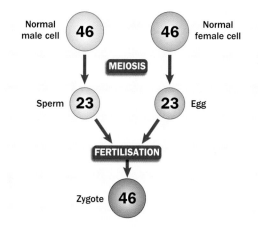

14.18 *Relationship between meiosis and fertilisation*

MEIOSIS ALLOWS FOR VARIATION

The cells resulting from meiosis are not identical. Their genes vary due to the exchange of genetic material which takes place during meiosis.

The variation in the genes (genetic variation) produced in meiosis results in variations or differences in the organisms resulting from sexual reproduction. This is why brothers (or sisters), while they may resemble each other, are rarely identical.

Variations produced in this manner are part of the basis of evolution, as detailed in Chapter 18.

The differences between mitosis and meiosis	
Mitosis	**Meiosis**
1 The number of chromosomes in each resulting cell is the **same** as the number of chromosomes in the parent cell.	The number of chromosomes in each resulting cell is **half** the number of chromosomes in the parent cell.
2 The genes present on the chromosomes in the resulting cells are identical.	The genes present on the chromosomes in the resulting cells are different.
3 One cell divides to form two new cells.	One cell divides to form four new cells.

THE CELL

THE CELL

Detailed study of mitosis

The account of mitosis that follows is for a similar cell to that outlined earlier in this chapter (i.e. an animal cell with four chromosomes).

The four stages of mitosis are called prophase, metaphase, anaphase and telophase. The sequence of these stages may be recalled by using the first letters of either of the phrases:

Passed	My	Algebra	Test	or
Party	Monday	And	Tuesday	

Prophase

- At the end of interphase and early in prophase chromatin starts to contract.
- In time the chromosomes become visible as double-stranded structures. The point at which the strands are held together is called a **centromere**. The two strands in a chromosome have identical genes at this stage. In fact, each strand **is** a chromosome.

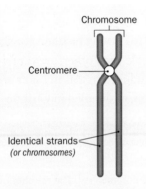

14.19 *A double-stranded chromosome*

- In addition, the nucleolus disappears. The nucleolus is a region in the nucleus where ribosomes are made. Some cells have more than one nucleolus.
- The fibres that appear in the cytoplasm at this stage are called spindle fibres. All the spindle fibres collectively form a structure called the spindle.
- The nuclear membrane starts to break down.

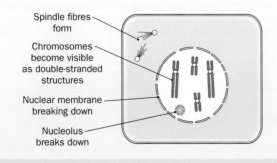

14.20 *Prophase*

Metaphase

- In metaphase the nuclear membrane completes its breakdown.
- A spindle fibre from each end (or pole) of the cell attaches to each centromere.
- The chromosomes line up across the middle or equator of the cell.

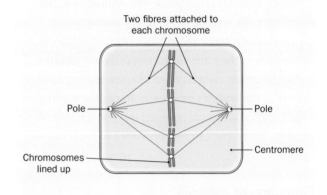

14.21 *Metaphase*

Anaphase

- The spindle fibres contract at anaphase. This causes the centromeres to split.
- One strand (or chromosome) from each double-stranded chromosome is pulled to opposite poles of the cell.
- This means the cell has eight chromosomes at this stage. The four chromosomes pulled to each pole have identical genes.
- Anaphase is the shortest phase in mitosis. It often lasts only a few minutes, compared with about 30 minutes for each of the other phases.

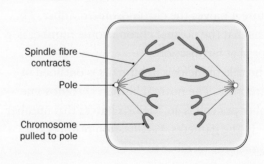

14.22 *Anaphase*

Telophase

- The four chromosomes at each pole begin to lengthen and become hard to distinguish.
- The spindle fibres break down.

- One or more nucleolus (plural nucleoli) begin to re-form.
- A nuclear membrane forms around each clump of chromatin at each of the two poles. The original nucleus has divided into two identical nuclei. Mitosis is now complete.

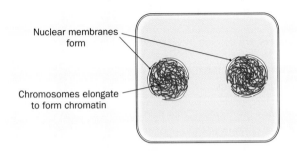

14.23 *Telophase*

Cell division

Cell division follows immediately after mitosis. The process of cell division proceeds differently in animal and plant cells.

Cell division in animal cells

Cell division occurs in animals by a process called cleavage. A shallow groove, called a **cleavage furrow**, appears around the cell, lining up with the position occupied by the equator during metaphase.

The cleavage furrow becomes deeper, until it eventually divides the cytoplasm and the cell splits into two.

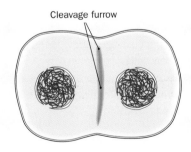

14.24 *Cell division in an animal cell*

Cell division in plant cells

In plant cells, the rigid cell wall prevents a cleavage furrow from forming.

Instead, a number of small membrane-enclosed sacs, called vesicles, gather in the area between the two nuclei. The vesicles contain the material, mainly cellulose, that forms the new cell walls. These vesicles form a structure called the **cell plate**.

The cell plate enlarges and its membranes join with the plasma membrane of the original cell. Two cell walls form within the cell plate, one for each of the daughter cells. The region between two adjacent plant cell walls is called the **middle lamella**.

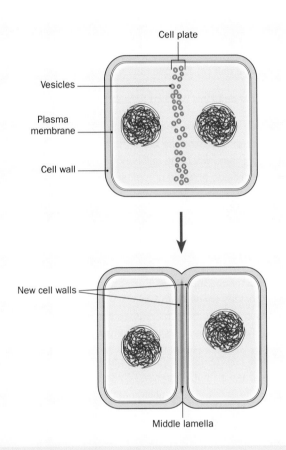

14.25 *Cell wall formation in plants*

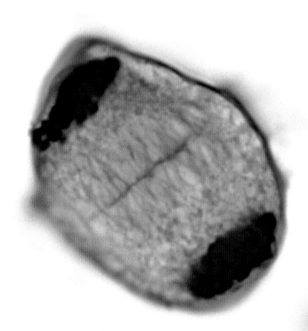

14.26 *Cell plate and spindle fibres*

THE CELL

Summary

Cell continuity means that all cells develop from existing cells.

Chromosomes are made of DNA and protein.
- Chromatin consists of chromosomes in an elongated form.
- Chromosomes contain genes.

A gene is a section of DNA which controls the formation of a protein.

A haploid cell (n) has one set of chromosomes.

A diploid cell (2n) has two sets of chromosomes.

The cell cycle is the changes that occur in a cell between one cell division and the next. The cell cycle includes:
- interphase, when the cell is not dividing
- cell division (mitosis or meiosis)

Interphase is an active phase because:
- new cell organelles are formed
- single-stranded chromosomes form double-stranded copies of themselves

Mitosis means that:
- a nucleus divides into two
- the chromosome number in each resulting nucleus remains the same as in the parent nucleus

Mitosis can be divided into four stages:
- **In stage 1** double-stranded chromosomes become visible in the nucleus, fibres appear in the cytoplasm and the nuclear membrane starts to break down.
- **In stage 2** the nuclear membrane breaks down fully, chromosomes line up along the middle of the cell and two fibres attach to each chromosome.
- **In stage 3** the fibres contract and pull one strand from each chromosome to each pole.
- **In stage 4** the chromosomes elongate and a nuclear membrane forms around each set of chromosomes.

Immediately after mitosis the cell divides into two new cells.

The functions of mitosis are:
- It allows single-celled organisms to reproduce
- In multicelled organisms it allows for growth and repair

A tumour results when one or more cells lose the ability to control the rate of mitosis and cell division.
- Benign tumours are not life-threatening.
- Malignant tumours are called cancers.

Cancer occurs when cells lose the ability to control the rate and the number of times mitosis takes place.

The group of disorders called cancers are dangerous because:
- the cells never stop dividing
- they invade other tissues
- they may spread from one body part to another

Cancers are caused by agents called carcinogens.

Meiosis halves the number of chromosomes in each resulting nucleus.

Gametes are haploid cells that are able to fuse with another gamete of the opposite sex.

The functions of meiosis are:
- to halve the number of chromosomes so that the normal number may be restored at fertilisation (i.e. to allow for sexual reproduction)
- to produce chromosomes with genetic variations that will result in variations in the organisms produced by sexual reproduction

The stages of mitosis are:
- **Prophase**: chromatin contracts, chromosomes are seen as two strands held together at the centromere, the nucleolus disappears, spindle fibres appear, the nuclear membrane breaks down.
- **Metaphase**: the nuclear membrane is broken, two spindle fibres attach to each centromere, the chromosomes line up along the equator of the cell.
- **Anaphase**: the spindle fibres contract, an equal number of identical chromosomes is pulled to each pole.
- **Telophase**: the chromosomes elongate to form chromatin, the spindle fibres break down, nucleoli re-form, two nuclear membranes form.

Cell division follows both mitosis and meiosis.
- In animal cells, a cleavage furrow forms and deepens to form two new cells.
- In plant cells, vesicles gather to form a cell plate. The cell plate forms new cell walls, which are separated by a middle lamella.

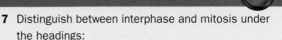

Revision questions

1 Explain what is meant by **(a)** cell continuity, **(b)** the continuity of life, **(c)** the cell cycle.

2 With regard to chromosomes:
   (a) Name the substances of which they are made.
   (b) Say where in a cell they are located.
   (c) What is their function?
   (d) How many chromosomes are present in a normal human cell?

3 **(a)** What is a gene?
   (b) Name the substance of which genes are made.
   (c) Use a diagram to explain the relationship between genes and chromosomes.
   (d) State the function of genes.
   (e) What is a genome?

4 Draw simple diagrams to show each of the following cells:
   (a) The chromosomes are single-stranded and the cell has a haploid number of four.
   (b) The chromosomes are single-stranded and the cell has a diploid number of eight.
   (c) The chromosomes are double-stranded for a cell where n = 3.
   (d) The chromosomes are double-stranded for a cell where 2n = 4.

5 **(a)** Name the main periods in the cell cycle.
   (b) Explain why interphase is not a resting phase in the cell cycle.

6 Refer to Figure 14.27 and answer the following:

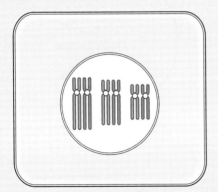

14.27

   (a) How many centromeres are shown in the diagram?
   (b) Is the cell shown haploid? Give a reason for your answer.
   (c) Name two events that should occur immediately after this stage of mitosis.
   (d) When this cell has finished mitosis, how many chromosomes will be in each nucleus?
   (e) Draw a labelled diagram of the cell immediately before this stage.

7 Distinguish between interphase and mitosis under the headings:
   (a) duration
   (b) chromosome appearance
   (c) what happens to organelles and chromosomes

8 With regard to mitosis, state:
   (a) why the nuclear membrane must break down
   (b) why fibres form
   (c) how the chromosomes are pulled apart
   (d) how many chromosomes will be in each resulting nucleus

9 Explain why the cells in a person's body are all identical genetically.

10 A cell has a chromosome number of 4. Draw a labelled diagram to show this cell in the second stage of mitosis.

11 **(a)** State two functions for mitosis.
   (b) Explain why the rate of mitosis in humans:
      (i) slows down after about 20 years of age
      (ii) speeds up at the site of a cut

12 **(a)** What is a tumour?
   (b) Distinguish between benign and malignant tumours.
   (c) What is cancer?
   (d) Give two reasons why cancer cells are said to be abnormal cells.

13 **(a)** What are carcinogens?
   (b) Name two common carcinogens.

14 A cell has 46 chromosomes. How many chromosomes will be in the nuclei resulting from **(a)** mitosis, **(b)** cancer, **(c)** meiosis?

15 If meiosis did not occur, why would sexual reproduction be a problem?

16 A chimpanzee has 48 chromosomes per cell. How many chromosomes are in each of the following:
   (a) chimpanzee eggs, **(b)** chimpanzee sperm, **(c)** chimpanzee zygote, **(d)** chimpanzee mouth cell?

17 Name the stages in mitosis associated with the following events:
   (a) the formation of spindle fibres
   (b) nuclear membrane formation
   (c) contraction of spindle fibres
   (d) lining up of chromosomes
   (e) movement of chromosomes to the poles
   (f) the division of the nucleus

18 Draw a labelled diagram of a plant cell at prophase of mitosis. Show the chromosome number as 2n = 6.

19 If the chromosome number in a nucleus at early interphase is given as 10, give the chromosome number in each cell at the following phases of mitosis:
   (a) late interphase
   (b) prophase
   (c) metaphase
   (d) anaphase

THE CELL

20 State which of the following options, (i), (ii), (iii), or (iv), is the correct answer.

  (a) In human liver cells, the correct chromosome number is:

  (i) 23, **(ii)** 24, **(iii)** 92, **(iv)** 46

  (b) Genes are made from:

  (i) chromosomes   **(ii)** DNA

  (iii) chromatin   **(iv)** proteins

  (c) The cell cycle consists of:

  (i) four stages   **(ii)** three states

  (iii) two stages   **(iv)** thousands of stages

  (d) Chromatin consists of:

  (i) cytoplasm   **(ii)** centromeres

  (iii) chromosomes   **(iv)** spindle fibres

  (e) A cleavage furrow develops after:

  (i) prophase   **(ii)** metaphase

  (iii) anaphase   **(iv)** telophase

  (f) A cell plate develops in:

  (i) metaphase   **(ii)** plant cells

  (iii) cancer cells   **(iv)** animal cells

Sample examination questions

Section A

21 The diagram shows a stage of mitosis.

  (a) Name A and B.

  (b) What is happening during this stage of mitosis?

  (c) How many cells are formed when a cell divides by mitosis?

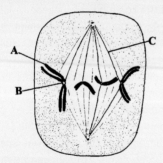

  (d) For what purpose do single-celled organisms use mitosis?

  (2005 OL Q 4)

22 Study the diagram of a stage of mitosis in a diploid cell and then answer the questions below.

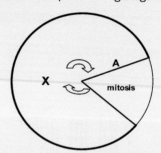

  (a) Name A, B and C.

  (b) What stage of mitosis is shown?

  (c) What is the diploid number of this nucleus which is undergoing mitosis?

  (e) Some cells in the human body undergo meiosis. Give one function of meiosis.

  (2007 HL Q 3)

23 **(a)** Draw a diagram of a nucleus during metaphase of mitosis where 2n = 6. Label the spindle and a centromere in your diagram.

  (b) State a function of mitosis in a single-celled organism.

  (c) State a function of mitosis in a multicellular organism.

  (d) State one way in which mitosis differs from meiosis.

  (e) When the normal control of mitosis in a cell is lost, cancer may result. Suggest **two** possible causes of cancer.

  (2005 HL Q 5)

24 The diagram represents the cell cycle.

  (a) What stage of the cycle is represented by X?

  (b) Give the names of the **two** processes involving DNA which take place during stage X.

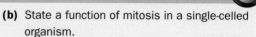
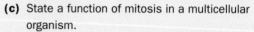

  (c) For convenience of study, mitosis is divided into four stages. List these in order, starting at A.

  (d) In which of the stages of mitosis that you have listed in **(c)** would you expect to see the spindle fibres contracting?

  (e) Explain the term diploid number.

  (f) What term is used to describe a group of disorders of the body in which cells lose the normal regulation of mitosis?

  (2008 HL Q 2)

Previous examination questions

Ordinary level	Higher level
2003 Sample Q 6	2005 Q 5
2005 Q 4	2007 Q 3
	2008 Q 2

*For latest questions go to **www.edco.ie/biology***

Chapter 15 Classification and heredity

Classification

There is a vast variety of living things on our planet. There is no way of counting, never mind studying, every single individual organism alive today.

In order to simplify the study of organisms, and to allow scientists to communicate with each other, a system of classifying organisms is necessary.

Classification means placing objects into similar groups or categories. For example, DVDs in a shop are classified under the headings of thriller, humour, romance etc.

Placing organisms into similar groups simplifies their study. It is far simpler to study the features of a group such as flowering plants, than to learn the details of every type of flowering plant (about 250 000 in total).

The science of classifying organisms is called **taxonomy**. Organisms are classified according to similarities in structure, function and development. These similarities exist because organisms are related to each other, having arisen from common ancestors by evolution. The basic unit of classification is the species.

15.1 *Mules and a horse: a mule is the offspring of a male donkey and a female horse. Horses and donkeys are different species as their offspring (mules) are unable to reproduce.*

Species

> A **species** is a group of similar organisms that are capable of naturally interbreeding with each other, but not with other such groups, to produce fertile offspring.

All domestic (tame) dogs are members of the same species. All such dogs can interbreed with each other to produce offspring, which themselves can reproduce. Domestic cats are members of a different species. Dogs and cats cannot naturally interbreed with each other. For the same reason, oak and ash trees are different species.

So far about 1.5 million species have been identified on Earth. Interestingly, insects alone make up about 750 000, or half, of all known species.

Thousands of previously unidentified species are discovered every year. Estimates of the total number of all species on Earth range between 5 and 100 million.

Variation within species

> **Variation within a species** means that in a group of successfully interbreeding organisms the individual members show different characteristics.

All living humans are members of the same species. Despite their many similarities humans may differ in features such as hair colour, skin colour and height. In the same way individual plants of the same species (such as roses) may differ in traits such as flower colour, leaf shape or size of thorns.

These differences mean that each individual organism (such as a person) is unique. The individual variations do not hinder the ability of the organisms to interbreed successfully.

There are two types of variation, as outlined on the following page.

THE CELL

THE CELL

ACQUIRED VARIATION

Acquired variations are not inherited. They are not genetically controlled, but are learned or developed during life. Examples include the ability to walk, speak a language, ride a bicycle or use a computer.

INHERITED VARIATION

Inherited variations are controlled by genes, as outlined below.

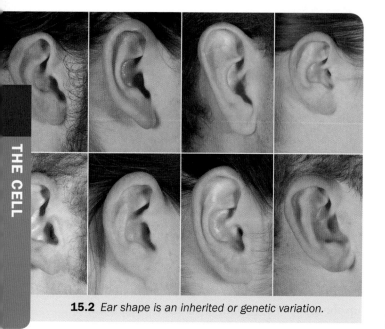

15.2 *Ear shape is an inherited or genetic variation.*

Heredity

> **Heredity** is the passing on of features from parents to offspring by means of genes.

Heredity is also called **genetic inheritance**.

Humans inherit genes to control features such as the number of fingers, the production of nails and the ability to form tears. Plants inherit genes to control the number of petals, the colour of the petals and the shape of the leaves.

Characteristics are traits or features that are inherited genetically.

Genes

> A **gene** is a section of DNA that causes the production of a protein.

Many of the proteins produced by genes are enzymes. Genes are said to control a cell because many of the enzymes they produce control cell activities.

Genes are the units (or structures) of heredity.

Gene expression

> **Gene expression** is the precise way in which the genetic information in a gene is decoded in the cell and used to make a protein.

In other words, gene expression refers to the way in which genes work. It describes the sequence of events that occur so that a gene on a chromosome in the nucleus can cause the production of, for example, an enzyme in the cytoplasm of the same cell.

It is the expression of genes that produces the characteristics or traits that are inherited. A child may inherit genes for tallness, for instance, but if the child's diet lacks the correct nutrients, the genes may not be able to cause tallness, i.e. the genes may not be expressed.

In the same way, leaf cells have genes to control the production of the green pigment, chlorophyll. However, if the plant grows in a dark place these genes do not work and chlorophyll is not made.

Characteristics such as those listed above arise from the interaction between the genes that are inherited (heredity) and the environment.

> Characteristics = heredity + environment

Chromosomes

Chromosomes are composed of about 60% protein (called histone) and 40% DNA.

The protein is responsible for holding the DNA in a tightly packed configuration so that it can fit into the nucleus. For example, a typical human chromosome has a DNA strand that could extend to about 6 cm long. This is far too large to fit into a nucleus that is much smaller than the full stop at the end of this sentence.

Genes are arranged along the DNA of a chromosome in linear order, just as railway stations are spread out along a railway track. Sometimes a number of genes are located close together on the chromosome. Other genes are widely separated along the chromosome.

This means that large sections of the chromosome are not made up of working genes. In fact it is known that about 97% of the DNA in a human cell does not consist of genes. This DNA is said to be non-coding (i.e. it does not carry the code for the formation of a protein).

At present, the function, if any, of non-coding DNA is not yet known. It is often called **junk DNA**. If this DNA is found to have a function, the term junk DNA will be shown to be mistaken.

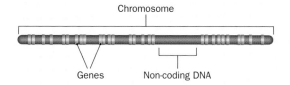

Chromosome

Genes   Non-coding DNA

15.3 *Relationship between genes and a chromosome*

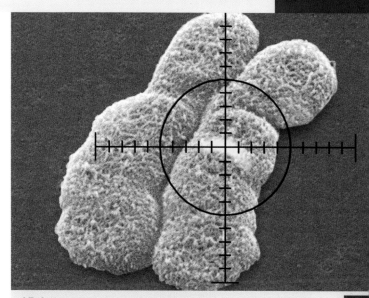

15.4 *Targeted gene on a chromosome*

THE CELL

Summary

Classification means placing organisms into similar groups. Classification is necessary in order to:
- simplify the study of organisms
- allow scientific communication

Taxonomy is the study of classification.

A species is a group of organisms capable of interbreeding naturally to produce fertile offspring.
- The members of a species, although similar in some respects, may show many differences.

Variation means that the members of a species show different characteristics.

Heredity (or genetic inheritance) is the passing on of features from parents to offspring by means of genes.

Characteristics arise from the interaction of genes and their environment.

Chromosomes are made of DNA and protein.

A gene is a section of DNA that controls the production of a protein.
- Genes only comprise about 3% of the DNA in human cells. The rest of the DNA is said to be non-coding.

Gene expression is the way in which a gene works to produce a protein.

Revision questions

1 Explain what is meant by:
 (a) classification
 (b) taxonomy.
2 Give two reasons why biologists classify organisms.
3 (a) What is a species?
 (b) Name two animal and two plant species.
 (c) Why are lions and tigers considered to be different species?
4 The members of a species show variations.
 (a) Name three variations that are visible in (i) humans, (ii) a named plant.
 (b) Why are all humans considered to be in the same species?
5 (a) What is heredity?
 (b) Name the key chemical that is inherited by organisms.
 (c) Name three inherited characteristics in (i) humans, (ii) plants.
6 (a) Distinguish between inherited and acquired variations.

 (b) Say which type of variation the following features represent:
 swimming, curly hair, long eyelashes, writing, tying a lace, red hair, reading, wearing make-up, dark eyes.
7 (a) Distinguish between a gene and a characteristic.
 (b) What is meant by gene expression?
8 (a) Name the materials of which chromosomes are made.
 (b) Give a function for each of these materials.
 (c) Show, by means of a diagram, the relationship between genes and chromosomes.
 (d) Explain what is meant by (i) coding, and (ii) non-coding, DNA.
9 Pick out the four pairs of organisms in this list that belong to the same species:
 house fly, giraffe, greyhound, black cat, zebra, horse chestnut tree, long-eared hamster, tiger, red tulip, guinea pig, ash tree, long-haired hamster, tortoiseshell cat, cheetah, yellow tulip, moth, highland terrier

Sample examination questions

Section A

10 Indicate whether each of the following statements is true (T) or false (F) by drawing a circle around T or F.

Chromosomes are made of DNA and lipid   **T   F**

Organisms of the same species can usually produce fertile offspring   **T   F**

(2004 OL Q 3)

Section C

11 (i) Explain briefly what is meant by a gene.

(ii) Where in the nucleus would you find genes?

(2007 OL Q 11c)

12 Explain the following terms as used in genetics: species, variation.

(2006 HL Q12a)

Previous examination questions

Ordinary level	Higher level
2004 Q 3	2006 Q 12a
2007 Q 11c	

*For latest questions go to **www.edco.ie/biology***

Chapter 16 **DNA and RNA**

Structure of DNA (deoxyribonucleic acid)

About 40 human cells would fit beside one another across the full stop at the end of this sentence. The DNA from just one of these cells would stretch to about 3 metres if it was fully unwound from the nucleus. This means that DNA must be a very long molecule in comparison to the size of a cell.

To enable DNA to fit into a nucleus, it is heavily coiled and folded, very similar to an elastic band twisted repeatedly until it forms a solid ball. Proteins (called histones) are responsible for holding the DNA in its folded state.

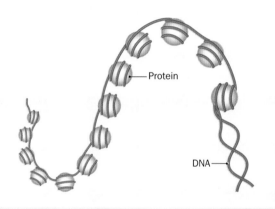

16.1 Chromosome structure

The structure of DNA is similar to that of a ladder. DNA has two strands, just like the sides of a ladder. The strands are linked by pairs of chemicals, called bases. Each pair of bases forms a 'rung' on the DNA molecule.

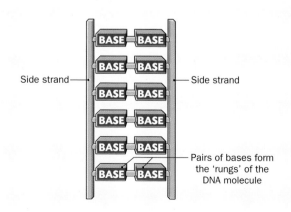

16.2 Basic structure of DNA

There are only four different bases used in DNA. The four bases are known by the first letter of their names, i.e. adenine (A), thymine (T), guanine (G) and cytosine (C).

Each of the four bases can only join or bond with one other base, i.e. A joins with T and G joins with C. The pairs of bases, A/T and G/C, are said to be complementary.

16.3 Complementary base pairs

The four bases, and the way they combine, can be recalled using the phrase:

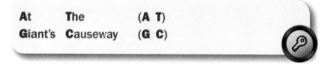

At   The   (A T)
Giant's Causeway   (G C)

DNA can be thought of as a rope ladder, with pairs of complementary bases forming the rungs of the ladder, as shown in Figure 16.4.

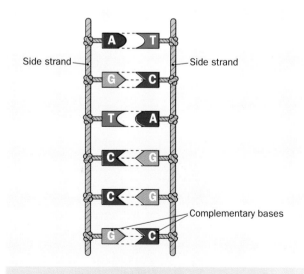

16.4 Simplified structure of DNA

The pattern of complementary base pairing means that if one strand of a DNA molecule has the sequence TAGCAT, then the sequence on the partner strand must be ATCGTA.

If the rope ladder is twisted to form a spiral structure each of the side strands will form a spiral or helix. DNA is arranged in this way to form a double helix shape.

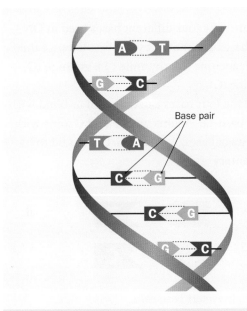

16.5 *DNA double helix*

Chromosomes and genes

A chromosome consists of many base pairs arranged into a double helix. For example, the DNA in the longest human chromosome (number 1) contains about 300 million base pairs.

A gene is a sequence of many bases. The precise sequence of bases is called the genetic code. A gene works, or is expressed, when this code is sent into the cytoplasm (using RNA) to form a protein.

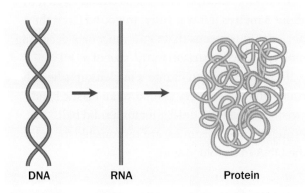

DNA   RNA   Protein

16.7 *Gene expression*

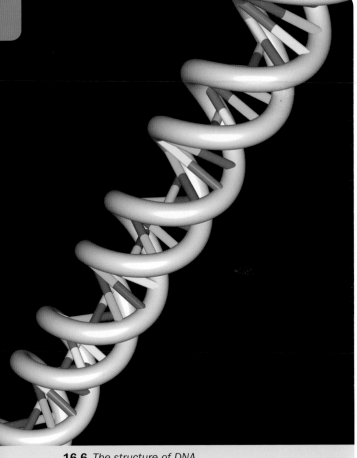

16.6 *The structure of DNA*

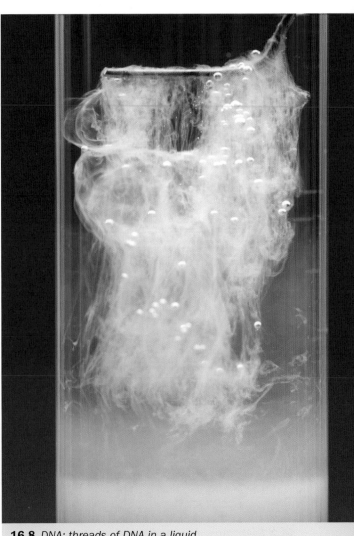

16.8 *DNA: threads of DNA in a liquid*

THE CELL

Activity 15 To isolate DNA from a plant tissue

1 Add 3 g of sodium chloride to 10 cm³ of washing-up liquid.

2 Add distilled water so that the solution is made up to 100 cm³.

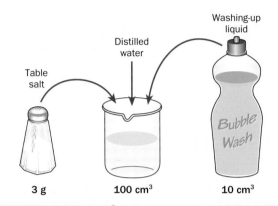

Table salt — 3 g
Distilled water — 100 cm³
Washing-up liquid — 10 cm³
Bubble Wash

16.9a *Steps 1 and 2*

3 Cut an onion into small cubes (each side should be about 0.5 cm).

4 Add the chopped onion to a beaker containing the salt/detergent solution and stir the mixture. (*The detergent causes the cell membranes to break, which releases DNA from the cells. The salt causes DNA molecules to clump together.*)

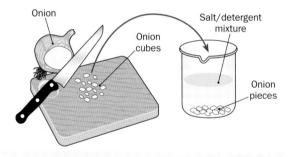

Onion
Onion cubes
Salt/detergent mixture
Onion pieces

16.9b *Steps 3 and 4*

5 Put the beaker in a water bath at 60°C for 15 minutes. (*This inactivates (denatures) enzymes that would normally digest the DNA. If left any longer than 15 minutes DNA itself would break down.*)

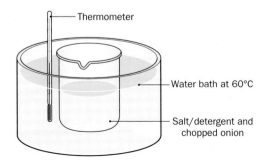

Thermometer
Water bath at 60°C
Salt/detergent and chopped onion

16.9c *Step 5*

6 Cool the mixture by placing the beaker in an ice water bath for 5 minutes, stirring frequently. (*This slows down the breakdown of the DNA.*)

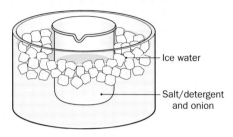

Ice water
Salt/detergent and onion

16.9d *Step 6*

7 Pour the mixture into a domestic food blender and blend it for only 3 seconds on high speed. (*This breaks down the cell walls and releases DNA. Blending it for too long would break down the DNA strands.*)

Blender
Salt/detergent and chopped onion

16.9e *Step 7*

8 Filter the mixture through coffee filter paper into a second beaker. Do not add the foam from the top of the mixture to the filter paper. (*Cell parts are retained in the filter paper. The filtered material, called filtrate, contains DNA and proteins. Normal laboratory filter paper is not used as its pores are too small and the process would be very slow.*)

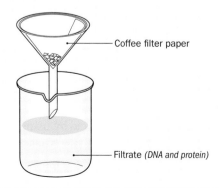

Coffee filter paper
Filtrate *(DNA and protein)*

16.9f *Step 8*

9 Use a 10 cm³ syringe, without a needle, to place 6 cm³ of the onion filtrate into a boiling tube.

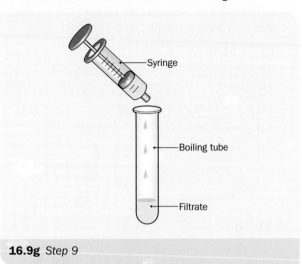

16.9g *Step 9*

10 Add 4 drops of protease enzyme (such as pepsin or trypsin) to the contents of the boiling tube and mix well. *(The protease breaks down the proteins around the DNA.)*

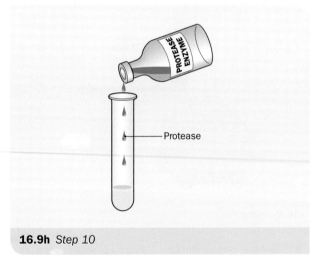

16.9h *Step 10*

11 Pour 9 cm³ of ice-cold 95% ethanol or methylated spirits (stored in a freezer overnight) carefully down the side of the boiling tube. The ethanol should form a layer on top of the onion filtrate. *(Alcohol removes water from DNA, which causes DNA to float to the top of the water. DNA is insoluble in ice-cold alcohol and so it precipitates at the alcohol-filtrate boundary. The DNA forms white threads in the alcohol.)*

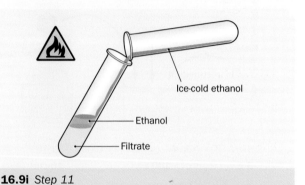

16.9i *Step 11*

12 Gently twist a small glass rod or a wire loop in the alcohol. Strands of DNA should attach to the rod or wire. Do not mix the two layers or damage the DNA which is very easily broken. *(The DNA forms a clear mesh of what looks like stringy mucous.)*

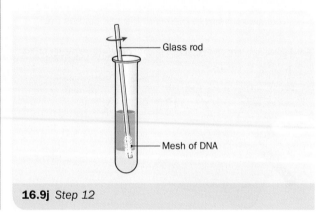

16.9j *Step 12*

The genetic code

Genes are made of DNA. A gene is a section of DNA required for the production of a particular protein molecule.

Proteins are made up of combinations of hundreds or thousands of amino acids joined together in a specific sequence. Up to 20 different types of amino acids are used in proteins. This means that a gene must carry a different code to control the assembly of each of the 20 different amino acids.

DNA codes for each amino acid by using a sequence of three consecutive bases. Such a sequence of three bases is called a **triplet** (or **codon**).

This is similar to the way in which Morse code uses a sequence of three dots or dashes to specify a letter. A long stretch of triplets that produce a protein forms a gene.

Did you know?

The DNA triplet CAA is the code for an amino acid called valine, and CGA is the triplet for an amino acid called alanine. If these triplets form part of a gene they will cause a protein to form with the relevant amino acids in sequence, as outlined in Figure 16.10.

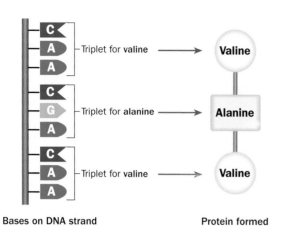

Triplet for valine ⟶ Valine

Triplet for alanine ⟶ Alanine

Triplet for valine ⟶ Valine

Bases on DNA strand   Protein formed

16.10 *DNA triplets code for particular amino acids*

The genetic code can be compared with the English language as follows:

- The four DNA bases represent the letters in the language.
- Each triplet or codon forms a word.
- A sequence of many triplets forms a gene or paragraph of instruction in how to make a protein.
- All the genes in a cell (called its genome) form the book of life for that cell.

The genetic code compared with the English language	
Genetic code	**English equivalent**
Base	Letter
Triplet or codon	Word
Gene	Paragraph
Genome	Book

Non-coding DNA

As mentioned in Chapter 15, up to 97% of the DNA in human cells does not carry the code for the production of proteins. This so-called junk DNA is of two types: some of it occurs between genes and the rest is found within genes.

The exact function of non-coding DNA is not known. However, the sequence of bases in non-coding DNA varies greatly from one person to another. It is the DNA in these non-coding sections that is used to prepare DNA profiles.

Replication of DNA

At the end of mitosis each new cell has single-stranded chromosomes. Before these cells can divide again, the DNA in each chromosome must produce an exact copy of itself. The single-stranded chromosomes must become double-stranded chromosomes. This process is called DNA replication and it takes place in the nucleus during interphase (Figure 16.11).

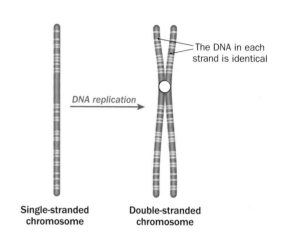

The DNA in each strand is identical

DNA replication ⟶

Single-stranded chromosome   Double-stranded chromosome

16.11 *An overview of DNA replication*

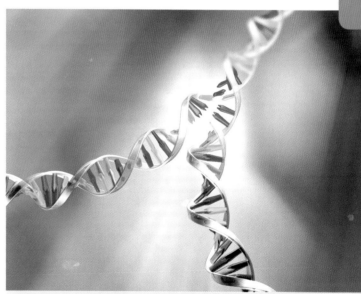

16.12 *DNA replication*

THE CELL

MECHANISM OF DNA REPLICATION (FIGURE 16.13)

1 The double helix unwinds (or uncoils).
2 An enzyme breaks the bonds between the base pairs.
3 DNA bases that are normally present in the cytoplasm enter the nucleus. The incoming bases attach to the exposed complementary bases (i.e. base pairing occurs). In this way, each side of the

DNA molecule acts as a mould or template for the new DNA that is formed.
4 Each new strand is:
   (a) half new DNA and half old DNA
   (b) identical to the original DNA strand and to the other new partner strand

Each new piece of DNA rewinds to form a double helix.

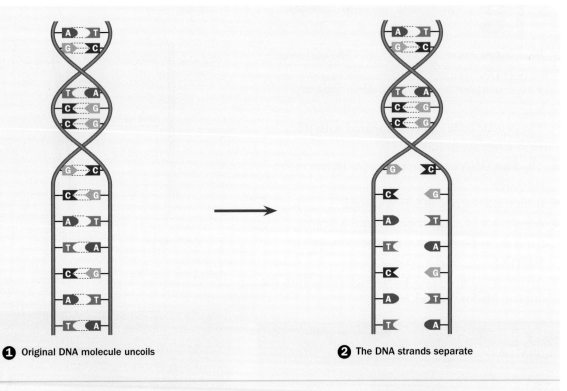

❶ Original DNA molecule uncoils

❷ The DNA strands separate

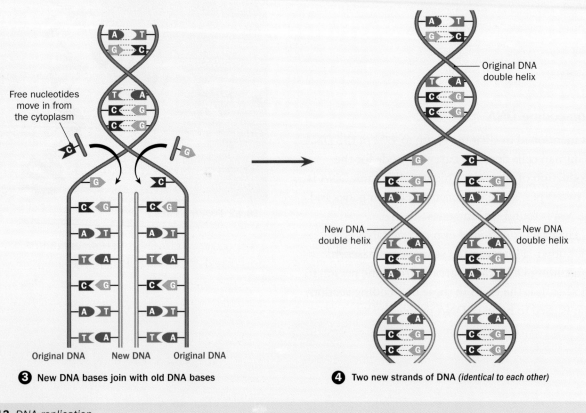

Free nucleotides move in from the cytoplasm

Original DNA   New DNA   Original DNA

❸ New DNA bases join with old DNA bases

Original DNA double helix

New DNA double helix

New DNA double helix

❹ Two new strands of DNA *(identical to each other)*

16.13 *DNA replication*

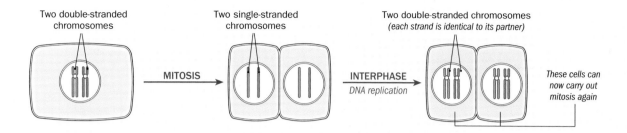

16.14 *The significance of DNA replication in a cell with one pair of chromosomes*

SIGNIFICANCE OF DNA REPLICATION

Each new DNA double helix (chromosome) will have exactly the same sequence of bases as the original (see Figure 16.14).

DNA is able to produce **exact** copies of itself (hence the term replication is used to describe its manner of reproducing). This means that the same DNA is passed on to each new generation of cells.

For example, a human zygote is a single cell with 46 chromosomes. These chromosomes contain a certain sequence of bases. The same sequence of bases is passed on, in the form of new chromosomes, to each body cell in a person due to DNA replication (and mitosis).

DNA profiling

DNA profiling (also called DNA or genetic finger-printing) is a method of making a unique pattern of bands from the DNA of a person, which can then be used to distinguish that DNA from other DNA.

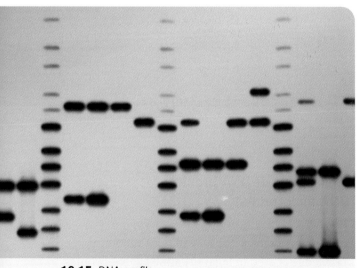

16.15 *DNA profile*

Method of preparing a DNA profile

Preparing a DNA profile involves four steps. Firstly, the DNA is released from cells. Secondly, the DNA is cut into fragments of different lengths. Then, the DNA fragments are separated according to their sizes. Finally, the patterns produced by the fragments are compared or analysed.

The following describes these four procedures in more detail.

1. DNA IS RELEASED

In order to produce a DNA profile, cells are broken down to release their DNA (as in Activity 15).

Did you know?

If the amount of DNA available is too small to work with, it can be increased or amplified. A common technique used to amplify small quantities of DNA is a process called the polymerase chain reaction (PCR).

2. DNA IS CUT INTO FRAGMENTS

The isolated DNA is cut into fragments using special enzymes. These enzymes are called restriction enzymes. They were first isolated from bacteria where they are used to destroy the DNA of invading viruses.

Different restriction enzymes cut DNA at specific base sequences. For example, one restriction enzyme will always cut DNA at the base sequence GAATTC, while another only cuts at the sequence GATC.

By using the GAATTC restriction enzyme, a long strand of DNA will be cut into sections, each section starting with the base sequence AATTC (the enzyme cuts the DNA between the G and the A bases).

The sections of DNA that are cut will be of different lengths because the base sequences being cut may be close together or far apart on the DNA strands.

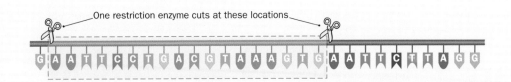

One restriction enzyme cuts at these locations

G A A T T C C T G A C G T A A A G T G A A T T C T T A G G

16.16 *The action of a restriction enzyme*

This means that if two GAATTC sequences are close together (as in Figure 16.16), then a short section of DNA results.

If two GAATTC sequences are very far apart, then the DNA section that is cut out will be much longer.

3. THE FRAGMENTS ARE SEPARATED

The sections of DNA that have been cut out are separated on the basis of their size. They are separated by a process called gel electrophoresis.

This involves placing the invisible DNA fragments in a small glass tank containing a sugar-based gel. An electric current is applied along the gel. The current draws the negatively charged DNA to one end of the gel.

Small DNA fragments move faster through the porous gel than do the larger fragments. In this way bands of small fragments are separated from bands of larger fragments.

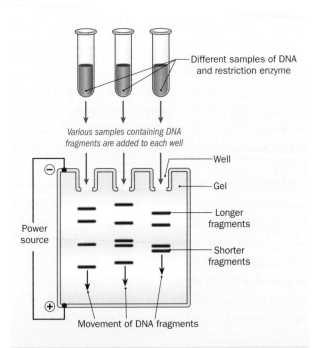

Different samples of DNA and restriction enzyme

Various samples containing DNA fragments are added to each well

Well

Gel

Longer fragments

Power source

Shorter fragments

Movement of DNA fragments

16.17 *Gel electrophoresis*

When the electrophoresis is finished a permanent record of the results is obtained. This may involve adding radioactive material, which combines with

DNA fragments to produce a flourescent image. A photographic copy of the final pattern of DNA bands is then obtained.

4. PATTERNS ARE COMPARED

In the same way that no two people have the same fingerprints, it is highly unlikely that any two people will have the same DNA profile (unless they are identical twins).

If the pattern of bands from two different DNA samples is the same, then the two samples must have come from the same person.

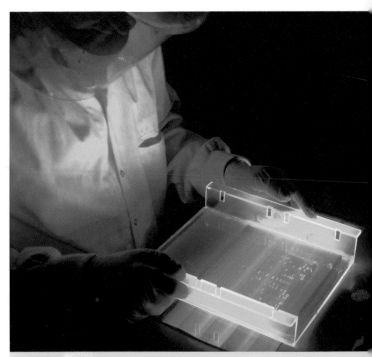

16.18 *DNA gel analysis: DNA fragments as seen under ultraviolet light*

Applications of DNA profiles (DNA fingerprints)

CRIME

Forensic medicine is the way in which medical knowledge is used in legal situations. DNA profiles are often used in forensic (legal) cases.

If biological material such as blood, hair, saliva or semen is left at the scene of a crime it can be collected and a DNA profile prepared.

If the pattern of the DNA profile is compared with those of the victim and a suspect it may be seen that it matches that of the suspect but not that of the victim. This would be strong evidence to associate the suspect with the crime scene. Of course the profile may not match that of the suspect, which might eliminate the suspect from the inquiry.

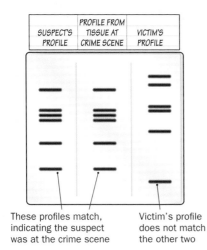

SUSPECT'S PROFILE	PROFILE FROM TISSUE AT CRIME SCENE	VICTIM'S PROFILE

These profiles match, indicating the suspect was at the crime scene

Victim's profile does not match the other two

16.19 *Forensic use of DNA profiles*

The bands differ in thickness due to there being more or less bands of this type present, e.g. a thick band represents many DNA fragments of a particular length. This is clear in Figure 16.20.

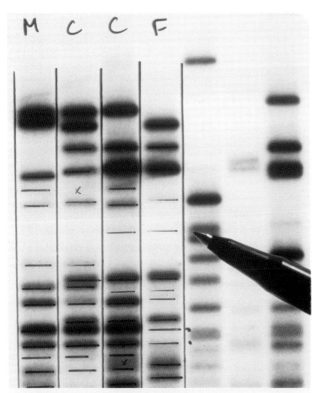

16.20 *The results of DNA fingerprinting: M represents the mother, each C represents a child and F represents the father*

16.21 *Bloodstained clothing analysis in a forensic lab*

MEDICAL

DNA profiles can be used to determine whether a particular person is, or is not, the parent of a child. In this way the paternity (father) or maternity (mother) can be established.

This information can apply in property or financial inheritance cases, or in immigration cases where a person can enter a country if his/her parent or child is already in that country.

To decide if a man is the father of a child, blood samples are taken from the child, the mother and the man. DNA profiles are prepared and examined.

If all the bands in the child's profile match with bands in either the mother's or the man's profile, then the man is shown to be the natural father of the child – see Figure 16.22(a).

If some of the child's bands match those of the mother, but the rest do not match with the man's bands, then the man is not the father of the child – see Figure 16.22(b).

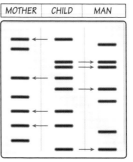

MOTHER	CHILD	MAN

(a) The child's bands match with either the mother's bands or the man's bands. The man is the father of the child.

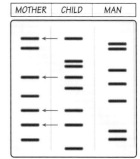

MOTHER	CHILD	MAN

(b) Some of the child's bands match with the mother but the rest do not match with the man's bands. The man is not the father of the child.

16.22 *Using DNA profiles to determine the father of a child*

THE CELL

Genetic screening

Sometimes the process of DNA replication does not work exactly as it should. In these cases, a gene (or a number of genes) may be incorrectly copied. In addition, DNA can be altered by mutations (see Chapter 18).

If genes are altered in any way they will not carry the correct code for the protein that they were intended to produce. This may have severe effects on a person who inherits such genes.

Did you know?

Genetic disorders caused by defective genes include albinism (where the pigment melanin cannot be made), cystic fibrosis (where there is a build-up of mucous in the lungs and intestines), haemochromatosis (where too much iron accumulates in the body and has to be removed by regular bleeding) and sickle cell anaemia (where abnormal haemoglobin is produced).

Genetic screening means testing DNA for the presence or absence of a particular gene or an altered gene.

Genetic screening often involves adding a radioactive section of DNA (called a DNA or genetic probe) to a sample of DNA from the person being tested. The DNA probe will only attach to a normal gene. If the probe does not attach then the gene is altered.

Genetic screening can be carried out in two main ways: adult screening and foetal screening.

Adult screening

Screening is sometimes carried out on adults who, although they do not suffer from a genetic disorder, may carry a defective gene in each of their cells. People who carry defective genes, without having the disorder themselves, are said to be carriers for the condition.

It is now possible to identify (genetically screen) individuals who are carriers for disorders such as sickle cell anaemia and the most common form of cystic fibrosis.

The benefit of these tests is that it gives people information regarding the chances of them having a child with the disorder.

Foetal screening

In foetal screening, cells can be removed from the placenta or the fluid around the foetus. These cells can be tested to detect if the child has any one of a number of genetic disorders.

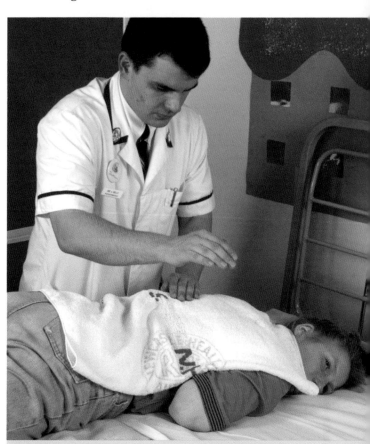

16.23 *A cystic fibrosis patient receiving physiotherapy to aid breathing*

Did you know?

Ethics of genetic screening
Ethics relates to whether behaviour is proper or improper. Genetic screening may cause ethical problems.

If the results of genetic tests become public, the people concerned may suffer embarrassment or be treated unfairly. For example, they may be isolated and treated as if they had a disease even if they do not. Employers and insurance companies may be reluctant to get involved with them.

Genetic screening presents other ethical dilemmas. For instance, would people wish to know that they have a genetic disorder that will develop in later years? This is especially problematic if the disorder is untreatable.

In relation to genetic screening or testing in the foetus, would knowledge of a genetic disorder help to prepare the family for the future, or encourage a termination of the pregnancy?

RNA (*ribonucleic acid*)

DNA and RNA are both nucleic acids. RNA (ribonucleic acid) also consists of four bases. However, RNA differs from DNA in the following ways:

◾ RNA contains the base uracil instead of thymine. This means that the bases in RNA are A, U, G and C. The bases A and U are complementary, as are the bases G and C.

16.24 *Base pairs in RNA*

◾ RNA is a single-stranded molecule, unlike DNA, which is a double strand (helix).
◾ The sequence of bases in RNA is determined by the sequence of bases in DNA. The bases in RNA are complementary to those in a section of DNA.

    For example, if a strand of DNA has the sequence GGAATC along one side, then the RNA produced will have the sequence CCUUAG.

◾ RNA can move out of the nucleus into the cytoplasm. DNA is always in the nucleus.

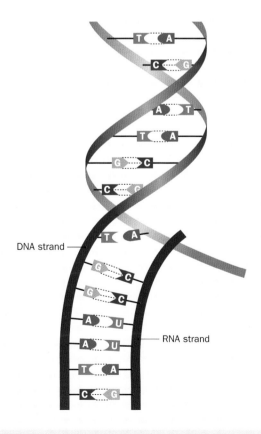

16.25 *Base pairing between DNA and RNA*

Differences between DNA and RNA

DNA	RNA
1 The bases are AT GC (thymine)	The bases are AU GC (uracil)
2 Double-stranded (i.e. double helix)	Single-stranded
3 Found in the nucleus	Found in the nucleus and cytoplasm

The difference between the bases in DNA and RNA are simplified below:

CATGUT

Bases in DNA ⎯⎯⏐   ⏐⎯⎯ U replaces T in RNA

Protein synthesis

Genes control cell activities by producing proteins, many of which are enzymes. Proteins are composed of amino acids. It is important that the amino acids are assembled in the correct sequence, in order to produce the correct protein.

    To understand the vital role carried out by genes (or DNA), it is essential to understand how genes work (i.e. how genes are expressed). This means it is necessary to know how DNA makes proteins. The main steps in this process are as follows:

1 The sequence of bases on a DNA strand carries instructions in the form of a code to make a particular protein.
2 The bases in DNA and RNA work in groups of three. Each group of three bases causes one particular amino acid to become part of the protein being made.
3 The DNA strands separate. This step takes place in the nucleus. See Figure 16.26.

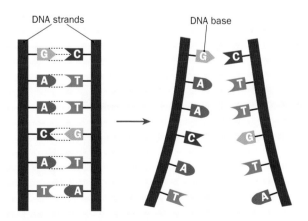

16.26 *DNA strands separate*

THE CELL

4 RNA bases attach to the exposed bases on one side of the DNA. This means that the code has been **transcribed** from DNA to a complementary strand of RNA. See Figure 16.27.

The RNA strand formed in this way is called messenger RNA (mRNA).

Transcription is the copying of a sequence of genetic bases from DNA onto messenger RNA (mRNA).

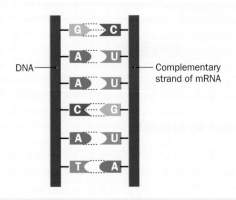

16.27 *Transcription of genetic code from DNA to RNA*

5 The mRNA strand detaches from the DNA and moves out of the nucleus into the cytoplasm.

6 The mRNA passes through a ribosome. As it passes through, each group of three bases causes a particular amino acid to be attached to the protein that is made in the ribosome.

In this way, the code on the mRNA is **translated** into the correct sequence of amino acids at a ribosome. See Figure 16.29.

Translation is the conversion of a sequence of genetic bases on messenger RNA into a sequence of amino acids.

7 The protein becomes folded as it emerges from the ribosome. This allows the protein to carry out its particular function.

16.28 *TEM of ribosomes*

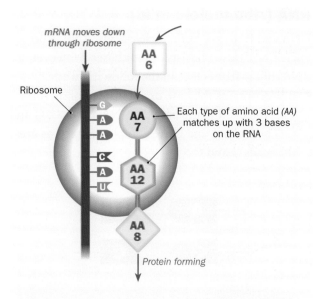

16.29 *Translation of genetic code from RNA to amino acids*

Detailed structure of DNA

The structure of DNA was worked out by James Watson and Francis Crick in 1953. They shared the Nobel prize in 1962 with Maurice Watkins for their discovery. Their findings were based on the earlier research of Rosalind Franklin, who unfortunately died in 1958.

The discovery of the structure of DNA is considered to be one of the outstanding advances in biology in the 20th century.

DNA is made up of units called nucleotides. These are arranged into very long chains called polynucleotides.

The detailed structure of DNA can be considered under three headings: nucleotides, base pairs and double helix.

1. Nucleotides

A nucleotide consists of three parts: a phosphate group, a sugar and a nitrogen-containing base. These are linked together as shown below.

16.30 *Structure of a nucleotide*

The sugar in DNA is deoxyribose (i.e. a 5-carbon sugar, similar to ribose but lacking an oxygen atom). Ribonucleic acid (RNA) contains the sugar ribose.

The phosphate group is PO$_4$, but this is normally represented as P. The phosphate and deoxyribose groups form the sides of the DNA strand.

There are four nitrogenous bases, two of which are classified as purines and two as pyrimidines.

The two purines (double-ring molecules) are adenine (A) and guanine (G). The pyrimidines (single-ring molecules) are thymine (T) and cytosine (C). This means that there are four distinct nucleotides.

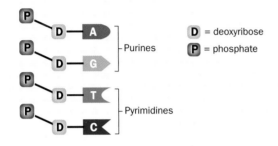

16.31 *The four DNA nucleotides*

The purine bases can be remembered by the phrase:

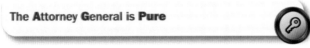

The **Attorney General** is **Pure**

The pyrimidines contain the letter '**y**':

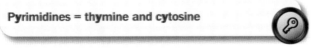

Pyrimidines = thymine and cytosine

The nucleotides join together, with a bond between the phosphate group of one and the sugar of the next, forming a polynucleotide.

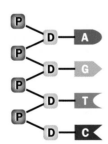

16.32 *A polynucleotide*

2. Base pairs

The bases join together in a very specific manner. Adenine and thymine each form two weak hydrogen bonds. This allows them to bond together. In a similar way guanine and cytosine each form three hydrogen bonds, so they can pair together.

The bases can be thought of as having opposite or complementary shapes, just like adjoining pieces of a jigsaw. Note that each base pair has a purine and a pyrimidine.

The forces holding the bases together are **hydrogen bonds**. These are weak bonds formed when a slightly positive hydrogen is attracted by another slightly negative atom (e.g. nitrogen or oxygen).

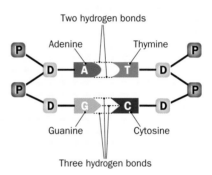

16.33 *Base pairs*

It is simpler to leave out the phosphates and sugars when drawing sections of DNA. In this case, only the base pairs are shown (see Figure 16.34).

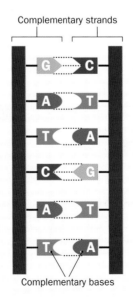

16.34 *Simplified structure of DNA*

3. Double helix

Crick and Watson discovered that DNA consisted of two helical or spiral chains of polynucleotides, as shown in Figure 16.35.

The outside strands of the double helix are made of deoxyribose and phosphate. The 'rungs' of the molecule are the base pairs on the inside.

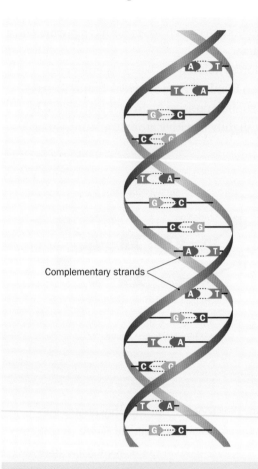

Complementary strands

16.35 *DNA double helix*

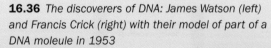

16.36 *The discoverers of DNA: James Watson (left) and Francis Crick (right) with their model of part of a DNA moleule in 1953*

Protein synthesis (extended study)

The process of protein formation proceeds as follows.

Initiation – Starting the process

1 Enzymes in the nucleus start to unwind the DNA double helix at the site of the gene that is going to produce a protein.

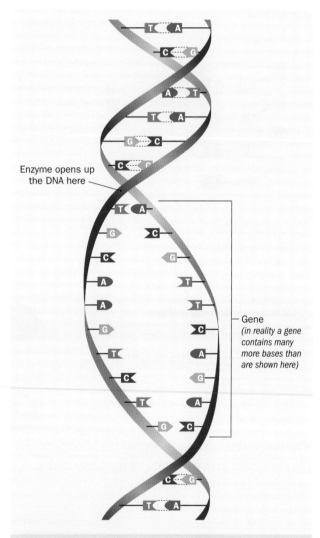

Enzyme opens up the DNA here

Gene
(in reality a gene contains many more bases than are shown here)

16.37 *The double helix unwinds at the site of a gene*

Transcription – rewriting the code from DNA to RNA

2 Complementary RNA bases bond with one of the exposed DNA strands.

3 The enzyme RNA polymerase joins the RNA bases together to form messenger RNA (mRNA). Each mRNA molecule has complementary bases to those on the DNA strand from which it was transcribed.

A sequence of three bases of DNA or RNA is called a triplet or codon. Each codon will eventually cause one amino acid to become part of the protein being made.

4 Each mRNA strand carries:
(a) a start codon (e.g. AUG)
(b) a series of codons to specify particular amino acids
(c) a stop codon (e.g. UAA)

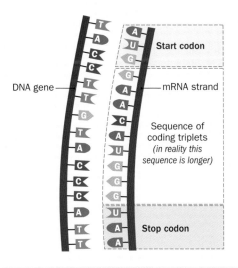

16.38 *Transcription (DNA → RNA)*

Translation – the production of a protein according to the RNA code

5 mRNA moves from the nucleus to the cytoplasm.
6 Ribosomes are made up of ribosomal RNA (rRNA) and protein.
7 The mRNA strand forms weak bonds with the rRNA in a ribosome. This will be the site of protein synthesis.

16.39 *mRNA in a ribosome*

8 The cytoplasm contains a supply of transfer RNA (tRNA) molecules. Each tRNA carries:
(a) a special triplet or anticodon
(b) a particular amino acid

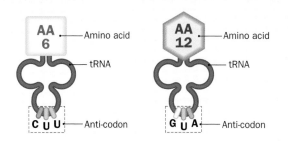

16.40 *tRNA molecules with amino acids attached*

9 tRNA molecules are attracted to the mRNA that is in the ribosome. Each anticodon on a tRNA is complementary to a codon on the mRNA. The tRNA molecules enter the ribosome.
10 The first tRNA molecule will attach to the mRNA just after the start codon (see left-hand side of Figure 16.41). In doing this it brings a particular amino acid to the ribosome.
11 The adjacent amino acids are detached from the tRNA and are bonded together by the ribosome to form part of the new protein.

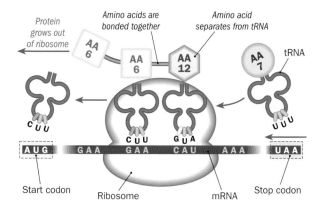

16.41 *Translation (RNA → protein)*

12 tRNA molecules leave the ribosome without any attached amino acids. In doing so they pull the mRNA strand through the ribosome.
13 tRNA molecules continue to bind with the mRNA until a stop codon is reached. At this point:
(a) the mRNA code sequence is complete, and
(b) the new protein is produced
14 Once the protein is formed it folds to allow it to have the correct shape.

THE CELL

THE CELL

Summary

DNA is a long, double-stranded molecule.
- The bases in DNA are adenine **(A)** and thymine **(T)**, guanine **(G)** and cytosine **(C)**.
- The genetic code consists of a sequence of three DNA (or RNA) bases repeated many times.
- Each group of three bases is the code for an amino acid.
- A sequence of bases that produce a protein is called a gene.

Most of the DNA in a chromosome does not code for any amino acids.
- Some of this non-coding DNA is found between the genes and some is found in the genes.

DNA makes exact copies of itself. This process is called DNA replication and it involves:
- each new strand being half new DNA and half old DNA
- each new strand being identical to its partner and to the original strand

To isolate DNA from onion cells:
- grind up onion tissue in a salt/detergent mixture (to clump DNA and break down cell membranes)
- filter the mixture (to remove cell parts); proteins and DNA form the filtrate
- add protease enzyme to the filtrate (to remove the protein)
- add ice-cold ethanol (to precipitate the insoluble DNA)

A DNA profile (or DNA or genetic fingerprint) is a unique pattern of bands of DNA from a person's cell(s). These bands can distinguish one person's DNA from another person's.

DNA profiles are obtained by:
- releasing DNA from cells
- cutting the DNA into fragments using restriction enzymes
- separating the fragments according to their size
- comparing the patterns of the bands

DNA profiles can be used to:
- establish whether biological tissue at a crime scene matches or does not match a suspect
- determine whether a person is or is not the parent of a child

Genetic or DNA screening means that a person's DNA can be tested to show the presence of normal or altered genes (which may cause disease).

Differences between DNA and RNA

DNA	RNA
Contains the base thymine (T)	Contains the base uracil (U)
Double-stranded (double helix)	Single-stranded
Found in the nucleus	Found in the nucleus and cytoplasm

DNA (or a gene) makes protein as follows:
- the DNA strands separate
- the bases on DNA link up with complementary bases to form mRNA (the code is transcribed)
- mRNA enters a ribosome
- the correct sequence of amino acids is linked together in the ribosome to form a protein (the code is translated)
- the protein folds into the correct shape

The detailed structure of DNA consists of:
- nucleotides, which contain phosphate, deoxyribose sugar and a base. The four bases are:
  - the purines adenine **(A)** and guanine **(G)**
  - the pyridimines thymine **(T)** and cytosine **(C)**
- nucleotide or base pairs, i.e. A=T or G≡C, join together due to hydrogen bonding
- a double helix, where the phosphates and sugars form the sides of the molecule and the base pairs are like rungs inside the double helix

H

The details of protein synthesis are as follows:
- enzymes open up the DNA at the site of a gene
- the DNA code is transcribed onto a complementary mRNA strand
- mRNA enters a ribosome in the cytoplasm
- every tRNA has a complementary triplet to the triplets on the mRNA
- tRNA molecules enter the ribosome
- every tRNA has a specific amino acid
- the amino acids are attached to each other at the ribosome to form a protein
- the protein folds into shape

H

Revision questions

1 (a) What do the letters DNA stand for?
(b) What name is given to the overall shape of DNA?
(c) Explain how a very long DNA molecule can fit into a tiny nucleus.

2 One strand of a DNA molecule has the base sequence GATTCGTA.
(a) What is the sequence of bases on the complementary DNA strand?
(b) Draw a diagram of this stretch of DNA as it would appear in a nucleus.

3 (a) Name the bases in DNA.
(b) What is a DNA triplet?
(c) How do DNA triplets relate to a gene?

4 (a) What is meant by junk DNA?
(b) State two places in a chromosome where non-coding DNA may occur.

5 (a) What is meant by DNA replication?
(b) What is the importance of DNA replication?
(c) At what stage of the cell cycle does DNA replication occur?
(d) Where in a cell does DNA replication occur?

6 In isolating DNA from plant tissue, give a reason for each of the following:
(a) using washing-up liquid
(b) using salt
(c) heating the salt, detergent and chopped tissue to 60°C
(d) using ice-cold water
(e) not grinding the tissues for too long in a blender
(f) using protease enzyme
(g) adding cold alcohol.

7 (a) What is genetic profiling?
(b) Give an outline account of how a genetic profile (or 'fingerprint') is obtained.
(c) Draw a labelled diagram of the results that might be obtained in a genetic profile.
(d) On a genetic profile, what does each band represent?
(e) Explain why some of the bands are thicker than others.

8 (a) Give two applications for genetic profiling.
(b) After a violent crime, genetic profiles were carried out on the victim's blood, the defendant's blood and some blood stains obtained from the clothing of the defendant. The results are given in Figure 16.42.
(i) What conclusions can be drawn from these results?
(ii) Do these results prove the innocence or guilt of the defendant? Explain your answer.

VICTIM'S BLOOD	BLOOD FROM CLOTHING	DEFENDANT'S BLOOD

16.42

9 (a) What is genetic screening?
(b) Name one human condition that may be identified in this way.
(c) State any possible benefit and problem associated with genetic screening.

10 (a) Outline two structural differences between DNA and RNA.
(b) Explain, with the help of a diagram, what occurs during translation in protein synthesis.

11 (a) If a stretch of DNA has the base sequence ATTGGCAT, what will the base sequence be on the complementary RNA strand?
(b) Distinguish between transcription and translation in protein formation.

12 (a) What is a gene?
(b) In what part of the cell are genes located?
(c) What material do genes produce in order to control the activities of a cell?

13 (a) What is meant by base pairing in DNA?
(b) Draw a diagram of a stretch of DNA comprising eight nucleotides so as to indicate base pairing involving all the possible base pairs. (There is no need to draw a double helix.)
(c) Who discovered the double helix structure of DNA?

14 Outline the functions of each of the following in protein synthesis:
(a) RNA polymerase
(b) a start codon
(c) a ribosome
(d) tRNA
(e) the protein folds into shape

15 (a) What is the full name for RNA?
(b) Name three types of RNA.
(c) State two places in a cell where RNA might be found.
(d) What is meant by the phrase 'DNA codes for messenger RNA'?

16 (a) Name the bases present in DNA.
   (b) What is a triplet?
   (c) How do triplets relate to genes?
   (d) Draw a labelled diagram of a section of DNA to show six bases. (There is no need to show deoxyribose, phosphates or a double helix.)
   On the same diagram show:
   (i) the complementary strand of RNA
   (ii) the two tRNA molecules that attach to the mRNA strand

17 Choose which of the options (i), (ii), (iii) or (iv) represents the correct answer in each case below.
   (a) A codon contains:
   (i) three base pairs
   (ii) three bases
   (iii) three triplets
   (iv) three genes
   (b) DNA is insoluble in:
   (i) washing-up liquid
   (ii) boiling water
   (iii) salt water
   (iv) ice-cold ethanol

(c) When the sequence of bases on DNA is coded onto an mRNA molecule, this is called:
   (i) translation
   (ii) replication
   (iii) transcription
   (iv) genetic fingerprinting
(d) DNA fragments can be obtained using:
   (i) bacteria
   (ii) protein synthesis
   (iii) restriction enzymes
   (iv) ribosomes
(e) DNA fingerprinting can be used to determine if a person:
   (i) has a disease
   (ii) is or is not the parent of a child
   (iii) has faulty RNA
   (iv) is a carrier for a disease
(f) During protein synthesis, the ribosome translates the code on mRNA, with the help of:
   (i) RNA polymerase
   (ii) tRNA
   (iii) DNA
   (iv) a double helix

THE CELL

Sample examination questions

Section A

18 The diagram represents a part of a DNA molecule. A and C represent nitrogenous bases.

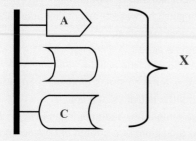

Complete the following in relation to DNA.
(a) Name the nitrogenous bases whose first letters are A and C.
(b) The structure labelled X is called a _____.
(c) Where in the cell would you expect to find most DNA?
(d) DNA contains the instructions needed to make protein. These instructions are called the _____ code.

(2008 OL Q 5)

Section B

19 (a) Explain each of the following terms in relation to DNA.
   (i) Replication
   (ii) Transcription
   (b) As part of your practical activities you extracted DNA from a plant tissue. Answer the following questions in relation to this experiment.

(i) What plant did you use?
(ii) It is usual to chop the tissue and place it in a blender. Suggest a reason for this.
(iii) For how long should the blender be allowed to run?
(iv) Washing-up liquid is normally used in this experiment. What is its function?
(v) Sodium chloride (salt) is also used. Explain why.
(vi) What is a protease enzyme?
(vii) Why is a protease enzyme used in this experiment?
(viii) The final separation of the DNA involves the use of alcohol (ethanol). Under what condition is the alcohol used?

(2005 HL Q 8)

Section C

20 (i) Name the four bases that are found in DNA.
   (ii) These bases form a triplet code. What is meant by a triplet code?
   (iii) The triplet code is transcribed into mRNA. What does this statement mean?
   (iv) To which structures in the cell does mRNA carry the code?

(2005 OL Q 13b)

21 (i) What is meant by DNA profiling?
   (ii) Describe briefly how DNA profiling is carried out.
   (iii) Give two uses of DNA profiling.

(2004 OL Q 12c)

22 (a) Copy the diagram into your answer book and then complete it to show the complementary base pairs of the DNA molecule. Label all parts not already labelled.

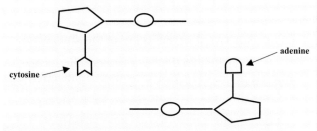

(b) The genetic code incorporated into the DNA molecule finds its expression in part in the formation of protein. This formation requires the involvement of a number of RNA molecules. List these RNA molecules and briefly describe the role of each of them.

(2004 HL Q 13a, b)

23 (a) (i) The DNA molecule is composed of two strands held together by paired bases.
1. Which base can link only to thymine?
2. Which base can link only to cytosine?
(ii) Name the type of bonding which occurs between members of a base pair.

(b) (i) Explain what is meant by the term DNA profiling.
(ii) Give a brief account of the stages involved in DNA profiling.
(iii) Give two applications of DNA profiling.
(iv) What is genetic screening?

(c) 'The same amount of DNA is present in nuclei of cells taken from the liver, heart, pancreas and muscle of a rat.'
(i) Use your knowledge of DNA and mitosis to explain this statement.
(ii) Name a cell produced by the rat which will contain a different amount of DNA in its nucleus to those mentioned above.
(iii) Briefly outline how you isolated DNA from a plant tissue.

(2007 HL Q 10)

24 (i) DNA is made of units called nucleotides. Draw a labelled diagram of a nucleotide to show its three constituent parts.
(ii) Which of the labelled parts in your diagram in **(i)** may vary from nucleotide to nucleotide?
(iii) The genetic code is contained within the DNA of chromosomes. Briefly describe the nature of this code.
(iv) What is meant by non-coding DNA?
(v) Give **one** structural difference between DNA and RNA.
(vi) Name a cell organelle, apart from the nucleus, in which DNA is found.

(2008 HL Q 14b)

THE CELL

Chapter 17 **Genetic crosses**

Gametes

All body cells except reproductive cells are called **somatic** cells. Somatic cells include cheek, liver, muscle, blood, leaf, stem and root cells.

The somatic cells in most organisms are diploid (or 2n), which means they contain a double set of chromosomes. If these cells were to join together, the number of chromosomes in the resulting cell would be double the normal number.

As outlined in Chapter 14, in meiosis the number of chromosomes in the nucleus is halved. This means that in meiosis the diploid number is reduced to a haploid number of chromosomes.

If the haploid cells formed in meiosis are capable of fusing together, they are called gametes or sex cells.

Gametes are haploid cells that are capable of fusion.

This means that gametes transmit genes from one generation to another in sexual reproduction. In humans, the gametes are the sperm and egg.

Fertilisation is the union of two gametes to form a single cell called a zygote.

The zygote normally grows (by mitosis) to form a new organism.

Genetic crosses

The mechanism of genetic crosses is best understood by the use of sample questions and their answers. Explanations for new terms are provided as they arise in the following examples.

Question 1

In cats, black coat (B) is dominant over white coat (b). Give the genotypes and phenotypes for the offspring of a cross involving two cats whose genotypes are (BB) and (bb).

EXPLANATION OF TERMS

Genes are represented by letters. Usually the first letter of the dominant trait is used (e.g. B).

Normally two different types of the same gene exist, i.e. a dominant version (symbolised by a capital letter, e.g. B) and a recessive version (small letter, e.g. b). These different versions are called alleles.

Alleles are different forms of the same gene.

Alleles are found at the same position (or locus) on similar chromosomes.

The locus of a gene is its position on a chromosome.

Dominant means that the allele prevents the working of the recessive allele.

When a dominant and recessive allele occur together it is the dominant allele that works. This means that cats which are BB or Bb are both black.

Recessive means the allele is prevented from working by a dominant allele.

Recessive alleles *recede* in the presence of a dominant allele. This means that cats which are Bb are black, although they contain the recessive allele (b) for white coat. For a cat to be white it has to be bb.

Genotype means the genetic make-up of an organism, i.e. the genes that are present.

Normally each characteristic is controlled by a gene that has a pair of alleles. For example, the genotypes may be BB, Bb or bb.

Phenotype means the physical make-up, or appearance, of an organism.

In Question 1 the phenotype is the coat colour of the cat (i.e. the phenotype is either black or white coat).

Genes are the instructions to the cell that help to produce the phenotype. However, genes are influenced by the environment. It is the interaction

THE CELL

of the genes with the environment that produces the phenotype.

Genotype + environment = phenotype

For instance, most people are born with the gene for the pigment melanin. However, the amount of melanin they produce will depend on their exposure to ultraviolet rays.

Did you know?

Amazingly, even gender can be influenced by the environment. In some reptiles and fish the sex of the individual will vary depending on heat or light acting on the genotype. Indeed, some organisms change from male to female every second year.

The relative importance of the genotype (nature) and the environment (nurture) has been argued for generations, especially with regard to intelligence.

This nature versus nurture argument has not been fully settled. Present-day opinion suggests that phenotype (e.g. intelligence) is a combination of inherited genes and the upbringing of the child.

Genetic crosses

When working out genetic crosses you should realise that:

- **A pair of alleles is present in the cells of an organism for each characteristic.**
- **Only one allele for each characteristic is carried in each gamete.**
- **As a result of gametes fusing, a pair of alleles is present in the progeny.**

These rules are applied in Figure 17.1. When writing the letters it is essential to distinguish *clearly* between capital and small letters.

Answer 1

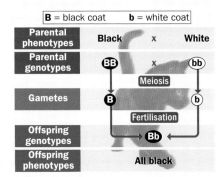

17.1 *Answer 1*

Question 2

In pea plants, green pods (G) are dominant to yellow pods (g). Show by means of diagrams the genotypes and phenotypes of the F₁ progeny that result from crossing two heterozygous plants.

EXPLANATION OF TERMS

Progeny refers to offspring that are produced.

The F₁ progeny means the first generation of offspring. F₁ is short for 'first filial generation'.

Homozygous means that two alleles are the same.

Remember *homo* means 'the same as'; think of homosexual.

Homozygous dominant = GG; homozygous recessive = gg. Pure breeding is another term for homozygous.

Heterozygous means that the alleles are different.

Hetero means 'different', as in heterosexual.

Heterozygous is also called hybrid. The genotype Gg (or gG) is heterozygous.

A **Punnett square** is a grid used to show the ratio of the genotypes of the progeny in a genetic cross.

Answer 2

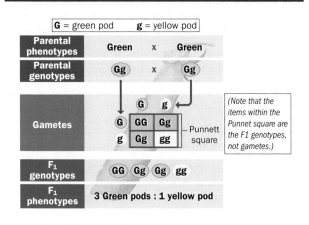

17.2 *Answer 2*

Question 3

In flies, long wing is dominant to short wing. If a homozygous dominant fly is crossed with a homozygous recessive fly:

(a) What letter should represent long wing?
(b) Give the genotype of the homozygous dominant parent.
(c) State the phenotype of the homozygous dominant parent.
(d) Give the genotypes of all the gametes produced.
(e) If 100 flies are produced, how many would you expect to be:
    (i) long winged,
    (ii) homozygous dominant?

Answer 3

The cross in this case can be represented as follows. Normally the first letter of the dominant trait is used to represent the gene.

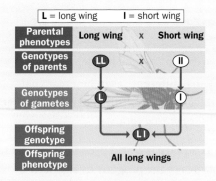

17.3 *Genetic cross for Question 3*

The specific answers are:
(a) Long wing = L.
(b) Genotype of homozygous dominant parent = LL.
(c) Phenotype of homozygous dominant parent = long wings.
(d) Gamete genotypes = L and l.
(e) (i) Expect 100 long-winged.
    (ii) Expect none of the flies to be homozygous dominant.

Question 4

In flies, straight wing (S) is dominant over curved wing (s). A homozygous dominant fly is crossed with a curved wing fly.

Show by diagrams the possible genotypes and phenotypes for the F_1 generation of this cross.

Answer 4

This cross involves crossing the homozygous dominant fly with the curved wing fly to produce the F_1 generation, as shown in Figure 17.4.

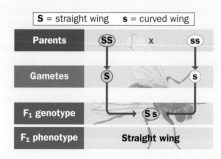

17.4 *Genetic cross to produce F_1 generation*

Question 5

In the fruit fly, *Drosophila*, body colour is controlled by two alleles. The allele for grey body (G) is dominant to the allele for black body (g).

If two heterozygous flies are crossed, show by diagrams that the ratio of flies with grey bodies to flies with black bodies is 3:1.

Answer 5

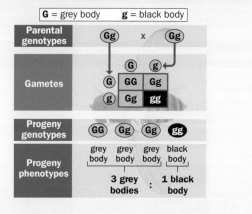

17.5 *Answer 5*

Incomplete dominance

Normally the characteristic controlled by a dominant allele is displayed in the heterozygous genotype. The characteristic controlled by a recessive allele is normally only displayed in the homozygous recessive genotype.

> **Incomplete dominance** means that neither allele is dominant or recessive with respect to the other. Both alleles work in the heterozygous genotype to produce an intermediate phenotype.

Incomplete dominance (also called codominance) is relatively rare.

- **Example 1.** One example of incomplete dominance occurs in shorthorn cattle. In this case the genotype RR produces a red coat and the genotype rr produces a white coat.

  The heterozygous condition Rr gives a roan coat (patches of red and patches of white coat).

- **Example 2.** Another example of incomplete dominance is flower colour in snapdragons. In this case RR produces red flowers, rr produces white flowers, but Rr produces pink flowers.

Question 6

Flower colour in snapdragons shows incomplete dominance, i.e. the heterozygous condition (Rr) is pink.

Give the phenotypes and genotypes for the progeny of the following crosses:
(a) a white-flowered plant and a red-flowered plant, and
(b) two pink-flowered plants.

Answer 6

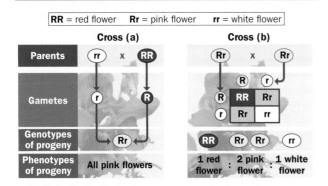

17.6 *Answers 6(a) and 6(b)*

Pedigree studies

A **pedigree** is a diagram showing the genetic history of a group of related individuals.

Question 7

In humans, the ability to produce the skin pigment melanin is controlled by a dominant allele (N). Lack of pigment (albinism) is controlled by the recessive allele (n).

The pedigree for a family is represented below.

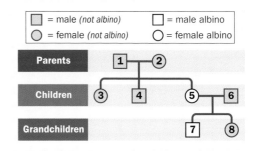

17.7 *Family pedigree for skin colour*

(a) Give the genotypes of persons 1, 2 and 5.
(b) Could person 6 be homozygous dominant? Give a reason for your answer.
(c) How many children had the parents 1 and 2?
(d) Give all the possible genotypes for person 4.

Answer 7

N = Normal pigment
n = Albino

(a) Person 5 must be nn, i.e. albino.
     Persons 1 and 2 have normal pigment but their child (person 5) is an albino.
     This means that persons 1 and 2 must both be Nn.
(b) Person 6 cannot be homozygous dominant. If person 6 was NN then all their children would have normal pigment. However, one of their children (person 7) is albino. Thus person 6 must be Nn.
(c) Parents 1 and 2 had three children (i.e. persons 3, 4 and 5).
(d) Person 4 could be NN or Nn.

Summary of the results of genetic crosses

Note: In the first four crosses below it is assumed that B (black coat) is dominant over b (white coat).
In the final cross the assumption is that RR = red coat, Rr = roan coat and rr = white coat.

Ratio	Example	Explanation
1 : 0 or **100%**	All offspring are black or 84 out of 84 of the offspring are black	BB × BB BB × Bb BB × bb
1 : 1 or **50% : 50%**	Equal numbers of black and white offspring were produced or 164 black and 159 white	Bb × bb
3 : 1 or **75% : 25%**	35 black and 11 white or 124 black and 41 white	Bb × Bb
1 : 2 : 1 or **25% : 50% : 25%**	19 red, 40 roan and 22 white offspring	Rr × Rr *(where alleles show incomplete dominance)*

Sex determination

The nucleus of each human somatic (or normal body) cell has 46 chromosomes (i.e. 2n = 46). These consist of 44 non-sex chromosomes called **autosomes** and two sex chromosomes.

The autosomes control features that are independent of whether a person is male or female. Examples of such gender-neutral features are skin colour, number of arms, formation of saliva and production of digestive enzymes.

17.8 *Human sex chromosomes: X-chromosome (left) and Y-chromosome (right)*

The two sex chromosomes are called the X and Y chromosomes. They contain genes that control gender in most species. The X chromosome is longer than the Y chromosome.

Humans

In humans every individual somatic cell nucleus should have two sex chromosomes. If these are XX the individual is female; if they are XY the individual is male.

The arrangement of XX for females and XY for males has the following two consequences:

- It is the male who determines the sex of the child.
- The ratio of male to female births should be 1:1.

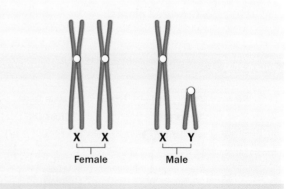

17.9 *The sex chromosomes in humans*

Other species

The pattern of sex determination in some species is the reverse of that in humans. For example, in birds, butterflies and moths males are XX and females are XY.

Question 8

Show by diagrams why in humans the father determines the sex of a child.

Answer 8

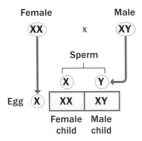

17.10 *Genetic cross for Question 8*

The female always donates an X chromosome (in the egg) to her children. The chance of a boy or a girl being formed depends on the sex chromosome in the sperm.

If a sperm containing an X chromosome fertilises the egg, a girl is produced. If the fertilising sperm carries a Y chromosome, a boy is formed.

This means that the sex of a child is determined by the genotype of the sperm that fertilises the egg, i.e. it is the father's sperm that determines the sex of the child.

Ratio of male to female births in humans

Figure 17.10 shows that the chance of an XX (girl) or XY (boy) offspring being formed is 50% (i.e. 1:1). This is because sperm containing an X chromosome and sperm containing a Y chromosome are produced in equal numbers. Therefore, if a woman is pregnant it is equally likely that her child will be a boy or a girl.

Did you know?

Despite the chance being equal in theory, equal numbers of boys and girls are not born. Large-scale worldwide studies suggest that boys are more likely to be born than girls (the figures are close to 106:100). This imbalance may occur to compensate for the fact that more males die early in life than females. The exact reason for the imbalance is not known.

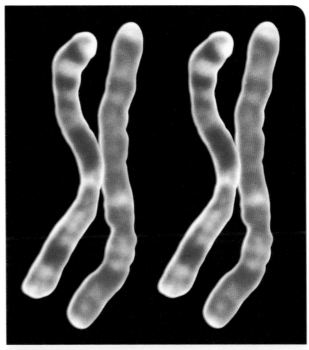

17.11 *The two X chromosomes of a human female*

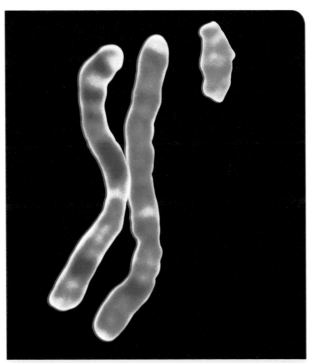

17.12 *The X and Y chromosomes of a human male*

THE CELL

THE CELL

The work of Gregor Mendel

Gregor Mendel is known as the father of genetics. He was born in Austria and became an Augustinian monk at the age of 21.

17.13 *Gregor Mendel (1822–84)*

Having twice failed his teacher's qualifying examination, he turned to the study of the edible or garden pea plant. He investigated the inheritance of seven characteristics of peas such as stem height, flower colour and seed shape.

Mendel carried out numerous experiments on garden pea plants. These experiments involved removing the pollen-producing structures (called anthers) from some flowers and transferring pollen from other flowers to the treated flowers by hand.

The treated flowers were then covered with bags to prevent any more pollen from reaching them. The seeds that formed were collected and grown in carefully labelled containers. The appearance (phenotype) of the resulting plants was studied and recorded.

The success of Mendel's work was largely due to two main features.

- Firstly, he only studied features (or characteristics) that displayed two forms (or traits). For instance, the plants were either tall or small and the pods were either green or yellow.
- Secondly, he counted the number of plants with each type of trait. He was able to detect mathematical ratios such as 1:1 or 3:1 from the numerical data he obtained.

Mendel's research was carried out around 1860 and resulted in two basic laws of inheritance (called Mendel's first and second laws). His results were ignored until 1900, when a number of researchers discovered the significance of his studies.

Mendel's first law

Figure 17.14 represents the results of one of Mendel's initial crosses. A true-breeding (now called homozygous) tall pea plant was crossed with a true-breeding small pea plant. The modern genotypes are shown alongside the diagrams of the plants.

In this cross, the first generation of progeny (called the F_1 or first filial generation) were all tall (Tt).

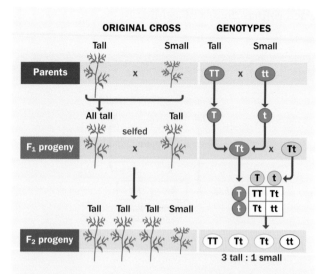

17.14 *One of Mendel's crosses (showing the genotypes)*

The F_1 plants were allowed to self-pollinate (i.e. they were selfed or crossed with their own genotype) to produce the second filial (F_2) generation. This is shown as (Tt) × (Tt).

When the seeds produced in this cross were sown the F_2 plants were counted and Mendel found that ¾ were tall and ¼ were small (i.e. a 3:1 ratio).

Mendel carried out a series of similar crosses, each involving a single pair of contrasting traits. In all cases the same ratio was obtained. The results led Mendel to forming his first law, the **law of segregation**.

Law of segregation

The **law of segregation** (Mendel's first law) states that:
- Inherited characteristics are controlled by pairs of factors.
- These factors segregate (or separate) from each other at gamete formation, with only one member of the pair being found in each gamete.

What Mendel called factors are now called **alleles**. In this law, Mendel predicted that a process had to occur which would halve the number of genes (i.e. meiosis).

At fertilisation, two gametes fuse to form a single cell called a zygote. Each gamete contains one factor or allele for each characteristic. Therefore, fertilisation means that the zygote (which is the first cell of the new organism) will contain two factors or alleles, one from each parent.

EXAMPLE OF THE LAW OF SEGREGATION

If, for a species of plant, T = tall and t = small, the height of the plant is controlled by a pair of alleles, e.g. TT, Tt or tt.

When gametes are formed, only one allele can enter each gamete (the alleles segregate or separate). This is shown by the diagram below.

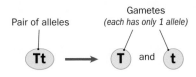

Pair of alleles   Gametes
                    (each has only 1 allele)

Tt → T and t

17.15 *Demonstration of Mendel's first law on alleles*

CHROMOSOMAL BASIS OF MENDEL'S FIRST LAW

1 In diploid organisms, chromosomes occur in matching pairs (homologous pairs).
2 Pairs of alleles occupy the same position (locus) on a homologous pair.
3 During meiosis, homologous chromosomes separate and go into different cells.
4 As a result, pairs of alleles also separate. (See Figure 17.16.)

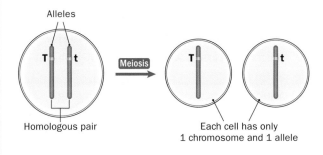

Alleles

T   t   Meiosis →   T   t

Homologous pair   Each cell has only
                       1 chromosome and 1 allele

17.16 *The behaviour of chromosomes due to Mendel's first law*

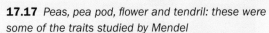

17.17 *Peas, pea pod, flower and tendril: these were some of the traits studied by Mendel*

Monohybrid and dihybrid crosses

A **monohybrid cross** involves the study of a single characteristic such as eye colour, seed shape or coat colour.

Each characteristic can display two variations or traits. This means that a characteristic such as eye colour can display two traits, such as brown eyes or blue eyes. All the examples given in this chapter so far are monohybrid crosses.

A **dihybrid cross** involves the study of two characteristics at the same time.

For example, Question 9 is a dihybrid cross because it involves two characteristics, plant size (tall or small) and pod colour (green or yellow).

Mendel's second law

Mendel carried out a range of dihybrid crosses. Having analysed his results, he formulated his second law, **the law of independent assortment**.

> **Law of independent assortment**
>
> The **law of independent assortment** states that:
> * when gametes are formed…
> * either of a pair of factors…
> * is equally likely…
> * to combine with either of another pair of factors.

As in the first law, the word alleles can be substituted for factors.

The second law means that in an organism with the genotype AaBb either of the As can combine with either of the Bs to form gametes. As a result, the four gamete types shown in Figure 17.18 are equally likely to be formed.

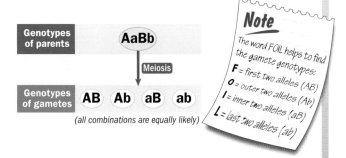

Genotypes of parents   **AaBb**
                        Meiosis
Genotypes of gametes **AB Ab aB ab**
                (all combinations are equally likely)

Note
The word FOIL helps to find the gamete genotypes:
F = first two alleles (AB)
O = outer two alleles (Ab)
I = inner two alleles (aB)
L = last two alleles (ab)

17.18 *Demonstration of Mendel's second law*

THE CELL

THE CELL

CHROMOSOMAL BASIS OF MENDEL'S SECOND LAW

As alleles are located on homologous chromosomes, Mendel's second law can be restated as:

- At gamete formation…
- either of a pair of homologous chromosomes…
- is equally likely…
- to combine with either chromosome of a second homologous pair.

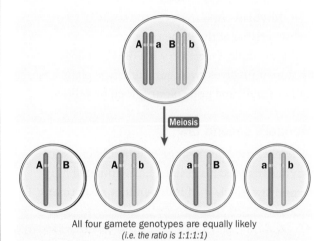

Meiosis

All four gamete genotypes are equally likely
(i.e. the ratio is 1:1:1:1)

17.19 *The behaviour of chromosomes due to Mendel's second law*

17.20 *Different flower colour in pea plants*

Examples of dihybrid crosses

Question 9

In pea plants, tall plant (T) is dominant over small plant (t). In addition, green pod (G) is dominant over yellow pod (g).

A tall plant with green pods (homozygous for both traits) is crossed with a small plant with yellow pods.

(a) Why is this a dihybrid cross?

(b) Show by diagrams the genotypes and phenotypes of the progeny of this cross.

Answer 9

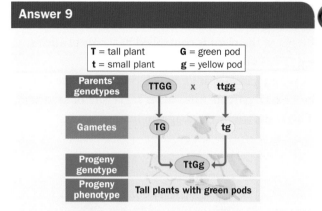

T = tall plant	**G** = green pod
t = small plant	**g** = yellow pod

Parents' genotypes	**TTGG** x **ttgg**
Gametes	**TG** **tg**
Progeny genotype	**TtGg**
Progeny phenotype	**Tall plants with green pods**

17.21 *Answer 9*

(a) This is a dihybrid cross because two characteristics are involved, i.e. plant height and pod colour. The cross is shown in Figure 17.21.

(b) Progeny genotypes = TtGg
Progeny phenotypes = all tall plants with green pods

Question 10

In guinea pigs, black coat (B) is dominant to white coat (b). Also short hair (S) is dominant to long hair (s).

(a) Show the genotypes and phenotypes of the F$_1$ progeny for a cross involving a black-coated, short-haired guinea pig (heterozygous for both traits) and a white-coated, long-haired animal.

(b) State the expected ratio of the offspring.

Answer 10

(a)

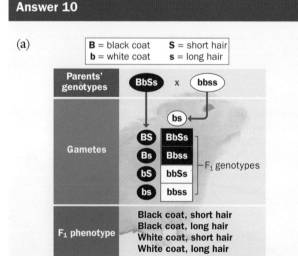

B = black coat	**S** = short hair
b = white coat	**s** = long hair

Parents' genotypes	**BbSs** x **bbss**
Gametes	**BS** → **BbSs**
	Bs → **Bbss**
	bS → **bbSs**
	bs → **bbss**

F$_1$ genotypes

F$_1$ phenotype	Black coat, short hair
	Black coat, long hair
	White coat, short hair
	White coat, long hair

17.22 *Answer 10(a)*

(b) The offspring are expected to occur in equal numbers (i.e. the ratio is 1:1:1:1).

Question 11

A homozygous purple-flowered, short-stemmed plant was crossed with a red-flowered, long-stemmed plant.

All the F$_1$ offspring were purple-flowered with short stems.

(a) State the dominant and recessive traits.
(b) Explain, using diagrams, why the F$_1$ plants all had the same phenotypes.
(c) Give the expected phenotype ratios if an F$_1$ plant is selfed.

Answer 11

(a) The cross can be summarised as shown below.

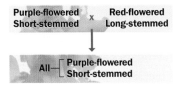

17.23 *Summary of cross in Question 11*

This means that purple-flowered and short-stemmed are the dominant traits. Red-flowered and long-stemmed are recessive.

Normally the first letter of the dominant trait is used to represent the gene. The alleles in this cross should be represented as:

P = Purple S = Short
p = Red   s = Long

(b)

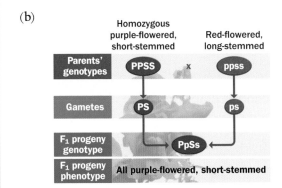

17.24 *Answer 11(b)*

Answer 11 continued

(c)

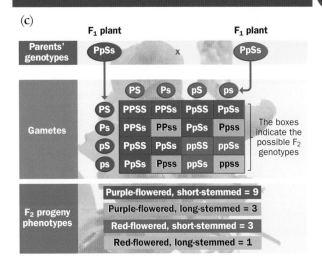

F$_2$ progeny phenotypes:
- Purple-flowered, short-stemmed = 9
- Purple-flowered, long-stemmed = 3
- Red-flowered, short-stemmed = 3
- Red-flowered, long-stemmed = 1

17.25 *Answer 11(c)*

Question 12

In fruit flies, body colour is controlled by one pair of alleles and length of antennae by another pair of alleles.

Three crosses were carried out and the results were as follows:

Cross 1 A black fly was crossed with a grey fly. All the offspring (402) were black.

Cross 2 A fly with normal antennae was crossed with one with dwarf antennae. All the offspring (443) had normal antennae.

Cross 3 A black fly with normal antennae was crossed with a grey fly with dwarf antennae. Of the resulting flies, 204 were black with normal antennae and 209 were grey with normal antennae.

(a) State whether each cross was monohybrid or dihybrid.
(b) Give the dominant phenotype in cross 1. Suggest suitable symbols for the alleles in this cross.
(c) Use suitable symbols to give the genotypes of the parents in crosses 1 and 2.
(d) For cross 2, give the genotypes of the gametes and of the progeny.
(e) For cross 3, state (i) the genotypes of the parents, (ii) the genotypes of the gametes, (iii) the genotypes of the progeny.

H

Answer 12

(a) Crosses 1 and 2 were monohybrid crosses. The single characteristic in cross 1 was fly colour. In cross 2 the characteristic was size of antenna.

Cross 3 is a dihybrid cross (i.e. the characteristics are fly colour and size of antenna).

(b) The dominant phenotype in cross 1 is black fly. Suitable symbols would be B = black fly, b = grey fly.

Before answering part (c) it is best to show the three crosses by means of diagrams.

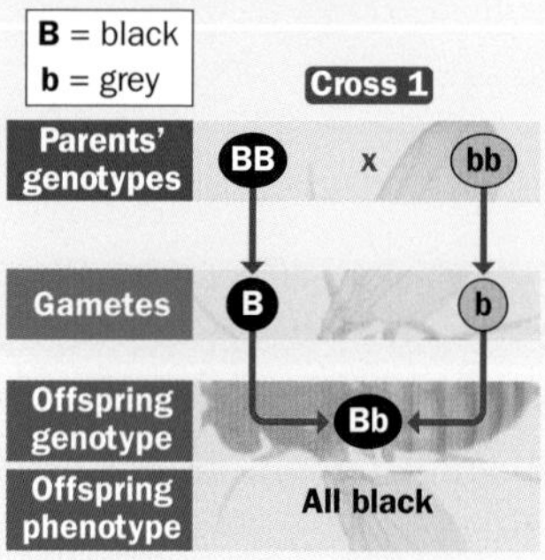

17.26 *Cross 1*

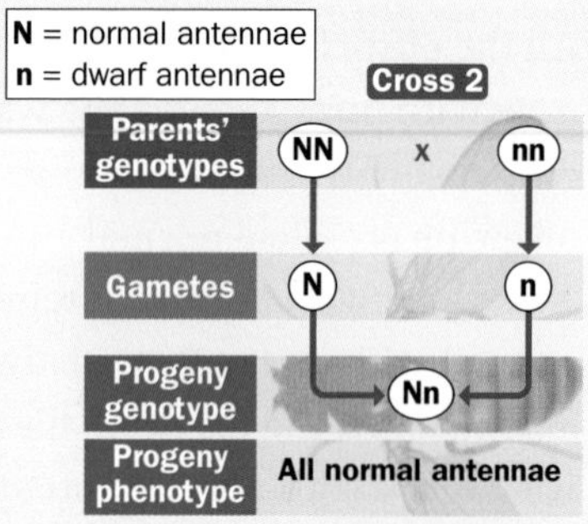

17.27 *Cross 2*

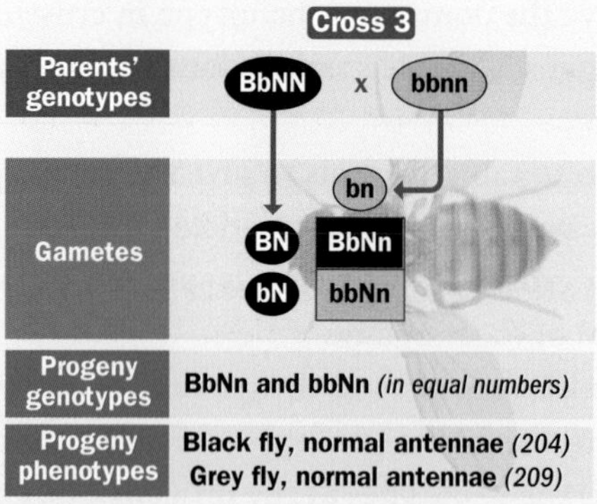

17.28 *Cross 3*

H

Answer 12 continued

(c) Genotypes of the parents in cross 1 are BB and bb.

Genotypes of the parents in cross 2 are NN and nn.

(d) Genotypes of the gametes in cross 2 are N and n.

Genotype of the progeny in cross 2 is Nn.

(e) (i) Genotypes of parents are: BbNN and bbnn.

(ii) Genotypes of gametes are: BN, bN and bn.

(iii) Genotypes of progeny are: BbNn and bbNn.

Expected ratios arising from Mendel's second law

In a dihybrid cross where one parent is heterozygous for both characteristics and the second parent is homozygous recessive (i.e. as in Question 10: BbSs × bbss), if the offspring are produced in the ratio 1:1:1:1 then independent assortment has occurred.

Equally if both parents are heterozygous (i.e. as in Question 11(c): PpSs × PsSs) and the offspring are in the ratio 9:3:3:1 then, again, independent assortment has occurred.

Linkage

Linkage means that genes are located on the same chromosome.

Linked genes tend to be passed on together to the next generation, i.e. they do **not** show independent assortment.

Chromosome diagrams

For simple chromosome diagrams, a chromosome is shown as:

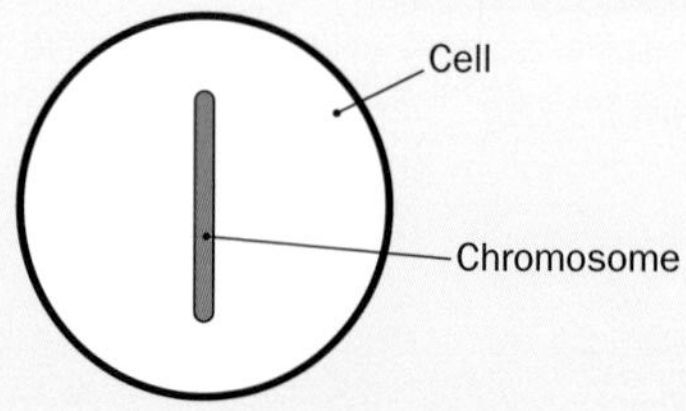

17.29 *Simple chromosome diagram*

H

The **locus** of a gene is its position on a chromosome. The locus (plural loci) of a gene is shown as:

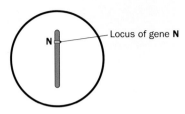

17.30 *The locus of a gene*

Alleles occupy similar loci on homologous chromosomes, e.g.

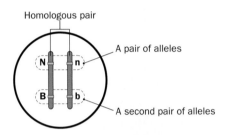

17.31 *The location of alleles*

Example of linked genes

In Figure 17.32 there are four chromosomes. The genes R and S are linked, as are the genes r and s. Nothing is linked to the genes T and t.

In addition, R and r (along with S and s as well as T and t) are alleles. However, R and S are *not* alleles, nor are R and s or R and T.

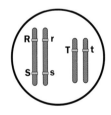

17.32 *A simple chromosome diagram showing linkage*

Draw simple chromosome diagrams to illustrate the following cells. In each case show the gametes that might be produced.

(a) The genes are not linked and the genotype is AaBb.
(b) The genes are linked (A to B and a to b) and the genotype is AaBb.

(a)

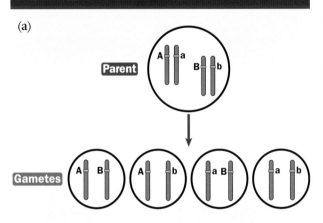

(b)

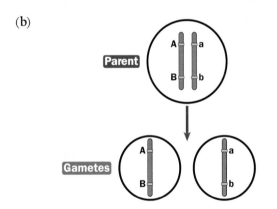

17.33 *Answer 13*

In part (a) the four gamete types are equally likely, i.e. the ratio is 1:1:1:1.

In the case of linked genes (part b), only two types of gametes are formed, i.e. the only gametes are (AB) and (ab).

This is a contradiction of the law of independent assortment. For this reason we can say that *linkage contradicts Mendel's second law of independent assortment.*

THE CELL

Question 14

Draw simple chromosome diagrams to show each of the following cells. In each case indicate the gametes that each cell might produce.

(a) Genotype RrSs, the genes are not linked.
(b) Genotype RrSs, the genes are linked (R to S and r to s).
(c) The genes are not linked, the cell is homozygous for R and heterozygous for S.
(d) The genes are linked and the cell is homozygous dominant for both genes.

Answer 14

(a)

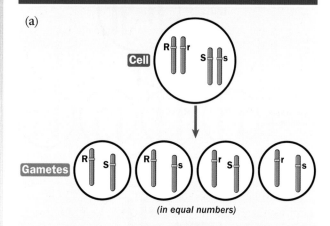

(in equal numbers)

(b)

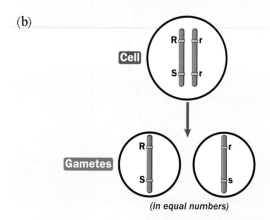

(in equal numbers)

(c)

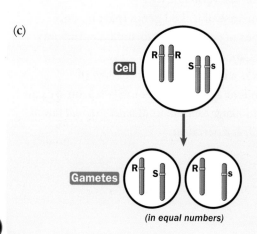

(in equal numbers)

Answer 14

(d)

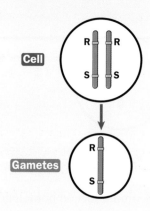

17.34 *Answer 14*

Question 15

Show the expected genotypes of the progeny for the following cross, AaBb × aabb:

(a) where there is no linkage
(b) where the genes are linked, A to B and a to b.

Answer 15

(a)

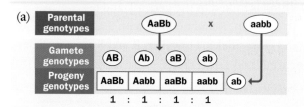

(b)

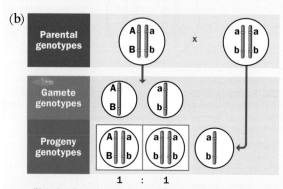

(Note that the expected ratios are different i.e. 1:1:1:1 vs 1:1)

17.35 *Answer 15*

The ratio of offspring in linked crosses

The ratios of the genotypes of the gametes produced by linked crosses are different from those produced in non-linked crosses. This results in linked crosses producing different ratios of offspring than might otherwise be expected.

Sex linkage

The sex chromosomes in humans are the X and Y chromosomes. The X chromosome carries a large number of genes. The Y chromosome is much shorter than the X and carries very few genes.

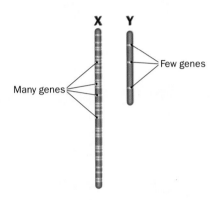

17.36 *The sex chromosomes*

> **Did you know?**
>
> The main gene isolated on the Y chromosome is the **sry** gene. This stands for the **s**ex-determining **r**egion of **Y**. It, and a small number of other genes on the Y chromosome, control the development of testes. These genes are thought to control maleness.

Sex linkage means that a characteristic is controlled by a gene on an X chromosome.

Sex-linked characteristics are also said to be X-linked.

In sex-linked characteristics, the recessive phenotype is more likely to occur in males, i.e. males suffer more often from sex linked characteristics.

Examples of sex- (or X-) linked characteristics are colour-blindness, haemophilia (inability to clot blood), Duchenne muscular dystrophy (where the muscles waste away, resulting in early death) and eye colour in *Drosophila* (the fruit fly, often used in genetics experiments).

All these characteristics are controlled by genes, or alleles, located on the X chromosome. In males there is no corresponding allele on the Y chromosome.

Examples of sex-linked characteristics

Colour-blindness

Normal individuals can detect three colours of light (red, green and blue). The allele for normal vision (N) is dominant. Colour-blindness (n) usually means an inability to distinguish red from green. The gene for colour vision is located on an X chromosome.

FEMALES

Females can have three distinct genotypes with respect to colour vision. These are shown in Figure 17.37.

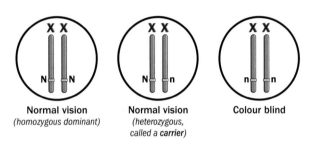

17.37 *The genes for colour vision in females*

Note that these genotypes can be represented as shown in Figure 17.37 or as XNXN or XXNn or XnXn.

For a female to be colour-blind, she needs two copies of the recessive allele (n). Since recessive alleles are usually relatively scarce, it is rare to have two recessives. The incidence of colour-blind females in Ireland is about 0.2%.

MALES

Males have only one allele for colour vision. This is on the X chromosome. The Y chromosome has no allele for colour vision.

This means there are only two genotypes for males, as shown in Figure 17.38. These genotypes can also be given as XNY– or XYn–.

17.38 *The genes for colour vision in males*

Males only need one recessive allele in order to be colour-blind. This means that males are more likely to be colour-blind than females. The incidence of colour-blindness in Irish males is 8%. Most of these males have some degree of colour vision. Complete colour-blindness is very rare in Ireland.

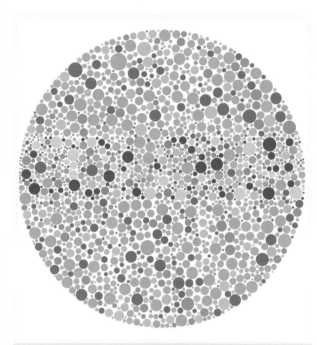

17.39 Colour-blindness test. A person with normal vision will be able to see the word 'colour'.

Haemophilia

Haemophilia is a bleeding disorder caused by the lack of a particular blood protein. Haemophiliacs suffer from frequent bleeding, often into the joints. Without treatment, some haemophiliacs may bleed to death after a small cut.

Did you know?

The ancient Jews did not insist on circumcision for sons whose families had a history of haemophilia. The royal families of Europe show a high frequency of haemophilia.

Haemophilia is treated by giving sufferers the missing protein. Unfortunately, in Ireland in the 1980s, some of the protein treatments given to haemophiliacs contained viruses for diseases such as hepatitis B and C and AIDS.

In recent years, the treatments are screened (checked) and treated to remove these viruses. The development of an artificially produced (genetically engineered) version of the protein totally eliminates any fear of contamination.

Haemophilia is caused by a gene that is located on the X chromosome. The allele (N) for the production of the clotting protein is dominant. The recessive allele (n) does not carry the correct genetic code for the production of the protein.

As with all sex-linked traits, haemophilia is more common in males (0.01%) than in females, where it is extremely rare. Males only need a single copy of the recessive allele (n) to be haemophiliac, but females need two copies of the recessive allele.

Question 16

The gene for haemophilia is located on an X chromosome. Normal blood clotting (N) is dominant over haemophilia (n).

Show the genotypes and phenotypes of the offspring of a cross between a mother who is a carrier and a father who is normal for this trait.

Answer 16

| N = normal |
| n = haemophilia |

	Mother		Father
Parents' genotypes	XNXn	x	XNY–

Gametes:

	XN	Y–	
XN	XNXN	XNY–	Offspring genotypes
Xn	XNXn	XnY–	

Offspring phenotypes	Female, normal clotting
	Female, normal clotting (carrier)
	Male, normal clotting
	Male, haemophiliac

17.40 Answer 16

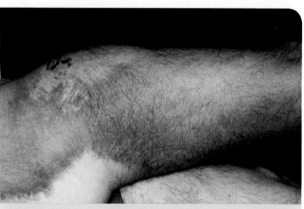

17.41 Large bruise (haematoma) on the leg of a male haemophiliac

Summary of the results of (dihybrid) genetic crosses

Note: *In the crosses below it is assumed that B (black coat) is dominant over b (white coat) and L (long tail) is dominant over l (short tail).*

Ratio	Example	Explanation
1 : 0 or **100%**	All offspring were black coated with long tails	BBLL × bbll or BBll × bbLL *(other explanations exist, but the two shown are the most commonly asked)*
1 : 1 : 1 : 1 or **25% : 25% : 25% : 25%**	All four offspring genotypes were formed in equal numbers or Black coat, long tail = 18 Black coat, short tail = 17 White coat, long tail = 19 White coat, short tail = 17	BbLl × bbll *(where the genes are **not** linked)*
9 : 3 : 3 : 1	Black coat, long tail = 176 Black coat, short tail = 62 White coat, long tail = 59 White coat, short tail = 20	BbLl × BbLl
1 : 1	Equal numbers of black-coated, long-tailed and white-coated, short-tailed or Black coat, long tail = 76 White coat, short tail = 75	BbLl × bbll *(where the genes **are** linked)*

Non-nuclear inheritance

Most of the DNA (and genes) in a cell is located in the nucleus. However, non-nuclear or extra-nuclear genes are present as small circles of DNA in mito-chondria and chloroplasts. Both of these organelles reproduce by themselves and pass on their genes to the resulting organelles.

17.42 *Cutaway computer model of mitochondrial DNA*

Did you know?

Mitochondria and chloroplasts are normally passed on to the next generation in the cytoplasm of the egg. Pollen does not contain these organelles.

While mitochondria are in the tail of the sperm, only the head of the sperm joins with the egg. This means that mitochondria from the sperm are not passed on to the zygote.

This means that mitochondria and chloroplasts follow a maternal line of inheritance, i.e. they are inherited from the female in the cytoplasm of the egg.

For example, in some plants, the genes controlling the production of pigments are located on DNA in the chloroplasts. In these plants, variegated (striped or spotted pigmentation) leaves are inherited only from the parent plant that produced the egg and never from the plant that provided the pollen.

Mitochondrial DNA (mtDNA) in humans is inherited only from the mother.

A number of rare human disorders are inherited only from the mother because they are controlled by non-nuclear genes located on mtDNA. These disorders normally involve a lack of energy (ATP) and affect systems with high energy demands, such as the muscular and nervous systems.

THE CELL

THE CELL

Summary

Somatic cells are body (or non-sexually reproductive) cells.

Gametes (sex cells) are haploid cells capable of fusion.

Fertilisation is the union of two gametes to form a zygote.

Genetics is the study of the mechanisms of heredity and variation.

Alleles are different forms of the same gene.
- A dominant allele stops another allele from working.
- A recessive gene does not work in the presence of a dominant allele.

Genotype means genetic make-up.

Phenotype means physical make-up or appearance.

The phenotype is formed by the action of the environment on the genotype.

Progeny means the offspring of a cross.

F_1 means the first filial generation, i.e. the first generation of offspring.

Homozygous means two alleles are the same.

Heterozygous means two alleles are different.

Incomplete dominance means there is no dominant or recessive allele and the heterozygous condition produces an intermediate phenotype.

A pedigree is a diagram that shows the genetic history of a family.

Autosomes are chromosomes that do not determine sexuality.

The sex chromosomes are the X and Y chromosomes. In humans:
- XX = female
- XY = male

Gregor Mendel is known as the father of genetics.
- He studied pea plants.
- He only studied characteristics that showed one of two traits.
- He counted the numbers of offspring produced.

Mendel's first law (the law of segregation) states that:
- Inherited traits are controlled by two alleles.
- The alleles separate at gamete formation, with each gamete only having one allele.

A monohybrid cross involves the study of only one characteristic.

A dihybrid cross involves two characteristics.

Mendel's second law (the law of independent assortment) states that:
- Either of a pair of alleles...
- is equally likely...
- to combine with either of another pair of alleles...
- when gametes are being formed

Linkage means genes are on the same chromosome and are likely to be passed on together to the next generation.
- Linkage contradicts Mendel's second law of independent assortment.

A cross between AaBb and aabb produces four offspring genotypes.
- If the genes are not linked, four genotypes are found in equal numbers (i.e. 1:1:1:1).
- If the genes are linked, the two genotypes will be AaBb and aabb (i.e. 1:1).

The locus of a gene is its position on a chromosome.

The sex chromosomes are the X and Y chromosomes
- the X chromosome contains many genes
- the Y chromosome is shorter and has very few genes

A sex-linked (or X-linked) **trait** is controlled by a gene on the X chromosome.
- In sex-linked traits, the recessive phenotype is more common in males than in females.

Non-nuclear DNA:
- is found in chloroplasts and mitochondria
- is passed on only from the female
- allows organelles to reproduce independently of the cell

Revision questions

1 Explain what is meant by **(a)** somatic cells, **(b)** gametes, **(c)** diploid, **(d)** haploid, **(e)** fertilisation.

2 Name the process in each case responsible for converting **(a)** diploid cells into haploid cells, **(b)** haploid cells into diploid cells.

3 In corn plants, yellow seed (Y) is dominant to green seed (y). A pure breeding (homozygous) yellow-seeded corn plant is crossed with a green-seeded corn plant.
  (a) Show by diagrams the F$_1$ genotype and phenotype.
  (b) From your diagrams state:
    (i) the genotypes of the parents
    (ii) the genotypes of the gametes
    (iii) the genotype and phenotype of the F$_1$ generation.
  (c) State the genotypes of the gametes that could be produced by the F$_1$ progeny.

4 In humans, the gene for brown eyes (B) is dominant to that for blue eyes (b). If both parents are heterozygous for the trait:
  (a) Give the genotypes of the parents.
  (b) Give the genotypes of the gametes produced.
  (c) Give the possible genotypes and phenotypes of the children.
  (d) What percentage of the children would you expect to be:
    (i) homozygous dominant?
    (ii) homozygous recessive?
    (iii) heterozygous?
    (iv) homozygous?

5 In a flower, red petal is dominant to white petal. A plant, homozygous for the dominant gene, is crossed with a plant with white petals.
  (a) Suggest suitable symbols for the two alleles.
  (b) Give the genotypes of each parent.
  (c) Give the genotypes of the gametes produced by each parent.
  (d) Give the gentoype of the F$_1$ progeny.
  (e) Give the phenotype of the F$_1$ progeny.

6 In peas, green seed (G) is dominant to yellow seed (g). A pea plant, pure-breeding for green seed, is crossed with a yellow-seeded plant.
  Find the genotypes and phenotypes produced in this cross.

7 In cats, black coat (B) is *dominant* to white coat (b). The *genotype* of the male cat is *heterozygous*. The female cat has the *phenotype* white coat. Half of the progeny of these two cats are *homozygous recessive*.
  (a) Explain the meaning of each of the italic terms.
  (b) Show this cross diagrammatically.
  (c) Use each of the *italic* terms at least once to label your diagrams.
  (d) What is the phenotype of the kittens that are not homozygous recessive?

8 In humans, normal skin colour (N) is dominant to albinism (n).
  (a) State the phenotypes of individuals who are (i) homozygous dominant, (ii) homozygous recessive, (iii) heterozygous.
  (b) Give the genotypes of the three individuals at (a) above.
  (c) Show by diagrams how two parents with normal skin colour can have an albino child.
  (d) An albino man has a daughter with normal skin colour. The daughter marries another albino man. Show by diagrams the percentage chance of their child having normal skin colour.

9 In a species of organism the allele **D** is dominant over the allele **d**. The chromosome diagrams show the genotypes of two members, A and B, of the species of organism.

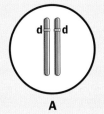 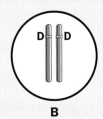

A   B

17.43 *Question 9*

  (a) Do these two organisms have the same phenotype? Explain your answer.
  (b) Give the possible genotypes of the gametes produced by each organism.
  (c) If A was crossed with B could any of the offspring have the genotype **dd**? Explain your answer.

10 In cucumber plants, the character non-bitter fruit (n) is recessive to bitter fruit (N). If two heterozygous plants are crossed, show by diagrams that the ratio of bitter to non-bitter fruit is 3:1.

11 In shorthorn cattle, coat colour shows a lack of dominance; the heterozygous condition is roan. Show the genotypes and phenotypes of the progeny for each of the following crosses:
  (a) a red male and a white female
  (b) two roan parents

12 Coat colour in collies shows incomplete dominance. The gene for black coat (B) shows equal dominance with the gene for white coat (b). The heterozygous condition is called mixed coat.
  (a) State the genotypes of a (i) black collie and (ii) white collie.
  (b) State the genotypes and phenotypes of the F$_1$ offspring that would result from crossing a black and a white collie.
  (c) State the genotype and phenotype of the progeny of a cross between two mixed-coated collies.

13 Blue eyes are recessive to brown eyes. Figure 17.44 shows the pedigree for eye colour in a family. Answer the following, using B to represent the dominant gene.

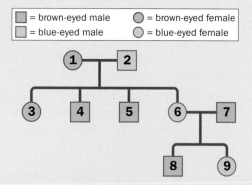

= brown-eyed male   = brown-eyed female
= blue-eyed male   = blue-eyed female

17.44 *Question 13*

(a) What is the relationship between persons (i) 3 and 5, (ii) 3 and 7, (iii) 1 and 8.

(b) What are the genotypes of persons 1, 6 and 8?

(c) If person 8 married a brown-eyed female, could they have any blue-eyed children? Explain your answer by means of diagrams.

14 Name the sex chromosomes in human (a) males, (b) females, (c) eggs, (d) sperm.

15 'A mother's chromosomes cannot determine the gender of her child.'

Is this statement valid? Support your answer by including a diagrammatic cross.

16 Explain, giving an example in each case, what is meant by: (a) allele, (b) genotype, (c) phenotype, (d) homozygous, (e) heterozygous, (f) dominant, (g) recessive, (h) incomplete dominance, (i) autosomes.

17 Some of the results of Mendel's crosses carried out on pea plants are given below.

Trait	Original cross	F1 progeny
Seed form	Round × wrinkled	Round
Seed colour	Yellow × green	Yellow
Flower position	Axial × terminal	Axial
Pod form	Inflated × constricted	Inflated

(a) Use suitable letters to show the genotypes of each of the following:
(i)   a green seeded plant
(ii)   homozygous dominant for seed form
(iii) heterozygous for flower position
(iv)   homozygous recessive for pod form.

(b) Give the phenotypes for the plants at (ii) and (iv) above.

(c) Give the genotypes of the gametes that could result from (ii) and (iv) above.

(d) Two plants, each with inflated pods, were crossed. All the progeny had inflated pods. What does this indicate about the genotypes of the parent plants?

(e) Show the results you would expect for the F_2 generation for the original cross involving seed form.

18 (a) State Mendel's first law of segregation.

(b) Show how this law applies to a cell with the genotype Tt.

19 (a) State Mendel's second law of independent assortment.

(b) Show how it applies to a cell with the genotype TtRr.

(c) What is the expected ratio of the gametes produced by the cell in part (b)?

20 Relate Mendel's first and second laws to the behaviour of chromosomes at gamete formation.

21 In pea plants, the trait tall (T) is dominant to short (t) with regard to plant height. Yellow (Y) is dominant to green (y) with regard to seed colour.

(a) Give the genotype of a pea plant that is heterozygous for height and seed colour. State the genotypes of the gametes that this plant could produce.

(b) Give the genotype of a pea plant that is homozygous for tallness and has green seeds. State the genotype of the gametes that this plant could produce.

(c) Show the phenotype(s) and genotype(s) of the progeny that could result from a cross between the plants described in (a) and (b) above.

22 In peas, the character round seed (R) is dominant over wrinkled seed (r) and yellow seed (Y) is dominant over green (y). Describe the genotypes and phenotypes found in the F_2 generation of the cross RRYY × rryy, when the F_1 generation is self-fertilised.

23 In the flour beetle, *Tribolium castaneum*, black eye (P) is dominant over pearl eye (p) and brown body (B) is dominant over sooty body (b). The genes governing these characters are located on different chromosomes.

A black-eyed, brown-bodied beetle, heterozygous for both genes, was crossed with a beetle with pearl eyes and sooty body. Describe the genetic constitution of the gametes formed and the genotypes and phenotypes of the progeny produced in this cross.

24 In snapdragons, flower colour can be red (RR), white (rr) or, in the heterozygous condition, pink. Also, tall (T) is dominant over dwarf (t). A dwarf red snapdragon plant was crossed with a homozygous tall white snapdragon plant.

State:

(a) the genotypes of the parents

(b) the genotypes of the gametes

(c) the possible genotypes and phenotypes of the offspring.

25 In shorthorn cattle, the colours red and white show incomplete dominance. In addition, the polled condition (without horns) is dominant over the horned condition. Show the results of a cross between a horned roan male and a polled white female. (*Note:* this question involves two crosses.)

26 Draw simple chromosome diagrams to illustrate each of the following, given that the allele A is dominant over the allele a and that the allele B is dominant over b.
  (a) The genes for A and B are not linked and the organism is heterozygous for both genes.
  (b) The genes are linked, A to B and a to b, and the organism is heterozygous for both genes.
  (c) The genes are not linked and the organism is heterozygous for A and homozygous for B.

27 In humans, tongue rolling is governed by a single pair of allelic genes, **R** and **r**. The allele **R** is the dominant allele that allows tongue rolling; the allele **r** does not. Another pair of allelic genes, which are *not linked* to the tongue-rolling gene, govern hair colour. In this second pair, brown hair, **B**, is dominant to red hair, **b**.
  Answer the following using the above information.
  (a) Draw a simple chromosome diagram to show the genotypes of all the possible gametes that a person, who is heterozygous in respect of tongue rolling *and* hair colour, can produce.
  (b) State briefly how these gamete genotypes demonstrate the principle of independent assortment.
  (c) State the phenotype of the person. What other genotypes would give rise to this phenotype?

28 Draw a large diagram of a cell nucleus with two pairs of chromosomes, each pair of chromosomes to be visibly distinguishable from the other pair.
  Indicate on the chromosomes the alleles A/a and R/r so that the nucleus is heterozygous for both genes and the genes are not linked.

29 With reference to Figure 17.45, state:
  (a) the genotype of the cell
  (b) what genes are linked
  (c) the three pairs of alleles
  (d) the number of chromosomes
  (e) the number of homozygous alleles
  (f) the number of recessive alleles
  (g) two non-allelic genes
  (h) the number of chromosomes in the gametes produced by this cell.

30 An organism of genotype SsTt was crossed with one of genotype sstt. Show the progeny genotypes that could be produced if:
  (a) the genes were linked
  (b) the genes were not linked
    In each case, indicate the expected ratio of each genotype.

31 **(a)** What is meant by sex linkage?
  (b) Give two examples of sex-linked traits in humans.

32 Colour-blindness is said to be a sex-linked characteristic. Show by means of diagrams why colour-blindness is more likely to affect males than females.

33 Colour-blindness is caused by a gene located on an X chromosome. Normal vision (N) is dominant to colour-blindness (n). Two parents with normal vision have a colour-blind son.
  (a) Give the genotypes of both parents and their son.
  (b) Did the son inherit the recessive allele from the mother or the father?
  (c) What is the chance of this couple having a colour-blind daughter? Explain your answer using diagrams.

34 In humans, red-green colour-blindness is a sex-linked trait. A colour-blind man and his wife have two sons. One of the sons is colour-blind and the other is not.
  (a) What is the genotype of the mother? Outline your reasoning.
  (b) If a future child of this couple is male, what is the chance that he will be colour-blind? Outline your reasoning.

35 Explain the meaning of the following terms:
  (a) sex-linked
  (b) linked genes
  (c) locus.

36 **(a)** Distinguish between nuclear and non-nuclear DNA.
  (b) State two places where non-nuclear genes may be found.
  (c) 'Non-nuclear DNA is only inherited from our mothers.' Explain why this statement is true for humans.

THE CELL

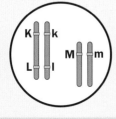

17.45 *Question 29*

THE CELL

Section A

37 (i) In tomato plants the allele responsible for purple stem (**P**) is dominant to that for green stem (**p**) and the allele for cut leaf (**C**) is dominant to the allele for potato type leaf (**c**). A plant with a purple stem and cut leaves was crossed with a plant with a green stem and potato type leaves. A total of 448 seeds was obtained. When the seeds were germinated four types of progeny resulted and they had the following phenotypes:

110 purple stem and cut leaves
115 green stem and potato type leaves
114 purple stem and potato type leaves
109 green stem and cut leaves
What were the genotypes of the tomato plants that gave rise to these progeny?

(ii) Do the progeny of this cross illustrate the Law of Independent Assortment? Explain your answer.

(2004 HL Q 3)

Section C

38 (a) Explain the following terms that are used in genetics: dominance, genotype, phenotype.

(b) In Aberdeen Angus cattle, the polled (**P**) condition (absence of horns) is dominant to the horned (**p**) condition. A heterozygous polled bull was crossed with a horned cow. Use the following layout in your answer book to find the possible genotypes and phenotypes of the calves that may result from this cross.

	Heterozygous polled bull	X	Horned cow
Genotypes of parents	....		....
Gametes	....		....
Genotypes of calves	....		....
Phenotypes of calves	....		....

(2004 OL Q 12)

39 The diagram shows some of the chromosomes in the nucleus of a cell taken from a small mammal.

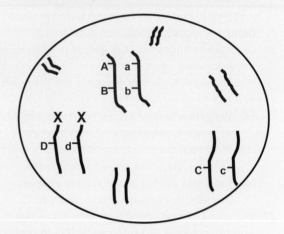

(i) What is the sex of this individual?

(ii) How many loci are marked in the diagram?

(iii) 'A is linked to B but not to C.' Is this statement correct? Explain your answer.

(iv) Is D linked to d? Explain your answer.

(v) What term is used to describe the allele pair Dd?

(vi) Draw a diagram, similar to the one above, but in which A, B and C are homozygous and the cell is taken from an individual of the opposite sex.

(2006 HL Q 12)

40 (a) (i) What is a chromosome?

(ii) The <u>haploid number</u> of chromosomes is found in the human egg and sperm. Explain the underlined term.

(b) Hair colour in humans is genetically controlled. The <u>allele</u> for brown hair (**B**) is <u>dominant</u> to the allele for red hair (**b**).

(i) Explain the underlined terms.

(ii) For hair colour Seán is heterozygous (**Bb**) and Máire is homozygous (**bb**).
1. What colour is Seán's hair?
2. What colour is Máire's hair?

(continued)

(iii) Use a Punnet square or other means to show the following:
1. the genotypes of all the gametes that Seán and Máire can produce.
2. the genotypes of the children that Seán and Máire may have.

(iv) What is the probability that one of their children may have red hair? (Give your answer as a ratio or a percentage.)

(2008 OL Q 11)

41 (a) Explain the following terms which are used in genetics: homozygous, recessive, phenotype.

(b) In the fruit fly, *Drosophila*, the allele for grey body (**G**) is dominant to the allele for ebony body (**g**) and the allele for long wings (**L**) is dominant to the allele for vestigial wings (**l**). These two pairs of alleles are located on different chromosome pairs.

(i) Determine all the possible genotypes and phenotypes of the progeny of the following cross:
grey body, long wings (heterozygous for both), X ebony body, vestigial wings.

(ii) What is the significance of the fact that the two allele pairs are located on different chromosome pairs?

(c) Haemophilia in humans is governed by a sex-linked allele. The allele for normal blood clotting (**N**) is dominant to the allele for haemophilia (**n**).

(i) What is meant by sex-linked?

(ii) Determine the possible genotypes and phenotypes of the progeny of the following cross:
haemophilic male X heterozygous normal female.

(2008 HL Q 11)

Previous examination questions

Ordinary level	Higher level
2003 Sample Q 11b	2003 Sample Q 11a, 11b
2004 Q 12a, 12b	2004 Q 3
2005 Q 13a	2005 Q 10a, 10c
2006 Q 11a, 11b	2006 Q 12b
2007 Q 4, Q 11c	2007 Q 5
2008 Q 11	2008 Q 11

*For latest questions go to **www.edco.ie/biology***

Chapter 18 Variation and evolution

Variation

Variation means that there are differences between the members of a species. As outlined in Chapter 15, variations may be acquired or inherited.

This chapter will deal only with inherited, or genetic, variations. Inherited variations are caused by sexual reproduction and by mutations.

Sexual reproduction

Sexual reproduction is responsible for most of the variations that arise in each generation of offspring. Sexual reproduction causes genetic variation for three reasons:

- Variations arise because of the way in which the chromosomes enter into the gametes at meiosis (i.e. the independent assortment of chromosomes). For a cell with four chromosomes there are four different combinations of chromosomes after meiosis, as shown in Figure 18.1. Each different gamete may result in a variation in the offspring produced.

  Human cells have 46 chromosomes. This means there are about 8 million different combinations of chromosomes available as a result of meiosis.

- During meiosis, a process called crossing over takes place. This produces chromosomes that are a combination of the genes the mother and father inherited from their parents. Therefore, crossing over is another source of variation in genes.

- Finally, at fertilisation each egg and sperm represents a one in eight million combination of chromosomes. Therefore the zygote will have at least a 1 in 64 000 000 000 000 (8 million × 8 million) combination of chromosomes. From this calculation alone it is clear that sexual reproduction produces a huge range of genetic variation.

18.2 *Colour variation in peppered moths: light (lower left) and dark (upper right)*

Mutations

> A **mutation** is a change in the amount or structure of DNA.

Mutations can arise anywhere at random on a chromosome. This means that any gene, or group of genes, can be affected by mutations. However, cells contain enzymes that have a great ability to repair damage to DNA. This means that the number of mutations that survive is very low.

Meiosis

Four different combinations of chromosomes at meiosis

18.1 *Variation due to the behaviour of chromosomes at meiosis*

If a gene is altered it is very likely that the change in its sequence of bases will mean that the correct protein is no longer formed. The new version of a gene formed in this way by mutation is called a recessive allele.

Many mutations produce no change in the characteristics of a diploid organism. This is because the dominant allele on the second homologous chromosome can still produce the original protein.

A very small number of mutations may be beneficial in that they produce an even better protein than the original one. However, many mutations are harmful.

Mutations in somatic (non-reproductive) cells may not be harmful. This is because the gene that is altered may not be active in the particular body cell affected.

For example, if a skin cell suffers a mutation in a gene for saliva production, the cell will not suffer because saliva is not produced by skin cells. However, some somatic mutations are harmful. If the mutation causes an increase in the rate of mitosis, then a tumour may result.

Mutations in a gamete are often very serious. This is because the mutation may be inherited by the zygote and passed on to *all* the cells in the developing child. This may give rise to genetic defects in the child or even in the following generation.

Causes of mutations

Mutations may arise naturally when DNA does not produce exact copies of itself or when it fails to repair properly. Mutations such as these are called **spontaneous mutations**.

Mutagens are agents that cause mutations.

If mutagens are present, the spontaneous rate of mutation is speeded up. A mutagen that causes cancer is called a carcinogen. The main categories of mutagens are:
- Ionizing radiation such as x-rays, gamma rays, cosmic rays and ultraviolet (UV) radiation.
- Chemicals such as formaldehyde, tobacco smoke, dioxins, caffeine and many drugs, preservatives and pesticides.

Did you know?

To protect against mutation when being x-rayed, a heavy lead shield is used to absorb stray x-rays.

When sun bathing, a high sun protection factor cream should be used. This may reduce the risk of developing skin cancer in later life due to exposure to UV rays from the sun.

Tobacco smoke contains about 400 harmful substances, which are responsible for 90% of lung cancer deaths (they also cause many other diseases). Even passive smokers have a 35% increased risk of developing lung cancer.

Types of mutation

GENE (OR POINT) MUTATIONS

Gene (or **point**) **mutations** are changes in a single gene.

Very often gene mutations are caused by changes in a single pair of bases. The altered gene is called an allele.

Examples of gene mutations are cystic fibrosis (the inability to remove mucous from the lung), haemophilia (the inability to form proper blood clots), albinism (lack of the skin pigment melanin), cancers and sickle cell anaemia.

EXAMPLE OF A GENE MUTATION

Sickle cell anaemia is an inherited blood disorder caused by a mutation in the haemoglobin gene. The mutated gene forms a recessive allele. A single copy of this mutation is found in about 10% of black Africans (who are healthy), but up to 1% have a double copy (i.e. they are homozygous recessive) and suffer from the disorder. It is also fairly common in people born near the Mediterranean.

18.3 *Sickle cell anaemia: note the misshaped red blood cells*

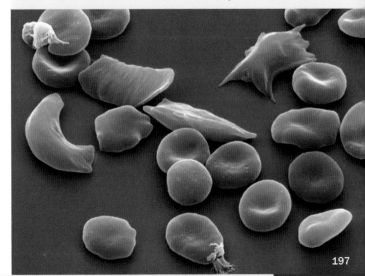

A person with two copies of the recessive allele produces haemoglobin with one incorrect amino acid. This results in an insoluble form of haemoglobin that causes the red blood cells to take on a curved or sickle shape. This causes the breakdown and clumping of red blood, which in turn leads to paleness, weakness, heart failure, severe pains, damage to the brain and other organs and, very often, death.

Apart from treating the symptoms of the disorder, the most common treatment involves total blood transfusions. Such a treatment is only temporary and is not easily available in many parts of Africa. There is some hope that bone marrow transplants may someday provide a permanent cure for sickle cell anaemia.

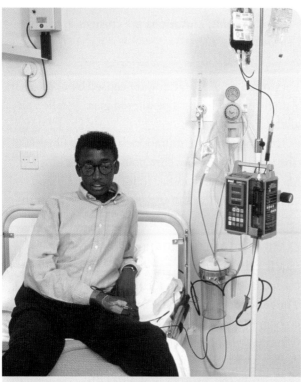

18.4 *A sickle cell anaemia patient undergoing a blood transfusion*

CHROMOSOME MUTATIONS

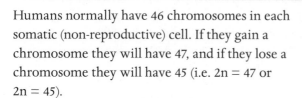

Chromosome mutations are large changes in the structure or number of one or more chromosomes.

Humans normally have 46 chromosomes in each somatic (non-reproductive) cell. If they gain a chromosome they will have 47, and if they lose a chromosome they will have 45 (i.e. 2n = 47 or 2n = 45).

EXAMPLE OF A CHROMOSOME MUTATION

Down's syndrome is an example of a chromosome mutation caused by the presence of one extra chromosome.

Down's syndrome (formerly known as mongolism) is usually caused by three number 21 chromosomes so that 2n = 47 (whereas a normal person has only two number 21 chromosomes). This disorder often arises from a fault in meiosis where the egg has two number 21 chromosomes (instead of one), with the sperm adding one more.

The presence of the single extra chromosome produces a range of physical and mental features associated with Down's syndrome. Down's syndrome is more common in children born to older mothers. The exact reason for this is not yet known.

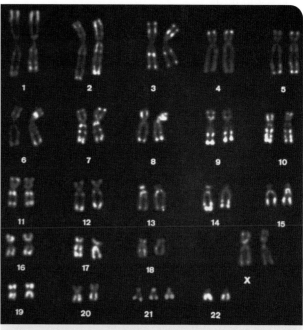

18.5 *Chromosomes for Down's syndrome*

Summary of mutations

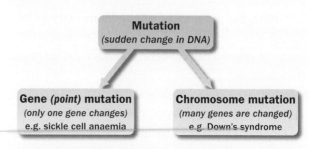

18.6 *Summary of mutations*

Evolution

> **Evolution** is the way in which living things change genetically to produce new forms of life over long periods of time.

Up until the early 1800s many people believed that species were fixed and unchanging. Since the start of the 19th century a number of theories of evolution have been suggested.

The most widely accepted modern theory of the mechanisms by which evolution takes place is based on the work of Charles Darwin.

Darwin initially studied theology but later became a naturalist. He formulated many of his ideas aboard a research ship, the HMS *Beagle*. Much of his work was done in the Galapagos Islands, which are located in the Pacific Ocean, west of South America.

18.7 *Charles Darwin (1809–82)*

Darwin's theory was first presented in 1858, largely due to pressure from another naturalist, Alfred Russel Wallace, who had come up with the same ideas as Darwin while living in Borneo.

In 1859 Darwin published these ideas in his book *On the Origin of Species by Means of Natural Selection*. Since then this theory has been known as natural selection.

Although almost everyone accepts that evolution takes place (i.e. that living things have changed over many millions of years), not everyone agrees that these changes take place by natural selection. For instance, many people believe that the changes were due to some form of divine intervention.

18.8 *Alfred Russel Wallace (1823–1913)*

It is important to realise that natural selection does not contradict mainstream religious beliefs and is widely accepted by most religions.

Theory of natural selection

The theory of evolution by means of natural selection is based on three observations and two conclusions derived from these observations. These ideas are outlined in the table below.

Outline of the theory of natural selection	
Observations	**Conclusions**

1. Overbreeding
Darwin noted that organisms produce large numbers of offspring.
  For example, trees produce thousands of seeds and oysters lay millions of eggs.
	1. There is a struggle for existence
	If more offspring are formed and the environment cannot support all of them, then there must be competition for scarce resources.
	  This means that animals compete for food, water, shelter, and mates.
	  Plants compete for space, light, water, and minerals.

2. Population numbers remain constant
The number of organisms of the same species (called a population) in an area will continue to increase until the environment can no longer support any more. Then the number of organisms stays more or less the same.
 	
3. Inherited variations occur in populations
The members of a population or species show genetic or inherited differences.
  These variations may arise from sexual reproduction, mutations or genetic engineering (variations arising due to the environment are not passed on, e.g. broken legs, learned abilities).
	2. Natural selection
	Those organisms that have variations which enable them to adapt better to their environment will survive and reproduce. They will pass their variations on to the next generation. Organisms with unfavourable variations will not survive and they will not be able to pass on their variations to the next generation.
	  Natural selection is also called survival of the fittest, but this expression is misleading. Natural selection is not about fitness in terms of physical or mental abilities. Instead, it relates to the suitability of a species (or organism) to its environment.
	  The essence of natural selection is how well adapted organisms are to their environment.

THE CELL

Speciation

If organisms are formed that can obtain more food, resist disease or produce more offspring, then they will be 'selected' by nature. This means they may live longer and reproduce more often and so be allowed to pass on their genes.

In time, the accumulation of slight changes results in the formation of organisms that can no longer interbreed. A new species is said to have formed. Speciation is said to have occurred.

The formation of new species does not mean that evolution ceases to take place. Evolution is a continual process and is taking place in all species (including humans) at present.

Natural selection is the process by which those organisms with genetically controlled characteristics that allow them to be well adapted to their environments will survive and reproduce to pass on their genes to following generations.

18.9 *Darwin's* On the Origin of Species *introduced the theory that populations evolve over the course of time through a process of natural selection.*

Evidence for evolution

Syllabus

Evidence in support of evolution comes from three main areas: the study of fossils, comparative anatomy (comparing structures in different organisms) and the study of embryos. The syllabus requires evidence from only one of these sources.

The rest of this chapter will outline how fossil evidence may be used to indicate evolution (particularly in relation to the height of horses).

18.10 *A 40-million-year-old fossil of an insect in amber: amber forms from solidified tree resin*

The study of fossils

One of the best sources of evidence for evolution is **palaeontology** (the study of fossils).

A fossil is the remains of something that lived a long time ago (or some indication of something that lived a long time ago).

Examples of fossils include entire organisms, shells, bones, teeth, seeds, pollen grains, leafprints, footprints and even the remains of faeces.

FOSSIL EVIDENCE FOR EVOLUTION

Fossils provide evidence for evolution in the following ways. The information outlined below indicates that organisms have changed over time. It does not prove that these changes were due to the theory of natural selection.

- Fossils can be aged. This can be carried out by reference to the depth at which they are found in a rock or soil formation, or by measuring the amount of radioactive decay. This allows fossils to be compared according to a time scale.
- Fossils discovered to date show changes when compared to modern organisms. These changes can be related to the time difference between when the fossilised organisms existed and the present.

Some fossilised organisms no longer occur as living organisms (they are extinct, e.g. the dodo and dinosaurs).

In other cases, there is no fossil record of modern species. This could be due to the modern organism being recently formed and therefore having no fossil record.

18.11 *Dinosaur footprints in Colorado*

- The more modern fossils show increased complexity.
- Very often the fossil evidence can be linked to environmental change, i.e. organisms had new environments to which they had to adapt.

    For example, 65 million years ago dinosaurs and many plants became extinct. At this time a layer of dust (rock) containing the element iridium was laid down. Iridium is rare on Earth but common in meteorites. This suggests there may have been a huge meteorite impact, creating large amounts of dust.

    The dust is thought to have reduced the amount of heat and light entering the Earth's atmosphere from the Sun. This may have resulted in the sudden, mass extinction of plants and animals.

EVOLUTION OF THE HORSE

The fossil record of the modern horse is very well documented. It covers a time span of about 60 million years and involves many hundreds of species, most of which are now extinct.

There are many trends to be seen in the evolution of modern horses. The following account deals with one change: the height of the animal.

- The ancestor of the modern horse developed about 60 million years ago. These animals were about the size of a fox (0.4 m high).
- Fossils from about 30 million years ago show that the ancestors of the horse were larger (about the size of a German shepherd, 0.6 m high).
- Fossils from 15 million years ago show the existence of creatures that were the size of a Great Dane (1 m high).
- The modern horse first evolved about 1 million years ago. Horses are normally about 1.6 m high.

TIMESCALE	HEIGHT
1 million years ago to the present	1.6 m
15 million years ago	1.0 m
30 million years ago	0.6 m
60 million years ago	0.4 m

18.12 *Evolution of the modern horse*

18.13 *Artist's impression of what is thought to be the first true horse species. It lived between 60 and 45 million years ago and was about 40 cm high at the shoulder.*

THE CELL

Summary

Variation means differences.
- Acquired variation is learned during life.
- Inherited variation is caused by genes.

Inherited variations are caused by sexual reproduction and by mutations.

Sexual reproduction causes genetic variation due to:
- the way in which the chromosomes enter into gametes at meiosis
- crossing over, which happens during meiosis
- the way in which sperm and eggs with many combinations of chromosomes may combine at fertilisation

A mutation is a change in the amount or structure of DNA. Mutations may produce:
- new alleles
- beneficial phenotypes
- no noticeable effect (i.e. no change in phenotype)
- benign tumours (relatively harmless)
- malignant tumours (cancer)
- genetic defects in the offspring

Mutations in a gamete are more serious than mutations in a somatic cell.

Mutations may be:
- spontaneous (i.e. arise naturally)
- caused by mutagens

Mutagens include some types of radiation and some chemicals.

A gene (or point) mutation is a tiny change in a single gene (often it only involves a single incorrect base).
- Sickle cell anaemia is caused by a gene mutation.

Chromosome mutations are larger changes in the structure or number of one or more chromosomes.
- Down's syndrome is caused by three number 21 chromosomes.

Evolution is the way in which genetic changes produce different types of organisms over long periods of time.

Darwin's (and Wallace's) theory of natural selection attempts to explain the mechanism by which evolution occurs. The theory of natural selection states:
- **Observation 1**
  Organisms overbreed.
- **Observation 2**
  Population numbers tend to remain static.
- **Conclusion 1**
  Not all organisms in a population can survive, so there is a struggle for existence.
- **Observation 3**
  Inherited variations arise in a population.
- **Conclusion 2**
  Nature selects those organisms most suited (or best adapted) to their environment.

Evolution leads to the formation of new species (called speciation).

A species is a group of organisms capable of interbreeding successfully.

Fossils provide evidence for evolution.

Palaeontology is the study of fossils.

A fossil is the remains of (or is produced by) an ancient organism.

Fossils can be formed as:
- entire organisms
- preserved parts
- seeds
- pollen grains
- imprints

Fossil evidence indicates:
- life has changed over time
- life has become more complex
- the changes can be linked to environmental change

The evolution of the horse shows that over 60 million years they have grown in size.

Revision questions

1. (a) What is meant by biological variation?
   (b) Distinguish, giving two examples in each case, between acquired and inherited variation.
2. Name two sources of inherited variation.
3. (a) What is a mutation?
   (b) Explain why many mutations may not be serious.
   (c) Mutations can result in tumours.
      (i) What is a tumour?
      (ii) Distinguish between benign and malignant tumours.
      (iii) Why are malignant tumours a greater health risk?
4. (a) What are mutagens?
   (b) Name two types of mutagens.
   (c) Why should suncreams with a high protection factor be used during sunbathing?

5 Ozone is a gas that absorbs ultraviolet radiation in the atmosphere.
  (a) Why does a reduction in the amount of ozone in the atmosphere represent a threat to human life?
  (b) What are the likely consequences of depleting ozone levels on the rate of evolution?
6 (a) Distinguish between a gene mutation and a chromosomal mutation.
  (b) Give one example from each of the categories of mutations named in part (a) and give details of the effects of the named condition.
7 What is evolution?
8 A population of rabbits living on an island experience a struggle for existence.
  (a) What two observations did Darwin make to suggest a reason for such a struggle?
  (b) Suggest four resources for which the rabbits might struggle.

9 (a) What is a fossil?
  (b) Give four examples of different types of fossils that have been discovered.
  (c) State two methods used to date fossils.
10 Explain three ways in which the theory of evolution is supported by the study of fossils.
11 Outline any way in which fossils show how the modern horse has evolved.
12 State the significance of each of the following in the theory of evolution by natural selection.
  (a) Organisms produce more offspring than their environment can support.
  (b) Organisms show genetically controlled variations.
  (c) A variation that does not improve the organism's ability to reproduce is of no value in terms of evolution.
  (d) Organisms that reproduce asexually (using only mitosis) tend to evolve more slowly.

Sample examination questions

Distribution of human heights

(bar chart: y-axis "numbers of men" from 0 to 200; x-axis "height/cm" ranging from 156 to 198)

Section A

13 (a) (i) The diagram above shows the distribution of heights in a group of men between the ages of 18 and 23.
  (ii) What term is used by biologists to describe differences within a population with respect to features such as height?
  (iii) State **two** factors that could be responsible for the differences shown.
  (iv) Would you expect a similar distribution if the students were weighed instead of being measured for height?
(b) (i) Give an example of a condition, found in the human population, that results from a mutation. Explain your answer.
  (ii) What is a mutation?
  (iii) State **one** cause of mutation.

(2004 HL Q 2)

Section C

14 (i) What is meant by evolution?
  (ii) Name **one** of the scientists associated with the Theory of Natural Selection.
  (iii) Give a brief account of the Theory of Natural Selection.
  (iv) Outline the evidence for evolution from any **one** named source.

(2008 OL Q 11)

Previous examination questions

Ordinary level	Higher level
2003 Sample Q 11c	2003 Sample Q1a
2005 Q 13c	2004 Q 2
2008 Q 11	2006 Q 12c

*For latest questions go to **www.edco.ie/biology***

THE CELL

Chapter 19 **Genetic engineering**

Introduction

> **Genetic engineering** is the artificial manipulation or alteration of genes.

The process of genetic engineering normally involves cutting a small section of DNA (usually containing a single gene called the target gene) from one organism and inserting it into the DNA of a second organism. In this respect it is really a 'cut and paste' process.

The altered DNA is called **recombinant DNA** because it recombines after the small section of DNA is inserted into it. The recombinant DNA is placed back into an organism. The organism with the altered DNA is called a genetically modified organism (GMO).

If this organism reproduces asexually, the altered DNA is also reproduced, so that all of the offspring get a copy of the recombinant DNA containing the target gene.

The organism with the altered DNA produces the substance for which the target gene codes, given the correct nutrients and conditions.

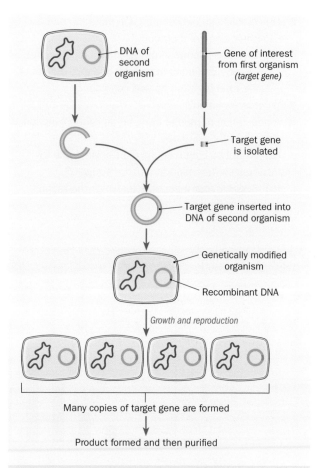

19.2 *General method of genetic engineering*

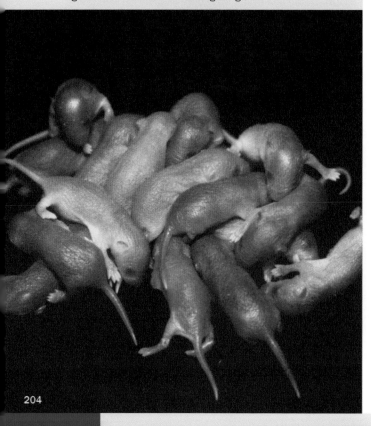

19.1 *A litter of mice: some of the mice have a jellyfish gene which causes them to glow green*

Genetic engineering breaks the species barrier

Genetic engineering means that DNA from different species can be joined together.

This often results in combinations of DNA that would never be possible in nature, where the two organisms would be prevented from reproducing together because they are from different species. For this reason, genetic engineering is not a natural process. Examples of this cross-species transfer of genes are:

- human genes can be inserted into bacteria
- bacterial genes can be placed into plants
- human genes can be inserted into other animals

Alternative names for genetic engineering

Genetic engineering is known by a number of other names. These include genetic manipulation, genetic modification, recombinant DNA technology, genetic splicing (to splice means to join two overlapping strands together) and gene cloning.

Gene cloning refers to the idea that many identical copies (clones) of the target gene are formed when the organism reproduces. Genetic engineering is the basis for most of the developments in the area of biotechnology.

Tools used in genetic engineering

Certain tools and materials are needed in order to cut and paste pieces of paper. These include the original document, the new material that is to be pasted on to the original document, scissors and some glue or paste.

In much the same way, genetic engineering requires the following materials and tools:

- **A source of DNA.** This is DNA (or a gene) that is taken from one organism to be placed into the DNA of a second organism. The inserted or target DNA can be thought of as 'foreign' DNA.
- **A cloning vector.** This is a special kind of DNA that can accept foreign DNA and replicate (reproduce exactly) itself and the foreign DNA.

   The most common cloning vector is a bacterial plasmid. This is a loop of DNA found in bacteria (in addition to the larger loop of DNA that acts as a bacterial chromosome).

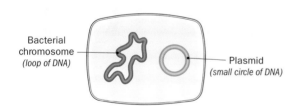

Bacterial chromosome *(loop of DNA)* — Plasmid *(small circle of DNA)*

19.3 *Bacterial cell DNA*

- **Restriction enzymes.** These are enzymes that cut DNA at specific places. They act as the genetic 'scissors'.
- **DNA ligase.** This is an enzyme that is used to get the foreign DNA to join with the DNA of the cloning vector. In this way it acts as the genetic 'glue' or 'paste'.

Restriction enzymes

Restriction enzymes will cut DNA only at particular sites. These enzymes recognise a specific sequence of DNA bases and will only cut the DNA where these sequences occur.

For example, one restriction enzyme will cut DNA whenever the base sequence (recognition site) GAATTC arises. This combination of bases only arises about every four thousand bases, i.e. it is found infrequently along a stretch of DNA.

If DNA from two different organisms is cut with the same restriction enzyme, the cut ends from both sources will be complementary.

If the cut sections are mixed together, they will form base pairs and combine, but they are only joined in a very weak manner.

DNA ligase

DNA ligase is an enzyme that is used to stick DNA molecules from different sources firmly together. This enzyme will only work if the DNA from the two sources has been cut with the same restriction enzyme. In this case, the ends of the cut DNA will be complementary to each other.

For example, DNA ligase allows sections of human DNA to be combined with plasmid DNA that has been cut open. In this way, DNA ligase forms the recombinant DNA.

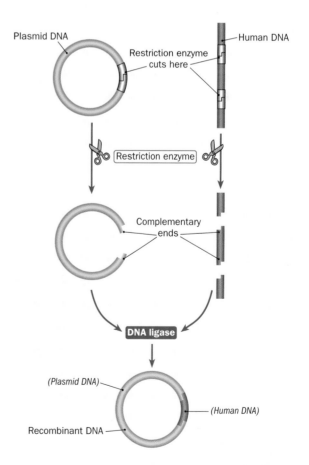

Plasmid DNA — Human DNA
Restriction enzyme cuts here
Restriction enzyme
Complementary ends
DNA ligase
(Plasmid DNA)
(Human DNA)
Recombinant DNA

19.4 *The production of recombinant DNA*

The process of genetic engineering

Genetic engineering is used in a vast and rapidly growing number of applications. The techniques used in most of these applications may include some or all of the five steps outlined in the following sections.

In this example, a human gene is to be inserted into a bacterium. The human gene is the target gene and is referred to as foreign DNA, because it is foreign to the bacterial cell in which it is placed.

1. Isolation

Isolation refers to the need to remove both human DNA containing the target gene from its chromosome, and plasmid DNA from the bacterium.

2. Cutting

The human DNA and the plasmid DNA are cut open using the same restriction enzyme.

The plasmid normally will be cut open at a single site.

The human DNA (chromosome) will be cut into thousands of sections. Only one of these sections will contain the target gene.

Figure 19.5 shows a single plasmid and a single chromosome being cut. In reality large numbers of each are cut at this stage.

3. Ligation

Ligation means that the target gene is placed into the DNA of the plasmid or cloning vector and joins onto it.

The cut plasmids are mixed with the human DNA sections. This allows the cut ends to combine.

The intention is that the cut ends of the plasmid should combine (by base pairing) with the complementary ends of the human DNA that contains the target gene. This happens, but many other combinations stick together as well.

For example, the plasmids may stick to each other, a plasmid may stick to several human DNA sections in a row, or a plasmid may stick to a section of human DNA that does not carry the target gene (see Figure 19.6).

19.5 *Cutting DNA with a restriction enzyme*

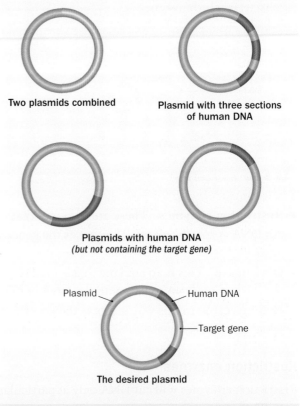

Two plasmids combined

Plasmid with three sections of human DNA

Plasmids with human DNA (but not containing the target gene)

Plasmid — Human DNA

— Target gene

The desired plasmid

19.6 *The different possible combinations of DNA (note that only the final combination is required)*

Ligation is the joining or splicing of the over-lapping cut ends of the DNA sections. DNA ligase is used to form strong bonds within the recombinant DNA (i.e. between the plasmid DNA and the human DNA).

In this way a base sequence change is introduced into the section of DNA that receives the target gene.

4. Transformation

Transformation is the uptake of DNA into a cell.

The bacteria are treated in such a way that they can take in plasmids (composed of recombinant DNA) from a surrounding solution.

The vast majority (up to 99%) of the bacterial cells normally fail to take up the plasmids or only take up a plasmid that does not contain the target gene. These bacteria will be of no further use because they do not contain the target gene.

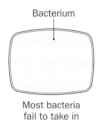 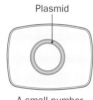

Bacterium	Plasmid	Target gene
Most bacteria fail to take in a plasmid	A small number of bacteria take in a plasmid without a target gene	Only a small number of bacteria take in the target gene

19.7 *Bacterial cells after transformation*

Special techniques are used to identify the small number of bacteria that have taken up a plasmid containing the target gene (i.e. the bacteria containing the recombinant DNA).

5. Cloning

Cloning means that identical copies of the bacterium are produced.

The bacteria containing the target gene are grown (or cloned) using a nutrient medium. As the bacteria reproduce, they produce copies of the plasmid with the target gene.

6. Expression

Expression means getting the organism with the recombinant DNA to produce the desired product (or protein).

Trying to express plant and animal genes in bacteria poses many problems. These problems do not arise to the same extent if the host cells are yeast, plant or animal cells. However, it is more difficult to get these cells to take up DNA from their surroundings, i.e. transformation is difficult.

Once the product has been formed (or expressed) in sufficient amounts, it has to be isolated from the culture and the bacteria that produced it. After it has been isolated the product is purified.

Applications of genetic engineering

Syllabus

You are required to know three applications: one involving a plant, one animal and one for a micro-organism.

Plants

WEEDKILLER-RESISTANT CROPS

Many types of crop plants have bacterial genes added to them. These crop plants are then resistant to particular weedkillers (or herbicides). This means that when the herbicide is sprayed on the crop it will kill the weeds but will not kill the transgenic plants.

Animals

There is a growing trend to experiment with inserting human genes into the DNA of other mammals. The transgenic animals formed in this way will then produce a human protein and secrete it into their milk or even into their eggs (in the case of hens).

SHEEP PRODUCE A PROTEIN TO TREAT EMPHYSEMA

Some people have a faulty gene which means they cannot produce a protective protein in their lungs. This leads to the collapse of the alveoli, a condition known as emphysema. A human gene for this protein (known as AAT) has been inserted into sheep DNA. These sheep produce the protein in their milk.

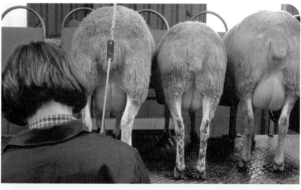

19.8 *Sheep with human gene being milked*

THE CELL

Micro-organisms

BACTERIA MAKE INSULIN

One of the first genetically engineered proteins to be produced commercially was human insulin.

This involved inserting the gene for human insulin into a bacterium (called *E. coli*). The bacterium then produced large quantities of insulin.

This meant that people with diabetes (who have a shortage of insulin) could inject themselves with human insulin. Prior to this development, insulin was obtained from animals, which caused problems because many diabetics are allergic to animal insulin.

Ethical issues in genetic engineering

The use of genetically modified organisms provides undoubted benefits. Nevertheless, these techniques raise safety and ethical issues for people and the environment. These issues centre around concerns such as:

- the release of genetically modified organisms (GMOs) into the environment
- the use of GMOs as a food source
- the fear that animals will suffer as a result of being genetically modified
- the fear that humans (especially human zygotes) may be genetically modified

---

Summary

Genetic engineering is the artificial manipulation or alteration of genes.
- Genetic engineering allows genes from different species to be combined.
- Genetic engineering is also called recombinant DNA technology (amongst other names).

Genetically modified organisms (GMOs) are living things whose DNA has been altered artificially.

Transgenic organisms contain genes from another species.

To form recombinant DNA, the following are required:
- a source of DNA called the target gene
- a piece of DNA (called a cloning vector) that can accept the target gene and replicate
- a restriction enzyme to cut DNA at specific places
- the enzyme DNA ligase to cause the target gene to join with the DNA of the cloning vector and form recombinant DNA

The most common cloning vector is a plasmid.
- A plasmid is a small circle of DNA found in bacteria.

Restriction enzymes cut DNA whenever they find a specific sequence of bases.
- Restriction enzymes cut DNA in such a way that the cut ends of the DNA will stick to each other.

The process of genetic engineering using bacteria usually involves most of the following steps:
- isolation of a chromosome (containing the target gene) and a plasmid
- cutting the chromosome and plasmids with a restriction enzyme
- ligation (or joining) of the target gene into the plasmid
- transformation of bacterial cells, i.e. getting bacterial cells to take up plasmids
- cloning or reproducing identical copies of the new genetically engineered bacterium
- expression or production of the required protein by the bacteria with the recombinant DNA

Applications of genetic engineering include:
- inserting a bacterial gene for herbicide resistance into crop plants, so that the herbicide kills weeds but does not affect the plant
- producing transgenic sheep by inserting a human gene for a lung-protecting protein into sheep DNA so that the sheep produce the protein in their milk
- inserting the gene for human insulin into a bacterium which then produces human insulin for use by diabetics

Genetic engineering raises many ethical and moral questions regarding procedures that may be considered right or wrong.

Revision questions

1 Explain what is meant by the following terms:
   (a) genetic engineering, (b) target gene,
   (c) recombinant DNA, (d) splicing, (e) transgenic.
2 Suggest one reason why genetic engineering is not a natural process.
3 Give one use for each of the following: (a) a cloning vector, (b) a restriction enzyme, (c) DNA ligase, (d) a plasmid.

4 Explain the meaning of each of the following terms in relation to forming a genetically modified bacterium containing the gene for human growth hormone (HGH): (a) isolation, (b) cutting, (c) ligation, (d) transformation, (e) expression.
5 State the reason for each of the following procedures in the formation of recombinant DNA.
   (a) using the same restriction enzyme for the target gene and the plasmid (or cloning vector)

(b) using a splicing enzyme

(c) after the transformation process is carried out most of the bacteria are of no use.

6 Explain, with the aid of a diagram, why genetic engineering can be considered to be a 'cut and paste' process.

7 What are **(a)** genetically modified organisms and **(b)** transgenic organisms?

8 Give one example and state a benefit for each of the following:

(a) inserting a human gene into a bacterium

(b) inserting a bacterial gene into a plant

(c) inserting a human gene into an animal.

9 Human growth hormone (HGH) is produced in the pituitary gland. People who do not produce sufficient amounts of HGH do not grow properly. The gene for HGH can be extracted from a human chromosome and inserted into a loop of DNA in a bacterium as shown in Figure 19.9.

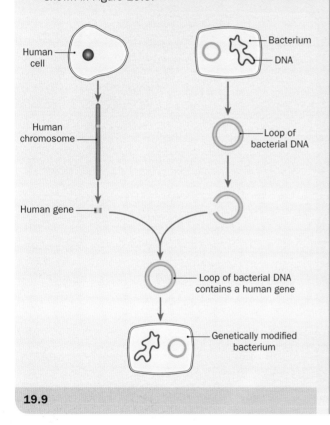

19.9

This procedure allows the hormone to be produced by bacteria using genetic engineering techniques.

(a) What is a hormone?

(b) Where in the body is the pituitary gland located?

(c) What are chromosomes made of?

(d) What biomolecules are used to extract a gene from a chromosome?

(e) Explain why the same biomolecule must be used to extract the gene and to open the loop of DNA in the bacterium.

(f) What substances should be added to a bioreactor to enable bacteria to grow?

10 Choose which of the options (i), (ii), (iii) or (iv) represents the correct answer in each case below.

(a) Genetic engineering:

(i) is a natural process

(ii) only takes place in micro-organisms

(iii) happens when cells divide

(iv) involves combining DNA from different species

(b) This most common cloning vector used in genetic engineering is:

(i) RNA

(ii) an enzyme

(iii) a plasmid

(iv) DNA ligase

(c) Which of the following is not associated with genetic engineering?

(i) translation

(ii) transformation

(iii) cloning

(iv) expression

(d) Genetically modified organisms:

(i) are always harmful

(ii) are always micro-organisms

(iii) may be beneficial

(iv) arise naturally

Sample examination questions

Section C

11 **(i)** What is genetic engineering?

(ii) Give one example of genetic engineering involving an animal and one example involving a plant.

(2006 OL Q 11c)

12 **(i)** What is meant by genetic engineering?

(ii) State two applications of genetic engineering, one involving a micro-organism and one involving a plant.

(2005 HL Q10a)

Previous examination questions

Ordinary level	Higher level
2006 Q 11c	2005 Q 10a

*For latest questions go to **www.edco.ie/biology***

UNIT 3
THE ORGANISM

THE ORGANISM

SEM of a garden spider eating a fly (green). The spider injects poison into its prey through fangs (red), which paralyse the fly and cause its insides to liquefy, so that the spider can suck it dry. Six of the spider's eight eyes (blue) are visible.

Chapter 20 Classification of organisms

The five kingdoms of life

As outlined in Chapter 15 there is a need to classify the vast range of living things into different groups or categories.

The original classification system was developed by the Greek philosopher and naturalist Aristotle about 350 BC. This system divided living things into two kingdoms: plants and animals. This division was later based mainly on the presence or absence of cell walls.

With the discovery of microscopic organisms, especially bacteria and fungi, the two-kingdom system was found to be increasingly unsatisfactory. In 1969 the American biologist Robert Whittaker proposed that life should be divided into five kingdoms. This five-kingdom system of classification gained widespread acceptance.

The five kingdoms are: **Monera**, **Protista**, **Fungi**, **Plantae** (plants) and **Animalia** (animals).

Each of these kingdoms is subdivided into many other categories, with each successive category containing organisms that are more and more similar. This is similar to the way in which the pupils in a school are classified into years, classes and individuals.

The final and most basic unit of biological classification is the species. The organisms in a species are similar enough to be able to interbreed successfully.

Note that viruses are not allocated to any of the five kingdoms because it is unclear whether or not they are living things. Viruses will be discussed in Chapter 39.

Monera (Prokaryotae)

The organisms in the kingdom Monera are also called Prokaryotes. This kingdom includes about 10 000 identified species of bacteria. It is thought that there may be up to four million species of bacteria on Earth. Bacteria were the first organisms on Earth (about 4000 million years ago) and were the only organisms for about 2000 million years.

Monerans (or bacteria) are found everywhere on Earth. They are in the air, soil, water, animal bodies, acidic environments, alkaline environments, deserts and mountain tops.

They are too small to be seen, but their numbers are absolutely colossal. They are by far the most numerous organisms on Earth. For example, there are more bacteria on the skin of one person than the total number of humans that have ever lived.

Although some bacteria cause disease, the vast majority are essential to life on Earth. One of their main roles is to decompose dead organisms. In this way they return minerals to the soil for use by other organisms.

We can get an idea of the importance of bacteria from the fact that if all the other four kingdoms of life were wiped out, the bacteria could still survive. However, if bacteria were to become extinct, life on earth would cease within about 30 years.

Main features of Monerans

- do not have a membrane-enclosed nucleus, i.e. they do not possess a distinct nucleus
- do not have membrane-enclosed organelles such as mitochondria and chloroplasts
- are mainly small, microscopic and single-celled organisms
- normally reproduce asexually

20.1 *Bacteria on the surface of a human tongue (SEM)*

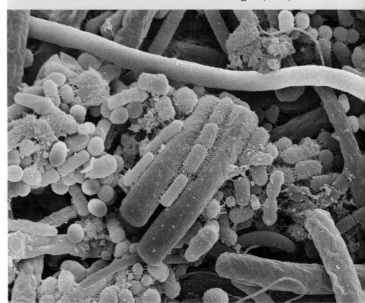

THE ORGANISM

212

Protista (Protoctista)

The kingdom Protista is also called Protoctista. This kingdom contains about 60 000 species such as plant-like algae (both microscopic algae or plankton as well as larger visible seaweeds), single-celled animal-like protozoans such as *Amoeba* (see Chapter 23) and fungus-like slime moulds.

The first of these organisms evolved about 2000 million years ago. They were the ancestors of the fungi, plants and animals that evolved many millions of years later.

Protists are found almost anywhere water is present. For example, they occur in damp soil, decaying organic material, puddles, pools, ponds, lakes and oceans. In the latter cases they are often found on or in the mud at the bottom of the water.

Interestingly, plankton and larger algae account for more than half of all the photosynthesis that takes place on Earth.

The protists are a very diverse group of organisms. In fact, they are so diverse that it is difficult to state the general features of the organisms in this kingdom.

Protists are often considered to be simple organisms that cannot be identified with any of the other four kingdoms.

Main features of protists

- have a membrane-enclosed nucleus, i.e. a true nucleus
- are mainly single-celled, but those that contain many cells are simple organisms (i.e. they do not form tissues)

20.3 *Diatoms – single-celled algae – are protists.*

20.4 *Seaweeds are protists.*

20.2 *A slime mould covering and feeding on a dead beetle (SEM)*

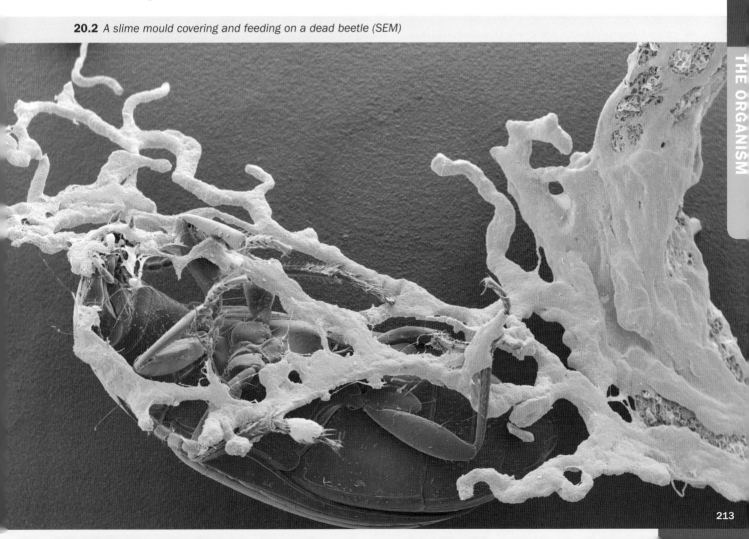

THE ORGANISM

Fungi

More than 100 000 species of fungi have been identified, but it is thought that this only represents one-tenth of all the fungi on Earth. Examples of fungi include mushrooms, moulds, mildews, lichens and yeasts.

Fungi are essential for life on Earth because (like bacteria) they break down dead organisms and allow minerals to recycle. In addition, most plants depend on fungi to allow their roots to absorb minerals and water from the soil.

Many fungi are of economic value, e.g. some are edible, some produce antibiotics, yeasts are used in baking and for producing alcohol. Some fungi cause diseases to plants, humans and other animals.

It is thought that fungi and animals evolved from a common ancestor about 700 million years ago. In many respects, fungi are more closely related to animals than to plants.

Main features of fungi

- do not make their own food but get their nutrients by absorbing food from an outside source
- mainly multicelled, composed of threads called hyphae which combine to form a visible fluffy mass called a mycelium
- cell (or hyphal) walls are made of a carbohydrate called chitin
- reproduce by spores

20.6 *Fungi growing on dead wood in a forest*

20.7 *Fungus growing on the surface of a strawberry*

20.5 *Fungi on the surface of a piece of decomposing melon in a compost heap (SEM)*

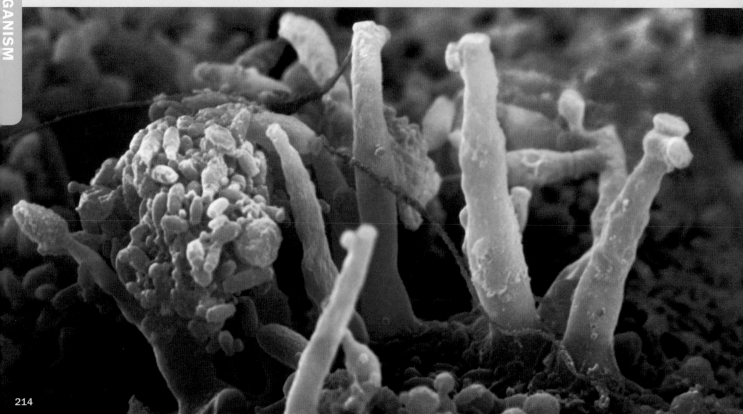

THE ORGANISM

Plants

It is thought that plants evolved from green algae about 500 million years ago. The evolution of plants allowed life to exist for the first time on land around this time.

The major groups of plants are mosses, ferns and seed-producing plants. The seed-producing plants consist of non-flowering plants such as pine trees and flowering plants such as grasses, cereals, flowers and many trees.

The flowering plants comprise the greatest number of plant species (about 250 000) compared to about 30 000 species for all the other types combined.

The emergence of plants on land provided food for the animals that were to evolve soon after them on land.

Main features of plants

- are complex, multicellular organisms
- are photosynthetic
- cell walls are made of cellulose
- cells often contain large vacuoles
- are non-motile
- reproduce asexually and sexually
- protect the embryo for a time within the structure of the parent plant

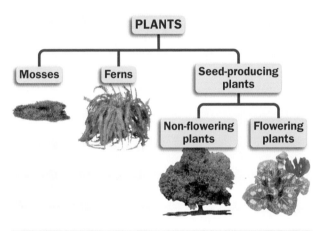

20.8 *The plant kingdom*

20.10 *Wildflowers*

20.9 *Ferns (green, centre) and mosses (grey, on left and right)*

THE ORGANISM

Animals

The first animals evolved in the sea about 700 million years ago. Animals later evolved to live in fresh water, and eventually they emerged to live on land.

Animals range from simple sponges and jellyfish, through flatworms, roundworms and segmented worms, to snails, insects and animals with backbones (vertebrates) such as fish, birds and humans.

Trying to define an animal is not easy. There is such a variety of animal species that there is normally an exception to every general animal feature.

Main features of animals

- are multicelled organisms that take in food (i.e. they do not make their own food)
- do not have cell walls
- have a nervous system (to allow fast responses) and a muscular system (to allow movement)
- normally reproduce sexually
- have a large egg that cannot move by itself (i.e. it is non-motile) and a small sperm that can swim (i.e. it is motile) by using a tail or flagellum (plural flagella)

20.12 *Birds and fish are vertebrates.*

20.13 *The bonobo – genetically our closest living relative*

20.11 *Insects are invertebrates.*

Summary

Living things were originally divided into two kingdoms: plants and animals

Life is now classified into five kingdoms:
■ Monera (or Prokaryotes), Protists (or Protoctists), Fungi, Plants and Animals.

Monera include bacteria and their main features are:
■ they lack a true nucleus and membrane-enclosed organelles
■ they are microscopic and single-celled
■ they reproduce asexually

Protists include plankton, seaweeds, *Amoebae* and slime moulds and their features are:
■ they have a true nucleus (i.e. it is surrounded by a membrane)
■ they are single-celled or simple multicelled organisms

Fungi include mushrooms, moulds, mildews and yeasts and their features are:
■ they absorb their food from outside
■ they are composed of multicelled hyphae which form mycelia
■ they have walls made of chitin
■ they reproduce by spores

Plants include mosses, ferns and seed-producing plants (some without and some with flowers). Their features include:
■ they are complex and multicelled
■ they make their own food by photosynthesis
■ they have cellulose cell walls
■ their cells have large vacuoles
■ they do not move
■ they reproduce asexually and sexually
■ they protect the embryo for a short time

Animals have most of the following features:
■ they are multicelled and take in their food
■ they have no cell walls
■ they have nervous and muscular systems
■ they reproduce sexually
■ they have large non-motile eggs and small motile sperm

Revision questions

1 (a) Name the kingdoms in the old two-kingdom system of classification.
  (b) What was the main basis for placing organisms in either of these kingdoms?
  (c) State one major flaw with the old system.
2 (a) Who first proposed the five-kingdom system of classification?
  (b) Name the five kingdoms.
  (c) Name the four kingdoms in which the organisms have a membrane around their nucleus.
3 Place each of the following organisms into its correct kingdom:
  (a) a mushroom
  (b) a frog
  (c) a daisy
  (d) a bacterium
  (e) an alga
  (f) *Amoeba*
  (g) yeast
  (h) a pine tree
  (i) a tulip
  (j) seaweed
  (k) a sponge.
4 With which kingdom is each of the following features associated?
  (a) cellulose cell walls
  (b) absence of a true nucleus
  (c) reproduction by spores
  (d) possessing a nervous system
  (e) complex, photosynthetic organisms
  (f) composed of hyphae
  (g) lacking mitochondria
5 (a) How many years ago (approximately) did each kingdom first evolve?
  (b) Arrange the kingdoms from the oldest to the most recently evolved.
6 (a) Distinguish between a kingdom and a species.
  (b) In which of the two categories named in part (a) are the organisms (i) most similar, (ii) able to interbreed, (iii) most numerous?

Previous examination questions

Ordinary level	Higher level
n/a	n/a

For latest questions go to www.edco.ie/biology

THE ORGANISM

Chapter 21 Monera (bacteria)

Distribution of micro-organisms in nature

Micro-organisms are small living things. They are so small that they can only be seen individually with the help of a microscope. They include bacteria, some fungi, and some protists such as plankton and slime moulds.

The study of micro-organisms (also called microbes) is called microbiology.

As outlined in Chapter 20, bacteria and fungi occupy a wide range of habitats in both terrestrial (land) and aquatic (water) environments. Fungi, however, are mainly associated with terrestrial habitats.

Bacteria are found in salt water, fresh water, soil, dust, air, plants and animals. They can be found in extreme environments such as hot springs where the temperatures are over 100°C, ponds of high salt concentration, sewage, swamps and human intestines.

Some species can even exist in the human stomach at a pH of 2, and some are found in sulfur springs with a pH as low as 1.

Bacteria can survive under extreme pressures and temperatures, and may be found anywhere from deep-sea vents to mountain tops.

21.1 *Morning Glory Pool, Yellowstone National Park: red and yellow algae colour the edges*

Basic structure of bacterial cell

Bacteria are very small, single-celled organisms. They range in size from 0.1 to 10 µm in length. (There are 1 000 000 micrometres (µm) in a metre and 1000 micrometres in a millimetre. Micrometres were formerly called microns).

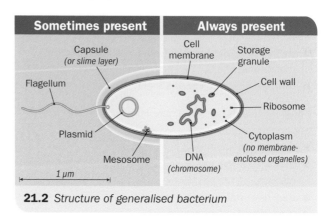

21.2 *Structure of generalised bacterium*

Bacteria are surrounded by a cell membrane, outside of which is a strong cell wall. The cell membrane often has infoldings called mesosomes. These carry out respiration and help during cell division.

The cell wall is made of a complex mixture of sugars and protein. The wall prevents bacteria from swelling with water and bursting when they are in solutions that are less concentrated than their cytoplasm (which is normally the case).

Outside the wall there may be further protection in the form of a semi-solid capsule or a more liquid slime layer. They have one bacterial chromosome consisting of a circular strand of DNA (deoxyribonucleic acid), without any surrounding membrane. The chromosome does not contain any associated protein.

The total number of genes (the genome) of a bacteria is quite small. They normally contain about 5000 genes (compared with humans who have about five or six times more).

Most bacteria also have one or more small DNA loops, called plasmids, in the cytoplasm. Plasmids contain genes that are responsible for bacterial resistance to antibiotics and are used in genetic engineering.

Bacterial genes are located on both the chromosome and the plasmid(s). This means that their genome (or genomic material) consists of a chromosome and one or more plasmids.

The material surrounding the chromosome is called the cytoplasm. It contains ribosomes, numerous storage granules (for food or waste), but no mitochondria or chloroplasts.

Many bacteria are motile (can move by themselves) due to having one or more flagella.

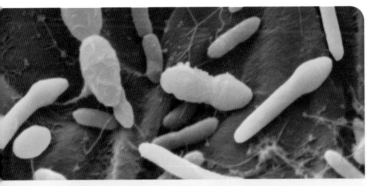

21.3 *Bacteria from human faeces (SEM)*

Bacterial types

Bacteria are classified into three groups depending on their shape.

Although only a small number of bacteria cause disease, the different types of bacteria associated with some common diseases are shown in Figures 21.4, 21.6 and 21.8.

1. ROUND

Round bacteria are called coccus (plural cocci). They can be found in pairs, chains or clusters as shown in Figure 21.4.

Capsule

Pneumonia   Sore throat   Food poisoning and boils

21.4 *Round bacteria*

21.5 *MRSA: round bacteria*

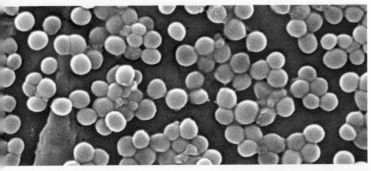

2. ROD

Rod-shaped bacteria are called bacillus (plural bacilli).

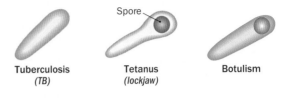

Spore

Tuberculosis (TB)   Tetanus (lockjaw)   Botulism

21.6 *Rod-shaped bacteria*

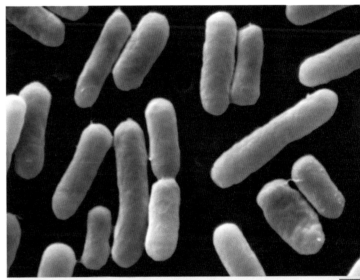

21.7 *Salmonella: rod-shaped bacteria*

3. SPIRAL

Spiral bacteria are called spirillum (plural spirilla).

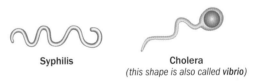

Syphilis   Cholera (this shape is also called *vibrio*)

21.8 *Spiral bacteria*

21.9 *Treponema: spiral-shaped bacterium that causes syphilis (TEM)*

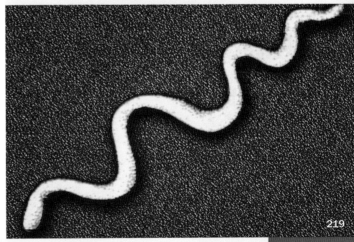

Reproduction

Bacteria reproduce asexually, by a method called **binary fission**.

When a bacterial cell gets to a certain size the DNA strand (chromosome) replicates itself. This means that there are now two identical strands of DNA. The cell elongates with a strand of DNA attached to each end. Finally the cell splits into two similar sized cells.

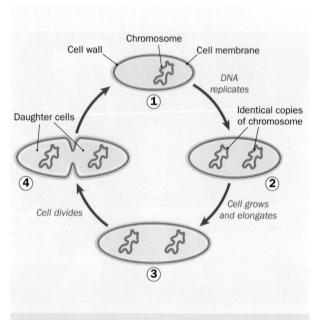

21.10 *Binary fission*

Bacteria can divide every 20 minutes if conditions are suitable. This means a single bacterium could produce over a million bacteria in 7 hours. This is why bacterial infection can produce symptoms so quickly.

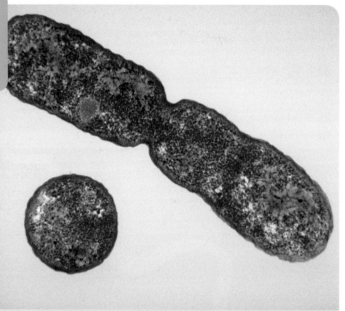

21.11 *Binary fission in a bacterial cell (TEM)*

Bacteria reproduce asexually, so their offspring are genetically identical. This means that they do not display the genetic variety that arises in plants and animals as a result of sexual reproduction. Consequently, bacteria would be slow to evolve due to their method of reproduction.

However, bacteria can evolve very fast due to the speed at which new mutations can spread within the rapidly growing bacteria.

The short life cycles of bacteria mean that any new variation produced by a mutation can be passed on very quickly to a large number of bacteria. This is how bacteria evolve (and will continue to evolve) resistance to new antibiotics.

Endospores

Some bacteria can withstand harsh and unfavourable conditions by producing **endospores**. These are formed when the bacterial chromosome replicates, with one of the new strands becoming enclosed by a tough-walled endospore formed inside the parent cell. The parent cell then breaks down and the endospore can remain dormant for a long time.

When conditions are suitable the endospore absorbs water and the tough wall breaks down. The chromosome is replicated and a normal bacterium forms again. This bacterium can then reproduce by binary fission.

Endospores are very difficult to kill. They can withstand lack of food and water, high temperatures and most poisons. They are normally not even killed by boiling water. Some endospores can survive for hundreds of years.

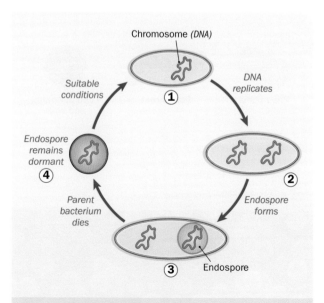

21.12 *The formation and growth of an endospore*

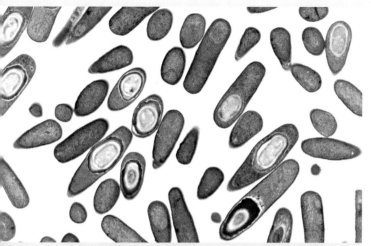

21.13 *C. diff bacteria are resistant to many antibiotics (note the endospores)*

Nutrition

Nutrition is the way an organism gets its food. Food supplies the energy and chemicals needed for survival and growth.

Bacteria get their food in four different ways. These four methods are grouped in pairs, under the headings **autotrophic** and **heterotrophic**.

Autotrophic

Autotrophic means an organism makes its own food.

The source of the energy needed to do this can be either sunlight (i.e. photosynthesis) or energy released from chemical reactions (i.e. chemosynthesis).

Photosynthetic bacteria often have chlorophyll on membranes within the cell (i.e. not in chloroplasts) and use the same type of light as plants.

Some photosynthetic bacteria have different pigments than plants and use mostly red light (almost invisible to humans). Some do not use water, but live on hydrogen sulfide gas (the gas found

in stink bombs). These are called purple sulfur bacteria.

Chemosynthetic bacteria make food using energy from reactions involving ammonia, sulfur compounds and iron compounds. Examples of these are nitrifying bacteria in the nitrogen cycle.

Heterotrophic

Heterotrophic means an organism takes in food made by other organisms.

Most bacteria are heterotrophic. These bacteria secrete enzymes into their environment and absorb the digested food. They are divided into two groups, saprophytes and parasites.

Saprophytes are organisms that take in food from dead organic matter.

Saprophytes are also called decomposers because they cause the source of their food to decay. Examples are bacteria of decay in the soil.

Did you know?

Some saprophytic bacteria can even use petrol and oil products as a food source. These bacteria are used to clean up oil spills.

Parasites are organisms that take in food from a live host and usually cause harm.

Examples include the disease-causing bacteria shown earlier in this chapter.

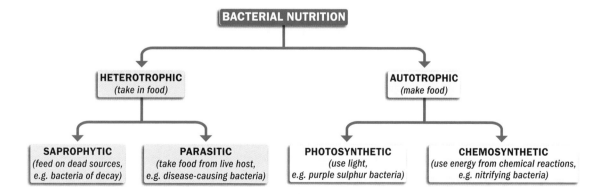

21.14 *Summary of bacterial nutrition*

Factors affecting growth

The growth of bacteria is affected by five factors. Too much or too little of any one of these factors will slow down, or stop, the growth of the bacteria.

Factors that slow down a process when in short supply are called **limiting factors**. Most of these factors relate to the way in which bacterial enzymes work. Bacterial growth factors include the following.

1. TEMPERATURE

The rate of bacterial reactions is affected by temperature.

* Although most bacteria grow well at temperatures between 20°C and 30°C, some bacteria can tolerate much higher temperatures without their enzymes being denatured.
* Low temperatures slow down the rate of bacterial growth.

Did you know?

Genes from high-temperature bacteria are often added to bacteria that are used in biotechnology. This allows bioreactors to be run at higher temperatures, which results in faster bacterial metabolism and a higher rate of product formation.

2. OXYGEN CONCENTRATION

* **Aerobic bacteria** require oxygen for respiration. Most bacteria are aerobic, e.g. *Streptococcus* bacteria.

    A low concentration of oxygen can often slow down bacterial growth, especially in liquids. This is why cultures in bioreactors often have oxygen bubbled through them and are stirred constantly.
* **Anaerobic bacteria** do not require oxygen to respire, e.g. *Clostridium*, which causes tetanus or botulism.
* **Facultative anaerobes** can respire with or without oxygen, e.g. *Escherichia coli* found in the intestines.
* **Obligate anaerobes** can only respire in the absence of oxygen (e.g. *Clostridium tetani* causes tetanus (or lockjaw) by infecting deep cuts where there is a poor oxygen supply).

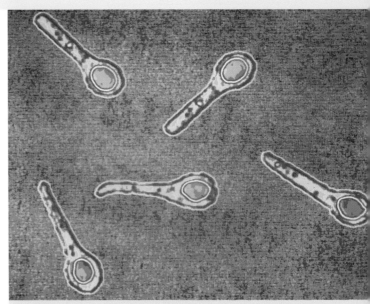

21.15 *Anaerobic tetanus-causing bacteria with spores*

3. PH

Bacterial enzymes are designed to work at specific pH values. If the bacterium is placed in an unsuitable pH its enzymes will be denatured.

* Most bacteria grow at or near neutral pH (i.e. pH 7).
* However, some bacteria can tolerate very low (acidic) or very high (alkaline) pH values.

For example, a bacterium called *Helicobacter* is found in the stomach of about half the Irish population. This bacterium can tolerate a pH of 2 and often causes stomach ulcers.

4. EXTERNAL SOLUTE CONCENTRATION

The growth of bacteria is affected by the external solute concentration. This is because bacteria gain or lose water by osmosis.

* If the external solution has a higher solute (e.g. salt or sugar) concentration than the bacterial cytoplasm, water will move out of the bacteria.

    This dehydrates the bacteria and stops their enzymes from working. This principle is behind the basis of methods of food preservation – salting and sugaring (as used for bacon and marmalade or jam).
* If the external solution has a lower solute (e.g. salt or sugar) concentration than the bacterial cytoplasm, water will enter the bacteria.

    The cell walls of bacteria can normally prevent bacterial cells from bursting in these circumstances. Most bacteria live in less concentrated solutions.

THE ORGANISM

5. PRESSURE

- The growth of most bacteria is inhibited by high pressures. This is because the bacterial walls are not strong enough to withstand the high pressure.
- However, some bacteria can withstand very high pressures, such as those found in deep-sea vents.

The use of bacteria in biotechnology often requires that they are able to grow in pressurised bioreactors. To allow this to happen, pressure-tolerant bacteria are formed by genetic engineering techniques.

Economic importance of bacteria

Syllabus

You are required to know two economic benefits and two economic disadvantages of bacteria.

Benefits

- Bacteria such as *Lactobacillus* are used to convert milk to products such as yoghurt and cheese. Other bacteria are involved in the production of vinegar, silage, pickles and antibiotics.

- Genetically modified bacteria (especially the bacterium *Escherichia coli* or *E. coli*) are used to make products such as insulin, drugs, enzymes, amino acids, vitamins, food flavourings, alcohols and a growing range of new substances.

21.16 *Round and rod-shaped bacteria in yoghurt*

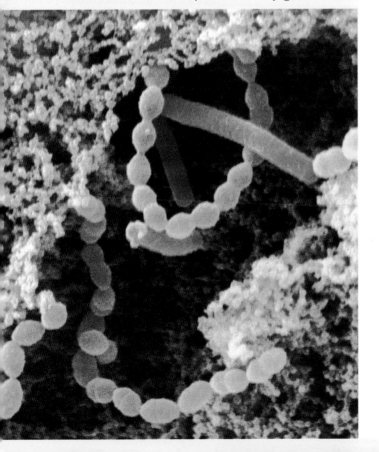

Disadvantages

- Bacteria cause human, animal and plant diseases such as tuberculosis, whooping cough, septic throats, meningitis (one type), typhoid, cholera, diphtheria, dysentery, food poisoning, mastitis and brucellosis.

Pathogens are micro-organisms that cause disease.

Pathogens include some bacteria and some fungi.

- Bacteria cause food to decay. For example, *Lactobacilli* cause milk to turn sour.

  Bacteria in the mouth convert sugars to acid, which then dissolves the outer layer of enamel on teeth, causing tooth decay.

21.17 *Round bacteria (blue) and red blood cells (red) on the surface of a human tooth (SEM)*

Antibiotics

Antibiotics are chemicals produced by micro-organisms that stop the growth of, or kill, other micro-organisms without damaging human tissue.

Antibiotics are normally used to control bacterial infection, but they can treat some fungal diseases. Note that antibiotics do not affect viruses.

Originally antibiotics were isolated from fungi. (Penicillin was first isolated in 1928 from a fungus by Sir Alexander Fleming.) Now antibiotics are mostly produced by genetically engineered bacteria.

Since the 1940s antibiotics have been widely used to treat bacterial infections. Many new antibiotics have been discovered, e.g. streptomycin, neomycin and tetracycline.

THE ORGANISM

21.18 *Sir Alexander Fleming (1881–1955), who discovered penicillin by accident. See also page 7.*

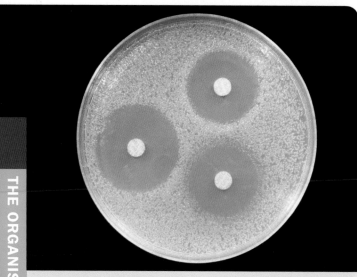

21.19 *The effects of three antibiotics on typhoid bacteria*

21.20 *Bacterial cell on left has burst due to an antibiotic; the cell on the right is dividing.*

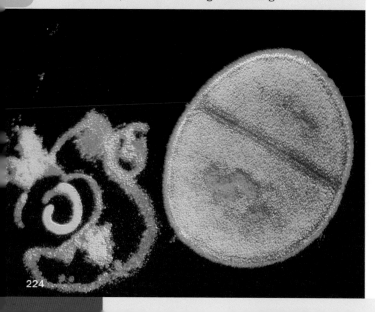

Antibiotic resistance

When an antibiotic is used to treat a bacterial infection most of the bacteria are killed. However, antibiotic-resistant bacteria have developed (and continue to do so) by mutations.

These bacteria are not affected by the antibiotic that is being used. This means that new antibiotics must be produced continually to treat newly resistant bacteria.

If a person is taking antibiotics, then all the bacteria in that person are killed. If antibiotic-resistant bacteria evolve or enter that person's body, then these bacteria have no competitors. They reproduce very fast and take over the person's body.

If a pathenogenic bacteria then enters the person, the antibiotic-resistant gene may be passed on to it. The person will then develop an infection for which the antibiotic is not an effective treatment.

In recent times bacterial strains have emerged that are resistant to almost all known antibiotics. These bacteria are said to be **multi-resistant**. Examples of such 'superbugs' are MRSA and C. difficile. These bacteria are becoming widespread, especially in hospitals.

Potential abuse of antibiotics in medicine

- The overuse of antibiotics (in both medicine and agricultural foods) results in the increased growth of antibiotic-resistant bacteria (because they have no competition). For instance, in some countries it is legal to buy antibiotics over the counter (without a doctor's prescription).
- The failure of some patients to complete their treatment of antibiotics allows the bacteria to survive and regrow. This leads to the need for more antibiotics (along with the increased risk of the growth of resistant bacteria).

Bacteria are prokaryotes

Bacteria belong to the kingdom Monera. The organisms in this kingdom are also called Prokaryotes.

As outlined in Chapter 7, prokaryotes are organisms that lack a membrane-enclosed nucleus or membrane-enclosed cell organelles such as mitochondria and chloroplasts.

Apart from the kingdom Monera, all other kingdoms contain eukaryotes (i.e. organisms whose nuclei and organelles are enclosed by membranes).

THE ORGANISM

Growth curve

Binary fission results in a very fast increase in bacterial numbers. The growth curve for a typical population of bacteria growing on nutrient agar in a warm environment is given in Figure 21.21.

Note that the numbers of bacteria are represented on a logarithmic or exponential scale. This is to allow huge numbers of bacteria to be represented on the graph.

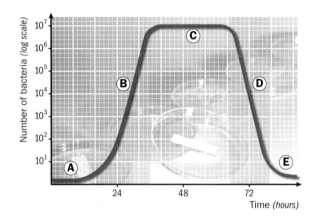

21.21 *Growth curve for bacteria*

The graph can be divided into five phases, labelled A, B, C, D and E. These phases are explained as follows.

Lag phase (A)

During the lag phase the bacteria are adapting themselves to their new environment. For example, they may be producing new enzymes to digest the nutrients on which they are to grow.

There is little, if any, increase in bacterial numbers during the lag phase.

Log phase (B)

The log phase is also called the exponential phase. The bacteria are reproducing at their maximum rate and their numbers are doubling in every new generation. This is due to ideal conditions (e.g. plenty of food, moisture, space or oxygen).

Stationary phase (C)

In the stationary phase there is no increase in bacterial numbers. The production of new bacteria is compensated for by the death of equal numbers of bacteria. The rate of growth slows down due to factors such as:

- lack of food
- lack of space

- lack of moisture
- lack of oxygen
- the build-up of toxic waste products

Decline phase (D)

Bacteria numbers fall when the death rate is greater than the rate of reproduction. The slow rate of reproduction is caused by the same factors as caused the stationary phase.

Death or survival phase (E)

Note that normally not all the bacteria die. A small number may survive as spores. Spores can survive by remaining dormant until conditions are again suitable.

Food processing

The production of useful products using enzymes was discussed in Chapter 12.

Modern bioprocessing methods involve the use of bacteria (and other organisms) to produce a wide range of foods and related products. These include dairy products such as yoghurts and cheeses, artificial sweeteners, amino acids, vitamins, flavourings, flavour enhancers and alcohol products such as wines and beers.

There is a growing trend towards the use of micro-organisms themselves as a food source, especially as a source of protein. The use of bacteria (as well as yeasts, other fungi and algae) to produce edible forms of protein is called **single-cell protein** (SCP) production.

There are two main methods of production: batch culture (or fermentation) and continuous flow culture (or fermentation).

21.22 *Quorn: a protein produced from the fermentation of a fungus is used as a meat substitute by vegetarians.*

THE ORGANISM

Batch culture

In batch culture, a fixed amount of sterile nutrient is added to the micro-organisms in the bioreactor. The micro-organisms go through the lag, log, stationary (and sometimes decline and survival) stages of a typical growth curve. As this happens the nutrients are used up and the product is formed.

The product normally forms at the log or stationary stage. The process is often stopped before the decline phase because there is very little product formed at this stage. In addition, there is a danger of the micro-organism bursting or of unwanted side products forming at this stage.

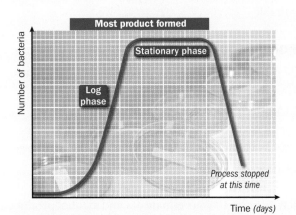

21.23 *The formation of product in batch culture*

The bioreactor (see Figure 21.24) may or may not have oxygen added (depending on whether the micro-organisms are aerobic or anaerobic). Also the mixture is usually, but not always, stirred.

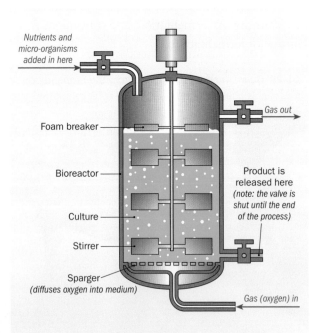

21.24 *A bioreactor for batch culture*

At the end of the production run the bioreactor is emptied. The product is then separated from the solution and purified. The bioreactor is cleaned, resterilised and the process can then be repeated.

Many antibiotics are made by batch culture.

Continuous flow

In continuous flow culture, nutrients are continuously fed into the bioreactor. At the same time the culture medium (containing some micro-organisms) is continuously withdrawn. In this way the volume of material in the bioreactor remains constant.

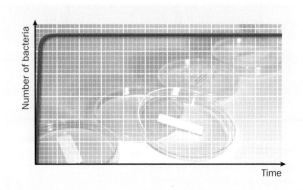

21.25 *The formation of product in continuous flow culture*

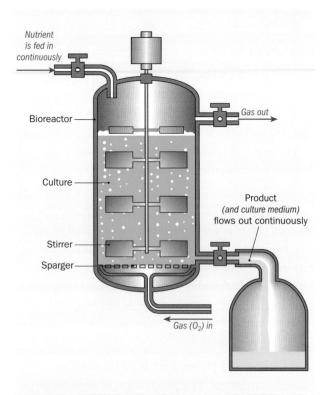

21.26 *A bioreactor for continuous flow processing*

In continuous flow culture the micro-organisms are maintained more or less constantly in the log stage of growth. This means they are growing rapidly and producing the product at a fast rate. Factors such as pH, temperature, the rate of stirring and the concentrations of nutrients, oxygen and waste products are kept constant. For this reason the organisms are said to grow under steady state (unchanging) conditions.

Maintaining constant conditions is very difficult. For this reason continuous flow processing is limited to a small number of applications. These include the production of single-cell protein (and some methods of waste water treatment; see Chapter 4).

Differences between batch and continuous flow culture	
Batch	**Continuous flow**
Fixed amount of nutrient added at the start	Nutrients added all the time
Micro-organisms go through the lag, log, stationary (and sometimes, decline) phases	Micro-organisms maintained in the log phase all the time
Product formed for a short time (and the process may then start again)	Product formed all the time for a long period of time

Summary

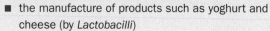

Micro-organisms are small living things.
- Micro-organisms include bacteria, some fungi and plankton.
- Micro-organisms are found in a wide range of habitats.

Bacteria are:
- microscopic
- single-celled
- have a cell wall
- do not have a nucleus or membrane-enclosed organelles
- have a single loop of DNA

Bacterial shapes are round, rod or spiral

Bacterial reproduction is asexual, by binary fission.

Bacteria evolve rapidly by mutating.

Endospores are tough-walled spores capable of surviving harsh conditions.

Nutrition can be:
- **Autotrophic** (make their own food)
  - (i) photosynthetic (use light as an energy source to make food)
  - (ii) chemosynthetic (use chemical reactions as an energy source to make food)
- **Heterotrophic** (take in food)
  - (i) saprophytic (feeding from a dead source)
  - (ii) parasitic (feeding from a live host)

Bacterial growth is affected by:
- temperature
- oxygen concentration
- pH
- external solute concentration
- pressure

Aerobic bacteria use oxygen; anaerobic bacteria do not use oxygen for respiration.
- Obligate aerobes are obliged to use oxygen.
- Facultative aerobes have the facility to use or not to use oxygen.

The economic benefits of bacteria include:
- the manufacture of products such as yoghurt and cheese (by *Lactobacilli*)
- the use of genetically engineered bacteria (such as *E. coli*) to produce insulin, drugs and enzymes

The economic disadvantages of bacteria include:
- they cause human, animal and plant diseases
- they cause food decay

Pathogens are micro-organisms that cause disease.

Antibiotics are chemicals made by fungi or bacteria to kill or stop the growth of bacteria (but not viruses).
- Bacteria can develop immunity (resistance) to antibiotics by mutations.
- Multi-resistant bacteria have evolved that are not affected by most antibiotics.

Prokaryotes do not have membrane-enclosed nuclei or organelles.
- Bacteria are prokaryotes.

Bacterial growth shows five phases:
- the lag phase (no increase in numbers)
- the log phase (numbers increase very rapidly)
- the stationary phase (no increase in numbers)
- the decline phase (rapid fall in numbers)
- the survival phase (some bacteria survive as spores)

Bacteria are used in food processing to form many types of food products.
- The growth of micro-organisms in a liquid medium is called fermentation.
- Fermentation takes place in a bioreactor.
- Sterile means the absence of living things.

(continued overleaf)

Batch culture means that:
- a certain amount of nutrient is added to the micro-organisms in a bioreactor
- the bacteria go through the lag, log and stationary stages of growth
- the process is stopped
- the bioreactor is emptied and sterilised so that the process can be repeated

Continuous flow culture means that:
- nutrients are continuously added to the bioreactor
- bacteria, culture medium and product are continuously removed
- the bacteria are maintained at the log stage of growth
- conditions in the bioreactor are kept constant

Batch culture is used more often than continuous flow culture.

Revision questions

1 (a) What are micro-organisms?
  (b) Name three types of micro-organisms.
  (c) State six habitats where micro-organisms may be found.
2 Figure 21.27 represents a bacterium.

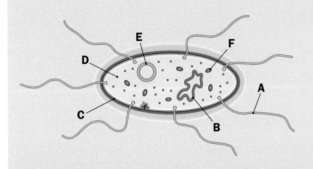

21.27

  (a) Name the parts labelled A to F and give one function for each part.
  (b) State the shape of the cell in Figure 21.27.
  (c) Name the other two bacterial shapes.
3 (a) Name the method of reproduction used by bacteria.
  (b) Describe, with the aid of labelled diagrams, this method of reproduction.
4 (a) Name the method by which bacteria evolve.
  (b) Give one reason why bacteria evolve so rapidly.
  (c) Suggest one disadvantage of bacterial evolution.
5 (a) What is an endospore?
  (b) Under what conditions do endospores develop?
  (c) State one advantage of endospores.
  (d) Suggest why endospores are not methods of reproduction.
6 (a) Distinguish between: **(i)** heterotrophic and autotrophic, **(ii)** a saprophyte and a parasite, **(iii)** photosynthesis and chemosynthesis, **(iv)** aerobic and anaerobic bacteria.
  (b) Name one type of bacterium in each of the eight categories listed in part (a) of this question.
7 Give one reason for each of the following.
  (a) Bacteria grow faster at 20°C than at 5°C.
  (b) Oxygen is bubbled into some bioreactors.
  (c) Bacterial growth is inhibited by unsuitable pH.

  (d) Most bacteria are prevented from growing by placing them in high salt concentrations.
  (e) The growth of many bacteria is inhibited by high pressure.
8 (a) Explain what is meant by **(i)** a pathogen, **(ii)** an antibiotic.
  (b) Suggest one way in which antibiotics have been abused.
  (c) How do antibiotic-resistant bacteria develop?
  (d) What is the danger with multi-resistant bacteria?
9 Sir Alexander Fleming, when growing pure cultures of the bacterium *Staphylococcus*, found that one of his agar plates of the bacterium was contaminated with the fungus *Penicillium notatum*. Figure 21.28 represents the contaminated plate. (Note: At the start of the experiment the bacterial suspension had been spread evenly over the agar surface.)

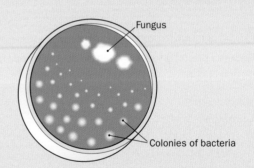
Fungus
Colonies of bacteria

21.28

  (a) What observation can you make about the distribution of the bacterial colonies on the plate in relation to the position of the fungus?
  (b) What deduction do you think Fleming made from his discovery of this plate that resulted in the discovery of antibiotics?
  (c) Why is Fleming's antibiotic less useful now than in previous years?
10 (a) Name the kingdom in which bacteria are placed.
  (b) Why are bacteria referred to as prokaryotes?
  (c) Why are fungi considered to be eukaryotes?

11 Figure 21.29 represents the number of bacteria growing on an agar dish over a period of time.

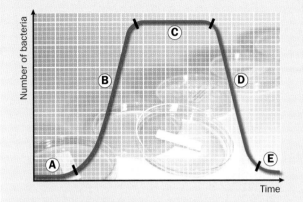

21.29

(a) Name the phases labelled A to E.

(b) State what is happening to the number of bacteria at each phase.

(c) Give a reason for the events in each phase.

(d) Does the graph show that all the bacteria die?

(e) Explain your answer to part (d) and give a reason why the bacteria behave as shown.

12 (a) Name two methods of food processing using bacteria.

(b) Explain what is meant by:

(i) a bioreactor

(ii) sterile conditions.

13 Distinguish between batch and continuous flow culture in terms of:

(i) how the nutrients are added

(ii) the stage(s) of growth at which the bacteria are found

(iii) the length of time for which the process can continue

(iv) when the products are obtained.

Sample examination questions

Section A

14 (a) Bacterial cells have three main shapes. Two of these are shown below. Name each shape.

(i)

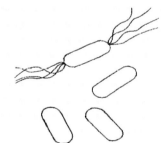

(ii)

(b) Bacteria reproduce asexually by dividing in two. What term is used for this form of asexual reproduction?

(c) What do bacteria form when environmental conditions become unfavourable?

(d) What does the term pathogenic mean in relation to bacteria?

(2003 Sample OL Q 2)

Section C

15 (a) The diagram shows a typical bacterial cell.

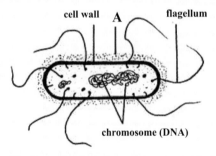

(i) Some bacteria have a layer outside the cell wall (labelled A in diagram). Name this layer and state its function

(ii) Name a structure, other than A, which is not found in all bacteria.

(b) The table below shows ways in which bacteria obtain their food. Study the table and then answer the questions that follow.

Autotrophic	Heterotrophic
Photosynthetic	Parasitic
Chemosynthetic	Saprophytic

(i) Distinguish between autotrophic and heterotrophic nutrition.

(ii) What is saprophytic nutrition?

(iii) Why are saprophytic bacteria important in nature?

(iv) Briefly explain chemosynthesis.

(v) What term is used for the organism from which a parasite obtains its food?

(vi) Give examples of **two** harmful bacteria.

(2007 OL Q13a, b)

16 Answer the following in relation to bacteria.

   (i) Distinguish between photosynthetic and chemosynthetic bacteria. Give an example of each type.

   (ii) Name **two** forms of heterotrophic nutrition found in bacteria.

   (iii) What are antibiotics? For what purpose are they used?

   (iv) Explain what is meant by antibiotic resistance and suggest how it may develop.

   (2006 HL Q 15b)

17 (i) Draw and label a diagram to show the basic structure of a typical bacterial cell.

   (ii) Other than being prokaryotic, state **two** ways in which a typical bacterial cell differs from a typical human cell (e.g. cell from cheek lining).

   (iii) Describe how some bacteria respond in order to survive when environmental conditions become unfavourable.

   (iv) What is meant when a bacterium is described as being pathogenic?

   (v) What are antibiotics? Use your knowledge of the Theory of Natural Selection to explain the possible danger involved in the misuse of antibiotics.

   (2005 HL Q 15b)

18 The diagram shows a bacterial growth curve.

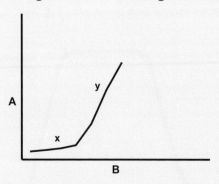

   (i) **A** and **B** represent the labels on the axes. What does each of them stand for?

   (ii) What term is applied to the part of the curve labelled **x**? What is happening during **x**?

   (iii) What term is applied to the part of the curve labelled **y**? What is happening during **y**?

   (iv) Copy the diagram into your answer book and continue the curve to show the next phase. Explain why you have continued the curve in this way.

   (v) Distinguish between batch and continuous flow food processing using micro-organisms in the food industry.

   (2008 HL 15c)

Previous examination questions	
Ordinary level	**Higher level**
2003 Sample Q 2	2005 Q 15b
2005 Q 6b	2006 Q 15b
2007 Q 13a, b	2007 Q 14b(v), (vi)
	2008 Q 15c

For latest questions go to www.edco.ie/biology

Chapter 22 Fungi

Introduction

There are over 100 000 different species of fungi, including mushrooms, mildews, moulds and yeasts. Fungi have membrane-enclosed nuclei and mitochondria. They also have cell walls, usually made of a carbohydrate called chitin. The study of fungi is called mycology.

Fungi have the following main characteristics:
- They reproduce by means of spores.
- They lack chlorophyll and are always heterotrophic. They do not ingest food, but secrete enzymes onto the food and absorb the digested molecules.
- They have cell walls, usually made of chitin.
- The body structure often consists of tubes called hyphae, which form a visible mycelium.

> A **hypha** is a tube or filament in a fungus.
> A **mycelium** is a (usually) visible mass of hyphae.

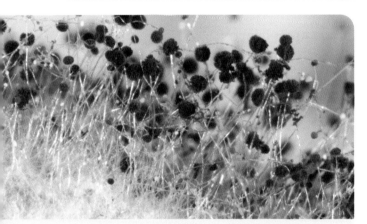

22.1 *Mycelium and sporangia-bearing spores of* Rhizopus *(bread mould)*

Nutrition

As fungi are heterotrophs they are either parasites (absorbing food from live hosts) or saprophytes (absorbing food from dead organic matter).

Parasites

Parasitic fungi mostly take their food from plants. The fungus penetrates between the cells of the plant from which it absorbs food. Some fungal parasites live on animals, e.g. athlete's foot and ringworm.

Obligate parasites (e.g. fungi causing mildews, smuts and rust diseases) can only live on live hosts and do not normally kill their host. Facultative parasites (e.g. fungi causing soft rots in fruit) may kill the host and feed on the dead remains.

Saprophytes

Most fungi are saprophytes. They are commonly found in the soil and on rotting leaves, trees and dead animals. Examples are mushrooms and moulds.

As the material is digested, minerals are released and recycled. For this reason saprophytic fungi are vital in the environment.

Edible and poisonous fungi

Some fungi are edible, but many are highly poisonous. Because it is difficult to distinguish edible fungi from the poisonous species, wild fungi should only be eaten with great caution.

Edible fungi include the standard field mushroom and morels. Both of these fungi grow above the ground.

Another edible fungus is the truffle. These highly priced fungi are formed underground, normally near the roots of trees. They have a very distinctive smell and in the past pigs were used to 'sniff them out'. In more recent times dogs have been trained to find truffles.

22.2 *A selection of edible mushrooms*

THE ORGANISM

22.3 *Death cap: the most poisonous mushroom known*

Poisonous fungi are numerous. Some species can cause death if only a single fungus cap is eaten. The most common poisonous mushrooms are the death cap and the destroying angel (both fungi are *Amanita* species). These fungi damage cells in the lining of the intestine and liver. Death normally results from liver failure.

Common bread mould (*Rhizopus*)

Nutrition

The common bread mould is a saprophyte of starchy foods, e.g bread, vegetable peelings and stored fruits such as apples.

The fungus secretes enzymes out into the starchy substrate. Digestion takes place outside the fungus and the digested nutrients are then absorbed.

Structure

Bread mould fungus appears as black circular patches. It is often called a **pin mould** because the reproductive structures look like pins sticking out from the surface.

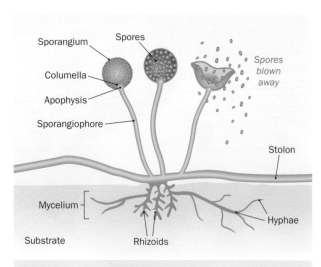

22.4 *Structure of Rhizopus*

Rhizopus consists of threadlike structures called hyphae (singular hypha). These have no cross walls (i.e. they are **aseptate**) and are multinucleate, each nucleus being haploid. A mass of hyphae is called a **mycelium**.

The hyphae digest and absorb the substrate on which they grow. A stolon is an aerial hypha which allows the fungus to spread more rapidly. Rhizoids are hyphae that provide extra surface area for absorption.

Life cycle of *Rhizopus*

ASEXUAL REPRODUCTION

After a few days growth, some hyphae grow up from the surface of the substate. These are called sporangiophores. Their tip swells to produce a sporangium whose contents divide by mitosis to form numerous spores. Each spore has at least one haploid nucleus. The base of the sporangium is a wall called the columella.

In dry conditions, the black sporangium dries out and opens to release many spores. Each spore blows away and grows into a new hypha and mycelium if it lands on a suitable substrate.

Sporulation is the process of making spores.

SEXUAL REPRODUCTION

Rhizopus exists as two separate strains called plus and minus strains. Both strains look identical but sexual reproduction can only occur between a plus and minus strain.

Sexual reproduction occurs as follows (refer to Figure 22.5).

1 Hyphae from opposite strains grow close together.
2 Swellings form opposite each other.
3 The swellings touch.
4 Nuclei (which are the sex cells, or gametes) move into each swelling, forming progametangia.
5 Cross walls form to produce gametangia (singular gametangium), which are held in place by suspensors.
6 The walls between the gametangia dissolve.
7 Many fertilisations produce a number of diploid zygote nuclei.
8 A tough-walled, black zygospore forms around these nuclei.
9 The zygospore can remain dormant for months.

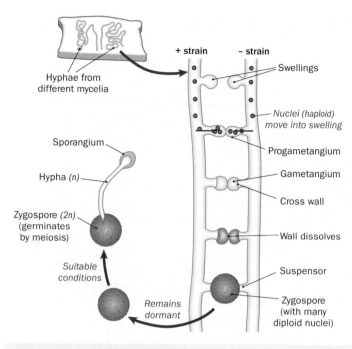

22.5 *Sexual reproduction in* Rhizopus

10 When conditions are suitable the zygospore germinates by meiosis.
11 A haploid hypha grows out of the zygospore and produces a sporangium at the tip.
12 The sporangium releases many haploid spores which produce new hyphae and mycelia.

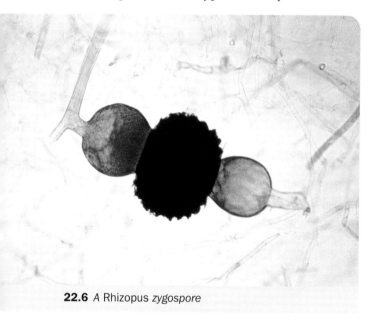

22.6 *A* Rhizopus *zygospore*

Yeast (*Saccharomyces*)

Structure

Yeasts are single-celled (unicellular) fungi. Many different fungi can be induced to form a yeast stage.

Yeast cells are round or oval. They are tiny cells (about 10 μm long) and are only clearly seen using an electron microscope.

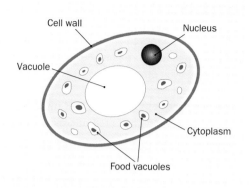

22.7 *Yeast*

Yeast cells have thin walls made of the carbohydrate chitin and a dense cytoplasm that contains many food storage vacuoles. This is why the cytoplasm appears granular or grainy. Usually one large vacuole is present. Each cell has one nucleus.

Yeasts respire anaerobically, breaking down sugars and producing ethanol and carbon dioxide, according to the equation:

Glucose ⟶ 2 ethanol + 2 carbon dioxide

Reproduction

Asexual reproduction in yeast occurs by **budding**. The parent cell divides by mitosis and one nucleus and some cytoplasm enters a small bud. This bud may separate or remain attached.

In the latter case each new bud may divide again. Eventually a colony can form. This often occurs when yeasts are growing rapidly. The colony is temporary and later divides to form single cells again.

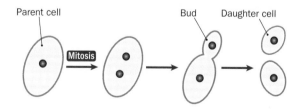

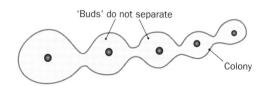

22.8 *Asexual reproduction in yeast*

General precautions when growing micro-organisms

In general you should assume that all micro-organisms are potentially harmful, unless it is stated or proven otherwise.

> **Aseptic** or **asepsis** means that measures are taken to exclude unwanted micro-organisms.
>
> **Sterile** means that all micro-organisms are destroyed, i.e. there is nothing living.

Aseptic techniques involve the creation of a germ-free environment, mainly by the use of sterilisation. Aseptic methods include the following procedures.

1 Wash your hands before and after each experiment.
2 Wash the bench with disinfectant before and after each experiment.
3 Do not put fingers, food, drink or equipment in or near your mouth.
4 Keep all containers closed where possible.

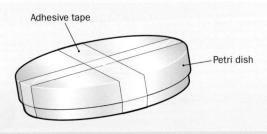

Adhesive tape

Petri dish

22.9 *A sealed petri dish*

5 When micro-organisms are in a petri dish seal the dish with adhesive tape as shown in Figure 22.9.
6 Sterilise all equipment before and after use. This can be done by placing the equipment (except plastic) in a pressure cooker (or autoclave) at 120°C for 15 minutes. Alternatively, immerse all equipment and cultures in Dettol for 24 hours.
    After being sterilised, the material can be put in a dustbin or, in the case of glassware and metal, cleaned and reused as usual.
7 Use the following techniques for safety and to avoid contamination by unwanted micro-organisms.
    (a) Sterilise all glassware, equipment and growth media by heating in a pressure cooker or autoclave at high pressure (120°C) for 15 minutes or by placing it in an oven at 160°C for an hour.
    (b) Flame all needles or loops by heating them in the flame of a bunsen burner.
    (c) Pass the neck of test tubes through a flame.
    (d) Open all containers (i) for the shortest possible time and (ii) open lids the shortest possible distance (minimal opening).
    (e) Flame all needles and loops again after they are used.

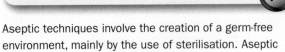

Activity 16   *To investigate the growth of leaf yeast using agar plates*

Micro-organisms are widely found in nature. This activity shows that, although they are not visible to the naked eye, leaves have many yeasts growing on their surfaces. These yeasts do not harm the leaves.

1 Collect some leaves from an outdoor plant – privet, ash or sycamore leaves are ideal. *(These will be tested for the presence of leaf yeasts.)*
2 Wash your hands with an aseptic soap solution. *(This reduces the chance of micro-organisms being on your hands.)*
3 Wash the bench or worktop with disinfectant. *(Again this eliminates micro-organisms.)*
4 Sterilise a forceps by heating it in the flame of a bunsen burner for a few seconds. *(This means there will be no micro-organisms on the forceps.)*
5 Obtain two sterile petri dishes containing prepared sterile nutrient agar. *(Agar is a material derived from seaweed. It is used to form a solid growth medium. The nutrient agar allows micro-organisms to grow.)*

6 Use the forceps to pick up one of the leaves, which should be small enough to fit across a petri dish. *(This prevents micro-organisms getting on to the leaf from your hands.)* Alternatively, for large leaves, you may flame a cork borer or scissors, allow it to cool and use it to cut a number of leaf discs.
7 Place a small spot of *Vaseline* or *Blue Tac* on the inside lid of the petri dish. *(This will be used to attach the leaf to the lid of the petri dish.)*
8 Reflame the forceps and allow it to cool.

Forceps

Bunsen flame

22.10 *Flaming a forceps*

9 Barely open the lid of one of the petri dishes – in terms of (a) the distance it is opened and (b) the time for which it is opened – and use the forceps to attach the leaf to the lid of the petri dish. Close the lid of the petri dish. The lower surface of the leaf is now facing down onto the agar. *(There are more micro-organisms on the lower surface of the leaf than on the upper surface. Leaf yeasts can expel their spores down onto the surface of the agar.)*

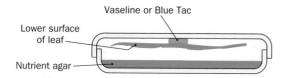

22.11 *Leaf attached to lid of petri dish*

10 Reflame the forceps. *(This will kill any micro-organisms on it.)*

11 Seal a sterile nutrient agar petri dish containing no leaf. *(This dish will act as a control or comparison. The only difference between the two petri dishes is that one contains a leaf and the other does not.)*

12 Seal the petri dishes with tape or parafilm. *(This prevents them from opening by accident.)*

13 Label the petri dishes on the undersurface with a marker. *(This allows the dishes to be identified, without further blocking the view of the agar surface.)*

14 Leave the petri dishes at room temperature or in an oven or incubator at 25°C. *(Leaf yeasts grow well at room temperature, but a higher temperature will speed up their growth.)*

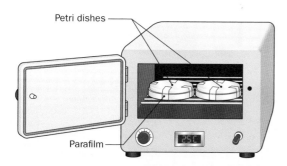

22.12 *Incubating petri dishes*

15 The dishes should be incubated upside down. *(This prevents condensation forming on the lids.)*

16 Observe the surfaces of the agar each day for two or three days *(to see if any yeast colonies are forming.)*

17 You should see yeast as red or pink circles or colonies growing on the surface of the agar.

18 The dish with the leaf should show yeast colonies on the surface of the agar. These colonies will form a pattern similar to the shape of the leaf. Very few other micro-organisms will grow on the agar, unless part of the leaf is touching the agar. *(The yeast can expel spores from a distance onto the agar; most other micro-organisms cannot grow across the space.)*

Note that the growth of leaf yeasts is inhibited by air pollution. If the leaves are collected from a location with polluted air there may be few, or no, yeasts on the agar. The agar in the control dish should have nothing growing on it. *(This shows that the yeasts did not arise from any other source except the untreated leaf.)*

19 At the end of the experiment dispose of the agar and yeasts by sterilising it in an autoclave or pressure cooker for 15 minutes. Alternatively it can be immersed in disinfectant (such as *Dettol* or *Milton*) for 24 hours and then put in a bin.

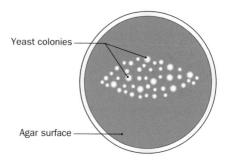

22.13 *Yeast colonies growing on agar*

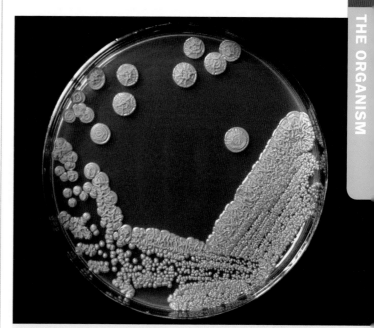

22.14 *Leaf yeast growing on nutrient agar*

Economic importance of fungi

Benefits

- Yeasts are used to produce alcohols such as beers and wines.
- Fungi such as mushrooms can be grown as a source of food.

Disadvantages

- Fungi destroy a wide range of materials. These include:
  - food (yeasts grow on fruits and sweet liquids; bread mould grows on bread)
  - crops (potato blight fungus destroys potatoes; smuts and rusts are fungal diseases of cereals)
  - paper (mildew grows on damp paper)
  - timber (dry rot and Dutch elm fungus both grow on wood)
- Fungal diseases of plants, humans and animals can result in financial losses.

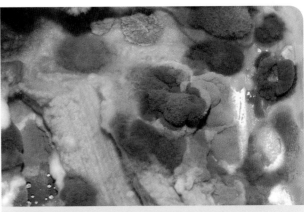

21.15 *Mould growing on composting kitchen waste*

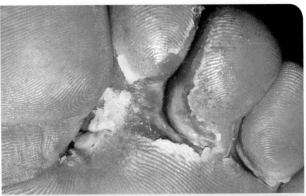

21.16 *Skin infected by Athlete's foot. This is the most common form of ringworm, a fungal infection of the surface of the skin. The fungi feed on keratin, a protein found in the skin. It is highly contagious.*

21.17 *Button mushrooms being grown commercially*

Summary

Fungi:
- reproduce by spores
- are heterotrophic (i.e. do not have chlorophyll)
- have cell walls made of chitin and often consist of hyphae, forming a mycelium

Fungi can be:
- parasites of plants (mildews, smuts, rusts, soft rots) and animals (athlete's foot, ringworm)
- saprophytes that cause decay (decomposers)

Edible fungi (mushrooms and truffles) are hard to distinguish from poisonous fungi (death cap fungus).

Rhizopus (black bread mould) is a saprophyte. It:
- has tubes called hypha(e) (forming a visible mycelium)
- reproduces asexually by spores
- reproduces sexually when nuclei from different mycelia fuse to form zygospores. These remain dormant until conditions are suitable for growth

Yeast:
- is a single-celled fungus
- reproduces asexually by budding
- respires anaerobically to form ethanol and carbon dioxide

General precautions that should be taken when working with micro-organisms include:
- use aseptic techniques to exclude unwanted micro-organisms
- sterilise (kill all micro-organisms) the work area, equipment and growth material before and after use
- flame any relevant equipment before and after use
- dispose of all material safely

The presence of yeast on leaves can be shown by:
- attaching the top surface of a leaf to the lid of a petri dish containing nutrient agar
- observing the colonies of yeast that form on the agar (as a control use a nutrient agar plate with no leaf)
- no yeast colonies form on the agar in the control dish

Economic benefits of fungi include:
- yeasts produce alcohol
- mushrooms are edible

Economic disadvantages of fungi include:
- they destroy food (*Rhizopus* destroys bread), crops and a wide range of other materials
- they cause human (athlete's foot and ringworm), animal and plant diseases

Revision questions

1 Name three characteristics of fungi that distinguish them from animals.

2 Name one feature of fungi, in each case, that they share with **(a)** plants, **(b)** animals.

3 What is the ecological benefit of fungi growing on dead leaves?

4 **(a)** Why are fungi obliged to be heterotrophic?
   (b) Name, giving two examples in each case, the two modes of heterotrophic nutrition used by fungi.

5 **(a)** Why may it be dangerous to eat wild fungi?
   (b) Give one example of an edible and a non-edible fungus.

6 Explain what is meant by:
   (a) hypha
   (b) mycelium
   (c) aseptate
   (d) multinucleate

7 Sexual reproduction in *Rhizopus* never occurs between hyphae of the same mycelium.
   (a) Explain why this statement is true.
   (b) Give an illustrated account of sexual reproduction in *Rhizopus*.

8 Give an account of yeast under the headings:
   (a) structure
   (b) reproduction
   (c) respiration

9 List **(a)** three similarities, and **(b)** three differences, between yeast and *Rhizopus*.

10 Outline the economic importance of fungi.

11 When growing micro-organisms, give one reason for each of the following practices:
   (a) using aseptic techniques
   (b) not eating food in the laboratory
   (c) keeping all containers with micro-organisms closed
   (d) using a pressure cooker or autoclave
   (e) using nutrient agar
   (f) only opening petri dishes briefly
   (g) sterilising the cultures after use.

12 When investigating the growth of leaf yeasts, give a reason for each of the following:
   (a) flaming the forceps
   (b) using vaseline
   (c) using a control
   (d) labelling the petri dishes on their undersurface
   (e) soaking the petri dishes in disinfectant overnight at the end of the investigation.

13 Suggest a reason for each of the following:
   (a) It may be dangerous to eat wild mushroms.
   (b) Some fungi inhibit the growth of bacteria.
   (c) Athlete's foot is not treated with antibiotics.
   (d) Fungus does not grow well on the surface of jams.
   (e) *Rhizopus* normally forms zygospores when all its food is used up.

(continued overleaf)

THE ORGANISM

(f) *Rhizopus* does not grow on most biscuits.

(g) Leaf yeasts are more common on the undersides of leaves (compared to the upper surfaces).

(h) Leaf yeasts are more abundant on leaves in rural rather than city environments.

(i) Leaf yeasts are more common on older leaves than younger leaves.

14 Choose which of the options (i), (ii), (iii) or (iv) represents the correct answer in each case below.

(a) On nutrient agar, leaf yeast colonies appear:
(i) white
(ii) red or pink
(iii) creamy
(iv) fuzzy

(b) Spores of *Rhizopus* are contained in a structure called a:
(i) sporangium
(ii) gametangium
(iii) colony
(iv) apophysis

(c) *Rhizopus* is:
(i) autotrophic
(ii) parasitic
(iii) saprophytic
(iv) photosynthetic

(d) Yeast is:
(i) unicellular
(ii) a bacterium
(iii) multicelled
(iv) poisonous

Sample examination questions

Section A

15 The diagram shows a yeast cell which is undergoing asexual reproduction.

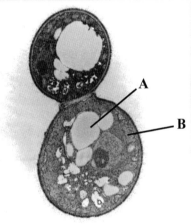

A.B. Dowsett/Science Photo Library

(a) Name A and B.

(b) What type of asexual reproduction is shown in the diagram?

(c) Which type of division, mitosis or meiosis, is involved in this form of reproduction?

(d) If yeast cells are kept under anaerobic conditions, alcohol (ethanol) and another substance are produced.
(i) What are anaerobic conditions?
(ii) Name the other substance produced.

(2006 OL Q 6)

Section B

16 (a) (i) Name a fungus, other than yeast, that you studied during your course.
(ii) Give one way in which the fungus that you have named in (i) differs from yeast.

(b) Answer the following questions in relation to your investigation of the growth of leaf yeast.
(i) It was necessary to use a nutrient medium. What is a nutrient medium?
(ii) Name the nutrient medium that you used.
(iii) The nutrient medium should be sterile. Explain the underlined term.
(iv) Describe, in words and/or labelled diagram(s), how you conducted the investigation.
(v) What was the result of your investigation?

(2007 HL Q 8)

17 It is important to use sterile apparatus when working with micro-organisms.

(a) (i) What is meant by sterile?
(ii) How may apparatus be sterilised?

(b) Answer the following questions about an investigation that you carried out to show the growth of leaf yeast.
(i) Name the container in which you grew the leaf yeast.
(ii) What was present in this container to provide food for the yeast?
(iii) Describe how you put leaf yeast into the container.
(iv) How long did it take for the leaf yeast to appear?
(v) Describe the appearance of the leaf yeast in the container.

(2008 OL Q 7)

Section C

18 The diagram shows part of the mycelium of *Rhizopus*.

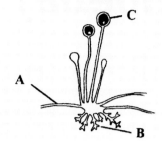

(i) Identify A, B, C.
(ii) State a function of B.
(iii) State a function of C.
(iv) What term is used to describe the nutrition of *Rhizopus*? Explain the importance of this type of nutrition in nature.
(v) To what kingdom does *Rhizopus* belong?
(vi) Name another organism that you have studied in your biology course that belongs to the same kingdom as *Rhizopus*.

(2005 OL Q 15c)

19 (i) Draw a labelled diagram to show the structure of *Rhizopus*.
(ii) *Rhizopus* uses both sexual and asexual reproduction. Give a brief account of its asexual reproduction, using diagrams.
(iii) The diagrams show stages of sexual reproduction of *Rhizopus*. Name the parts labelled A and B.
(iv) What is the function of B?

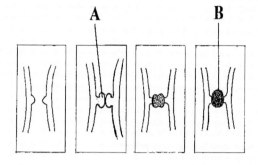

(2007 OL Q 13c)

20 Saprophytic and parasitic fungi are widespread in nature.
(i) Explain each of the underlined terms.
(ii) State a role of each of these types of fungus in the overall scheme of nature.
(iii) Give **one** example of a beneficial fungus and **one** example of a harmful fungus.
(iv) State a function for each of the following structures that are found in fungi: rhizoid, sporangium, gametangium, zygospore.

(2005 HL Q 15c)

Previous examination questions	
Ordinary level	**Higher level**
2003 Sample Q 15b	2003 Sample Q 8
2005 Q 15c	2004 Q 15c
2006 Q 6	2005 Q 9, 15c
2007 Q 13c	2006 Q 6c
2008 Q 7	2007 Q 8

*For latest questions go to **www.edco.ie/biology***

Chapter 23 **Protista (*Amoeba*)**

Introduction

Amoeba is in the kingdom Protista. It is a microscopic organism that lives at the bottom of shallow freshwater ponds and streams. (Other species of *Amoeba* are found in seawater.)

Each *Amoeba* consists of just a single cell. Each cell is about 0.1 mm in diameter (about five *Amoeba* cells would fit across the full stop at the end of this sentence).

Amoeba is a heterotroph (takes in food) and is omnivorous, i.e. it eats other single-celled protists, plants and animals.

It is important to realise that *Amoeba* can carry out all the life processes of larger organisms, even though it is only a single cell.

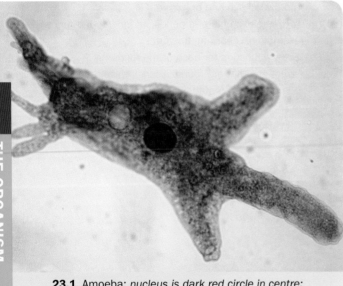

23.1 Amoeba: *nucleus is dark red circle in centre; contractile vacuole is lighter circle above left of nucleus*

Structure of *Amoeba*

The living material in the cell (protoplasm) is surrounded by a flexible membrane. The shape of the cell is constantly changing to allow it to move from place to place.

The nucleus can move about within the cytoplasm, which itself is constantly flowing within the cell.

The outer cytoplasm (ectoplasm) is clear and relatively stiff. The inner cytoplasm (endoplasm) is grainy due to food vacuoles and waste materials. The endoplasm is more fluid than the ectoplasm.

The endoplasm contains a variable number of food vacuoles, fat droplets and crystals of waste products. There is usually a single, large contractile vacuole present. Sometimes a number of these vacuoles are found.

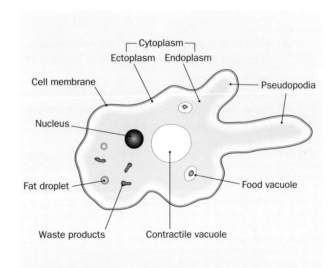

23.2 Structure of Amoeba

Functions of cell structures

- The cell membrane retains the cell contents in place. In addition, gases diffuse in and out through the cell membrane.
- The nucleus controls the cell.
- Food vacuoles secrete acids to kill the prey. They then produce enzymes to digest the prey. Digested material is absorbed from the food vacuole into the cytoplasm.
- The pseudopodia extend in the direction *Amoeba* wishes to move. The cytoplasm (in particular the endoplasm) moves or flows into the pseudopodia causing the cell to move. The pseudopodia are also used to surround (engulf) its prey.
- *Amoeba* lives in fresh water. This means its cytoplasm is more concentrated than its external environment. As a result water enters *Amoeba* by osmosis.
- The contractile vacuole collects water that enters *Amoeba*. It then expands, touches the cell membrane and bursts to expel the water. It is said to be responsible for osmoregulation. Without a contractile vacuole, *Amoeba* would expand and burst.

THE ORGANISM

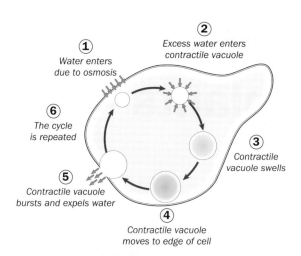

① Water enters due to osmosis
② Excess water enters contractile vacuole
③ Contractile vacuole swells
④ Contractile vacuole moves to edge of cell
⑤ Contractile vacuole bursts and expels water
⑥ The cycle is repeated

23.3 *Osmoregulation in* Amoeba

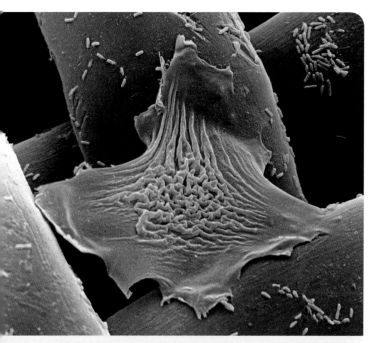

23.4 *An* Amoeba *and rod-shaped bacteria on a piece of nylon cloth (SEM)*

Plant and animal kingdoms

Chapter 21 dealt with organisms (bacteria) from the kingdom Monera. Chapter 22 dealt with organisms (fungi) from the kingdom fungi. This chapter deals with an organism (*Amoeba*) from the kingdom Protista.

The plant and animal kingdoms will be outlined by reference to flowering plants and humans in most of the following chapters.

Previous examination questions

Ordinary level	Higher level
2005 Q 6a	n/a

*For latest questions go to **www.edco.ie/biology***

Summary

Amoeba is in the kingdom Protista.
- The habitat for *Amoeba* is fresh water.
- The protoplasm consists of the nucleus and surrounding cytoplasm.
- The cytoplasm consists of the outer firm ectoplasm and the inner fluid endoplasm.
- The cell membrane retains the cell contents and allows for gas exchange.
- The nucleus controls the cell.
- The pseudopodia are used for movement and to engulf prey.
- The contractile vacuole eliminates water and prevents the cell from bursting.

Revision questions

1. (a) State the kingdom to which *Amoeba* belongs.
   (b) What are the main features of this kingdom?
   (c) Why is *Amoeba* considered to be a simple organism?
2. (a) Describe the typical (i) habitat, and (ii) size, of *Amoeba*.
   (b) Draw a large, labelled diagram of *Amoeba*.
3. Name the structures used by *Amoeba* for each of the following: (a) movement, (b) digestion, (c) water control, (d) absorbing oxygen, (e) controlling the cell.
4. State three differences in each case between *Amoeba* and (a) bacteria, (b) fungi.
5. Distinguish between:
   (a) ectoplasm and endoplasm
   (b) food vacuole and contractile vacuole.
6. (a) Name the five kingdoms of living things.
   (b) Name one type of organism that you are required to study from each phylum.

Sample examination questions

Section A

7. The diagram shows the structure of *Amoeba*.

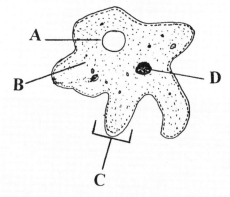

(i) Name A, B, C, D.
(ii) To which kingdom does *Amoeba* belong?

2005 OL Q 6a

THE ORGANISM

Chapter 24   Structure of flowering plants

Introduction

In Chapter 2 we saw that the need for organisation is one of the characteristics of life. Chapter 8 described how cells were organised into tissues, organs, organ systems and, finally, organisms. Chapter 4 showed that organisms are arranged into populations.

This chapter will examine the way in which flowering plants are organised.

External structure of a flowering plant

There are about 300 000 species of flowering plants (also called angiosperms). This section will deal with the general structure of a flowering plant such as a buttercup or wallflower. Generally these plants are composed of an underground root system and an overground shoot system.

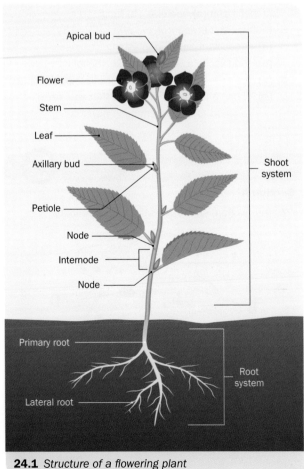

24.1 *Structure of a flowering plant*

Roots

TYPES OF ROOTS

Tap roots consist of a main root that develops from the initial root that emerged from the seed (called a radicle). This main root is called the primary or tap root.

Lateral or secondary roots emerge from the primary root. The tips of the lateral roots have thousands of tiny, invisible root hairs. Tap roots are present in most dicots, e.g. dandelion, wallflower, ash.

Fibrous roots form when the radicle dies away to leave a group of equal-sized roots. These roots emerge from the base of the stem. They are most common in monocots, e.g. grasses and daffodils.

Adventitious roots are roots that do not develop from the radicle. They are sometimes said to grow in strange places. Examples include fibrous roots, the roots at the base of an onion and the gripping roots of ivy.

FUNCTIONS OF ROOTS

Plant roots:

- anchor the plant in the soil
- absorb water and mineral salts from the soil – the root hairs carry out this function
- transport the absorbed materials to the shoots
- store food in some plants, e.g. carrots, turnips, radish

24.2 *Types of roots*

24.3 *Tap roots (left) and fibrous roots (right)*

THE ZONES IN A ROOT

If a root tip is examined it is seen to have four zones, each with a distinct function, as shown in Figure 24.4.

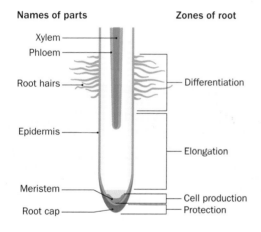

24.4 *Longitudinal section (LS) of root tip*

1 **Zone of protection.** The root cap protects the root cells as they push through the soil.
2 **Zone of cell production** or **meristematic zone.**

> A **meristem** is a plant tissue capable of mitosis.

Meristems allow plants to grow. **Apical meristems** are found in the root tip and in the shoot tip. Other meristems are found around the edge of some plant stems and in leaves and fruits.

Cells in the root meristem are constantly dividing by mitosis to produce new cells for root growth.

3 **Zone of elongation.** When new cells are formed by the meristem they are very small. In the zone of elongation, plant growth regulators (such as auxins) stimulate the cells to grow longer.

4 **Zone of differentiation.** In this region, the elongated cells, which are all similar or undifferentiated, develop into different types of tissues. These are:
  • **dermal tissue** (such as epidermis), which protects the plant
  • **ground tissue**, which is found between the dermal and vascular tissues
  • **vascular tissue** (such as xylem and phloem), which transports materials

These tissues are outlined more fully on the following page.

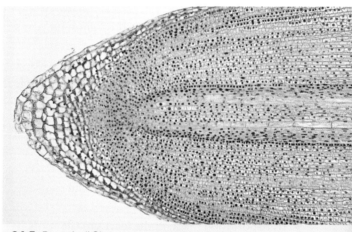

24.5 *Root tip (LS)*

Stems

The stem is the main part of the shoot. In herbaceous plants (e.g. daffodil) it is usually soft and green and does not contain wood. In woody plants (e.g chestnut tree) it is hard, woody and brown.

> **Herbaceous** plants do not contain wood (or lignin).
> **Woody** plants contain wood (or lignin).

The stem carries leaves, which emerge from points called **nodes**. The part of the stem between two nodes is called an internode.

The tip of the stem has a terminal or **apical bud** (from the Latin *apex*, meaning *tip*). This causes the stem to grow at the growing tip. If the growth tip is removed, a low bushy plant will form.

The **axil** is the angle between a leaf and a stem. Axillary or lateral buds are located at each axil. These buds produce new growth such as branches or flowers.

A **lenticel** is an opening for gas exchange found in the stems of plants such as trees and shrubs.

The structure of a typical shoot is shown in Figure 24.1.

THE ORGANISM

STEM IN WINTER

In winter a woody stem may appear as shown in Figure 24.6 below.

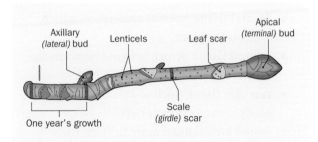

24.6 *Structure of a stem in winter*

The apical bud will produce the following year's growth. The scale scars mark the locations of previous apical buds. The distance between two sets of scale scars represents one year of growth. The leaf scars indicate where a leaf has fallen.

FUNCTIONS OF STEMS

Plant stems:

- support the aerial parts of the plant
- transport water and minerals from the roots to the leaves and flowers
- transport food made in the leaves to the roots
- carry out photosynthesis (when they are green)
- may store food

Leaves

LEAF STRUCTURE

Leaves are attached to stems at a node. The stalk of the leaf is called the petiole. Some leaves do not have a petiole (i.e. they are joined directly to the stem). Such leaves are said to be sessile.

The leaf is normally flattened into a thin leaf blade or lamina. The petiole continues through the lamina as the midrib. Veins emerge from the midrib and are clearly seen in the lamina. The petiole, midrib and veins contain transport tissues called xylem and phloem.

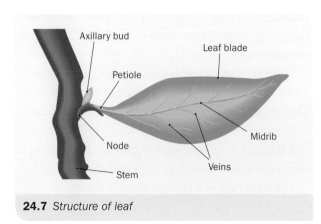

24.7 *Structure of leaf*

VENATION

The pattern of veins in a leaf is called venation. Two types of venation are common.

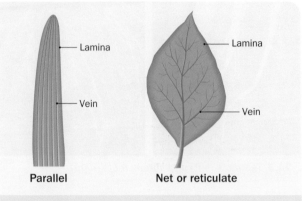

24.8 *Leaf venation*

1 **Parallel venation** means that the veins run alongside each other. This pattern is found in most monocots, e.g. grasses, daffodils and tulips.
2 **Net** or **reticulate venation** means that the veins form a branching network throughout the lamina. This pattern is most common in dicots, e.g. horse chestnut, rose and buttercup.

24.9 *A monocot leaf: parallel veins*

24.10 *A dicot leaf: note the branching veins*

FUNCTIONS OF LEAVES

- Leaves make food (i.e. carry out photosynthesis).
- Leaves exchange gases with the atmosphere. They take in carbon dioxide and release oxygen and water vapour.
- Leaves lose water (in a process called transpiration). This allows fresh water and mineral salts to be taken into the plant. It may also cool the plant.
- Leaves store food (this is why the leaves of plants such as grasses, lettuce and cabbage are often consumed by animals and humans).

Flowers

The structure and functions of flowers and their parts will be discussed in Chapter 40, *Sexual Reproduction in Flowering Plants*.

Tissues in flowering plants

When meristematic tissue divides, it produces new cells. Initially, these cells are unspecialised or undifferentiated.

They differentiate into three categories of plant tissue: dermal, ground and vascular tissue. These tissues are continuous throughout the plant, but their exact structure and arrangement may vary.

Dermal tissue

Dermal tissue forms the covering layer on a plant. In many respects it is similar to the skin of humans. It is normally called epidermis.

Its main function is to protect the plant. It may have secondary functions, depending on its location. For example, the root hairs are extensions of the epidermis at root tips and are designed to absorb water and minerals.

The epidermis of leaves and most stems is coated with a waxy cuticle to prevent water loss from the plant.

Ground tissue

Ground tissue occupies the area between the dermal and vascular tissues in a plant.

Ground tissue makes up most of the bulk of a young plant. It carries out a range of functions such as photosynthesis, storage of food and wastes, and gives strength and support to the plant.

Vascular tissue

Vascular tissue consists of xylem and phloem. The main function of vascular tissue is to transport materials throughout the plant. The two main vascular tissues are xylem and phloem.

XYLEM

Xylem is made up of two main types of cells, vessels and tracheids. The living contents of tracheids and vessels die before they reach maturity. For this reason, xylem is a dead tissue.

- *Appearance:* **Xylem tracheids** are long, tapering cells whose insides are hollow at maturity. They overlap and allow water to pass from tracheid to tracheid through thin parts of the wall called pits.

Tracheids are more primitive than vessels. They are the only type of xylem found in coniferous trees such as pine trees.

Xylem vessels are tubular structures formed when a number of cells join end-to-end. They are wider than tracheids and their end walls break down to form a continuous tube. They have pits in their side walls to allow water to pass from one vessel to another. They are more efficient at transporting water than tracheids and are very common in flowering plants.

Lignin is a hard, strong chemical. It is found in some plant cell walls and makes these walls very strong.

Both tracheids and vessels have thick, lignified (lignin-containing) cell walls. This gives them great strength. Lignin is laid down in definite patterns, the most common of which is spiral. Lignified xylem forms the wood in trees.

- *Function:* Xylem transports water and mineral salts from the roots to the leaves. It also gives mechanical support to the plant.
- *Location:* Xylem is found in roots, stems, leaves and flowers. It is usually found in vascular bundles (special groups of transporting cells).

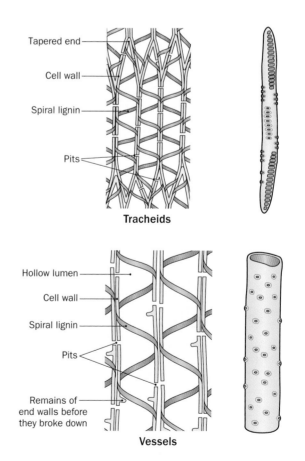

Tapered end

Cell wall

Spiral lignin

Pits

Tracheids

Hollow lumen

Cell wall

Spiral lignin

Pits

Remains of end walls before they broke down

Vessels

24.11 *LS of xylem*

PHLOEM

Phloem is mainly composed of sieve tubes and companion cells.

- *Appearance:* **Sieve tubes** are long, tubular structures. They form when individual cells, called sieve tube elements, join end-to-end.

    The end walls develop pores, which allow the passage of materials from one element to another. The end walls are called **sieve plates** because they resemble plates with numerous pores in them. The cytoplasm of each element remains, although the nucleus degenerates. The walls are made of cellulose, but lignin is not present.

    Each sieve tube element has an accompanying **companion cell** on its outside. These have a nucleus and dense cytoplasm. Phloem forms a living tissue because of the companion cells.

- *Function:* Sieve tubes transport food made by photosynthesis from the leaves to the rest of the plant. Companion cells control the activities of the sieve tube elements.

- *Location:* Phloem is found in the vascular bundles of roots, stems, leaves and flowers.

Main differences between xylem and phloem	
Xylem	**Phloem**
Carries water and minerals	Carries food
Is living	Has dead
Has lignin	No lignin
Has no companion cells	Has companion cells

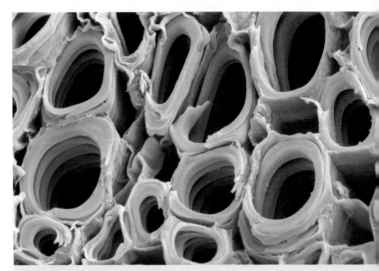

24.14 *Xylem in a stem (SEM)*

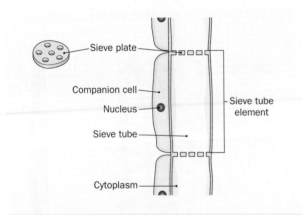

24.12 *LS of phloem*

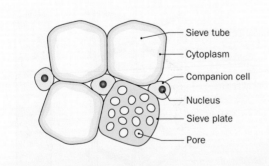

24.13 *TS of phloem*

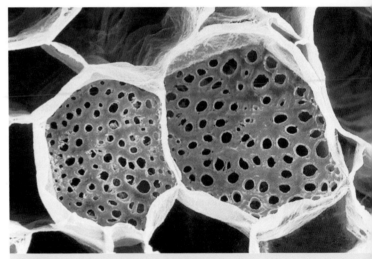

24.15 *TS of a plant stem, showing phloem sieve plates*

Location of plant tissues in roots, stems and leaves

Roots

In a longitudinal section of a root (as shown in Figure 24.4), the dermal tissue forms the epidermis and root hairs. The vascular tissue consists of the xylem and phloem in the centre of the root and the rest of the cells (apart from the meristem) make up the ground tissue.

    Figure 24.16 shows the arrangements of tissues in the transverse section (TS) of a root.

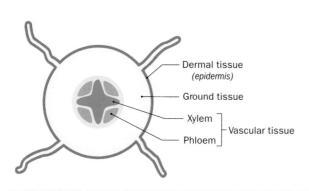

24.16 *TS of root*

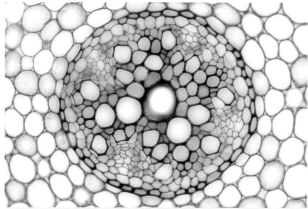

24.17 *TS of centre of a root: xylem is blue-green and phloem is pink*

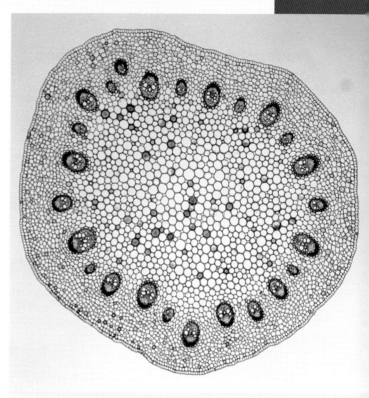

24.20 *Vascular bundles in a dicot stem*

Leaves

The location of the three plant tissues in the TS of a leaf is shown in Figure 24.21. A more detailed version of this diagram is shown in Figure 25.5.

Stems

The location of the three plant tissues in a stem LS and TS are shown in Figures 24.18 and 24.19.

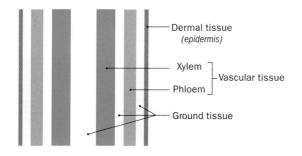

24.18 *LS of stem*

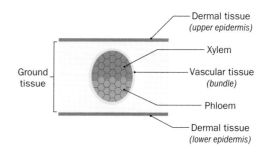

24.21 *TS of leaf showing plant tissues*

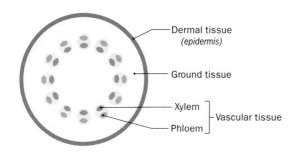

24.19 *TS of dicot stem*

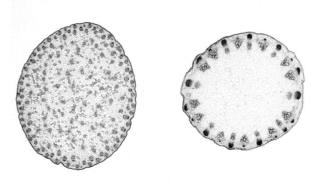

24.22 *Vascular bundles scattered in a monocot stem (left) and in a ring in a dicot stem (right)*

Monocotyledons and dicotyledons

Flowering plants are divided into two categories: monocotyledons and dicotyledons. These names are usually shortened to monocots and dicots.

Monocots include daffodils, tulips, grasses and cereals such as wheat and barley. Dicots include beans, peas, peanuts, sunflowers, roses and trees such as chestnut, oak and ash. There are greater numbers and varieties of dicots than there are of monocots.

24.23 *A dicot seed: note the two cotyledons in the seed at the top*

Monocot features

The following features are shown in Figure 24.24.

- Monocots take their name from the fact that they have one cotyledon in the seed. A **cotyledon** is a leaf in the seed (a seed leaf) specialised for food storage.
- Monocots are mostly **herbaceous** plants. This means they are soft, because they do not contain woody parts.
- Monocot leaves are long and narrow with veins that run parallel along the leaf (this is called parallel venation) as shown in Figs. 24.9 and 24.24.
- Monocot vascular bundles are scattered at random inside the stem.
- Monocot flowering parts are arranged in groups of three or multiples of three. For example there may be either three, six, nine etc. petals in the flower of a monocot.

Dicot features

Many of these features are shown in Figure 24.24.

- Dicots are so named because they have two cotyledons in each seed. See Figure 24.25.
- Dicots may be herbaceous (e.g. peas, sunflowers or tomatoes) or woody (roses, oak and ash trees).
- Dicot leaves are often broad and they have a network of veins (net venation), as seen in Figs. 24.10 and 24.24.
- The vascular bundles of dicots are arranged in a ring around the inside of the stem.
- Dicots' flowering parts are arranged in fours or fives, or multiples of these numbers.

MONOCOTS	DICOTS
Single cotyledon	Two cotyledons
Long, narrow leaf	Broad leaf
Veins are parallel	Network of veins
Vascular bundles scattered	Ring of vascular bundles
Flower parts in multiples of three	Flower parts in multiples of five (or four)

24.24 *Differences between monocots and dicots*

24.25 *Cotyledons are clearly visible when you eat peanuts. When the shell is cracked open each peanut is surrounded by a thin brown coat. When this is removed the peanut (which is really a seed) can be divided into two halves or cotyledons. In roasted peanuts the cotyledons have normally been separated in advance.*

Activity 17 *To prepare and examine a transverse section (TS) of a dicot stem*

1 Plants that are suitable for this purpose are celery (although celery is actually a petiole rather than a stem), busy Lizzy, begonia and sunflower. *(As these are herbaceous stems (i.e. non-woody) they are easier to cut.)*

2 Cut out a short section of the stem between two nodes using a scalpel or backed blade.

3 Wet the blade *(to reduce friction)* and cut thin sections of the stem *(cutting away from your fingers to prevent injury).*

4 Cut the sections at right angles to the stem (i.e. try and avoid wedge-shaped sections).

 If the stem is too soft and flexible, it can be placed into a slit that is cut in some elder pith or carrot, which can then be sectioned as shown in Figure 24.26.

5 Store the cut sections in a clock glass or petri dish of water *(to prevent them dehydrating).*

6 Transfer a thin section onto a microscope slide using a forceps or small paint brush.

7 Add a few drops of water and a cover slip at an angle *(to eliminate air bubbles).*

8 Observe the section under low power (× 100) and then under high power (× 400) of the microscope (as explained in Activities 6 and 7) and compare them to Figure 24.19.

9 Alternatively, the tissues can be stained after step 6. Suitable stains include iodine (stains starch a blue-black colour), anilinc sulfate (stains lignin yellow) or Schultz's solution (stains cellulose purple).

10 Draw a diagram of the TS of the stem. Label the position of the vascular tissue, dermal tissue and ground tissue.

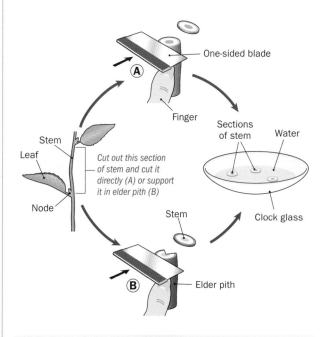

24.26 *Cutting sections of stem for microscopic investigation*

Summary

Flowering plants are divided into:
- underground root systems for anchorage and absorption of water and minerals
- overground shoot systems, which consist of stems, leaves and flowers

Roots can be:
- tap roots (where one main root grows down into the soil)
- fibrous roots (where a mass of small, branched roots emerge from the stem)

The zones in a root are:
- the zone of protection (root cap)
- the zone of cell production (meristem)
- the zone of elongation
- the zone of differentiation

The main functions of stems are:
- to support the aerial parts
- to transport materials to and from the leaves

Leaf venation (the pattern of veins on a leaf) is of two types:
- parallel (typical of monocots)
- reticulate or net (typical of dicots)

The main functions of leaves are:
- to make food
- to exchange gases
- to allow water loss (transpiration)

The three main categories of plant tissues are:
- dermal tissue (forms a protective covering layer)
- vascular tissue (xylem for water transport, phloem for food transport)
- ground tissue (found between the other two tissues, carrying out a range of functions)

Xylem is a dead tissue that transports water.

Phloem is a living tissue that transports food.

(continued overleaf)

Flowering plants are subdivided into monocots and dicots.

Monocots (such as daffodils and grasses) have:
- one seed leaf or cotyledon
- long, narrow leaves with parallel veins
- scattered vascular bundles in the stem
- flowering parts arranged in multiples of three

Dicots (such as beans and oak trees) have:
- two seed leaves or cotyledons
- broad leaves with a network of veins
- vascular bundles arranged in a ring in the stem
- flowering parts arranged in multiples of four or five

To prepare and examine a TS of a dicot stem:
- cut thin sections of a stem
- prepare a microscope slide using the sections
- examine the sections under low and then high power of the microscope
- draw a labelled diagram to show the three categories of tissue

Revision questions

1 (a) Arrange the following into the correct order, starting with the simplest: organ, cell, population, organ system, tissue, organism.
  (b) Give one example for four of these levels of organisation in a flowering plant.
2 (a) Name the parts labelled A to H on Figure 24.27.

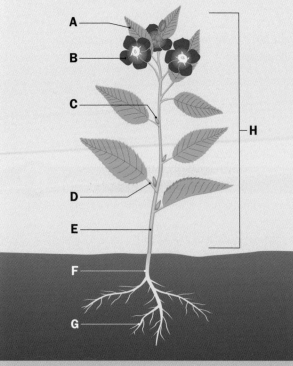

24.27

  (b) What evidence is there to suggest that this plant is: (i) photosynthetic or (ii) a dicot?
  (c) Describe the pattern of veins in the leaves.
  (d) Give the functions of the parts labelled A and C.
3 Distinguish between the following pairs of terms:
  (a) herbaceous and woody
  (b) node and internode
  (c) root and shoot
  (d) tap and fibrous roots

  (e) dermal and ground tissue
  (f) apical and axillary bud.
4 (a) What is meant by venation?
  (b) Draw labelled diagrams to show leaves with (i) parallel, and (ii) net, venation.
  (c) Name a plant with each type of venation.
5 Give one function for each of the following plant parts: (a) petiole, (b) apical bud, (c) root hairs, (d) stems, (e) leaf, (f) leaf blade, (g) meristem.
6 Plants have three main types of tissue.
  (a) Name the three plant tissues.
  (b) State one location in a root for each tissue.
  (c) State one function for each tissue.
  (d) Draw a TS of a stem to show the locations of these tissues.
7 (a) Name the zones of the root labelled A, B, C and D on Figure 24.28.

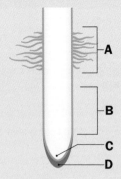

24.28

  (b) Which of the labelled parts do you associate with (i) absorption of water, (ii) the formation of xylem and phloem, (iii) mitosis, (iv) cells becoming longer?
8 (a) Name two types of vascular tissue in plants.
  (b) State the function of each of these tissues.

9 Distinguish between xylem vessels, xylem tracheids, phloem sieve tube cells and phloem companion cells in terms of:
   (a) whether they are living or dead
   (b) their functions
   (c) whether they have lignin or not
   (d) whether they have pits or not
   (e) whether they are tapered or not.

10 (a) Name a monocot plant.
   (b) Which of the leaves X or Y in Figure 24.29 is typical of a monocot?

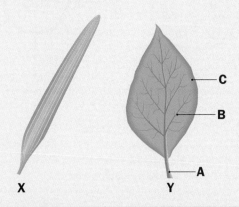

24.29

   (c) Name the parts A, B and C of leaf Y.
   (d) Name the type of venation shown by each of the leaves.
   (e) Draw a labelled diagram to show the arrangement of vascular bundles in a TS of the stem of plant X.

11 When examining the TS of a stem under a microscope, give one reason for each of the following:
   (a) wetting the blade or scalpel
   (b) cutting very thin sections of the stem
   (c) storing the cut sections under water
   (d) cutting the sections at 90° to the stem
   (e) adding the cover slip at an angle.

12 Choose which of the options (i), (ii), (iii) or (iv) represents the correct answer in each case below.
   (a) Fibrous roots are found in:
      (i) wheat
      (ii) dandelions
      (iii) carrots
      (iv) ash trees
   (b) Petioles are attached to:
      (i) petals
      (ii) phloem
      (iii) leaves
      (iv) internodes
   (c) Which of the following transports food?
      (i) xylem vessel
      (ii) phloem companion cell
      (iii) xylem tracheid
      (iv) phloem sieve cell
   (d) The tissue that transports water in a plant is called:
      (i) ground tissue
      (ii) epidermal tissue
      (iii) xylem
      (iv) phloem
   (e) Which of these cells contains lignin?
      (i) companion cells
      (ii) xylem vessels
      (iii) meristematic cells
      (iv) epidermis cells

Sample examination questions

Section A

13 The diagram represents a tomato plant.

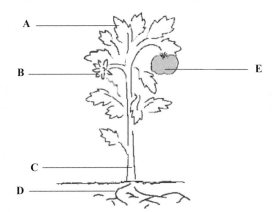

   (a) Name the parts labelled B, C and E.
   (b) Give one main function each for the parts labelled A and D.
   (c) What is the role of part E?
   (d) Name the tube-like tissue found in part C in which water moves through the plant.

(2007 OL Q 5)

THE ORGANISM

14 The diagrams represent two forms of a vascular plant tissue, as seen under the microscope.

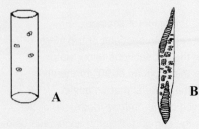

(a) Name this vascular tissue

(b) Identify the two forms of this tissue.

(c) The walls of A and B are reinforced with a hard material. Name this material.

(d) Where precisely is this vascular tissue found in the stem of a young dicotyledonous plant?

(e) Name another vascular tissue.   *(2007 HL Q 6)*

Section B

15 (a) Observation of a transverse section of a dicotyledonous stem reveals vascular and other tissues. Name **two** of the tissues that are not vascular tissues.

(b) Answer the following questions in relation to the preparation of a microscope slide of a transverse section of a dicotyledonous stem.

   (i) State **one** reason why you used an herbaceous stem rather than a woody one.

   (ii) Explain how you cut the section.

   (iii) Why is it desirable to cut the section as thinly as possible?

   (iv) Draw a diagram of the section as seen under the microscope. Label the vascular tissues that can be seen.

   (v) State one precise function of each of the vascular tissues labelled in your diagram.

(2008 HL Q 8)

Section C

16 (i) What is meant by ground tissue?

(ii) Give a function of ground tissue.

(iii) What is a meristem?

(iv) Give a location for a meristem.

(v) The diagram shows a transverse section through part of a plant. Is this part the root or the stem? Give **two** reasons for your answer.

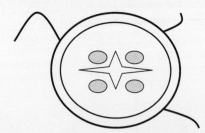

(vi) Copy the diagram into your answer book. Place an X where you would find vascular tissue and place a Y where you would find ground tissue.

(2007 OL Q 14a)

17 (i) Which of the two diagrams 1 or 2 represents a transverse section of a young root?

(ii) State **two** features of the diagram that indicate it is a root.

(iii) The letters A, B, C in the diagram represent three different tissue types. State which tissue type in the following list is represented by each letter: ground tissue, vascular tissue, dermal tissue.

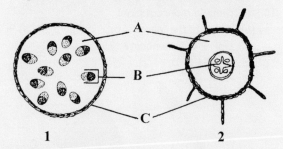

(iv) Name **two** vascular tissues and give **one** way in which they differ.

(v) State a function of ground tissue.

(2005 OL Q 15a)

18 The diagram shows part of a transverse section through a dicotyledonous stem.

(i) Copy the diagram into your answer book and identify each of the following by placing the appropriate letter on your diagram:
phloem P,
ground tissue G, xylem X,
dermal tissue D.

(ii) In which of the tissues that you have identified are sugars mainly transported?

(iii) State a function of D.

(iv) In the course of your practical work you cut and observed a transverse section of a stem. Answer the following in relation to that procedure.

   1. What did you use to cut the section?

   2. How did you support the stem while you were cutting the section?

   3. How did you transfer the section to a microscope slide?

(v) State one way in which a transverse section through a monocotyledonous stem differs from the one that you cut.

(2006 HL Q 14)

Previous examination questions	
Ordinary level	**Higher level**
2003 Sample Q 12	2004 Q 8
2005 Q 15c	2005 Q 3ii
2005 Q 15a	2006 Q 14c
2006 Q 14a, 14b	2007 Q 6
2007 Q 5, 14a	2008 Q 8

For latest questions go to www.edco.ie/biology

THE ORGANISM

Chapter 25 Transport, food storage and gas exchange in flowering plants

The need for a transport system in plants

Plants make their own food in the process of photosynthesis. Organisms that make their own food are said to be autotrophic.

Metabolism refers to all the reactions in an organism. Plant metabolism refers to reactions such as photosynthesis and respiration, and to reactions that occur in other processes such as cell division, growth and reproduction.

To allow these processes to occur, plants need to be able to acquire and transport water, carbon dioxide, oxygen and certain minerals. The following sections will deal with how plants acquire and transport these materials.

25.1 *Root hairs greatly increase the surface area of the root for uptake of water and nutrients.*

Water uptake by roots

Many root hairs are found near the tip of small roots.

Root hairs are extensions of root epidermis cells and have thin walls that are not covered by a cuticle. For these reasons they are suited to absorption.

The large number of root hairs increases the surface area over which absorption can take place.

Roots are greatly assisted in this absorption by the presence of fungal hyphae, which project out of the roots. These fungi do not harm plants but increase the surface area for the absorption of water and minerals, which they pass on to the plant.

The absorption of water into root hairs takes place by osmosis.

Osmosis

Soil particles are enclosed by a layer of relatively pure water called capillary water. The cytoplasm of root hairs contains many dissolved solutes. This means that the cytoplasm is more concentrated than the water in the soil. As a result, water enters the cytoplasm of the root hairs by osmosis.

Movement of water into xylem

Water diffuses from the root hair cells into the ground tissue (which in this location is called cortex). It continues to diffuse across the ground tissue until it reaches the xylem in the centre of the root. See Figure 25.2 overleaf.

Xylem vessels form a continuous hollow pipeline from the roots to all parts of the plant. In particular, water can flow in xylem from the roots, up through the stem, into the petiole and from there into the leaves.

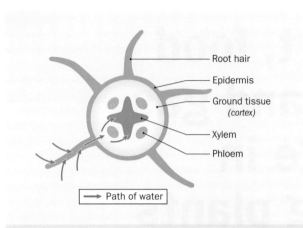

25.2 *Transverse section (TS) of a root to show the movement of water*

Upward movement of water

There are two mechanisms that combine to cause the movement of water from the roots to the upper parts of a plant: root pressure and transpiration.

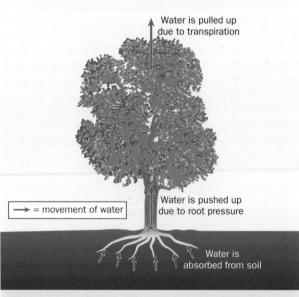

25.3 *Reasons for the upward movement of water in plants*

Root pressure

When water is drawn into roots by osmosis, the build-up of water causes a pressure. Root pressure pushes water up through the xylem.

However, root pressure does not fully explain how water rises in stems, especially in very tall trees. Root pressure has been measured and it is not strong enough to push water to the top of very high plants. Also, root pressure is very low in summer, yet this is when most water passes up through the stem.

25.4 *A cut stem showing the effect of root pressure, which is forcing water out of the cut end*

Transpiration

Transpiration is the loss (by evaporation) of water vapour from the leaves and other aerial parts of a plant.

Most transpiration takes place through openings called stomata (singular, stoma) on the underside of the leaf; see Figure 25.5.

Water evaporates from the ground tissue in the leaf into the air spaces. From the air spaces it diffuses out into the atmosphere through the stomata.

When the cells in the ground tissue lose water in this way they become less swollen and less turgid. As a result, they become more concentrated than the xylem cells. This means that water passes from the xylem into the ground tissue due to an osmotic gradient.

As each water molecule is 'pulled' from the xylem cells by osmosis it pulls the next water molecule. This pulling force is transmitted from water molecule to water molecule all the way down the stem and into the root. In this manner water is said to be pulled up through the plant by transpiration.

Transpiration exerts a pulling force. The upward pull of water due to transpiration is similar to the way water (or any other liquid) is sucked up through a drinking straw.

THE ORGANISM

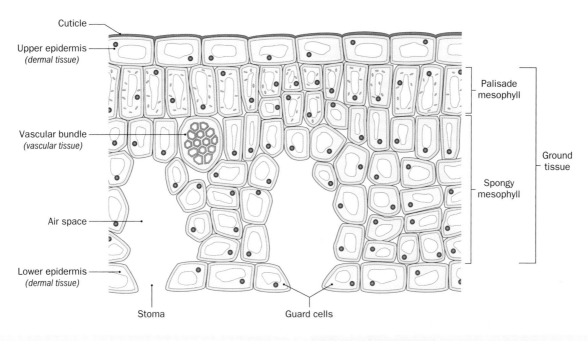

Cuticle

Upper epidermis
(dermal tissue)

Palisade
mesophyll

Vascular bundle
(vascular tissue)

Ground
tissue

Spongy
mesophyll

Air space

Lower epidermis
(dermal tissue)

Stoma

Guard cells

25.5 *Transverse section of a leaf*

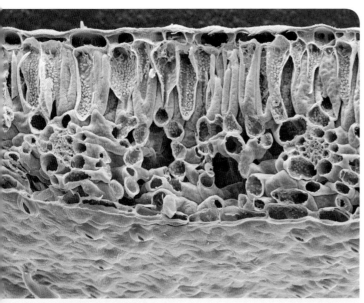

25.6 *TS of a leaf*

Control of transpiration in leaves

Leaves may lose more than their weight in water each day due to transpiration. If they do not replace this water they will wilt and may die. At certain times, especially in dry weather, plants may find it difficult to absorb water from the soil.

To prevent wilting it is necessary for plants to reduce their rate of transpiration. They can do this in the following ways.

- Leaves have a waxy cuticle through which water cannot pass. The cuticle is normally thicker on the upper surface of the leaf because more water can evaporate from the upper surface of a leaf

than from the lower surface. The cuticle does not cover the stomata on the lower surface of the leaf.

- Stomata are normally located on the lower surface of a leaf. This helps to reduce water loss by transpiration because the rate of evaporation is higher on the upper surface than on the lower surface.

- Each stoma is surrounded by two guard cells. The guard cells can open or close the stoma by changing shape.

    Normally stomata are open by day. This allows the leaf to exchange gases for photosynthesis during the day.

    Stomata generally close at night. This helps to reduce water loss from the leaves at night, when gas exchange is not necessary because there is no photosynthesis in the dark.

However, environmental conditions can cause stomata to close during the day. This happens due to the following conditions: (a) if the plant loses too much water, (b) high temperatures and (c) high wind.

In these cases the rate of transpiration is too great. By closing the stomata the plant reduces water loss.

In dry conditions (drought) the stomata will remain closed for much of the time. This is why food crop yields are normally substantially reduced in dry weather.

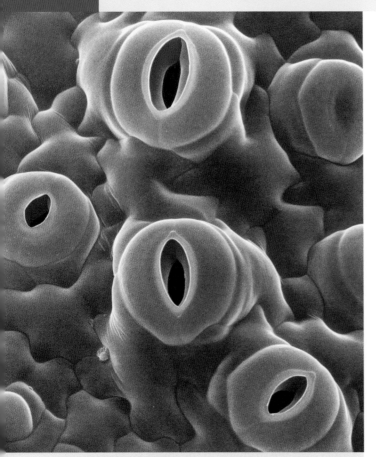

25.7 *Stomata (SEM)*

THE ORGANISM

Mineral uptake and transport

Plants require a variety of minerals to function normally. The functions of calcium and magnesium were outlined in Chapter 3. These minerals exist in the soil, dissolved in water. Minerals such as these, along with nitrates, phosphates and potassium ions, enter the root hairs from the soil, dissolved in water.

The entry of minerals into a root hair requires energy. Root hairs contain many mitochondria to supply this energy. Minerals enter root hairs by a process called **active transport**.

Once inside the root, the minerals are transported to all parts of the plant dissolved in water. This means that minerals (along with water) are transported throughout the plant by xylem.

Uptake and transport of carbon dioxide

Photosynthesis takes place mostly in the mesophyll cells of the leaf (both palisade and spongy mesophyll). There are two sources of carbon dioxide for photosynthesis.

- Most of the carbon dioxide comes in through the stomata from the atmosphere. This carbon dioxide diffuses into the air spaces in the leaf.

From here it diffuses into the photosynthesising cells in the ground tissue of the leaf. The rate of absorption or uptake of carbon dioxide is a measure of the *apparent* rate of photosynthesis.

- Carbon dioxide is produced in leaf cells by the process of respiration. This carbon dioxide may also be used in photosynthesis.

The production of carbon dioxide in this way is more substantial at higher temperatures due to increased rates of respiration at these temperatures.

The real or true rate of photosynthesis is calculated by combining the carbon dioxide taken in through the stomata with the carbon dioxide formed in respiration.

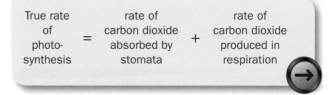

The fate of the products of photosynthesis

The leaf is the main photosynthetic organ in a flowering plant. Photosynthesis takes place in the chlorophyll containing cells of the leaf. Chlorophyll is contained in chloroplasts and these are mostly located in the ground tissue or mesophyll of the leaf.

- Oxygen produced in photosythesis can diffuse into the air spaces of the leaf. Oxygen can then diffuse out through the stomata into the atmosphere.

However, some of the oxygen formed in photosynthesis can be used in leaf cells for respiration.

- Glucose is the main carbohydrate produced in photosynthesis. Glucose may be used immediately for respiration, or converted to starch for storage. Some of this starch is stored in leaf cells, especially the spongy mesophyll cells.

Starch stored in leaves is an important part of the diet of leaf-eating animals such as horses, cattle, sheep, monkeys and apes.

Some of the glucose formed in photosynthesis is converted to another carbohydrate called sucrose (which is table sugar).

Sucrose enters the phloem sieve tube cells in the leaf and is then transported throughout the plant. The solution of sugary water carried in phloem is called phloem sap.

The precise mechanism(s) by which food moves in phloem are not yet fully known.

Phloem carries food to all parts of the plant. For example, some of the food is sent to the growth areas of the plant. These growth areas can include buds, leaves, stems, roots or flowers. The food can then be used for respiration, to form new structures in the plant or it can be stored as starch.

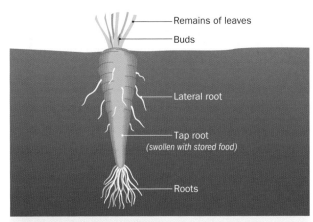

25.9 *Modified root of carrot*

Modified stem

Potato plants produce an underground stem system. The tips of some of these underground stems become swollen with stored starch. These swollen tips are called stem **tubers**. The standard edible potato is a modified stem or stem tuber.

In nature a potato tuber would remain dormant in the soil over winter. The following spring the tuber would grow to form a new potato plant. To allow this to happen, potato tubers have buds, which form part of the 'eye' of the potato.

Cultivated potato tubers are removed from the soil at the end of their first year of growth. This prevents their food from being used up the following year.

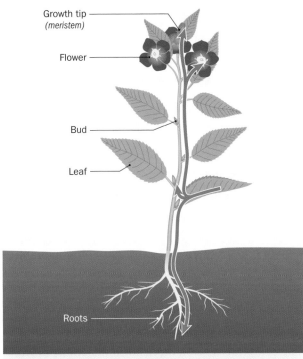

25.8 *Transport of food in phloem*

Food storage organs in plants

Plants can alter or modify their roots, stems and leaves to act as food storage organs.

Modified root

Some dicots produce a large, V-shaped root that penetrates deep down into the soil. This **tap root** serves to anchor the plant and to absorb water deeper in the soil.

In some plants, such as carrots, turnips and sugar beet, the tap root becomes swollen and fleshy with stored food. The stored food is used in the following year to produce flowers, seeds and fruits.

To prevent the food from being used up in this way, these tap root crops are harvested at the end of their first year of growth.

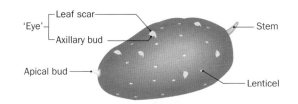

25.10 *Modified stem (potato tuber)*

25.11 *Enlarged brown lenticels on the surface of a potato*

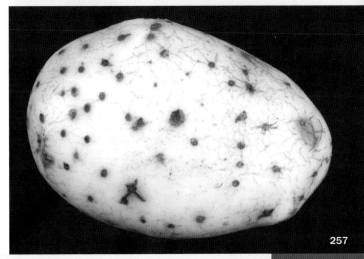

THE ORGANISM

Modified leaves

Plants such as onions, daffodils and tulips produce bulbs. A **bulb** contains an underground stem that is reduced in size. Swollen fleshy leaves, which are modified to store food, are attached to this stem.

The fleshy leaves surround a central apical bud. A number of lateral or axillary buds are located where the leaves meet the reduced stem. The entire bulb is protected by old, dry, scaly leaves on the outside.

Note that celery and rhubarb are leaf petioles that are modified to store food.

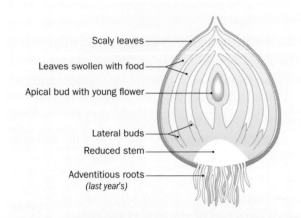

Scaly leaves

Leaves swollen with food

Apical bud with young flower

Lateral buds

Reduced stem

Adventitious roots
(last year's)

25.12 *An onion bulb (showing modified leaves)*

Did you know?

Although onion bulbs are edible, the bulbs of daffodils and tulips are poisonous. This is an adaptation to prevent them from being eaten by organisms while in the ground.

25.13 *Cross-section of a red onion*

The cohesion–tension model of water transport in xylem

Introduction

Some plants have to move large amounts of water very rapidly from their roots to their leaves. For example, in warm conditions a large tree may lose 200 litres of water in an hour. The rate at which this water flows up through the tree is in excess of 15 metres per hour.

As mentioned earlier, water moves up through a flowering plant partly by being pushed up by root pressure, but mostly by being pulled up due to transpiration. The cohesion–tension model explains how water is transported in plants to great heights against the force of gravity.

The cohesion–tension method was first put forward in 1894 by two Irish scientists, Henry Dixon (1869–1953) and John Joly (1857–1933), working in Trinity College, Dublin. It is now thought to be the main mechanism for the upward movement of water in plants.

Cohesion is the sticking of similar molecules to each other. Water has a high cohesion, i.e. water molecules tend to stick together.

Adhesion occurs when different molecules stick together. Water adheres to the walls of xylem, but this force is not as great as the cohesive forces of water.

Outline of the cohesion–tension model

The cohesion–tension model of water transport in xylem can be outlined as follows:

1 Water evaporates from the xylem into the air spaces of the leaf (and eventually out of the stomata into the air).

As transpiration pulls each water molecule out of the xylem, the next water molecule is pulled with it, due to their high **cohesion**. This is comparable to sucking water up through a straw.

Provided there is a continuous column of water in a xylem tube, this pull will be transmitted through the water right down the stem to the root. The ability of water to be pulled upwards in this way only works in narrow tubes such as xylem.

THE ORGANISM

2 When water molecules are pulled in this way the entire column of water in the xylem is stretched (like a piece of elastic). The water in the xylem is said to be under **tension**.

   The cohesive forces between the water molecules are great enough to hold water molecules in a column without breaking, even when tension is applied.

3 The tension in the xylem due to transpiration is great enough to pull water to a height of approximately 150 metres. As the tallest trees are only about 100 metres high, the cohesion–tension model can easily account for the upward movement of water in plants.

4 Stomata open in daylight and transpiration occurs. The tension produced in the water column causes xylem to become narrower. This in turn causes stems to become slightly narrower by day.

   To prevent xylem cells collapsing inwards, each xylem cell is strengthened with lignin. Wood is a mixture of cellulose and lignin.

5 When transpiration stops (i.e. at night when the stomata close), the lack of tension allows the xylem to return to its original wider shape. This happens due to the elasticity of the xylem walls.

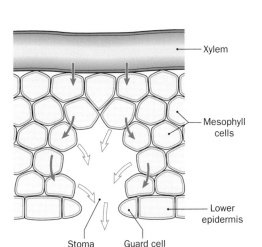

25.14 *Water movement in a leaf*

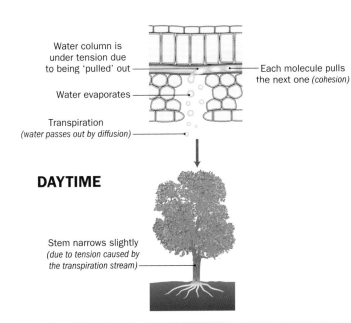
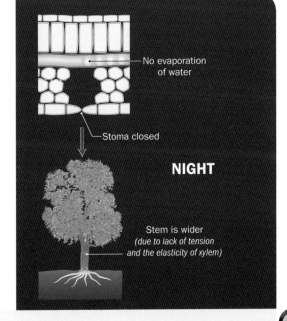

25.15 *Water movement in a leaf by day and by night*

THE ORGANISM

Gas exchange in the leaf

Carbon dioxide

Plants require carbon dioxide for photosynthesis. Carbon dioxide diffuses from the atmosphere into leaves through the stomata located on the lower surface of the leaf. The function of the stomata is gas exchange.

The underside of a leaf normally contains a huge number of stomata; many leaves have about 50 000 stomata per cm^2. The large number of stomata increase the rate of gas exchange.

Once inside the leaf, carbon dioxide diffuses to the mesophyll cells through the air spaces between these cells (intercellular air spaces).

The air spaces increase the internal surface area of the leaf. In most leaves the internal surface area is about 20 times greater than the outer, visible surface area of the leaf. The increased surface area allows carbon dioxide to diffuse more readily into the mesophyll cells.

Oxygen

Photosynthesis produces glucose and oxygen. Oxygen diffuses from the mesophyll cells, into the intercellular air spaces and out of the leaf through the stomata.

When the Earth was formed as a planet, the atmosphere did not contain any oxygen, i.e. it was anaerobic. Oxygen now makes up about 20% of the atmosphere. This oxygen has been produced by plants in photosynthesis and released out of the stomata.

Water vapour

Water vapour also diffuses out of the leaf through the stomata. The loss of water vapour from a plant is called transpiration.

Each stoma is enclosed by a pair of guard cells. The guard cells can open or close the stoma.

In general, stomata are open by day (to allow gas exchange for photosynthesis) and closed at night (to reduce water loss).

Gas exchange in stems

Cells on the inside of the stems (or trunks) of trees and shrubs require oxygen for respiration. In addition, they produce carbon dioxide as a result of respiration. Normally the epidermis or bark does not permit the passage of gases in or out of the stem.

> **Lenticels** are openings in the stems of plants that allow gas exchange.

Normally oxygen diffuses inwards through a lenticel; carbon dioxide and water vapour diffuse outwards.

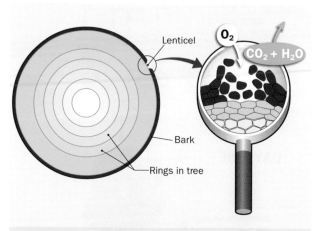

25.17 *TS of a stem of a tree (showing gas exchange in a lenticel)*

25.18 *Lenticels on birch bark*

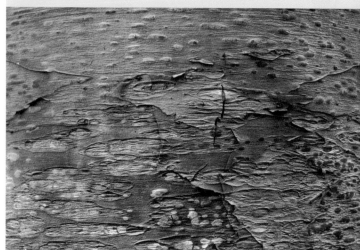

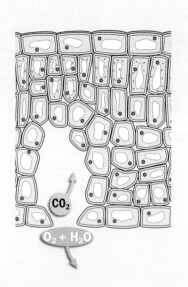

25.16 *Transverse section of a leaf (showing gas exchange in daylight)*

Stomatal opening and closing

Each stoma is enclosed by a pair of kidney-shaped guard cells. The guard cells open and close the stoma by changing shape.

The walls of the guard cells are especially thickened on the insides. This causes the cells to curve when they absorb water and swell.

When water enters the guard cells by osmosis, they become swollen or turgid. The guard cells are joined at their tips. The increase in size of the guard cells causes them to buckle outwards. The gap between them (which is the stoma) increases in size.

When the guard cells lose water they shrink in size. This causes the gap between them (the stoma) to close.

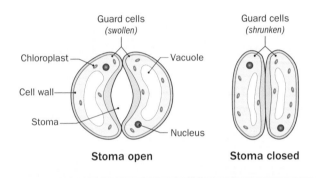

25.19 *Stomatal opening and closing (as viewed from the underside of a leaf)*

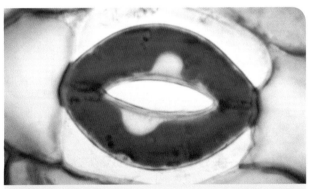

25.20 *An open stoma*

25.21 *A closed stoma*

Control of stomatal opening and closing

A major factor in the process of stomatal opening and closing is the concentration of carbon dioxide in the air spaces of the leaf.

HIGH CONCENTRATION OF CO_2

High levels of carbon dioxide in the air spaces cause the stomata to close.

The rate of photosynthesis falls in the evenings due to decreasing light intensity. As the rate of photosynthesis reduces, less carbon dioxide is absorbed by mesophyll cells. In fact, respiration in these cells may increase the level of carbon dioxide. This means that carbon dioxide levels can build up in the air spaces. As a result the stomata close in the evenings.

LOW CONCENTRATION OF CO_2

Low levels of carbon dioxide cause the stomata to open. In the mornings photosynthesis resumes in the leaf. The level of carbon dioxide falls because it is absorbed by the mesophyll cells. This results in the stomata opening.

If a plant is placed into a dark chamber with no carbon dioxide present, the stomata will open. This shows that carbon dioxide levels (and not light) trigger stomatal opening.

> High concentration of CO_2 ⟶ stomata close
> Low concentration of CO_2 ⟶ stomata open

The exact mechanism responsible for stomatal opening and closing is not yet certain. Although carbon dioxide levels play a major role in the process, other factors may be involved.

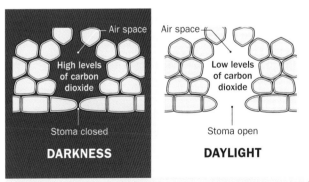

25.22 *CO_2 levels controlling stomatal opening*

THE ORGANISM

THE ORGANISM

Summary

Plants make their own food and are autotrophic.

Plants need to transport:
- water
- carbon dioxide
- oxygen
- minerals for their metabolism

Root hairs absorb water by osmosis.

Minerals dissolved in water are absorbed into roots by active transport and transported in xylem.

Water diffuses from root hairs into root xylem.

Xylem vessels transport water from the roots to all parts of the plant.

The transport of water in a plant is caused by:
- root pressure, which pushes water up from the roots
- transpiration (the loss of water from a plant), which pulls water out of the leaves.

The loss of water from leaves is controlled by:
- a waterproof cuticle covering the top and bottom of leaves
- stomata being on the lower surface of a leaf
- the closing of the stomata at night, and during the day when transpiration rates are high

Carbon dioxide for photosynthesis can be:
- absorbed from the atmosphere through the stomata
- obtained from respiration in leaf cells

Photosynthesis mainly takes place in the chlorophyll containing ground tissue
- in the mesophyll (both palisade and spongy mesophyll) of the leaf

The products of photosynthesis are glucose and oxygen.

Oxygen formed by photosynthesis may:
- diffuse out through the stomata
- be used by leaf cells for respiration

Glucose formed in photosynthesis may be:
- used directly in respiration
- stored as starch
- transported around the plant as sucrose in phloem sieve tubes

Modified plant food storage organs include:
- modified roots such as carrot tap roots
- modified stems such as potato tubers
- modified leaves such as those found in onion bulbs

The function of stomata is gas exchange.
- Carbon dioxide diffuses inwards through the stomata in daylight.
- Oxygen and water vapour diffuse outwards through the stomata during daylight.

Air spaces increase the surface area for gas exchange inside a leaf.

Lenticels are openings in the stems of plants for gas exchange.

Guard cells change shape to open and close the stoma:
- When the guard cells are full of water they swell to open the stoma.
- When the guard cells lose water they shrink to close the stoma.

High levels of carbon dioxide (at night) cause the stomata to close. (H)

Low levels of carbon dioxide (by day) cause the stomata to open.
- Carbon dioxide is a controlling factor in gas exchange in leaves.

The main method by which water rises in plants is the cohesion–tension model.
- Cohesion means similar molecules sticking together (water has a high cohesion).
- Adhesion means different molecules sticking together (water and xylem have a lower adhesion).
- Water is pulled out of xylem (and leaves) because it evaporates into the air (i.e. transpiration).
- Each water molecule pulls the next one behind it, creating tension in the xylem.
- This tension is caused by transpiration.
- The tension is transmitted down to the root xylem due to cohesion between water molecules.
- Tension in the water column causes xylem to become narrow during transpiration.
- When transpiration stops, xylem cells return to their normal wider shape, due to the elasticity of their walls.

Lignin prevents xylem from collapsing inwards. (H)

Revision questions

1 (a) Name four substances transported by plants.
  (b) For each substance named state:
    (i) where it originates,
    (ii) a place to where it is transported.
2 (a) List three adaptations of root hairs for maximum absorption.
  (b) Name the process by which water enters root hairs.
  (c) Name the process responsible for the movement of water from root hairs to root xylem.
3 Draw a labelled diagram of the TS of a root to show:
  (a) where water enters the root
  (b) the position of the vascular tissue in the root
  (c) the path of water across the root.
4 (a) What is transpiration?
  (b) Name two adaptations of leaves to reduce the rate of transpiration.
  (c) Distinguish between transpiration and root pressure.
5 The apparatus shown in Figure 25.23 was set up to investigate water movement in a dicot plant.

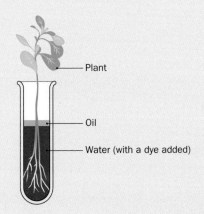

- Plant
- Oil
- Water (with a dye added)

25.23

  (a) Why is a dye added to the water?
  (b) What is the purpose of the oil layer?
  (c) What will happen to the level of water in the test tube? Give a reason for your answer.
  (d) Draw simple diagrams to show the areas where the dye will appear in a TS of (i) the root, and (ii) the stem, of this plant.
6 Name two forces responsible for the movement of water against the force of gravity in a plant.
7 (a) Name two minerals required by plants.
  (b) Give one function for each of these minerals in plants.
  (c) How do these minerals enter a plant?
  (d) State how these minerals get into a leaf.
8 Give two possible fates for each of the following:
  (a) carbon dioxide produced in respiration in leaves
  (b) oxygen formed in photosynthesis in leaves
  (c) glucose formed in photosynthesis in leaves.

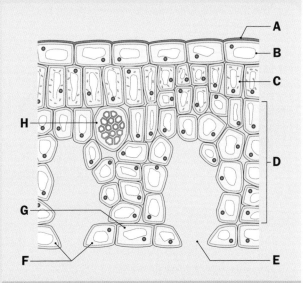

A, B, C, D, E, F, G, H

25.24

9 (a) Name the parts labelled A to H in Figure 25.24.
  (b) Which labelled part(s) represent (i) dermal, (ii) ground, (iii) vascular tissue?
  (c) In which labelled parts does photosynthesis take place?
  (d) In which labelled parts are chloroplasts mostly found?
10 Give one reason for each of the following.
  (a) Chloroplasts are mostly concentrated near the upper surface of a leaf.
  (b) There are no stomata on the upper surface of most leaves.
  (c) Stomata tend to open during the day.
  (d) Stomata close at night.
  (e) Air spaces are located directly over stomata.
  (f) Leaves have a cuticle but roots do not.
  (g) Stomata are enclosed by guard cells.
  (h) Leaves contain veins.
11 Draw labelled diagrams of (a) a root, (b) a stem and (c) leaves, modified for food storage.
12 (a) Who first proposed the cohesion–tension model of water movement in xylem?
  (b) Is this model a push or a pull effect? Explain your answer.
13 Explain, giving examples, the difference between cohesion and adhesion.
14 Why must the water column be continuous for the cohesion–tension model to work?
15 In the cohesion–tension model, explain what causes:
  (a) the tension
  (b) the xylem to become narrow
  (c) the xylem to become wider again
  (d) the xylem not to collapse inwards.

THE ORGANISM

263

16 The diameter of a tree trunk was measured and found to vary as shown by the graph in Figure 25.25. The time between X_1 and X_2 represents 24 hours.

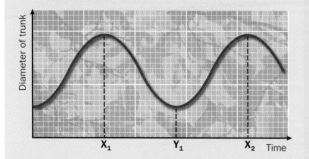

25.25

(a) What time of day is represented by X_1 and Y_1?
(b) Describe the results shown in the graph.
(c) What causes the changes in the diameter of the trunk?

17 (a) Name the tissue responsible for carrying food in plants.
(b) Name the carbohydrate that is normally carried in this tissue.
(c) Give one example in each case of food moving (i) downwards, and (ii) upwards, in plants.

18 Name the carbohydrate used by plants for:
(a) respiration, (b) storage, (c) cell walls.

19 (a) Why does a leaf require carbon dioxide?
(b) Why do leaves produce oxygen?
(c) How do these gases get in and out of leaves?

20 Name two structures in plants whose function is gas exchange.

21 (a) Draw labelled diagrams to show the structure of the guard cells (i) in bright light, (ii) in darkness.
(b) What causes the change in size of the guard cells?

22 (a) Why is the level of carbon dioxide in the air spaces of a leaf (i) high at night, (ii) low by day?
(b) What are the results on stomatal opening or closing of (i) high, and (ii) low, CO_2 concentrations?
(c) What is the benefit to a plant of the stomata closing at night?

23 Choose which of the options (i), (ii), (iii) or (iv) represents the correct answer in each case below.
(a) Mesophyll is an example of:
(i) vascular tissue
(ii) ground tissue
(iii) dermal tissue
(iv) meristematic tissue
(b) Stomata are found mostly in the:
(i) stem
(ii) tree
(iii) leaf
(iv) bud
(c) Water enters root hairs by a process known as:
(i) translocation
(ii) cohesion
(iii) osmosis
(iv) diffusion
(d) During drought conditions, stomata are usually:
(i) turgid
(ii) open
(iii) closed
(iv) waxy

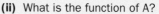
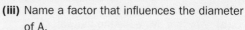
Sample examination questions

Section A

24 (a) The diagram shows part of the under surface of a leaf as seen through the microscope. A is an aperture. B and C are cells.
(i) Name A, B, C.
(ii) What is the function of A?
(iii) Name a factor that influences the diameter of A.
(iv) Name the apertures in stems that are equivalent to A. (continued)

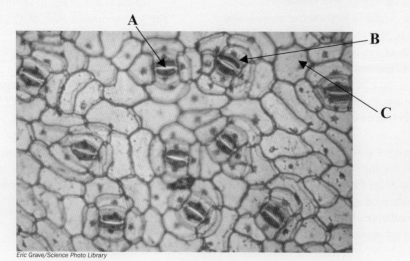
Eric Grave/Science Photo Library

(b) In some species of flowering plants the leaves are modified for the storage of food.
   (i) Name a plant in which the leaves are modified for food storage.
   (ii) Name a carbohydrate that you would expect to find in the modified leaves of the plant that you named above.
   (iii) Name a type of modified stem that functions in food storage.

(2004 HL Q 4)

Section C

25 (i) Draw a diagram of a section through a leaf. Label a stoma and a guard cell.
   (ii) Give a function of the guard cell.
   (iii) Name two gases that enter or leave the leaf.
   (iv) Name the process by which the gases move in or out of the leaf.

(2007 OL Q 15b)

26 The passage of water through a plant is known as the transpiration stream. Answer the following questions in relation to the transpiration stream.
   (i) Explain how water enters the plant at the root hair.
   (ii) Do minerals enter the plant by the process that you have indicated in (i)? Explain your answer.
   (iii) How is xylem adapted for its role in water transport?
   (iv) Strong forces of attraction exist between water molecules. Give an account of the importance of these forces in raising water to great height in trees.

(2004 HL Q 14a)

27 (i) Name the tissue that transports water from the root to the leaves.
   (ii) Mention **one** way in which the tissue you have named in (i) is adapted for the transport of water.
   (iii) The diagram below shows another tissue that is involved in transport in plants. Name this tissue and name a substance that is transported in it.

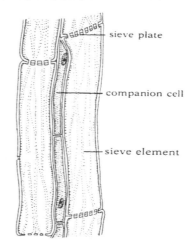

(2008 OL Q 15a)

28 Name the openings in the leaf which allow the entry of carbon dioxide for photosynthesis. State a factor which influences the diameter of these openings.

(2008 HL Q 14a(i))

29 (i) Draw a large, labelled diagram of a transverse section through a young root.
   (ii) Describe how minerals such as nitrates enter the root of a plant from the soil.

(2008 Q 14c(i), (v))

Previous examination questions	
Ordinary level	**Higher level**
2006 Q 4	2003 Sample Q 15a
2007 Q 15b	2004 Q 4
2008 Q 15a	2005 Q 3b, 14a
	2006 Q 6a, 6d, 11c
	2008 Q 14a(i), 14c(i), (v)

For latest questions go to **www.edco.ie/biology**

THE ORGANISM

Chapter 26 **Blood**

Composition of blood

Blood has four parts: plasma, red blood cells (corpuscles), white blood cells and platelets.

Plasma

Plasma is a pale, golden liquid that comprises about 55% of the blood. The remaining 45% consists of blood cells and platelets.

If blood is specially treated so that it cannot clot and is then left to settle, it will appear as shown in Figure 26.1.

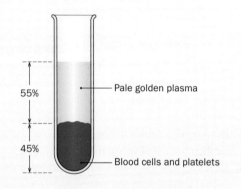

55% ——— Pale golden plasma

45% ——— Blood cells and platelets

26.1 *Result of separating plasma from blood*

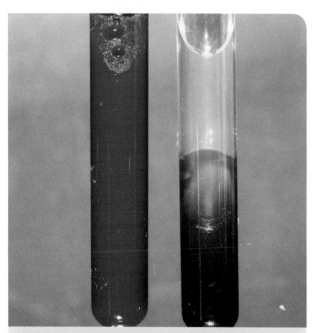

26.2 *Blood samples: the plasma is pale orange and the blood cells appear red. Blood is a complex fluid that makes up about 8% of our normal body weight. Most people have 5 to 6 litres of blood (10–12 pints).*

Plasma is made of:
- 90% water
- 7% proteins
- 3% dissolved materials which are being transported

The main plasma proteins are:
- **antibodies**, which are produced by white blood cells in order to combine with and neutralise foreign substances
- **clotting proteins**, which are acted upon to form blood clots. As these proteins are too large to pass easily through the walls of blood vessels they help ensure that blood plasma has the same concentration as the blood cells.

ROLE OF PLASMA

The role (or function) of plasma is to transport dissolved materials such as glucose, amino acids, minerals, vitamins, salts, carbon dioxide, urea and hormones. Plasma also carries heat.

Serum is plasma from which the clotting proteins have been removed. Serum contains the other plasma-soluble materials (including antibodies). It is sometimes used in injections to give someone resistance to disease.

Red blood cells (erythrocytes)

Red blood cells (also called red blood corpuscles) are produced in the marrow of bones such as the ribs, breast bone, the long bones in the arms and legs, and the vertebrae of the backbone.

Red blood cells are round and very small – about 5 million are found in 1 cubic millimetre (mm^3) of blood. They consist of a flexible membrane containing almost 300,000 molecules of a red protein called haemoglobin.

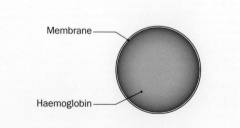

Membrane

Haemoglobin

26.3 *Red blood cell*

THE ORGANISM

Red blood cells are broken down (and replaced) at the amazing rate of 3 million cells per second. This is because they become damaged by constantly changing shape in order to pass through narrow blood vessels. Red blood cells cannot repair themselves and so they live for only about 4 months.

Dead red blood cells are broken down in the liver and spleen. The iron from the haemoglobin is stored in the liver and may be recycled to make new haemoglobin in bone marrow. The rest of the red blood cell and haemoglobin is converted to bile pigments such as biliverdin and bilirubin.

ROLE OF RED BLOOD CELLS

The role (or function) of red blood cells is to transport oxygen.

Haemoglobin is based on molecules of iron and can join with oxygen in areas of high oxygen concentration (e.g. the lungs) and release oxygen in areas of low oxygen (e.g. the body cells).

Did you know?

Anaemia is a lack of haemoglobin (or red blood cells). The symptoms of anaemia are pale skin colour and a loss of energy.

White blood cells (leucocytes)

White blood cells are larger than red blood cells, have no definite shape, live for a few days and are less numerous (700 red : 1 white). They are made in bone marrow (and some of them mature in the lymphatic system).

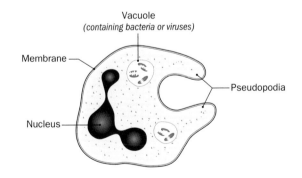

Vacuole
(containing bacteria or viruses)

Membrane

Pseudopodia

Nucleus

26.4 *White blood cell*

ROLE OF WHITE BLOOD CELLS

The role (or function) of white blood cells is to defend the body against infection and to fight infections.

There are many types of white blood cells. The majority of white blood cells attack bacteria in the body. They surround (engulf) the bacteria (and other invading particles such as viruses) and digest them, similar to the way in which *Amoeba* takes in its food.

The way in which a cell 'eats' solid particles is called phagocytosis. As a result these white blood cells are called **phagocytes**.

Some white blood cells (called lymphocytes) react to invading particles, such as bacteria and viruses, by producing antibodies. Antibodies play an important role in defending the body against infection and are dealt with more fully in Chapter 38.

Did you know?

Leukaemia is a form of cancer in which white blood cells are produced too rapidly and are immature. They crowd out other blood cells and may cause anaemia, increased risk of infection and reduced ability to clot the blood. Leukaemia may be treated by radiation or drugs.

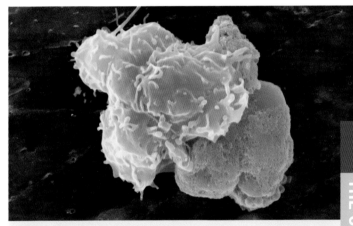
26.5 *A phagocyte (green) engulfing a foreign particle (purple)*

26.6 *Red blood cells (red), white blood cells (yellow) and platelets (pink)*

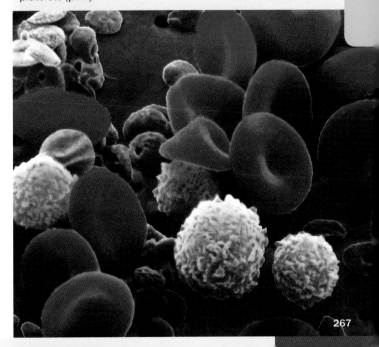

Platelets (thrombocytes)

Platelets are made in bone marrow from large cells called megacytes. These megacytes break down to produce cell fragments called platelets. A platelet is smaller than a red blood cell.

ROLE OF PLATELETS

The role (or function) of platelets is to clot the blood. A clot results when damaged body cells produce chemicals that stimulate platelets to form a clot.

Blood clots have two main functions:
- they reduce the loss of blood, and
- they prevent the entry of micro-organisms.

Haemophiliacs are unable to produce one or more of the clotting chemicals (usually Factor VIII). As a result, haemophiliacs cannot form blood clots and may suffer from excessive bleeding.

Clots do not usually form in healthy, undamaged blood vessels. However, if the vessel walls are damaged, a blood clot may form and may block the blood vessel. This is called thrombosis. Examples include clots forming in blood vessels in the brain (causing strokes) or in the vessels of the heart (causing heart attack).

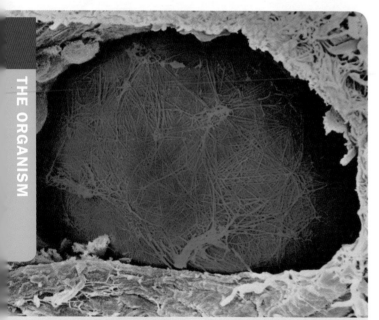

26.7 *A blood clot (red) in a tiny blood vessel*

Functions of blood

- Transport of food, waste products and hormones by plasma
- Transport of heat from internal organs by plasma. This helps to maintain a constant body temperature
- Transport of oxygen by red blood cells

- Defence against disease. This is due to:
  - (a) White blood cells (phagocytes), which engulf and digest bacteria
  - (b) White blood cells (lymphocytes), which produce antibodies to destroy 'foreign bodies' such as bacteria and viruses
  - (c) Platelets clotting the blood, which prevents blood loss and the entry of disease-causing organisms

Blood groups

ABO groups

Around 1900 an Austrian-American called Karl Landsteiner (1868–1943) discovered that humans have four major blood groups (the ABO blood groups). He won a Nobel prize for his work in 1930.

Landsteiner found that most red blood cells contain a complex carbohydrate and protein chemical on the surface of their membranes.

Red blood cells can be placed in four different categories (or blood groups), depending on the types of chemicals (if any) attached to their cell membranes. The four main (ABO) blood groups are A, B, AB and O.

When blood transfusions are given it is important to match the incoming blood group to the blood group of the recipient. Failure to do this may result in blood clumping in the recipient.

Did you know?

*The four common **blood groups** and their frequency in the population of Ireland are shown in the table below.*

Blood groups in Ireland	
Blood group	**% of the population**
O	55
A	31
B	11
AB	3

Blood group O is called the universal donor because it can be given safely to all the other four blood groups. This is why hospitals often request donations of blood group O at times of crisis.

The rhesus factor

Apart from the ABO blood groups there are about 400 other blood types. The best known of these is the rhesus factor. This is named after rhesus

THE ORGANISM

monkeys in whom it was first discovered by Landsteiner in the 1940s.

About 85% of Irish people have a chemical called the rhesus factor on the surface of their red blood cells. Those people who have this chemical are said to be rhesus positive (Rh+). The 15% of the population who do not have the rhesus chemical on their red cells are said to be rhesus negative (Rh–).

People of blood group A may be A positive (also called A+ and A Rh+). This means they are in blood group A and have the rhesus chemical on their red blood cells. Those who are A negative (A– or A Rh–) do not have the rhesus chemical. A similar situation applies for those who are B+ and B–, AB+ and AB–, O+ and O–.

Did you know?

Rhesus negative blood can be given safely to a rhesus positive person. If rhesus positive blood is given to a rhesus negative person it may cause a serious reaction if the recipient had received transfusions of rhesus positive blood before.

The rhesus factor may also lead to complications if a rhesus negative mother is pregnant with a rhesus positive baby. Her first rhesus positive baby will be safe, but any further rhesus positive babies may have their red blood cells damaged. This may cause the baby to be anaemic or, in severe cases, brain damaged or even stillborn.

Further details of red blood cells

When red blood cells (erythrocytes) are first made they have a nucleus. They lose their nuclei within a few days so that mature red blood cells have no nuclei. They are then called red blood corpuscles. They also lack mitochondria.

Red blood cells are said to have a biconcave shape. This gives them a larger surface area over which they can exchange oxygen.

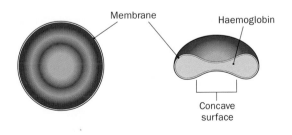

26.8 *Shape of red blood cells*

Haemoglobin has an amazing ability to form a loose chemical union with oxygen. In the lungs haemoglobin combines with four oxygen molecules to form oxyhaemoglobin. Haemoglobin is a purple colour; oxyhaemoglobin is a bright red colour.

Fortunately, haemoglobin loses oxygen very readily, which allows it to supply the cells in the body with oxygen.

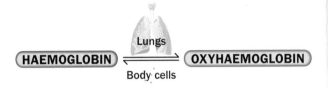

26.9 *Relationship between haemoglobin and oxyhaemoglobin*

Types of white blood cells

There are a number of categories of white blood cells or leucocytes. Two of the categories are lymphocytes and monocytes.

Lymphocytes

Lymphocytes are made in bone marrow. Some of them mature and all of them are later stored in parts of the lymphatic system such as the spleen, lymph nodes, tonsils, adenoids and thymus gland.

Lymphocytes comprise 25% of white blood cells. Each lymphocyte has a large round nucleus, with very little cytoplasm. Lymphocytes can survive for between three months and ten years.

The main function of lymphocytes is to make antibodies. Antibodies help the body to resist infection by micro-organisms (they are discussed in more detail in Chapter 38).

26.10 *A lymphocyte (left) and a monocyte (right)*

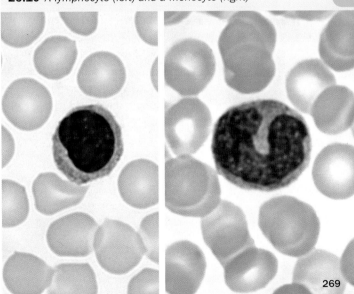

Monocytes

Monocytes are large cells that scavenge throughout the body and digest bacteria and other particles. In this way they act as phagocytes.

Monocytes are also called **macrophages**. They are formed in the bone marrow, comprise about 5% of white blood cells and survive for 6–9 days. They have kidney-shaped nuclei. The remaining (about 70%) white blood cells act as phagocytes, but they are not on the Leaving Certificate syllabus.

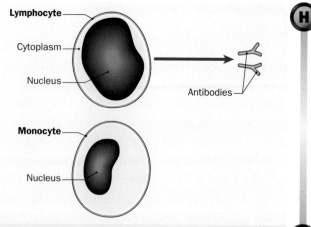

26.11 *Lymphocyte and monocyte*

Summary

Plasma:
- is the liquid part of blood
- transports foods, salts, hormones, waste and heat

Serum:
- is plasma without the clotting proteins

Red blood cells (erythrocytes):
- are made in bone marrow
- contain haemoglobin
- carry oxygen

Dead red blood cells:
- are broken down in the liver and spleen

Haemoglobin:
- is broken down to form bile

White blood cells (leucocytes):
- have no definite shape
- are bigger than red cells but less numerous
- defend the body against infection

Platelets (thrombocytes):
- are cell fragments
- are formed in bone marrow
- help to clot the blood

The main functions of blood are:
- transport
- body defence

The human blood groups are:
- O, A, B, AB

Blood groups can be rhesus positive or rhesus negative.

Red blood cells have:
- no nuclei
- no mitochondria
- a biconcave shape

Haemoglobin:
- gains oxygen in the lungs, forming oxyhaemoglobin

Oxyhaemoglobin:
- loses oxygen to body cells forming haemoglobin

Two categories of white blood cells (leucocytes) are:
- lymphocytes (25% of white blood cells, made in bone marrow but found in the lymphatic system, make antibodies)
- monocytes (5% of white blood cells, made in bone marrow, engulf bacteria)

Revision questions

1. (a) Name the four parts of blood.
   (b) Which of these parts are made of or from cells?
   (c) State one function for each part named.
2. Contrast red blood cells and white blood cells under these headings:
   (a) number of types
   (b) shape
   (c) function
   (d) ratio of each type
   (e) contents
   (f) site(s) of production.

3. Explain the two methods by which white blood cells defend the body against infection.
4. The virus responsible for AIDS attacks and inhibits white blood cells. Suggest why AIDS victims may suffer from increased infections.
5. (a) Name two advantages of blood clotting.
   (b) What causes blood to clot?
   (c) Explain why blood within the circulatory system does not normally clot.
6. (a) Where are red blood cells made?
   (b) Name the main pigment in red blood cells.
   (c) What mineral is essential for this pigment.

THE ORGANISM

7 Name the part of blood responsible for each of the following:
(a) clotting
(b) transporting glucose
(c) transporting oxygen
(d) attacking bacteria
(e) making antibodies
(f) carrying wastes
(g) transporting carbon dioxide.

8 (a) Name the four main blood groups.
(b) What is the basis by which people are allocated to a particular blood group?
(c) What are rhesus factors?

9 (a) What shape are red blood cells?
(b) What is the advantage of this shape?
(c) Suggest two reasons why red blood cells have short lives.
(d) Where are red blood cells broken down?
(e) Name the end product made from the breakdown of red blood cells.

10 (a) Name two categories of white blood cells.
(b) Discuss them in terms of their:
(i) site of production
(ii) % of the total number of white cells
(iii) shape of nucleus
(iv) function
(v) lifespan.

11 Draw labelled diagrams of each of the following:
(a) red blood cell
(b) lymphocyte
(c) monocyte.

12 (a) Name seven components of human blood.
(b) Give one function for each of the components named.
(c) Distinguish between:
(i) the nucleated (i.e. having a nucleus) and non-nucleated parts of blood
(ii) the cellular and non-cellular components of blood

13 Choose which of the options (i), (ii), (iii) or (iv) represents the correct answer in each case below.
(a) Serum is known as:
(i) plasma plus clotting protein
(ii) plasma minus platelets
(iii) plasma minus clotting protein
(iv) plasma minus white blood cells
(b) The rhesus factor is a chemical structure found on the surface of:
(i) white blood cells **(iii)** all body cells
(ii) platelets **(iv)** red blood cells
(c) The metallic element in haemoglobin is:
(i) copper **(iii)** sodium
(ii) calcium **(iv)** iron
(d) Anaemia may result from a lack of:
(i) iron **(iii)** sleep
(ii) platelets **(iv)** energy
(e) The shape of the nucleus in a lymphocyte is:
(i) granular **(iii)** kidney-shaped
(ii) round **(iv)** biconcave
(f) The lifespan of a monocyte is:
(i) 4 months
(ii) a few days
(iii) 3 months to 10 years
(iv) 6–9 days

Sample examination questions

Section C

14 (i) Name the liquid part of blood.
(ii) Name **two** substances that are dissolved in the liquid part of blood.
(iii) State **one** function of the liquid part of blood.
(iv) Blood contains red cells and white cells. State one function for each of these.
(v) Name two common blood-grouping systems.
(2003 OL Sample Q 10c)

15 (i) State a precise location in the human body at which red blood cells are made.
(ii) State **two** ways in which red blood cells differ from typical body cells, e.g. from the cheek lining.
(2006 HL Q 13a)

16 Answer the following questions in relation to blood.
(i) What is blood plasma? Give a role for blood plasma.
(ii) Name **two** types of cell found in the blood and give a function for each of them.
(iii) The ABO blood group system has four blood groups. What are these **four** groups?
(iv) Suggest a reason why it is important to know a person's blood group. *(2008 OL Q 15b)*

Previous examination questions

Ordinary level	Higher level
2003 Sample Q 10c	2005 Q 3f
2008 Q 15b	2006 Q 13a
	2007 Q 13a(ii)

*For latest questions go to **www.edco.ie/biology***

THE ORGANISM

Chapter 27 The heart and blood vessels

The need for a circulatory system

Small organisms such as *Amoeba* have no need for a circulatory system. Nutrients and oxygen are supplied to their cells and wastes are removed by diffusion. Diffusion is adequate provided that the organisms are only a few cells thick.

However, larger organisms need a circulatory system to supply their cells with all the materials they require.

Open and closed blood systems

There are two forms of circulatory systems: open systems and closed systems.

In an **open circulatory system** the heart pumps blood into vessels that are open-ended. The blood leaves these vessels and flows around all the cells of the animal's body.

The blood flows back to the heart, entering it through openings in the heart wall.

Animals with open circulatory systems include crabs, lobsters, insects, spiders, snails and slugs.

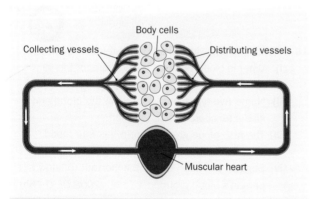

27.1 *An open circulatory system*

In a **closed circulatory system**, blood remains in a continuous system of blood vessels, i.e. blood is always enclosed in blood vessels. Materials are exchanged between the blood and cells through the thin walls of the smallest blood vessels.

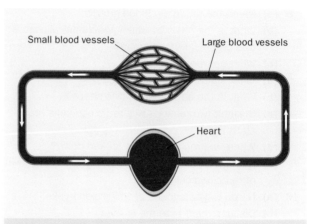

27.2 *A closed circulatory system*

The human circulatory system is a closed system. A closed system is more efficient than an open system, for two main reasons:

- Firstly, the blood can be pumped around the body faster. This allows nutrients and, especially, oxygen to be distributed faster to the cells. This in turn allows the animal to be more active (i.e. have a higher metabolic rate).
- Secondly, a closed system allows the flow of blood to different organs to be increased or decreased. For example, more blood can be supplied to the leg muscles when the animal is running.

Composition of the closed circulatory system of humans

The human circulatory system consists of:
- blood (as described in Chapter 26)
- the heart (which pumps the blood)
- blood vessels (which carry the blood to and from the heart)

Blood vessels

The three main types of blood vessel are:
- **Arteries**, which carry blood **away** from the heart. Arteries divide into smaller vessels called arterioles.

'a' for artery and for **away**

- **Veins** carry blood **to** the heart. Small veins are called venules.
- **Capillaries** are tiny vessels that link arteries and veins.

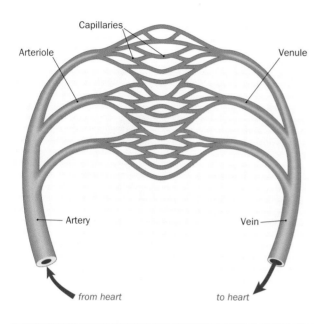

27.3 *Relationship between blood vessels*

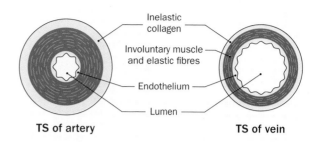

27.4 *Structure of artery and vein*

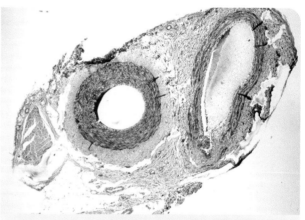

27.5 *A thick-walled artery (on left) and a thin-walled vein*

Arteries and veins

Arteries and veins both have three similar layers in their walls. The main difference is that veins have a thinner middle layer. This results in veins having larger lumens (Figure 27.4). The three layers are:

1 An outer layer of tough, **inelastic protein** (called collagen), which prevents the walls from over-expansion.

2 A middle layer of **muscle and elastic fibres**. The muscle is involuntary and can alter the size of the vessel.

   For example, during exercise the arteries leading to muscles expand and allow up to ten times more blood to flow into the muscle. Also, when we are too hot, blood vessels in the face expand (or dilate), causing blushing. This allows more blood to enter the vessels. As a result more heat is lost, allowing us to cool.

   The elastic fibres bring the vessel back to shape when the muscle relaxes. The recoil of the artery also helps to pump blood.

3 An inner single layer of living cells called the **endothelium**, which surrounds the lumen.

Blood pressure and valves

Blood pressure is the force the blood exerts against the wall of a blood vessel.

Blood pressure is highest in arteries when the heart contracts. This pressure causes the artery to expand slightly. The expansion can be detected as a pulse.

   Pressure in veins is very low. Physical activity helps to push blood in the veins back to the heart. This happens when ordinary body muscles (skeletal muscles) contract. They squeeze the veins and help to return blood to the heart.

   People who are stationary often get weak because their muscles do not contract. Blood then collects in veins and the brain suffers from a shortage of blood (and oxygen).

   The pressure that forces blood through the veins is low. In order to prevent backflow, and to ensure blood flows only towards the heart, veins have valves.

Valves control the direction of blood flow.

   When the veins in the forearm are bulging the valves can be felt at 2 cm intervals.

THE ORGANISM

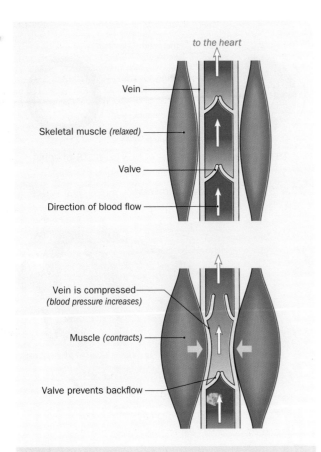

27.6 *Role of skeletal muscle in blood circulation*

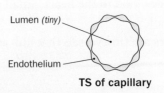

TS of capillary

27.7 *Structure of a capillary*

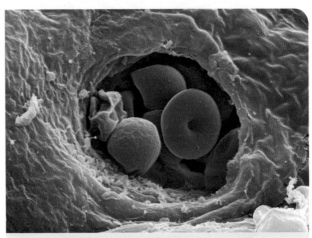

27.8 *Red blood cells in a capillary*

The main differences between arteries and veins are shown in the table below.

Summary of arteries and veins	
Artery	**Vein**
Carries blood away from the heart	Carries blood to the heart
Blood under high pressure	Blood under low pressure
Thick walls	Thin walls
Small lumen	Large lumen
Blood flows in pulses	Blood flows smoothly (no pulses)
Valves absent	Valves present
Blood rich in oxygen (except pulmonary artery)	Blood low in oxygen (except pulmonary vein)

Capillaries

Capillaries are tiny, much-branched vessels. Their walls are made of a single layer of endothelium cells.

Capillary walls are permeable so they allow exchange of materials between the blood and body tissues.

The body has so many capillaries (100 000 km) that there is a capillary close to all body cells.

The heart

The heart is located between the two lungs (slightly to the left-hand side of the chest, or thorax) and just above the diaphragm.

It is made of cardiac muscle and surrounded by a double membrane called the pericardium. Pericardial fluid between these membranes helps to reduce friction when the heart beats.

Cardiac muscle is a special type of muscle that is slow to fatigue.

Did you know?

The human heart is about the size of a clenched fist. It contracts about 100 000 times every day and pumps between 5 and 20 litres of blood per minute.

Structure of the heart

The heart is divided into two sides by a wall called the septum. There are four chambers in the heart.

ATRIA

The two upper chambers are the atria (singular **atrium**). The atria pump blood to the lower chambers or ventricles. Because the distance is so short the atria have thin walls.

THE ORGANISM

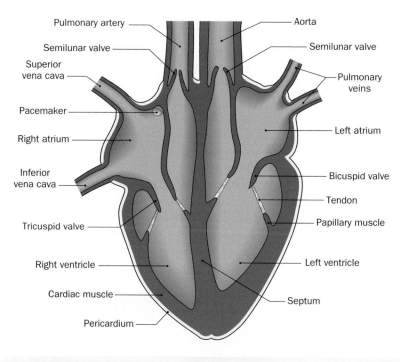

27.9 *Structure of the heart and major blood vessels*

VENTRICLES

The **ventricles** pump blood out of the heart. The right ventricle pumps blood to the lungs. The left ventricle pumps blood to the head and body. As this is a much longer circuit, the wall of the left ventricle is much thicker (and stronger) than the wall of the right ventricle.

The atria and ventricles are separated by valves. These are held in place by tough cords ('heart strings') called tendons. The tendons are attached to the walls of the heart by projections called papillary muscles.

VALVES

The valves ensure that blood can only flow from the atria to the ventricles (i.e. they prevent backflow of blood). The valve on the right-hand side of the heart is the **tricuspid valve** (i.e. it has three flaps). The valve on the left is the **bicuspid valve** (i.e. it has two flaps).

Semilunar valves (named because their flaps are shaped like half moons) allow blood to flow out of the heart into the two main arteries (i.e. the pulmonary artery and the aorta). They prevent blood returning to the heart.

Blood flow in the heart

DEOXYGENATED BLOOD

Blood that is low in oxygen (deoxygenated) enters the heart through the two venae cavae. The inferior vena cava carries blood from the lower part of the body. The superior vena cava carries blood from the head, arms and chest.

The blood enters the right atrium. This chamber contracts and forces blood down through the tricuspid valve. The venae cavae close to prevent blood flowing back out of the heart.

The blood now enters the right ventricle. When this chamber contracts the tricuspid valve closes. Blood is forced out of the heart to the lungs through the semilunar valve in the pulmonary artery.

OXYGENATED BLOOD

Oxygen-rich (oxygenated) blood returns to the heart from the lungs. It enters the left atrium through the pulmonary veins. It is pumped down, through the bicuspid valve, to the left ventricle. When this chamber contracts, the bicuspid valve closes and blood is pumped out to the body through the semilunar valve in the aorta.

The semilunar valves allow blood to pass out of the heart. When the ventricles relax, these valves close to stop blood flowing back into the ventricles.

The oxygen content of the blood in the two sides of the heart can be recalled as follows:

LORD
Left Oxygenated Right Deoxygenated

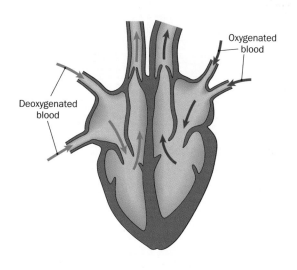

27.10 *Blood flow in the heart*

Activity 18 *To dissect, display and identify the parts of a heart*

A sheep's heart is smaller than an ox (or cow's) heart. Your teacher will demonstrate how to dissect an ox or sheep's heart and attached vessels.

 Dissect an ox or sheep's heart in the following manner.

1. Rinse the heart in cold water. Wash out any dark-coloured, jelly-like clumps or blood.
2. Place the heart on a dissecting board or tray.
3. Distinguish between the front (ventral) and back (dorsal) surface of the heart. The front is more rounded and the thick-walled arteries are on this side.

   Also the lower part of the left side feels much firmer than the lower part of the right side. (Note: very often the butcher will have removed most of the vessels).
4. Identify the four major blood vessels that enter and leave the heart. Notice how thick-walled the arteries are compared with the veins. Notice the coronary arteries and veins on the surface of the heart. These vessels supply blood to the heart itself.
5. Locate the four chambers of the heart. (Note that the upper chambers or atria are quite small and are very high up.)
6. Draw a labelled diagram of the external structure of the undissected heart.
7. ⚠ Make eight cuts in the front of the heart using a scalpel, in the positions shown in Figure 27.11.

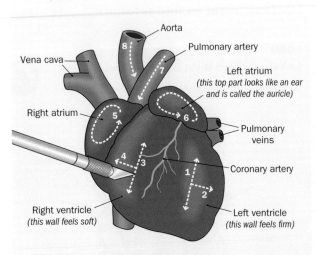

27.11 *Ventral view of heart showing the cuts to be made*

8. **Cut 1.** Open up the left ventricle. In this chamber you should observe:
   - a very thick wall
   - white 'strings', which are the tendons
   - the two flaps of the bicuspid valve

9. **Cuts 3 and 4.** Open up the right ventricle. In this chamber you should observe:
   - a thinner wall
   - white 'strings', which are the tendons
   - the three flaps of the tricuspid valve

10. **Cuts 5 and 6.** Open up the atria. In these chambers you should observe:
    - very thin walls
    - the bicuspid and tricuspid valves

11. **Cut 7.** Cut down the length of the pulmonary artery. This should allow you to see:
    - the semi-lunar valve (at the point where the artery emerges from the heart).

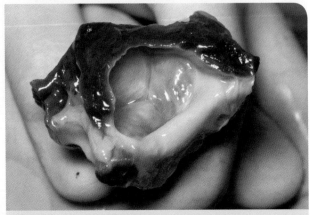

27.12 *A semi-lunar valve*

12. **Cut 8.** Cut down the length of the aorta. This should allow you to see:
    - the second semi-lunar valve
    - the origin of the coronary artery (just above the semi-lunar valve). If you squirt water (or a dye) into the coronary artery you will see it flow down to the heart.
13. Identify the septum between the ventricles.
14. Draw a diagram of the dissected heart. This will be similar to Figure 27.9.
15. Using small pins, flag-label the parts you have identified (Figure 27.13).

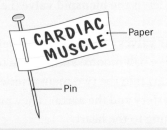

27.13 *A flag label*

16. Wash your hands and sterilise the board and dissecting instruments.

Double circulation

The human heart is really a double pump (see Figure 27.14). The two sides of the heart are separated by the septum. The septum is necessary to separate deoxygenated and oxygenated blood. This separation is a vital part of the two-circuit circulatory system in humans: the pulmonary circuit and the systemic circuit.

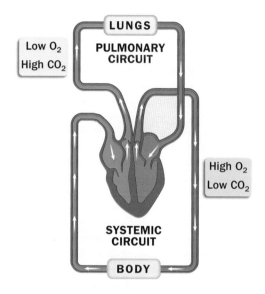

27.14 *Double circulation in humans*

PULMONARY CIRCUIT (HEART → LUNGS → HEART)
The right ventricle pumps blood around the pulmonary circuit. In this circuit, blood gains oxygen (and loses carbon dioxide) in the lungs. This circuit is relatively short, so the walls of the right ventricle are fairly thin.

SYSTEMIC CIRCUIT (HEART → BODY → HEART)
The left ventricle pumps oxygenated blood to the head, arms, trunk and legs. This is a much longer route than the pulmonary circuit so the walls of the left ventricle are thicker and stronger than those of the right ventricle.

DOUBLE VERSUS SINGLE CIRCULATION
A double-circulation system allows oxygen-rich and oxygen-poor blood to be kept separate. It also ensures that the blood pressure is high enough to reach all parts of the body.

In contrast to double circulation, some animals display single circulation. This means that blood is pumped from their hearts, around the body and back to the heart again in a single circuit.

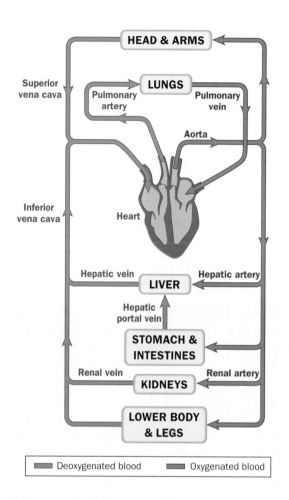

27.15 *The circulatory system*

A single-circulation system can only produce low blood pressure around most of the body. This restricts the activities (metabolism) of the animal. Examples of animals with single circulation are earthworms and fish.

Portal system

A **portal system** is a blood pathway that begins and ends in capillaries.

The vessel(s) in a portal system do not connect directly to the heart.

The hepatic portal vein connects the stomach and intestines to the liver. The hepatic portal vein is an example of a portal system.

Blood supply to the heart

The muscle of the heart is supplied with blood by the coronary (or cardiac) arteries. These branch from the aorta at the point where it leaves the heart.

Blood is drained from the muscle of the heart by the coronary (or cardiac) veins. These return the blood directly to the right atrium (i.e. not to the venae cavae).

Blockage of the coronary arteries is a common cause of heart attack. Such attacks are often preceded by chest pains called angina.

The cardiac arteries sub-divide to form numerous cardiac capillaries. These capillaries exchange materials with the muscular walls of the heart. The cardiac capillaries re-join to form cardiac veins.

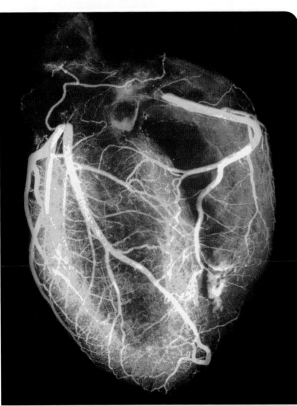

27.16 *Coronary arteries in the heart (highlighted using an x-ray dye)*

Control of heartbeat

If a heart is removed from a body and kept in a nutritive, oxygen-rich fluid it will continue to beat. This shows that heartbeat can occur independently of the brain.

Heartbeat is controlled by a small bundle of specialised tissue called the **pacemaker**. This is located in the wall at the top of the right atrium.

The pacemaker sends out regular electrical impulses, which initially cause the atria to contract. These impulses then cause the ventricles to contract.

This means that blood is first pumped from the atria to the ventricles and, a split second later, it is pumped from the ventricles out of the heart. The frequency of these impulses can be increased or decreased by the brain (i.e. the brain can cause the pacemaker to speed up or slow down the rate of heartbeat).

Heartbeat is controlled in the following way:
1 The pacemaker (also called the SA or sino-atrial node) pulses and causes the atria to contract.
2 The electrical impulse from the pacemaker stimulates the AV (atrio-ventricular) node. This is similar to the pacemaker but is located further down in the right atrium.
3 The AV node sends an impulse down special muscle fibres located in the septum.
4 The impulse is passed out to the walls of the ventricles by thin fibres. The impulses from these fibres cause the ventricles to contract.

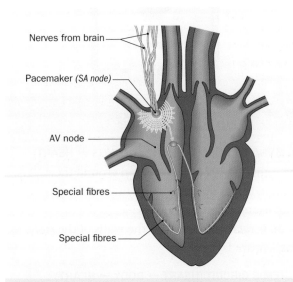

27.17 *Path of nerve impulses in the heart*

The pacemaker controls the rate of heartbeat. However, nerves from the brain (along with hormones) can change the rate at which the pacemaker (and therefore the heart) operates.

Factors that increase the rate of heartbeat include exercise, temperature, emotions and shock. Factors such as relaxation, sleep and alcohol decrease the rate of heartbeat.

Did you know?

*Electrodes placed on the chest can measure the electrical activity of the heart. A record of this activity is called an **ECG** (electrocardiogram).*

The stages of heartbeat (cardiac cycle)

The events that take place during one heartbeat occur in three stages.

> **Diastole** is when heart chambers relax; **systole** is when the heart chambers contract.

1 Blood enters the heart.

The atria and ventricles are both relaxed (diastole). Blood enters the atria. All valves are closed.

2 Blood is pumped from the atria to the ventricles.

Electrical impulses from the pacemaker cause the atria to contract (atrial systole). This pumps blood to the ventricles.

The tricuspid and bicuspid valves open. The venae cavae and pulmonary veins close to stop blood entering the atria.

The semi-lunar valves remain closed.

3 Blood leaves the heart.

The atria relax and impulses from the AV node cause the ventricles to contract (ventricular systole). This forces blood out of the heart into the pulmonary artery and the aorta.

The pressure forces open the semilunar valves and closes the tricuspid and bicuspid valves.

The ventricles now relax again. Closing of the semilunar valves prevents blood from flowing back into the heart (or ventricles).

The venae cavae and pulmonary veins open and the cycle starts again.

Did you know?

The sounds of heartbeat

The characteristic double sound of heartbeat (called the 'lub-dub' sound) is caused by the valves being forced shut. The low-pitched, quieter, long-lasting 'lub' sound is due to the bicuspid and tricuspid valves being forced shut when the ventricles contract. The higher-pitched, louder, much shorter 'dub' sound is due to the semi-lunar valves snapping shut.

A heart murmur is any abnormal sound associated with heartbeat. A heart murmur may indicate damage to one or more of the valves.

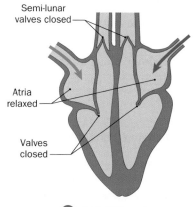

1 Atrial Diastole *(atria fill with blood)*

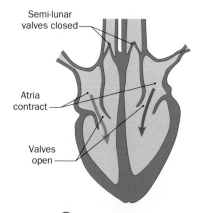

2 Atrial Systole *(blood pumped to ventricles)*

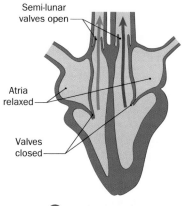

3 Ventricular Systole *(blood pumped out of heart)*

27.18 *Stages of heartbeat*

THE ORGANISM

Pulse

When the left ventricle contracts, the pressure of the blood forced into the aorta causes the aorta to expand. A wave of expansion (followed by contraction) passes down along all the arteries. The contraction is caused by the elastic walls of the arteries.

> A **pulse** is the alternate expansion and contraction of the arteries.

The pulse can be felt most easily in the wrist or neck. The pulse rate is an indication of the heart rate.

The average adult pulse (or heart) rate is 72 beats per minute. Most people have rates between 60 and 100 beats per minute.

27.19 *Measuring pulse rate*

Blood pressure

Blood entering the aorta is under high pressure due to the contraction of the left ventricle. As the blood passes from the aorta to the arteries, arterioles, capillaries, venules, veins and back to the right atrium of the heart, the pressure of the blood falls. Blood pressure is the force exerted by the blood against the walls of the blood vessels (mainly the arteries).

Human blood pressure is taken (using a device called a sphygmomanometer) in an artery in the upper arm. The amount of pressure required to stop the flow of blood in this artery is measured.

Blood pressure readings are given as two values. Normally the higher value records the pressure of blood as a pulse passes through the artery (i.e. when the ventricles contract, or are in systole). It is called the systolic pressure.

The lower value usually records the pressure when there is no pulse (i.e. when the ventricles are not contracting, or are in diastole). It is called the diastolic pressure.

Typical blood pressure for a young adult is about $^{120}/_{80}$ mm of mercury (or mm of Hg, the units used to record blood pressure). These values normally rise with age.

Activity 19a   To investigate the effect of exercise on the pulse rate of a human

You have a choice between this activity and investigating the effect of exercise on the breathing rate of a human (Activity 19b on page 309).

1 Work in pairs, one person recording the results.
2 Locate a strong pulse in your neck or wrist (just below the thumb).
3 Count the number of pulses per minute while at rest.
4 Repeat this four times and calculate your average pulse rate per minute at rest. Record your results. *(This value is used as a control.)*
5 Walk slowly for 5 minutes.
6 Count your pulse rate per minute immediately after walking. Repeat this until your pulse rate returns to (or below) normal.
7 Exercise strenuously for 2 minutes (e.g. step up and down on a chair every 3 seconds).
8 Count your pulse rate per minute immediately after exercising.
9 Repeat this every minute for 6 minutes or until the pulse returns to the resting rate.
10 Compare your resting rate with the rate immediately after exercise. Calculate how long it took you to return to a normal pulse rate.
11 Present your aims, methods, results and conclusions in a written report.

THE ORGANISM

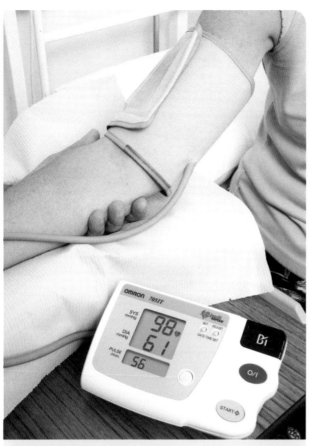

27.20 *Measuring blood pressure*

Did you know?

*If the lower of the two values (the diastolic pressure) is over 95 mm of Hg the person is said to suffer from **high blood pressure** (called hypertension).*

High blood pressure is most often caused by blockages in arterioles and small arteries. These blockages mean that the heart has to pump harder and this may lead to a stroke (lack of blood in the brain), heart attack and death.

27.21 *Fatty plaques (yellow) block a coronary artery, leading to a heart attack.*

The effects of smoking, diet and exercise on the circulatory system

Smoking

Tobacco contains about 400 harmful chemicals. These include nicotine – a drug that is more addictive than heroin – and carbon monoxide.

- Nicotine causes increased heart rates and raises blood pressure, both factors that increase the workload of the heart.
- Carbon monoxide reduces the amount of oxygen carried by the blood. This results in lower energy production by the body.
- Other chemicals in tobacco smoke increase the likelihood of blood clots in blood vessels (thrombosis). Note that smoking also causes lung cancer, bronchitis and many other lung ailments.

In Ireland about 7000 people a year die from smoking-related causes. On average, smokers die 10 to 15 years earlier than non-smokers.

Diet

The three main dietary factors affecting the circulatory system are fat intake, salt and being overweight.

- Harmful fats are mostly found in animal products such as red meat and dairy foods (milk, cream, butter and cheese). These fats are high in cholesterol. Cholesterol increases the risk of forming blockages (called plaques) in arteries, especially the coronary arteries and those leading to the brain. These blockages result in heart attacks and strokes.

  It is healthier to eat low-fat products (such as low-fat milk and low-fat cheese) and less-harmful fats that are found in margarine, sunflower oil, soya bean oil and oily fish. In addition, it is better to bake or grill food than to fry it.
- High salt intake also causes high blood pressure. Very often a single helping of packaged food contains more salt than the recommended salt intake for an entire day. Instead of salting food we should use pepper or other herbal seasonings.
- Obesity means being more than 20% overweight. Obesity is a contributory factor to causing high blood pressure and heart attacks.

THE ORGANISM

Exercise

Sportspeople who exercise regularly tend to have visibly larger body muscles. In the same way, exercise enlarges and strengthens the heart. Exercise also improves our overall circulation and helps to reduce body weight.

The most beneficial forms of exercise are aerobic exercises. These speed up our intake of oxygen and are maintained for long periods of time. Aerobic exercises include fast walking, jogging, running, cycling, swimming and dancing.

27.22 *Regular aerobic exercise is good for your heart.*

Summary

Diffusion is sufficient for transport of materials in small animals; large animals need a circulatory system.

An open circulatory system means that blood leaves blood vessels.

A closed circulatory system:
- means that blood is always in blood vessels
- moves blood around the body faster
- allows alterations in blood flow to body organs

Arteries:
- carry blood away from the heart
- have high pressure
- have thick walls
- do not have valves
- have narrow lumens
- carry oxygen-rich blood (except for the pulmonary artery)

Veins:
- carry blood to the heart
- have low pressure
- have thin walls
- have valves
- have large lumens
- carry oxygen-poor blood (except for the pulmonary vein)

Capillaries connect arteries to veins, have thin walls and allow exchange of materials.

Valves prevent backflow of blood.

Double circulation means that blood flows:
- from the heart to the lungs and then back to the heart (pulmonary circuit)
- from the heart to the rest of the body and back to the heart (systemic circuit)

Although heartbeat is usually controlled by the pacemaker, it can be altered by nervous stimulation from the brain or by hormones.

Heartbeat is controlled by:
- the pacemaker (SA node) in the wall of the right atrium, which causes the atria to contract
- the atrio-ventricular (AV) node, which sends the electrical impulses down the septum
- the ventricles, which contract

Diastole is when the heart is relaxed.

Systole is when the heart contracts.

The stages of heartbeat are:
- diastole: blood enters the atria
- atrial systole: blood is pumped to the ventricles
- ventricular systole: blood is pumped out of the heart

A pulse:
- is caused by the expansion and contraction of an artery as blood is forced through it
- is caused by ventricular systole

The effects of exercise on heartbeat are investigated by comparing the pulse rate at rest and after exercise.

Blood pressure is the force of blood against the walls of the arteries. Normally the higher value is a measure of the systolic pressure; the lower value is a measure of the diastolic pressure.

Smoking damages the heart and blood vessels by:
- increasing heart rate
- increasing blood pressure
- increasing the risk of blood clots

The main dietary factors affecting the circulatory system are:
- saturated fats (causing blocked arteries)
- high salt intake (raising blood pressure)
- being greatly overweight (raises blood pressure and causes heart attacks)

Aerobic exercise (high oxygen intake over a long period):
- strengthens the heart
- improves blood circulation
- reduces body weight

THE ORGANISM

Revision questions

1 (a) Name the method of transport in small organisms that do not have a circulatory system.

 (b) Why can humans not rely on the transport method used in small organisms?

 (c) How do humans overcome this problem?

2 (a) Distinguish between an open blood system and a closed blood system.

 (b) Name one animal with each type of circulation system.

 (c) Give one advantage of a closed blood system compared to an open blood system.

3 (a) State two structural differences between an artery and a vein.

 (b) Give two other differences between an artery and a vein.

 (c) State two ways in which a capillary differs from both an artery and a vein.

4 Name the material which **(a)** gives strength to an artery, **(b)** allows arteries and veins to change size, **(c)** lines all blood vessels.

5 (a) Arteries and veins are unsuited to exchanging materials with surrounding tissues. Explain why this is the case.

 (b) Give two reasons why capillaries are suited to exchanging materials.

6 (a) Name the structures labelled A to G in Fig. 27.23.

 (b) What structure is located at X?

 (c) Give the functions of the structures labelled D, E, G and X.

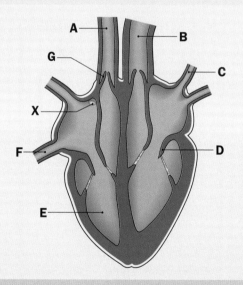

27.23

7 (a) What is a portal system?

 (b) Name a portal system in humans.

 (c) Suggest why the coronary arteries and veins do not form a portal system.

8 (a) Why are the walls of the atria thinner than the walls of the ventricles?

 (b) Why are the walls of the left ventricle thicker than the walls of the right ventricle?

9 (a) Draw a diagram of the heart, about the size of your fist. Label: **(i)** the four chambers, **(ii)** four major blood vessels, **(iii)** four valves, **(iv)** any other four parts associated with the heart.

 (b) Indicate on your diagram the direction of blood flow through the heart. Use blue to show deoxygenated blood and red for oxygen-rich blood.

10 Describe in words the path taken by a blood cell from the time it enters the heart at the vena cava until it leaves the heart in the aorta (e.g. *vena cava → right atrium → ...*)

11 Distinguish between the pulmonary and systemic circuits.

12 (a) Explain the roles of the pacemaker and the brain in controlling heartbeat.

 (b) Why should a person with an artificial pacemaker avoid strenuous exercise?

13 With regard to heartbeat, answer the following:

 (a) What structure causes it?

 (b) Where is this structure located?

 (c) What effect has exercise on heartbeat?

 (d) How is heartbeat normally measured?

14 Outline the stages of heartbeat under these headings:

 (a) Where the blood is flowing

 (b) The chambers that are contracted (if any)

 (c) The valves that are closed.

15 (a) Distinguish between systole and diastole.

 (b) What is meant by blood pressure?

 (c) How is blood pressure measured?

16 (a) What causes a pulse?

 (b) In terms of blood vessels, why is a pulse often taken at the wrist?

 (c) Why do those who exercise regularly usually have lower pulse rates than those who do not exercise?

 (d) What is the danger in having a very high resting pulse rate?

17 A person's blood pressure is found to be $^{180}/_{120}$ mm of Hg.

 (a) Why are two values given?

 (b) What does this reading indicate about this person?

18 Outline two negative effects on the circulatory system of each of the following: **(a)** smoking, **(b)** poor diet, **(c)** lack of exercise.

19 Give a reason for each of the following:

 (a) Standing still may cause a person to feel faint.

 (b) A person with a hole in the heart (septum) often lacks energy.

 (c) Pulses are felt in arteries but not in veins.

 (d) Turning red in the face after exercise.

 (e) Recording the pulse rate a number of times when calculating resting heart rates.

(continued overleaf)

THE ORGANISM

(f)   Arteries blocked with fatty plaques are bad for the heart.

(g)   Smokers are at risk of having strokes.

(h)   Avoiding eating saturated fats.

20   In investigating the effects of exercise on pulse rate, the following results were obtained:

Pulses per minute after exercise		
	Person 1	Person 2
1st minute	70	98
2nd minute	62	90
3rd minute	58	86
4th minute	56	83
5th minute	55	80
6th minute	55	78

Pulses per minute at rest		
	Person 1	Person 2
Trial 1	54	78
Trial 2	56	80
Trial 3	54	76
Trial 4	56	78
Average	55	78

(a)   How were the pulse rates measured?

(b)   Why were the resting pulse rates taken four times?

(c)   Which person had the higher resting rate?

(d)   Which person's heart rate returned to normal soonest after exercise?

(e)   What do these results suggest about the fitness of the two individuals?

21   What is unusual about blood in the:

(a)   pulmonary artery

(b)   pulmonary vein

(c)   hepatic portal vein?

22   (a)   What is the average resting rate of the human heart in beats per minute?

(b)   State **one** factor that decreases heart rate and **one** factor that increases it.

23   Figure 27.24 (right) shows the circulatory system of a mammal.

(a)   Name the structures labelled A to H.

(b)   Name the vessel in each case marked on the diagram which has the highest concentration of **(i)** oxygen, **(ii)** carbon dioxide, **(iii)** glucose, soon after a meal.

(c)   Which labelled vessels in the diagram have no valves?

(d)   Name the chambers of the heart to which the vessels marked B, C, G and H are connected.

24   (a)   Name the liquid part of blood.

(b)   Name **two** substances that are dissolved in the liquid part of blood.   *(continued)*

(c)   State **one** function of the liquid part of blood.

(d)   Blood contains red cells and white cells. State **one** function for **each** of these.

(e)   Name two common blood-grouping systems.

25   Choose which of the options (i), (ii), (iii) or (iv) represents the correct answer in each case below.

(a)   Pulmonary circulation involves:

(i)   an open circulatory system

(ii)   the lungs and kidneys

(iii)   the hepatic portal vein

(iv)   the pulmonary artery and the pulmonary vein

(b)   Inelastic collagen is found in:

(i)   only veins

(ii)   only capillaries

(iii)   arteries and veins

(iv)   only arteries

(c)   The hepatic portal vein contains:

(i)   blood rich in glucose

(ii)   blood rich in hormones

(iii)   blood lacking glucose

(iv)   blood rich in oxygen

(d)   The semi-lunar valves can be seen:

(i)   in the aorta only

(ii)   in the septum

(iii)   in the pulmonary artery only

(iv)   in both the aorta and pulmonary artery

(e)   Smoke that enters the blood in the lungs next enters the:

(i)   liver   (ii)   right atrium

(iii)   vena cava   (iv)   pulmonary artery

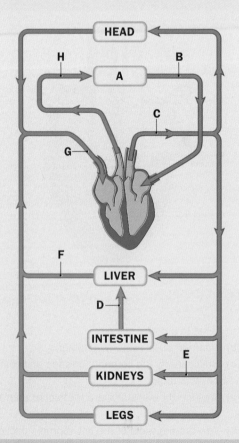

27.24

Section A

26 (a) The diagram shows a section of human tissue containing an artery and a vein.

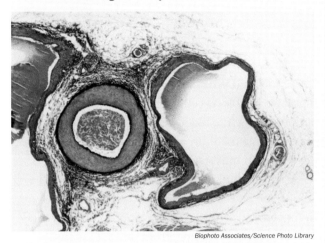

Biophoto Associates/Science Photo Library

   (i) Make a copy of the diagram and identify the artery by writing A on it and the vein by writing B on it.

   (ii) State **two** features of the artery that can be seen in the diagram which allowed you to identify it.

(b) Name **two** tissues that are present in the walls of arteries and veins and give a function of each of these tissues.

(c) Veins contain valves whereas arteries do not. What is the function of the valves?

(2003 Sample HL Q 3)

Section B

27 (a) (i) Name the chamber of the heart that receives blood back from the lungs.

   (ii) Name the blood vessels that bring this blood back from the lungs.

(b) Answer the following in relation to the dissection of a heart.

   (i) What instrument did you use for the dissection?

   (ii) Describe how you carried out the dissection.

   (iii) Draw a diagram of the dissected heart and on it label the following: bicuspid valve, left ventricle, right atrium, tricuspid valve.

(2006 Q 7 OL)

28 (a) (i) Cardiac muscle may be described as a <u>contractile</u> tissue. Explain the meaning of the underlined term.

   (ii) Which chamber of the heart has the greatest amount of muscle in its wall?

(b) Describe how you dissected a mammalian heart in order to investigate the internal structure of atria and ventricles.

   (i) Draw a labelled diagram of your dissection to show the location and structure of the bicuspid and tricuspid valves.

   (ii) State the procedure that you followed to expose a semilunar valve.

   (iii) What is the function of a semilunar valve?

   (iv) Where in your dissection did you find the origin of the coronary artery?

(2004 HL Q 9)

Section C

29 (a) (i) What is the average resting rate of the human heart in beats per minute?

   (ii) State **one** factor that decreases heart rate and **one** factor that increases it.

(b) The diagram shows a vertical section through the human heart.

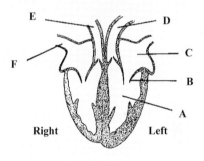

   (i) Name the parts A, B, C, D, E and F.

   (ii) To where does E carry blood?

   (iii) What is the function of B?

   (iv) Name the artery that supplies the heart muscle with blood.

(2003 Sample OL Q 10a, b)

Ordinary level	Higher level
2003 Sample Q 10a, 10b	2003 Sample Q 3
2004 Q 9	2004 Q 9
2005 Q 12a, 14c	2006 Q 5a, 5b
2006 Q 7	2007 Q 13a(i)
2008 Q 4, 8	

*For latest questions go to **www.edco.ie/biology***

Chapter 28 The lymphatic system

Introduction

Along with the blood circulatory system, mammals have a second circulatory system called the lymphatic system. The lymphatic system is a one-way system of dead-ending vessels. These lymph vessels collect the fluid that surrounds each cell in the body and return it to the blood.

Lymph nodes are swellings in the lymph vessels. Lymph nodes help to fight infection in the body.

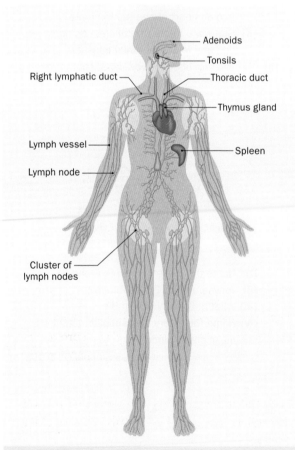

28.1 *The lymphatic system*

Formation of lymph

Blood in arteries is under higher pressure than blood in veins. This causes some fluid and small proteins to be forced out of blood plasma in capillaries at the arteriole side. This fluid is called **tissue fluid** (or interstitial fluid or extra cellular fluid, ECF). It surrounds all the cells of the body.

Tissue fluid is similar to plasma except it does not have red blood cells or platelets and has small amounts of white blood cells and proteins. It acts as an exchange medium whereby materials entering or leaving cells must pass through it.

As tissue fluid is continuously being formed (i.e. about one litre an hour is produced) it must be removed and returned to the blood. This prevents swelling (called oedema) from developing in the tissues. Tissue fluid is drained away by two routes:

- Most (90%) of it is drawn back into plasma in the capillaries near the veins. This occurs by osmosis and is helped by the reduced blood pressure in the veins.

- About 10% of the fluid enters dead-ending tubes called lymph vessels (or lymphatics). The fluid is now called lymph. Lymph contains large amounts of white blood cells, proteins and fats.

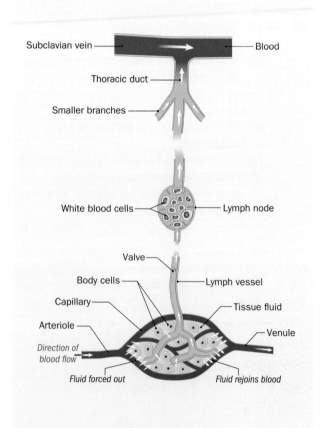

28.2 *Formation and path of lymph*

Lymph vessels

Lymph vessels are found throughout the body. Lymph is moved slowly through lymph vessels by:

- the muscular walls of the vessels
- general body movements pressing on the vessels

A system of valves ensures that lymph can only flow towards the shoulder regions.

Smaller lymph vessels join together to form two main vessels: the thoracic duct on the left side of the body and the right lymphatic duct at the right shoulder. These ducts empty lymph into the bloodstream at the subclavian veins located near the collar bones at the shoulders.

Lymph nodes

Lymph nodes are small swellings found along the lymph vessels. They contain large numbers of white blood cells (lymphocytes) with many channels through which lymph flows.

Lymph nodes are found in clusters, which form glands, in areas of the body such as the tonsils, adenoids (in the back of the nose), neck, armpits, thymus (a gland in the chest), spleen and groin (where the legs join the body).

Lymph nodes fight infection in two ways:

- They filter bacteria and other harmful material from lymph as it passes through.
- They also mature and store large numbers of white blood cells called lymphocytes. Some of these lymphocytes kill micro-organisms directly, others make antibodies, which help to neutralise micro-organisms.

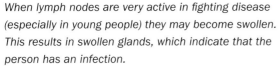

Did you know?

When lymph nodes are very active in fighting disease (especially in young people) they may become swollen. This results in swollen glands, which indicate that the person has an infection.

If lymph vessels become blocked (or if a person is inactive for several hours), swelling (oedema) may result. This is often seen in the ankles where gravity adds to the excess tissue fluid.

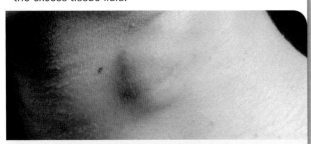

28.3 *A swollen lymph node in the neck*

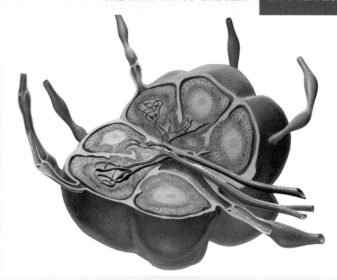

28.4 *Artwork showing the internal structure of a lymph node*

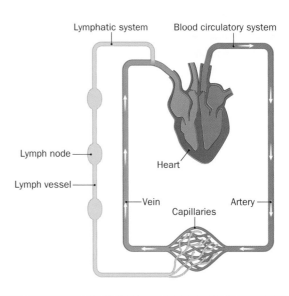

28.5 *Relationship between the blood and lymphatic circulatory systems*

Functions of the lymphatic system

The lymphatic system forms a link between different parts of the blood (i.e. plasma produces tissue fluid, tissue fluid forms lymph and lymph returns to the plasma).

The lymphatic system has the following functions:

- To collect tissue fluid and return it to the blood.
- To defend the body against infection. It does this by:
  (a) filtering out micro-organisms in lymph nodes
  (b) maturing and storing lymphocytes
  (c) destroying micro-organisms by engulfing and digesting them or by antibody production
- To absorb and transport fats in the digestive system. Lymph is found in the lacteals (which are in the villi of the small intestine). Lymph often has a milky appearance because of its high fat concentration.

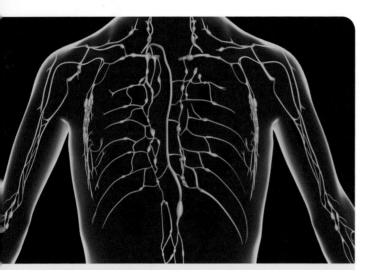

28.6 *Lymph supply in the upper body*

Summary

The lymphatic system:
- is a secondary transport system
- returns tissue fluid from around cells to the blood

Tissue fluid:
- is plasma without red cells, platelets or large proteins
- surrounds all body cells and helps transport materials in and out of cells

Tissue fluid returns to the plasma in two ways:
- most enters blood capillaries
- some enters dead-ending lymph vessels where it is called lymph. Lymph is later returned to the bloodstream

Lymph is made from tissue fluid and contains white blood cells, proteins and fats.

Lymph moves in lymph vessels due to:
- muscles in the vessel walls
- general body movements

Valves in lymph vessels control the direction of lymph flow.

Lymph returns to the blood in the subclavian veins (near the collar bones).

Lymph nodes:
- are swellings found along lymph vessels
- filter bacteria
- store lymphocytes (white blood cells). Some of these kill micro-organisms and others produce antibodies.

The lymphatic system's functions are:
- to return tissue fluid to the blood
- to defend the body against infection
- to transport fat

Revision questions

1. Name two circulatory systems in a human.
2. **(a)** How is tissue fluid made?
   (b) Give one function for tissue fluid.
   (c) What happens to this fluid to prevent too much from accumulating?
3. Give one difference in each case between:
   (a) plasma and tissue fluid
   (b) tissue fluid and lymph
   (c) a lymph vessel and a lymph node
4. If plasma is leaving the blood at the rate of 1 litre every hour, explain why the volume of blood does not normally fall.
5. Distinguish between blood and lymph in terms of:
   (a) colour, **(b)** contents, **(c)** cause of movement.
6. **(a)** Name the items labelled A to D in Figure 28.7.
   (b) State, giving a reason, whether X or Y on the diagram represents the arteriole side of the capillary.
   (c) State two pieces of evidence from the diagram which indicate that structure B is not a blood capillary.

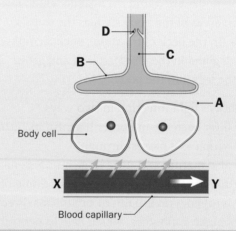

Body cell

Blood capillary

28.7

7. **(a)** Where are lymph nodes mostly located in the body?
   (b) What is their main function?
   (c) State two ways in which they achieve this function.
   (d) Why do they sometimes become swollen?

Sample examination questions

Section C
8. **(i)** Describe the structure of the lymphatic system.
   (ii) Give an account of **three** functions of the lymphatic system.   *(2006 HL Q 13c)*

Previous examination questions

Ordinary level	Higher level
n/a	2006 Q 13c

*For latest questions go to **www.edco.ie/biology***

THE ORGANISM

Chapter 29 **Human nutrition**

Types of nutrition

Nutrition is the process by which an organism obtains and uses its food.

Autotrophic means an organism can make its own food.

Most autotrophs are green plants. They make their food using carbon dioxide, water and sunlight as a form of energy. This process is called photosynthesis.

Heterotrophic means that an organism cannot make its own food, but must obtain its food from the environment.

Animals, fungi and some bacteria are heterotrophs. If an organism gets it food from a live source it is said to be a parasite, e.g. disease-causing bacteria and potato blight fungus. If the food is taken from a dead host the organism is a saprophyte, e.g. bread mould fungus.

Depending on what they eat, heterotrophs can be categorised as follows:

> **Herbivores** are animals that feed exclusively on plants, e.g. cattle, sheep, deer.
>
> **Carnivores** are animals that feed on other animals. They are often called flesh-eaters, e.g. dogs, cats, seals.
>
> **Omnivores** are animals that feed on plants and animals, e.g. humans, bears, badgers.

Digestion

Digestion is the breakdown of food into particles that are small enough to pass into body cells. Digestion may be physical (or mechanical) or chemical (using enzymes).

The need for a digestive system

Some animals, such as sponges, have no digestive system. In these cases each cell has to digest its own food. Consequently each cell produces a range of enzymes to digest different types of food. This is unnecessarily repetitious.

Most animals have a digestive system. This means that food is only processed once, before being transported to all the cells of the body.

A digestive system allows the materials needed to process the food to be localised in a single place, e.g. teeth in the mouth, acid in the stomach. The digestive system prevents each cell having to contain a full range of all the digestive enzymes.

The digestive system

In humans, the digestive system consists of the **alimentary canal** or gut. This is a long tube starting at the mouth and ending at the anus. Attached to the alimentary canal are the associated glands. These are the salivary glands, the liver and the pancreas.

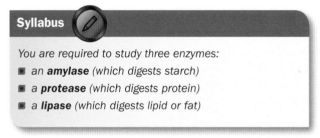

Syllabus

You are required to study three enzymes:
- an **amylase** (which digests starch)
- a **protease** (which digests protein)
- a **lipase** (which digests lipid or fat)

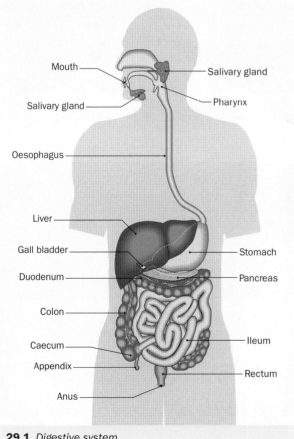

29.1 *Digestive system*

Sequence of events in human nutrition

The intake and use of food involves the following steps:

1 **Ingestion**. This is the taking of food into the alimentary canal, i.e. putting food into the mouth.
2 **Digestion**. This is the mechanical (or physical) and chemical breakdown of food. Food is mechanically broken down by teeth, peristalsis and muscular churning. This allows a greater surface area for enzymes to chemically digest the food.

   Digestion is essential to allow for absorption. If food was not broken down, the chemicals in the food would not pass from the digestive system into the body tissues.
3 **Absorption**. Food in the digestive system is not considered to be in the body. It is absorbed into the blood and enters the body when it passes across the membranes lining the alimentary canal.
4 **Egestion**. This is the removal of unabsorbed and undigested material from the digestive system (through the anus).

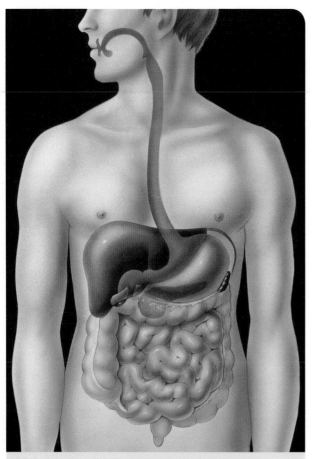

29.2 *Artwork of the human digestive system*

Mouth

Mechanical digestion is carried out by the chewing action of the **teeth**. Humans have four types of teeth. Each type of tooth is specialised to carry out a specific function. Starting at the front of the mouth and working back, the types and functions of teeth are:

- **Incisors** – chisel shaped, with sharp edges for cutting, slicing or biting.
- **Canines** – long, pointed teeth (fangs). They are poorly developed in humans but well developed in carnivores. They grip, stab and tear food.
- **Premolars** – teeth with projections on the surface called cusps. They crush and chew food.
- **Molars** – the large teeth located at the back of the jaws. They also crush and chew food.

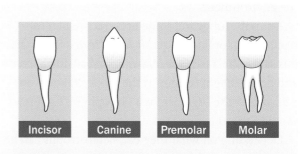

| Incisor | Canine | Premolar | Molar |

29.3 *Types of teeth*

HUMAN DENTAL FORMULA

There are 32 teeth in a full set of human permanent teeth. The arrangement of the different types of teeth can be given in the dental formula. The dental formula for an adult human is:

$$2 \left(I\frac{2}{2} \ C\frac{1}{1} \ PM\frac{2}{2} \ M\frac{3}{3} \right)$$

In this formula the letters represent the four types of teeth. The upper numbers refer to the number of each type of tooth in the upper jaw on one side of the mouth. The lower numbers refer to the number of each type of tooth in the lower jaw on the same side of the mouth.

For example, the right-hand side of the mouth has a maximum of two upper and two lower incisors, one upper and one lower canine, two upper and two lower premolars, and three upper and three lower molars.

DIGESTION IN THE MOUTH

- **Mechanical** or **physical digestion** of food is carried out by the action of the teeth. This results in smaller particles of food that are easier to swallow and have a greater surface area for enzymes to act on.
- **Chemical digestion** takes place due to the action of the enzyme amylase. This is found in saliva, which is a liquid secreted by three pairs of salivary glands. These are located under the tongue, at the back of the jaws and in the cheeks. They secrete about one litre of saliva every day.

Saliva consists of water, salts, mucous (also called mucin) and the enzymes amylase (also called ptyalin) and lysozyme. Saliva helps to soften and dissolve food so that we can taste and swallow it.

Lysozyme helps to destroy micro-organisms (it is also found in sweat and tears).

Amylase digests starch into maltose. Amylase is produced in the salivary glands and travels through small tubes (or ducts) into the mouth where it carries out its action. The ideal pH of the mouth is 7. Amylase only acts for a short time because it is inhibited by acid in the stomach.

In the mouth, food is formed into a ball, or bolus, and pushed backwards into the pharynx. A flap called the **epiglottis** closes over the trachea (or windpipe) and ensures the bolus passes down the oesophagus.

Oesophagus (or foodpipe)

The oesophagus carries food to the stomach by an involuntary wave of muscular contraction called **peristalsis**.

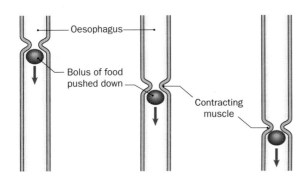

29.4 *Peristalsis*

The movement of the bolus is assisted by mucous found in saliva and by mucous produced by the inner lining of the oesophagus. The process of peristalsis continues throughout the length of the alimentary canal.

PERISTALSIS

Peristalsis moves food through the alimentary canal. In the stomach, peristalsis helps to break down food mechanically. It also mixes food with the secretions of the stomach and then forces the mixture into the small intestine.

In the small intestine, peristalsis forces food forwards and backwards, which helps the food to be absorbed. Finally, about every thirty minutes strong waves of peristalsis in the large intestine force waste into the rectum.

ROLE OF FIBRE

Dietary fibre (also called roughage) consists of cellulose from plant cell walls. Humans cannot digest cellulose. Good sources of fibre in our diet include wholemeal bread, cereals, vegetables and fruit.

Fibre absorbs and stores water. This causes the unabsorbed wastes to expand, especially in the large intestine. The physical bulk of the waste stimulates the muscles of the intestine to work. In this way fibre stimulates peristalsis.

Did you know?

A high-fibre diet is thought to be helpful in reducing the risk of cancer of the colon. This is because wastes move more rapidly through the colon, which means that cancer-causing chemicals have less time in contact with the colon.

Stomach

The stomach is a muscular bag that stores and digests food. Food enters from the oesophagus when the cardiac sphincter muscle at the top of the stomach opens. A sphincter muscle is a circular muscle that opens and closes (like the top of a duffel bag).

The stomach can hold about 1 litre of food for up to 4 hours. The lining of the stomach (the mucosa) is heavily folded, forming millions of gastric glands. These glands produce a range of secretions, collectively called gastric juice. This consists of the following:

- **Mucous**, which coats the stomach and prevents self-digestion in the stomach.

- **Pepsinogen**, which is an inactive enzyme and therefore does not digest the cells in the stomach lining that produce it. Pepsinogen is converted to the active enzyme pepsin by acid in the stomach.

  Pepsin converts proteins to smaller peptides:

Proteins $\xrightarrow{\text{Pepsin}}$ Peptides

  Pepsin is said to be a protease, i.e. it is an enzyme that digests protein.

- **Hydrochloric acid** (**HCl**) gives the stomach a pH of 1 to 2. The acid kills many bacteria, loosens fibrous and cellular foods, activates pepsinogen and denatures salivary amylase.

Did you know?

An overproduction of acid in the stomach can lead to heartburn. This occurs when the acid rises up the oesophagus, which is not as well covered in mucous as the stomach. It may be controlled by neutralising the acid with alkali, such as Alka-Seltzer or Rennies.

The contraction of the stomach walls helps to churn and digest the food mechanically. This turns it into a thick, soupy mixture called chyme. Chyme leaves the stomach in small amounts when the pyloric sphincter at the base of the stomach opens briefly.

PROTECTION FROM SELF-DIGESTION

Gastric juice (especially pepsin and HCl) could potentially digest the stomach wall. This is prevented in a number of ways:

- Mucous lines the stomach.
- Mucous is alkaline and reduces the acidity near the stomach wall.
- Pepsin is released as the inactive pepsinogen. Thus pepsin does not come into contact with the cells as it enters the stomach cavity.
- The cells that line the stomach are tightly packed and can be replaced very rapidly; typically half a million are formed per minute.

Did you know?

If these mechanisms fail, an ulcer results. Ulcers in the stomach are called peptic ulcers (duodenal ulcers are more common). Ulcers cause bleeding and may dissolve all the way through the stomach wall to form a perforated ulcer. In this case bacteria could pass into the body, leading to death.

Glands associated with the small intestine

Pancreas

The pancreas secretes the hormone insulin (see Chapter 36) and digestive materials, which form pancreatic juice.

Pancreatic juice consists mainly of the salt sodium hydrogen carbonate (or sodium bicarbonate), which neutralises chyme from the stomach, and a range of enzymes such as amylase and lipase. These enzymes act on food in the duodenum.

Pancreatic amylase is similar to salivary amylase. It converts starch to maltose.

Starch $\xrightarrow{\text{Amylase}}$ Maltose

Pancreatic lipase converts lipids (or fats) to fatty acids and glycerol.

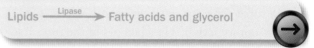

Lipids $\xrightarrow{\text{Lipase}}$ Fatty acids and glycerol

Lipase and amylase, which are made in the pancreas, enter the duodenum through the pancreatic duct. Lipase acts on lipids in the duodenum, while amylase digests starch, also in the duodenum. Both enzymes function best at a pH of between 7 and 8, which is the pH of the duodenum.

Liver

The liver is a complex organ with many functions. Among the most important functions of the liver are:

- making bile
- detoxifying the body, i.e. breaking down poisons such as alcohol and drugs
- breaking down excess amino acids to form urea
- converting glucose to glycogen for storage
- converting excess carbohydrates to fat
- storing vitamins such as vitamin D
- storing minerals such as iron (Fe), copper (Cu) and zinc (Zn)
- making plasma proteins such as fibrinogen (used in blood clotting)
- making cholesterol, which is needed to form many hormones
- producing heat to warm the blood (and the body)

THE ORGANISM

BILE

Bile is partly formed from the remains of dead red blood cells. It is a yellow-green viscous liquid. It consists of water, bile salts and bile pigments (it does not contain any enzymes).

Bile is made in the liver and stored in the gall bladder. Gallstones can form in the bile duct and prevent the release of bile.

29.5 *Gall stones*

Bile enters the duodenum through the bile duct. The functions of bile are as follows:

- It emulsifies lipids, i.e. it breaks down large fats and oils into tiny droplets. This increases the surface area for enzyme digestion. (If you put oil and water in a test tube and shake it, a cloudy emulsion forms, consisting of fat droplets in water.)
- It contains sodium hydrogen carbonate, which helps to neutralise chyme from the stomach.
- It excretes the pigments biliverdin and bilirubin, which are made from dead red blood cells.

Small intestine

The small intestine consists of two main parts.

- The first 25 cm is the duodenum. This is the area where most digestion occurs.
- The remaining 5.5 metres comprise the ileum. This is the region where the absorption of digested foods into the body takes place.

Food remains in the small intestine for between 1 and 6 hours.

Duodenum

The main function of the duodenum is digestion.

The cells lining the duodenum produce a range of digestive enzymes. In addition, the products of the pancreas and liver enter the duodenum.

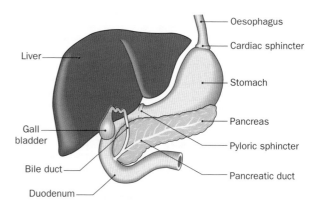

29.6 *Relationship between the alimentary canal and the liver and pancreas*

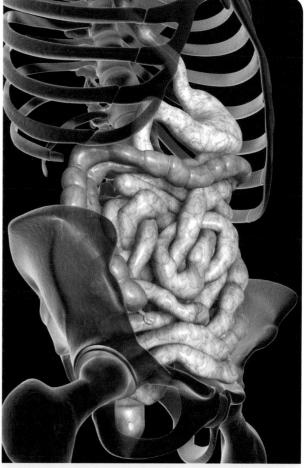

29.7 *The position of the intestines relative to the skeleton*

The inner lining of the small intestine contains many infoldings called villi (singular villus). This gives the lining a velvety texture. In addition, each villus has about 600 microvilli.

The numerous foldings increase the surface area for either digestion (in the duodenum) or absorption (in the ileum).

Intestinal glands are located between the villi. These glands produce a range of enzymes called intestinal juice.

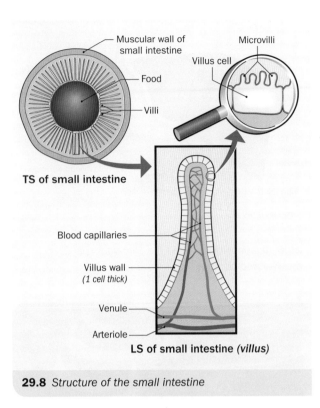

TS of small intestine

LS of small intestine *(villus)*

29.8 *Structure of the small intestine*

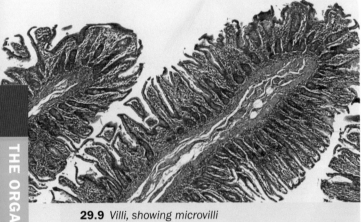

29.9 *Villi, showing microvilli*

A summary of the digestive process is given in the table below.

Ileum

The food entering the ileum is almost fully digested. The function of the ileum is to absorb nutrients. The end products of digestion are given below.

End products of digestion	
Food	**Digested to**
Carbohydrates	Monosaccharides (e.g. glucose)
Proteins	Amino acids
Lipids	Fatty acids and glycerol

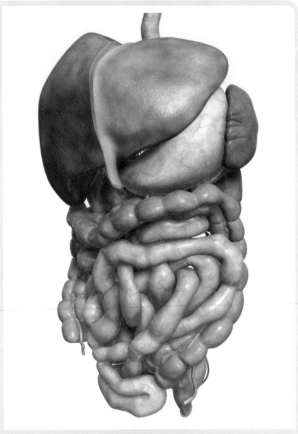

29.10 *The liver and intestines*

Summary of the digestive process (the enzymes are highlighted)					
Substance	**Made in**	**Active in**	**Preferred pH**	**Substrate**	**Product**
Amylase (enzyme)	**Salivary glands**	**Mouth**	**7 to 8**	**Starch**	**Maltose**
Pepsin (enzyme)	**Stomach lining**	**Stomach**	**2**	**Protein**	**Peptides**
Hydrochloric acid	Stomach lining	Stomach	–	Bacteria and fibrous foods	Dead bacteria and softened food
Sodium hydrogen carbonate	Pancreas	Duodenum	–	Acid	Neutralises acid
Amylase (enzyme)	**Pancreas**	**Duodenum**	**7 to 8**	**Starch**	**Maltose**
Lipase (enzyme)	**Pancreas**	**Duodenum**	**7 to 8**	**Lipids**	**Fatty acids and glycerol**
Bile salts	Liver	Duodenum	–	Lipids	Lipid droplets
Sodium hydrogen carbonate	Liver	Duodenum	–	Acid	Neutralises acid

VILLUS (PLURAL VILLI)

The lining of the duodenum and ileum contains many villi. As mentioned earlier, these increase the surface area for absorption. In addition, their walls are only one cell thick. There is a rich blood supply just inside each villus. The capillaries in each villus absorb water and soluble nutrients such as glucose, amino acids, vitamins and minerals.

The capillaries carry the nutrients to the hepatic portal vein, which takes them to the liver. The liver acts as a warehouse, storing some nutrients and releasing others for use throughout the body.

Amino acids cannot be stored in the body (they tend to become toxic). Any amino acids not used by the body are broken down in the liver, forming urea. This process is called **deamination**.

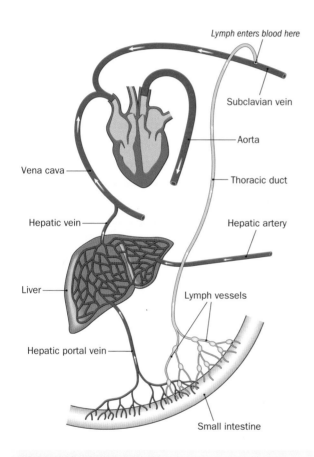

29.11 *Role of the liver*

Urea and other waste leaves the liver in the hepatic vein and eventually passes to the kidney. Here it forms part of urine, which is then excreted (see Chapter 32).

LACTEAL

Inside each villus is a **lacteal** (see Figure 29.12). Each lacteal contains a liquid called lymph. Fatty acids and glycerol are absorbed into the cells of the villus lining. Here they re-form into fats. These fats are coated with protein and pass into the lymph in the lacteals.

The fats are transported by the lymph, which carries them to the bloodstream. It takes lymph about 18 hours to rejoin the bloodstream at the subclavian veins near the base of the neck. The protein coat is dissolved in the blood and the fats are absorbed into cells.

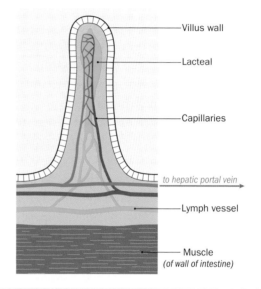

29.12 *Section through villus and lacteal (TS of small intestine)*

ADAPTATIONS OF THE SMALL INTESTINE FOR ABSORPTION

- It is very long.
- It has numerous villi and microvilli.
- The walls of the villi are very thin.
- There is a rich blood supply to carry away water-soluble products.
- Each villus has a lymph supply (lacteal) to carry away the fats.

29.13 *Numerous villi (lacteals are visible in some of these villi)*

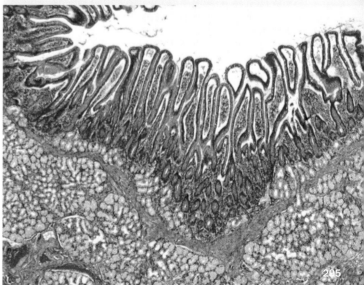

THE ORGANISM

Large intestine

The large intestine is only about 1.5 metres long (compared with the small intestine, which is about 6 metres long). It is called 'large' due to its greater diameter (about 6 cm, compared to 3 cm for the small intestine).

Food stays in the large intestine for between 10 hours and a few days.

Caecum and appendix

The part of the large intestine below its junction with the small intestine is called the caecum. The appendix is found at the end of the caecum.

The functions of the appendix and caecum in humans are not known. In many herbivores (e.g. rabbits) they contain bacteria capable of digesting cellulose. It is thought that our ancestors once needed them for the same reason.

We no longer need to digest cellulose as we get our carbohydrate supplies from more easily digested sources such as starch. The caecum and appendix are now **vestigial** organs (i.e. they have lost their former use).

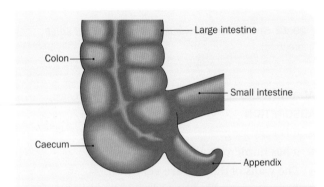

29.14 *Junction of small and large intestine*

Colon

The function of the colon is to reabsorb water. The liquid waste that enters the large intestine is thus converted to a semi-solid waste called faeces. The colour of faeces is due to bile.

Faeces are stored in the rectum before being egested through the anus (Note: faeces are not excreted, as excretion is the removal of waste products of metabolism (in cells) from the body. Faeces were never absorbed into the body cells).

Diarrhoea occurs when unabsorbed material moves too rapidly through the colon. Less water is then reabsorbed and the faeces contain more liquid.

Constipation is the reverse. It results from unabsorbed material passing too slowly through the colon so that too much water is reabsorbed. It may

be controlled by eating more fibre, which stimulates peristalsis.

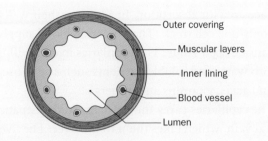

29.15 *TS of large intestine*

Symbiotic bacteria in the digestive system

- Bacteria in the colon feed on the waste and produce some B group vitamins and vitamin K. We absorb these vitamins from the colon. Bacteria such as these obtain food from humans and provide useful vitamins in return. They are said to be symbiotic bacteria.

- In addition to producing vitamins in the colon, bacteria in the digestive system break down food, especially cellulose. Some of the digested nutrients are absorbed into the body from the intestines. These bacteria are also symbiotic.

- The presence of beneficial bacteria prevent the growth of disease-causing (pathogenic) bacteria and fungi.

Did you know?

*Sometimes bacteria gather and grow in the **appendix**. Their waste products may produce painful inflammation of the appendix. The pain is felt between the navel and the lower right-hand side of the abdomen. If the pain appears and disappears it is called a 'grumbling appendix'.*

If not treated the appendix may burst and bacterial infection of the abdomen lining results (called peritonitis). This is a very serious condition.

29.16 *The caceum and appendix (mid left), with the ileum in the background*

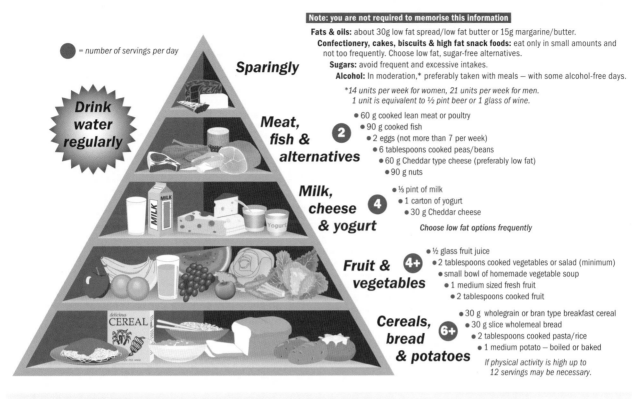

● = *number of servings per day*

Drink water regularly

Sparingly

Fats & oils: about 30g low fat spread/low fat butter or 15g margarine/butter.
Confectionery, cakes, biscuits & high fat snack foods: eat only in small amounts and not too frequently. Choose low fat, sugar-free alternatives.
Sugars: avoid frequent and excessive intakes.
Alcohol: In moderation,* preferably taken with meals — with some alcohol-free days.

*14 units per week for women, 21 units per week for men.
1 unit is equivalent to ½ pint beer or 1 glass of wine.

Meat, fish & alternatives

2
- 60 g cooked lean meat or poultry
- 90 g cooked fish
- 2 eggs (not more than 7 per week)
- 6 tablespoons cooked peas/beans
- 60 g Cheddar type cheese (preferably low fat)
- 90 g nuts

Milk, cheese & yogurt

4
- ⅓ pint of milk
- 1 carton of yogurt
- 30 g Cheddar cheese

Choose low fat options frequently

Fruit & vegetables

4+
- ½ glass fruit juice
- 2 tablespoons cooked vegetables or salad (minimum)
- small bowl of homemade vegetable soup
- 1 medium sized fresh fruit
- 2 tablespoons cooked fruit

Cereals, bread & potatoes

6+
- 30 g wholegrain or bran type breakfast cereal
- 30 g slice wholemeal bread
- 2 tablespoons cooked pasta/rice
- 1 medium potato — boiled or baked

If physical activity is high up to 12 servings may be necessary.

29.17 *Food pyramid. Note: you are not required to memorise the information in small print on the right.*

Balanced human diet

A balanced diet contains seven components, i.e. carbohydrate, protein, lipid, vitamins, minerals, fibre and water. These components must be present in our diet in the right amounts and should come from a variety of sources, in order to ensure that the body gets all the necessary energy and nutrients.

The total amount of food a person requires depends on:

- age (young people need more food than older individuals)
- activity levels
- gender (males need more food than females)
- health

Food groups

Foods that contain similar nutrients are arranged into four food groups. These groups are:

- cereals, bread and potatoes
- fruit and vegetables
- milk, cheese and yogurt
- meat, fish and poultry

We should eat a variety of foods from each of these food groups. Suggested numbers of servings of each food group are given in the food pyramid in Figure 29.17.

29.18 *A balanced diet: the proportions relate to the amount of each food group that should be eaten*

Summary

NUTRITION

- **AUTOTROPHIC** *(make food)*
  - **PHOTOSYNTHESIS** *(use light energy)*
  - **CHEMOSYNTHESIS** *(use chemical energy)*
- **HETEROTROPHIC** *(take in food)*
  - **HERBIVORES** *(eat plants)*
  - **CARNIVORES** *(eat animals)*
  - **OMNIVORES** *(eat plants & animals)*

29.19 *Types of nutrition*

Heterotrophic nutrition involves ingestion (taking in), digestion (breaking down), absorption (food entering the body) and egestion (removing waste).

Mouth:
- The four types of teeth are incisors, canines, premolars and molars.
- The enzyme amylase digests starch to maltose.

Oesophagus:
- is a muscular pipe
- moves food by peristalsis

Peristalsis is a wave of muscular action that forces food through the intestines.

Fibre stimulates peristalsis.

The stomach:
- stores and digests food
- is a muscular bag; churns food to make chyme
- stomach lining makes
  - (i)   mucous
  - (ii) pepsinogen (becomes pepsin in acid; pepsin digests protein to peptides)
  - (iii) hydrochloric acid (pH 1–2), which kills bacteria and softens food

The pancreas makes:
- sodium hydrogen carbonate (neutralises acid from stomach)
- the enzymes
  - (i) amylase (starch to maltose)
  - (ii) lipase (lipid to fatty acid and glycerol)

The digestive roles of the liver:
- makes bile which emulsifies fat
- makes sodium hydrogen carbonate to neutralise acid
- stores many nutrients

The duodenum is the main location for digestion. It makes a range of digestive enzymes.

The ileum absorbs food:
- the ileum is lined with numerous villi to increase surface area
- glucose and amino acids are absorbed into the bloodstream and taken to the liver
- fatty acids and glycerol enter the lacteals and are transported in lymph and returned to the bloodstream for distribution around the body

The appendix and caecum are vestigial (i.e. have lost their former use).

The colon:
- reabsorbs water from the waste, forming faeces
- symbiotic bacteria in the colon
  - (i)   make vitamins and digest cellulose
  - (ii) prevent harmful micro-organisms from growing
  - (iii) prevent the growth of disease-causing organisms

The rectum stores faeces.

There are seven components of a balanced diet:
- carbohydrate
- lipid
- protein
- minerals
- vitamins
- fibre
- water

The amount of food a person requires depends on age, activity, gender and health.

The four food groups and their average number of servings per day are:
- cereals, bread and potatoes (6+)
- fruit and vegetables (4+)
- milk, cheese and yogurt (4)
- meat, fish and poultry (2)

THE ORGANISM

Revision questions

1 (a) What is nutrition?
   (b) Distinguish between autotrophic and heterotrophic nutrition.
2 (a) Name the four stages in heterotrophic nutrition.
   (b) Give the location for each stage in humans.
3 (a) Name the parts of the alimentary canal in sequence and give a function for each part.
   (b) Name the associated glands.
4 Distinguish between:
   (a) mechanical and chemical digestion
   (b) autotrophic and heterotrophic
   (c) parasite and saprophyte
   (d) incisor and canine
   (e) herbivore and carnivore
5 (a) Name the four types of teeth.
   (b) Describe the shape of each type of tooth.
   (c) Give the function for each tooth type.
   (d) Give the full human dental formula.
6 Why is salivary amylase inactive in the stomach?
7 (a) Name the material that makes up the wall of the stomach.
   (b) What enzyme in the stomach digests this substance?
   (c) How does the stomach prevent self-digestion?
   (d) Why does stomach acid not damage the duodenum?
8 What are the functions of each of the following:
   (a) duodenum, (b) ileum, (c) colon, (d) rectum.
9 (a) Where is bile made?
   (b) What is it made from?
   (c) Where is it stored?
   (d) Where does it act?
   (e) What are its functions?
10 List four features of the small intestine which are adaptations to help it absorb food.
11 (a) Name a digestive enzyme that is secreted in an inactive form.
   (b) State where the enzyme is (i) made, and (ii) activated.
   (c) Name the substance that causes activation.
12 Give a biological reason for each of the following:
   (a) Chewing food well.
   (b) Certain tablets relieve heartburn.
   (c) An astronaut in space can still swallow.
   (d) Ulcers forming in the stomach.
   (e) Pepsin is not secreted in an active form.
   (f) Chocolate provides energy very rapidly compared to potatoes.
   (g) A person can survive without an appendix.
13 For each of the substances pepsin, bile, amylase and lipase, state:
   (a) where they are produced
   (b) where they act
   (c) what they act on
   (d) the result of their action
   (e) their preferred pH (if any).

14 (a) Redraw Figure 29.20 at twice its present size.
   (b) Name the parts labelled A to M.

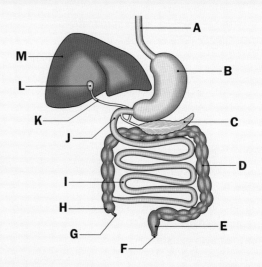

29.20

   (c) Name a part of the diagram:
      (i)   that is acidic
      (ii) where chyme is formed
      (iii) where bile is stored
      (iv) where glycogen is stored
      (v)   where bacteria are killed
      (vi) where bacteria live
      (vii) where villi are found.
15 Copy out and complete the table below.

Enzyme	Substrate	Product
Amylase		
	Lipid	
		Peptides

16 (a) State the end products of digestion.
   (b) Name the end products of food digestion that are (i) soluble and (ii) insoluble in water.
   (c) Explain what happens to the (i) water-soluble end products and (ii) water-insoluble end products.
17 Choose which of the options (i), (ii), (iii) or (iv) represents the correct answer in each case below.
   (a) Proteins are chemically digested in the:
      (i)   mouth
      (ii) stomach
      (iii) liver
      (iv) large intestine
   (b) Lacteals are used to absorb:
      (i)   starch
      (ii) amino acids
      (iii) lipids
      (iv) proteins

(continued)

THE ORGANISM

(c) The substance produced by the pancreas to neutralise stomach acid is called:

(i) chyme

(ii) maltose

(iii) vitamin D

(iv) sodium hydrogen carbonate

(d) Gastric juice contains:

(i) chyme, pepsin and hydrochloric acid

(ii) mucosa, proteins and hydrochloric acid

(iii) mucous, pepsinogen and hydrochloric acid

(iv) amylase, mucous and pepsin

(e) Symbiotic bacteria in the colon produce:

(i) Vitamins A and D

(ii) Vitamins A and B

(iii) Vitamins D and K

(iv) Vitamins B and K

Sample examination questions

Section A

18 Answer the following questions in relation to the human alimentary canal.

(a) What is peristalsis?

(b) State **one** reason why a low pH is important in the stomach.

(c) Why is fibre important?

(d) Name an enzyme that is involved in the digestion of fat.

(e) What are the products of fat digestion?

(f) What is the role of bile in fat digestion?

(g) State a role of beneficial bacteria in the alimentary canal.

(2004 HL Q 6)

19 Study the diagram and then answer the following questions.

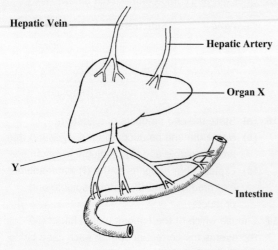

(a) Name X and Y

(b) Place arrows on Y, the hepatic artery and the hepatic vein to indicate the direction of blood flow.

(c) State the precise location of organ X in the human body.

(f) State a role that organ X plays in the digestive process.

(2006 HL Q 5)

20 The diagram shows part of a section of the human small intestine.

(a) Name A, B, C.

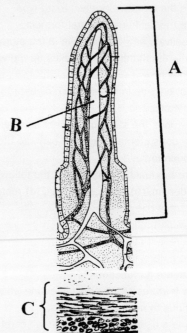

(b) State two ways in which A is adapted for the absorption of soluble foods.

(c) Name a process by which soluble foods are absorbed into the blood from the small intestine.

(d) What type of food is mainly absorbed into B?

(2005 HL Q 6)

21 The graph shows how the rate of reaction of a carbohydrate-digesting enzyme in the human alimentary canal varies with pH.

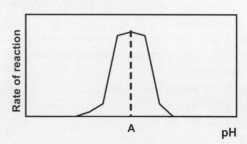

(continued)

(a) Name a carbohydrate-digesting enzyme in the human alimentary canal.

(b) Where in the alimentary canal does this enzyme act?

(c) State the enzyme's product(s).

(d) What is the pH at A?

(e) A is said to be the enzyme's _____ pH.

(f) Suggest a temperature at which human enzymes work best.

(g) What term best describes the shape of an enzyme?

(2007 HL Q3)

Section C

22 (a) Bile is involved in digestion in the human body.

    (i) 1. Where is bile produced?

        2. Where is bile stored?

    (ii) Where does bile act in the alimentary canal?

(b) The diagram shows the digestive system of the human.

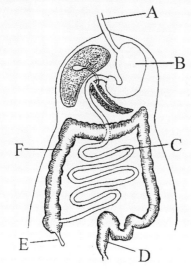

(i) Name the parts labelled A, B, C, D, E and F.

(ii) What is the role of peristalsis in the digestive system?

(iii) Where do the products of digestion enter the blood?

(iv) How do these products of digestion pass into the blood?

(c) (i) For each of the parts labelled B and C in the diagram above, state whether the contents are acidic, neutral or alkaline.

    (ii) Amylase is an enzyme that is found in saliva. State the substrate and the product of this enzyme.

    (iii) State **two** functions of symbiotic bacteria in the alimentary canal.

    (iv) What is meant by egestion? From which labelled part of the diagram does egestion occur?

(2008 OL Q 13)

23 (a) (i) Distinguish between mechanical and chemical digestion.

    (ii) Name a structure in the human digestive system, other than teeth, which is involved in mechanical digestion.

(b) The diagram shows the human digestive system.

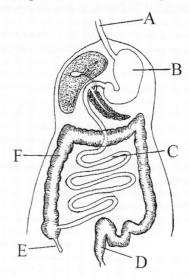

(i) Name the parts A, B, C, D, E and F.

(ii) Describe **two** functions of bile in relation to digestion.

(iii) Answer the following in relation to a lipase:

    1. Where is it secreted?

    2. Where does it act?

    3. What is the approximate pH at its site of action?

(c) (i) What are symbiotic bacteria?

    (ii) Give **two** activities of symbiotic bacteria in the human digestive system.

    (iii) Name the part(s) of the digestive system in which the following are absorbed into the blood.

    1. the products of digestion,

    2. water.

    (iv) Name a process involved in the passage of the products of digestion into the blood.

    (v) Explain how the structure that you have named in (iii) 1. is adapted for the absorption of the products of digestion.

(2008 HL Q 12)

Previous examination questions

Ordinary level	Higher level
2006 Q 12	2004 Q 6
2007 Q 15c	2005 Q 6
2008 Q 13	2006 Q 3a, b, c, 5
	2008 Q 12

For latest questions go to **www.edco.ie/biology**

THE ORGANISM

Chapter 30 Homeostasis

External and internal environments

The term external environment refers to the surroundings in which an organism lives. The external environment for *Amoeba* is fresh water; for humans it is the air around us. Most organisms (apart from humans) have relatively little ability to control their external environment.

Internal environment refers to the surroundings of the cells in a multicelled organism. The internal environment of humans is tissue fluid (or intercellular fluid). Tissue fluid surrounds every cell in the human body. All organisms have the ability to control their internal environment, or their cell conditions, to some extent.

> **Homeostasis** is the ability of an organism to maintain a constant internal environment.

Homeostasis involves a combination of many processes acting together to control the internal environment of an organism. Examples of homeostasis in humans include:

- maintaining body temperatures very close to 37°C, despite widespread changes in external temperatures
- keeping the pH of the blood and tissue fluid very close to pH 7.4
- preventing the build-up of toxic chemicals in the body
- maintaining sufficient levels of oxygen in the body
- regulating the level of glucose in the blood plasma so that it stays close to 0.1%

The control of features such as those listed above requires the involvement of many organs and organ systems. For example:

- Body temperature is controlled mainly by the skin (as described in Chapter 32).
- Blood plasma and, consequently, tissue fluid pH, is controlled by the kidneys (as described in Chapter 32).
- The prevention of the build-up of toxic wastes is controlled by the liver and kidneys (Chapter 32).

- Heart rate and blood pressure have to be regulated (Chapter 27).
- Prevention of infection is carried out by the defence system (Chapter 38).

In humans, the brain co-ordinates the activities of these organs and systems. To allow this to happen, the brain must be continuously informed of conditions, both inside and outside the body, so that it can cause the relevant change(s) to be made.

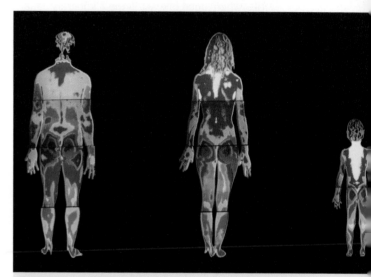

30.1 *A thermal image showing skin temperatures: white is hottest; red, orange, green, blue and purple are cooler*

Diffusion and exchange

In many cases, homeostasis is dependent on an organism exchanging materials with its environment by diffusion. For example, materials such as gases, nutrients and toxic wastes have to be exchanged between cells and their external environment.

The rate and efficiency at which exchange can take place depends on the amount of material to be exchanged and the surface area available for diffusion.

For small, single-celled organisms (such as *Amoeba*), special organs are not required for exchange. This is because there is a large surface area over which a relatively small amount of material can be exchanged.

THE ORGANISM

In larger, multicellular organisms, such as plants and animals, the problems of diffusion and exchange are overcome by a range of methods. Some of these methods require the development of exchange systems such as respiratory and excretory systems, as outlined in the following.

30.2 *The common frog hibernates in winter to avoid low temperatures.*

Methods used to improve diffusion and exchange

- The organ or organism may be flattened, as is the case in the leaves of a plant. This reduces the distance between the two surfaces and allows sufficient materials to be exchanged by diffusion.
- Respiratory systems provide increased surface area for the exchange of gases by diffusion. This is seen in the development of alveoli in the human lungs (see Chapter 31).
- Respiratory and excretory systems take materials to the body surface. This happens in humans where gases pass in and out of the lungs and waste products are excreted from the body (e.g. when salts and water are removed from the body in the form of sweat).

In addition to the methods outlined above, large organisms have another problem. Diffusion is only effective over short distances (about 0.5 mm). Therefore large active animals such as humans have to develop a circulatory system.

The circulatory system transports materials such as gases, nutrients and toxic wastes over long distances. For example, gases are transported by the blood circulatory system from all over the body to and from the lungs. In addition, waste products from all parts of the body are taken to the kidneys in the bloodstream.

The need for homeostasis

Homeostasis allows organisms to function efficiently

Homeostasis controls the environment surrounding the cells. This allows the cells to maintain constant conditions, thus enabling them to function under the most suitable (optimal) conditions. If the cells operate under ideal conditions then the organism will function most efficiently.

For example, if the temperature of the cells in the human body falls below 37°C, the reactions in the cells will slow down (because the rate of enzyme reactions slows down). This will result in the metabolism of the person slowing down.

If the temperature of human cells rises above 37°C, the reactions will also slow down (because human enzymes begin to lose their shape and work less efficiently at high temperatures). Each human cell (and as a consequence the human body) works most efficiently at 37°C.

Homeostasis allows organisms to function independently of their external environment

Homeostasis allows organisms to function most efficiently in adverse external conditions. For example, humans can continue to function when the external temperature drops in winter because they can control their internal temperature (i.e. they are endothermic).

However, frogs, for example, cannot control their internal temperature – they are ectothermic. Their temperature rises and falls with the temperature of their external environment. As a result, low temperatures cause frogs to slow down their metabolism. In order to avoid slowing down (and dying) in the cold of winter, frogs are forced to hibernate in order to conserve energy.

30.3 *The temperature of a sick person may rise due to infection.*

THE ORGANISM

Homeostasis allows slight changes in internal environments

It is important to realise that conditions in the internal environment of any organism have to be allowed to change or fluctuate *slightly*.

■ For example, human body temperature falls (by about 1°C) at night when we sleep. In contrast, our temperatures rise when we get an infection (this is called a fever and is an attempt by the body to destroy whatever is causing the infection).

■ Also, the internal environment of the body changes due to hormonal changes during the menstrual cycle and at puberty and the menopause.

In the short term, homeostasis maintains a relatively constant internal environment. However, homeostasis can be adapted to allow for the changing requirements of the body over longer periods of time.

Summary

The external environment surrounds the outside of an organism.

The internal environment surrounds the cells in an organism.

Homeostasis:
■ is the ability of an organism to maintain a constant internal environment
■ involves many organs and organ systems acting together, co-ordinated by the brain
■ often requires an organism to exchange materials with its environment

Cells exchange materials with their environment by diffusion.

Special organs of exchange are not needed in small organisms because diffusion is adequate.

To improve their rate of exchange, large organisms require special features such as:
■ flat structures
■ a respiratory system with a large surface area
■ respiratory and excretory systems, which take materials from within the body to the body surface

Large organisms require a circulatory system to carry materials over long distances.

Homeostasis allows:
■ cells, and therefore organisms, to function at their most efficient rate
■ organisms to function independently of external conditions
■ slight changes in internal conditions when necessary

Revision questions

1 (a) What is homeostasis?
   (b) Distinguish between the external and internal environment of an organism.
   (c) Name the internal environment for humans.
2 (a) Name three organs involved in homeostasis in humans.
   (b) Briefly explain the role of each of the organs you have named.
   (c) State the immediate consequences for a person if each of the named organs ceased to function.
3 (a) What is diffusion?
   (b) Name any two exchange systems in humans.
   (c) Why do small animals not have exchange systems?
4 (a) Name one method in each case by which large plants and animals improve their rates of exchange.
   (b) Name one substance in each case that is exchanged by these methods.
5 (a) Why are circulatory systems found in large animals but not in small ones?
   (b) Suggest one method by which an animal without a circulatory system might transport materials.
6 (a) Outline one benefit of homeostasis.
   (b) What is the likely result in an organism of the failure of any one named homeostatic organ?
7 Name the organ that co-ordinates homeostasis.
8 'Homeostatic mechanisms allow for temporary changes in the internal environment.' Give two examples in support of this statement.

Sample examination questions

Section C

9 What is homeostasis? Note **one** reason why it is important in the human body.   *(2007 HL Q 15c(i))*
10 What is homeostasis? State the role of the kidneys in homeostasis.   *(2004 HL Q 12a)*

Previous examination questions

Ordinary level	Higher level
n/a	2003 Sample Q 6
n/a	2004 Q 12a
n/a	2007 Q 15c

*For latest questions go to **www.edco.ie/biology***

Chapter 31 Human breathing

The human respiratory system

The human respiratory system consists of a pair of lungs and a series of tubes. The lungs are located in the chest or **thorax** (also called thoracic cavity).

A sheet of muscle called the diaphragm forms the floor of the thorax. The ribs (surrounded by the intercostal muscles) form the walls of the thorax.

Contractions of the diaphragm and the intercostal muscles alter the size of the thorax and cause ventilation (i.e. the movement of air into and out of the lungs).

Parts of the respiratory system

NOSE

Air can be inhaled through the mouth (also called the buccal cavity) or the nose. The openings into the nose are called nostrils. Each nostril leads to the nasal chambers, or passages. The nostrils are separated by the nasal septum, which is made of cartilage at its lower end and bone near the face.

Breathing in through the nose is beneficial because the air is:

- filtered by hairs and mucous in the nose
- moistened
- warmed as it passes across the nasal passages

Moist, warm air diffuses more easily from the lungs into the bloodstream.

PHARYNX

In the pharynx (or throat), a flap of tissue called the epiglottis closes off the trachea (windpipe) when we swallow. This prevents food and drink entering the windpipe.

Just below the epiglottis is the larynx (voicebox or Adam's apple). It contains two vocal cords. These vibrate when we force air across them. The vibrations produce sound, which our tongue and lips convert to speech.

The area at the top of the windpipe containing the larynx (and vocal cords) is called the glottis.

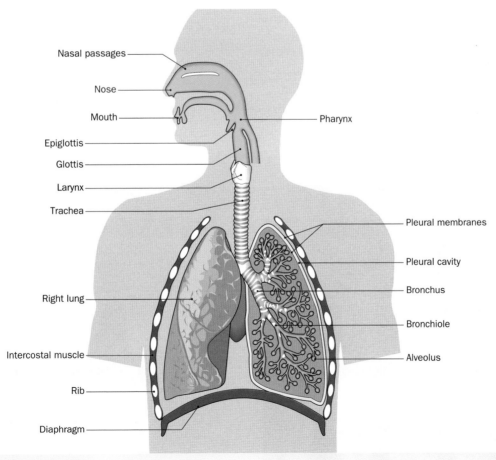

31.1 The respiratory system

Labels: Nasal passages, Nose, Mouth, Epiglottis, Glottis, Larynx, Trachea, Right lung, Intercostal muscle, Rib, Diaphragm, Pharynx, Pleural membranes, Pleural cavity, Bronchus, Bronchiole, Alveolus

THE ORGANISM

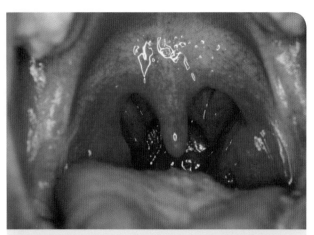

31.2 *A healthy throat: the tonsils are on both sides at the back*

TRACHEA AND SUBDIVISIONS

The trachea (or windpipe) and its subdivisions (the bronchi and the higher bronchioles) are all made of muscle and elastic fibres with incomplete (C-shaped) rings of cartilage. Cartilage is a strong material and it prevents these tubes from collapsing as air is drawn in.

The walls of the smaller (lower) bronchioles are made of muscle and elastic fibres only. These are the bronchioles that become narrow during an asthma attack.

All these airpipes are lined with mucous-secreting cells and tiny hairs called cilia. The sticky mucous traps particles such as dust, bacteria and viruses.

The cilia beat and create an upward current. This moves the mucous up and into the oesophagus, through which it passes to the stomach. We often clear our throats to help force the mucous upwards and away from the vocal cords.

31.3 *Cilia (pink) and mucous (green) in the windpipe*

LUNGS

The lungs are large, spongy structures in which gas exchange takes place. Each lung is enclosed by a pair of pleural membranes (the pleura).

The outer pleura lines the chest wall and diaphragm. The inner pleura lines the lungs. The gap between these membranes is the pleural cavity and it is full of liquid. This liquid lubricates the membranes and reduces friction during breathing.

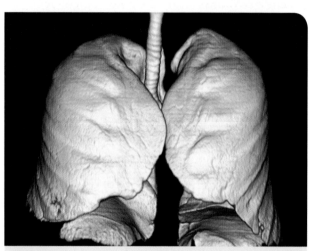

31.4 *A CT scan of healthy lungs*

ALVEOLI

Each bronchus subdivides into about a million bronchioles. These end in hollow, balloon-like air sacs called alveoli (singular alveolus). There are over 700 million alveoli in the two lungs. This gives a very large surface area for gas exchange (about the size of a tennis court).

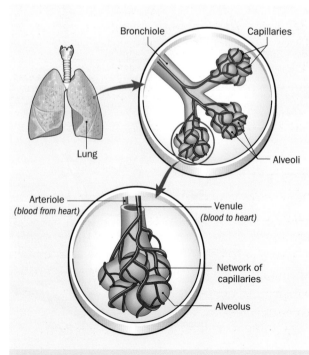

31.5 *Alveoli*

THE ORGANISM

Each alveolus is thin-walled (only one cell thick), moist and enclosed in a network of blood capillaries. This means that gases only have the membranes of the alveolus and capillary wall to pass through when they are exchanged.

The function of the alveoli is gas exchange.

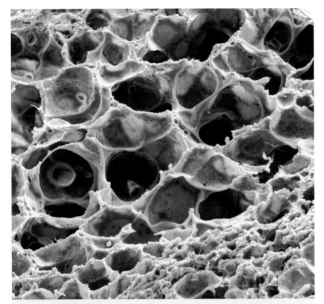

31.6 *Alveoli: some red blood cells are visible through the thin walls*

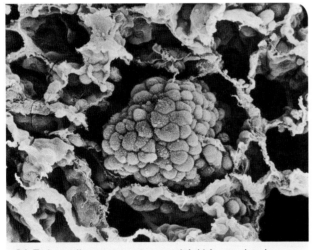

31.7 *A small cancerous tumour (pink) in an alveolus*

Gas exchange

Respiration occurs in the cells of the body in order to supply them with energy. As a result, body cells use up oxygen and produce carbon dioxide and water.

Carbon dioxide and water diffuse out of body cells and into the blood plasma because the cytoplasm has a higher concentration of carbon dioxide and water compared with the blood.

In the lungs, carbon dioxide and water diffuse out of the blood plasma into the alveolus, i.e. from a high to a low concentration.

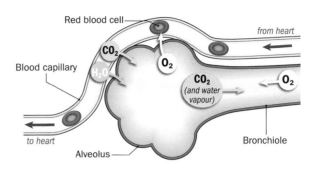

31.8 *Gas exchange in an alveolus*

In the same way, oxygen diffuses from the alveoli into the blood and then from the blood into the body cells. In each case, oxygen is passing from a high to a low concentration.

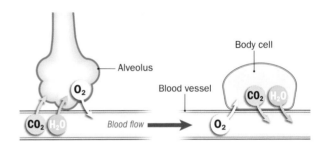

31.9 *Exchange in alveolus and body cell*

Adaptations to improve gas exchange

The alveoli and capillaries have the following adaptations to enable them to exchange gases more effectively:

- alveoli have thin walls
- alveoli are very numerous
- alveoli are moist
- capillaries have thin walls
- capillaries are numerous

Transport of gases

Haemoglobin is a red pigment found in red blood cells. Plasma is the liquid part of blood.

Oxygen is mostly transported by haemoglobin (97%), with only 3% carried, dissolved, in the plasma.

Carbon dioxide is carried by the blood, dissolved in plasma. Water is also carried in the plasma.

INHALED VS. EXHALED AIR

The composition of inhaled and exhaled air for a person at rest is given in the following table.

THE ORGANISM

Inhaled and exhaled air – person at rest		
	Inhaled	Exhaled
% Oxygen	21	14
% Carbon dioxide	0.04	5.6
Water concentration	Low	Higher

31.10 *Lungs: a healthy lung on the left and a smoker's lung on the right*

Mechanism of breathing

Breathing (or ventilation) is normally an involuntary process. An adult at rest breathes about 15 times per minute. Breathing in is called inhalation or inspiration. Breathing out is called exhalation or expiration.

The processes involved in a normal breath are as follows:

Inhalation

1 The brain controls the rate of breathing.
2 Normally a message is sent from the brain to the diaphragm and intercostal muscles between the ribs.
3 These muscles contract. For this reason inhalation is said to be an active process.
4 The ribs are pulled up and out, and the diaphragm moves down.
5 The volume of the chest cavity (thorax) increases.
6 The pressure in the chest cavity falls.
7 External air pressure is now higher than the pressure of air in the chest. As a result air is forced into the lungs. This is called inhalation or inspiration.

Exhalation

8 In exhalation steps 3 to 7 are reversed and air is forced out of the lungs as described below.
9 The intercostal muscles and diaphragm relax.
10 The ribs move down and in, and the diaphragm moves up.
11 The volume of the chest (or thoracic) cavity decreases.
12 The thoracic pressure increases.
13 Air is forced out of the lungs.

Exhalation is said to be passive because the muscles only have to relax. Nervous control is not needed for exhalation.

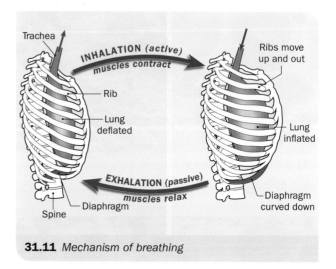

31.11 *Mechanism of breathing*

Effect of exercise on the rate of breathing

Exercise increases the rate of respiration, especially in muscle cells. The brain detects this increased level of exercise and increases the rate of breathing. Exhalation, which is normally passive, becomes an active process as a result of exercise. In addition, extra muscles are used to increase the depth of breathing.

The rate of breathing can be controlled consciously for a short time. This takes place in speech, singing or swimming when we control the timing of our breathing. However, breathing is normally under unconscious control.

Activity 19b   *To investigate the effect of exercise on the breathing rate*

1 Work in pairs, with one person counting and recording for the other.
2 Breathing in and breathing out is considered as one breath.
3 Record the number of inhalations or exhalations a person takes per minute for three minutes while resting.
4 Calculate the average number of inhalations or exhalations per minute. Record your results. Sample results are given in the table below. *(The resting rate is used as a control.)*

Breaths per minute at rest

	Person 1	Person 2
Trial 1	16	14
Trial 2	15	12
Trial 3	17	13
Average	16	13

5 Exercise gently by walking for 5 minutes.

6 Count the number of inhalations or exhalations per minute until the rate returns to (or below) the resting rate.
7 Exercise vigorously (i.e. run) for 5 minutes.
8 Count the number of inhalations or exhalations per minute until the rate returns to (or below) the resting rate.
9 The results might appear as shown below.

Breaths per minute after gentle exercise

	Person 1	Person 2
1st minute	60	40
2nd minute	52	28
3rd minute	39	15
4th minute	22	13
5th minute	17	12

10 Note how the rate of breathing increases after exercise. The breathing rate returns to normal faster in fitter individuals.

 After exercise the rate of breathing often falls below the resting rate (as happened with person 2 in the sample results above). This is due to deeper breathing.
11 The conclusion that can be drawn from this activity is that exercise increases the rate of breathing.

Breathing disorders

Asthma

SYMPTOMS

The symptoms (or signs) of asthma include noisy, wheezy breathing and a feeling of breathlessness.

CAUSE – EXTERNAL

The exact causes of asthma are not clear, but attacks may be triggered by substances called allergens that are inhaled. Common allergens include pollen, animal dander (tiny scales from skin, hair or feathers), house dust and dust mites.

 Lung infections, exercise (especially in cold air), stress or anxiety can also contribute to causing asthma.

CAUSE – INTERNAL

In an asthma attack the lower bronchioles become narrow (or constricted).

About 10% of children are asthmatic and the incidence of asthma seems to be rising in developed countries. More than half of children affected by asthma grow out of it in their teenage years.

31.12 *A partially and a fully constricted bronchiole*

PREVENTION

Asthmatic attacks may be prevented by identifying and avoiding those allergens or conditions that trigger attacks. Tests can be undertaken to identify the precise allergens that affect an individual.

In addition, preventative inhalers may be used. These prevent the bronchioles from reacting to allergens.

TREATMENT

The normal treatment for asthma is to inhale drugs that cause the bronchioles to widen (or dilate; hence they are called bronchodilators). In addition, steroids may be inhaled to reduce inflammation. In severe cases these drugs are given by injection.

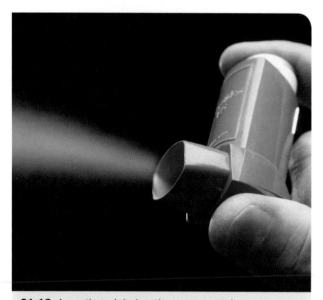

31.13 *An asthma inhaler: the spray contains a bronchodilator*

Control of human breathing

Earlier in this chapter we saw that the rate of human breathing is controlled by the brain. The brain controls breathing by monitoring the levels of carbon dioxide in the blood that passes through it.

Carbon dioxide is a slightly acidic gas. It dissolves in water to form a weak acid called carbonic acid. Carbonic acid causes the pH of the blood and tissue fluid to fall slightly.

Special centres in the brain detect the slight drop in pH and react by sending out impulses to the diaphragm and intercostal muscles that cause us to breathe. Breathing allows gas exchange to take place in the lungs.

If we exercise vigorously the level of carbon dioxide in our blood will increase (due to respiration). This will result in a drop in blood pH. The brain will detect this change and cause our breathing rate to increase.

Our brain does not normally respond to low levels of oxygen. It is interesting to note that we breathe in response to high levels of carbon dioxide, rather than responding to low levels of oxygen.

Carbon dioxide controls gas exchange

In Chapter 25 we saw that carbon dioxide causes the opening and closing of the stomata in leaves. We now know that carbon dioxide also causes the rate of breathing in humans to increase.

For both of these reasons, we can say that carbon dioxide operates as a controlling factor in gas exchange in both plants and animals.

Summary

The respiratory system is located in the chest cavity (also called the thorax or thoracic cavity).

- Breathing in through the nose causes the air to be filtered, moistened and warmed.
- The epiglottis prevents food and drink entering the trachea.
- The larynx contains vocal cords for speech.
- The trachea (windpipe), bronchi and larger bronchioles are made of muscle, elastic fibres and rigid cartilage.
- Smaller (lower) bronchioles have muscle and elastic fibres only.
- Mucous traps dust and micro-organisms.
- Cilia are tiny hairs that beat to sweep the mucous out of the airpipes (and into the oesophagus).
- Each lung is enclosed by a pair of pleural membranes. These are separated by the pleural cavity.

Alveoli are tiny, thin-walled air sacs that allow gas exchange.

- Oxygen diffuses from the alveoli to the red cells in the blood. Carbon dioxide diffuses from the blood plasma into the alveoli.
- These gases diffuse in the reverse direction in the cells of the body.

Breathing in is called inhalation or inspiration.
Exhaling is called exhalation or expiration.

Inhalation involves the following:

- The brain controls the rate of breathing.
- The intercostal muscles and diaphragm contract.
- The chest cavity gets bigger.
- The pressure falls in the chest cavity.
- Air is forced into the lungs by the higher external air pressure.

THE ORGANISM

Exhalation is the reverse of inspiration.

Exercise increases **(a)** the rate, and **(b)** the depth of breathing.
■ The effect of exercise on breathing rate can be shown by comparing breathing rates at rest with those after exercise.

Asthma is:
■ a breathing disorder
■ triggered by outside agents called allergens
■ due to the smaller bronchioles becoming narrower
■ controlled by avoiding known allergens
■ treated by drugs (usually taken from inhalers)

Human breathing is controlled by the brain.

High levels of carbon dioxide in the blood or tissue fluid:
■ form an acid
■ decrease the pH
■ trigger the brain to cause breathing

Carbon dioxide is a controlling factor in gas exchange in leaves and in human breathing.

Revision questions

1 Distinguish between:
 (a) nose and nostril
 (b) pharynx and larynx
 (c) oesophagus and trachea
 (d) bronchus and bronchioles
 (e) pleural membranes and pleural cavity
 (f) lungs and thorax
 (g) glottis and epiglottis.
2 List two ways by which the respiratory system protects itself from infection.
3 (a) What are the functions of (i) the epiglottis, (ii) alveoli, (iii) intercostal muscles, (iv) nasal passages?
 (b) Why are there so many alveoli?
4 'Gas exchange in the alveoli is the reverse of gas exchange in muscle cells.' By reference to two named gases explain why this statement is true.
5 Name four adaptations shown by the alveoli that enable them to exchange gases efficiently.
6 (a) Name the parts labelled A to H in Figure 31.14.
 (b) What are the functions of A and G?
 (c) What have E and F in common?
 (d) Does the position of F suggest it is contracted? Explain your answer.

7 Name the type of blood vessel taking blood (a) to the lungs, (b) around the alveoli, (c) from the lungs.
8 Referring to diffusion in the alveoli, suggest why slow, deep breaths are more efficient than short, shallow ones.
9 Why is exhalation usually a passive process, but inhalation is active?
10 Why is the right lung bigger than the left lung?
11 Figure 31.15 represents the respiratory system.
 (a) What parts of the respiratory system do the following represent: (i) the balloon, (ii) the bell jar?
 (b) What happens to the balloon when air is withdrawn through the hollow pipe?
 (c) Explain your answer to part (b).
 (d) What phase of breathing does this represent?

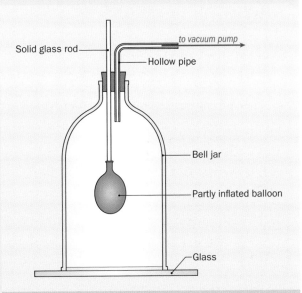

31.15

12 In investigating how exercise affects the rate of breathing:
 (a) How is the breathing rate measured?
 (b) Why should the rate/minute be taken a number of times? *(continued)*

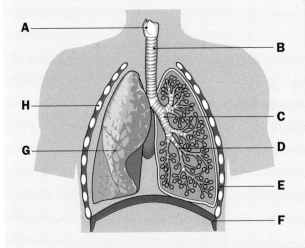

31.14

THE ORGANISM

(c) State the expected results of the experiment.

(d) Some time after exercise the rate of breathing is often lower than it was before the exercise started. Suggest a reason for this.

13 (a) Explain what happens to the smaller bronchioles to cause asthma.

(b) Why does this not happen to larger (higher) bronchioles in an asthma attack?

14 (a) What are the symptoms of asthma?

(b) What are allergens?

(c) Name three common substances that may trigger asthma.

(d) Give details regarding any **(i)** cure, **(ii)** prevention or **(iii)** treatment, for asthma.

15 (a) Name the gas that causes humans to breathe.

(b) What process **(i)** increases, and **(ii)** decreases, the concentration of this gas in the bloodstream?

(c) What effect has this gas on the pH of the blood?

(d) Where in the body is the concentration of this gas monitored?

(e) What is the result of high levels of this gas in the body?

16 'We breathe to get rid of carbon dioxide, not to take in oxygen.' Give one reason in support of this statement.

17 Choose which of the options (i), (ii), (iii) or (iv) represents the correct answer in each case below.

(a) Another name for the voicebox is:
  (i) larynx
  (ii) pharynx
  (iii) thorax
  (iv) epiglottis

(b) The correct percentage of CO_2 in exhaled air for a person at rest is about:
  (i) 0.04%
  (ii) 20%
  (iii) 5.6%
  (iv) 78%

(c) The rate of breathing is controlled by:
  (i) the lungs
  (ii) the thoracic cavity
  (iii) the brain
  (iv) the diaphragm

(d) The flap of tissue that prevents food 'going down the wrong way' is called:
  (i) the pleura
  (ii) the larynx
  (iii) the epiglottis
  (iv) the oesophagus

Sample examination questions

Section B

18 (a) (i) Answer the following in relation to human breathing rate **or** pulse rate. State which of these you will refer to.

  (ii) What is the average rate at rest?

  (iii) State a possible effect of smoking on the resting rate.

(b) (i) How did you measure the resting rate?

  (ii) Describe how you investigated the effect of exercise on this rate.

  (iii) Using the axes below draw a graph to show how rate is likely to vary as the exercise level increases.

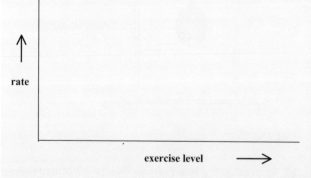

(2004 OL Q 9)

19 (a) State the location in the human body of the following muscles which are used for breathing:
  (i) diaphragm
  (ii) intercostals

(b) Answer the following questions about an activity that you carried out to investigate the effect of exercise on the breathing rate or pulse of a human.

  (i) At the start of the investigation you asked the person who was about to do the exercise to sit down for a few minutes. Explain the purpose of this.

  (ii) How did you measure the breathing rate or the pulse?

  (iii) Describe how you conducted the investigation after the period of rest.

  (iv) State the results of your investigation.

(2008 OL Q 8)

Section C

20 (a) (i) Name the major blood vessels that carry blood
  1. from the heart to the lungs
  2. from the lungs to the heart.

  (ii) What gas is released from the blood when it reaches the lungs?

(b) The diagram shows part of the human breathing system.

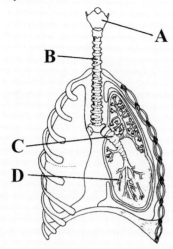

(i) Name A, B, C, D.

(ii) D ends in a small sac. What is the name of this sac?

(iii) What is the function of A?

(iv) B contains rings of cartilage. Suggest a function of this cartilage.

(v) Where is the epiglottis? What is its function?

(c) (i) Name the muscles that are used in breathing.

(ii) Breathing causes pressure changes in the thoracic cavity. Describe briefly how these pressure changes are brought about.

(iii) Name a breathing disorder. Give a possible cause of this disorder and suggest a means of prevention **or** treatment.

(2005 OL Q 12)

21 (a) (i) Name the blood vessel that returns blood to the heart from the lungs.

(ii) Name the main gas transported in the blood vessel that you have named in **(i)**. How is this gas transported?

(b) (i) Draw a large diagram of the human breathing system. Label the trachea, bronchus and lung.

(ii) State the function of the following: epiglottis, larynx.

(iii) Describe briefly the role of the diaphragm and intercostal muscles in inhalation. In your answer refer to volume and thoracic air pressure.

(c) (i) Give **three** ways in which an alveolus is adapted for efficient gas exchange.

(ii) Name the process involved in the passage of gas between the alveolus and the blood.

(iii) Name a breathing disorder.

(iv) In the case of the breathing disorder that you have named in **(iii)** state:

1. a cause,

2. a means of prevention,

3. a treatment.

(2007 HL Q 13)

THE ORGANISM

Chapter 32 **Excretion**

Excretion in plants

Excretion is the elimination of metabolic waste from the body. It is a term that is generally applied to animals.

Plants do not have as great a need for excretion as animals, because plants make their own food. Consequently, they do not produce surplus amounts of food (which reduces the amount of waste they produce).

In addition, the products of some plant reactions are reused by the plant. For example, some of the oxygen produced in photosynthesis is used in respiration. Also, carbon dioxide and water produced in respiration are used in photosynthesis.

Many plant waste products are stored in vacuoles in living plant cells and within dead cells (such as old xylem) in the plant. Sometimes these stored waste products are removed when the plant loses its leaves, bark, petals, seeds and fruit.

Role of stomata and lenticels in excretion

However, plants do lose oxygen and water vapour, especially during daylight. These products are mostly lost through the stomata on the lower surface of the leaf, but also through lenticels on the stem. At night-time plants lose carbon dioxide through the same openings.

Homeostasis

Homeostasis is the maintenance of a constant internal environment in an organism. In particular, this means that humans must maintain a constant temperature, fluid balance and chemical composition.

Temperature regulation in animals

The need to control body temperature is determined by the fact that temperature regulates the rate of chemical (especially enzyme-controlled) reactions. High temperatures can damage enzymes; low temperatures will slow down reactions.

Animals use two different methods to control their temperatures.

> **Ectotherms** gain or lose heat from or to their external environment.

Ectotherms were formerly known as cold-blooded animals. Examples include fish, frogs, snakes and lizards.

> **Endotherms** generate their own heat from metabolic reactions.

Endotherms generate most of their own heat from respiration and were formerly called warm-blooded animals. Examples include birds and mammals such as dogs, cats, mice and humans.

Temperature regulation in humans

The skin plays a major part in regulating human body temperature.

The skin

The skin consists of two layers, the outer epidermis and the inner dermis. Beneath these layers is the subcutaneous tissue, which contains fat-rich cells called adipose tissue.

Epidermis

Cells in the Malpighian layer (see Figure 32.1) are constantly dividing by mitosis to produce new epidermis cells. As the new cells move out through the granular layer, they produce a waterproof protein called keratin (this is the material from which nails, claws, hooves, horns, scales, feathers and hair are made).

The build-up of keratin causes the cells to become hardened or cornified. Excess keratin, along with a lack of blood capillaries, causes the cells in the cornified layer to die as they reach the surface of the skin. The dead outer cells are continuously worn away (as skin flakes or dandruff).

Specialised cells in the Malpighian layer produce a brown or black coloured pigment called **melanin**. This gives colour to the skin, hair and the coloured part of the eye (the iris). Freckles and moles are areas where melanin is very concentrated.

Melanin protects the skin against the harmful effects of ultraviolet radiation. Production of melanin increases following exposure to sunlight.

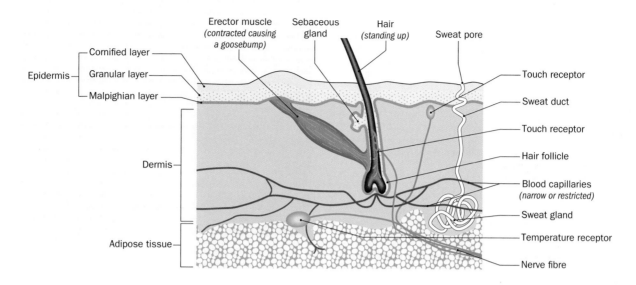

32.1 *Vertical section of skin (in cold conditions)*

Dermis

The dermis consists of connective tissue containing a strengthening protein called collagen. The dermis contains a variety of specialised structures such as sweat glands, hair follicles, sebaceous glands (which produce an oil called sebum), blood vessels and nerve receptors.

Functions of the skin

Protection

- The **epidermis** protects the body from damage, and acts as a barrier to prevent the loss of water and the entry of pathogens.
- The **dermis** protects internal organs from damage due to bumps and bangs.
- **Melanin** protects the skin from ultraviolet radiation (which can cause skin cancers).
- **Sebum** is an oil produced by sebaceous glands that are located alongside hair follicles. Sebum passes out of the hair follicle and onto the epidermis. Sebum keeps hair moist and flexible, and also prevents the skin from drying-up and becoming cracked. For this reason sebum can be considered to protect the body.

Did you know?

Sebaceous glands are especially concentrated on the face and scalp of humans. At puberty excessive production of sebum, due to hormonal influences, may cause acne.

Vitamin production

Vitamin D is produced in the skin following exposure to ultraviolet radiation. This vitamin helps to absorb calcium in the intestines.

Food store

Fat in the adipose tissue acts as a food store.

Sense organ

The skin contains a variety of receptors that allow it to act as an organ of touch. For example, the skin can detect sensations of touch and temperature.

Excretion

Sweat glands act as organs of excretion. Sweat contains water and salts. When sweat passes out of the skin these wastes are removed from the body.

Temperature regulation

COLD CONDITIONS (see Fig. 32.1)
In cold conditions, the skin helps to retain heat in two ways.

- Erector muscles contract (forming goose bumps). This causes the hairs to stand up on the skin – a process called **piloerection**. A layer of warm air is trapped close to the skin by the hairs. This air helps to reduce heat loss from the body.
- Blood vessels in the skin contract when we are cold. This is called **vasoconstriction**. It reduces heat loss through the skin.

THE ORGANISM

315

A third mechanism also helps us to maintain our temperature in cold conditions. A part of the brain responds to low blood temperature by causing muscles throughout the body to contract and relax very rapidly. This results in shivering, which produces heat to raise our temperature.

Note that fat stored under the skin insulates the body from heat loss.

Did you know?

Many animals produce large amounts of insulating fat, e.g. seals, polar bears and water birds such as ducks. This is why duck meat is very fatty.

WARM CONDITIONS (see Fig. 35.1, page 349)

In warm conditions, the skin acts in two ways to reduce our temperature.

- Sweat is produced and released onto the skin. When the water evaporates it lowers our body temperature. At normal room temperature we can lose as much as one litre of sweat in a day. During exercise, the loss of water and salts in the form of sweat is much greater.

    It is important to drink water and salts before, during and after exercise to maintain the salt/water concentration of the body. Salt tablets are often taken before competing in sports events in very warm weather to replace salt that will be lost in sweat.

- When we are too hot, blood vessels in the skin (especially in the face) expand (or dilate). This increases heat loss through the skin and reduces body temperature. This is why we turn red in the face after exercise.

Did you know?

Our temperature also rises when we are embarrassed; we then try to cool down by opening blood vessels in our face, which causes blushing.

Excretion and homeostasis

The role of the excretory system in homeostasis can be summarised as:

- regulating body temperature
- controlling osmosis (i.e. controlling the salt and water balance of the body)
- controlling the concentration of body fluids
- removing waste products of metabolism from the body

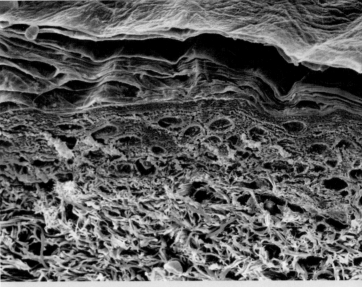

32.2 *The layers in human skin*

Organs of excretion

The main organs of excretion are:

- **Lungs**. These excrete water and carbon dioxide (see Chapter 31).
- **Skin**. The skin excretes water and salts in the form of sweat.
- **Kidneys**. These are the main excretory organs in humans. They excrete water, salts and urea in the form of urine.

    By controlling the amount of water and salts that are excreted, the kidneys play a major role in the homeostasis of the fluid and chemical composition of the blood (and of the body).

The urinary system

Kidneys

The urinary system consists of two kidneys, two ureters, the bladder and the urethra.

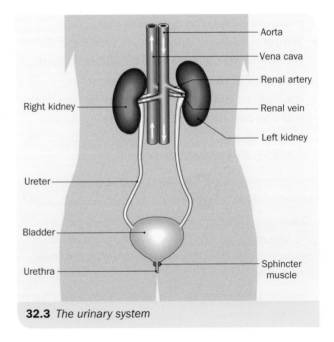

32.3 *The urinary system*

The kidneys are fist-sized organs located just below the diaphragm in the small of the back. They are bean-shaped and the depression in each kidney is called the hilum.

Blood in the aorta contains waste products collected from all over the body. Some of this blood enters the kidneys through the two renal arteries. Every minute about 20% of our blood passes into the kidneys.

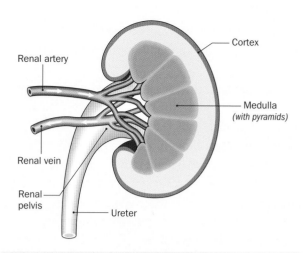

32.5 *Location and structure of the kidneys*

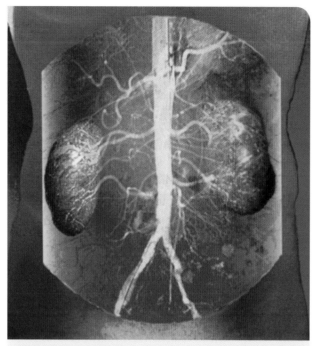

32.4 *An angiogram of the kidneys and their blood supply*

Urine

Urine is typically composed of 96% water, 2.5% nitrogenous waste (mostly urea) and 1.5% salts. Urea is produced in the liver. It is formed when excess proteins are broken down (de-aminated).

> **Did you know?**
>
> *Normal urine is sterile, but it is easily decomposed by bacterial action outside the body. This results in the formation of ammonia, which is the cause of nappy rash in young children.*

FILTRATION
In the kidneys the incoming blood is filtered. This takes place in the outer cortex of each kidney. Filtration results in small substances (both useful and waste) being forced out of the bloodstream into the kidney.

REABSORPTION
Some of the useful materials are then taken back into the blood. This is called reabsorption. It occurs in the cortex and medulla of each kidney.

SECRETION
Some substances are secreted from the blood into the cortex of the kidney. These substances include potassium and hydrogen ions. (Too much potassium in the body prevents nerve impulses travelling correctly and reduces the strength of muscular contraction.) By controlling the hydrogen ion concentration of the blood, the kidneys control blood pH.

Only unwanted waste and toxic products are left in the kidney. These form the liquid called urine.

Purified blood leaves the kidneys through the renal veins. The renal veins take the blood to the vena cava.

Urine flows from the medulla into the renal pelvis. This is shaped like a funnel and collects waste and carries it into the ureter. The waste (called urine) is then carried by the two ureters to the bladder.

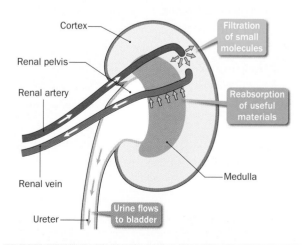

32.6 *Simplified diagram of filtration and reabsorption in the kidney*

Bladder

The adult bladder can store up to 800 ml of urine. It is a muscular organ that is not under voluntary control.

Two sphincter muscles are located at the junction of the bladder and urethra. In babies, these muscles open automatically by reflex action when the bladder becomes about half full. The bladder then contracts to force urine out into the urethra.

The urethra emerges through the penis in males and close to the vagina in females.

Control of urination is caused by the ability to control the sphincter reflex. Up to about 2 years of age children cannot control this reflex and urination is automatic. Once the reflex is controlled then, even though the bladder may be very full, urine can be retained for some time.

Functions of the kidneys

Excretion

As outlined earlier, the kidneys remove waste products from the bloodstream and convert them to urine. Urine is sent to the bladder for storage and excreted through the urethra.

Osmoregulation

WATER CONTENT

Kidneys control the water content of the body. They do this by varying the water content of the urine. For example, on hot days the kidneys conserve water by producing low volumes of urine.

SALT CONCENTRATION

Kidneys control the salt concentration of the body fluids. They achieve this by varying the amount of salt released in the urine. For example, if we consume too much salt the kidneys will increase the amount of salt excreted in urine.

In controlling water and salt concentrations, the kidneys ensure that the blood plasma (and, as a result, all body fluids) has the same concentration as normal body cells. This means that the cells bathed by these fluids do not have problems gaining or losing water by osmosis. For this reason the kidneys are said to regulate osmosis or to be osmoregulatory.

pH control

Kidneys control the pH of the body fluids. They do this by producing urine that is either more or less acidic. This allows the pH of the blood to remain at its normal value of 7.4.

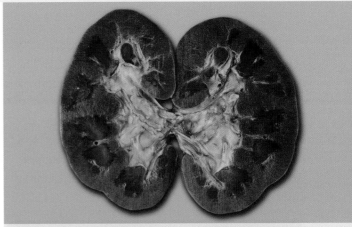

32.7 *A dissected kidney: the cortex and medulla are red; the pelvis is pale coloured*

The nephron

Each kidney contains more than a million nephrons. A nephron is a tube about 3 cm long, located in the cortex and medulla of the kidney as shown in Figure 32.9.

Nephrons are the functional units of the kidney, i.e. they make urine. To understand the workings of the kidney it is necessary to understand what happens in each nephron.

Blood supply to nephron

Blood enters each kidney through the renal artery. Once inside the kidney, this vessel divides to form many renal arterioles, which then split, forming many smaller afferent (incoming) arterioles.

Each afferent arteriole in turn divides to form a cluster of capillaries called the glomerulus. A glomerulus is found in each Bowman's capsule, which is a cup-shaped structure at one end of the nephron.

Blood leaves the glomerulus in the efferent (outgoing) arteriole. This then divides to form the capillaries that surround the rest of the nephron.

These capillaries eventually rejoin to form renal venules, which then combine and emerge from the kidney as the renal vein.

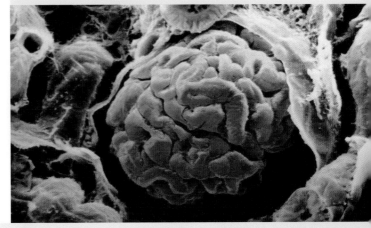

32.8 *A glomerulus, shown in red, with part of Bowman's capsule, in white-brown (SEM)*

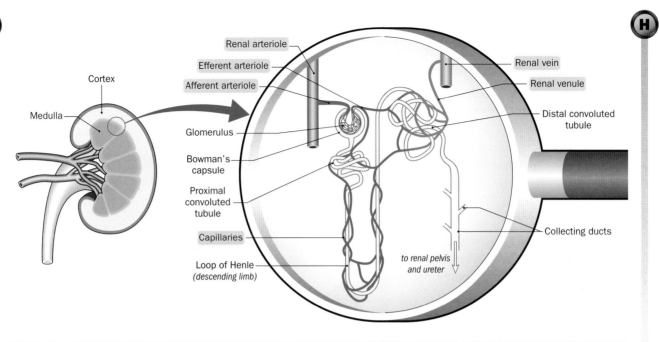

32.9 *Structure of the nephron and its associated blood supply (shown as* *)*

Urine production

Urine is produced in the nephron. There are three main processes involved in urine production: filtration, reabsorption and secretion.

FILTRATION

1 Blood entering the nephron in the afferent arteriole contains waste products.

2 Filtration takes place in the glomerulus. Small molecules such as glucose, amino acids, vitamins, some hormones, urea, salts and water are forced out of the plasma and into Bowman's capsule (Figure 32.10). Here they form a dilute solution called **glomerular filtrate**.

3 The structure of the glomerulus helps filtration in three ways:

- The pressure in the glomerulus is greater than normal blood pressure. This is caused by the already high pressure of the afferent arteriole being increased due to the efferent arteriole being narrower.

- The surface area of capillaries in the glomerulus is large. This increases the area for filtration.

- The walls of the glomerular capillaries are more porous than normal capillaries.

    In addition, the wall of Bowman's capsule is only one cell thick.

4 Larger substances do not enter the glomerular filtrate. These include red and white blood cells, platelets, antibodies, clotting proteins and some hormones.

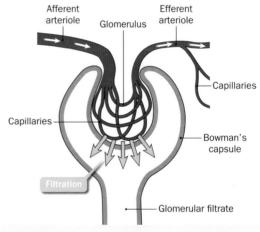

32.10 *Bowman's capsule and related blood vessels*

Did you know?

About 180 litres of glomerular filtrate are formed every 24 hours. This is 4.5 times the fluid content of the body. Obviously not all of this liquid can leave the body as urine.

32.11 *Bowman's capsule (pale) containing a glomerulus with the proximal convoluted tubule on the right*

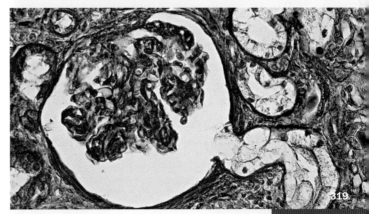

THE ORGANISM

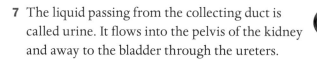

REABSORPTION

1   In the rest of the nephron (beyond Bowman's capsule), water, most salts and useful substances are reabsorbed into the blood. About 99% of the glomerular filtrate is reabsorbed. This leaves about 1.5 litres of urine to be excreted in a normal day.

2   In the proximal convoluted tubule most of the water is reabsorbed by osmosis. All of the glucose, amino acids and vitamins pass from the filtrate into the capillaries by a combination of diffusion and active transport.

> **Active transport** means that energy is used to move molecules, often against a concentration gradient, i.e. from low concentrations to high concentrations.

In addition, most of the salts are reabsorbed by active transport or diffusion. To help in the process of reabsorption the proximal tubule:
- is thin-walled, only one cell thick
- is long (14 mm)
- has numerous infoldings (called microvilli) in its cells
- has a high concentration of mitochondria to provide energy for active transport

3   The descending limb of the loop of Henle is permeable to water. In this section of the loop of Henle a small amount of the water is reabsorbed by osmosis.

4   The ascending limb of the loop of Henle is permeable to salts. In this region salts move out of the nephron into the fluid of the medulla. Initially the movement of salts is by diffusion, but at the top of the ascending limb sodium is pumped out by active transport.

The addition of salts makes the medulla more concentrated than the fluid in the tubule. This helps to remove water (by osmosis) from both the descending limb of the loop of Henle and the collecting ducts. For this reason, the function of the loop of Henle is to reabsorb water.

5   The distal convoluted tubule is involved in the delicate, precise control of the water, salt and pH values of the blood.

Some water and salts can be reabsorbed from the tubule into the blood in this region.

6   The collecting duct is permeable to water. A small amount of the water in the filtrate can pass out of the collecting duct. This occurs by osmosis, due to the high salt concentration in the medulla.

7   The liquid passing from the collecting duct is called urine. It flows into the pelvis of the kidney and away to the bladder through the ureters.

SECRETION

Secretion means that some substances pass from the blood into the nephron.

Summary of nephron functions

The functions of the regions of the nephron, and the materials reabsorbed in each, are summarised in the following table and Figure 32.13.

Functions of the regions of a nephron		
Location	**Amount of water reabsorbed**	**Salts reabsorbed**
Proximal tubule	Most	Most (as well as glucose, amino acids and vitamins)
Descending limb of loop of Henle	A little	None
Ascending limb of loop of Henle	None	Some
Distal tubule	Some	Some
Collecting duct	A little	None

Glomerular filtrate differs from urine in the following ways:
- it has more water (i.e. is more dilute) than urine
- it contains many useful molecules, e.g. glucose and amino acids that are not normally found in urine.

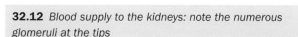

32.12 *Blood supply to the kidneys: note the numerous glomeruli at the tips*

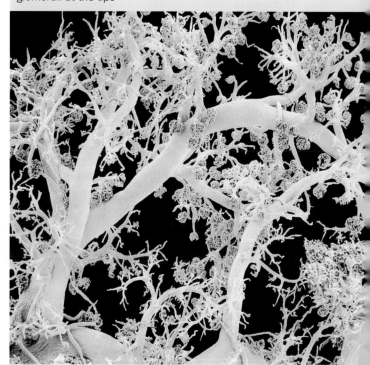

THE ORGANISM

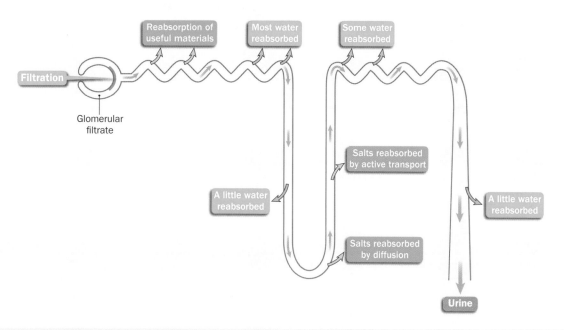

32.13 *Summary of the functions of a nephron*

Control of urine volume

BLOOD PLASMA TOO CONCENTRATED

1 When we drink too little water, or if we lose too much water as sweat or faeces, the salt concentration of the plasma may rise. This may cause the plasma to become more concentrated than blood cells (see Figure 32.14).

2 Receptors in the brain are triggered. They send a message to the pituitary gland, causing it to release the hormone ADH (**anti-diuretic hormone**, also called vasopressin).

3 ADH travels to the kidneys in the bloodstream. In the kidneys, ADH causes the walls of the distal tubule and the collecting ducts to become more permeable to water.

4 Due to ADH, more water is reabsorbed from the nephron. This reduces the salt concentration of the plasma so that it eventually has the same concentration as the blood cells.

5 ADH also causes a lower volume of urine to be produced.

BLOOD PLASMA CONCENTRATION NORMAL OR TOO DILUTE

1 In the reverse situation, where a great deal of water is consumed, the plasma becomes diluted (or less concentrated than the blood cells).

2 In this situation, ADH is not produced, and the distal tubules and collecting ducts become relatively impermeable to water.

3 This means that water is not reabsorbed from the distal tubules and collecting ducts.

4 As a result, a larger volume of dilute urine is produced.

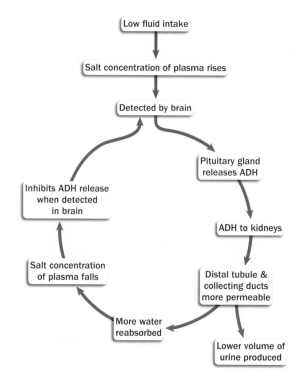

32.14 *Control of urine volume*

The effects of different conditions on urine production are shown in the following table.

Effects of different conditions on urine production

Condition	Effect on blood	ADH	Distal tubule & collecting duct	Urine
Thirsty or **Salty diet** or **Hot day** or **Exercise**	Low water content and high salt concentration	Produced	More permeable to water	Low volume of water; Higher salt concentration (i.e. a low volume of concentrated urine)
Excessive water intake or **Very low salt diet**	High water content and low salt concentration	Not produced	Less permeable to water	High volume of water; Lower salt concentration (i.e. a high volume of dilute urine)
High protein diet	Normal water content and increased concentration of urea	No effect	No effect	Same volume of water; Increased urea concentration (i.e the same volume of concentrated urine)

Summary

Excretion is the getting rid of waste products of metabolism.

Plants:
- produce very little waste
- store some wastes and lose more when dead structures fall off
- lose waste gases through their stomata and lenticels

Homeostasis is the maintenance of a stable internal environment in an organism.

Ectotherms are animals that obtain their heat from external sources.

Endotherms generate their heat with their own body reactions.

Skin is composed of:
- **Epidermis**
  - The outer layer is dead, cornified, and full of waterproof keratin.
  - The inner layer has living, granular cells.
  - The base of the granular layer is the Malpighian layer. This makes new cells and contains many pigment (melanin) cells.
- **Dermis**
  - These cells contain a strong protein called collagen.
  - This layer has many blood vessels, sweat glands, hairs, sebaceous glands, and nerve receptors.
- **Subcutaneous layer** contains fat in adipose tissue.

The functions of skin are:
- **protection**:
  - epidermis protects against damage, water loss, and the entry of pathogens
  - melanin protects against UV radiation
  - sebum (oil) keeps the epidermis intact

- **vitamin production** (vitamin D is made in the skin)
- **food store** (fat stores energy)
- **sense organ** (the skin is an organ of touch, e.g. it senses touch and temperature)
- **excretion** (sweat removes water and salts from the body)
- **temperature regulation**:
  - Cold conditions cause
    - hairs to stand up to keep skin warm
    - blood vessels narrow (constrict) to retain heat
    - shivering
  - Warm conditions cause
    - sweating, which cools the body due to evaporation
    - blood vessels to widen (dilate) to lose heat

The main excretory organs are:
- lungs (water and carbon dioxide)
- skin (water and salts)
- kidneys (water, salts, and urea)

The urinary system consists of two kidneys, two ureters, the bladder, and urethra.

The kidneys make urine in the following way:
- blood (containing waste) enters the kidneys through the renal arteries
- the kidneys filter waste and useful materials from the blood
- useful materials are reabsorbed from the kidneys back into the blood
- some materials are secreted from the blood into the kidneys
- urine formed in the kidneys flows to the bladder through the ureters
- blood (low in waste) leaves the kidneys in the renal veins

THE ORGANISM

The bladder stores urine.

Urine is excreted through the urethra.

The functions of the kidneys are:
- excretion of water, salts, and urea
- osmoregulation:
  - control the water content of the blood (and body fluids)
  - control the salt concentration of the blood (and body fluids)
- control the pH of the blood (and body fluids)

(H) Nephrons:
- carry out the functions of the kidneys
- are located in the cortex and medulla of the kidney.

A nephron makes urine as follows:
- **filtration**:
  - blood enters the nephron in the afferent arteriole
  - this forms many capillaries called the glomerulus
  - high pressure in the glomerulus forces water and small molecules out of the blood
  - glomerular filtrate is a dilute solution of waste and useful molecules
- **reabsorption** takes place in the following parts of the nephron:
  - **proximal tubule** = water by osmosis, useful molecules and most salts by diffusion and active transport
  - **loop of Henle**
    - (i) descending limb = water by osmosis
    - (ii) ascending limb = salts by diffusion and then by active transport
  - **distal tubule** = water by osmosis and some salts by active transport
  - **collecting ducts** = water by osmosis
- **secretion** into the nephron of some substances
- **urine flows** from the collecting ducts to the ureters and then to the bladder

A hormone (ADH):
- is released from the pituitary gland
- controls the volume of urine formed

Lack of water in the plasma stimulates ADH.
- ADH causes increased reabsorption of water in the distal tubule and collecting ducts.
- Water is returned to the plasma and less urine is released.

(H)

Revision questions

1. What is meant by **(a)** excretion, **(b)** metabolism, **(c)** the urinary system, **(d)** homeostasis?
2. **(a)** Why have plants less need for excretion than animals?
   (b) Name two places in each case where plants **(i)** store, and **(ii)** reuse, the products of metabolism.
   (c) Name three materials released from openings in plants.
   (d) Name the two openings from which these materials are released.
3. **(a)** Why do living things need to control their temperatures?
   (b) Distinguish, naming two animals in each case, between **(i)** ectotherms, and **(ii)** endotherms.
4. **(a)** Name the parts of the skin labelled A to J on Figure 32.15.
   (b) In which labelled region would you expect to find the greatest rate of mitosis?
   (c) Explain how the parts labelled B, D, E, and G help to regulate the temperature of the body.
   (d) How do parts C and I help the body to resist infection?

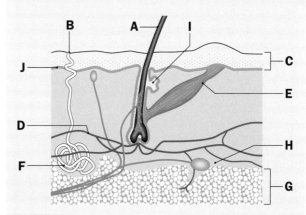

32.15

5. **(a)** State six functions carried out by the skin.
   (b) Name one part of the skin associated with each of the functions listed and explain how each part named carries out its function.
6. Give a biological reason for each of the following:
   (a) We shiver when we are cool.
   (b) We blush when we are embarrassed.
   (c) Whales have a lot of blubber.
   (d) We sweat heavily after exercise.
   (e) A boxer is fanned with a towel between rounds.
7. **(a)** Name three human excretory organs.
   (b) State the main substances excreted by each organ.
   (c) Why is faeces not considered to be excreted?

8 (a) Name the parts labelled A to I in Figure 32.16.
   (b) State the part in Figure 32.16 that carries out
        each of the following: **(i)** makes urine, **(ii)** stores
        urine, **(iii)** carries blood to the kidney, **(iv)** takes
        blood from the kidney, **(v)** controls the release of
        urine, **(vi)** excretes urine.

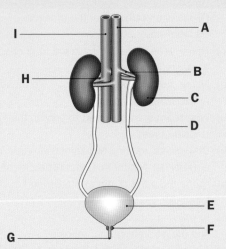

32.16

9 Why are the kidneys referred to as osmoregulatory
   structures?
10 (a) Name two ways by which the body gains water.
   (b) Name six ways by which water is lost from the
        body.
11 (a) From what food type is urea made?
   (b) Where is urea made?
   (c) Where does urea enter the blood?
   (d) Where does urea leave the blood?
   (e) Where does urea leave the body?
12 Where in the body is urine **(a)** made, **(b)** stored,
   (c) excreted?
13 (a) Redraw Figure 32.17 twice the size shown here.
   (b) Name the parts A to M labelled on the diagram.
   (c) Give one function carried out by each part
        labelled.

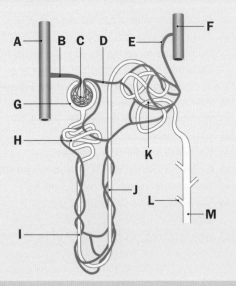

14 Draw a labelled diagram to show the location of a
   nephron in the kidney.
15 Why do the cells lining some parts of the nephron
   contain many mitochondria?
16 Why is the blood pressure in the glomerulus higher
   than normal?
17 (a) Name three substances common to plasma,
        glomerular filtrate, and urine.
   (b) Name three substances in plasma, but not in
        glomerular filtrate.
   (c) Name three substances in glomerular filtrate but
        not in urine.
18 The table below shows the composition of plasma,
   glomerular filtrate, and urine.

Substance	% in plasma	% in glomerular filtrate	% in urine
Protein	8	0	0
Glucose	0.2	0.2	0
Urea	0.03	0.03	2
Salts	0.7	0.7	1.5

   (a) Why is there no protein in the filtrate or urine?
   (b) Explain why the urine has no glucose.
   (c) According to these figures, the urea
        concentration in the urine is much greater than
        that in the glomerular filtrate. Explain why this
        is so.
   (d) Why does the salt concentration only increase
        by a factor of about 2 (i.e. 0.7% to 1.5%) while
        urea concentration increased by a factor of 67
        (i.e. 0.03% to 2%).
19 Describe the effects on the composition and volume
   of urine of the following: **(a)** a hot day,
   (b) drinking a lot of water quickly, **(c)** eating a
   protein-rich meal.
20 (a) Name a hormone that controls urine volume.
   (b) From which gland is this hormone released?
   (c) What part of the body triggers its release?
   (d) State two situations that might cause it to be
        released.
   (e) Name the parts of the nephron affected by the
        hormone.
   (f) What effect has a high level of the hormone on
        (i) urine, **(ii)** blood plasma?
21 Name three features of the nephron that improve its
   ability to carry out filtration.
22 The functions of the nephron can be summarised as
   <u>filtration</u>, <u>reabsorption</u>, and <u>secretion</u>.
   (a) Explain the meaning of each of the underlined
        terms.
   (b) State a location and name two substances
        involved in filtration and reabsorption.

23 Choose which of the options (i), (ii), (iii) or (iv) represents the correct answer in each case below.

(a) A seal is:
- **(i)** cold-blooded
- **(ii)** an ectotherm
- **(iii)** an endotherm
- **(iv)** an ectoplasm

(b) Piloerection is associated with:
- **(i)** sweating
- **(ii)** blushing
- **(iii)** goosebumps
- **(iv)** cooling

(c) Which one of the following is not associated with the production of urine?
- **(i)** transpiration
- **(ii)** secretion
- **(iii)** reabsorption
- **(iv)** filtration

(d) Filtration in the kidney occurs in:
- **(i)** the cortex
- **(ii)** the medulla
- **(iii)** the pyramids
- **(iv)** the pelvis

(e) The hormone ADH is released from:
- **(i)** the hypothalamus
- **(ii)** the pituitary gland
- **(iii)** the cortex
- **(iv)** the collecting duct

(f) Most reabsorption occurs in:
- **(i)** Bowman's capsule
- **(ii)** proximal tubule
- **(iii)** loop of Henle
- **(iv)** distal tubule

Sample examination questions

Section A

24 The diagram shows a section through human skin.

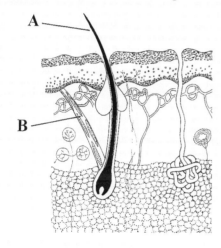

(a) Name parts A and B.

(b) Place X on the diagram to show where sweat reaches the skin surface.

(c) Apart from water, name **one** other substance which is found in sweat.

(d) Describe briefly **one** way by which the skin helps to retain heat in cold conditions.

(2008 OL Q 6)

Section C

25 Use your knowledge of the human vascular and excretory systems to answer the following.

(i) Explain the terms, plasma, glomerular filtrate.

(ii) Explain why red blood cells are normally absent from glomerular filtrate.

(iii) The concentration of glucose is the same in plasma and glomerular filtrate. Why is this?

(iv) Why is glucose normally absent from urine?

(continued)

(v) Following a period of heavy exercise an athlete may produce only a small volume of concentrated urine. Explain this observation and give an account of the process that concentrates the urine.

(2006 HL Q 13)

26 (i) What is meant by excretion?

(ii) Name **two** products excreted by the human.

(iii) Name **one** organ of excretion, other than the kidney, in the human body.

(iv) What is meant by osmoregulation?

(v) Study the diagram of a section through the kidney and answer the following questions.

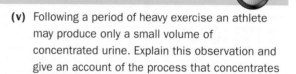

1. Where does filtration of blood take place?
2. Where does reabsorption of salt take place?
3. To what organ does the ureter link the kidney?
4. To which main blood vessel does the renal artery link the kidney?

(vi) Name the fluid present in the ureter.

(2007 OL Q 14)

27 (a) (i) Draw a labelled diagram of a nephron. Include blood vessels in your diagram.

(ii) Filtration and reabsorption are vital processes that take place in the nephron. Describe how each of these processes occurs.

(continued)

THE ORGANISM

(b) Answer the following questions in relation to human body temperature.

  (i) What is the source of the heat that allows the body to maintain a constant internal temperature?

  (ii) State **two** ways in which the body is insulated against loss of heat.

  (iii) Describe the ways in which the body responds when its internal temperature rises above the normal level.

  (iv) Describe briefly the hormonal and nervous responses that occur when internal body temperature drops.

(2004 HL Q 12)

28 (a) The diagram shows a vertical section through human skin.

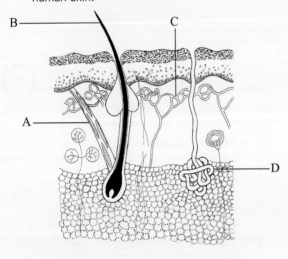

  (i) Identify parts A, B, C and D on the diagram.

  (ii) The human being is an endotherm. What does this mean?

  (iii) What is the main source of body heat in endotherms?

  (iv) Describe the role of D in relation to body temperature.

  (v) What happens to the small arteries (arterioles) in the skin when the external temperature drops?

(2006 OL Q 15)

29 (a) (i) What is meant by excretion?

  (ii) Urea and carbon dioxide are excretory products of the human body. In the case of each product name a substance from which it is derived.

(b) The diagram shows the structure of a nephron and its associated blood supply.

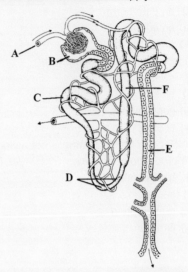

  (i) Name the parts A, B, C, D, E and F.

  (ii) From which blood vessel is A derived?

  (iii) Where in the kidney is B located?

  (iv) Give the part of the nephron in which each of the following takes place:
1. filtration, 2. reabsorption of amino acids.

  (v) Give **two** features of the nephron that aid filtration.

  (vi) Name a group of biomolecules in the blood which are too large to pass through the filtration system of the nephron.

(c) (i) Suggest **two** situations which may result in a drop in the water content of the blood.

  (ii) When the water content of the blood drops a hormone is released. Name this hormone and the endocrine gland from which it is secreted.

  (iii) Give a precise target area for this hormone. How does the hormone reach the target area?

  (iv) Explain the role of the hormone at its target area, when the water content of the blood is low.

(2008 HL Q 13)

Previous examination questions	
Ordinary level	**Higher level**
2003 Sample Q 15a	2003 Sample Q 6
2005 Q 14a	2004 Q 12
2006 Q 15a	2005 Q 3a
2007 Q 14b	2006 Q 13b
2008 Q 6	2007 Q 15c
	2008 Q 13

*For latest questions go to **www.edco.ie/biology***

THE ORGANISM

Chapter 33 **Plant responses**

Stimulus and response

A **stimulus** (plural stimuli) is anything that causes a reaction in an organism or in any of its parts.

Animal stimuli include hearing a loud noise, seeing a pleasant sight, smelling nice perfume, or feeling pain or hunger. Plant stimuli include light, gravity and temperature.

A **response** is the activity of a cell or organism as a result of a stimulus.

Animal responses include movement, production of enzymes or hormones, and feeding. Plant responses include growth, flowering, and production of plant enzymes and hormones.

The structures required for response

The structures needed by organisms in order to allow them to respond include:
- a chemical or hormonal system (present in plants and animals)
- a nerve and sense organ system (only found in animals)
- a method of movement, which includes growth, and muscular and skeletal systems (a muscular and skeletal system is only found in animals)
- a defence or immune system

The structures required by animals for responding will be dealt with in Chapters 34–38.

Plants do not possess nervous systems. Instead, they depend on chemical coordination for their responses. Chemical coordination is much slower than nervous coordination.

Plant responses often involve growth and changes in growth. These responses cause plants to move, but their movement is much slower than that of animals.

Responses in flowering plants

Growth regulation

The growth of flowering plants can be controlled by external and internal factors. Normally the external factors operate by causing, or controlling, the production of internal factors.

EXTERNAL FACTORS
- Light affects plant growth by providing the energy needed for photosynthesis. This in turn supplies the energy-rich molecules needed by plants for growth. In addition, light is needed to produce chlorophyll, fully formed chloroplasts, normal-sized leaves and strong stems.
- Day length plays a very significant role in causing plants to flower. It may also have a role in fruit and seed formation, dormancy, leaf loss and germination of some seeds.
- Gravity can cause roots to grow down into the soil, while shoots grow upwards, away from gravity.
- Temperature affects the growth of plants mainly by affecting the rate of enzyme reactions. As a result, plants grow faster at higher temperatures. In addition, some plants will only produce flowers if they are exposed to low temperatures for a number of days or weeks.

INTERNAL FACTORS
Plants produce a number of chemicals called growth regulators. These growth regulators are produced in the meristematic regions of the plant, such as in the root tip or shoot tip regions.

33.1 *Geotropism: the stem is growing away from gravity*

Tropisms

> A **tropism** is a change in the growth of a plant in response to an external stimulus.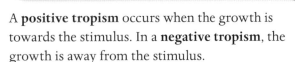

A **positive tropism** occurs when the growth is towards the stimulus. In a **negative tropism**, the growth is away from the stimulus.

The main advantage of tropisms is that they allow plants to obtain more favourable growing conditions. For example, stems grow towards light so they can produce more food by photosynthesis. Roots grow towards gravity so they can penetrate deeper into the soil for better anchorage and absorption.

The main types of tropisms are outlined below.

PHOTOTROPISM

> **Phototropism** is the change in growth of a plant in response to light, usually from one direction (i.e. unidirectional light).

Stems are positively phototropic (i.e. they grow towards light). This allows the stem (and the leaves) to get more light. In this way they can carry out more photosynthesis and produce more food.

Many roots are negatively phototropic. This is clearly seen in the roots of climbing plants such as ivy, where the roots grow away from light and towards the wall.

33.2 *Positive phototropism*

GEOTROPISM (GRAVITROPISM)

> **Geotropism** (or gravitropism) is the change in growth of a plant in response to gravity.

Roots usually grow towards gravity (positively geotropic) and stems grow away from gravity (negatively geotropic).

By growing away from gravity, stems grow towards the light. This allows the plant to produce more food. If the roots grow towards gravity they can anchor the plant more efficiently in the soil. In addition they can absorb more water and minerals.

THIGMOTROPISM

> **Thigmotropism** is the change in growth of a plant in response to touch.

Climbing plants (e.g. ivy, vines, peas, tomatoes) produce specialised parts, called tendrils, which wrap around supporting structures. Tendrils exhibit positive thigmotropism, i.e. they grow around any object they touch.

33.3 *Thigmotropism: tendrils wrapped around a support*

HYDROTROPISM

> **Hydrotropism** is a change in growth of a plant in response to water.

Roots and pollen tubes grow towards water.

CHEMOTROPISM

> **Chemotropism** is a change in growth of a plant in response to chemicals.

Roots grow towards minerals, (e.g. fertilisers such as nitrogen, phosphorous and potassium) in the soil. Pollen tubes grow towards chemicals released by the ovule. These are examples of positive chemotropism.

However, most roots are negatively chemotropic to acids or heavy metals (e.g. lead and zinc) in the soil.

Growth regulators

> A **growth regulator** is a chemical that controls the growth of a plant.

Most growth regulators are produced in small amounts in one part of a plant (mainly in meristems) and transported to another part where they cause an effect. For this reason they are often called hormones.

The exact way that growth regulators are transported is not known. Most, however, are transported in the vascular tissues (xylem and phloem).

It is difficult to establish the exact role of plant regulators. This is due to the following reasons:

- They are active in very small amounts.
- Their effects depend on their concentration. This means the same regulator can have opposite effects at high or low concentrations.
- Their effects depend on the location in the plant in which they are acting. For example, the same concentration of plant regulator can have opposite effects in the stem and root.
- Different regulators interact in different ways. Some regulators support each other to produce a greater effect. Others interfere with each other and the combination may have no effect.

Some regulators, such as auxins, are growth promoters. They increase the rate of growth of the plant. Other regulators act to slow down or inhibit growth. These are called growth inhibitors (e.g. abscisic acid and ethylene).

Growth promoters

Auxins

There are a number of auxins, the most important of which is indoleacetic acid (IAA). IAA, which is often simply called auxin, is made in shoot tips, young leaves and seeds. It moves down the stem by an unknown mechanism.

Auxins cause stem and root growth, along with fruit formation (at certain concentrations).

Auxin as an example of a growth regulator

PRODUCTION SITES

Auxin is produced in the meristematic tissue in the tips of shoots. It is also produced in young leaves and in developing seeds.

FUNCTIONS OF AUXIN

The functions of auxin include:

- stimulating stem elongation
- stimulating root growth
- causing cells to form into different structures
- developing fruit
- inhibiting side branching in stems
- causing phototropism
- causing geotropism

EFFECTS OF AUXINS

- **Tropisms**. Auxins cause cell elongation and growth or bending, as described later in this chapter.
- **Apical dominance**. The apex is the tip (top) of the plant. If it is intact, auxin produced in the tip will pass down the stem and inhibit (prevent the growth of) lateral buds. This means the apex will grow at the expense of side branches.

  This form of growth is clearly seen in cacti (which have very few side branches) and conifers (where the inhibition decreases down the stem, allowing lower branches to grow more strongly).

  If the apex or apical tip is removed side branches are allowed to develop. The plant will then develop as a low, bushy form.

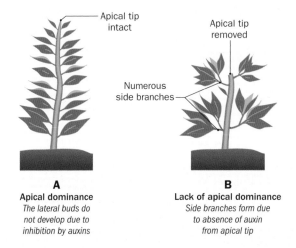

A	**B**
Apical dominance	Lack of apical dominance
The lateral buds do not develop due to inhibition by auxins	*Side branches form due to absence of auxin from apical tip*

33.4 *Effect of the apical tip on plant growth*

- **Fruit formation**. IAA is made in developing seeds. It stimulates food to form in the fruit that surrounds the seed(s).
- **Root growth**. At low concentrations, IAA causes roots to grow. IAA can be applied artificially to stimulate rooting. However, artificial growth promoters (i.e. synthetic ones) are more efficient at this process.

THE ORGANISM

(H) The mechanism of a plant response to light (i.e. of phototropism)

Auxin and cell elongation

Auxin loosens cell walls, which allows them to expand. Cell elongation is essential for normal growth and tropisms.

Role of auxin (IAA) in phototropism

1 IAA is produced in the growth tips (meristems) of the stem.
2 If the stem is exposed to light from one side IAA will diffuse down the shaded side.
3 The concentration of IAA present in the shaded cells causes them to elongate more than the cells on the bright side of the stem.
4 As a result of the uneven elongation, the stem bends towards the light.

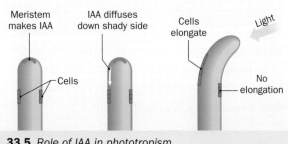

Meristem makes IAA   IAA diffuses down shady side   Cells elongate   Light   Cells   No elongation

(H) 33.5 *Role of IAA in phototropism*

Growth inhibitors

Ethene (ethylene)

Ethene is the only growth regulator that is a gas. It is made by plants in stem nodes, ripe fruits and decaying leaves. It plays a major role in ripening fruits, stimulating leaves to fall in autumn and the ageing of plants.

It causes fruit colour to form, fruit flavour to develop and fruit tissues to soften. It also has the effect of stimulating more ethene production (i.e. ethene stimulates more ethene).

Ethene is used commercially to ripen bananas. Bananas are harvested while they are still green and exported to consumer countries. They are exposed to ethene to stimulate ripening (i.e. they turn yellow and soften) just before distribution to shops.

Abscisic acid

Abscisic acid is produced in leaves, stems and root caps. It is often called the stress regulator of plants because it causes plants to respond to harmful conditions.

In dry conditions it causes stomata to close (conserving water). It causes the production of bud scales, which protect the buds in winter. Its presence in seeds inhibits germination, which allows the seeds to remain dormant in the soil during winter.

Although it was thought to cause leaf fall (abscission) in autumn, this is now known to be caused by ethene (in combination with auxins).

Did you know?

*The saying 'one bad apple rots the barrel' is true because damaged fruit releases **ethene**, which will ripen (and soon over-ripen) surrounding fruit. If ripe fruit is put in a plastic bag with green tomatoes, ethene will cause the tomatoes to turn red faster than normal.*

Commercially prepared growth regulators

Syllabus

You are required to know two uses of commercially prepared plant growth regulators.

Plant growth regulators can be produced outside of plants by artificial or synthetic methods.

- **Rooting powders** often contain a synthetic growth regulator such as NAA (naphtylacetic acid). This stimulates rapid root formation on stem cuttings.
  Horticulturists use NAA to produce roots on cuttings more quickly than would naturally be the case.
- In **tissue culturing**, pieces of plant material are grown to form entire new plants.
  If a piece of plant tissue is grown in a high auxin concentration, it will develop into a mass of similar (undifferentiated) cells, called a callus. By adding different concentrations of auxins, the callus can be stimulated to form roots, shoots or an entire plant, whichever is required.
- **Ethene** ripens bananas.

33.6 *Applying rooting powder to a cutting*

Activity 20   *To investigate the effect of IAA growth regulator on plant tissue*

Preparing a stock solution

1 Dissolve 100 mg of IAA in 2–3 ml of ethanol. Note that although pure IAA may be toxic, dilute solutions do not carry much risk. Ethanol is flammable. *(IAA is dissolved in ethanol first because it does not easily dissolve in water.)*

2 When the IAA is fully dissolved in the ethanol, bring the volume up to 1 litre using distilled water. This stock solution has an IAA concentration of 100 mg /litre (Figure 33.7a).

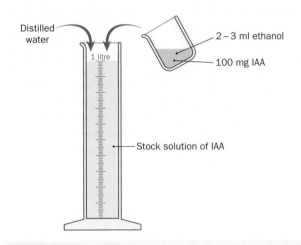

Distilled water
1 litre
Stock solution of IAA
2 – 3 ml ethanol
100 mg IAA

33.7a

Carrying out a serial dilution

3 Label eight petri dishes A to H.

4 Pipette 10 ml of the stock solution (100 mg/litre) into dish A.

5 Using a clean pipette, place 9 ml of distilled water into each of the dishes labelled B to H. (Note: do not add any distilled water to dish A.)

6 Use a suitable pipette to transfer 1 ml of IAA solution from dish A to dish B and stir to mix thoroughly.

7 Using a clean pipette, transfer 1 ml of IAA solution from dish B to C and stir to mix thoroughly.

8 Using a clean pipette each time, and stirring to mix the contents thoroughly, transfer 1 ml of IAA solution from C to D, from D to E, E to F and F to G (see Fig. 33.7b). Remove 1 ml of solution from dish G and dispose of it down the sink. *(The procedure carried out in steps 4 to 8 is called a serial dilution. It produces a range of IAA solutions, each one of which is $\frac{1}{10}$ the concentration of the previous solution.)*

9 Do not transfer any IAA solution to dish H. It acts as a control (containing only distilled water).

10 The final concentration of IAA in each dish is shown in the table below.

(continued overleaf)

Dish	A	B	C	D	E	F	G	H
IAA conc. (mg/litre)	100	10	1	0.1	0.01	0.001	0.0001	0

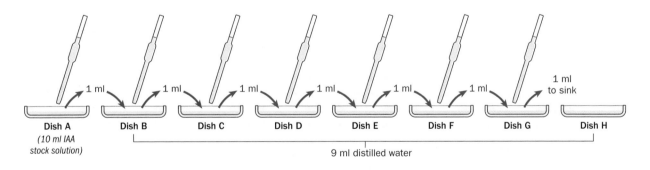

Dish A *(10 ml IAA stock solution)*   Dish B   Dish C   Dish D   Dish E   Dish F   Dish G   Dish H

1 ml   1 ml   1 ml   1 ml   1 ml   1 ml   1 ml to sink

9 ml distilled water

33.7b

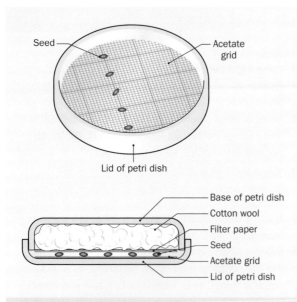

Labels (top): Seed, Acetate grid

Label (bottom): Lid of petri dish

Labels (second diagram): Base of petri dish, Cotton wool, Filter paper, Seed, Acetate grid, Lid of petri dish

33.7c

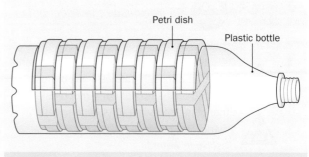

Labels: Petri dish, Plastic bottle

33.7d

Investigating the effect of IAA on plant tissue

11 Photocopy a sheet of graph paper on to acetate sheets. *(The acetate will be used to measure the length of the roots or shoots.)*

12 Place a circular acetate grid in the lid of each of the petri dishes.

13 Place five radish, cress or larger seeds along one of the lines on the acetate sheets.

14 Place filter paper on top of the seeds in the lid of the petri dishes.

15 Use a clean dropper to add about one-quarter of each IAA solution to each filter paper.

16 Cover the filter papers with layers of cotton wool.

17 Add the remaining solution to each piece of cotton.

18 Put the base of the petri dish over the cotton wool and tape it shut.

19 Stand the petri dishes on their edges. *(This ensures that the roots grow down and the shoots grow up.)* A slot can be cut in a large plastic bottle to stand the dishes in.

20 Incubate the dishes at 25°C for two or three days.

Observing the results

21 Use the acetate grid to measure the lengths of the seedlings. Record the results as shown in the table at the bottom of the page. The possible results are:
- The roots and shoots in the control dish are seen to have grown (due to IAA produced by the seeds themselves).
- Depending on the concentration the roots may grow longer or shorter than the roots in the control.
- Depending on the concentration the shoots may grow longer or shorter than the shoots in the control.
- At some concentrations the roots or the shoots (or both) may not grow at all.

22 Calculate the percentage increase or decrease according to the formula:

$$\frac{\% \text{ increase}}{\text{or decrease}} = \frac{\text{average length} - \text{average length of controls}}{\text{average length of controls}} \times \frac{100}{1}$$

23 Draw a graph (using graph paper) of the % increase or decrease vs. IAA concentration. Put IAA on the horizontal axis.

Note: *IAA may cause cell elongation or inhibition in roots and shoots. Roots are much more sensitive to IAA than shoots. The elongation of root cells occurs at very low concentrations of IAA, but IAA levels that cause shoot cells to elongate will cause root cells to contract.*

Dish	Concentration of IAA		Length of roots (mm)					Total length	Average length	% increase (+) or decrease (−)
	(mg/litre)	(ppm*)	Seed 1	Seed 2	Seed 3	Seed 4	Seed 5	(mm)	(mm)	
A	100	10^2								
B	10	10^1								
C	1	$10^0 = 1$								
D	0.1	10^{-1}								
E	0.01	10^{-2}								
F	0.001	10^{-3}								
G	0.0001	10^{-4}								
H (control)	0	0								

*ppm = parts per million

THE ORGANISM

Plant adaptations for protection

Plants are subject to a large range of potentially harmful environmental conditions. These include being eaten by herbivores, being infected with disease-causing micro-organisms, loss of water and the danger of overheating.

To protect themselves, plants have a large number of adaptive features. Some of these features are anatomical (or structural); others are chemical.

Anatomical protective features

- Plants are enclosed by a physical barrier consisting of epidermis or bark. These layers prevent the entry of pathogens and reduce the loss of water from the plant.

  In addition, the epidermis is often covered with a protective cuticle. In some plants, the epidermis cells are adapted to form thorns (e.g. blackberry bushes) or stinging hairs (e.g. nettle leaves).

- A shortage of water in a plant causes the guard cells to shrivel. This has the effect of closing the stomata and therefore reduces any further loss of water. This process can be enhanced when the mesophyll cells in the leaf produce abscisic acid. Abscisic acid also causes the stomata to close and helps to conserve water.

33.8 *SEM of grey thorns on a leaf (the pale-brown projections produce a smell to deter insects)*

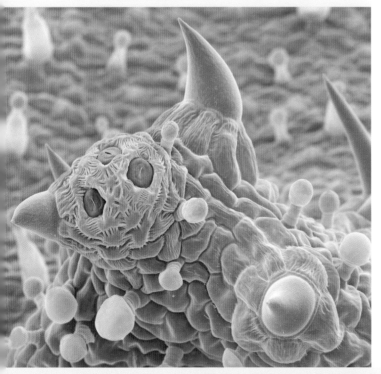

Chemical protective features

- Excessive heat may cause plant enzymes to lose shape and become denatured. This may harm or even kill plants.

  Many plants form special heat-shock proteins once the temperature rises above about 40°C. These heat-shock proteins normally surround other proteins (especially enzymes) and help them to maintain their shapes.

  Heat-shock proteins are also formed by animals and micro-organisms that are subjected to high temperatures (such as during fevers in humans).

- When a plant is infected by a micro-organism the plant is sometimes able to produce stress proteins. Some of these stress proteins are called **phytoalexins**. Stress proteins act in different ways, some of which include:
  - damaging the micro-organisms by attacking their cell walls
  - stimulating the formation of specialised plant cell walls that prevent the spread of the micro-organism
  - stimulating nearby plant cells to respond to the micro-organism

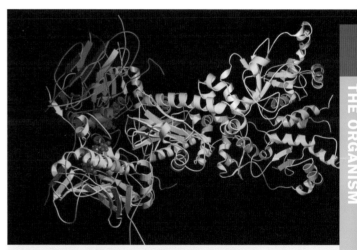

33.9 *Computer model of a heat shock protein*

THE ORGANISM

Summary

A stimulus is anything that causes a reaction in an organism or in any of its parts.

A response is the activity of a cell or organism as a result of a stimulus.

Plant responses often involve growth and changes in growth due to:
- external factors such as light, day length, gravity and temperature
- internal factors such as growth regulators

A tropism is the change in growth of a plant in response to an external stimulus.
- A positive tropism means the growth is towards the stimulus.
- A negative tropism means that the growth is away from the stimulus.

The benefit of tropisms is that they help the plant to achieve the best growing conditions.

The most common tropisms are:
- phototropism (response to light)
- geotropism or gravitropism (response to gravity)
- thigmotropism (touch)
- hydrotropism (water)
- chemotropism (chemicals)

Growth regulators are chemicals that control growth in a plant.
- Growth promoters (auxins) cause plant growth.
- Growth inhibitors (ethene and abscisic acid) slow down or stop growth.

Auxins are the best known growth promoters.

Indoleacetic acid (IAA) is the best known auxin.

The effects of auxins are to cause:
- tropisms (i.e. growth and bending responses)
- apical dominance (i.e. they allow the tip of the stem to grow, but inhibit side branches)
- fruit formation (even when fertilisation has not taken place, i.e. parthenocarpic fruit)
- root formation and growth

IAA affects phototropism as follows:
- IAA is made in the tip of the stem
- it diffuses down the stem
- it causes stem cells to elongate
- it diffuses down the shaded side of a stem
- the cells on the shaded side elongate, causing the stem to bend towards light

Growth inhibitors include:
- ethene (or ethylene), which is a gas that ripens fruit, and causes ageing and leaf fall
- abscisic acid, which responds to stress in plants by closing stomata, forming bud scales and inhibiting seed germination

Commercial growth regulators are used to:
- stimulate root formation in cuttings
- stimulate the formation of new plants in tissue culturing
- ripen bananas

To investigate the effect of IAA on plant tissues:
- different concentrations of IAA are prepared
- seeds are grown in the IAA concentrations
- changes in length of the seedlings are recorded

Plant protective methods may be:
- anatomical or structural (epidermis, bark, cuticle, closure of stomata)
- chemical (heat-shock proteins, stress proteins)

Revision questions

1. **(a)** What is meant by a **(i)** stimulus, **(ii)** response?
   (b) Give two examples in each case for animal and plant stimuli and responses.
2. Name two external factors that control growth in plants.
3. **(a)** What is a tropism?
   (b) Distinguish between positive and negative tropisms.
4. Name two positive tropisms in each case that affect **(a)** shoots, **(b)** roots.
5. What is the significance of tropisms for plants?
6. Outline one benefit to a plant in each case of:
   (a) phototropism, **(b)** geotropism or gravitropism.
7. **(a)** What is a growth regulator?
   (b) How are growth regulators transported in plants?

   (c) Give three reasons why it proved difficult for scientists to discover the role of growth regulators.
8. **(a)** Distinguish between growth promoters and growth inhibitors.
   (b) Name one growth promoter and one growth inhibitor, and give one function for each.
9. With regard to auxin, state:
   (a) a precise location where it is produced
   (b) two ways in which it acts as a growth regulator
   (c) one way in which it acts as a growth inhibitor
   (d) its effects on **(i)** fruit formation and **(ii)** side branching
10. Describe, with the aid of a labelled diagram, the role of auxin (IAA) in the change in growth of a stem in response to light from one side.

THE ORGANISM

11 Some oat seedlings were grown in the dark and then treated as follows:

Group A: no treatment given, left intact.

Group B: tips of seedlings covered with metal foil.

Group C: tips of seedlings cut off.

The seedlings were then exposed to light from one side as shown in Figure 33.10.

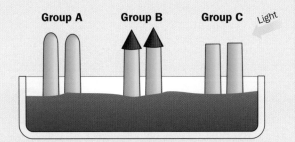

33.10

(a) Which group of seedlings will respond to the light?

(b) Explain why the other groups will not respond.

(c) Name the response that is produced.

(d) What is the value of this response to a plant?

(e) Name the substance causing the response.

12 In an experiment three groups of oat seedlings were set up and illuminated from one side only (unilateral light). Group A were untreated; members of group B had black paper sleeves around them except at their tips; group C had black paper caps over their tips. The results are shown in Figure 33.11.

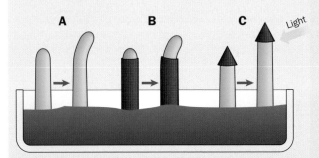

33.11

(a) Explain the reason for the results in group A.

(b) Why do the stems in group C not bend?

(c) What result would you expect for group C if the caps were transparent?

(d) Why do the stems in group B bend?

13 Give a biological reason for the following:

(a) placing a ripe fruit in a bag of hard pears

(b) treating a plant cutting with NAA

(c) subjecting green bananas to ethene gas

(d) growing plant cells on agar containing a high concentration of auxins

(e) removing the tips of plants in a hedgerow

14 (a) State two ways in which plant growth regulators may be used commercially.

(b) State the benefit for each example given.

(c) Say whether each regulator is acting as a growth promoter or growth inhibitor.

15 In investigating the effect of a growth regulator on plant tissue:

(a) Name the growth regulator used.

(b) Name the plant used.

(c) Why was the growth regulator dissolved in ethanol first?

(d) Why were five seedlings (rather than a single seedling) placed in each dish?

(e) Why was there no growth regulator in one dish?

(f) How was the effect of the regulator on the plant tissue judged?

16 (a) Name four factors that plants may protect themselves against.

(b) Give two examples in each case of anatomical and chemical methods by which plants protect themselves.

(c) Explain why a nettle sting is a combination of anatomical and chemical protection.

17 The graph in Figure 33.12 shows the effect of IAA concentration on roots and shoots.

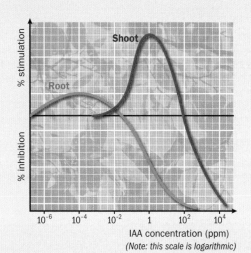

33.12

(a) What concentration of IAA:

(i) has the same effect on roots and shoots?

(ii) causes maximum root elongation?

(iii) causes no effect on shoots?

(b) Suggest the effect of the following IAA concentrations:

(i) 10^4 ppm on roots

(ii) 1 ppm on shoots

(iii) 10^{-2} ppm on roots

(iv) 10^{-4} ppm on roots and shoots

18 From the information given in the graph in Question 17, state the two factors that influence the effects of IAA.

THE ORGANISM

19 Choose which of the options (i), (ii), (iii) or (iv) represents the correct answer in each case below.

(a) The growth regulator that causes leaves to fall off trees in autumn is called:
   (i) auxin
   (ii) ethene
   (iii) abscisic acid
   (iv) IAA

(b) The response of a plant to touch is called:
   (i) thermotropism
   (ii) chemotropism
   (iii) thigmotropism
   (iv) geotropism

(c) Phototropism is caused by cell elongation in:
   (i) the bright side of the stem tips
   (ii) the shady side of the stem tips
   (iii) the base of the stem
   (iv) all the cells in the stem

(d) Phototropism is caused by cell elongation in:
   (i) the bright side of the stem tips
   (ii) the shady side of the stem tips
   (iii) the base of the stem
   (iv) all the cells in the stem

Sample examination questions

Section B

20 Growth regulators in plants can promote growth or inhibit it.

(a) Give an example of each of the following:
   (i) A growth regulator that promotes growth.
   (ii) A growth regulator that inhibits growth.

(b) In the course of your studies you investigated the effect of a growth regulator on plant tissue. Answer the following questions in relation to that investigation.
   (i) Name the plant that you used.
   (ii) Describe how you carried out the investigation.
   (iii) Give a safety precaution that you took while carrying out the investigation.
   (iv) State the results that you obtained.

(2008 HL Q 8)

21 (a) (i) State a location in a flowering plant where a growth regulator is secreted.
   (ii) Give an example of the use of a synthetic growth regulator.

(b) The diagram shows apparatus that may be used to investigate the effect of the growth regulator IAA.

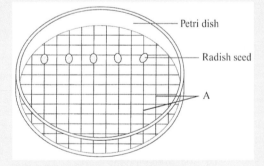

(i) Name A.
(ii) What is the purpose of A in this experiment?
(iii) How would you make up solutions of different concentrations from a stock solution of IAA?

(continued)

(iv) After preparation the dishes are placed standing on their edges for a number of days. What is the reason for this?
(v) Describe the results that you would expect in this experiment.

(2003 Sample HL Q 9)

Section C

22 The graph shows the effect of varying auxin concentration on the root and shoot of a plant.

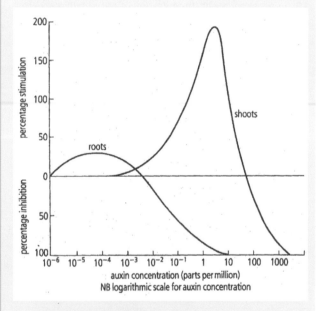

(i) What is an auxin?
(ii) At what approximate auxin concentration does the root receive maximum stimulation?
(iii) At what approximate auxin concentration does the shoot receive maximum stimulation?
(iv) What is the effect on the root of an auxin concentration of 10–2 parts per million?
(v) Give two examples of uses of synthetic (man-made) auxins.
(vi) Describe three methods used by plants to protect themselves from adverse external environments.

(2005 HL Q 14b)

23 (i) What is an auxin? State a site of auxin secretion. How may the action of an auxin be considered similar to the action of a hormone in the human body?

(ii) Define tropism. List three types of tropism.

(iii) Relate the role of an auxin to one of the tropisms that you have listed in (ii).

(2004 HL Q 15b)

*For latest questions go to **www.edco.ie/biology***

Chapter 34 The nervous system

Introduction

In animals, the nervous system and the endocrine system (Chapter 36) are responsible for the coordination of activities in the body. They allow the animal to respond to internal and external changes called stimuli.

The nervous system is specially adapted for the rapid responses that an animal makes. It is divided into:

- the **central nervous system** (**CNS**), which consists of the brain and spinal cord
- the **peripheral nervous system** (**PNS**), which consists of a vast network of nerves that carry messages between the CNS and the rest of the body

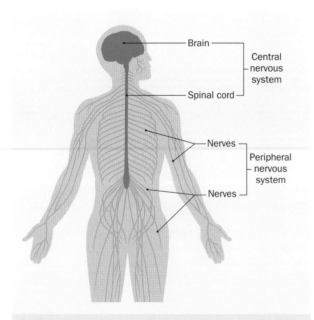

Brain

Central nervous system

Spinal cord

Nerves

Peripheral nervous system

Nerves

34.1 *The parts of the nervous system*

In order to make the correct response to a stimulus, four processes are involved.

- **Reception**. The stimulus must be detected. This is the function of neurons (nerve cells) and sense organs.
- **Transmission**. The message passes along the neurons. The neurons in the PNS carry messages from receptors to the CNS and from the CNS to effectors, such as muscles.

- **Integration**. The incoming messages are sorted and processed and a response decided upon. This occurs in the CNS, especially in the brain.
- **Response**. This is carried out by the effectors (i.e. muscles or glands) when they are stimulated by neurons.

Neurons

A **neuron** (or neurone) is a nerve cell.

Neurons are the basic units of the nervous system and are specialised to carry information (as electrical impulses) from one place to another.

There are three types of neurons:

- **Sensory** (or afferent) **neurons** take messages from sense organs to the CNS.
- **Motor** (or efferent) **neurons** take messages from the CNS to muscles and glands, causing them to respond.
- **Interneurons** (also called intermediate, relay or association neurons) carry information between sensory and motor neurons. They are only found in the CNS.

Not only do neurons vary in type, they also differ in size. Neurons in the brain are very tiny, whereas neurons connecting the spine and the feet may be over 1 metre long.

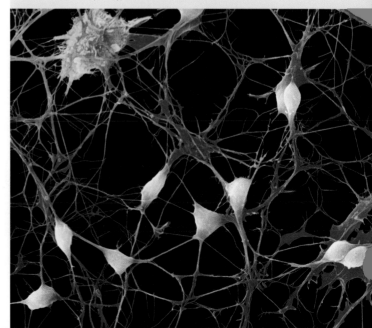

34.2 *Neurons (blue), axons and thinner dendrites*

THE ORGANISM

Structure of neurons

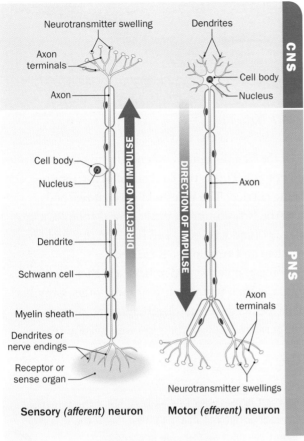

34.3 Sensory and motor neurons

Functions of the parts of neurons

- A receptor is a cell or group of cells that detects a stimulus.
- Nerve endings connect sensory neurons to receptor cells or sense organs.
- Dendrites are fibres (often highly branched) that carry impulses **toward** the cell body.
- Axons carry impulses **away from** cell bodies.
- Schwann cells are located along the length of neurons. They make the myelin sheath.
- The myelin sheath is a fat-rich membrane that insulates the electrical impulses.

Did you know?

*In **multiple sclerosis (MS)**, patches of myelin degenerate in the central nervous system. As a result, the passage of nerve impulses is impeded and the person suffers symptoms ranging from numbness and tingling to paralysis and loss of bladder control.*

- The cell body contains a nucleus and cell organelles. It forms the dendrites and axons that may emerge from it as well as neurotransmitter

chemicals. A group of cell bodies located outside the CNS is called a **ganglion** (plural ganglia).

- The cell bodies of sensory neurons are located outside the CNS. The cell bodies of motor neurons are located within the CNS.
- The end of each axon breaks up into many axon terminals. Each of these small branches ends in a swelling called a neurotransmitter swelling.

These swellings release chemicals that carry the impulse from one nerve cell to another. The chemicals are called neurotransmitters. Neurotransmitters are stored in vesicles in the swellings.

Nerve fibres

Many axons often combine to form nerve fibres (sometimes simply called a nerve). Axons can be quite long – those that run from the spine to the feet may be over 1 metre in length.

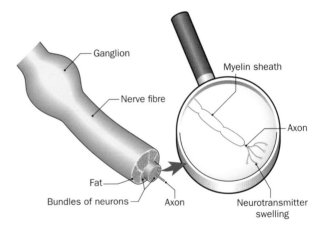

34.4 Relationship between nerve fibres and neurons

34.5 Nerve fibres: connective tissue (yellow), myelin (pink) and axon (brown)

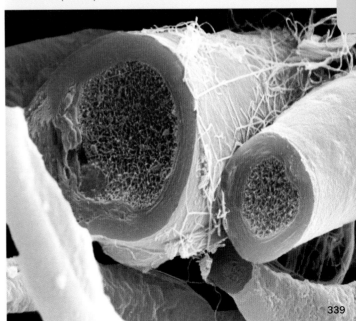

Interneurons

Interneurons are short neurons found in the CNS. They are not enclosed in myelin sheaths. They connect motor and sensory nerves.

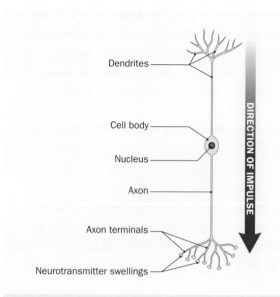

34.6 *An interneuron*

Transmission of nerve impulses

When a neuron receives a stimulus of sufficient strength, an electrical current or impulse travels along the dendrite and axon to the neurotransmitter swellings. The movement of the electrical impulse along a neuron involves the movement of ions (charged particles).

Features of nerve impulses

Resting neuron

When a neuron is not carrying an impulse, ions (charged particles) are pumped in and out of the axon. This results in the inside of the axon being negative and the outside positive.

Threshold

> The **threshold** is the minimum stimulus needed to cause an impulse to be carried.

A stimulus below the threshold has no effect, but one that is at or above the threshold causes an electrical impulse to travel along the axon.

The transmission of a nerve impulse can be compared to a set of dominoes lined up, as shown in Figure 34.7.

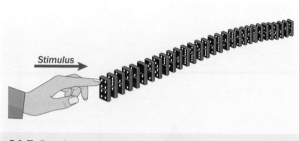

34.7 *Dominoes*

If the first domino is touched lightly the dominoes do not fall. This is the equivalent of no impulse being carried. The threshold was not reached.

If the first domino is pushed hard enough, it and all the other dominoes will fall. The threshold was reached and an impulse is carried.

Some people are said to have a higher threshold for pain, high temperature or some other stimulus. This means they can tolerate more pain or higher temperatures before their nervous system reacts.

'All or nothing' law

> The **'all or nothing law'** states that if the threshold is reached an impulse is carried, but if the threshold is not reached no impulse is carried.

The 'all or nothing' law means that an impulse is either carried or not carried.

In the case of the dominoes, either they all fall when the first one is pushed over or none fall if the first one is not pushed over.

If the threshold is reached a message is sent. No matter how strong the stimulus is, once it is above the threshold level, the same impulse is carried. This means that a mild stimulus or a severe stimulus will cause the same impulse to be sent along any axon.

Sensitivity to different degrees of stimulation (e.g. mild versus severe pain) depends on the number of neurons stimulated and the frequency with which they send their impulses.

Movement of impulse

Once the threshold is reached the axon (or dendron) changes its permeability to ions. At the site of stimulation the inside of the axon becomes positive and the outside becomes negative.

This change in the charge causes the next section of the axon to alter its permeability in a similar way. A chain reaction is set up and a movement of positive charge runs along the inside of the axon. Energy (ATP) is needed to cause these changes.

Once the impulse has moved along, the area behind is restored to the resting state (i.e. inside negative, outside positive).

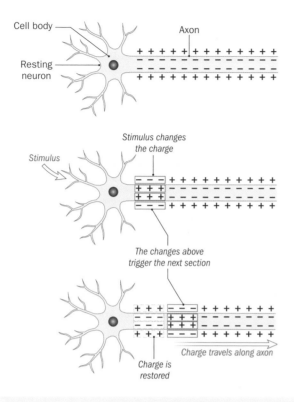

34.8 *Passage of an impulse along a neuron*

Refractory period

The **refractory period** is a short timespan after a neuron has carried an impulse during which a stimulus fails to cause a response.

While the ions are moving in and out of each section of the neuron, the region affected cannot carry another impulse. There has to be a slight delay of about 5 ms ($\tfrac{5}{1000}$ of a second) between any two impulses. This time span is called the refractory period.

This delay can be compared to the time needed to stand the dominoes up again after they have fallen down.

Speed of impulse

The speed at which an electrical impulse travels along a neuron depends on whether myelin is present or absent around the neuron.

If myelin is absent, the changes in positive and negative charge occur all along the dendrite or axon. The speed of the impulse is reduced (typically to about 2 m/sec).

In a myelinated neuron the charges can only move in and out at the gaps in the myelin. The impulse jumps from gap to gap and is transmitted more rapidly (typically about 120 m/sec).

The speed at which the electrical impulse travels is also dependent on the diameter of the dendrite or axon. The larger the diameter, the faster the impulse travels.

Synapse

A **synapse** is a region where two neurons come into close contact.

Synapses are commonly found between the axon terminals of one neuron and the dendrites of another neuron.

A **synaptic cleft** is the tiny gap between the two neurons at a synapse.

Normally the gap is as small as 0.00002 mm (20 nanometres, nm). The number of synapses associated with each neuron is very large, ranging from 1000 for a cell body in the spinal cord up to 10 000 for cell bodies in the brain.

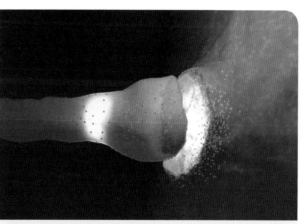

34.9 *An image of a synapse*

ACTIVATION OF NEUROTRANSMITTER

Electrical impulses cannot cross a synapse. Instead, the ions stimulate the neurotransmitter swellings in the presynaptic neuron to release a chemical substance that diffuses rapidly across the synaptic cleft. These chemicals are called **neurotransmitters**.

Some neurotransmitters are made in the cell bodies of the neurons, and others are formed in the neurotransmitter swellings. The enzymes needed to make these latter neurotransmitters are made in the cell body and transported to the swellings.

Neurotransmitters are contained in vesicles in the neurotransmitter swellings.

Over 60 different neurotransmitters are known, the most common being acetylcholine (ACh) and noradrenalin (also called norepinephrine).

The neurotransmitter diffuses across the synaptic cleft. It then combines with receptors on the postsynaptic neuron. This causes the electrical impulse to be regenerated.

INACTIVATION OF NEUROTRANSMITTER

The neurotransmitter is then broken down by enzymes. The digested neurotransmitters are reabsorbed back into the neurotransmitter swellings. This allows them to be recycled.

At a synapse the following interchange occurs:

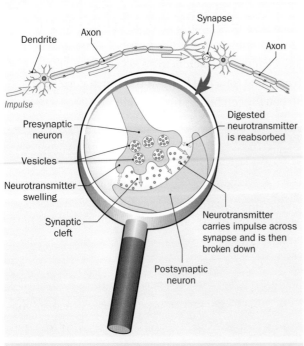

34.10 *Structure of a synapse*

Functions of synapses

1 They transmit impulses from one neuron to another neuron or to an effector (muscle or gland).
2 They control the direction of the impulse. This is due to neurotransmitter swellings only being found on the presynaptic side of the synapse. In this way they act as valves (i.e. they only allow a one-way flow).

3 They prevent overstimulation of effectors. This happens when the neurotransmitter ceases to be produced due to constant stimulation. The impulse is therefore inhibited and the effector ceases to be stimulated.

This means we tend to get used to stimuli such as pain and noise, and are stimulated only by changes in these inputs.
4 The impulse can be blocked by certain chemicals (drugs). This is important in controlling pain and some psychiatric disorders.

The central nervous system (CNS)

The brain

The senses and individual sensory neurons act as receptors for incoming stimuli. Electrical impulses are passed along the sensory neurons (dendrites and axons) to the CNS and in particular to the brain. The brain acts as an interpreting centre to sort and process the incoming impulses and decide on a response.

The human brain is composed of about 12 000 million neurons. The cell bodies and synapses form the grey matter of the brain, with the nerve fibres (dendrites and axons) forming the white matter. The brain uses about 20% of the body's energy.

Both the brain and spinal cord are protected by bone and are covered by three membranes called **meninges**.

The space between the inner two meninges is filled with cerebrospinal fluid. This fluid acts as a protective shock absorber and as an exchange medium between the blood and brain. There is about 100 cm³ (⅙ pint) of cerebrospinal fluid in the CNS.

34.11 *A CAT scan of the brain*

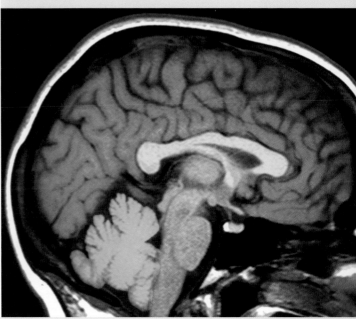

Meningitis *is an inflammation of the meninges. (The meninges enclose the brain and they also enclose the nerves in the spinal cord.) Meningitis occurs more commonly in children than adults, but can occur at any age. There are two causes of meningitis, a virus and a bacterium.*

*   **Viral meningitis** *is a more common and less severe infection. It causes irritability, headache and fever. In severe cases it results in neck ache. There is no specific treatment and the symptoms normally disappear within a week or two.*

*   **Bacterial meningitis** *is much more dangerous. Along with the symptoms described above, it causes skin rash, vomiting, intolerence of bright light, inability to bend the neck down, convulsions, and even coma and death.*

Bacterial meningitis is treated with antibiotics. Vaccines are available for some forms of bacterial meningitis.

Structure of the brain

CEREBRUM

The cerebrum is the largest part of the brain. It contains about 75% of the neurons in the brain. It is divided into two halves, the right and left cerebral hemispheres.

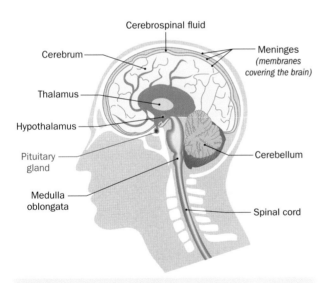

34.12 *Structure of the brain*

The functions of the cerebrum include controlling voluntary movements, receiving and interpreting impulses from the sense organs, thinking, intelligence, memory, language, emotions, judgement and personality.

The right hemisphere controls the left-hand side of the body. Neurons from the left hemisphere control the right-hand side of the body. This is why

a stroke (a blood clot in the brain) may paralyse only one side of the victim.

Each hemisphere is specialised to function in different ways. In general, the left side is dominant for hand use (i.e. most people are right-handed), language, mathematics, analysis and logic. The right side specialises in art, music, shape recognition and emotional responses.

The functions associated with different parts of the cerebrum are shown on Figure 34.13.

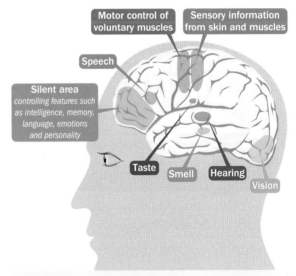

34.13 *Functions of cerebrum*

The outer part of the cerebrum, called the cerebral cortex, is grey.

The inner, white matter of the cerebrum contains millions of nerve fibres. These connect different areas of the cortex and the two sides of the brain (which are connected by a structure called the corpus callosum).

CEREBELLUM

The cerebellum is the second largest section of the brain. It is heavily folded. The cerebellum controls muscular coordination and allows smooth, refined muscular action. It also controls balance.

The responses of the cerebellum are involuntary, once the process has been learned. For example, walking is originally controlled by the cerebrum, but once we learn to walk the cerebellum takes over and walking is controlled involuntarily.

MEDULLA OBLONGATA

The medulla oblongata connects the spinal cord with the rest of the brain. It contains clusters of nerve cells that control involuntary actions such as breathing, blood pressure, swallowing, coughing, salivation, sneezing and vomiting.

THE ORGANISM

THALAMUS AND HYPOTHALAMUS

The thalamus is located below the cerebrum. It acts as a sorting centre for the brain and relays all incoming messages to the relevant part of the brain.

The hypothalamus lies below the thalamus. It regulates the internal environment of the body (homeostasis) by monitoring body (blood) temperature, appetite, thirst, osmoregulation and blood pressure. It also links with the pituitary gland to regulate the production of many hormones.

The hypothalamus is thought to be the link between the mind (or brain) and the body.

PITUITARY GLAND

The pituitary gland is not a part of the brain. It is located below the hypothalamus, to which it is attached. It produces numerous hormones and is described in Chapter 36.

Nervous system disorder

Syllabus

You are required to study a nervous system disorder: either Parkinson's disease or paralysis.

Parkinson's disease

CAUSE

Parkinson's disease is a disorder of the nervous system. It is caused by the failure (for reasons unknown) to produce a neurotransmitter called **dopamine** in a part of the brain. Lack of dopamine results in the inability to control muscle contraction.

This results in symptoms such as trembling of the hands and/or legs. Later the muscles and body become stiff and rigid and the person walks with a shuffling unbalanced gait. The face often has a fixed, unblinking stare. Everyday activities such as dressing, washing and eating become difficult. Thought processes are not affected until late in the course of the disease.

Parkinson's disease is normally found in the elderly and is more common in males than in females.

PREVENTION

There is no known way to prevent Parkinson's disease.

TREATMENT

Initial treatment involves physiotherapy and special exercises, and the provision of special aids and home help to patients. Treatment with drugs to stimulate

or mimic dopamine can reduce the symptoms but cannot stop the degeneration of the brain.

Recent research suggests that electrical stimulation or implanting dopamine-secreting tissue (stem cells) into the brain may prove beneficial.

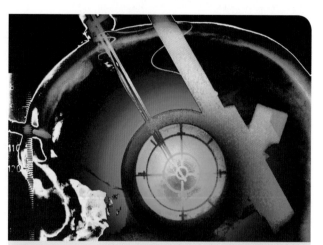

34.14 *An x-ray of the head (forehead on left) showing electrodes being positioned to treat Parkinson's disease*

Spinal cord

The spinal cord is composed of nerve tissue. It is surrounded by bony vertebrae, which protect it. The spinal cord transmits impulses to and from the brain. It also controls many reflex actions.

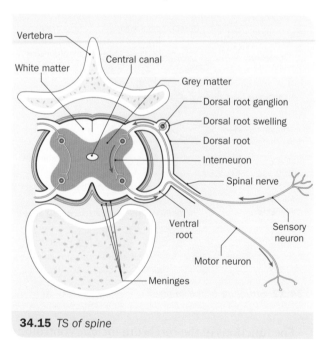

34.15 *TS of spine*

The spinal cord is located in the neural canal of the vertebrae. The neural canal is lined by the meninges.

In cross-section the spinal cord appears as an outer ring of white matter (axons only) surrounding an inner H-shaped region of grey matter (cell bodies and dendrites). At the centre of the grey matter is the central canal, which contains cerebrospinal fluid.

The dorsal root carries sensory neurons into the spinal cord and the ventral root carries motor neurons out. These neurons are usually linked by numerous interneurons in the grey matter.

The dorsal root swellings contain ganglia, i.e. groups of cell bodies of sensory neurons.

The dorsal and ventral roots combine to form 31 pairs of spinal nerves, which take impulses to and from the spinal cord.

Peripheral nervous system

The PNS mostly consists of nerve fibres outside the brain and spinal cord. These are made up of long dendrites or axons taking impulses to or from the CNS.

The cell bodies of sensory nerves are located in ganglia in the PNS (i.e. in the dorsal root ganglia just outside the spinal cord). Cell bodies of motor neurons are found in the CNS (i.e. in the grey matter of the brain and spinal cord).

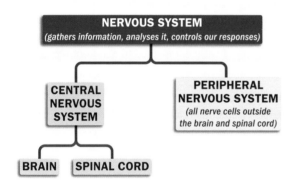

34.16 Parts of the nervous system

Reflex action

The simplest form of activity in the nervous system is a reflex action.

> A **reflex action** is an automatic, involuntary, unthinking response to a stimulus.

The neurons forming the pathway taken by nerve impulses in a reflex action make up a reflex arc. A reflex arc is the unit of function of the nervous system.

Examples of reflex actions

Many of the activities of the body are reflex and are controlled by reflex arcs, e.g. the grasp reflex

in children, the movement of the iris of the eye, blinking our eyes for protection, breathing, control of blood pressure and the protective actions we take when falling.

Advantages of reflex action

The advantage of reflex actions is that they are fast responses and so can protect the body from damage. This is best understood by considering a relatively simple, 3-neuron withdrawal reflex, such as pulling the hand back from a hot flame.

Withdrawal reflex

1 Receptors in the fingers are stimulated by the hot flame.
2 Sensory neurons carry an impulse into the spinal cord.
3 In the spinal cord numerous synapses are made with other neurons.
   (i) An interneuron carries the impulse across the spinal cord to a motor neuron.
   (ii) Another neuron takes the impulse up to the brain.
4 Motor neurons take the impulse straight out of the spine to the effector (i.e. a muscle or gland). This causes us to pull our hand back from the hot flame.
5 At the same time as the hand withdraws, the impulse reaches the brain. This makes us aware of what has happened and we feel some pain.

This account is a simplification of the process. Extra connections and pathways exist to add further complexity to the process.

For example, we pull our arm *up* from a hot cooker, but *down* when changing a hot overhead bulb. Also reflex actions can be inhibited, e.g. we drop a hot plate but we attempt to place an expensive hot dish down gently.

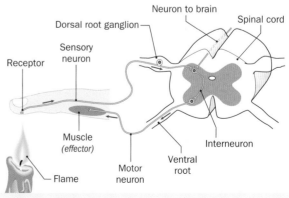

34.17 A reflex arc

Summary

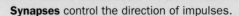

The nervous system is divided into:
- the central nervous system (CNS) = brain and spinal cord
- the peripheral nervous system (PNS) = the nerves outside the CNS

Nervous coordination involves:
- reception (detecting a stimulus)
- transmission (movement of the impulse)
- integration (impulses are sorted, processed and decisions made)
- response (a muscle or gland carries out the effect)

A neuron is a nerve cell. There are three types of neurons.
- Sensory (afferent) neurons take messages to the CNS.
- Motor (efferent) neurons take messages from the CNS.
- Interneurons connect motor and sensory neurons in the CNS.

The main parts of a neuron:
- Nerve endings connect to receptors or sense organs.
- Dendrites (can be long or short, and branched) carry impulses to a cell body.
- Axons carry nerve impulses away from cell bodies.
- Schwann cells make myelin.
- Myelin insulates the electrical impulses.
- The cell body forms neurotransmitters and the different parts of the neuron.

Nerve impulse transmission:
- A resting neuron has negative ions on the inside and positive ions on the outside.
- The threshold is the minimum stimulus needed for an impulse to travel.
- The 'all or nothing' law says that:
    - if the threshold is reached, an impulse travels
    - if the threshold is not reached, no impulse travels
- There is a delay (or refactory) period between two impulses.
- The myelin sheath speeds up the passage of an impulse.

A synapse is the region where two neurons come into close contact.

A synaptic cleft is a tiny gap between one neuron and either another neuron or an effector.

A nerve impulse involves the following:
- Neurotransmitter swellings (or synaptic knobs) produce neurotransmitters such as acetylcholine (ACh).
- ACh diffuses across the synapse.
- ACh causes the production of an electrical impulse at the other side where it is broken down by enzymes.

Synapses control the direction of impulses.

Functions of the parts of the brain

Part of brain	Function
Cerebrum	Controls voluntary muscles. Receives impulses from sense organs. Intelligence, memory, language, emotions, judgement & personality.
Cerebellum	Controls muscular coordination, balance.
Medulla	Controls involuntary actions.
Thalamus	Sends messages to different parts of the brain.
Hypothalamus	Controls internal environment of the body.

Parkinson's disease:
- is a nervous disorder caused by a lack of dopamine in the brain
- results in trembling limbs, a rigid body and inability to walk properly
- cannot be prevented
- is treated by physiotherapy and drugs

The spinal cord carries impulses to and from the brain and controls many reflex actions.

In the spinal cord:
- sensory neurons enter through dorsal roots
- the dorsal root ganglion contains the cell bodies of the sensory neurons
- white matter contains axons
- grey matter contains cell bodies and dendrites
- interneurons connect sensory and motor neurons
- motor neurons emerge through ventral roots

The peripheral nervous system is mostly made of nerve fibres (i.e. long dendrites or axons).

A reflex action is an automatic response to a stimulus. Reflex actions are:
- fast responses
- designed to protect the body

A reflex arc is the basic unit of function of the nervous system.
- Reflex arcs consist of receptors, nerves and effectors.
- The route taken along a reflex arc is:
  receptor → sensory neuron → spinal cord → interneuron → motor neuron → effector.
- At the interneuron stage an impulse is also sent to the brain. The brain is made aware of the action, but does not control it.

THE ORGANISM

Revision questions

1 In relation to the nervous system, explain the terms **(a)** stimulus, **(b)** response and **(c)** impulse. (See Chapter 33.)

2 **(a)** Name the four stages involved in producing nervous responses.
   (b) Give one location or structure associated with each stage.

3 **(a)** Name the three types of neurons.
   (b) Distinguish between the three types of neurons in terms of where they carry impulses to and from.

4 **(a)** Name the type of neuron shown in Figure 34.18.

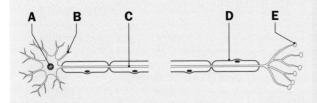

34.18

   (b) Name, and give one function for, all the parts labelled A to E.
   (c) In what form does the impulse travel along structure C?
   (d) In what direction does the impulse travel at C?
   (e) Name the other two types of neurons and draw similar labelled diagrams for each.

5 Distinguish between:
   (a) the central and peripheral nervous system
   (b) afferent and efferent neurons
   (c) dendrites and axons
   (d) synapse and synaptic cleft.

6 **(a)** What is a synapse?
   (b) Give two benefits of synapses.

7 Describe how an impulse arriving at a synapse can continue across the synapse.

8 **(a)** What is the function of neurotransmitters?
   (b) Name two neurotransmitters.

9 **(a)** Name the parts of the CNS labelled A, B, C and D in Figure 34.19.

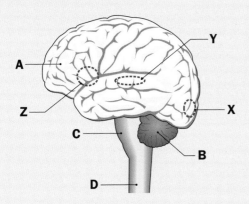

34.19

   (b) Give two functions for each part named in answer **(a)**.
   (c) Assign each of the following abilities to one of the regions labelled X, Y or Z: memory, eyesight, speech, hearing.

10 Give a location and function for each of the following: **(a)** meninges, **(b)** cerebrospinal fluid, **(c)** corpus callosum, **(d)** hypothalamus, **(e)** pituitary gland.

11 **(a)** Name a disorder of the nervous system.
   (b) Give three symptoms of this disorder.
   (c) Name one way in which the disorder may be treated.

12 **(a)** Name the parts labelled A to K in the TS of the spinal cord shown in Figure 34.20.

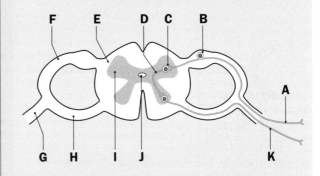

34.20

   (b) Name the structures contained in B.
   (c) Describe the direction of the impulse in each of the structures labelled A, D and K.
   (d) How many structures similar to G emerge from the spinal cord?
   (e) Name the substance in the part labelled J.

13 **(a)** Give three examples of reflex actions.
   (b) What is the advantage of a reflex action?
   (c) What is the difference between a reflex action and a reflex arc?

14 'Reflex actions are not brain controlled and yet the brain is aware of the response.' Explain, using a diagram, why this is true.

15 Choose which of the options (i), (ii), (iii) or (iv) represents the correct answer in each case below.
   (a) The part of the brain that controls body temperature is called:
      (i) cerebrum
      (ii) cerebellum
      (iii) thalamus
      (iv) hypothalamus
   (b) Which of the following is not a neurotransmitter?
      (i) adrenaline
      (ii) noradrenaline
      (iii) dopamine
      (iv) acetylcholine

(c) The myelin sheath of an axon is composed of:
  (i) ATP
  (ii) vesicles
  (iii) fat
  (iv) ions

(d) The decision to take off a sweater on a very hot day is a function of:
  (i) the cerebellum
  (ii) the involuntary nervous system
  (iii) the peripheral nervous system
  (iv) the medula oblongata

(e) Thinking is associated with which area of the brain?
  (i) hypothalamus
  (ii) cerebrum
  (iii) cerebellum
  (iv) medulla oblongata

(f) The white matter of the spinal cord is found in:
  (i) the central canal
  (ii) the dorsal root
  (iii) the outer ring
  (iv) the H-shaped region

Sample examination questions

Section A

16 The diagram shows a motor neuron.

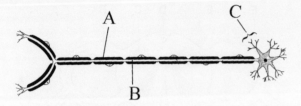

(a) Identify parts A, B and C.
(b) Give a function of A.
(c) Place an arrow on the diagram to show the direction of the impulse.
(d) Give a function of C.
(e) Place an X on the diagram at a point at which a neurotransmitter substance is secreted.
(f) What is the role of the motor neuron?

(2008 HL Q 4)

Section C

17 (i) What is a neuron?
(ii) Distinguish between sensory, motor and interneurons (association neurons).
(iii) Briefly explain the role of neurotransmitter substances.
(iv) State a function for:
  1. Schwann cells,
  2. Myelin sheath.
(v) In relation to Parkinson's disease or paralysis give:
  1. A possible cause,
  2. A method of treatment.

(2006 HL Q 14b)

18 The diagram shows part of a reflex arc.

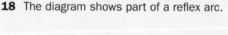
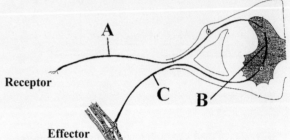

(i) Name neurons A, B and C.
(ii) In which direction is the impulse transmitted A→B→C or C→B→A?
(iii) Name the small gaps between neurons.
(iv) Neurons produce neurotransmitter substances. What is their function?
(v) Give an example of a reflex action in humans.
(vi) Why are reflex actions important in humans?

(2007 OL Q 15a)

19 (i) Draw and label sufficient of two neurons to show a synaptic cleft.
(ii) Describe the sequence of events that allows an impulse to be transmitted across a synapse from one neuron to the next.
(iii) Suggest a possible role for a drug in relation to the events that you have outlined in (ii).

(2004 HL Q15a)

Previous examination questions

Ordinary level	Higher level
2007 Q 15a	2004 Q 15a
	2005 Q 3b, 14c(iii)
	2006 Q 14b
	2008 Q 4

For latest questions go to www.edco.ie/biology

THE ORGANISM

Chapter 35 **The senses**

Introduction

Humans were said to have five senses: touch, taste, smell, sight and hearing. It is now thought that balance is also a sense.

In addition, touch is seen as a complex sense because its functions include detecting pressure, pain, hot and cold. This chapter will focus on the five senses: touch, taste, smell, sight and hearing.

The senses are based on receptor cells or groups of receptors that form a sense organ. Receptor cells may be neuron endings or specialised cells in close contact with neurons.

Receptors are specialised to respond to various stimuli such as heat, light, pressure and chemicals. All these stimuli are forms of energy that the receptors absorb. They convert this energy into electrical impulses that travel along neurons.

All neurons carry similar electrical impulses. We distinguish between sight or hearing due to the part of the brain to which the neuron connects. The brain interprets the impulses arising from the appropriate sense organ. Sensations occur in the brain.

Touch

The structure of the skin is shown in Figure 35.1. The skin contains receptors for touch and temperature.

These receptors are found in different concentrations in skin at various locations around the body. For example, there are few touch receptors in the skin at the heel of the foot, but there are many temperature receptors at the elbow (which is why the elbow is often used when testing the temperature of a baby's bath).

Taste

Receptors for taste are located in taste buds. These are found on the top and sides of the tongue and in some parts of the lining of the throat.

35.2 *Taste reception on the tongue*

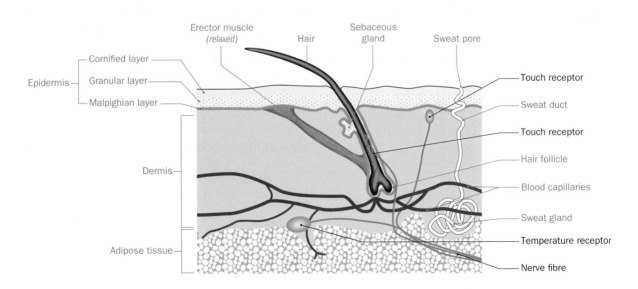

35.1 *Vertical section of skin (in warm conditions)*

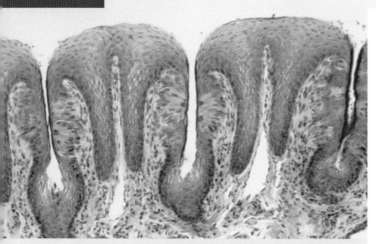

35.3 *Taste buds are visible on either side of the grooves on the tongue.*

There are four basic taste receptors: sweet, sour, bitter and salt. Different areas of the tongue have greater numbers of each of these receptors, as shown in Figure 35.2 (previous page).

Did you know?

Recently a fifth taste, called umami, has been suggested. This is exemplified by MSG, the flavour enhancer sometimes used in Chinese cooking and processed snack foods such as crisps.

Tastes often persist due to substances dissolving and lodging in the grooves of the taste buds.

The flavour of food is a combination of taste, smell, texture and temperature. When we have a cold the sense of smell is reduced and food loses much of its flavour.

Smell

The roof of the nasal cavity has about 20 million neurons to detect smell (olfactory neurons). These neurons respond to about fifty different chemicals in the gaseous state. The responses combine to produce about 10 000 different smells (as opposed to only four different tastes).

Did you know?

Smell receptors are extremely sensitive. They also adjust very quickly to a smell and stop responding. Within the first second of detecting a new smell about 50% of the sensations disappear. This is why we get used to smells so quickly.

Sight

Structure of the eye

Figure 35.4 shows the structure of the eye.

Functions of the parts of the eye

Conjunctiva. This is a thin membrane protecting the sclera. Inflammation of this membrane is called conjunctivitis.

Sclera (or sclerotic coat). This is the white of the eye. It is very tough and opaque (lets no light through). It holds the eye in shape.

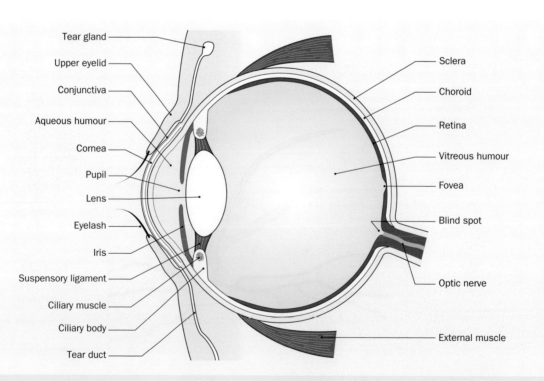

Tear gland
Upper eyelid
Conjunctiva
Aqueous humour
Cornea
Pupil
Lens
Eyelash
Iris
Suspensory ligament
Ciliary muscle
Ciliary body
Tear duct

Sclera
Choroid
Retina
Vitreous humour
Fovea
Blind spot
Optic nerve
External muscle

35.4 *Structure of the eye*

THE ORGANISM

Cornea. This is the transparent part of the sclera at the front of the eye. It lets light into the eye and bends it towards the retina.

Choroid. This layer has blood vessels to nourish the eye and black pigment (melanin) to absorb light in the eye. It ensures that there is no internal reflection of light inside the eye. The choroid is a dark-coloured layer.

Retina. It is here that the light receptors (rods and cones) are located.

Comparison of rods and cones	
Rods	**Cones**
120 million per eye	6 million per eye
Detect black & white	Detect colours (red, green, blue)
Work in dim light	Work in bright light
Found all over retina	Found mostly at fovea

The pigment in rods is called rhodopsin. Cones have three pigments that detect red, green and blue light respectively.

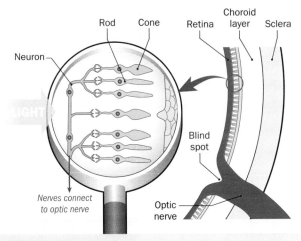

35.5 *Structure of the retina*

35.6 *Rods (green) and cones (blue) with the choroid (brown) beneath them*

Fovea. This area of the retina only contains cones. It is the region of sharpest vision and it is here that most images are focused. When we stare at or concentrate on an object, its image forms on the fovea (also called the yellow spot).

Blind spot. Nerve fibres from the rods and cones are located on the surface of the retina. This means that they impede incoming light rays and therefore obstruct vision. The reason why the eye is structured in this way is not known (it is thought to be an evolutionary 'mistake').

Nerve fibres leave the eye through a part of the retina called the blind spot. There are no rods or cones at the blind spot and it is not sensitive to light.

Optic nerve. This contains 126 million axons that carry impulses from the rods and cones to the back of the brain (cerebrum). The optic nerve is white and about the diameter of a ballpoint refill.

Lens. This is an elastic transparent structure. It changes shape to focus light on the retina.

Did you know?

The lens contains a clear protein. Cataracts occur when this protein becomes cloudy, just as egg white becomes less transparent when cooked.

35.7 *Longitudinal section (LS) of the eye*

THE ORGANISM

Ciliary muscle. This surrounds the lens and causes the shape of the lens to change when we look at near or far objects. The changing of shape of the lens is a reflex action and is called **accommodation**. The ciliary muscle (which is part of the ciliary body) is connected to the lens by suspensory ligaments.

Iris. This is a coloured, muscular part of the eye. The amount of light entering the eye is controlled by the iris. It may be pigmented with melanin (i.e. giving the person dark-coloured eyes). Blue-eyed people have no melanin in the iris.

Pupil. The opening in the iris is called the pupil. It lets light into the eye. The pupil is black because no light normally emerges from the inside of the eye (i.e. all the incoming light is absorbed by the retina or the choroid).

The changing of shape of the iris is a reflex action carried out in response to light intensity. In bright light, the size of the pupil is reduced so that less light can enter the eye.

In dim light, the size of the pupil enlarges (dilates) to allow more light to enter the eye.

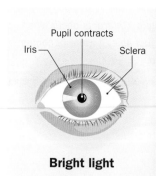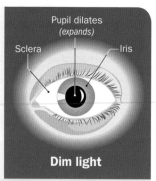

35.8 *Response of the iris to light*

Aqueous humour. This is a salt solution that holds the front of the eye in shape.

Vitreous humour. This is a more viscous fluid (similar to raw egg white). It supports the eye by exerting an outward pressure on the eyeball.

External muscle. The eye is moved by the use of six external muscles.

 Did you know?

The size of the pupil has psychological significance. When we observe an object that we admire, our pupils dilate (for example, mothers observing their babies). Also, large pupils are considered a warm, friendly sign. Advertisements often have faces with large, dark pupils to highlight the appeal of the person's face.

Syllabus

You are required to know corrective measures for either long and short sight or a hearing defect. We will examine a hearing defect (glue ear) later in this chapter.

Hearing

Functions of the ear

The functions of the ear are hearing and balance. The ear is composed of three sections: the outer, middle and inner ear. The outer and middle ear are filled with air; the inner ear is filled with a fluid called lymph.

Structure of the ear

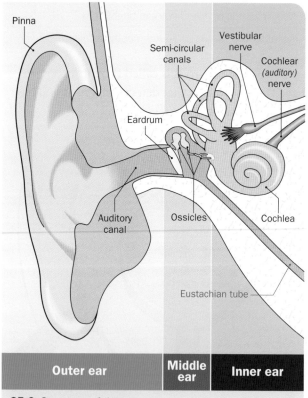

35.9 *Structure of the ear*

The ear and hearing

Sound is caused by vibrations in the air (or in the medium in which an organism is located, e.g. water). Vibrations are collected by the outer ear, passed through the middle ear (where the vibrations are amplified or increased) and transferred to fluid (lymph) in the cochlea of the inner ear.

The cochlea contains receptors that are stimulated by pressure waves in lymph. These receptors cause electrical impulses to be sent to the brain, which interprets them as sound.

Pinna. This is mostly made of cartilage. It helps to collect and channel vibrations into the auditory canal.

Auditory canal. This tube carries vibrations to the eardrum. Wax is secreted outside the eardrum to trap dust particles and protect the ear.

Eardrum (tympanic membrane). This is a small, tightly stretched membrane that separates the outer ear from the middle ear. It vibrates due to the air vibrations that reach it.

Ossicles. The ossicles are three tiny bones in the middle ear called the hammer, anvil and stirrup (or malleus, incus and stapes). The stirrup is the smallest bone in the body.

These bones transmit vibrations from the outer to the inner ear and amplify (increase) the vibrations.

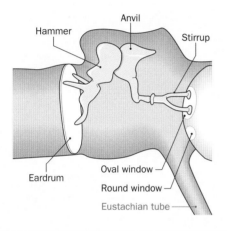

35.10 *Structure of middle ear*

35.11 *Computer artwork of the middle and inner ear*

Eustachian tube. Strictly speaking, the Eustachian tube is not part of the ear. It runs from the middle ear to the pharynx (throat). It equalises pressure on either side of the eardrum. This prevents damage to the eardrum caused by differences in pressure between the outer and middle ear.

Did you know?

The Eustachian tube is usually closed, but opens with a 'pop' when we yawn or swallow. For example when we go up a mountain the external air pressure falls. As a result there is a danger that the eardrum might be forced outwards. In this case the Eustachian tube opens and air moves out of the middle ear.

If we dive underwater the reverse happens, i.e. air moves into the middle ear to equalise the increased pressure caused by the water.

It is common for infections to travel between the throat and middle ear along the Eustachian tube. This results in an association between ear, nose and throat infections (which is why hospitals have ENT departments).

Cochlea. This is a spiral tube, 3.5 cm long, which resembles a snail's shell. It is responsible for hearing because it converts pressure waves caused by sound vibrations into electrical impulses that travel to the brain. The cochlea works in the following manner.

- Vibrations arrive at the cochlea from the stirrup. This bone attaches to a membrane in the cochlea called the oval window.
- The vibrations pass through the oval window and form pressure waves in lymph in the cochlea.
- The pressure waves stimulate receptors in the cochlea. These receptors are hairs that are attached to 24 000 sensory cells. The sensory cells collectively form part of a structure called the organ of Corti.
- The receptors cause electrical impulses to be sent to the brain. These impulses travel along the auditory or cochlear nerve.
- The round window allows the pressure waves to dissipate out of the cochlea into the air of the middle ear.

THE ORGANISM

The ear and balance

Balance is largely detected in the vestibular apparatus in the inner ear. The vestibular apparatus mainly consists of three semicircular canals.

However, balance is also maintained due to vision, receptors in muscles, ligaments and tendons and pressure receptors in the soles of the feet.

A person suffering damage to the vestibular apparatus loses his/her sense of balance. After some time the person may learn to use other receptors to redevelop a sense of balance.

The structure of the vestibular apparatus is shown in Figure 35.12.

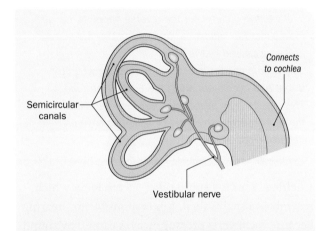

Connects to cochlea

Semicircular canals

Vestibular nerve

35.12 *Structure of the vestibular apparatus*

The vestibular apparatus is filled with liquid. Receptors located in different parts of the vestibular apparatus detect whether the head is vertical or not. Other receptors in the vestibular apparatus can detect movements of the head. All these receptors send impulses to the cerebellum of the brain through the vestibular nerve.

Corrective measures for a hearing disorder

DISORDER

Glue ear is a common hearing disorder in children. It is caused by surplus sticky fluid collecting in the middle ear (often due to overproduction of fluid as a result of infection or blockage of the Eustachian tubes).

The fluid prevents the free movement of the eardrum and of the small bones in the middle ear. This results in some degree of deafness.

CORRECTION

In mild cases, nose drops are taken to decongest and unblock the Eustachian tube.

In more severe cases, small tubes called grommets are inserted into the eardrum. Grommets allow air into the middle ear and this forces fluid down the Eustachian tube. In time the grommets fall out of the eardrum by themselves.

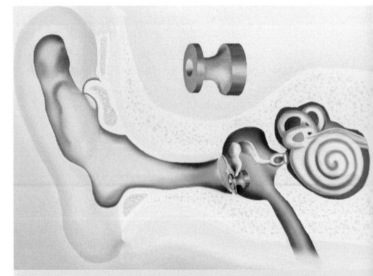

35.13 *Artwork of the ear showing grommets (orange)*

Summary

The five traditional senses are:	The nose is the organ of smell. Olfactory neurons in the nose detect many smells.

The five traditional senses are:
- touch
- smell
- taste
- sight
- hearing

The skin is the organ of touch and temperature.

The tongue is the organ of taste. Taste buds in the tongue can detect the following tastes:
- sweet (at the tip)
- salt (at the sides, near the front)
- sour (at the sides, near the back)
- bitter (across the back)

The nose is the organ of smell. Olfactory neurons in the nose detect many smells.

The eye is the organ of sight. The main parts of the eye and their functions are:
- The **conjunctiva** is the membrane around the eye. It protects the eye.
- The **sclera** is a tough, white coat that holds the eye in shape.
- The **cornea** is the front part of the sclera. It allows light into the eye and bends it to help focus it on the retina.
- The **choroid** nourishes the eye and prevents internal reflection of light.

THE ORGANISM

- The **retina** is light sensitive. It contains light receptors, rods (for black and white vision, work in dim light) and cones (for colour vision, work in bright light).
- The **fovea** is the part of the retina where most images are focused.
- The **blind spot** is where the optic nerve leaves the retina. It has no rods or cones.
- The **optic nerve** carries impulses to the brain.
- The **lens** focuses light on the retina.
- The **iris** is the coloured part of the eye. It controls the amount of light entering the eye.
- The **pupil** is the black circle at the front of the eye. It lets light into the eye.
- **Ciliary muscles** change the shape of the lens (called accommodation) to focus the image on the retina.
- The **aqueous** and **vitreous humours** keep the eye in shape.

The ear is the organ of hearing. The functions of the parts of the ear associated with hearing are:
- The pinna collects vibrations.
- The auditory canal carries vibrations to the eardrum.
- The eardrum carries the vibrations to the middle ear.

- The ossicles (the hammer, anvil and stirrup) amplify (increase) the vibrations and pass them on to the oval window.
- The Eustachian tube, although not part of the ear, connects the middle ear with the pharynx and equalises pressure between the middle and outer ear.
- The cochlea is responsible for hearing. It converts vibrations into electrical impulses that are sent to the brain along the auditory nerve.
- The organ of Corti in the cochlea contains receptor cells that allow hearing.

Balance is detected by the vestibular apparatus in the inner ear.
- The main parts of the vestibular apparatus are the semi-circular canals, which are responsible for balance.

Glue ear is:
- a hearing disorder
- caused by too much sticky fluid in the middle ear
- corrected by decongestants or grommets

Revision questions

1 **(a)** Name the five senses.
   (b) Name the organ responsible for each sense.
   (c) A sixth sense is now thought to exist in humans. Name this sense.
2 Give a biological explanation for each of the following:
   (a) A parent often tests the temperature of a baby's milk on the inside of the wrist.
   (b) A pin sticking into the toe causes more pain than a pin in the heel.
   (c) Pain receptors are very numerous in the extremities of the body, e.g. toes and fingertips.
   (d) The taste of food can remain in the mouth long after the food is swallowed.
   (e) Colds and flu reduce our appetite.
   (f) A person does not notice the smell of his/her own deodorant but a stranger can.
   (g) A clean lollipop stick that touches different parts of the tongue may taste sweet, sour, salty or bitter.
3 **(a)** Name four tastes to which the tongue is sensitive.
   (b) Draw a labelled diagram to illustrate the part of the tongue that is most sensitive to each taste.
4 **(a)** Name the parts of the eye labelled A to N in Figure 35.14.
   (b) Give one function for each of the labelled parts.
   (c) Name the types of receptor in structure G.
   (d) To what part of the brain does structure I connect?

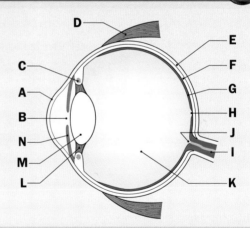

35.14

5 Figure 35.15 represents the front view of an eye.
   (a) Name the parts labelled A, B and C.
   (b) What is the evidence that this eye is adapted to dim light?
   (c) Draw a similar diagram to show how this eye would appear in bright light.

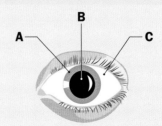

35.15

THE ORGANISM

6   Distinguish between rods and cones in terms of **(a)** numbers, **(b)** shape, **(c)** location, **(d)** operating conditions, **(e)** what they detect.

7   Explain the likely results of damage to the following structures:
   (a) the optic nerve
   (b) suspensory ligaments
   (c) the fovea
   (d) the iris.

8   Give a reason for each of the following:
   (a) The pupil is normally black.
   (b) People with cataracts have obscured vision.
   (c) A person may be born with blue eyes but later develops dark-coloured eyes.
   (d) It is difficult to detect colour at dusk.
   (e) Sunglasses increase the size of the pupils.

9   **(a)** State the two functions of the ear.
   (b) Name the parts of the inner ear associated with each of the stated functions.

10 Name **(a)** three parts of the outer ear, **(b)** three parts of the middle ear, **(c)** two parts of the inner ear.

11 **(a)** Name the parts labelled A to I on Figure 35.16.

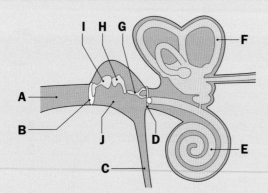

35.16

   (b) Give a function for each part named.
   (c) Draw a similar diagram of the ear, twice this size, and mark on it:
      (i) the outer, middle and inner ear
      (ii) the auditory and vestibular nerves
      (iii) the pinna
      (iv) the oval window.
   (d) Name two structures on the diagram that contain fluid.
   (e) What substance is found in the part labelled J?
   (f) Suggest the likely effect(s) of damage to the parts labelled E and F.

12 How can throat infections gain entry to the ear?

13 **(a)** Name a hearing disorder.
   (b) What is the cause of the disorder you named?
   (c) What are the effects of the disorder?
   (d) How may the disorder be corrected?

14 Choose which of the options (i), (ii), (iii) or (iv) represents the correct answer in each case below.
   (a) The function of the lens in the eye is:
      (i) vision
      (ii) reflection
      (iii) focus
      (iv) dilation
   (b) Protection of the eyeball is the function of:
      (i) the fovea
      (ii) the sclera
      (iii) the cornea
      (iv) the choroid
   (c) The inner ear is filled with:
      (i) fluid
      (ii) air
      (iii) protein
      (iv) lipid
   (d) Which of the following is connected to the brain by the olfactory nerve?
      (i) the ear
      (ii) the skin
      (iii) the eye
      (iv) the nasal cavity
   (e) The flavour of glucose can be detected by taste receptors in which part of the tongue?
      (i) the back
      (ii) the bottom
      (iii) the sides at the front
      (iv) the tip

THE ORGANISM

Section C

15 The diagram shows a vertical section through the human eye.

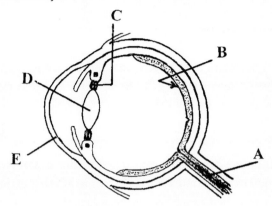

(i) Name A, B, C, D and E.

(ii) In which of these parts would you find rods and cones?

(iii) Give **one** function of rods and **one** function of cones.

(iv) What is the function of A?

(2006 OL Q15b)

16 (i) Copy the diagram of the front of the eye into your answer book and label the iris and the pupil.

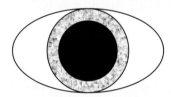

(ii) Is the eye shown in the diagram above adapted for dim light or bright light? Explain your answer.

(iii) Where in the eye is the retina located?

(iv) Two types of cells that receive light are found in the retina. Name each of these.

(v) Give **one** difference between the two types of cell that receive light.

(vi) The optic nerve is attached to the eye. What is the function of the optic nerve?

(2008 OL Q 14b)

17 The diagram shows the structure of the human ear.

(i) Name the parts A, B, C, D, E, F.

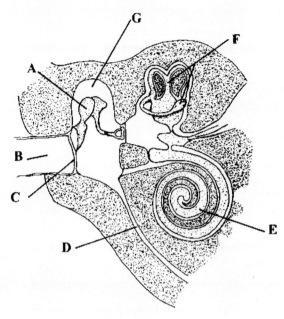

(ii) What is connected to the ear by D?

(iii) Which is present in G, gas or liquid?

(iv) State the function of E.

(v) State the function of F.

(2004 OL Q15a)

Ordinary level	Higher level
2003 Q 1d	n/a
2004 Q 15a	
2006 Q 15b	
2008 Q 14b	

*For latest questions go to **www.edco.ie/biology***

THE ORGANISM

Chapter 36 The endocrine system

Nervous and endocrine coordination

Two systems are used to coordinate body responses, the nervous and endocrine (hormonal) systems. These systems interact in the manner shown in the table at the foot of the page.

Glands

Glands are structures that secrete substances. There are two types of gland, exocrine and endocrine.

> **Exocrine glands** release their product into ducts or tubes.

Examples include salivary glands, sweat glands, tear (or lacrimal) glands in the eye, gastric glands in the stomach, sebaceous glands in the skin and mammary glands in the breasts.

> An **endocrine gland** is a ductless gland that produces hormones which are released directly into the bloodstream.

Endocrine glands secrete hormones into tissue fluid and from there the hormones pass into the bloodstream. For this reason endocrine glands have a rich supply of capillaries because their hormones are transported by the blood.

Hormones

> A **hormone** is a chemical messenger produced by an endocrine gland and carried by the bloodstream to another part of the body where it has a specific effect.

Although hormones are carried to all parts of the body in the bloodstream, they only affect specific areas, called target tissues or organs. Hormones are sometimes said to be chemical messengers.

Most hormones are made of protein. However, some hormones are steroid-based (especially male and female reproductive hormones). A steroid is a form of lipid.

As shown in the table at the foot of the page, hormones are usually slow to act. For example, sex hormones may take many years to cause all the changes that occur around puberty.

Once produced, however, hormones remain active for long periods of time. Hormones are said to be slow-acting but sustained in their effects.

Endocrine glands

> **Syllabus**
>
> *For each of the principal endocrine glands you must know the location and name and function of one hormone.*

Comparison of nervous and endocrine system		
Feature	**Nervous system**	**Endocrine system**
Speed of response	Fast-acting (e.g. catching an object)	Slower (e.g. growth)
Method by which messages are carried	Mostly electrical	Chemical
Speed of message	Fast transmission (electrical)	Slow transmission (in blood)
Duration of response	Short-lived	Long-lasting
Location affected	Localised (i.e. one effector reacts)	Effects may be widespread

THE ORGANISM

Traditionally there are ten major endocrine glands. In addition, hormones can be made by other organs such as the stomach, intestines, kidneys, heart, brain and placenta.

The locations of the ten major endocrine glands are shown below.

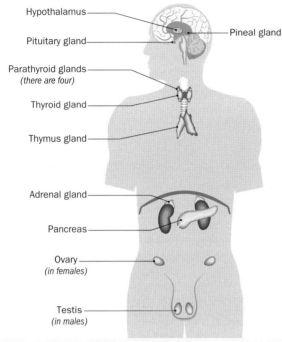

36.1 *Location of endocrine glands*

Role of principal endocrine glands

Pituitary

The pituitary is often called the master gland. This is because it produces a range of hormones that regulate other endocrine glands.

The pituitary gland produces hormones such as follicle stimulating hormone (FSH) and luteinising hormone (LH). These hormones regulate the activity of other glands and are described in Chapter 42.

Among a range of other hormones produced by the pituitary gland is **growth hormone (GH)**. This causes body cells to absorb amino acids and form proteins. In this way it causes growth. In particular, it causes the elongation of the bones of the skeleton.

36.2 *Robert Wadlow, 8 feet 8½ inches tall. At the time of his death in 1940 he was the tallest person ever, at 8 feet, 11 inches. His height was due to an over-production of growth hormone.*

Hypothalamus

The hypothalamus links the nervous and endocrine systems. It secretes hormones that control the pituitary gland in response to messages from the brain and other hormones.

An example of a hormone produced in the hypothalamus is **anti-diuretic hormone (ADH)**. This hormone is then stored in the pituitary and released from there when needed.

ADH causes water to be reabsorbed in the kidneys (it controls osmoregulation).

Pineal

The pineal is a tiny gland located within the brain. It was once thought to be the site of the soul. It produces a number of hormones, the best known of which is **melatonin**. This hormone is mainly produced when we are asleep.

The function of melatonin is not fully understood, but it seems to be involved in biological rhythms such as ovulation, sleep and activity patterns, and sexual maturity.

THE ORGANISM

For one hormone you must give a description of its deficiency symptoms, excess symptoms and corrective measures.

Thyroid

The thyroid is a H-shaped gland located on the trachea in the neck. It produces the hormone **thyroxine**. This is made when an amino acid (tyrosine) combines with iodine. Thyroxine controls the rate of all the body's reactions, i.e. it controls metabolism.

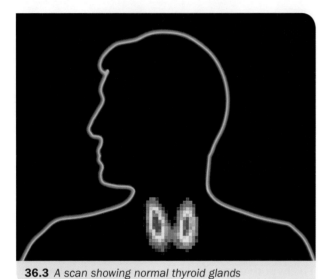

36.3 *A scan showing normal thyroid glands*

Thyroxine deficiency

SYMPTOMS

- Under-production of thyroxine in young children results in low metabolic rates and retarded mental and physical development. This condition is called cretinism.
- Deficiency of thyroxine in an adult results in a reduced metabolic rate. This is seen as tiredness, lack of energy, slow mental and physical activity and weight gain caused by the build-up of fluid under the skin. These symptoms are collectively called myxoedema. It also causes the thyroid gland to swell, a condition known as goitre.

CORRECTIVE MEASURES

- New-born babies are tested for low thyroxine levels as part of what is called the 'heel test'. If necessary, thyroxine can be administered to prevent the occurrence of cretinism.
- In adults, thyroxine tablets or iodine can be taken to prevent myxoedema.

Thyroxine excess

SYMPTOMS

Over-production of thyroid hormone results in an increased metabolic rate (often 60% higher than normal). This causes symptoms such as bulging eyes, hunger, loss of weight, heat production, nervousness, irritability and anxiety. The condition is called Graves' disease.

CORRECTIVE MEASURES

Graves' disease can be cured by surgically removing part of the thyroid or by killing part of the gland using radioactive iodine.

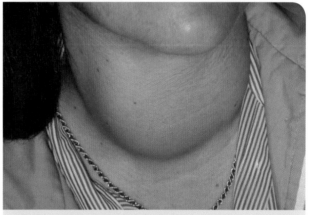

36.4 *A woman suffering from goitre*

Parathyroids

The four parathyroid glands are embedded in the thyroid gland. They make **parathormone**, which stimulates the release of calcium from bones into blood plasma.

Thymus

The two lobes of the thymus gland are located behind the breastbone in the upper chest. The thymus gland produces a hormone called **thymosin**, which causes lymphocytes (white blood cells) to mature and become active. The activated white blood cells are involved in the body's immune system.

The thymus begins to degenerate around puberty (which is why it is associated with childhood) but some tissue remains until middle age.

Adrenals

The two adrenal glands are located on top of the kidneys. They produce hormones that help the body cope with stress.

The adrenal glands produce **adrenaline**. This is called the fright/fight/flight hormone.

Adrenaline is produced when we are frightened or in an emergency. It affects the body in a number of ways that help us to respond more efficiently to stress.

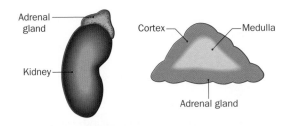

36.5 *Location and structure of adrenal gland*

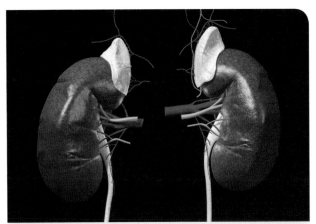

36.6 *Artwork showing the kidneys and the adrenals (pale yellow)*

Pancreas

The pancreas is both an exocrine and an endocrine gland.

EXOCRINE FUNCTION
The bulk of the pancreas cells produce enzymes (such as amylase). These flow to the duodenum through ducts. In this respect, the pancreas is an exocrine gland.

ENDOCRINE FUNCTION
The pancreas also contains about a million groups of cells called **islets of Langerhans** (after the German biologist Paul Langerhans). These cells produce the hormone **insulin**, which is carried away by the bloodstream. In this respect, the pancreas (or the islets of Langerhans) is an endocrine gland.

Insulin is a vital hormone, because it is the only hormone that reduces blood glucose levels. It causes cells, especially muscle and fat cells, to absorb glucose from the blood. The absorbed glucose is either used in respiration or converted to glycogen. Glycogen is mostly stored in the liver and muscles.

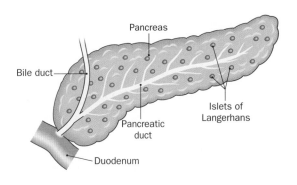

36.7 *The pancreas*

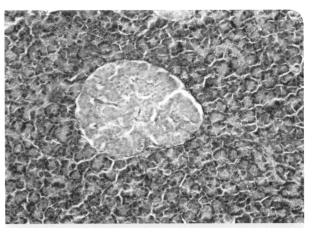

36.8 *An islet of Langerhans in the pancreas*

Ovaries and testes

The role of these glands will be discussed in Chapter 42 in the context of human reproduction.

Hormone supplements

Insulin

Low insulin production, or an inability of cells to take up insulin, results in a disorder called diabetes. If this develops in young people, it is normally caused by the failure of the islets of Langerhans in the pancreas to work properly.

The symptoms of diabetes are high glucose concentration in the blood and urine, the production of large amounts of urine, severe thirst, loss of weight and tiredness.

Severe diabetes is controlled by regular (between one and four times daily) injections of insulin. In addition, the intake of carbohydrate is controlled, physical activity is increased and normal weight is maintained.

Insulin cannot be taken into the digestive system because it is a protein and would be broken down by digestive enzymes.

THE ORGANISM

Anabolic steroids

Anabolic steroids are drugs that build up protein (or muscle). They are similar to the male sex hormone testosterone.

Anabolic steroids build up muscle, speed up muscle recovery after injury and help to strengthen bones. For these reasons they allow for more severe training methods and increase the size and strength of muscles.

These drugs have been widely abused in sport (particularly in track and field events, body-building and weight lifting). Their use is illegal because they give an unfair advantage and they endanger the health of those who take them.

Risks associated with abuse of anabolic steroids include liver and adrenal gland damage, infertility (the inability to produce offspring), failure of males to achieve erections (impotence) and the production of male traits in female abusers.

Anabolic steroids are sometimes given to animals to promote increased muscle (meat) mass. They also produce low-fat (lean) meat. This procedure is banned in EU countries because of the risk of the hormones entering the human food chain.

36.9 *A bodybuilder injecting anabolic steroids*

Control of thyroxine level

Control of thyroxine level (and of many other hormones) is similar to the control used in a central heating system. If the temperature of the water in the system falls too low, the thermostat causes the boiler to switch on. If the temperature is sufficiently high the boiler shuts off.

This method of control is called **negative feedback**, i.e. the correct level of one item has a negative effect on a previous step in the cycle.

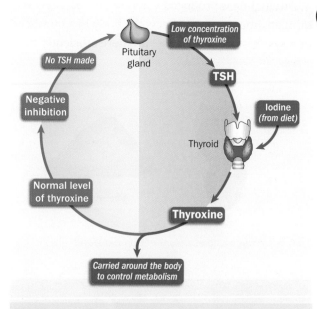

36.10 *Negative feedback*

NORMAL CONCENTRATIONS OF THYROXINE

If thyroxine concentration is normal, it inhibits the pituitary from releasing thyroid stimulating hormone (TSH). This means no further thyroxine is made.

LOW CONCENTRATIONS OF THYROXINE

When thyroxine concentrations fall below the required level, the pituitary gland produces thyroid stimulating hormone (TSH). This causes more thyroxine to be made by the thyroid gland, until thyroxine concentration is returned to normal again.

GOITRE

Goitre is an enlargement of the thyroid gland (see Figure 36.4, page 360). It normally indicates the underproduction of thyroxine. This is usually caused by a lack of iodine in the diet (sources of iodine are seafood and iodised table salt).

A low concentration of thyroxine in the blood causes the pituitary to produce thyroid stimulating hormone (TSH). This hormone is carried by the blood to the thyroid.

Normally TSH combines with iodine in the thyroid to produce thyroxine. However, if this cannot happen (due to a shortage of iodine) then TSH is stored in the thyroid. This causes the thyroid to swell, causing goitre.

This form of goitre can be treated by increasing the intake of iodine in the diet.

THE ORGANISM

Summary

Body coordination is controlled by the nervous and endocrine systems.

The endocrine system:
- is slow-acting
- is based on chemicals (hormones)
- has a slow transmission rate around the body
- produces long-lasting, widespread effects

Exocrine glands have ducts.

Endocrine glands are ductless and make hormones.

A hormone is:
- a protein or steroid
- produced by endocrine glands
- carried in the blood to other parts where they cause their effects

The location and main functions of the major hormonal glands are summarised in the table at the bottom of the page.

Deficiency of thyroxine:
- causes cretinism in young children (mental and physical retardation)
- causes goitre, myxoedema and reduced rates of metabolism in adults (slow responses, lack of energy, excess weight, fluid build-up under skin)
- is controlled by taking thyroxine or iodine

Excess thyroxine:
- causes increased rates of metabolism, weight loss, large appetite, nervousness (Graves' disease)
- is controlled by removing part of the thyroid or killing it with radioactive iodine

The pancreas is:
- an exocrine gland (releases enzymes into pancreatic duct)
- an endocrine gland (releases insulin into bloodstream)

Inability of the islets of Langerhans to make sufficient insulin is called diabetes.
- Diabetes can be controlled by regular injections of insulin (and by controlling the intake of carbohydrates).

Anabolic steroids are sometimes used in sport and agriculture to enhance muscle growth.
- Abuse of anabolic steroids can result in liver and adrenal disorders and a number of sexual disorders.

Hormone levels are often controlled by negative feedback mechanisms.
- Normal concentrations of thyroxine inhibit TSH production. This means no more thyroxine is made.
- Reduced concentrations of thyroxine allow TSH to be made. New thyroxine is then produced until its concentration returns to normal.

Goitre is a swelling of the thyroid gland in the neck. It is normally caused by:
- a lack of iodine, which results in an underproduction of thyroxine. In this case the thyroid swells due to storing large amounts of TSH.

Major hormonal glands

Gland	Location	Hormone	Function
Pituitary	Beneath brain	Growth hormone	Causes bone elongation (growth)
Hypothalamus	Base of brain, above pituitary	Anti-diuretic hormone (ADH)	Causes water to be reabsorbed in the kidneys
Pineal	Within brain near the hypothalamus	Melatonin	Controls body rhythms
Thyroid	On trachea, in the neck	Thyroxine	Controls metabolism
Parathyroids (4)	In the thyroid	Parathormone	Controls release of calcium from bones into plasma
Thymus	Top of chest	Thymosin	Matures white blood cells
Adrenals (2)	Top of kidneys	Adrenaline	Causes emergency responses (fight/flight)
Pancreas (islets of Langerhans)	In the abdomen, below stomach	Insulin	Reduces blood sugar levels

THE ORGANISM

Revision questions

1 Distinguish between the nervous and endocrine systems in terms of: **(a)** speed of action, **(b)** method by which the message is carried, **(c)** speed of transmission, **(d)** duration of effect, **(e)** areas affected.

2 **(a)** Distinguish between exocrine and endocrine glands, giving two examples of each type.
  (b) Name a gland that is both exocrine and endocrine and name a product in each case.

3 Suggest why endocrine glands have rich blood supplies.

4 **(a)** Name the glands labelled A, B and C in Figure 36.11.

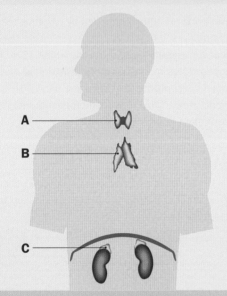

36.11

  (b) Name one hormone produced by each of these glands, and give a function for this hormone.
  (c) Make a copy of this diagram and indicate on it the positions of the following glands:
  (i) pituitary
  (ii) parathyroids
  (iii) pancreas.

5 In the case of the thyroid:
  (a) Name a hormone it secretes.
  (b) Give the function of this hormone.
  (c) Name two disorders associated with abnormal activity of this gland.
  (d) Give three symptoms for each disorder.
  (e) Suggest a cure for each disorder.

6 Name one endocrine gland in each case that **(a)** develops, **(b)** degenerates, at puberty.

7 **(a)** Name a hormone that lowers blood sugar concentration.
  (b) Name the cells that produce this hormone.
  (c) Name the condition associated with a lack of this hormone.
  (d) People with this condition often carry a sugar sweet or some chocolate. Explain why this is so.

8 **(a)** Name one endocrine gland in each case located in the **(i)** head, **(ii)** thorax, **(iii)** abdomen.
  (b) Name one endocrine gland found only in males and one found only in females.

9 **(a)** Name two hormone supplements that can be taken by humans.
  (b) State one reason why each hormone is taken.

10 State a biological reason for each of the following:
  (a) Taking extra iodine in the diet.
  (b) Testing newborn babies for thyroxine levels.
  (c) Testing urine samples for glucose.
  (d) Insulin is not taken in tablet form.

11 **(a)** Name two substances needed to produce thyroxine.
  (b) What hormone causes thyroxine to be produced?
  (c) Where is the hormone you have named produced?
  (d) Under what condition is the named hormone made?
  (e) What normally prevents the production of the named hormone?
  (f) Name the process by which thyroxine concentrations are controlled.

12 **(a)** What is goitre?
  (b) Describe the normal cause of goitre.
  (c) Historically goitre was associated with inland areas or countries. Explain why this was the case.

13 Control of thyroxine production can be compared to a central heating system. In our bodies, what acts as the **(a)** thermostat, **(b)** boiler?

14 Choose which of the options (i), (ii), (iii) or (iv) represents the correct answer in each case below.
  (a) Adrenalin is produced by:
    (i) the thymus gland
    (ii) the parathyroid gland
    (iii) the adrenals
    (iv) the testes
  (b) Which of the following glands has both an exocrine and an endocrine function?
    (i) ovary
    (ii) pituitary
    (iii) adrenal
    (iv) pancreas
  (c) Hormones are sometimes called:
    (i) biological catalysts
    (ii) stimulators
    (iii) coordinators
    (iv) chemical messengers
  (d) The hormone thyroxine contains:
    (i) salt   **(ii)** iodine
    (iii) iron   **(iv)** calcium
  (e) One of the following glands is sometimes called 'the gland of childhood':
    (i) thyroid   **(ii)** pancreas
    (iii) pineal   **(iv)** thymus

Section C

15 **(i)** What is a hormone?

(ii) Draw an outline diagram of the human body and indicate on it the location of the following hormone-producing glands by using the following letters:

W Pituitary

X Thyroid

Y Pancreas (Islets of Langerhans)

Z Adrenals

(iii) In the case of **one** of the hormone-producing glands that you have located in your diagram, state:

1. the gland and a hormone that it produces.

2. a function of this hormone.

3. a deficiency symptom of this hormone.

(iv) State **one** way in which hormone action differs from nerve action.

(2004 OL Q15b)

16 **(i)** Other than the secretion of hormones, how does an endocrine gland differ from an exocrine gland?

(ii) State **two** ways in which hormone action differs from nerve action.

(iii) Copy the following table into your answer book and fill each of the empty boxes.

Endocrine gland	Location	Hormone	Role of hormone
	Pancreas	Insulin	
Thyroid gland			
			'fight or flight'

(iv) In the case of a **named** hormone give:

1. a deficiency symptom,

2. a corrective measure.

(2007 HL Q15b)

17 Answer the following questions in relation to systems of response to stimuli in the human body.

(i) The pancreas is both an <u>exocrine</u> gland and an <u>endocrine</u> gland. Explain the underlined terms.

(ii) Name a product of the endocrine portion of the pancreas and state one of its functions.

(2005 HL Q 14)

Previous examination questions

Ordinary level	Higher level
2004 Q1a, 15b	2005 Q 1c, 14c(i)
	2007 Q 15b

For latest questions go to **www.edco.ie/biology**

Chapter 37 The skeleton and muscles

Introduction

The skeletal and muscular systems work together in most animals to form the musculoskeletal system. This system is controlled by the nervous system.

Muscles associated with the skeleton are called skeletal muscle. Other types of muscles are found in the heart (cardiac muscle) and in places such as blood vessels, intestines, the bladder and the uterus (smooth muscle).

Functions of the skeleton

- **Support.** The bones of the skeleton provide a rigid framework that holds the body upright.
- **Protection.** The skull protects the brain, vertebrae protect the nerves of the spinal cord and the ribs protect the heart and lungs.
- **Movement.** Bones provide a system of rigid levers against which muscles can pull. Without rigid bones movement would not be possible.
- **Shape.** The shape of the body is determined to a large extent by the skeleton. If a person has long bones they are tall; the bones in the feet determine the width of the foot.
- **Manufacture of blood components.** Bone marrow makes red blood cells, white blood cells and platelets.

Structure of human skeleton

The human skeleton has 213 bones and is divided into the axial and appendicular skeleton (Figure 37.1).

The axial skeleton consists of the skull, spine, ribs and sternum (breastbone).

The appendicular skeleton is composed of the limbs (arms and legs), the pectoral (shoulder) girdle and the pelvic (hip) girdle.

Parts of the axial skeleton

Skull

The skull or cranium consists of over 20 bones fused together.

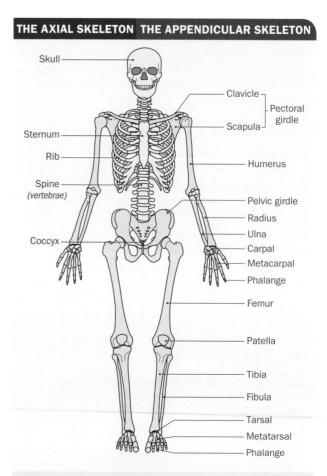

THE AXIAL SKELETON   THE APPENDICULAR SKELETON

Skull
Clavicle
Pectoral girdle
Scapula
Sternum
Rib
Humerus
Spine (vertebrae)
Pelvic girdle
Radius
Ulna
Coccyx
Carpal
Metacarpal
Phalange
Femur
Patella
Tibia
Fibula
Tarsal
Metatarsal
Phalange

37.1 *The human skeleton*

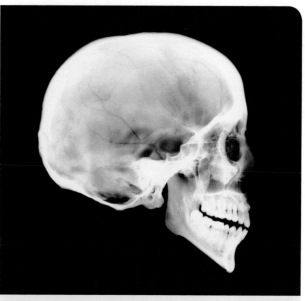

37.2 *An x-ray of a human skull*

Spine

The spine is made of 33 bones called **vertebrae**. These are arranged into five regions, as shown in Figure 37.4.

The top 24 vertebrae are held together by ligaments and can move slightly relative to one another. They are separated by (intervertebral) discs of cartilage. These discs have a hard outer layer and a soft, jelly-like centre. They act as shock-absorbers and protect the vertebrae.

The last nine vertebrae are fused together and there are no discs between them. No movement occurs between these vertebrae.

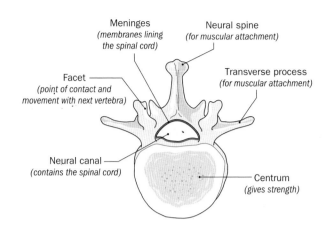

37.5 *TS of vertebra*

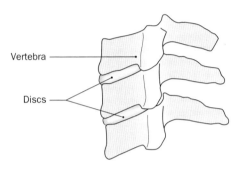

37.3 *The position of discs in relation to vertebrae*

Vertebrae have different shapes, depending on where they are located in the spine. The general shape of a vertebra is shown in Figure 37.5.

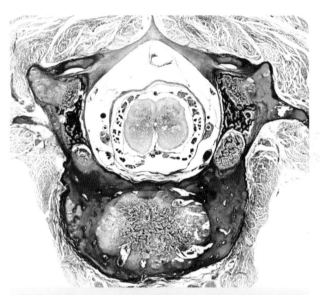

37.6 *TS of vertebra: bone is purple, spinal cord is yellow, the neural canal is white*

Number of vertebrae	Region
7	Cervical (neck)
12	Thoracic (chest)
5	Lumbar (back)
5	Sacrum (hip)
4	Coccyx (tail)

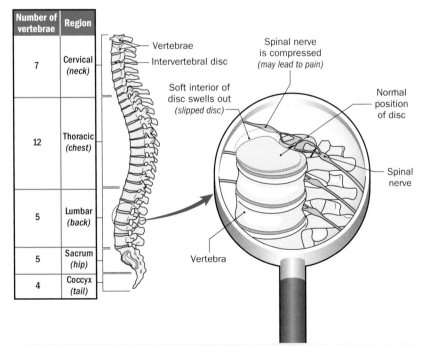

37.4 *Regions of the spine (showing a normal and slipped disc)*

Did you know?

Sometimes the soft centre of a disc bulges out and compresses some spinal nerves. This may result in pain in the back or leg (i.e. the region to which the nerve is attached). This condition is often called a 'slipped disc'.

In addition it is known that people are taller in the mornings when their discs are fully expanded. During the day the discs become compressed (due to gravity) and people become slightly shorter.

THE ORGANISM

Rib cage

The rib cage consists of the sternum (breastbone) and twelve pairs of ribs. All ribs are attached to the vertebrae of the spine.

The top seven ribs are attached to the breastbone at the front of the body. They are called **true ribs**.

The next three ribs (i.e. numbers 8, 9, 10 from the top) are attached to each other at the front of the chest by cartilage. They are called **false ribs**.

The bottom two ribs, called **floating ribs**, are only attached to the spine (i.e. they do not attach to anything at the front of the body).

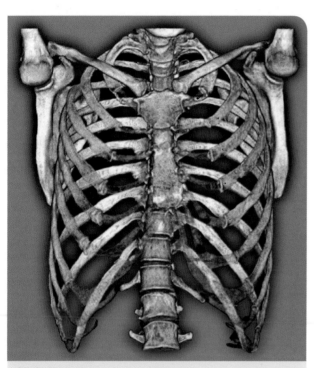

37.7 *CT scan of a normal rib cage*

Parts of the appendicular skeleton

Pectoral girdle

The pectoral girdle consists of the collarbone (or clavicle) and the shoulder blade (or scapula). It forms a connection with the vertebral column and with the arms (i.e. the humerus, radius, ulna, carpals, metacarpals and digits (fingers), which contain the phalanges).

Pelvic girdle

The pelvic girdle is composed of two halves joined at the front by a band of flexible cartilage. Each half consists of three fused bones.

The pelvic girdle is fused (joined firmly) to the spine (at the sacrum). The hollow cavity where the hip bones attach to the sacrum is called the pelvis.

The pelvic girdle consists of the hip bones and the sacrum, and is connected to the legs (the femur, patella, tibia, fibula, tarsals, metatarsals and digits (toes), which contain the phalanges).

Limbs

The arms and legs have a similar design pattern, as shown in Figure 37.8. Each limb ends in five digits (fingers or toes). For this reason they are called **pentadactyl limbs**.

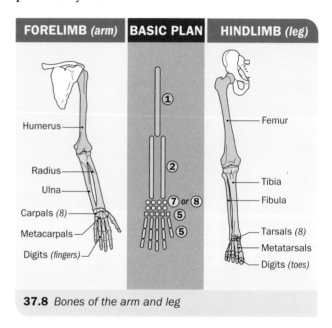

37.8 *Bones of the arm and leg*

The phalanges are the individual bones of the fingers and toes. Each finger and toe has three phalanges, except the thumb and big toe, which only have two phalanges.

> **Did you know?**
>
> *An important feature of the limbs of great apes (orang-utan, gorilla and chimpanzee) and humans is that they have **opposable thumbs**. This means that the thumb can be pushed against all the other four digits. This gives much greater powers of grip and manipulation.*

Cartilage

Cartilage contains a firm but flexible fibrous protein called collagen.

Cartilage is lacking in blood vessels and nerves. For transport it depends on materials diffusing through to the cells that form it (compared to bone, which has a rich blood supply). This is why cartilage is slower to heal than bone.

Cartilage is found in the pinna of the ear, the nose, trachea and in discs between the vertebrae. Cartilage also covers the ends of bones.

Function of cartilage

Cartilage protects bones (by acting as a shock absorber) and allows friction-free movement.

Types of bone

There are three types of bone: compact bone, spongy bone and bone marrow.

INTERNAL STRUCTURE

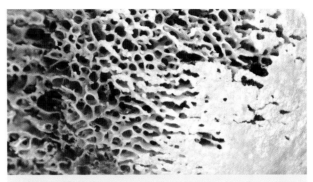

LS of long bone

37.9 *Internal structure of a long bone*

Compact bone

Compact bone is made of bone cells (called osteoblasts) embedded in a matrix, composed of 70% inorganic (non-living) salts such as calcium phosphate and 30% protein (called collagen).

Bone cells are supplied with nutrients by blood vessels. Nerve fibres also run throughout a bone.

Compact bone is mostly found in the shaft (diaphysis) of a bone. It is also located as a layer around the ends of a bone.

FUNCTION OF COMPACT BONE

Compact bone (calcium salts) give bone its strength, and protein gives bone its flexibility. Bone cells and protein are both organic (living) materials.

Spongy bone

Spongy bone is like compact bone that contains numerous hollows (similar to *Aero* chocolate). Spongy bone consists of a network of thin, bony bars separated by different-sized spaces.

The spaces in spongy bone are filled with red bone marrow that produces blood cells. Spongy bone is found mostly in the ends (epiphyses) of bones.

FUNCTION OF SPONGY BONE

Spongy bone also gives strength and rigidity to the skeleton.

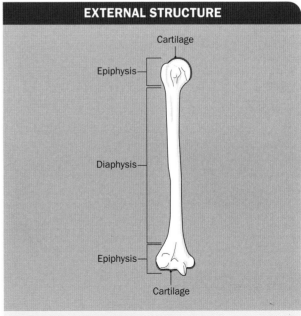

37.10 *A section of the femur: compact bone is at lower right and spongy bone is at top left*

Bone marrow

Bone marrow is a soft fatty substance found in the medullary cavity and within spongy bone.

In young people, bone marrow is full of active, red marrow. Red marrow makes blood components.

In adults, active marrow is confined to the spongy bone. The medullary cavity of adults contains inactive, yellow, fat-rich marrow. This marrow can convert to red marrow if the body requires increased blood cell formation.

Structure of long bone

Long bones such as the femur are enclosed by a membrane called the periosteum. This membrane contains blood vessels and nerves. The long shaft of a bone is the diaphysis and the head of a bone is called the epiphysis.

EXTERNAL STRUCTURE

Cartilage

Epiphysis

Diaphysis

Epiphysis

Cartilage

37.11 *External structure of a long bone*

Bone growth

Embryonic cartilage begins to be replaced with bone around the eighth week of development in the uterus.

Bone-forming cells called **osteoblasts** produce the protein collagen. A hard compound (mainly calcium phosphate) forms around the collagen fibres. The osteoblasts become trapped in this hard compound and become dormant bone cells.

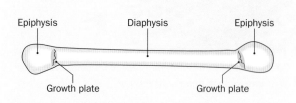

Epiphysis   Diaphysis   Epiphysis

Growth plate   Growth plate

37.12 *The location of the growth plates in a bone*

The increase in the length of a bone is due to a **growth plate** made of cartilage. This plate is found between the epiphysis and diaphysis of the bone.

In this plate, cartilage is continually formed and turned into bone (ossified). The growth plate ceases to function when the person becomes an adult. This limits the growth of the bones and the height of the individual.

The inactivation of the growth plate is said to terminate the development of adult height.

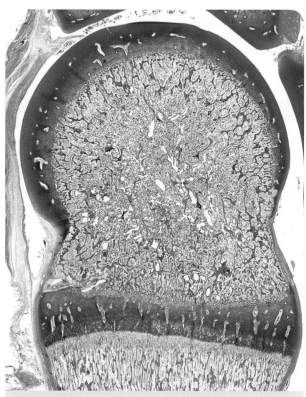

37.13 *The top of a long bone: cartilage (blue) is at the top; the growth plate is the horizontal (blue) strip*

Bone development

Throughout life bone is being dissolved and replaced. This happens at least ten times during the life of each bone.

The restructuring of bone involves bone material being removed from the interior of the medullary cavity and extra bone material being deposited on the outside of the bone. This ensures that as bones become larger they do not become too heavy.

Large bone-digesting cells (called **osteoclasts**) move about in the medullary cavity. They digest the bone that lines the cavity and deposit calcium from the bone into blood vessels.

These cells are catabolic cells. The activity of bone-digesting cells alone would cause bones to become thin and weak.

Osteoblasts form new bone to replace the bone that is destroyed. Bone-digesting cells and osteoblasts work in conjunction to enlarge the medullary cavity and thicken the compact bone lining it.

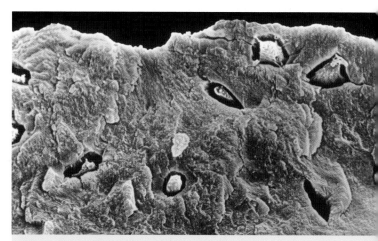

37.14 *Osteoblasts surrounded by bone matrix*

RENEWAL OF BONE

Continual renewal of bone is dependent on physical activity, hormones and diet.

- When bones are stressed by physical activity they become thicker and stronger (the osteoblasts are stimulated). This happens especially at the sites where muscles attach to the bone. Lack of stress on bones causes them to become thin.
- The main hormones affecting bone development are growth hormone, sex hormones and parathormone.

  Growth hormone and many sex hormones increase the size of bones. This can be seen clearly at puberty when bone mass in the body may increase rapidly.

THE ORGANISM

Parthormone removes calcium from bone. This happens so that the level of calcium in the blood can be raised (a constant level of calcium in the blood is essential for muscles and nerves to work properly).

- It is essential to have sufficient supplies of calcium in the diet.

Osteoporosis is the loss of protein (collagen) material from bone. It causes bones to become brittle and easily broken. (It should not be confused with osteomalacia, which is the loss of minerals (calcium) from bone due to the lack of vitamin D.)

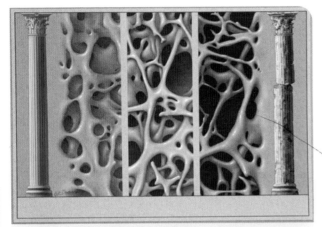

37.15 *Artwork representing normal healthy bone (left) and osteoporosis (right)*

Joints

A joint is where two or more bones meet. Joints may be classified according to the degree of movement they allow.

Immovable

Immovable (fixed or fused) joints include the skull and pelvic girdle. The junction between fused bones is called a suture. These joints provide strength, support and protection.

Slightly movable

The joints between vertebrae in the upper spinal column are slightly movable. In these joints the bones are separated by pads of cartilage.

The vertebrae are separated by a disc of cartilage and the bones are held in place by ligaments. These ligaments limit the amount of movement possible in order to protect the nerves of the spinal cord.

Freely movable (synovial)

In synovial joints, the ends of the bones are covered with cartilage and the bones are separated by a cavity.

The bones are held in place by ligaments, which prevent excessive movement of bones at joints.

Inside the ligaments the joint is enclosed in a synovial membrane. This membrane secretes synovial fluid, a clear sticky liquid resembling egg white. This fluid lubricates the joint and reduces friction in the joint. The entire joint is enclosed in a protective capsule.

Did you know?

*Excessive fluid in joints often occurs due to an injury. As a result, the synovial membrane secretes more fluid and the joint swells. The usual treatment for this is summarised by the word **RICE** (i.e. **R**est; **I**ce or cold treatment applied as soon as possible; **C**ompression with a bandage or sock; **E**levation of the limb to allow the fluid to drain away). Occasionally anti-inflammatory drugs may be needed.*

Examples of synovial joints include:

- **Ball and socket joints**, e.g. shoulder and hip. These allow movement in all directions. They are unable to support heavy loads.
- **Hinge joints**, e.g. elbow and knee. These allow movement in one direction only. They can support heavy loads.

The structure of a typical synovial joint is shown in Figure 37.18 (overleaf).

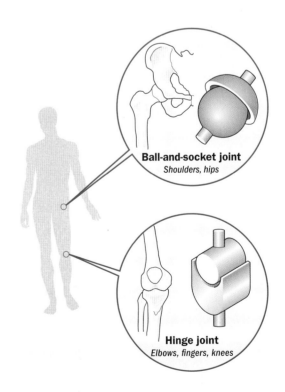

Ball-and-socket joint
Shoulders, hips

Hinge joint
Elbows, fingers, knees

37.16 *Types of synovial joint*

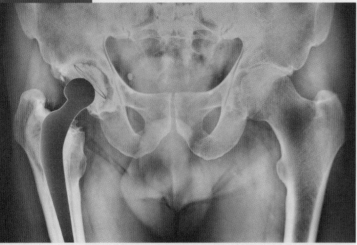

37.17 *X-ray of a male pelvis with a false hip implant (orange)*

Ligaments

Ligaments are strong, fibrous, slightly elastic tissues that connect bone to bone.

Ligaments are more flexible when warm; hence the need for warming-up exercises before physical activities, to prevent ligaments from being damaged.

Tendons

Tendons are strong, flexible, inelastic fibres that connect muscle to bone.

Tendons are mostly composed of collagen and contain some blood vessels.

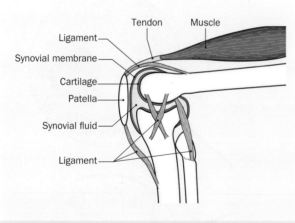

37.18 *Typical synovial joint (the knee)*

Musculoskeletal disorders

Syllabus

You are required to study either arthritis or osteoporosis as an example of a musculoskeletal disorder.

Arthritis

CAUSE

Arthritis is a skeletal disorder resulting from inflammation (swelling) of a joint. There are over one hundred types of arthritis.

- The most common type of arthritis is **osteoarthritis**. This usually occurs from 50 years of age onwards. It is caused by the cartilage in synovial joints wearing down. The underlying bones enlarge and more synovial fluid forms. The joint(s) become sore and stiff. Osteoarthritis affects about half a million people in Ireland.
- **Rheumatoid arthritis** is the most severe form of joint inflammation. It is caused genetically by the body's immune system turning on itself (i.e. it is an auto-immune disease).

  The synovial membranes are attacked first. The joint swells and, in time, may become damaged and deformed. Up to 3% of Irish people have some signs of this disease (75% of these being females). It can occur at any age.

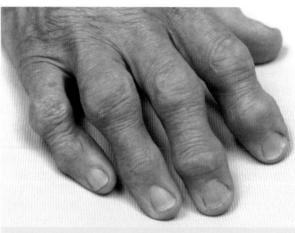

37.19 *Osteoarthritis*

Prevention

As osteoarthritis is caused by wear and tear on the cartilage in joints, it may be prevented by reducing damage to joints. This may involve using proper footwear when running, avoiding running on hard surfaces (especially roads) and perhaps exercising by walking or swimming instead of running.

Treatment

There is no cure for either form of arthritis. Treatments include rest, exercises to maintain mobility and strength, weight loss, anti-inflammatory medications, steroids, drugs to reduce the immune response and possibly surgery to replace the joint.

THE ORGANISM

Muscles

There are three types of muscle: skeletal, smooth and cardiac muscle.

Skeletal muscle

Skeletal muscle is also called striated, striped or voluntary muscle. There are over six hundred skeletal muscles in the body and they make up 50% of body weight.

Skeletal muscle is concerned with body movements. It can contract quickly, but tires very easily (try opening and closing your fist for one minute). It is under voluntary or conscious control.

Smooth muscle

Smooth muscle is also called unstriped or involuntary muscle. It is found in internal structures such as the digestive system, blood vessels, bladder and uterus. It contracts slowly and is slow to tire. It is under involuntary or unconscious control.

Cardiac muscle

Cardiac muscle is found in the heart. It is involuntary, i.e. not under conscious control. Cardiac muscle has many mitochondria, contracts strongly and does not tire as easily as skeletal muscle.

Antagonistic pairs

Muscular contraction is an active process and requires energy in the form of ATP.

Muscles are connected to bones by tendons. When the muscle contracts, the tendon pulls on the bone, causing it to move.

Muscles can only pull (by contracting). They cannot push. For example, in the forearm a muscle on top of the humerus called the **biceps** contracts to pull the lower arm up.

To straighten the lower arm a second muscle is required. This is a smaller, weaker muscle (called the **triceps**), located at the back of the humerus. It contracts to straighten the arm.

An **antagonistic pair** is two muscles that have opposite effects to each other.

In the example above, the biceps is a flexor (i.e. it closes the joint) and the triceps is an extensor (it opens the joint).

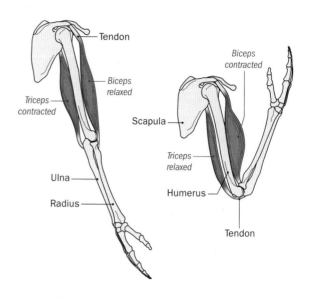

37.20 *Antagonistic muscles in the arm*

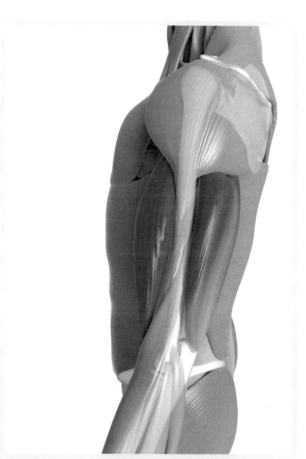

37.21 *A model showing the biceps (left) and the triceps*

Did you know?

Generally flexors are stronger than extensors. The palm of the hand has many flexors (i.e. the front of the hand is fleshy), but the back of the hand has smaller, weaker extensors (the back of the hand has less 'padding'). The same effect is seen on the back and front of the shins and thighs.

Summary

Muscles and the skeleton work together to form the musculoskeletal system.

The functions of the skeleton are:
- support
- protection
- movement
- shape
- blood cell manufacture

The axial skeleton is made up of the:
- skull
- spine
- ribs
- breastbone (sternum)

The appendicular skeleton contains the:
- arms
- legs
- pectoral (shoulder) girdles
- pelvic (hip) girdles

The regions of the spine and the number of vertebrae in each are:
- cervical or neck (7)
- thoracic or chest (12)
- lumbar or back (5)
- sacrum, near the hips (5)
- coccyx or tail (4)

Vertebrae are separated by discs of cartilage.

The twelve pairs of ribs are arranged as follows:
- The top seven are true ribs (attached to the spine and breastbone).
- The next three are false ribs (attached to the spine and a higher rib).
- The lowest two are floating ribs (only attached to the spine).

The long shaft of a bone is the diaphysis. The enlarged end of a bone is called the epiphysis.

There are three types of bone:
- Compact bone is hard and strong. It has bone cells (osteoblasts) in a matrix of salts (strength) and protein (flexibility).
- Spongy bone is more porous. It has hollow spaces containing bone marrow.
- Bone marrow is a soft material. Red marrow makes blood cells; yellow marrow is inactive.

The medullary cavity is a hollow tube located at the centre of the shaft of a bone.

Osteoblasts are cells that form bone.

Bones grow longer due to a growth plate between the epiphysis and diaphysis.

Bones change during life due to:
- bone-digesting cells (osteoclasts) removing bone material from inside the medullary cavity
- osteoblasts making new bone material

Renewal of bone is affected by:
- physical activity
- certain hormones
- diet

A joint is where bones meet.

The types of joints are:
- Immovable (fixed or fused) joints such as the skull
- Slightly movable joints such as those between vertebrae
- Freely movable (synovial) joints, which include:
  - ball and socket (shoulder and hip)
  - hinge (elbow and knee)

Cartilage:
- protects the ends of bones
- forms structures such as the ear, nose and trachea

Ligaments join bone to bone.

Tendons join muscle to bone.

There are three types of muscle:
- Skeletal, striped or striated muscle is attached to bones. It is under voluntary control.
- Smooth, unstriped muscle is involuntary. It is found in internal organs.
- Cardiac muscle is in the heart.

Arthritis:
- is a disorder of the musculoskeletal system
- results from inflammation in joints
- may be prevented by reducing damage to joints in sports
- is treated by rest, exercise, drugs and surgery

Muscle contraction needs energy (ATP).

An antagonistic pair is two muscles that produce opposite effects.
- The biceps contracts to raise the forearm. It is a flexor.
- The triceps contracts to straighten the forearm. It is an extensor.

THE ORGANISM

Revision questions

1 Name three systems in the human body involved in movement.

2 (a) State the functions of the skeleton.
  (b) Explain briefly how each function is carried out.

3 Name the parts of the (a) axial, (b) appendicular, skeleton.

4 (a) Name the parts labelled A to D in the TS of a vertebra shown in Figure 37.22.
  (b) What is the common function of the structures labelled A and B?
  (c) What is found in C during life?
  (d) What is the function of E?

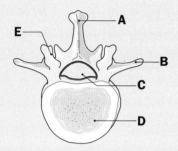

37.22

5 Distinguish between:
  (a) true, false and floating ribs
  (b) pectoral and pelvic girdles
  (c) compact and spongy bone
  (d) ligament and tendon
  (e) red and yellow marrow.

6 (a) What are vertebrae?
  (b) Name the regions of the spine and say how many vertebrae are located in each region.
  (c) Name the material located between the vertebrae.
  (d) What is the function of this material?

7 (a) Name the bones labelled A, B, C and D shown in Figure 37.23.
  (b) What types of joint are found at X and Y?
  (c) Draw a similar diagram and include the positions of the biceps and triceps. Say if each muscle is contracted or relaxed.
  (d) Name the two bones to which the biceps attach.
  (e) Why is the biceps called a flexor?

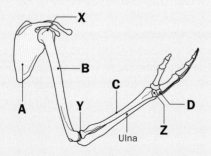

37.23

8 (a) How many ribs are normally present in a complete ribcage?
  (b) Outline the attachment of the ribs (i) at the back, and (ii) in the chest region.

9 Figure 37.24 represents the hip.
  (a) Name the parts labelled A to D.
  (b) What function is common to parts B and C?
  (c) What type of joint is represented by the diagram?

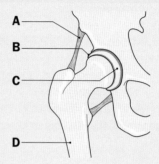

37.24

10 Draw a long section of a bone to show the positions of:
  (a) compact bone
  (b) spongy bone
  (c) medullary cavity
  (d) red marrow
  (e) periosteum
  (f) epiphysis
  (g) diaphysis.

11 (a) Name the parts labelled A to F in Figure 37.25 of the knee.
  (b) What type of joint does the knee represent?
  (c) Is the muscle, labelled M, a flexor or extensor? Explain your answer.
  (d) Is the antagonistic partner of muscle M located at position X, Y or Z?

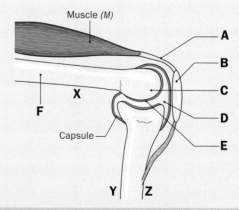

37.25

12 In adults bone is continually being broken down and replaced.
  (a) Explain how this process takes place.
  (b) Suggest one reason why this happens to bone.

THE ORGANISM

13 (a) Name the structure that causes bones to grow longer.

(b) Why does bone stop growing in length in adults?

14 (a) Why is exercise good for bones?

(b) Name one hormone that increases and one that reduces bone mass.

15 (a) What is arthritis?

(b) Name and distinguish between two types of arthritis.

(c) Name two methods by which the effects of arthritis may be relieved.

16 Give a biological reason for each of the following:

(a) A slipped disc in the back often causes pain in the leg.

(b) Ligaments and tendons are slow to heal.

(c) People may be slightly shorter in the evenings than they are in the mornings.

(d) Osteoporosis causes bone to become more brittle.

(e) In the jaw, flexor muscles are stronger than extensor muscles.

(f) Loss of cartilage may lead to arthritis in the knee.

17 Suggest one benefit for each of the following:

(a) The joints between vertebrae are not freely movable.

(b) Synovial joints are freely movable.

(c) Wearing proper shoes when running on roads.

18 (a) What is meant by an antagonistic pair?

(b) Name an antagonistic pair of muscles.

(c) Why must muscles usually work in pairs?

(d) Distinguish between a flexor and an extensor.

19 Choose which of the options (i), (ii), (iii) or (iv) represents the correct answer in each case below.

(a) The human forelimb contains the following number of long bones:

(i) 3 (iii) 30

(ii) 8 (iv) 5

(b) The function of a transverse process is for:

(i) articulation (iii) muscular attachment

(ii) ossification (iv) strength

(c) Osteoporosis is a skeletal disorder caused by a loss of:

(i) collagen (iii) marrow

(ii) calcium (iv) cartilage

(d) The wall of the alimentary canal contains which type of muscle?

(i) striped (iii) cardiac

(ii) smooth (iv) antagonistic

(e) The shin bone is usually called the

(i) humerus (iii) fibula

(ii) femur (iv) tibia

Sample examination questions

Section A

20 Study the diagram of a synovial joint and then answer the following questions.

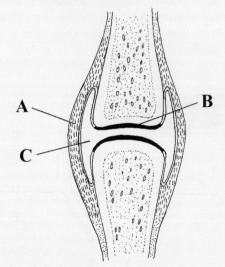

(a) Name tissue A.

(b) Give a function of A.

(c) Name tissue B.

(d) Name the fluid in C.

(e) Give a function of the fluid in C.

(2007 OL Q 6)

Section C

21 (i) State **two** functions of the human skeleton.

(ii) The vertebrae form part of the axial skeleton. Name the vertebrae found in:

1. The neck,

2. The small of the back.

(iii) Name the part of the central nervous system that runs through the vertebrae.

(iv) Name the **three** bones that form the human arm.

(v) Write a short note (about five lines) on **one** of the following:

arthritis or osteoporosis.

(2006 OL Q 15c)

22 (i) Draw a diagram to show the structure of a synovial joint. Label **three** parts of the joint that you have drawn, other than bones.

(ii) Explain the functions of the three parts that you have labelled.

(iii) Name a disorder of the musculoskeletal system.

(iv) Give a possible cause of the disorder that you have named in (iii) and suggest a treatment for it.

(2006 HL Q15a)

23 Answer the following questions in relation to the human musculoskeletal system.

(i) Give **three** roles of the skeleton.

(ii) Explain what is meant by the axial skeleton.

(iii) Give a function for each of the following:
1. Red marrow, 2. Cartilage, 3. Tendon.

(iv) Explain what is meant by an antagonistic muscle pair and give an example in the human body.

(v) Suggest a treatment for a **named** disorder of the musculoskeletal system.

(2008 HL Q 15a)

Previous examination questions

Ordinary level	Higher level
2003 Sample Q 1d	2005 Q 3d
2004 Q 1b, 4	2006 Q 15a
2006 Q 15c	2008 Q 15a
2007 Q 6	

For latest questions go to ***www.edco.ie/biology***

THE ORGANISM

Chapter 38 The human defence system

Introduction

The human body defends itself against bacteria, fungi and viruses that cause disease.

> A **pathogen** is an organism that causes disease.
>
> **Immunity** is the ability to resist infection.

The human defence system allows the body to resist infection. It has two parts: the general defence system and the specific defence system.

GENERAL DEFENCE SYSTEM

The **general defence system** is non-specific. This means that it acts against all pathogens. There are two parts to the general defence system.

- The first part consists of the skin, mucous membranes and their secretions. These attempt to prevent the entry of all pathogens.
- The second part consists of white blood cells and chemicals that destroy any pathogens that penetrate into the body.

SPECIFIC DEFENCE SYSTEM

The **specific defence system** is also called the immune system. It attacks particular (or specific) pathogens, either by producing antibodies against them or by killing infected cells.

General defence system

> The **general defence system** acts as a barrier to all pathogens attempting to gain entry to the human body.

First line of general defence

The first line of general defence consists of the skin, mucous membranes that line the respiratory, digestive, urinary and reproductive tracts, and secretions produced by the skin and mucous membranes.

Examples of how the first line of the general defence system operates include the following.

SKIN. This provides a structural barrier to infection. This means it is a physical barrier that prevents pathogens from passing through.

CLOTTING. If the skin is broken, blood clotting prevents the entry of further pathogens (as well as preventing blood loss).

LYSOZYME. This is an enzyme found in sweat, tears and saliva. It attacks and dissolves the cell walls of many bacteria.

SEBACEOUS GLANDS in the skin produce chemicals that kill bacteria. These chemicals are released in sebum (oil).

MUCOUS. Many body systems are lined with sticky mucous. Pathogens are trapped by this mucous and prevented from entering the body.

CILIA. The respiratory system is lined with tiny hairs called cilia. These beat and create a current, which moves mucous back up the respiratory system so that it can be swallowed into the stomach. When we cough to clear our throats we are assisting this process and clearing mucous from the larynx.

ACID. Hydrochloric acid in the stomach kills many pathogens.

BENEFICIAL BACTERIA in the vagina produce lactic acid. This acid prevents the growth of pathogens.

38.1 *Cilia in the trachea with pollen (pink) and dirt*

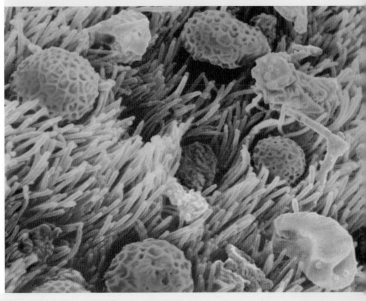

Second line of general defence

The second line of general defence consists of the destruction of pathogens by white blood cells, the production of a series of proteins that kill or prevent pathogens from reproducing, and the inflammatory response. The ways by which these mechanisms work are outlined below.

PHAGOCYTIC WHITE BLOOD CELLS. When cells are damaged by invading micro-organisms they release a large number of chemicals. These chemicals attract white blood cells from the bloodstream. The white blood cells engulf (surround) and destroy any bacteria, viruses or other micro-organisms that they meet.

These white blood cells are called **phagocytes** because they surround and ingest pathogens.

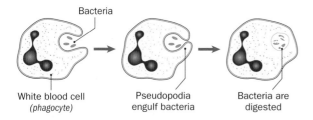

38.2 *Phagocytosis by a white blood cell*

Some phagocytes are very large and are called **macrophages**. Some macrophages move around the body in body fluids and act as scavengers for pathogens.

Other macrophages remain fixed in places such as the spleen, lymph nodes and other lymphatic tissues such as the tonsils, adenoids and appendix. These macrophages filter out and destroy any pathogens that are present in lymph.

38.3 *A phagocyte (blue) engulfing a yeast cell (yellow)*

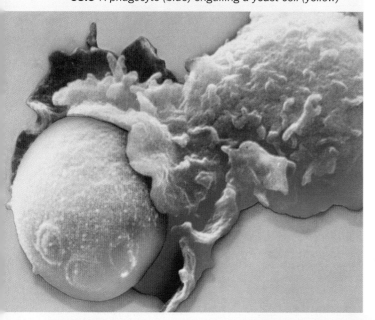

DEFENCE PROTEINS. Complement is a set of about 20 proteins found in the blood plasma. The proteins in complement are activated by infection, and they destroy viruses and other pathogens.

Interferons are another set of defence proteins. They prevent viral multiplication and help to limit the spread of virus infections such as colds and influenza.

INFLAMMATION. When cells are infected they release a chemical that results in blood capillaries opening wider (dilating) and becoming more porous. This causes localised swelling, redness, heat and pain. In addition, it brings more white blood cells to the area to fight the infection.

Sometimes inflammation occurs over the whole body. In this case it causes increased body temperature, called fever. This interferes with the ability of some bacteria and viruses to reproduce.

Specific defence system (the immune system)

> The **specific defence system** attacks particular (or specific) pathogens.

The specific defence system works either by the production of antibodies or when white blood cells destroy body cells that are infected with a particular pathogen.

Lymphocytes and monocytes

Lymphocytes and monocytes are two types of white blood cell (or leucocyte). Both lymphocytes and monocytes are formed in bone marrow.

Once they are produced, these cells move from the bone marrow into blood vessels and into parts of the lymphatic system such as lymph vessels, lymph nodes, the spleen and thymus gland in the chest. Lymphocytes and monocytes both react to pathogens in different ways.

MONOCYTES develop into white blood cells called macrophages. Macrophages recognise foreign molecules (called antigens) that are present on the surface of pathogens.

When a macrophage digests a pathogen, antigens from the pathogen are normally displayed on the surface of the macrophage. These antigens then stimulate the production of antibodies.

THE ORGANISM

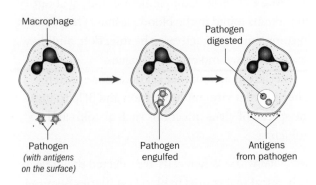

38.4 *The response of a macrophage to antigens*

Macrophage
Pathogen
(with antigens
on the surface)
Pathogen
engulfed
Pathogen
digested
Antigens
from pathogen

LYMPHOCYTES fight infection in two different ways.

■ Some lymphocytes attack body cells that contain antigens on their surface. These cells may be infected with a pathogen or they may be cancerous cells (cancer cells produce abnormal molecules that are identified as 'foreign' by lymphocytes).

■ Other lymphocytes produce antibodies.

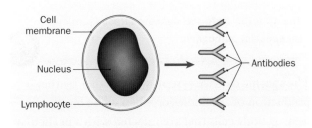

Cell
membrane
Nucleus
Lymphocyte
Antibodies

38.5 *A lymphocyte forms antibodies*

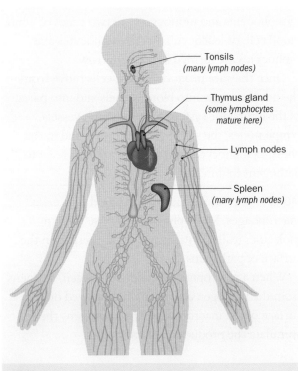

Tonsils
(many lymph nodes)
Thymus gland
(some lymphocytes mature here)
Lymph nodes
Spleen
(many lymph nodes)

38.6 *Organs of the immune system*

Antigens and antibodies

> An **antigen** is a foreign molecule that stimulates the production of antibodies.

The word **antigen** is based on the words **anti**body-**gen**erating.

Antigens include molecules from the coats of viruses and the cell walls of bacteria, fungi and other micro-organisms. Antigens are also found in parts of foreign cells such as pollen grains, incompatible blood transfusions, transplanted tissues or organs, and cancer cells.

> An **antibody** is a protein produced by white blood cells (called lymphocytes) in response to an antigen.

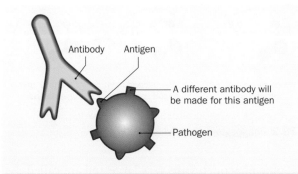

Antibody   Antigen
A different antibody will be made for this antigen
Pathogen

38.7 *The antigen–antibody reaction*

A large number of antigens are displayed on the surface of a pathogen. Many similarly shaped antibodies normally bind to the antigens on the pathogen.

38.8 *Computer model of a virus (green and red) covered in antibodies (blue)*

THE ORGANISM

The antigen–antibody reaction is a highly specific reaction. This means there is a precise fit between the antigen and the antibody. Each antigen stimulates the production of only one specific antibody.

Antibodies help to dispose of pathogens in the following ways (see Figure 38.8):

- In some cases, antibodies prevent viruses and bacteria from entering new host cells. The pathogens are then destroyed by phagocytes.
- In other cases, antibodies inactivate pathogens by causing them to clump together. This allows phagocytes to destroy the pathogens.
- Antibodies trigger the complement system, which results in the pathogenic cells being burst.

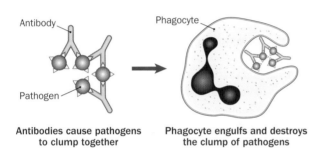

Antibodies cause pathogens to clump together

Phagocyte engulfs and destroys the clump of pathogens

38.9 *Disposal of antigens by antibodies*

Duration of immunity

After an infection is overcome, some of the antibody-producing lymphocytes remain in the body for a long time. These long-lived cells are called memory cells.

If a second, similar antigen enters the body later, these memory lymphocytes can rapidly produce large amounts of the specific antibody. This is why we usually do not suffer from the same infection for a second time.

On first contact with an antigen (or pathogen), the body takes about 14 days to produce the maximum number of antibodies. On subsequent contact with the same antigen, antibodies are produced in large numbers in about 5 days.

We can suffer from colds or influenza more than once. This is because there are many different forms of cold and flu viruses (each with different antigens). New cold and flu viruses develop by mutations.

GENERAL (NON-SPECIFIC) DEFENCE SYSTEM		SPECIFIC DEFENCE (IMMUNE) SYSTEM
First line of defence	Second line of defence	Third line of defence
Skin	Phagocytes	Monocytes destroy pathogens
Mucous membranes	Defence proteins	Antibodies
Secretions of skin & mucous membranes	Inflammation	

38.10 *Overview of the human defence system*

Induced immunity

Induced immunity is the ability to resist disease caused by specific pathogens by the production of antibodies.

There are two types of induced immunity: active and passive immunity.

Active immunity

Active immunity involves the production of a person's own antibodies in response to antigens that enter the body.

Active immunity develops after a person is infected by a virus or bacterium or after vaccination.

Active immunity is long-lasting because the lymphocytes responsible for producing the particular antibody live for a long time in the body.

Active immunity can occur in two ways: naturally or artificially.

NATURAL ACTIVE IMMUNITY

Natural active immunity occurs when a pathogen enters the body in the normal way.

For example, when we get a cold, flu or chickenpox, we develop natural resistance to these infections by producing antibodies against them.

ARTIFICIAL ACTIVE IMMUNITY

Artificial active immunity occurs when a pathogen is medically introduced into the body.

This form of immunisation is often called vaccination. A vaccine is taken in oral form or by injection.

> A **vaccine** is a non disease-causing dose of a pathogen (or its toxin), which triggers the production of antibodies.

A vaccine may contain pathogens that are killed or treated so that they cannot reproduce. In some cases only the outer wall or coat of the pathogen is used, as these contain the antigens needed to produce antibodies.

The person who receives a vaccine produces antibodies without suffering the full symptoms of the infection. The ability to form these antibodies persists in the body, conferring long-term immunity (often for life).

Children are usually vaccinated (or immunised) for tuberculosis (BCG injection), diphtheria, whooping cough and tetanus, polio (given by mouth on a sugar lump) and measles, mumps and rubella (MMR injection). Vaccinations for influenza and some forms of meningitis are also available. Booster vaccinations strengthen the effect of the first treatment.

Passive immunity

> **Passive immunity** occurs when individuals are given antibodies that were formed by another organism.

In this case an individual does not have to be infected with the pathogen.

Passive immunity provides short-term resistance to infections. The immunity lasts until the antibodies are broken down in the recipient's body. This usually happens somewhere between a few weeks and about 6 months.

Passive immunity can occur in two ways: naturally or artificially.

NATURAL PASSIVE IMMUNITY

> **Natural passive immunity** occurs when a child gets antibodies from its mother.

These antibodies can be passed to the child either across the placenta while the child is in the womb, or in the mother's milk if the child breast feeds.

These antibodies give the child immunity to most common diseases for the first few months of life.

ARTIFICIAL PASSIVE IMMUNITY

> **Artificial passive immunity** occurs when a person is given an injection containing antibodies made by another organism.

These antibodies act very fast to control the disease. However, they do not last very long in the recipient.

An example of artificial passive immunity is when a person gets an anti-tetanus injection. The antibodies are extracted from blood samples taken from horses that have been infected with tetanus bacteria. The horse antibodies are then given to an infected human.

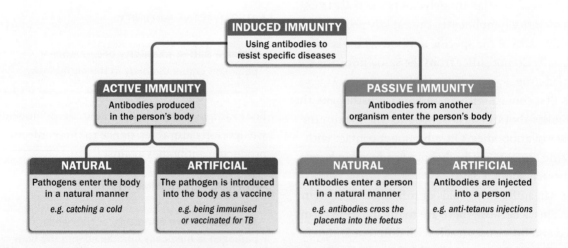

38.11 *The categories of induced immunity*

Role of lymphocytes in the immune system

Lymphocytes are white blood cells or leucocytes. They are formed in bone marrow. Each lymphocyte has a large, round nucleus with very little cytoplasm.

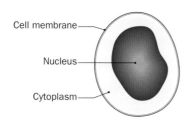

38.12 *Lymphocyte*

There are two types of lymphocytes: B-lymphocytes (B-cells) and T-lymphocytes (T-cells). These lymphocytes are distinguished according to the location in which they mature.

B-cells continue to mature in the bone marrow. T-cells move from the bone marrow and mature in the thymus gland, which is located in the top of the chest. The difference between the two types of lymphocytes can be recalled by the first letters, B and T:

> **B**-cells mature in **B**one marrow
> **T**-cells mature in the **T**hymus gland

B-cells

When they have matured in the bone marrow, B-cells move out into lymphatic tissue, especially the spleen and lymph nodes.

There are many millions of different B-cells. However, each B-cell is adapted to recognise only one specific antigen, which is usually present on the surface of a macrophage. Each B-cell produces only one type of antibody.

When a B-cell comes into contact with the antigen to which it is targeted, it multiplies to produce large amounts of the required antibody.

Antibodies inactivate antigens by attaching to them. This allows the cell that carries the antigen to be disposed of by phagocytes or by activating the complement system, which causes the cells to burst.

MEMORY B-CELLS

Most of the B-cells die off once the infection has been overcome. However, some remain alive for many years. It is these surviving memory B-cells that allow the body to respond if the same antigen enters the body again.

This so-called secondary response is much more effective for the following reasons:

- It produces antibodies in response to much smaller amounts of antigen.
- It produces antibodies much faster (in 5 days rather than 14 days).
- It produces much greater numbers of antibodies than is the case with a first-time infection.

These three factors prevent us from being infected more than once by the same pathogen.

B-cells are particularly active in controlling bacterial infections (but can also control some virus infections).

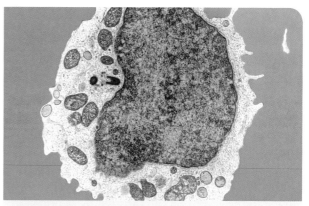

38.14 *A B-lymphocyte: the nucleus is green and mitochondria are red*

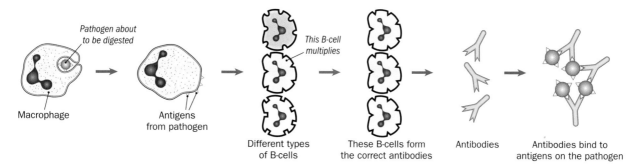

Pathogen about to be digested

Macrophage | Antigens from pathogen | Different types of B-cells | This B-cell multiplies | These B-cells form the correct antibodies | Antibodies | Antibodies bind to antigens on the pathogen

38.13 *How B-cells work*

T-cells

T-cells move from the bone marrow into the thymus gland where they become activated.

This process is especially important in the early months and years of life. The thymus gland is most active in the first few weeks before and after birth. It remains relatively active (and enlarges) up to puberty, when it begins to shrink in size.

T-cells do not produce antibodies. Instead they act against most viruses and some bacteria in one of four ways. The functions of T-cells are explained by reference to the four types of T-cells: helper T-cells, killer T-cells, suppressor T-cells and memory T-cells.

Helper T-cells

Helper T-cells recognise antigens on the surface of other white blood cells, especially macrophages.

Helper T-cells stimulate the multiplication of the correct B-cells. These, in turn, produce the correct antibodies.

Helper T-cells are the main types of cells that are infected by HIV (human immunodeficiency virus).

HIV severely reduces the efficiency of the entire immune system by preventing helper T-cells from functioning properly. In this way HIV is responsible for the condition known as AIDS (see Chapter 39).

Along with stimulating B-cells, helper T-cells also stimulate killer T-cells to reproduce.

Killer T-cells

Killer T-cells attack and destroy abnormal body cells. Abnormal body cells include virus-infected cells or cancer cells. Killer T-cells are stimulated by chemicals that are produced by helper T-cells.

Killer T-cells release a protein called **perforin**, which forms pores in the membrane of the abnormal cell. Water and ions (charged particles) flow into the abnormal cell through these pores. The abnormal cell swells and bursts; see Figure 38.15.

Killer T-cells are said to be cytotoxic cells (from the Greek *kytos* meaning hollow or cell and *toxikon* meaning poison).

Suppressor T-cells

Suppressor T-cells are stimulated to grow by specific antigens. They grow more slowly than the other T- or B-cells. Suppressor T-cells usually become active after the antigen (and pathogen) has been destroyed.

Suppressor T-cells inhibit B-cells, other T-cells (such as helper T-cells and killer T-cells) and macrophages. In this way they turn off the immune response when the infection is over.

Memory T-cells

Memory T-cells can survive for a long time; many of them often survive for life. If the same pathogen re-enters a person's body, the memory T-cells very quickly stimulate memory B-cells to produce huge amounts of the correct antibody. Memory T-cells also trigger the production of killer T-cells.

Memory T-cells (along with memory B-cells) are responsible for lifelong immunity from infections.

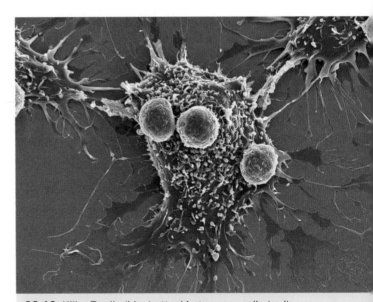

38.16 *Killer T-cells (blue) attacking cancer cells (red)*

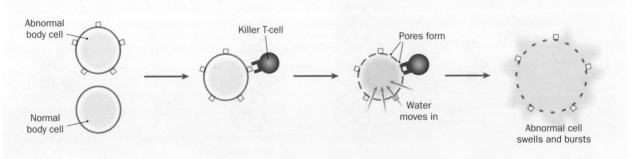

38.15 *The role of killer T-cells*

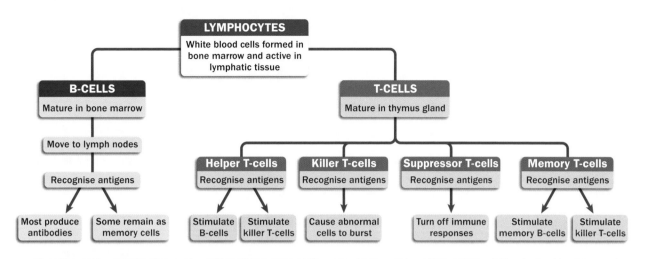

38.17 *The roles of lymphocytes in immunity*

Summary

A pathogen is an organism that causes disease.

The general defence system:
- acts against all pathogens
- is not specific to any one pathogen

The specific defence system:
- acts against only one particular type of pathogen
- is called the immune system
- acts by forming antibodies and by killing infected cells

The general defence system involves two lines of defence:
- skin, blood clotting, lysozyme, chemicals in sebum, mucous membranes, cilia, stomach acid and lactic acid in the vagina
- white blood cells that act by phagocytosis, defensive proteins (interferons and complement) and inflammation

Lymphocytes and monocytes:
- are white blood cells
- are found in lymphatic tissue
- both react to antigens

Monocytes (which develop into macrophages) destroy pathogens and display antigens on their membranes

Lymphocytes:
- attack body cells displaying antigens
- produce antibodies

The organs of the immune system are the spleen, thymus and lymph nodes.

An antigen is a foreign molecule that stimulates the production of antibodies.

An antibody is a protein produced by lymphocytes in response to an antigen.
- Each type of antibody is highly specific to a single antigen.

Antibodies inactivate antigens and allow them to be destroyed.

Some lymphocytes survive for many years as memory cells, allowing long-term immunity.

Induced immunity is the ability to resist disease (by producing antibodies) caused by specific antigens.

Active immunity means that a person makes his/her own antibodies. This provides long-term immunity in two ways:
- when pathogens naturally enter the body
- when antigens are artificially placed in the body due to vaccination

Passive immunity occurs when foreign antibodies are introduced into the body. This provides short-term immunity in two ways:
- a child getting antibodies in a natural manner from the placenta or mother's milk
- getting an injection of foreign antibodies

B-cells (or B-lymphocytes) mature in the bone marrow.

T-cells (or T-lymphocytes) mature in the thymus gland.

B-cells:
- recognise an antigen
- produce antibodies
- control mostly bacterial infections (and some virus infections)

The four types of T-cells all recognise specific antigens:
- **helper T-cells** stimulate B-cells (to produce antibodies)
- **killer T-cells** (cytotoxic cells) produce perforin, which causes abnormal body cells to burst
- **suppressor T-cells** turn off immune responses
- **memory T-cells** survive a long time to trigger immunity to the same antigen in later years

THE ORGANISM

Revision questions

1 (a) Against what does the defence system protect the body?

  (b) Distinguish between the (i) general and specific defence systems, (ii) self and non-self cells.

2 Suggest one way in which each of the following help to defend the body:

  (a) skin

  (b) blood clotting

  (c) mucous membranes

  (d) cilia

  (e) acid in the stomach

  (f) phagocytes

  (g) complement

  (h) interferons

  (i) inflammation

  (j) lactic acid.

3 (a) Distinguish between (i) an antigen and an antibody, (ii) an antigen and a pathogen.

  (b) What type of cell makes antibodies?

  (c) Why do adults have a greater variety of antibodies than children?

4 (a) Why is the antibody–antigen reaction said to be specific? Explain your answer with the aid of a labelled diagram.

  (b) Outline two ways by which antibodies help to prevent infection.

5 (a) What is meant by induced immunity?

  (b) Distinguish between active and passive induced immunity.

  (c) Why does active immunity last longer than passive immunity?

6 (a) Explain what is meant by each of the following types of immunity:

   (i)   natural active immunity

   (ii) natural passive immunity

   (iii) artificial active immunity

   (iv) artificial passive immunity.

  (b) Which of the above types of immunity do not work in people with AIDS?

7 Give a biological reason for each of the following:

  (a) Young children do not normally get common infections for the first few months of life.

  (b) Breast-fed babies tend to get fewer infections than bottle-fed babies.

  (c) A person feels ill for a day or two after receiving a vaccination.

  (d) A sting becomes inflamed.

  (e) A dog licking a wound helps prevent infection.

  (f) Some forms of immunity last longer than others.

  (g) Booster injections are sometimes given.

  (h) People suffering from AIDS do not respond to vaccines.

  (i) Some people suffer allergic reactions.

(continued)

  (j) Transplant patients are given drugs to inhibit their immune systems.

  (k) People can suffer influenza infections more than once.

8 (a) Distinguish between B- and T-lymphocytes.

  (b) Outline the role of B-cells in fighting infection.

9 The graph in Figure 38.18 shows the response to injecting the same antigen at two different times labelled X and Y.

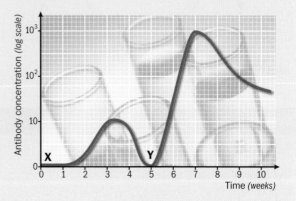

38.18

  (a) What is meant by (i) antigen, (ii) antibody?

  (b) Name the particular type of white blood cell responsible for the production of antibodies.

  (c) How long did it take to start producing antibodies (i) after injection X, (ii) after injection Y?

  (d) What evidence is there on the graph to indicate that the reaction to injection Y was (i) greater, (ii) more rapid?

  (e) Suggest one reason why the antibody concentration declined around the fourth week.

  (f) Copy the graph and show on it the graph you would expect if a different antigen was injected at time Y.

10 (a) Name four types of T-lymphocytes.

  (b) Give one function for each of the four types of T-lymphocytes.

11 Name one way in which helper T-cells are (a) stimulated, (b) inhibited.

12 Give two reasons why helper T-cells are considered to be crucial to the working of the specific defence system.

13 (a) Name the type of lymphocyte that attacks cancer cells.

  (b) Suggest one reason why these cells attack cancer cells but not other body cells.

14 What is the significance of memory cells in the immune system?

THE ORGANISM

15 Choose which of the options (i), (ii), (iii) or (iv) represents the correct answer in each case below.

(a) A pollen grain that enters a person's nose is an example of:
  (i) an antibody
  (ii) an antigen
  (iii) an antibiotic
  (iv) a pathogen

(b) Lysozyme is an enzyme found in:
  (i) lymph glands
  (ii) bacteria
  (iii) viruses
  (iv) tears

(c) Monocytes develop into:
  (i) micro-organisms
  (ii) lymphocytes
  (iii) antibodies
  (iv) macrophages

(d) B-cells become mature in the:
  (i) blood
  (ii) lymph
  (iii) thymus gland
  (iv) bone marrow

(e) Killer T-cells produce this chemical:
  (i) perforin
  (ii) allergen
  (iii) interferon
  (iv) lysozyme

Sample examination questions

Section C

16 (i) What is meant by the term immunity? Distinguish between active and passive immunity.

(ii) Describe two ways in which the skin helps to defend the body against pathogenic micro-organisms.

(iii) Lymphocytes play a vital role in the body's immune system. To which group of blood cells do lymphocytes belong? Name two types of lymphocyte and state a role of each.

(iv) What is the purpose of vaccination?

(2003 Sample HL Q 15b)

17 (i) Name two types of lymphocyte and state a role of each when viruses or other micro-organisms enter the blood.

(ii) 'Immunity that results from vaccination is effectively the same as the immunity that develops following an infection.' Do you agree with this statement? Explain your answer.

(2005 HL Q 15a)

18 (i) What is meant by the term immunity?

(ii) Outline briefly the role of B-lymphocytes in the human immune system.

(iii) Distinguish between active and passive immunity.

(iv) 'Vaccination gives rise to active immunity.' Explain this statement.

(v) In certain situations a person is given a specific antibody rather than being vaccinated.
  1. Is this an example of active or passive immunity?
  2. Under what circumstances might an antibody, rather than a vaccination, be given?
  3. Comment on the duration of immunity that follows the administration of an antibody.

(2007 HL Q 14c)

Previous examination questions

Ordinary level	Higher level
n/a	2003 Sample Q 15b
	2005 Q 15a
	2006 Q 6e
	2007 Q 14c

*For latest questions go to **www.edco.ie/biology***

THE ORGANISM

Chapter 39 **Viruses**

Introduction

Viruses are tiny, non-cellular structures. They cannot be seen with a light microscope, only with an electron microscope.

Viruses are measured in nanometres (nm). There are 1000 million nanometres in a metre, or one million nanometres in a millimetre (mm). Viruses are about 200 nm in size (i.e. about 50 times smaller than a bacterium).

Virus structure

Viruses have an outer protein coat called a capsid. In some viruses (e.g. the influenza virus) the capsid is enclosed in a complex outer membrane.

Inside the capsid is a nucleic acid: either DNA or RNA. In either case there are very few genes. Viruses contain from four to several hundred genes, unlike more complex organisms which have tens of thousands of genes. Viral genes carry instructions for the formation of new viruses.

Viruses do not have ribosomes, mitochondria or other cytoplasmic organelles. They do not carry out any metabolic reactions on their own. They require the organelles and enzymes of a host cell to carry out their limited number of reactions.

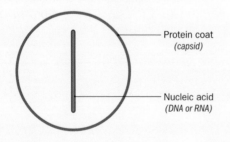

Protein coat
(capsid)

Nucleic acid
(DNA or RNA)

39.1 *General structure of a virus*

Viruses: living or dead?

Viruses are on the border between living and non-living. They show some features of living things but lack many others. The evidence relating to whether viruses are living or non-living is summarised in the table at the bottom of the page.

Viruses are not included in any of the five kingdoms of living things. This is because viruses are non-cellular and do not carry out any metabolic reactions on their own.

Shapes of viruses

Viruses are classified into three groups according to their shapes. Viruses may be round, rod-shaped or complex in shape.

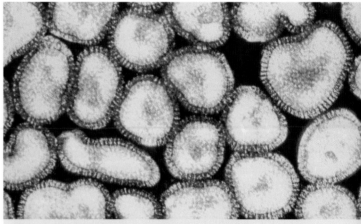

39.2 *Influenza viruses*

Replication

As viruses are not cells, the term replication is used instead of reproduction. Viruses cannot replicate themselves; they only multiply by using the energy and structures of a live host cell. For this reason viruses are said to be obligate parasites.

The living and non-living features of viruses	
Living	**Non-living**
1 Possess genetic material (either DNA or RNA)	**1** Are non-cellular
2 Posses a protein coat	**2** Cannot reproduce by themselves
3 Can replicate (inside a living cell)	**3** Do not possess ribosomes, mitochondria etc.
	4 Only have one type of nucleic acid (living things have both DNA and RNA)

THE ORGANISM

A **bacteriophage** (or phage) is a virus that infects bacteria.

Bacteriophages are the most complex and best-studied viruses. The replication cycle of a typical bacteriophage such as the T-phage takes about 30 minutes and is outlined in Figure 39.3. This is also the way in which most viruses infect human cells.

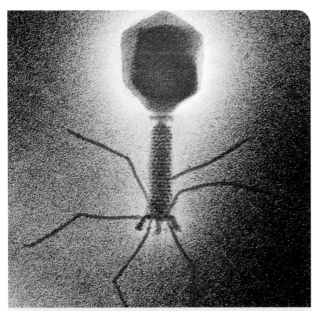

39.3 *A bacteriophage (TEM)*

Stages in virus replication

ATTACHMENT
The virus attaches to the host cell (Figure 39.4). Proteins on the virus match up with receptor sites on the host wall or membrane. This is why viruses are often specific to one host.

ENTRY
The virus forms a hole in the host cell and viral nucleic acid is pushed through. The protein coats of bacteriophages stay outside the bacterium cell. When viruses enter animal cells the protein coats also enter, but are digested.

SYNTHESIS
The host nucleic acid (DNA) is made inactive. The viral nucleic acid uses the host's organelles to produce new viral nucleic acid and proteins.

ASSEMBLY
New viruses are made inside the host cell using the viral molecules that have been produced.

RELEASE
The host cell bursts to release between 100 and 100 000 new viruses. The bursting of the host cell is called lysis.

> **Did you know?**
>
> *Retroviruses* contain RNA (instead of DNA) and an enzyme that converts the virus RNA to DNA. This DNA then makes new copies of the virus RNA and new viruses inside the host cell. The virus (HIV) that causes AIDS is a retrovirus.

Some viruses do not destroy the host DNA. Instead the viral DNA integrates (joins) with the host DNA and remains inactive (Figure 39.5). When the host DNA is copied, the virus DNA is copied also and passed on to the daughter cells. The resulting host cells may behave normally or may produce new chemicals, due to the presence of the virus.

Diphtheria, scarlet fever and botulism occur when a virus enters a bacterium in this manner. The virus causes the bacterium to release toxins that are responsible for the disease.

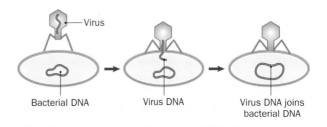

39.5 *Method of action of some viruses*

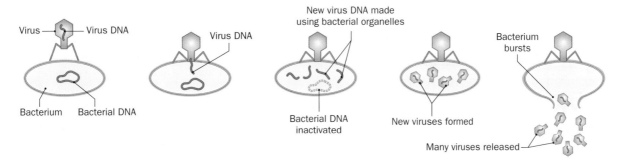

39.4 *Viral replication*

THE ORGANISM

Medical and economic importance of viruses

Syllabus

You are required to know two harmful examples and one beneficial example of viruses.

Disadvantages of viruses

1. HUMAN DISEASES

Viruses are responsible for causing a wide range of human diseases. These include common colds, influenza (flu), polio, rabies, mumps, measles, German measles (rubella), chickenpox, one form of meningitis, warts, cold sores, hepatitis, AIDS, and some cancers.

2. PLANT DISEASES

Plant diseases caused by viruses include tobacco mosaic disease (where the leaves of the plant develop a spotted, mosaic appearance), potato mosaic disease and tomato mosaic disease.

3. ANIMAL DISEASES

Common animal diseases caused by viruses are foot and mouth, rabies, distemper, cowpox and myxomatosis.

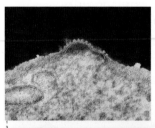
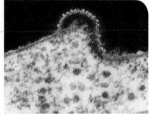
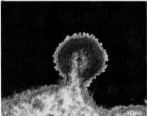
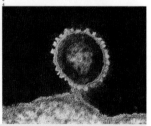

39.6 *A HIV particle (red-green) emerging from a T-cell*

Benefits of viruses

1. GENETIC ENGINEERING

Viruses are sometimes used to transfer genes from one organism to another in genetic engineering. Such viruses are called vectors.

2. CONTROL OF INFECTIONS

Bacteriophages may be used to control bacterial infections. In this way, they may help to reduce infections by antibiotic-resistant bacteria.

Did you know?

AIDS

Cause. *Acquired Immune Deficiency Syndrome is a disorder in which the person cannot make antibodies. This is due to infection with human immunodeficiency virus (HIV).*

Transmission. *HIV enters the body in fluids such as blood and semen. The most common methods of transmission are sexual intercourse, infected blood products and shared needles. It can also be passed from mother to child across the placenta or in breast milk.*

HIV is not contracted by touching, embracing, kissing where saliva is not exchanged, sharing utensils such as cups, or from toilet seats.

Effects. *Once the virus enters the body, it may enter a white blood cell and either remain dormant and produce no effects, or disable the white blood cell.*

When the virus is dormant a person can be identified as having HIV by testing his/her blood for antibodies against HIV. If these antibodies are present, it indicates that the person has the virus, and is said to be HIV-positive. Unfortunately these antibodies do not disable the virus. This is because the virus mutates (changes) very rapidly to a different form.

The type of white blood cell affected by HIV is a lymphocyte called a helper T-cell. The virus disables these cells, which results in the person being unable to produce antibodies.

The result of not producing antibodies is that the ability to resist infection is severly reduced. Consequently, AIDS sufferers die of opportunistic infections (e.g. pneumonia), which they would normally fight off.

While accurate figures are difficult to obtain, it is thought that over 33 million people worldwide suffer from AIDS. The number of AIDS cases is growing by about 2 million every year (especially in developing countries).

Control and prevention. *At present there is no cure or vaccine for AIDS. This means that prevention is vital in controlling the spread of the disease. The main methods of prevention are:*

- *Avoid sexual intercourse.*
- *Confine sexual intercourse to one faithful partner.*
- *Use a condom during intercourse.*
- *Do not use shared needles, toothbrushes or razors.*
- *Avoid contact with blood and body fluids (i.e. wear gloves when treating another person's wounds).*
- *Those with AIDS or who are tested positive for HIV antibodies should not donate blood, semen or body organs.*

Control and immunity

- Viruses are controlled by the body's general defence system (e.g. skin, mucous, stomach acid and phagocytes) and the specific defence system (i.e. antibodies are produced to disable viruses).
- In addition, immunity to many virus infections can be produced artifically by vaccination or by injecting antibodies.
- Antibiotics kill bacteria but do **not** affect viruses. However, some antiviral drugs exist. These interfere with viruses without affecting the host (a difficult objective as the two are so closely linked).

Interferon is a range of substances produced by virus-infected cells to protect healthy cells. It can be made artificially and can help to treat colds and viral hepatitis B.

Acyclovir helps to treat the herpes (cold sore) virus. AZT is another drug that has had some success in slowing the development of AIDS, especially when given in association with other antiviral drugs.

Summary

Viruses are tiny, consisting of a protein coat (capsid), and nucleic acid (either DNA or RNA).

- Retroviruses have a protein coat, RNA, and an enzyme to convert RNA to DNA.
- Viruses are non-cellular.
- They do not have cell organelles.

Viruses:
- are borderline between living or non-living
- can be round, rod-shaped or complex in shape
- are obligate parasites

A bacteriophage (or phage) is a virus that infects a bacterium.

A virus replicates by sending its nucleic acid into a live host cell and using the host to produce new viruses.

The disadvantages of viruses are that they cause:
- human diseases
- plant diseases
- animal diseases

The advantages of viruses are that they:
- transfer genes from one organism to another
- can be used to control bacterial infections

Viruses may be controlled by:
- the general body defences
- the production of antibodies
- vaccination or
- drugs (partially)

Revision questions

1. **(a)** In what units are **(i)** viruses, and **(ii)** bacteria, measured?
   (b) Relate these units to a millimetre.
2. Describe the structure of viruses.
3. 'Viruses have no ribosomes, but have got protein walls.'
   (a) Why is this statement an apparent contradiction?
   (b) Explain how it can be true.
4. List five differences between viruses and bacteria.
5. **(a)** What name is given to virus multiplication?
   (b) How does this process differ from reproduction?
   (c) Outline how viruses increase in numbers.
   (d) 'We give ourselves the flu.' Explain why this statement can be considered to be true.
   (e) Why are viral diseases so difficult to treat with drugs?
6. Explain **(a)** bacteriophage, **(b)** retrovirus, and **(c)** obligate parasite, in terms of viruses.
7. Explain why viruses are sometimes considered to be non-biological.

8. Say whether the following diseases are caused by a virus, bacterium or fungus:
   wheat rust, rabies, ringworm, diphtheria, colds, lockjaw, potato mosaic, apple mildew, cold sores, pneumonia, athlete's foot, AIDS, syphilis, thrush, mumps, measles, potato blight, foot and mouth
9. **(a)** Distinguish between HIV and AIDS.
   (b) How can AIDS be prevented?
   (c) Explain why a person could be HIV-positive but not suffer from AIDS.
   (d) Name the type of blood cell attacked by HIV.
   (e) Explain why AIDS patients suffer from so many other infections.
10. **(a)** Why do viruses not cause decay?
    (b) Why are viruses not grown on agar plates in laboratories?
    (c) Suggest why it might be dangerous to work with viruses in a laboratory.

THE ORGANISM

11 Choose which of the options (i), (ii), (iii) or (iv) represents the correct answer in each case below.

   (a) The protein coat surrounding a virus is made by:
     (i) the host's DNA
     (ii) the host's ribosomes
     (iii) viral DNA
     (iv) viral RNA

   (b) A retrovirus contains:
     (i) RNA only
     (ii) DNA only
     (iii) RNA and a protein coat
     (iv) only a protein coat

   (c) HIV in humans affects:
     (i) the lungs
     (ii) the sex organs
     (iii) the body fluids
     (iv) the white blood cells

   (d) Taking penicillin (an antibiotic) for the flu is:
     (i) very beneficial
     (ii) totally ineffective
     (iii) effective within 48 hours
     (iv) effective for life

   (e) Viruses are active:
     (i) only inside living cells
     (ii) only in sewage
     (iii) only in bacteria
     (iv) almost everywhere

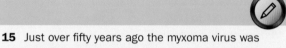

Sample examination questions

12 (i) Comment on the difficulty of describing a virus as a living organism.

  (ii) Name the two main chemical components of a virus.

  (iii) Describe how virus reproduction takes place in a host cell.

  (iv) Name a virus whose activity poses a major threat to human health. In the case of this virus explain the following:
     1. How it is transmitted
     2. How it affects the human body
     3. How its spread is controlled.

(2003 HL Sample Q 15c)

13 (i) Comment briefly on the difficulty in classifying viruses as living organisms.

  (ii) Name two diseases of humans caused by viruses.

(2005 HL Q 15a)

14 (i) Comment on the difficulty of defining viruses as living organisms.

  (ii) What are the two main biochemical components of a virus particle?

  (iii) Name two diseases caused by viruses.

  (iv) Give an example of a beneficial application of a virus.

  (v) What is an antibiotic?

  (vi) Antibiotics should not be prescribed for a person suffering from a viral infection. Suggest a reason for this.

(2007 HL Q 14b)

15 Just over fifty years ago the myxoma virus was brought to Ireland. The disease for which it is responsible in rabbits, myxomatosis, quickly decimated the wild population. Now, however, the disease is much less common and is responsible for far fewer deaths.

  (i) Why do you think that the rabbit population was decimated when the myxoma virus was first brought to Ireland?

  (ii) Suggest a reason why myxomatosis is no longer a major threat to the Irish rabbit population.

  (iii) The use of one species to control the population of another species is called biological control. Suggest one advantage and one disadvantage of biological control.

  (iv) The human immunodeficiency virus (HIV) is responsible for AIDS in the human population. Would you expect a similar trend to that shown by myxomatosis as time passes? Explain your answer.

  (v) Outline briefly how a virus replicates (reproduces).

(2008 HL Q 15b)

Previous examination questions

Ordinary level	Higher level
n/a	2003 Q 15c
	2005 Q 15a
	2007 Q 14b
	2008 Q 15b

*For latest questions go to **www.edco.ie/biology***

THE ORGANISM

Chapter 40 Sexual reproduction in flowering plants

Introduction

The ability to produce offspring of the same species as the parent is one of the characteristics of life. Reproduction ensures that the traits of the parent and species are transmitted to succeeding generations.

Reproduction has two basic functions. Firstly, it replaces those organisms that die. This maintains the continuity of the species. Secondly, it allows for an increase in numbers when conditions are suitable.

Asexual and sexual reproduction

There are two types of reproduction: asexual and sexual.

ASEXUAL REPRODUCTION

Asexual reproduction involves only one parent.

Asexual reproduction does not require meiosis and does not involve sex cells (gametes).

In asexual reproduction, the offspring are genetically identical to the parent. This is because all the cell divisions are by mitosis. Genetically identical offspring produced by asexual reproduction form a family called a **clone**.

SEXUAL REPRODUCTION

Sexual reproduction involves the union of two sex cells or gametes.

In this way it involves two parents. Each parent typically produces sex cells called gametes.

Gametes are haploid cells capable of fusion.

Two gametes fuse to form a diploid cell called a zygote.

In order to halve the chromosome number in the formation of gametes, meiosis is essential for sexual reproduction.

The offspring produced as a result of sexual reproduction show variations due to the mixing of genes from two parents. As variations are the basis for evolution, sexual reproduction is more advantageous to a species than asexual reproduction.

Structures and functions of the parts of a flower

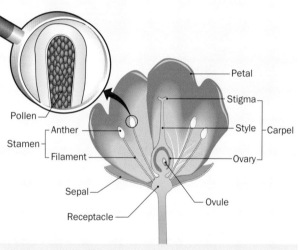

40.1 *Structure of a flower*

Receptacle. This is the part of the flower from which the floral parts arise. It supports these parts.

Sepals. These are usually green, leaf-like structures. Their function is to protect the flower when it is a bud.

Petals. In animal-pollinated plants, petals are large and brightly coloured to attract animals (especially insects). In wind-pollinated plants, petals are small (or absent) and green.

Stamens are the male parts of the flower.

Each stamen consists of a thin stalk or filament. This contains a vascular bundle to bring food and water up to the anther. The anther produces pollen grains on its inside as a result of meiosis.

Carpels are the female parts of the flower.

A flower may have more than one carpel. Each carpel has three parts: a **stigma** where the pollen lands, a **style** through which the pollen tube grows and an **ovary** which contains one or more ovules.

The embryo sac is produced in the ovule as a result of meiosis.

After fertilisation the ovule becomes the seed and the ovary becomes the fruit.

40.2 Carpel surrounded by stamens

Formation of sex cells (or gametes)

Male gamete formation

The cells lining the inside of the anther are diploid. Meiosis takes place in some of these cells to produce **pollen grains** containing a single haploid nucleus.

Each pollen grain divides by mitosis to form the male sex cells or gametes.

Pollen grains are formed on the inside of the anther. When the pollen grains are fully developed, the anther splits and peels back so that the pollen grains are exposed on the outside of the anther.

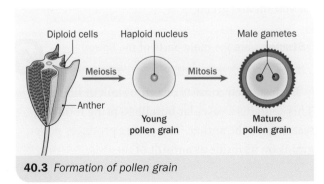

40.3 Formation of pollen grain

Pollen grain development

An anther consists of four chambers called pollen sacs. Each pollen sac is enclosed by a protective epidermis and fibrous layer. The tapetum is a layer of cells located just inside the fibrous layer. The tapetum is a food store and supplies the energy necessary for the cell divisions in the pollen sac.

Inside each pollen sac are a number of diploid microspore mother cells, also called pollen mother cells. These cells divide by meiosis to produce a cluster of four haploid cells called a tetrad. Each tetrad soon breaks up to form four separate haploid pollen grains. Pollen grains are also called microspores.

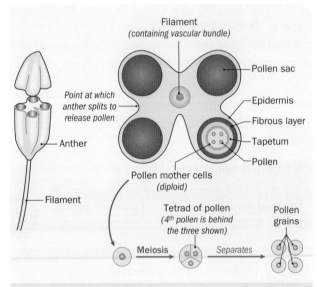

40.4 Structure of anther

Each pollen grain has a thick outer wall called the **exine**. The exine often has a very distinctive pattern, which is specific to the type of plant. The exine is made of a very durable material that allows it to survive for long periods of time. The **intine** is a thin, inner coat on a pollen grain.

While still in the pollen sac, the pollen may divide by mitosis to produce two haploid nuclei, the tube and generative nuclei. This division may also take place just after pollination.

40.5 Assorted pollen grains (SEM)

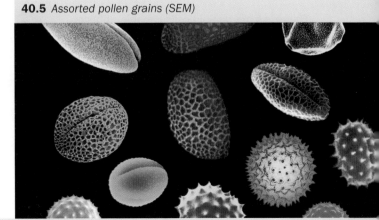

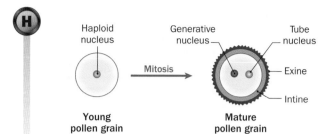

40.6 *Formation of pollen grain*

Both the tube and generative nucleus are haploid. The tube nucleus will form the pollen tube (as described later) and will then degenerate. The generative nucleus will form the male gametes (described later).

When the pollen grains have matured, the walls of the anther become dry and they shrivel. This results in the splitting (dehiscing) of the anther walls. The pollen grains are then exposed on the outside of the anther.

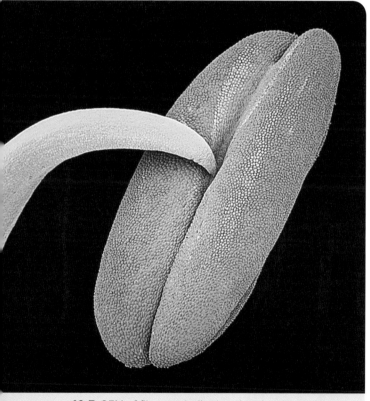

40.7 *SEM of filament (yellow) and anther (green)*

Female gamete formation

Each ovule is composed of a number of diploid cells. One of these cells divides by meiosis to form a single haploid cell. This cell undergoes mitosis three times to form a single large cell, called the **embryo sac**.

The embryo sac contains the egg cell and two polar nuclei.

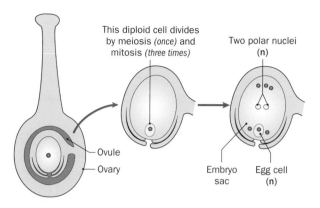

40.8 *Formation of embryo sac*

Development of the embryo sac

Each ovary contains one or more ovules. An ovule has two walls, called integuments. The integuments have a small opening, the micropyle, through which a pollen tube can enter.

The bulk of the ovule consists of diploid nucellus cells that supply nutrients for later growth in the ovule.

One cell, low down in the ovule, is called the megaspore mother cell (or the embryo sac mother cell). This cell is diploid and divides by meiosis to form four haploid cells (see Figure 40.9).

Three of these cells degenerate. The remaining cell is the embryo sac (also called the megaspore because it is large).

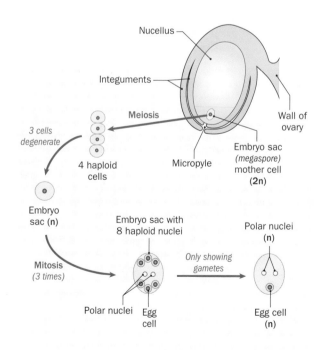

40.9 *Structure of ovule and development of the embryo sac*

(H) The haploid nucleus of the embryo sac divides by mitosis three times to form eight haploid nuclei. These are contained in the embryo sac, which swells using food supplied by the nucellus.

Of the eight nuclei, five take no further part in reproduction and degenerate. The three remaining nuclei form the female gametes.

Two of the female gametes form the polar nuclei in the embryo sac. The remaining female gamete forms a thin cell wall and becomes the egg cell. By the time the embryo sac is mature the carpel will appear as shown in Figure 40.10.

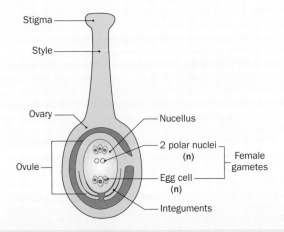

(H) **40.10** *LS of carpel with mature embryo sac*

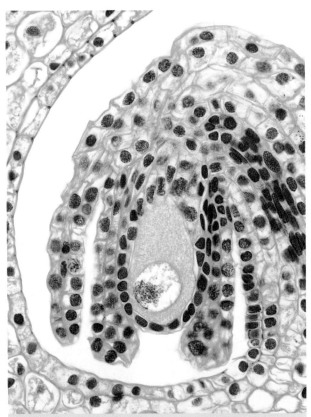

40.11 *Ovule: the megaspore mother cell is in the centre (green) and its nucleus (white) has some chromosomes (brown)*

Pollination

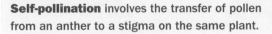
Pollination is the transfer of pollen from an anther to a stigma of a flower from the same species.

Self-pollination involves the transfer of pollen from an anther to a stigma on the same plant.

Self-pollination leads to self-fertilisation, which is an extreme form of inbreeding. The resulting seeds may be less sturdy and vigorous. Some cereals are self-pollinated.

Cross-pollination involves the transfer of pollen from an anther to a stigma on a different plant of the same species.

Cross-pollination results in cross-fertilisation and the seeds formed show more variation and vigour. Plants use many techniques to ensure cross-pollination occurs.

40.12 *Pollen (pink) on a stigma (yellow) (SEM)*

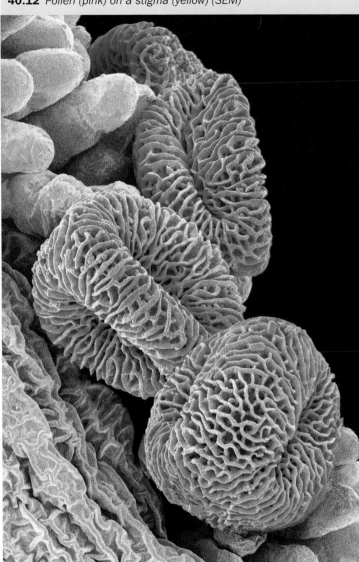

THE ORGANISM

Adaptations of flowers to wind or animal pollination

Wind pollination	Animal pollination
Petals: small (or absent), not brightly coloured (green), no scent, no nectaries.	**Petals:** large, brightly coloured, scented, have nectaries (these contain nectar, i.e. sugary water).
Pollen: large amounts, light, small, dry, smooth.	**Pollen:** small amounts, heavy, large, sticky, spiny.
Anthers: large, outside petals, loosely attached to filament.	**Anthers:** usually small, inside petals, firmly attached to filament.
Stigmas: large and feathery, outside petals.	**Stigmas:** usually small and sticky, inside petals.

Methods of pollination

Plants cannot move from place to place. In order to get the male gametes to reach the female gametes, plants use either wind or animals (self-pollination does not need any external agents in order to take place).

- **Wind** was the original form of pollination used by plants. It is very wasteful of pollen. Examples of wind-pollinated plants are conifers, grasses, oak, hazel and alder.
- **Animals** provide a more advanced form of pollination. They are more precise in carrying pollen directly to a stigma and so less pollen is wasted.

   The most common animal pollinators are insects. However, bats and birds can also carry pollen. Examples of insect-pollinated plants are orchids, dandelions, primroses, snapdragons, daisies and buttercups.

Flowers show many adaptations to suit their method of pollination. Some of these adaptations are outlined in the table above and shown in Figures 40.13 and 40.14.

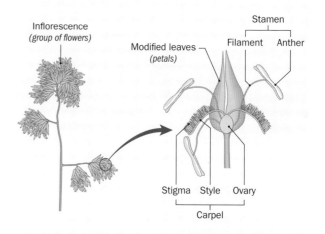

40.13 *A wind-pollinated flower*

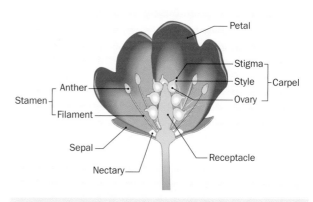

40.14 *An animal (insect) pollinated flower*

Did you know?

Hay fever *is an allergic reaction to the inhalation of particles of certain harmless substances. The substance that triggers the allergic reaction is called an allergen.*

The most common allergens are pollen grains, but others include fungus spores, animal skin or scales, house dust and house dust mites.

The normal symptoms of hay fever (also called allergic rhinitis) are inflammation of the mucous membranes in the nose, sneezing, a blocked and runny nose, along with watery and irritated eyes.

Hay fever affects up to 10% of the population. It can be reduced by avoiding the allergen (which can be identified by skin tests). Treatments include decongestant drugs to clear the nose, antihistamines to reduce inflammation and other drugs that partially inhibit the allergic response.

40.15 *Pollen from a birch tree: wind pollination involves huge amounts of pollen grains*

THE ORGANISM

40.16 *Pollen tubes growing from pollen grains*

Fertilisation

> **Fertilisation** is the union of the male and female gametes to form a diploid zygote.

When a pollen grain lands on a stigma it is stimulated to grow by sugars produced by the stigma. A pollen tube grows down through the style towards the ovule.

The growth of the pollen tube is controlled by a nucleus, which degenerates when the pollen tube reaches the opening of the ovule (the micropyle). The pollen tube grows towards chemicals released from the ovule. This is an example of chemotropism.

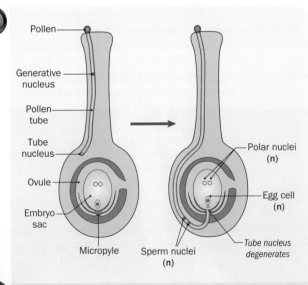

Pollen
Generative nucleus
Pollen tube
Tube nucleus
Ovule
Embryo sac
Micropyle
Sperm nuclei (n)
Polar nuclei (n)
Egg cell (n)
Tube nucleus degenerates

40.17 *Growth of a pollen tube*

The haploid generative nucleus divides by mitosis as it moves down the pollen tube. As a result, two haploid sperm nuclei are formed. These are the male gametes.

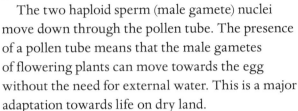

The two haploid sperm (male gamete) nuclei move down through the pollen tube. The presence of a pollen tube means that the male gametes of flowering plants can move towards the egg without the need for external water. This is a major adaptation towards life on dry land.

Double fertilisation

Flowering plants are unique in having a double fertilisation.

1 One sperm nucleus (n) joins with the egg nucleus (n) to form a diploid (2n) zygote. This zygote will develop into an embryo (i.e. young plant).
2 The second sperm nucleus (n) joins with the two polar nuclei (both n) to form a triploid (3n) endosperm nucleus.

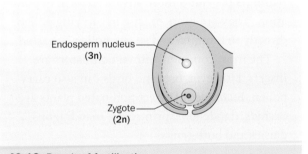

Endosperm nucleus (3n)
Zygote (2n)

40.18 *Result of fertilisation*

Seed formation

The fertilised ovule becomes the seed. The walls of the ovule (integuments) dry up to become the wall of the seed (testa).

The zygote (2n) grows repeatedly by mitosis. It forms a group of cells that give rise to the embryo (2n) or young plant. The embryo consists of the future root (radicle) and future shoot (plumule). Some of the embryo cells grow to form the seed leaves (cotyledons). These are simple leaves, which may become swollen with stored food, especially in dicots.

At the same time, the endosperm nucleus (3n) divides repeatedly by mitosis to produce many endosperm cells (3n). These expand and absorb the nucellus. The endosperm acts as a food store. The main foods stored by seeds are fats (or oils) and starch.

THE ORGANISM

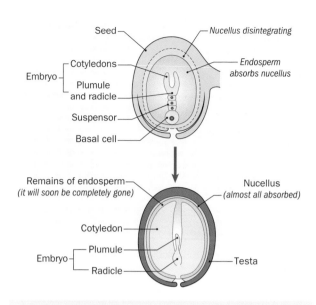

40.19 *Seed development*

Endospermic and non-endospermic seeds

In time, the cotyledons will continue to grow and absorb the endosperm. If all the endosperm is absorbed by the cotyledons, the seed is said to be **non-endospermic** (e.g. broad bean, peanut, sunflower).

> A **non-endospermic seed** has no endosperm when fully formed.

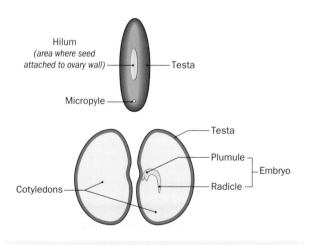

40.20 *A non-endospermic seed (broad bean)*

If the cotyledons only absorb some of the endosperm, the seed is said to be **endospermic**, i.e. some endosperm remains in the seed. Examples of endospermic seeds are maize and corn. The white material in popcorn is the endosperm.

> An **endospermic seed** contains some endosperm when fully formed.

Food stored in the nucellus is used to allow the growth of the endosperm and the embryo. In addition, food enters the seed from the parent plant.

When the seed is fully formed it loses most of its water. This slows down the development of the embryo and allows dormancy to begin.

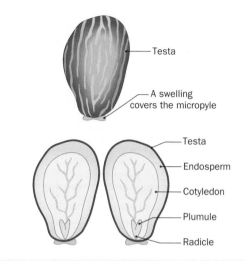

40.21 *An endospermic dicot seed (castor oil bean)*

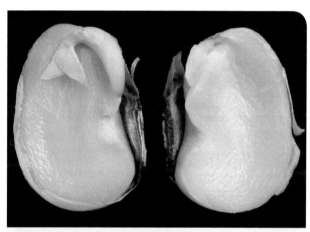

40.22 *Two cotyledons, one containing the embryo*

Monocot and dicot seeds

- As explained in Chapter 24, monocots (mono-cotyledons) are plants in which the seed has only one cotyledon, e.g. cereals, grasses, daffodils.

  Dicots have two cotyledons in each seed, e.g. peanuts, broad bean, sunflower.
- Monocots and dicots also differ in the way they store food in the seed. In monocots, food is rarely stored in the cotyledons. Instead, the growing embryo absorbs food stored in the endosperm.

  In dicots, food is stored in the cotyledons. This means that in a non-endospermic dicot (e.g. broad beans and most dicots), food is stored only in the cotyledons.

In an endospermic dicot (e.g. castor oil beans), food is stored in cotyledons and in the endosperm.

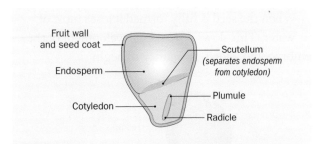

40.23 *LS of a monocot seed (maize). Note that maize is not a typical monocot seed in that it stores food in the cotyledon, as shown above.*

40.25 *Apricot fruit (orange) containing one seed (brown)*

Fruit formation

As the seed is developing, the surrounding ovary becomes the fruit. The process of fruit formation is stimulated by growth regulators (auxins) produced by the seeds.

The wall of the ovary becomes the wall of the fruit (the pericarp). Fruits are designed to protect the seed(s) and to help in seed dispersal.

Some fruits are succulent or fleshy, e.g. tomatoes, grapes, peaches and plums. Other fruits are dry. These include pea pods, green beans, monkey nuts (peanuts in the shell), popcorn grains and grass grains.

Grains (such as grass and cereals) are called fruits because they have an internal seed and the fruit wall is attached to the seed wall.

Once the fruit forms, the rest of the flower parts die and fall away.

False fruits

Although most fruits develop from an ovary that becomes swollen with food, there are some exceptions. False fruits develop from other parts of a flower besides the ovary.

For example, an apple is a false fruit that develops when the flower parts, at the base of the flower, join together and swell with stored food. The core of the apple derives from the ovary.

A strawberry is also a false fruit, because it develops from a swollen receptacle.

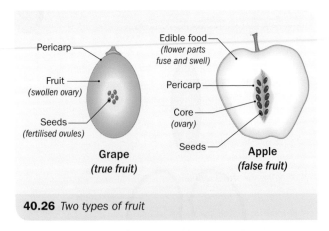

40.26 *Two types of fruit*

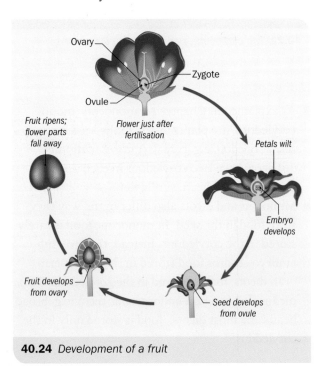

40.24 *Development of a fruit*

Changes in flower after fertilisation

Before fertilisation	After fertilisation
1 Ovule	Seed
2 Integuments	Testa *(seed coat)*
3 Nucellus	Endosperm → cotyledon(s)
4 Egg	Zygote → embryo *(plumule, radicle, cotyledon(s))*
5 Polar nuclei	Endosperm
6 Ovary	Fruit
7 Ovary wall	Pericarp *(fruit coat or wall)*

THE ORGANISM

Seedless fruit

The development of a fruit without a seed is called parthenocarpy (or parthenocarpic fruiting). This is a form of virgin birth, in that the egg is not fertilised. Seedless fruit can be formed in two ways.

- Seedless fruit can be formed genetically, either naturally or by special breeding programmes. Examples include bananas, grapefruit, pineapples, seedless oranges and grapes.
- Another way to produce seedless fruit is to spray plants with growth regulators. If large concentrations of growth regulators (e.g. auxins) are sprayed on flowers, fruits may form without fertilisation or the production of seeds. Examples include seedless grapes, peppers, cherries, apricots, peaches and some types of seedless tomatoes.

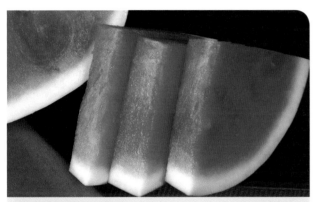

40.27 *Seedless watermelon*

In addition to stimulating seedless fruits, these growth regulators also cause fruits and vegetables to grow larger.

Along with the role of plant growth regulators in producing seedless fruits with more stored food, the plant growth regulator ethene (or ethylene) is used commercially to ripen many fruits.

For example, ethene gas is pumped into large storage containers where it ripens fruits such as bananas, melons and tomatoes. Ethene is also used to 'de-green' fruits by causing the breakdown of chlorophyll. This process takes place in the three previously named fruits as well as in oranges, lemons and grapefruit.

Did you know?

Carbon dioxide inhibits the production of ethene. For this reason fruits such as apples can be stored in containers through which carbon dioxide is circulated. This allows apples to be picked in autumn and stored for use in the following summer.

Fruit and seed dispersal

Dispersal is the transfer of a seed or fruit away from the parent plant.

Dispersal is necessary to:

- avoid large numbers of seeds competing with each other and with the parent plant
- increase the chance of survival for the plant
- find new areas for growth
- increase the numbers of the species

The main methods of seed dispersal are wind, water, animal and self dispersal.

Wind dispersal

- Orchids produce small, light seeds. This is an advantage because they are easily dispersed. However, the young plant (embryo) has very little food supply to nourish it in the early days of growth.
- Dandelions, thistles and clematis produce parachute devices that help to disperse the seeds more widely.
- Sycamore and ash produce fruit with wings. These spiral down to the ground and increase the distance over which the seeds may be dispersed.

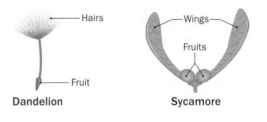

40.28 *Wind-dispersed seeds (fruits)*

40.29 *Wind dispersal in a dandelion: each 'parachute' has a fruit (or seed) attached*

Water dispersal

Coconut trees, alders and water lilies have light, air-filled fruits that float. This allows them to be dispersed by rivers or streams or even by the sea (as happens with coconuts).

Animal dispersal

Animal dispersal is very successful because animals can carry seeds or fruits long distances and tend to live where seeds have a chance of growing. Fruits dispersed by animals have either of two major adaptations.

STICKY FRUITS

Fruits with hooks (called burrs) may cling to an animal's hair or fur and be carried away. These seeds are dispersed by attaching to the external surface of the animal. Examples of these fruits include burdock, goose grass and buttercup.

40.30 *Animal dispersal: a burdock seed head stuck in dog's hair*

EDIBLE, FLESHY OR SUCCULENT FRUITS

These fruits attract animals by being brightly coloured with strong scents and plenty of food. The animal eats and digests the fruit but the seed passes through the intestine unharmed. These seeds are dispersed after passing through the digestive system of the animal.

The seeds are released with the faeces, which even acts as a fertiliser for them. Examples include strawberries, tomatoes, blackberries, acorns and other nuts (which are dispersed when they are accidently dropped).

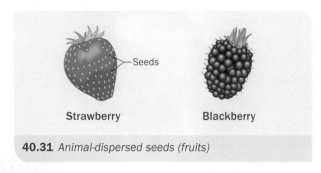

Strawberry   Blackberry

40.31 *Animal-dispersed seeds (fruits)*

40.32 *Succulent fruits: animals digest the fruits and disperse the seeds*

Self dispersal

Some fruits have explosive mechanisms that catapult the seeds away. These fruits often have pods that dry out and split open (dehisce). Examples are peas, beans and gorse.

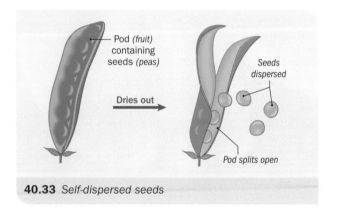

40.33 *Self-dispersed seeds*

Dormancy

> **Dormancy** is a resting period when seeds undergo no growth and have reduced cell activity or metabolism.

Dormancy is brought about in a number of ways.

- Growth inhibitors (such as abscisic acid) may be present in the outer part of the seed. Inhibitors delay growth until they are broken down by water, cold or decay.
- The testa may be impermeable to water or oxygen. Eventually the testa decays and breaks down, allowing water and oxygen to enter the seed.
- The testa may be too tough to allow the embryo to emerge.
- There may be a lack of a suitable growth regulator needed to stimulate growth. The regulator may be produced due to increased light or temperatures in spring.

Dormancy in agriculture and horticulture

Many seeds need a cold period to break dormancy. The cold may cause the breakdown of growth inhibitors or the production of growth promoters such as auxins.

Special conditions may be necessary to break dormancy in seeds before they are planted for agricultural or horticultural use. These conditions include soaking the seeds in water, physical damage (e.g. scraping them with fine sandpaper) that breaks the testa, exposing them to light or dark, exposing them to cold temperatures (e.g. placing them in a fridge).

Advantages of dormancy

- It allows the plant to avoid the harsh conditions of winter.
- It gives the embryo time to develop fully.
- It provides time for the seed to be dispersed.
- It maximises the growing season for the young seedling, i.e. by starting growth in spring the plant is well developed by autumn.
- It helps the survival of the species because the duration of dormancy varies. This means that some seeds always remain dormant in the soil and form what is called a **seed bank**. These dormant seeds can grow following the elimination of the mature plants by natural (or man-made) disasters.

Germination

> **Germination** is the regrowth of the embryo, after a period of dormancy, if the environmental conditions are suitable.

Germination involves the regrowth of the embryo, because the zygote initially grows to form the embryo, which then remains dormant for some time. When germination occurs, the embryo resumes its growth.

Conditions for germination

- Water is needed to allow enzyme reactions to occur. The seed absorbs water from the soil. This causes the seed to swell (and increase in weight) and allows enzymes to function.
- Oxygen is needed for aerobic respiration. It is absorbed from the soil.

- A suitable temperature is needed to allow enzyme reactions to take place. Each species has its own preferred temperature for germination. Suitable temperatures are usually between 5° and 30°C.
- Dormancy must be complete.

Events in germination

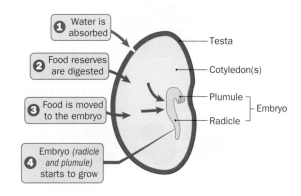

40.34 *Events in seed germination*

1 Seeds store food in the form of oils, starch (especially in cereals and grasses) and protein (especially in legumes such as peas and beans).
2 Germination begins when the seed absorbs water. Water is absorbed through a tiny hole called the micropyle (located near the hilum) and through the testa. Water allows enzymes to be activated in the seed.
3 In germinating seeds, oils are digested to fatty acids and glycerol, starch is digested to glucose and proteins are digested to amino acids.
4 The products of digestion are moved to the growing embryo (i.e. the plumule and radicle).
5 Glucose and amino acids are used to make new structures such as cell walls and enzymes.
6 The fats and some of the glucose are used in respiration to produce energy.
7 The dry weight (mass) of the seed falls due to the foods used in respiration.
8 As the weight of the food stores (i.e. the endosperm and/or cotyledon(s)) falls, the weight of the embryo increases.
9 The radicle bursts through the testa.
10 The plumule emerges above ground and leaves form.
11 Once the first leaves start to photosynthesise, the dry weight of the seedling increases again.

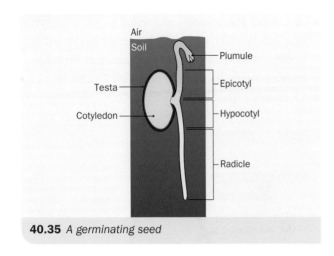

40.35 *A germinating seed*

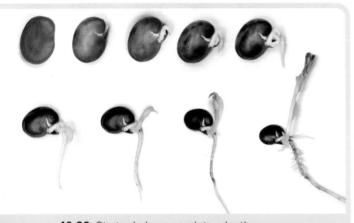

40.36 *Stages in bean seed germination*

40.37 *Bean seed germination and leaf formation*

Changes in the dry weights of germinating seeds

When weighing plant material, dry weight is normally used. This is the weight without water. Dry weight is measured by placing the plant in an oven at 100°C until the weight remains constant.

The changes in the dry weights of the parts of a germinating seed can be seen on graphs as shown in Figure 40.38.

In graph A, the weight (mass) of the seed falls from days 0 to 6, due to respiration. From day 6 on, it increases due to photosynthesis taking place in the newly formed leaves.

In graph B, the loss of weight of the endosperm is matched by a rise in weight of the embryo. This suggests that food is passing from the endosperm to the embryo.

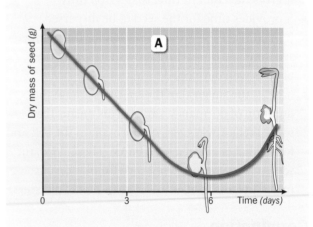

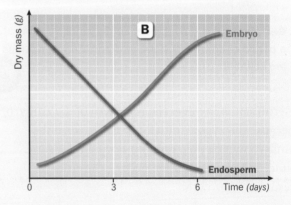

40.38 *Changes in dry weights of germinating seed parts*

THE ORGANISM

The stages in seedling growth

Cotyledons remain below soil

Broad beans are an example of this type of germination.

- In this type of germination, the seed absorbs water, enzymes become active and the radicle begins to grow.
- The radicle bursts out through the testa (seed coat) and grows down due to geotropism.
- The plumule emerges and the region between the cotyledon and the plumule (called the epicotyl) grows.
- The plumule grows up through the soil and its delicate leaves are protected by the plumule being hooked over.
- The cotyledons (and endosperm, if present) shrivel as food is transferred from them.
- The radicle develops into the primary (or tap) root, which forms many lateral roots.
- Once above the ground, the plumule straightens up and produces the first true leaves. These soon become green and start to photosynthesise.

Cotyledons move above the soil

Sunflower seeds are an example of this type of germination. (Sunflower 'seeds' are in fact fruits, with the fruit wall (pericarp) and the seed wall (testa) being fused.)

This form of germination is similar to the previous form of germination, with the following differences:

- The region between the emerging radicle and the cotyledons (called the hypocotyl) grows. This causes the cotyledons to be carried above the soil.
- Once above the soil, the fruit wall (pericarp) falls to the ground. The cotyledons open out, become green and photosynthetic. The plumule emerges from between the cotyledons and forms the first foliage leaves.

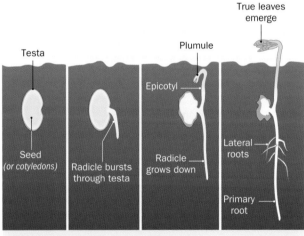

40.39 *Germination in broad bean*

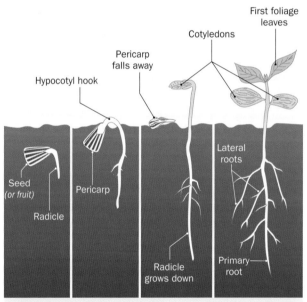

40.40 *Germination in sunflower*

THE ORGANISM

Activity 21   *To investigate the effect of water, oxygen and temperature on germination*

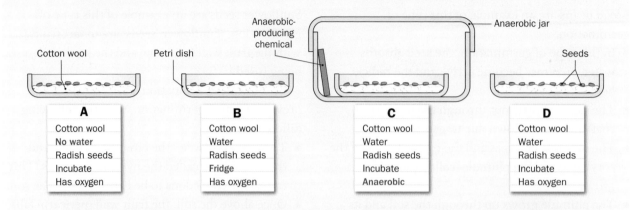

A
Cotton wool
No water
Radish seeds
Incubate
Has oxygen

B
Cotton wool
Water
Radish seeds
Fridge
Has oxygen

C
Cotton wool
Water
Radish seeds
Incubate
Anaerobic

D
Cotton wool
Water
Radish seeds
Incubate
Has oxygen

40.41 *To investigate germination*

1 Place equal amounts of cotton wool in the base of four petri dishes.
2 Label the dishes A, B, C and D.
3 Add water to the cotton wool in dishes B, C and D. Leave dish A dry.
4 Place ten radish seeds on the surface of the cotton wool in each dish.
5 Place dish B in a fridge (low temperature).
6 Place dish C in an anaerobic jar, activate the anaerobic-producing chemical and seal the jar.
7 Place dishes A, C (in the anaerobic jar) and D in an incubator at 25°C (or leave them at room temperature, 20°C). *(Dish D acts as the control.)*
8 Check the dishes each day for 2 to 3 days.
9 Record the results as shown below.

Note 1: *Test tubes can be used instead of petri dishes.*

Note 2: *Anaerobic conditions can be created in another way. To remove oxygen, boil water vigorously and allow it to cool. Place seeds in the boiled water and add a layer of oil to prevent oxygen diffusing into the water.*

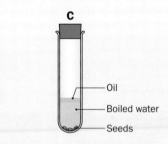

40.42 *Creating anaerobic conditions*

Activity 21 results

Dish	Conditions present	Conditions absent	Germination (yes/no)
A	Oxygen Suitable temperature	Water	
B	Water Oxygen	Suitable temperature	
C	Water Suitable temperature	Oxygen	
D	Water Suitable temperature Oxygen	None (control)	

THE ORGANISM

Activity 22  *To use starch agar or skimmed milk plates to show digestive activity during germination*

Note: *This activity allows the use of starch agar or skimmed milk plates. Starch agar plates are used in the following account.*

Seeds contain the enzyme amylase. In this activity, amylase breaks down starch in the agar plates.

Starch $\xrightarrow{\text{Amylase}}$ Maltose

1 Soak four broad bean seeds in water for a day or two.
2 Wash the bench with disinfectant (to kill bacteria and fungi).
3 Kill two of the seeds by boiling them in water for 5 minutes *(these will act as controls)*.
4 ⚠ Use a backed blade to split the four seeds in half.
5 Sterilise the half seeds by soaking them in alcohol or mild disinfectant for 10 minutes.
6 Wash off the alcohol or mild disinfectant with water.
7 Flame a forceps using a Bunsen burner and allow it to cool *(this sterilises it)*.
8 Barely open a petri dish containing starch agar *(to prevent bacteria or fungi from entering)*.
9 Using the forceps, place four of the cut, unboiled, half seeds face down onto the starch agar in one dish. Label this dish A.
10 Reflame the forceps and use it to place four cut, boiled, half seeds face down in another dish. Label this dish B. *(These act as controls.)*
11 Re-flame the forceps.
12 Place the covered dishes in a warm place for 2 days.
13 Remove the half seeds and add dilute iodine solution to the dishes *(to test for starch)*.
14 After 2 minutes pour off the iodine.
15 The areas of the agar containing starch will turn a dark (blue-black) colour.
16 Observe the results.
17 The result will be that the agar around the seeds in dish A will stay clear, while the rest of the agar turns blue-black. This is due to the digestive action of the enzyme amylase formed by the germinating seeds. The enzyme breaks down starch so that there is no reaction with iodine.

     In dish B there will not be any clear areas around the seeds because the enzymes were denatured by boiling (i.e. all the starch will turn blue-black).

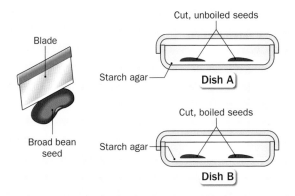

40.43 *To show digestion during germination*

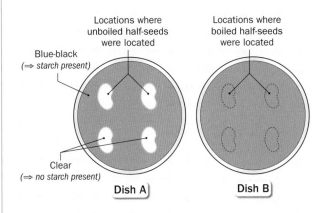

40.44 *Results after adding iodine*

THE ORGANISM

407

Summary

Asexual reproduction:
■ involves only one parent
■ produces identical offspring

Sexual reproduction:
■ involves the fusion of two sex cells (gametes)
■ produces non-identical offspring

The main parts of a flower:
■ The receptacle supports the flower parts.
■ Sepals protect the flower when it is a bud.
■ Petals may attract animals (especially insects).
■ Stamens (male) consist of a filament and anther. The anther produces pollen.
■ Carpels (female) consist of a stigma, style and ovary. The ovary contains the ovule(s), which produce(s) the embryo sac.

The pollen grain produces male gametes.

Pollen development involves:
■ meiosis occurring in the pollen sac (part of the anther) to produce haploid pollen grains
■ each pollen grain later producing two male gametes

The embryo sac produces female gametes called the egg cell and the (two) polar nuclei.

Embryo sac development involves:
■ meiosis occuring in the ovule to produce a haploid embryo sac
■ the embryo sac later producing eight haploid nuclei by mitosis:
    ■ five of these nuclei degenerate
    ■ two nuclei form the polar nuclei
    ■ the remaining nucleus forms the egg cell
    ■ the polar nuclei and egg cell are the gametes

The food supply in the ovule is the nucellus.

The integuments are the walls of the ovule.

Pollination is the transfer of pollen from an anther to a stigma.
■ Self-pollination occurs when the anther and stigma are on the same plant.
■ In cross-pollination, the anther and stigma are on different plants.

Methods of cross-pollination are wind and animals (especially insects).

Differences in flowering parts due to pollination methods

Wind pollination	Animal pollination
Small, green petals with no scent or nectar	Large, coloured petals with scent and nectar
Huge amounts of light, dry pollen	Small amounts of heavy, sticky pollen
Large, loosely held anthers, outside petals	Small, firmly held anthers, inside petals
Large, external feathery stigmas	Small, internal stigmas

Fertilisation is the union of male and female gametes.

The pollen tube grows down the style to the embryo sac.

Double fertilisation occurs in flowering plants as follows:
■ a sperm nucleus (n) + the egg nucleus (n) → zygote (2n)
■ the second sperm nucleus (n) + the two polar nuclei (n) → endosperm (3n)

After fertilisation:
■ The ovule becomes the seed.
■ The integuments become the testa.
■ The endosperm (3n) absorbs the nucellus (2n).
■ The zygote (2n) grows into the young plant (or embryo, 2n).
■ The ovary forms the fruit. The wall of the ovary forms the fruit wall (pericarp).

The embryo has two main parts:
■ the plumule (future shoot)
■ the radicle (future roots)
    (Cotyledon(s) – simple seed leaf or leaves – develop from the embryo.)

In monocots:
■ one cotyledon develops from the embryo
■ the food is normally stored in the endosperm

In dicots:
■ two cotyledons emerge from the embryo
■ the cotyledons usually absorb food from the endosperm
■ if all the endosperm is absorbed, the seed is non-endospermic
■ if some of the endosperm remains, the seed is endospermic

THE ORGANISM

Fruits protect and disperse seeds.

Fruits may be:
- fleshy or succulent (tomatoes, grapes, oranges)
- dry (pea pods, cereal grains)

Seedless fruits form due to:
- genetic breeding programmes
- treating flowers with growth regulators

Ethene is a growth regulator used to:
- remove the green colour from fruits
- ripen fruits

Dispersal is the carrying of the seed as far as possible from the parent plant.

The methods of seed dispersal are:
- wind
- water
- animal
- self

Dormancy is a resting period when seeds reduce their metabolism and do not grow.

Dormancy is brought about:
- by growth inhibitors
- if the testa is impermeable to water or oxygen
- if the testa is too tough
- by the lack of a growth promoter

The advantages of dormancy are:
- the seedling avoids growing in winter
- the embryo has time to develop
- there is time for dispersal
- it allows the seedling the maximum growing season
- it allows some seeds to survive in the soil

Germination is the regrowth of the embryo after dormancy, under suitable conditions. The conditions required for germination are:
- water
- oxygen
- suitable temperature
- dormancy completed

The main events in germination are:
- The seed absorbs water.
- Stored foods are digested to simpler forms by enzymes in the seed.
- Digested foods are transferred from the endosperm or cotyledon(s) to the embryo.
- Some digested foods make new structures; some are used in respiration.
- The radicle grows and bursts out through the testa.
- The plumule emerges above ground and new leaves form.

In one form of germination the cotyledons stay below ground, e.g. broad bean.

In another form of germination the cotyledons move above ground to form the first leaves e.g. sunflower.

To investigate the effect of water, oxygen and temperature on germination:
- Grow a number of radish seeds on damp cotton wool in a warm place (these seeds should germinate and act as a control).
- Grow three different sets of radish seeds (a) on dry cotton wool, (b) in a cold fridge, (c) in anaerobic conditions.
- The sets described at (a), (b) and (c) do not germinate due to the lack of water, a suitable temperature and oxygen, respectively.

To show that germinating seeds produce digestive enzymes:
- Place halved, sterile, soaked seeds on starch agar.
- Leave in a warm place.
- Remove the halved seeds and add iodine after a few days.
- The starch is digested by enzymes in live seeds (clear areas occur, surrounded by blue-black agar).
- The starch is not digested by dead (boiled) seeds (no clear areas occur, i.e. all the agar is blue-black).

THE ORGANISM

Revision questions

1 **(a)** Distinguish between asexual and sexual reproduction.

   (b) State the type of cell division involved in each type of reproduction.

   (c) Say which type of reproduction is more advanced and give a reason for your answer.

2 State whether the following parts are male or female: **(a)** stamen, **(b)** style, **(c)** ovary, **(d)** filament, **(e)** ovule, **(f)** stigma, **(g)** carpel, **(h)** anther.

3 **(a)** What is the function of a flower?

   (b) Name the structures labelled A to E on the diagram of a flower in Figure 40.45.

   (c) Is this flower wind- or insect-pollinated? Give two reasons, visible on the diagram, to support your answer.

   (d) In which two labelled parts does meiosis occur?

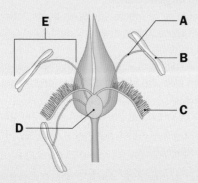

40.45

4 Name the cell in each case in which **(a)** male gametes, **(b)** female gametes, are formed.

5 Distinguish between:

   (a) microspores and megaspores

   (b) tapetum and tetrad

   (c) tube and generative nucleus

   (d) exine and intine.

6 **(a)** Name the cell division at X and Y in Figure 40.46.

   (b) What is the ratio between the chromosome number of the nuclei at A and B?

   (c) Name the nuclei at C and D.

   (d) One of the nuclei labelled C and D will divide again. Name the type of cell division involved and state the significance of the products.

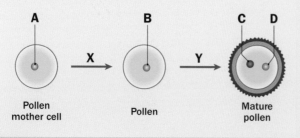

Pollen mother cell   Pollen   Mature pollen

40.46

7 Explain why cross-pollination is more advantageous than self-pollination.

8 Which of the three pollen grains shown in Figure 40.47 is most likely to be wind-pollinated? Explain your reasoning.

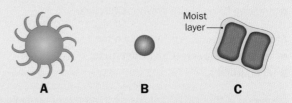

Moist layer

A   B   C

40.47

9 What structure in flowering plants has removed the need for external water in fertilisation?

10 **(a)** What is meant by double fertilisation in flowering plants?

   (b) Name the products of double fertilisation.

   (c) State the location of double fertilisation.

11 If a plant has a diploid number of 20 chromosomes, state how many chromosomes are present in each of the following:

   (a) a pollen nucleus

   (b) the egg nucleus

   (c) a cell from the stigma

   (d) the zygote

   (e) a nucellus cell

   (f) an endosperm nucleus

   (g) a cotyledon cell

   (h) a cell from the fruit.

12 **(a)** What is a cotyledon?

   (b) Distinguish between the **(i)** number, and **(ii)** role, of cotyledons in monocots and dicots.

13 **(a)** Name the parts labelled A to F in Figure 40.48 of an endospermic fruit.

   (b) Give one common function and one difference between the parts labelled B and C.

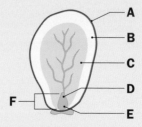

A
B
C
D
F
E

40.48

14 Name the structures from which each of the following develop prior to fertilisation: **(a)** seeds, **(b)** testa, **(c)** endosperm, **(d)** fruit, **(e)** pericarp.

15 **(a)** What is the advantage of seedless fruit to humans?

   (b) What is the disadvantage of such fruit to the plant?

16 Name one growth regulator in each case responsible for:

(a) forming seedless fruit

(b) breaking down chlorophyll in fruit walls

(c) producing larger fruit.

17 (a) What is seed dispersal?

(b) Suggest one advantage of seed dispersal.

(c) Name the methods of seed dispersal and name one plant example in each case.

18 (a) What is dormancy?

(b) State two methods used by plants to ensure their seeds remain dormant.

(c) List two advantages of dormancy.

19 Suggest one reason in each case for each of the following practices used in sowing seeds.

(a) placing the seeds in a fridge or cold place overnight

(b) making a small cut in the seed coat

(c) soaking the seeds in water

(d) not sowing the seeds too closely

(e) storing seeds for a year before sowing them.

20 (a) What is germination?

(b) Name the three main conditions necessary for germination.

(c) Suggest one reason why each of the named conditions is necessary.

21 When investigating the need for certain factors in germination:

(a) Name the three factors investigated.

(b) Outline how you removed each factor.

(c) What factors were present in the control apparatus?

(d) Why was a control apparatus necessary?

(e) Why were a number of seeds used in each apparatus rather than single seeds?

22 (a) Name the parts labelled A to E in Fig. 40.49.

(b) What have B and D in common?

(c) Name a plant that shows this type of germination.

(d) Name and draw similar labelled diagrams to show the other type of germination in a named plant.

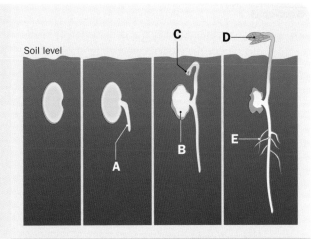

40.49

23 Choose which of the options (i), (ii), (iii) or (iv) represents the correct answer in each case below.

(a) The nucellus provides nutrients for:

(i) the nucleus   **(iii)** the ovary

(ii) the ovule   **(iv)** the integuments

(b) The wall of a fruit is called:

(i) testa   **(iii)** parthenocarpy

(ii) pod   **(iv)** pericarp

(c) In sunflower germination, the part of the seed that carries the cotyledons above the soil is:

(i) the epicotyl   **(iii)** the hypocotyl

(ii) the embryo   **(iv)** the micropyle

(d) The triploid part of a seed is called:

(i) the hilum   **(iii)** the cotyledon

(ii) the zygote   **(iv)** the endosperm

(e) During fertilisation, the tube nucleus degenerates as soon as the pollen tube arrives at:

(i) the micropyle

(ii) the cotyledons

(iii) the ovary

(iv) the style

Sample examination questions

Section A

24 The diagram shows the external structure of a stamen.

(a) Name A and B.

(b) Where is pollen produced, in A or in B?

(c) To which part of a flower is pollen carried?

(d) What is meant by cross-pollination?

(e) Name two methods of cross-pollination.

(2005 OL Q 3)

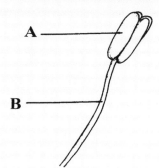

Section B

25 (a) (i) What is meant by the germination of seeds?

(ii) Seeds may remain inactive for a period before germination. What term is used to describe this period of inactivity?

(b) Answer the following questions about an investigation that you carried out on the effect of water, oxygen and temperature on germination.

(i) What seeds did you use?

(ii) Explain how you set up a control for the investigation.

(iii) How did you deprive some of the seeds of oxygen?

(iv) How did you ensure that some of the seeds were deprived of a suitable temperature for germination?

(v) State the results of the investigation, including those of the control.

(2008 OL Q 9)

Section C

26 The diagram shows the structure of a flower.

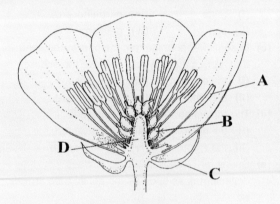

(i) Name the parts labelled A, B, C, D.

(ii) In which labelled part is pollen produced?

(iii) What is meant by pollination?

(iv) From the list below, choose **three** characteristics in each case of:
1. an insect-pollinated flower,
2. a wind-pollinated flower.
brightly coloured petals, feathery stigmas, anthers within petals, anthers outside petals, nectaries, petals reduced or absent.

(v) What process follows pollination in the life cycle of a flowering plant?

(2008 OL Q 14a)

27 The diagram shows a vertical section through a carpel.

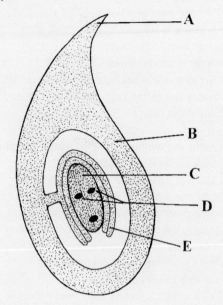

(i) Name A, B, C, D, E.

(ii) What happens to the two nuclei labelled D?

(iii) In the case of B and E state what may happen to each of them after fertilisation.

(iv) Copy the diagram into your answer book and add a pollen tube that has completed its growth. Label the nuclei in the pollen tube.

(2004 HL Q 14a)

28 Answer the following in relation to sexual reproduction in flowering plants.

(i) State a role for each of the following: sepal, anther, stigma, ovary.

(ii) Distinguish between pollination and fertilisation.

(iii) The two male gametes in the pollen tube are derived from the generative nucleus. Do these gametes form as a result of mitosis or meiosis? Explain your answer.

(iv) Describe the fate of each of the male gametes.

(v) State **one** method that is used to produce seedless fruits.

(2006 HL Q 14a)

29 (i) From what structure in the carpel does the seed develop?

(ii) State **two** locations in the seed where food may be stored.

(iii) The embryo plant within the seed has a number of parts. List **two** of these parts, apart from food stores, and give a role for each of them.

(iv) Following dispersal, the seed undergoes a period of dormancy. What is dormancy?

(v) Suggest **two** advantages of dormancy.

(2007 HL Q 14a)

30 **(i)** In the table below, which letter gives the correct order of events in the life cycle of a flowering plant – A, B, C, D or E?

A	germination	seed and fruit formation	growth	pollination	fertilisation	dispersal
B	germination	fertilisation	seed and fruit formation	growth	dispersal	pollination
C	germination	fertilisation	growth	seed and fruit formation	pollination	dispersal
D	germination	growth	pollination	fertilisation	seed and fruit formation	dispersal
E	germination	seed and fruit formation	growth	fertilisation	dispersal	pollination

(ii) Distinguish clearly between pollination and fertilisation.

(iii) State a location in the seed where food is stored.

(iv) What is germination?

(v) State **three** factors necessary for the germination of a seed.

(2007 OL Q 14c)

Previous examination questions

Ordinary level	Higher level
2003 Q 9, 15c	2003 Q 14a
2004 Q 14	2004 Q 14a
2005 Q 3, 9	2005 Q 3g, j
2006 Q 9, 14c	2006 Q 7, 14a
2007 Q 14c	2007 Q 14a
2008 Q 9, 14a	

For latest questions go to ***www.edco.ie/biology***

THE ORGANISM

Chapter 41 Vegetative propagation

Introduction

> **Vegetative propagation** (or vegetative reproduction) is asexual reproduction in plants.

Vegetative propagation does not involve gametes, flowers, seeds or fruits. Only one plant is involved, so the offspring are produced by a single parent plant.

Generally a specialised part of the plant separates from the parent and grows by mitosis to form a new plant. The offspring formed in this way are genetically identical with the parent.

41.1 *Strawberry plants and runners (red)*

Natural vegetative propagation

Vegetative propagation involves forming new plants from a stem, root, leaf, or bud, as outlined in the following sections. Sometimes the structures that are used are altered or modified for reproduction; sometimes they are not altered.

Methods of natural vegetative propagation

1. STEM

> **Runners** (e.g. strawberries and buttercups) are horizontal stems that run (or grow) above ground and from which new plants grow.

Runners normally have long internodes. Buds are formed at each node.

Each bud may give rise to a new plant, complete with its own root system. In time, the new plant will continue the process by producing its own runners.

Examples of plants with runners are strawberries and buttercups.

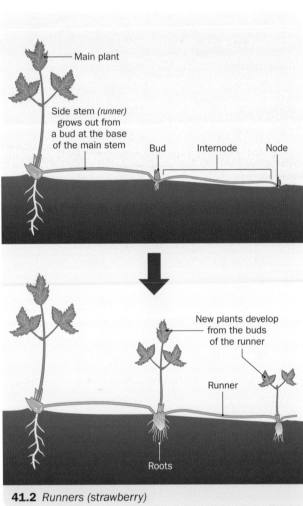

41.2 *Runners (strawberry)*

2. ROOT

> A **root tuber** is a swollen, underground root that remains dormant during winter and from which new plants may grow.

New shoots grow from the buds at the base of the old stem, which has withered away.

An example of a plant that has root tubers is the dahlia.

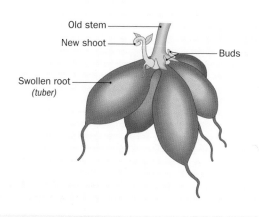

Old stem
New shoot
Buds
Swollen root
(tuber)

41.3 *Root tuber (dahlia)*

41.4 *Dahlia tubers*

3. LEAF

The leaves of some plants will readily grow into new plants if they are detached from the parent plant. This form of asexual reproduction is very common in begonia, cactus, and succulent plants.

In addition, plants such as *Kalanchoe* produce a large number of new small plants (plantlets) along the edge of their leaves. Hence this plant is also called the 'maternity plant' or 'mother of thousands'.

41.5 *Plantlets forming on the leaf of Kalanchoe*

4. BUDS

> A **bulb** is a modified bud.

A bulb (e.g. onion, daffodil and tulip) contains an underground stem reduced in size. Numerous leaves are attached to this stem. Each leaf is swollen with stored food.

The centre of the bulb has an apical bud, which can produce leaves and a young flower. Lateral buds are located between the stem and each leaf. These buds can each form a new shoot in spring.

Once the new shoot has finished flowering it should be left in position in the soil for about six weeks. This is necessary to allow it to form new food (by photosynthesis). This food is sent back down to form one or more new bulb(s) inside the old bulb.

The old leaves become dry and scaly and serve to protect the new bulb(s) inside.

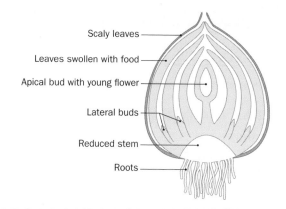

Scaly leaves
Leaves swollen with food
Apical bud with young flower
Lateral buds
Reduced stem
Roots

41.6 *A bulb (onion)*

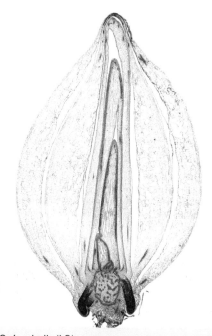

41.7 *Onion bulb (LS)*

Did you know?

Each bulb contains one or more buds. If more than one bud grows, each one will form a new shoot. Each new shoot will form a new bud at the end of its growing season. In this way, the bulbs show asexual reproduction.

    Gardeners often have to dig up bulbs in autumn and replant some of them, in order to prevent overcrowding when the plants emerge from the ground.

41.9 *Leaf cutting (note the rooting powder on the left)*

Artificial vegetative propagation

Apart from the natural methods of vegetative reproduction, a number of artificial methods are employed to reproduce plants by vegetative methods.

These methods are widely used in horticulture (growing plants) and agriculture to propagate (grow) new plants that are identical to the parent.

Syllabus

You are required to know any four methods of artificial vegetative propagation.

Methods of artificial vegetative propagation

1. CUTTINGS

Cuttings (e.g. busy Lizzie, geranium, willow) are parts of a plant (usually shoots) that are removed from the parent plant and allowed to form new roots and leaves. The shoot is cut at an angle and is often treated with rooting powder (a growth promoter) to speed up root formation.

Normally some leaves are removed from a cutting in order to reduce water loss. Plants produced from cuttings will be similar to the parents.

Propagation by cuttings is a simple, cheap method of producing large numbers of similar plants.

2. GRAFTING

Grafting is used to combine useful qualities or traits from two different plants into one plant.

When grafting plants such as roses and apple trees, part of one plant is removed and attached to a healthy, rooted part of a second plant. To be successful the graft has to achieve good contact between the growth areas (meristems) and vascular tissue of both plants.

In roses, a section with large flowers (but a poor root system) can be grafted to a wild rose with large roots (but with small, insignificant flowers). In this way the best features of both plants can be combined.

Eating-apple trees can be grafted to crab-apple plants. This produces well rooted plants that produce good quality eating apples.

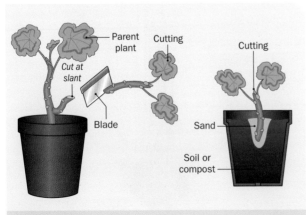

41.8 *Taking a cutting*

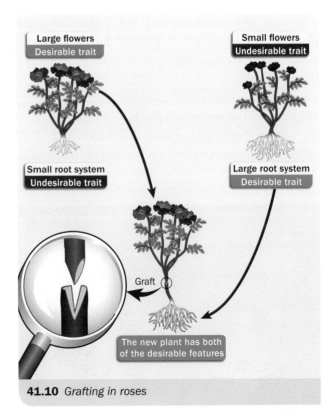

Large flowers
Desirable trait

Small flowers
Undesirable trait

Small root system
Undesirable trait

Large root system
Desirable trait

Graft

The new plant has both of the desirable features

41.10 *Grafting in roses*

41.11 *Grafting*

3. LAYERING

In layering, a branch of a parent plant is bent down and covered in soil, except at the tip (e.g. blackberries, roses and carnations). The covered part forms roots and the exposed tip forms new shoots. In time the two plants are separated.

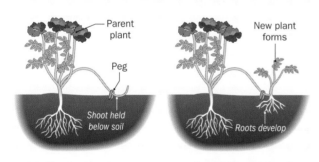

41.12 *Layering*

41.13 *Layering (the stem is held in place with a wire in the soil in the pot and a new plant will develop)*

4. MICROPROPAGATION

Micropropagation is also called tissue culturing. It involves growing large numbers of plants from small plant pieces. Very often, the new plants are grown from single cells taken from a parent plant. These cells are grown using tissue culturing techniques (as explained in Chapter 8).

The cells or small pieces of plant tissue are grown on an artificial medium (such as agar). Nutrients and growth regulators are added so that the growing cells form a group of similar cells called a callus.

Different growth regulators are then added so that the callus develops into a small plant with shoots and roots. These small plants may be grown in soil just like normal plants.

Micropropagation can be used to grow many vegetables and flowering plants. In particular, it is used to grow orchids and plants that have been produced by genetic engineering techniques. However, it is an expensive and specialised process, which means its use is limited.

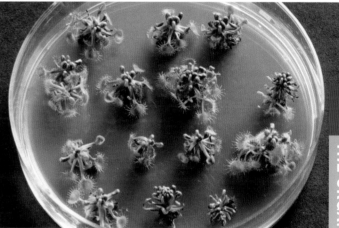

41.14 *Micropropagation: the new plants are growing on a soil substitute enriched with minerals*

Comparing sexual (seed) reproduction with asexual reproduction

Both sexual and asexual methods of plant propagation have their advantages and disadvantages.

SEXUAL REPRODUCTION

The main advantage of seed or sexual reproduction is that the offspring possess variations.

These variations may assist the new plants to survive in a habitat by being better adapted. For example, some of the seedlings may be resistant to a pathogen, or may be able to survive if climatic conditions change.

THE ORGANISM

Additional advantages of seed reproduction include the ability of seeds to be dispersed widely, and the possibility that some seeds may survive in the soil and grow when unsuitable environmental conditions improve.

ASEXUAL REPRODUCTION

Asexual reproduction allows plants to produce many copies of themselves in a short space of time.

This helps asexually reproducing plants to establish themselves very rapidly in new habitats.

In addition, the new plants are very strong because they can draw nutrients from the parent plant while they are still attached to it.

The advantages and disadvantages of each method of reproduction are outlined in the table below.

Comparison between sexual (seed) and asexual (vegetative) reproduction in plants	
Sexual (seed)	**Asexual (vegetative)**
Advantages	**Disadvantages**
Offspring show variations from parents (allowing evolution)	There are no variations (though this may be an advantage to the grower)
Some plants may be resistant to disease	If one plant is susceptible to a disease then all plants are susceptible
There is less competition due to seed dispersal	There is overcrowding and competition
Some seeds may remain dormant in the soil	No seeds are formed (i.e. no dormant structures in soil)
Disadvantages	**Advantages**
Complex process	Simple process
May depend on outside agents, e.g. for pollination and dispersal	No outside agents are needed
Slow growth of the young plants to maturity	Rapid growth, as young plants are attached to the parent
Wasteful (e.g. petals, nectar, pollen, fruit)	No waste

Summary

Vegetative propagation:
■ is asexual reproduction in plants
■ produces genetically identical offspring

Vegetative propagation may form new plants from the following structures:
■ **stems**, such as runners in strawberries
■ **roots**, such as root tubers in dahlias
■ **leaves**, in cacti
■ **buds**, in bulbs such as onions or daffodils

Artificial methods of vegetative propagation include:
■ **cuttings** – shoots that are removed from a plant and allowed to form new plants
■ **grafting** – a section from one plant is attached to a section of another plant
■ **layering** – a branch of a plant is fixed into the soil to allow it to form roots and a new plant
■ **micropropagation** – the growth of new plants from tiny pieces of a parent plant

The advantages of seed (sexual) reproduction are:
■ variation in offspring
■ more disease resistance
■ less overcrowding due to seed dispersal
■ dormant seeds survive in soil

The advantages of vegetative (asexual) reproduction are:
■ it is a simple process
■ no external agents are needed
■ young plants show fast growth
■ there is little waste

Revision questions

1 Explain what is meant by **(a)** asexual reproduction, and **(b)** vegetative propagation.
2 Name the type of cell division involved in vegetative reproduction.
3 Many fruits and vegetables are genetically identical.
   (a) State one way in which plants forming such fruits and vegetables are produced.
   (b) State two advantages of producing plants in this way.
4 Give three examples of natural vegetative propagation using different parts of named plants in each case.
5 **(a)** Name three methods of artificially propagating plants.
   (b) Name one plant in each case that is propagated by the methods named.

6 Suggest a biological reason for each of the following:
   (a) growing plants from cuttings rather than from seeds
   (b) removing leaves from a cutting before planting it in soil
   (c) using growth regulators when growing cuttings
   (d) grafting cultivated roses onto wild rose rootstock
   (e) cherry blossom trees may have white flowers on some branches and pink flowers on other branches
   (f) growing plants by micropropagation
   (g) plants that reproduce vegetatively in nature may become overcrowded.
7 Give three reasons why seed reproduction is more complex than vegetative reproduction.
8 Explain why seed-grown plants often show more resistance to disease than plants that arise from vegetative propagation.

Sample examination questions

Section C

9 **(i)** In relation to flowering plants explain what is meant by vegetative propagation.
   (ii) Clones are genetically identical individuals. Are the products of vegetative propagation clones? Explain your answer.
   (iii) Give **two** examples of natural vegetative propagation that involve different parts of a plant.
   (iv) Describe **two** techniques of artificial vegetative propagation that are used for flowering plants. Suggest a benefit of artificial propagation.
   (2003 Sample HL Q 14b)

10 **(i)** What is vegetative propagation?
   (ii) Give **one** example of vegetative propagation and state whether it involves a stem, a root, a leaf or a bud.
   (iii) How does vegetative propagation differ from reproduction by seed?
   (iv) Artificial propagation is widely used in horticulture. Give **two** examples of artificial propagation.
   (v) Suggest **one** advantage and **one** disadvantage of artificial propagation.
   (2005 OL Q 15b)

*For latest questions go to **www.edco.ie/biology***

Chapter 42 Human reproduction

Introduction

The human reproductive systems (male and female) are composed of three structural levels of organisation:

1 A pair of structures in both males and females to produce sex cells. The testes produce the male sex cells (gametes) called sperm. The ovaries produce the female gametes called eggs or ova (the singular is ovum).
2 A series of transport tubes.
3 A number of glands to secrete hormones that control human reproduction.

The male reproductive system

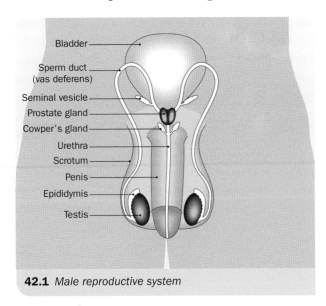

42.1 *Male reproductive system*

Testes

> A **gonad** is an organ that produces sex cells in animals.

The male gonads, called the testes, develop inside the body cavity. A few weeks before birth they descend out of the body cavity into a pouch called the scrotum.

The temperature in the scrotum is maintained at 35°C. At this temperature meiosis can occur, producing sperm. (Meiosis does not take place properly in males at normal body temperature, i.e. 37°C).

Each testis consists of a coiled mass of tubules (about 50 cm long in total). These tubules are lined with diploid sperm-producing cells. It is in these cells that meiosis occurs to produce haploid sperm.

Cells located between the tubules produce the hormone testosterone.

Epididymis

The tubules in the testes combine to form the epididymis, which is located outside each testis (see Figure 42.2). Sperm mature in the epididymis and are stored (for up to 6 weeks).

If sperm are not released they are broken down in the epididymis and taken back into the bloodstream, a process called resorption.

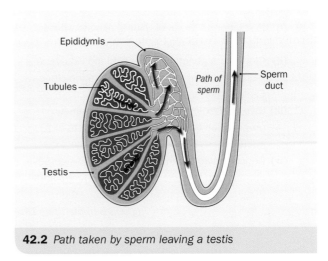

42.2 *Path taken by sperm leaving a testis*

Sperm duct

The epididymis leads into the sperm duct (or vas deferens). A vasectomy is an operation performed to cut the sperm ducts. This is a form of male sterilisation.

The sperm ducts carry sperm to the urethra. The urethra is the tube located in the centre of the penis. It has the dual function of carrying urine or sperm out of the body at different times.

Associated glands

The **seminal vesicles**, the **prostate gland** and **Cowper's glands** produce a liquid called seminal fluid. When seminal fluid is added to sperm cells the resulting liquid is called **semen**.

Seminal fluid provides a medium for the sperm to swim in and also nourishes the sperm (as it contains fructose).

Ejaculation is the release of semen from the penis.

Normally males release 200–300 million sperm at each ejaculation. However, recent evidence suggests that males are producing and therefore releasing fewer sperm in their semen.

Sperm

Sperm are produced by meiosis. Sperm-producing cells are diploid, i.e. they contain 46 chromosomes. They divide by meiosis to form sperm cells. Meiosis halves the number of chromosomes and so sperm cells (spermatozoa) are haploid, i.e. they contain only 23 chromosomes.

Sperm cells are first produced in the testes at the onset of sexual maturity, called **puberty**. This occurs at about 12 or 13 years of age in males. Sperm are formed continually throughout a man's lifetime.

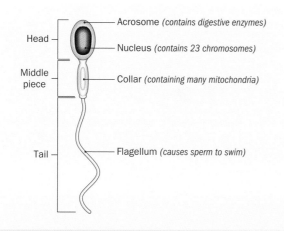

Head
Acrosome *(contains digestive enzymes)*
Nucleus *(contains 23 chromosomes)*
Middle piece
Collar *(containing many mitochondria)*
Tail
Flagellum *(causes sperm to swim)*

42.3 *Structure of sperm cell*

42.4 *Sperm cells in a testis (SEM)*

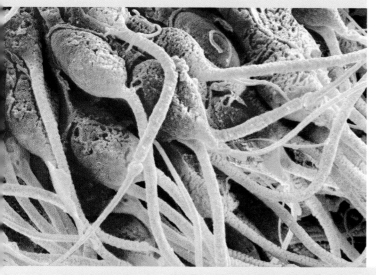

Penis

The penis is a structure adapted to introduce sperm into the female reproductive system. The swollen tip of the penis is called the glans. A fold of skin called the foreskin (or prepuce) partially covers the glans. Circumcision is the removal of the foreskin. This may be carried out for religious or health reasons.

During sexual arousal more blood flows into the penis than can flow out of it. This causes the penis to become erect. In this state it can be used to place sperm into the female system.

Hormones in the male reproductive system

At puberty two hormones are produced by the male pituitary gland:

- **FSH** (follicle stimulating hormone) causes the sperm-producing cells in the testes to divide by meiosis and produce sperm.
- **LH** (luteinising hormone) stimulates the testes to produce testosterone.

Testosterone

Androgens are male hormones. Testosterone is the main androgen. It is produced in small amounts by the testes before puberty (and by the female ovaries throughout life).

Testosterone causes the primary male sex characteristics early in life, i.e. the growth of the penis and other male reproductive parts and the descent of the testes into the scrotum.

The production of testosterone increases enormously at puberty, causing the enlargement of the penis, testes and other reproductive parts. Testosterone also causes the secondary male characteristics such as those listed below.

Secondary sexual characteristics are those features that distinguish males from females, apart from the sex organs themselves.

SECONDARY MALE CHARACTERISTICS

- growth of pubic, underarm, facial and body hair
- enlargement of the larynx, causing the voice to break and deepen
- increased muscular and bone development
- widening of the shoulders
- growth spurt (body weight may double)
- increased secretion of sebum in the skin

Male infertility (e.g. low sperm count)

> **Infertility** is the inability to produce offspring.

The main type of male infertility is the production of low numbers of sperm.

CAUSE
Low sperm counts may arise due to persistent smoking of cigarettes, alcohol abuse, use of marijuana or anabolic steroids or low levels of male hormones.

If males suffer from mumps in adult life, this may also destroy the ability of the testes to produce sperm.

Recent evidence suggests that contact with certain chemicals used in detergents and plastics may reduce sperm counts.

CORRECTIVE MEASURES
Treatment to correct a low sperm count consists of changes in diet and lifestyle. These include stopping smoking cigarettes, not taking any drugs, stopping or reducing alcohol consumption and reducing stress levels.

If the cause of the infertility is hormonal then the relevant hormone may be administered.

Sometimes *in vitro* (artificial) fertilisation can be tried. This process is described later in this chapter.

Female reproductive system

Ovaries

The ovaries produce eggs and female hormones. Eggs are produced by meiosis. Puberty, the onset of sexual maturity, occurs in females at about 11 or 12 years of age.

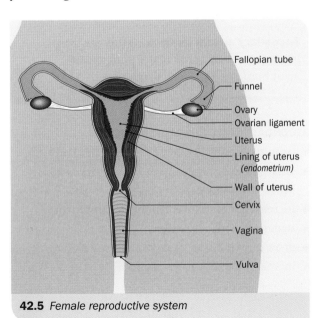

42.5 *Female reproductive system*

The ovaries of a female foetus may contain up to one million potential eggs at birth. These potential eggs have not yet divided by meiosis. As a result, they are diploid, containing 46 chromosomes.

By the age of puberty, the number of potential eggs has fallen to about 40 000. Each potential egg is enclosed in a cluster of cells, forming what is called a follicle in the ovary.

After puberty, about 20 eggs are produced by meiosis each month. Usually only one egg continues to grow; the rest die off.

Once meiosis is complete, a haploid egg (ovum) is surrounded by a **Graafian follicle**. The Graafian follicle produces the female hormone oestrogen.

As the Graafian follicle matures, it forms a swelling (like a blister) on the surface of the ovary. The follicle bursts at ovulation to release the egg.

> **Ovulation** is the release of an egg from the ovary.

After ovulation, the follicle fills with yellow cells and becomes the **corpus luteum** (or yellow body). This secretes the hormone progesterone.

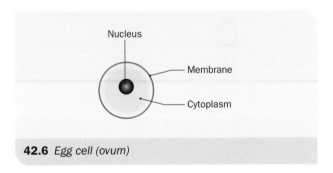

42.6 *Egg cell (ovum)*

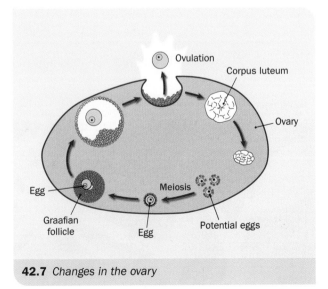

42.7 *Changes in the ovary*

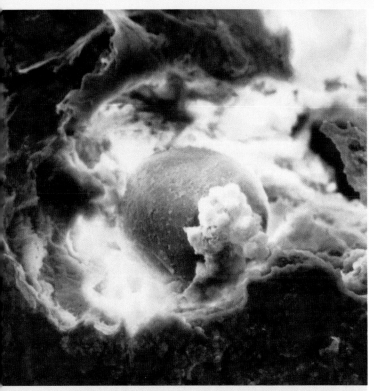

42.8 *Ovulation: the egg (pink) and some white fluid bursting out of the ovary (brown)*

Fallopian tubes

The **oviduct** is a collective term for the Fallopian tubes and uterus. The Fallopian tubes are muscular tubes about 12 cm long. Their ends have funnels that catch the egg after ovulation.

The egg is moved along the Fallopian tube by cilia and muscular peristalsis. The egg is either fertilised or dies in the Fallopian tube.

Uterus (womb)

The uterus is a muscular structure about the size of the fist. The outer wall is made of involuntary muscle. The inner lining is called the **endometrium**. This lining thickens each month with cells and blood vessels in order to nourish the embryo in the event of pregnancy. The opening into the uterus is called the cervix.

42.9 *Cilia (yellow) in the Fallopian tube (SEM)*

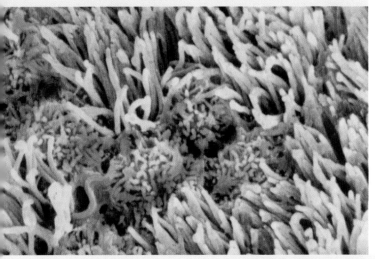

Vagina

The vagina is an elastic, muscular tube about 10 cm long. It allows the entry of sperm into the female system and also serves as the birth canal to allow the exit of the baby.

The vagina is lined with mucous-producing cells. The urethra, which carries urine from the bladder, opens near the vagina. The labia are folds of skin that protect the vagina. Collectively they form the vulva.

The hymen is a ring of tissue that may partially block the vagina entrance. It is stretched or torn by the use of tampons or at first sexual intercourse.

The menstrual cycle

> The **menstrual cycle** is a series of events that occurs every 28 days on average in the female if fertilisation has not taken place.

The menstrual cycle (*mensis* is the Latin for a month) begins at puberty and continues until the **menopause**, which is the end of a woman's reproductive life (usually between the ages of 45 and 55).

The events of a typical menstrual cycle can be summarised as follows:

DAYS 1–5
- The old lining of the uterus (endometrium) breaks down and is shed from the body. The loss of this blood and tissue through the vagina is called menstruation (or a period).
- Meiosis occurs in an ovary to produce a new egg. The new egg is surrounded by the Graafian follicle.

DAYS 6–14
The developing Graafian follicle produces the hormone oestrogen. This hormone causes the endometrium to thicken again. It also prevents new eggs from developing, so that normally only one Graafian follicle develops during each menstrual cycle.

DAY 14
Ovulation occurs when the Graafian follicle bursts to release the egg from the ovary. The egg passes into the abdomen of the female and on into the funnel of the Fallopian tube. The egg is then moved along the Fallopian tube.

The egg is normally only available for fertilisation for up to 48 hours after ovulation.

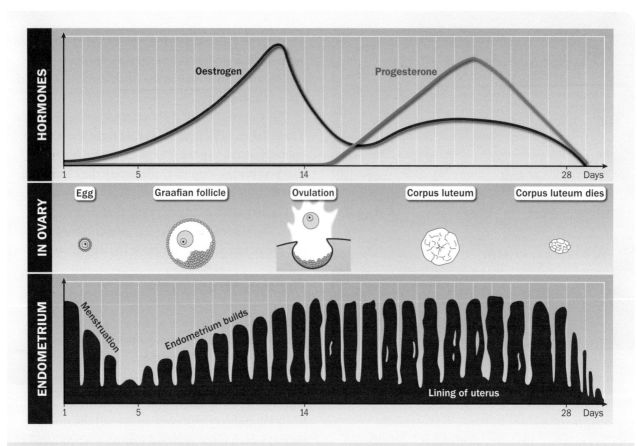

42.10 *Events during a single menstrual cycle*

DAYS 14–28

The remains of the Graafian follicle develop into the corpus luteum (or yellow body). This makes the hormone progesterone (and some oestrogen), which causes the endometrium to thicken even more. Progesterone also prevents new eggs from forming. The egg that was released will die by day 16 if it is not fertilised.

If fertilisation has not taken place, the corpus luteum starts to degenerate around day 22. This results in a reduction in progesterone levels, which causes the lining of the uterus to break down on day 28. Menstruation and a new cycle begins again.

The spongy, nutritive lining of the uterus breaks down and is released from the body through the vagina. This bleeding is called 'a period'. The bleeding lasts for about 5 days. The onset of bleeding marks the start of a new monthly (menstrual) cycle.

Functions of oestrogen and progesterone

Oestrogen causes the endometrium to thicken in the first half of the cycle. Progesterone continues this process in the second 14 days.

Both hormones prevent (inhibit) eggs from developing. For this reason they are used in contraceptive pills.

The high levels of oestrogen produced at puberty cause the primary female sexual characteristics. These are the growth of the sex organs.

The combination of oestrogens and progesterone at puberty cause the secondary female characteristics.

SECONDARY FEMALE CHARACTERISTICS

- the maturing and enlargement of the breasts
- widening of the pelvis to allow for birth
- increased body fat
- growth of pubic and underarm hair
- growth spurt (which is also stimulated by testosterone produced by the adrenal glands)

Female infertility (e.g. endocrine gland failure)

As mentioned earlier, infertility is the inability to produce offspring. The most common type of female infertility is the failure to ovulate (i.e. release the egg from the ovary).

CAUSE

Sometimes failure to ovulate seems to have no obvious cause. In other cases it may be caused by a hormonal disorder (i.e. endocrine gland failure), stress or problems with the ovary such as a tumour.

CORRECTIVE MEASURES

The treatment given for female infertility will depend on the cause of the problem. If the problem is associated with an endocrine gland failure (hormonal) then hormonal treatment is given. Other treatments involve stress relief or surgery on the ovary.

As a last resort, *in vitro* fertilisation may be used to achieve pregnancy (see later in this chapter).

Did you know?

Infertility problems are experienced by up to one in six couples. The causes are divided approximately evenly between the male partner, the female partner or both partners. Approximately 50% of couples with infertility problems go on to produce offspring when properly treated.

Hormonal control in menstrual cycle

There are four hormones involved in the menstrual cycle. Each one tends to cause the production of the hormone following it and to inhibit the preceding hormone.

In the following account, each hormone is dealt with under three headings: (a) site of production, (b) time of production and (c) functions.

FSH (FOLLICLE STIMULATING HORMONE)
(a) Produced by the pituitary gland.
(b) Produced early in the cycle (days 1 to 5).
(c) It stimulates a few potential eggs to develop, surrounded by Graafian follicles. Only one follicle normally survives.

FSH is sometimes used in fertility treatments to stimulate the ovaries to produce eggs. Often a number of eggs develop, resulting in multiple births.

Each Graafian follicle will secrete oestrogen, so that FSH can be said to cause the production of oestrogen.

OESTROGEN
(a) Produced by the Graafian follicle (in the ovary).
(b) Produced from days 5 to 14.
(c) It causes the endometrium to develop. It also inhibits FSH by negative feedback (ensuring no further eggs develop; hence its use in the contraceptive pill).

High levels of oestrogen just before day 14 stimulate the release of the next hormone, LH.

LH (LUTEINISING HORMONE)
(a) Produced by the pituitary gland.
(b) Produced on day 14.
(c) It causes ovulation. It then causes the remains of the Graafian follicle to develop into the corpus luteum.

The corpus luteum makes the final hormone in the cycle, progesterone (along with small amounts of oestrogen).

PROGESTERONE
(a) Produced by the corpus luteum (in the ovary).
(b) Produced from days 14 to 28.
(c) It maintains the structure of the endometrium. It inhibits (by negative feedback) the production of FSH, which prevents further eggs from developing. It also inhibits LH so that further ovulation and pregnancies are prevented. Progesterone also prevents contractions of the uterus.

If pregnancy does not occur, the corpus luteum starts to degenerate around day 22. By day 28, low levels of progesterone (and oestrogen) produce the following effects:

- FSH secretion by the pituitary gland is no longer inhibited. As the FSH level rises, new eggs begin to develop.
- The uterus contracts and the endometrium is shed from the body. Menstruation and a new cycle have begun.

Menstrual disorder (e.g. fibroids)

Fibroids are benign tumours of the uterus. This means they result from the overproduction of cells but they do not invade other tissues and do not spread. Fibroids are slow growing and range from the size of a pea to the size of a large grapefruit. They are most common between the ages of 35 and 45.

Small fibroids often produce no symptoms. As they enlarge they cause heavy and prolonged menstrual bleeding (which in turn leads to anaemia). They can also cause pain, miscarriage or infertility.

CAUSE

The cause of fibroids is uncertain. They may be abnormal responses to oestrogen. For this reason they tend to be larger in women taking the contraceptive pill.

THE ORGANISM

(H) **PREVENTION AND TREATMENT**
Small fibroids require no treatment apart from frequent examinations to check on their growth. Larger fibroids are removed by surgery. If there are large numbers of fibroids it may be necessary to remove the entire uterus, a process called
(H) hysterectomy.

The stages of copulation

Sexual arousal

Sexual arousal in the male causes the flow of blood into the penis to increase and the blood flow out of the penis to decrease. Spongy tissue in the penis fills with blood and the penis becomes erect. In this state the penis can be inserted into the vagina.

Arousal in females results in the vagina becoming lubricated, elongated and wider.

Copulation

Copulation is also called coitus or sexual intercourse. During this process, the penis moves inside the vagina. Breathing and heart rates increase in both partners.

Orgasm

Physical and mental sensations resulting from copulation may lead to a climax in sexual excitement called orgasm. This may last from a few seconds in males to up to a minute in females.

During orgasm, muscles in the pelvis of both partners contract and heart rates, respiration and blood pressures rise dramatically. In the female, the outer vagina and uterus contract.

In the male, the sphincter muscle from the bladder closes and contraction of the involuntary muscles in the epididymis, sperm ducts, glands and urethra discharge semen out of the penis. The propelling of semen from the penis is called ejaculation.

Behaviour of sex cells

Insemination is the release of semen into the vagina, just outside the cervix.

Contractions of the uterus and Fallopian tubes can move the sperm along the Fallopian tubes within 5 minutes of insemination.

If ovulation has occurred and an egg is present, it releases a chemical that attracts the sperm. The sperm swim towards the chemical released by the egg. This process is called **chemotaxis**.

Fertilisation

Events leading to fertilisation

Many of the sperm die in the female system. This is due either to the acidic conditions in the vagina or to being attacked (as foreign objects) by white blood cells in the female system. Some sperm enter the wrong Fallopian tube, i.e. the tube that does not contain an egg.

However, many sperm reach the egg in the Fallopian tube. Acrosomes at the front end of the sperm contain enzymes that are used to digest an opening through the membrane of the egg.

One sperm loses its tail and the head of the sperm enters the egg. Once the sperm has entered, the membrane of the egg undergoes a rapid chemical change, forming a fertilisation membrane. This prevents further sperm from entering.

Fertilisation occurs when the nucleus of the sperm fuses with the nucleus of the egg, forming a diploid zygote.

Fertilisation normally takes place in the Fallopian tube.

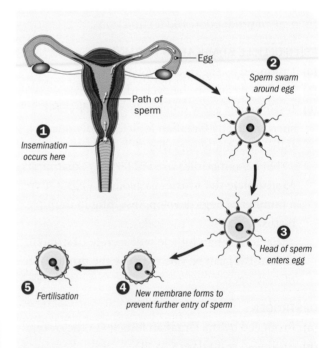

42.11 *Events leading up to fertilisation*

Fertilisation may normally result if copulation takes place in the interval from 3 days before ovulation (as the sperm can live for 3 days in the female system) to 2 days after ovulation (as the egg dies 2 days after ovulation).

In a typical menstrual cycle, this means the most fertile time is days 11 to 16. However, many women do not have regular menstrual cycles. It is common for irregular cycles to occur in women whose cycle is normally very regular. For these reasons, the fertile time is really days 9 to 18.

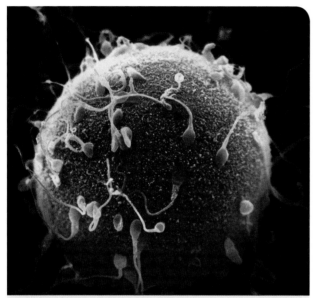

42.12 *Sperm and egg: just prior to fertilisation*

Birth control

> **Birth control** refers to methods taken to limit the number of children that are born.

Birth control may involve abortion or contraception.

> **Abortion** is the termination of a pregnancy.

The use of abortion as a method of birth control is controversial and is not normally carried out in many countries (including Ireland).

> **Contraception** is the deliberate prevention of fertilisation or pregnancy.

There are four methods of contraception: natural, mechanical, chemical and surgical methods.

Natural contraception

Natural contraception involves not having intercourse at those times in the menstrual cycle when pregnancy is possible. This is the only method of contraception approved by the Roman Catholic church.

Natural methods of contraception try to identify the time of ovulation based on:
- body temperature (which rises after ovulation)
- mucous secreted in the cervix (which changes its texture after ovulation)
- past menstrual cycles (this is called the rhythm method and it presumes that in women with regular 28-day cycles ovulation will occur 14 days after the last period, which cannot always be relied upon)

Mechanical contraception

Mechanical contraception involves using mechanical (physical) barriers to prevent sperm from reaching the egg. These barriers include:
- condoms (male condoms cover the penis, female condoms are placed in the vagina)
- diaphragms (which are dome-shaped rubber devices fitted into the vagina before intercourse)
- caps (small rigid rubber devices that cover the cervix)

Chemical contraception

Chemical contraception involves the use of spermicides or hormones.

Spermicides (substances that kill sperm) are normally used along with the mechanical methods of contraception.

Hormones such as progesterone and oestrogen prevent ovulation. These hormones may be taken in tablet form (the so-called 'pill') every day for the first 21 days in each menstrual cycle. They are not taken for the full cycle to allow one week for a 'false' menstruation to take place. Longer-acting hormones can be implanted under the skin or given by injection.

Hormonal contraceptives may produce side effects such as sickness, weight gain and headaches. More serious side effects include increased risk of blood clots, high blood pressure, heart disease and liver disorders.

42.13 *A variety of contraceptives*

Surgical contraception

Surgical methods of contraception involve sterilisation of the female and vasectomy for males. Both methods are difficult to reverse and so are considered to be permanent methods of contraception.

Female sterilisation involves cutting or tying (called tubal ligation) the Fallopian tubes so that sperm cannot reach an egg. In a vasectomy each vas deferens (sperm duct) in the male is cut. The male will continue to ejaculate but there are no sperm present in the semen.

Apart from never having sexual intercourse, sterilisation is the only method of contraception that is 100% guaranteed. All the other contraceptive methods have some level of failure.

Implantation

> **Implantation** is the embedding of the fertilised egg into the lining of the uterus.

Implantation happens about 6 to 9 days after fertilisation. By this time the zygote has grown to form an **embryo**.

During implantation a membrane called the amnion develops, around the embryo. The amnion secretes amniotic fluid, which will surround and protect the embryo (by acting as a shock absorber).

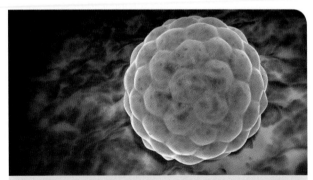

42.14 *Implantation: the blastocyst (pink) attaching to the lining of the uterus (orange-red)*

In vitro fertilisation and implantation

> ***In vitro*** **fertilisation (IVF)** involves removing eggs from an ovary and fertilising them outside the body.

IVF may be used for females whose Fallopian tubes are blocked or who fail to produce eggs naturally. It is also used to allow males with low sperm counts to have offspring.

In vitro fertilisation involves giving the female fertility drugs in the first week of her menstrual cycle. These drugs stimulate several eggs to develop.

On day 14 the eggs are surgically removed from the ovary. They are then mixed with sperm in a dish (often a glass petri dish is used). The term *in vitro* fertilisation (IVF) literally means fertilisation *in glass*. Two days later the eggs are examined microscopically to see if they have developed into embryos. If embryos have formed, a number of these embryos are put into the uterus to allow them to implant naturally.

The woman is checked regularly in the following days to ensure that implantation has occurred. Once implantation is successful the pregnancy normally proceeds in the usual way.

> **Did you know?**
>
> *Women treated with IVF often have multiple births (i.e. twins or triplets) because a number of the embryos implant and develop. Babies born as a result of IVF are often (wrongly) called test-tube babies. While fertilisation may take place 'in glass', the baby develops normally in the uterus for 9 months (exactly as naturally fertilised babies do).*

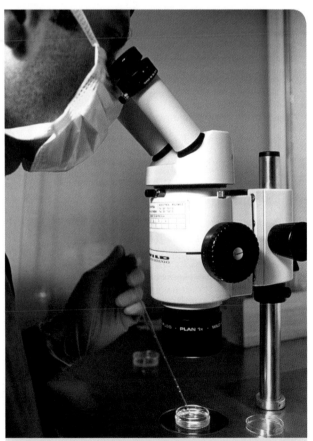

42.15 *In vitro fertilisation (IVF): embryos being selected for placement in the uterus*

THE ORGANISM

Placenta formation

1 Soon after implantation, the embryo forms an outer membrane called the chorion. This completely surrounds the amnion and the embryo.

The chorion develops large chorionic projections called villi which, together with the blood vessels of the mother in the endometrium, form the placenta.

The placenta becomes fully functional about three months into the pregnancy. The placenta is the only animal organ that is formed from the tissues of two different individuals (i.e. the embryo and the mother).

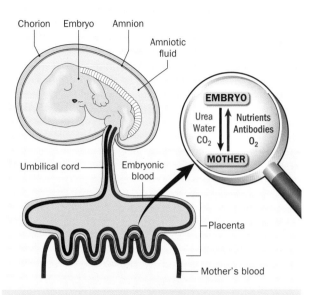

42.17 *Structure and function of the placenta*

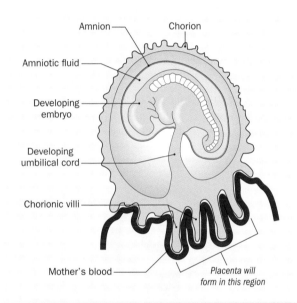

42.16 *Formation of the placenta*

2 The placenta allows gases, nutrients, waste, antibodies, drugs and some hormones and micro-organisms to be exchanged between the blood of the mother and of the embryo. The placenta also produces hormones.

3 The blood supplies of the mother and embryo do not mix. The separation of the two blood supplies is essential for two reasons.

Firstly, the blood groups might not be compatible, which would lead to damage to red blood cells. Secondly, the blood pressure of the mother's system would cause damage to the embryo.

4 The umbilical cord connects the embryo (at the navel) with the placenta. It contains blood vessels that take blood from the embryo out to the placenta and back to the embryo again.

Early development of zygote

1 The fertilised egg or zygote contains 46 chromosomes. Half of these are from the egg and half from the sperm. However, most of the cytoplasm in the zygote comes from the egg.

2 The zygote divides rapidly by a series of mitotic divisions to produce two cells, then four, eight, sixteen etc. cells.

After about 3 days, a solid clump of cells, called the **morula**, has formed.

A **morula** is a solid ball of cells formed from a zygote by mitosis.

3 Around 5 days after fertilisation, the morula forms a hollow ball of a few hundred cells called the **blastocyst**.

A **blastocyst** (or blastula) is a hollow ball of cells formed from a morula.

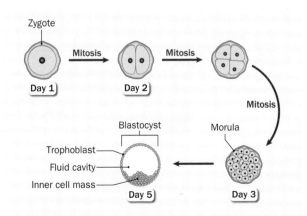

42.18 *Development of blastocyst*

The outer cells of the blastocyst form the tropho-blast. This will later form the membranes around the embryo. The inner cells of the blastocyst (called the inner cell mass) will later form the embryo (see Figure 42.18).

4 The blastocyst is pushed down the Fallopian tube into the uterus.

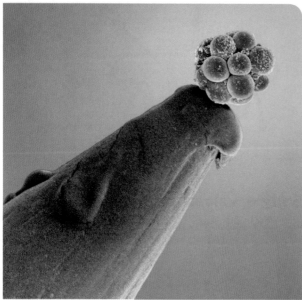

42.19 *SEM of 16-cell morula on the tip of a pin*

Did you know?

Stem cells are unspecialised (undifferentiated) cells that can give rise to many different types of tissue. They are found in the blastocyst (and also in red bone marrow and other places in the body). Research is ongoing into the use of stem cells to renew or repair damaged body parts.

42.20 *A four-day-old blastocyst (light microscope)*

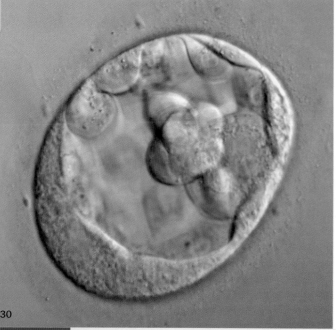

Embryonic development

1 About 10 days after fertilisation, the cells of the inner cell mass of the blastocyst form the embryonic disc. The cells of the disc give rise to three layers of cells called primary **germ layers**: the ectoderm, mesoderm and endoderm.

Germ layers are basic layers of cells in the blastocyst from which all adult tissues and organs will form.

Each germ layer gives rise to specific structures in the developing embryo. Animals (such as humans) that arise from three germ layers have more complex organ systems than those that arise from only two cell layers (e.g. jellyfish, which lack a mesoderm).

In humans, the middle layer of cells (the meso-derm) is divided into an outer and inner layer. The gap between them is called a coelom and it allows space for complex organs such as the heart, lungs and kidneys to develop.

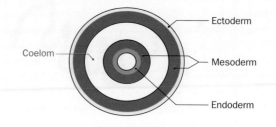

42.21 *The three germ layers of the embryo*

Each of the three germ layers gives rise to specific organs and systems in the developing embryo as shown in the following table.

Embryonic development	
Germ layer	**Organ or system produced**
Ectoderm	Skin, nails, hair, nervous system
Mesoderm	Muscles, skeleton, excretory system, respiratory system, circulatory system
Endoderm	Inner lining of digestive, respiratory and excretory systems; also the liver and pancreas

2 In the first 4 weeks after fertilisation, the heart forms and starts to beat in the embryo. The brain develops and the umbilical cord forms.

THE ORGANISM

3 By the 5th week, the internal organs and the limbs have started to form. The embryo is highly vulnerable to alcohol and drugs at this stage.

4 By the 6th week, the eyes are visible and the mouth, nose and ears are forming.

5 By the 8th week, the tail has diminished. The face is human and the major body organs are formed. Ovaries or testes are distinguishable. Bone is beginning to replace cartilage.

At this stage the embryo is recognisably human and is called a **foetus**.

6 From the 8th week onwards the foetus grows and refines the structures already formed. During the remainder of the pregnancy the foetus does not produce any more organs.

The last 7 months of the pregnancy involve the growth of the foetus (along with the enlargement of the mother's uterus and abdomen).

7 By the end of the third month (12 weeks) the eyes are low in the face and are widely spaced. Bones grow to replace cartilage (called ossification). The nerves and muscles become coordinated, allowing the arms and legs to move. The foetus sucks its thumb, kicks and forms milk teeth beneath the gums.

Although it is exchanging gases and excreting waste through the placenta, the foetus is seen to take amniotic fluid in and out of its mouth. It even urinates and releases faeces into the amniotic fluid.

At this stage the external sex organs have formed and the gender of the foetus can be seen in scans.

8 **Gestation** is the length of time spent in the uterus from fertilisation to birth.

In humans gestation lasts 266 days (38 weeks or 9 months) from the date of fertilisation.

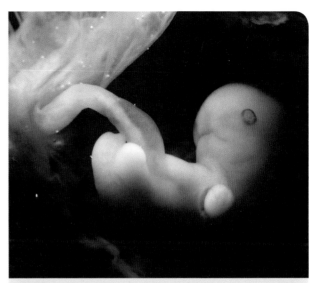

42.23 *A six-week-old human embryo: one eye (black) is visible, as are the arms, legs, umbilical cord and mouth*

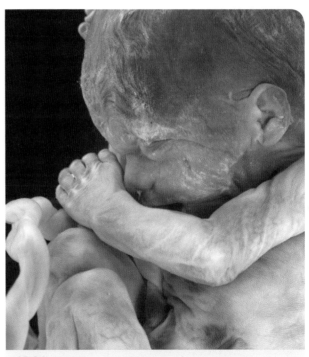

42.24 *A three-month-old human foetus: note the umbilical cord on the left*

THE ORGANISM

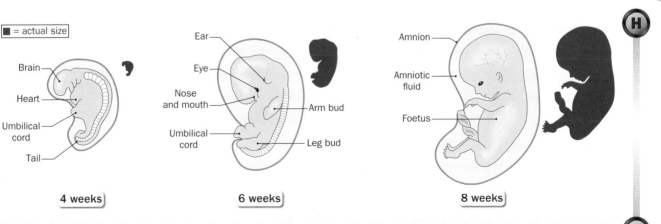

■ = actual size

4 weeks
- Brain
- Heart
- Umbilical cord
- Tail

6 weeks
- Ear
- Eye
- Nose and mouth
- Umbilical cord
- Arm bud
- Leg bud

8 weeks
- Amnion
- Amniotic fluid
- Foetus

42.22 *Development of the embryo*

Birth

1 Throughout pregnancy the hormones progesterone and oestrogen are produced in greater and greater amounts.

  For the first 10–12 weeks these hormones are made by the corpus luteum in the ovary of the mother. After 12 weeks they are made by the placenta, which means the placenta acts as an endocrine gland.

2 The factors that cause childbirth (also called parturition) to begin are not fully understood.

3 Immediately before birth the placenta stops producing progesterone. The walls of the uterus begin to contract when levels of progesterone are low.

4 At the same time, the pituitary gland of the mother produces a hormone called **oxytocin**. This causes contractions of the uterine muscle, resulting in the onset of labour. It is thought that many other hormones are involved in the onset of labour.

5 Labour begins when the uterus starts to contract involuntarily. Labour may be divided into three main stages.

6 **Stage 1** (normally lasts about 12 hours). The contractions of the uterus push the foetus down towards the cervix. A mucous plug that blocks the cervix is expelled, along with some blood. The membranes around the foetus break to allow the loss of about 1 litre of amniotic fluid from the vagina (the 'waters' are said to break).

7 **Stage 2** (normally lasts about 20 minutes to an hour). The cervix dilates (opens) enough to allow the baby to be born. The foetus is pushed out through the cervix and vagina of the mother, usually head first.

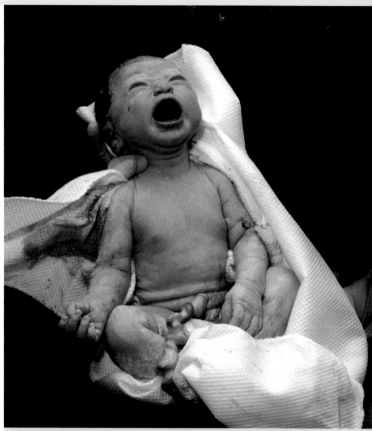

42.26 *Healthy newborn baby seconds after birth, before the umbilical cord has been cut*

The umbilical cord is still attached to the baby. The cord is clamped or tied (near the baby's body) and then cut. The baby is now independent of the mother.

8 **Stage 3.** Within 5 to 30 minutes of the birth, continuing uterine contractions expel the placenta and foetal membranes (called the afterbirth) from the mother.

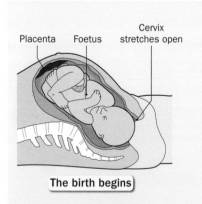

Placenta   Foetus   Cervix stretches open

The birth begins

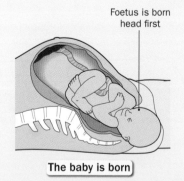

Foetus is born head first

The baby is born

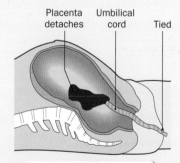

Placenta detaches   Umbilical cord   Tied

The afterbirth is expelled

42.25 *The process of birth*

THE ORGANISM

Lactation

Lactation is the secretion of milk by the mammary glands (breasts) of the female.

1. The breasts produce a thick, yellow fluid called colostrum for the first few days after birth. Mothers are encouraged to breast-feed, at least for a few days, because colostrum has less fat and sugar than breast milk, but is higher in minerals, proteins and antibodies. Colostrum helps to nourish the baby and provides protection against infection.

2. During pregnancy, progesterone prevents the production of a hormone called prolactin. Once the baby is born this inhibition is removed and the mother's pituitary gland produces **prolactin**.

   This hormone stimulates milk production. Prolactin (and therefore milk) continues to be produced as long as the baby breast-feeds.

3. Once breast-feeding stops, the breasts of the mother will soon cease to produce milk.

Biological benefits of breast-feeding

- Human milk contains the ideal balance of nutrients needed by the baby.
- Breast-feeding provides a continuing supply of antibodies in the milk produced by the mother. This means the baby has extra resistance to most common infections.
- Breast-feeding is safer for the baby, i.e. there is less danger of infection from micro-organisms than if bottles are used.
- It helps the mother's body to recover from the effects of pregnancy and birth. It does this by causing the uterus to contract and it may help her body to lose excess fat.
- It may help to reduce the risk of breast cancer in the mother.

42.27 *Mother breastfeeding her 2-week-old baby*

Summary

The male and female reproductive systems consist of:

- gamete-producing structures (ovaries and testes)
- gamete transport tubes
- hormone-secreting structures

The testes produce sperm and testosterone.

- Meiosis occurs in tubules in the testes. Haploid (23 chromosomes) sperm are produced.
- Cells between the tubules make testosterone.

The epididymis matures and stores sperm.

Sperm ducts carry sperm to the urethra in the penis.

The urethra allows the passage of either urine or sperm.

The associated glands (seminal vesicles, the prostate gland and Cowper's glands) produce seminal fluid that feeds the sperm and allows them to swim.

Sperm and seminal fluid form semen.

The male reproductive hormones are:

- **FSH**, which is made by the pituitary gland. It stimulates sperm production.
- **LH**, which is also made by the pituitary gland. It causes testosterone production to increase greatly.
- **Testosterone** causes:
  - the primary male characteristics (growth of penis and descent of testes from body cavity)
  - the secondary male characteristics (increased body hair, enlargement of the larynx, muscle and bone growth)

Infertility is the inability to produce offspring.

Male infertility:

- can be due to the production of low numbers of sperm
- can be caused by lack of hormones, smoking, drugs, mumps or chemicals
- can be treated by hormones or by treating the cause (smoking, alcohol or drugs) or by *in vitro* fertilisation

Puberty is the onset of sexual maturity (about 11 or 12 years of age in females and 12 or 13 in males).

The menopause is the time at which the reproductive life of a female ends.

After puberty, the ovary produces eggs and female hormones.

Each month the ovary allows one potential egg to mature (by meiosis) into an egg (ovum).

The egg is enclosed in a Graafian follicle, which makes oestrogen.

Ovulation is the release of an egg from the Graafian follicle in the ovary.

After ovulation, the empty follicle becomes the corpus luteum, which makes progesterone and some oestrogen.

The funnel of the Fallopian tube catches the egg; then cilia and muscles push it along the tube.

The uterus is a muscular structure with a spongy lining (called the endometrium) that is enriched with blood vessels to nourish the embryo.

The vagina allows the entry of sperm and the exit of the baby at birth.

The events of an average menstrual (monthly) cycle are:

- **Days 1–5**: Menstruation (loss of old endometrium). Meiosis occurs in the ovary, forming a new egg in the Graafian follicle.
- **Days 6–14**: The endometrium thickens (due to oestrogen).
- **Day 14**: Ovulation (i.e. an egg is released from the Graafian follicle in the ovary).
- **Days 14–28**: The endometrium continues to develop; the egg dies by day 16 if it is not fertilised.

If fertilisation does not occur, the cycle starts again.

Increased oestrogen at puberty causes the growth of the female sex organs (primary female traits).

Oestrogen and progesterone also cause the following effects:

- In the menstrual cycle they both cause the development of the endometrium and they both inhibit egg formation.
- At puberty they cause secondary female traits such as breast enlargement, widening of the pelvis, increase in body fat, body growth and production of body hair.

Female infertility (inability to produce offspring):

- is often due to the failure to release an egg from the ovary (ovulate)
- can be caused by hormonal imbalance, stress or a tumour on the ovary
- is treated by hormones, relieving stress or surgical removal of the tumour. *In vitro* fertilisation is sometimes used

Hormonal control in the menstrual cycle involves four hormones:

- FSH is made by the pituitary gland between days 1 and 5. It stimulates egg development.
- Oestrogen is made by the Graafian follicle on days 5 to 14. It causes the endometrium to develop, inhibits secretion of FSH, and high concentrations of oestrogen stimulate secretion of LH.
- LH is made by the pituitary on day 14. It stimulates ovulation and causes the corpus luteum to form.

(continued)

THE ORGANISM

- Progesterone and oestrogen are made by the corpus luteum on days 14 to 28. They continue the enlargement of the endometrium, inhibit the secretion of FSH and LH, and inhibit uterine contraction.
- If pregnancy has not occurred approaching day 28, the lack of progesterone allows contractions of the uterus (resulting in menstruation) and FSH to be formed (resulting in a new egg).

Fibroids are benign tumours of the uterus.

Fibroids:
- are of unknown cause (although they may be associated with oestrogen)
- produce no symptoms when small but cause heavy and prolonged periods, pain, miscarriage or infertility if they are large
- are not treated if they are small but are removed by surgery when they are large

The stages in copulation are:
- sexual arousal, which causes the penis to become erect and the vagina to enlarge and produce lubricants
- copulation (sexual intercourse)
- orgasm, which is the climax of sexual excitement
- ejaculation, which is the emitting of semen from the penis

Insemination is the release of sperm (semen) into the female.

Sperm are pushed (and swim) to an egg (if one is present) in the Fallopian tube.

Fertilisation is the union of the sperm and egg nuclei to produce a diploid zygote.

Birth control involves taking steps to reduce the number of children born. This includes:
- abortion (the termination of a pregnancy)
- contraception (using methods to prevent fertilisation)

Contraceptive methods include:
- natural methods, i.e. intercourse is avoided at times in the menstrual cycle when it may result in fertilisation
- mechanical methods use physical barriers to stop sperm and eggs from uniting
- chemical methods use chemicals to kill sperm or hormones to prevent ovulation
- surgical methods involve closing the Fallopian tubes or sperm ducts (sterilisation)

Implantation is the burrowing of the fertilised egg into the endometrium.

The placenta separates the blood of the embryo and mother.

The functions of the placenta include the exchange of materials between the embryo and mother. These include:
- oxygen, food, antibodies, drugs, some hormones and micro-organisms entering the embryo
- carbon dioxide, salts and urea entering the mother

Embryonic development includes (length of time since fertilisation given in brackets):
- rapid mitosis to form a solid ball of cells, called a morula (3 days)
- the formation of a hollow blastocyst (day 5)
- implantation, which is the burrowing of the blastocyst into the endometrium (day 7)
- the blastocyst forms three germ layers (day 10)
- each germ layer forms specific structures in the embryo
- the outer wall of the blastocyst (trophoblast) forms the chorion, which surrounds the embryo and the amnion (day 10)
- the heart, brain and umbilical cord form (by the 4th week)
- the chorion and the mother's blood vessels in the endometrium make the placenta (about 5th week)
- internal organs start to form (5th week)
- by the 8th week, all the organs and systems are formed. The shape is now recognisably human and the embryo is called a foetus
- by the 12th week bones are replacing cartilage; the foetus sucks its thumb and kicks its legs
- For the rest of the pregnancy (up to the 38th week), the foetus grows in size.

Gestation is the length of time spent in the uterus from fertilisation to birth (38 weeks or 9 months).

Birth (or parturition) has three stages:
- **Stage 1:** Contractions of the uterus push the head of the foetus towards the cervix. The amnion bursts and amniotic fluid is released.
- **Stage 2:** The head of the baby is forced out through the vagina.
- **Stage 3:** The afterbirth (placenta and foetal membranes) are expelled from the vagina.

The main hormones at birth are:
- a sudden drop in the level of progesterone, which allows the uterus to contract
- oxytocin (produced by the pituitary of the mother), which stimulates uterus contractions

Lactation is the production of milk by the mother's breasts. It is stimulated by breast-feeding.

Prolactin (produced by the pituitary of the mother after the birth of the child) stimulates milk production.

THE ORGANISM

Revision questions

1 (a) Name the parts labelled A to H in Figure 42.28 of the male reproductive system.

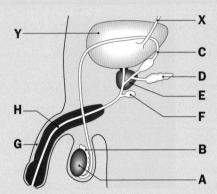

42.28

(b) Structure A is kept at a different temperature to body temperature.
   (i) State the ideal temperature for structure A.
   (ii) Why is this temperature necessary?
(c) Name four labelled parts that help to make semen.
(d) Name two liquids that can pass through part H.
(e) Name and give the functions of parts X and Y.
2 State three differences between a sperm and a normal body cell.
3 Give one function for each of the following:
   (a) the acrosome
   (b) prostate gland
   (c) testes
   (d) the epididymis
   (e) seminal fluid.
4 (a) Name two hormones made by the pituitary gland in the male at puberty
   (b) State one function for each of the named hormones.
5 (a) Draw a diagram of a sperm and label four major parts.
   (b) Give one function for each part named.
6 (a) Distinguish between primary and secondary male traits.
   (b) Name the hormone responsible for these traits.
7 (a) What is meant by infertility?
   (b) Name one type of male infertility.
   (c) Suggest two causes for your answer to part (b) of this question.
   (d) How may this disorder be treated?
8 State **(a)** two similarities, and **(b)** two differences between an egg and a sperm.

9 (a) Name the parts labelled A to G in the side view of the female reproductive system (Fig. 42.29).

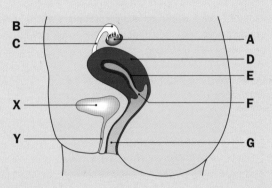

42.29

(b) (i) In which labelled part does meiosis occur?
   (ii) What does meiosis produce?
   (iii) Name two other substances produced in the same labelled part.
(c) Name and give the functions of the structures labelled X and Y.
10 (a) What is meant by the term menstrual cycle?
   (b) State one important event that occurs on the following days in a typical cycle: **(i)** day 1, **(ii)** day 14, **(iii)** day 28.
   (c) Name a hormone associated with: **(i)** days 5 to 14, **(ii)** days 14 to 28.
11 (a) State one function common to oestrogen and progesterone in the menstrual cycle.
   (b) Name the hormone that causes the primary female traits.
   (c) What hormones cause the secondary female traits?
   (d) Name three of these traits.
12 (a) State one type of female infertility.
   (b) State two possible causes for this type of infertility.
   (c) Outline two possible treatments for the disorder named.
13 Figure 42.30 shows the changes taking place in the reproductive system of a female over 28 days.
   (a) What name is given to the events of the 28 days shown?
   (b) What name is given to what happens to the lining of the uterus from days 1 to 5?
   (c) What structure causes oestrogen production up to day 14?
   (d) Name the event occuring in the Graafian follicle on day 14.
   (e) Why does the level of oestrogen fall just after day 14?
   (f) What structure makes progesterone after day 14?

(continued)

THE ORGANISM

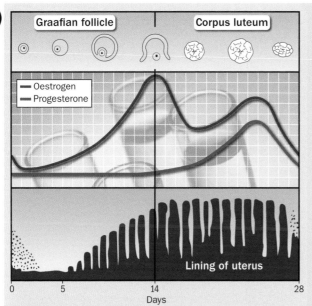

42.30

(g) Why does the level of progesterone fall just before day 28?

(h) What effect does this fall have on the lining of the uterus?

(i) Does this diagram indicate that pregnancy has occurred? Explain your answer.

14 (a) Name the four hormones involved in the menstrual cycle in the order in which they are produced.

(b) State the approximate days on which each hormone is produced.

(c) Outline two effects of each hormone within the cycle.

15 (a) Name one menstrual disorder.

(b) Suggest how the named example may affect the menstrual cycle.

(c) Suggest a treatment for this disorder.

16 (a) What do you understand by: (i) copulation, (ii) insemination, (iii) fertilisation, (iv) implantation?

(b) Draw a diagram of the female reproductive system to show the location of events (ii), (iii) and (iv) above.

17 List eight structures through which sperm must pass from where they are produced to where fertilisation takes place.

18 List three structures through which the egg must pass from where it is made to where fertilisation takes place.

19 State the normal survival times for (a) sperm in the female system, (b) an egg after ovulation.

20 (a) Name the normal location in the female reproductive system for fertilisation.

(b) State the events that occur from the time the sperm reaches an egg until fertilisation takes place.

21 (a) Distinguish between abortion and contraception.

(b) Give one example from each of the following categories of contraception and state how your named example works: (i) natural, (ii) mechanical, (iii) hormonal, (iv) surgical.

(c) Which of your named examples is foolproof in preventing fertilisation?

22 Explain the terms: (a) gamete, (b) zygote, (c) morula, (d) blastocyst, (e) trophoblast, (f) amnion, (g) chorion and (h) germ layer

23 (a) Name the three primary (germ) layers from which humans develop.

(b) Name two structures produced by each layer.

24 (a) What is *in vitro* fertilisation?

(b) Why is it given this name?

(c) Name two disorders that it is used to treat.

25 In carrying out *in vitro* fertilisation:

(a) Why is the female given hormonal treatment in advance?

(b) Why are several eggs removed from the ovary?

(c) Why are the fertilised eggs put back into the uterus?

(d) Why does the procedure often result in the birth of more than one baby?

26 (a) Name the parts labelled A to G in Figure 42.31.

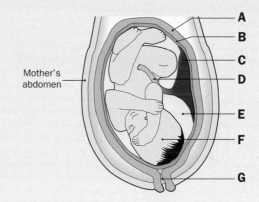

Mother's abdomen

42.31

(b) Who makes the part labelled C?

(c) What is the function of the liquid labelled E?

(d) To what part of the foetus does structure D attach?

(e) What flows through part D?

27 'The placenta acts as the foetal lungs and digestive system.' Explain this statement.

28 (a) Name three substances in each case that pass in the following directions: (i) from the foetus to the mother's blood, (ii) from the mother's blood to the foetus.

(b) Name two harmful substances that could pass from the mother to the foetus.

29 State two reasons why the blood of the mother and foetus should not mix.

30 Give a reason why the placenta can be considered to be an endocrine gland.

THE ORGANISM

31 State two hormonal changes that occur in a mother just before childbirth.

32 Suggest why breast-fed babies should get fewer infections than bottle-fed babies.

33 **(a)** What is colostrum?
   (b) What hormone causes milk production?
   (c) What causes this hormone to be produced?
   (d) For how long is this hormone produced?

34 **(a)** Name the hormone that prevents menstruation during pregnancy.
   (b) Name the structures that produce this hormone during pregnancy.
   (c) Explain the role of this hormone at the end of pregnancy.

35 Choose which of the options (i), (ii), (iii) or (iv) represents the correct answer in each case below.
   (a) After the 8th week of pregnancy, the baby is called:
      (i) an embryo
      (ii) a foetus
      (iii) a zygote
      (iv) a blastocyst

(b) Oxytocin is a hormone that causes:
   (i) ovulation
   (ii) meiosis
   (iii) labour
   (iv) milk production

(c) The structure that matures and stores sperm is the:
   (i) testis
   (ii) epididymis
   (iii) scrotum
   (iv) sperm duct

(d) In males, FSH is the hormone that is responsible for:
   (i) mitosis
   (ii) meiosis
   (iii) ejaculation
   (iv) secondary male features

(e) The lungs of the developing baby arise from cells in this layer:
   (i) endoderm
   (ii) periderm
   (iii) mesoderm
   (iv) ectoderm

Sample examination questions

Section A

36 The diagram shows the reproductive system of a human female.

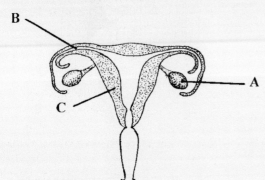

(a) Name parts A, B and C.
(b) In which of the parts A, B or C is the ovum (egg) formed?
(c) What is meant by fertilisation?
(d) In which of the parts A, B or C does fertilisation occur?
(e) Give one cause of female infertility.

(2006 OL Q 5)

37 The diagram shows the female reproductive system.
(a) Identify parts A, B and C.

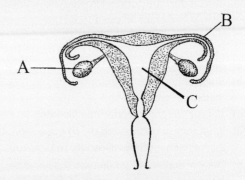

(b) Using the letters X, Y and Z and arrows, identify each of the following on the diagram: endometrium **(X)**, where fertilisation normally occurs **(Y)**, where meiosis occurs **(Z)**.
(c) Which part of the system is influenced by both FSH and LH?
(d) Give **two** biological advantages of breast-feeding.

(2008 HL Q 6)

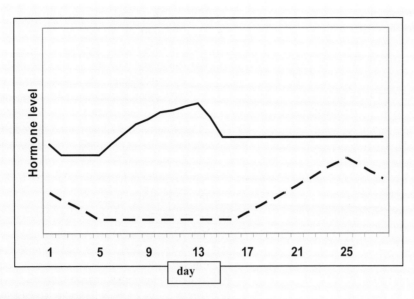

A _____

B _ _ _ _

38 The graphs above illustrate changes in the levels of two hormones, A and B, which are involved in the development of the endometrium, during the human female menstrual cycle.

(a) Name one of these hormones.

(b) What happens in the ovary around day 14 of the cycle?

(c) Apart from the two hormones illustrated, another hormone called FSH has a role in the cycle.
   (i) Where is FSH produced?
   (ii) Give one function of FSH.

(d) Which graph, A or B, represents the hormone secreted by the corpus luteum (yellow body)?

(e) Draw a line graph in the space above A and B to illustrate the changes that take place in the thickness of the endometrium over the course of the cycle.

(2007 HL Q 4)

Section C

39 (i) Draw a large labelled diagram of the reproductive system of the human female.

(ii) Indicate on your diagram where each of the following events takes place: fertilisation, implantation.

(iii) What is the menstrual cycle? Outline the main events of the menstrual cycle.

(2005 OL Q 14b)

40 (a) What are secondary sexual characteristics? Give an example of a human secondary sexual characteristic.

(b) The diagram (above right) shows the reproductive system of the human male.
   (i) Name the parts A, B, C, D, E.
   (ii) Where are sperm produced?
   (iii) What is the function of the prostate gland?
   (iv) State **one** way in which a sperm differs from an ovum (egg).

(continued)

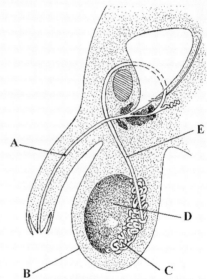

(c) (i) What is meant by infertility? State **one** cause of infertility in the human male.
   (ii) Name **three** methods of contraception and, in each case, explain how the method prevents conception.

(2004 OL Q 11)

41 (a) (i) Draw a labelled diagram of the reproductive system of the human female.
   (ii) What is fertilisation? Indicate where fertilisation normally occurs on your diagram.
   (iii) State **one** cause of infertility in the female and **one** cause of infertility in the male.
   (iv) What is meant by *in vitro* fertilisation? What is done with the products of *in vitro* fertilisation?

(b) Answer the following questions from your knowledge of human embryology.
   (i) What is a germ layer? List the **three** germ layers.
   (ii) Relate each of the germ layers that you have listed in **(i)** to an organ or system in the adult body.

(continued)

(iii) From what structures does the placenta develop? State **three** functions of the placenta.

(iv) Name a hormone associated with the maintenance of the placenta.

(v) Describe the amnion and state its role.

(2004 HL Q 14)

42 (a) (i) Where is testosterone secreted in the body of the human male?

(ii) Give a brief account of the role of testosterone.

(b) (i) Draw a large, labelled diagram of the reproductive system of the human male.

(ii) Where are sperm produced?

(iii) State **two** ways in which sperm differ from ova (eggs).

(iv) Name a gland that secretes seminal fluid.

(v) State a function of seminal fluid.

(c) (i) What is meant by contraception?

(ii) Give an example of a surgical method of male contraception. Suggest an advantage and a disadvantage of the method that you have named.

(continued)

(iii) List **three** methods of contraception other than surgical. In your answer you may refer to either or both sexes.

(iv) Suggest a possible effect on a human population that may result from an increased availability of contraception.

(2005 HL Q 13)

43 (i) Draw a detailed diagram of the reproductive system of the human male. Label the following parts on your diagram: testis, seminal vesicle, urethra, sperm duct (vas deferens), epididymis, prostate gland.

(ii) Place an X on your diagram where meiosis occurs.

(iii) Place a Y on your diagram where sperm are stored.

(iv) State two functions of testosterone.

(v) Give a cause of male infertility and suggest a corrective measure.

(2007 HL Q 15a)

Previous examination questions

Ordinary level	Higher level
2004 Q 11	2004 Q 14
2005 Q 14b	2005 Q 13
2006 Q 5	2006 Q 15c
	2007 Q 4, 15a
	2008 Q 6

*For latest questions go to **www.edco.ie/biology***

Glossary

abiotic factors non-living factors. *page 27*

abortion termination of a pregnancy. *page 427*

active immunity the production of a person's own antibodies in response to antigens that enter the body. *page 381*

active site the part of an enzyme that combines with the substrate. *page 103*

active transport where energy is used to move molecules, often against a concentration gradient, i.e. from low concentrations to high concentrations. *page 320*

adaptation any alteration that improves an organism's chances of survival and reproduction. *page 68*

alleles different forms of the same gene. *page 174*

all or nothing law states that if the threshold is reached an impulse is carried, but if the threshold is not reached no impulse is carried. *page 340*

anabolic reactions convert smaller molecules into larger ones. *page 20*

antagonistic pair two muscles that have opposite effects to each other. *page 373*

antibiotics chemicals produced by micro-organisms that stop the growth of, or kill, other micro-organisms without damaging human tissue. *page 223*

antibody a protein produced by white blood cells (called lymphocytes) in response to an antigen. *page 380*

antigen a foreign molecule that stimulates the production of antibodies. *page 380*

artificial active immunity occurs when a pathogen is medically introduced into the body. *page 381*

artificial passive immunity occurs when a person is given an injection containing antibodies made by another organism. *page 382*

aseptic or **asepsis** measures taken to exclude unwanted micro-organisms. *page 234*

asexual reproduction involves only one parent. *page 393*

autotrophic (organism) one that makes its own food. *page 221*

bacteriophage (or phage) a virus that infects bacteria. *page 389*

biology the study of living things. *page 2*

biomolecules chemicals that are made inside a living thing. *page 14*

bioprocessing the use of enzyme-controlled reactions to produce a product. *page 98*

bioreactor vessel or container in which living cells or their products are used to make a product. *page 98*

biosphere the part of the planet containing living organisms. *page 26*

biotechnology the use of living things or their components (especially cells and enzymes) to manufacture useful products or to carry out useful reactions. *page 122*

biotic factors living factors. *page 27*

birth control methods taken to limit the number of children that are born. *page 427*

blastocyst (or blastula) hollow ball of cells formed from a morula. *page 429*

blood pressure the force the blood exerts against the wall of a blood vessel. *page 273*

bulb modified bud. *page 415*

cancer a group of disorders in which certain cells lose their ability to control both the rate of mitosis and the number of times mitosis takes place. *page 144*

carnivores animals that feed on other animals. They are often called flesh-eaters, e.g. dogs, cats, seals. *page 289*

carpels the female parts of the flower. *page 394*

catabolic reaction one in which a complex molecule is broken down to simpler ones. *page 20*

catalyst substance that speeds up a reaction, without itself being used up in the reaction. *page 94*

cell continuity means that all cells develop from pre-existing cells. *page 140*

characteristics = heredity + environment *page 152*

chemotropism a change in growth of a plant in response to chemicals. *page 328*

chromatin the name given to chromosomes when they are not dividing. *page 80*

chromosomes coiled threads of DNA (which forms genes) and protein that become visible in the nucleus at cell division. *page 140*

chromosome mutations large changes in the structure or number of one or more chromosomes. *page 198*

climatic factors weather over a long period of time. *page 27*

community all the different populations in an area. *page 27*

competition where organisms actively struggle for a resource that is in short supply. *page 45*
- **contest competition** an active physical contest between two individual organisms. *page 45*
- **scramble competition** where all of the competing individuals get some of the resource. *page 45*

conservation the wise management of our existing natural resources, in order to maintain a wide range of habitats and prevent the death and extinction of organisms. *page 36*

consumers organisms that take in food from another organism. *page 30*

continuity of life means that living things arise from other living things of the same type. This is also called **biogenesis**. *page 11*

contraception the deliberate prevention of fertilisation or pregnancy. *page 427*

control a standard against which the actual experiment can be judged. *page 5*

cross-pollination the transfer of pollen from an anther to a stigma on a different plant of the same species. *page 396*

data the measurements, observations or information gathered from experiments. *page 3*

denatured enzyme one that has lost its shape and can no longer carry out its function. *pages 95, 104*

denitrification the conversion of nitrates to nitrogen gas. *page 34*

dental formula

$$2 \left(I\frac{2}{2} \ C\frac{1}{1} \ PM\frac{2}{2} \ M\frac{3}{3} \right)$$ *page 290*

diastole when heart chambers relax. *page 279*

diffusion the spreading out of molecules from a region of high concentration to a region of low concentration. *page 133*

diploid cell one that has two sets of chromosomes, i.e. it has two of each type of chromosome in the nucleus. *page 141*

dispersal the transfer of a seed or fruit away from the parent plant. *page 401*

DNA profiling (also called DNA or genetic fingerprinting) a method of making a unique pattern of bands from the DNA of a person, which can then be used to distinguish that DNA from other DNA. *page 161*

dominant means that the allele prevents the working of the recessive allele. *page 174*

dormancy a resting period when seeds undergo no growth and have reduced cell activity or metabolism. *page 402*

ecological niche (of an organism) the functional role it plays in the community. *page 32*

ecology the study of the interactions between living things (organisms) and between organisms and their environment. *page 26*

ecosystem a group of clearly distinguished organisms that interact with their environment as a unit. *page 26*

ectotherms gain or lose heat from or to their external environment. *page 314*

edaphic factors soil factors such as the soil pH, soil type and the moisture, air and mineral content of soil. *page 27*

ejaculation is the release of semen from the penis. *page 421*

endocrine gland a ductless gland that produces hormones which are released directly into the bloodstream. *page 358*

endospermic seed contains some endosperm when fully formed. *page 399*

endotherms generate their own heat from metabolic reactions. *page 314*

enzymes proteins that speed up a reaction without being used up in the reaction. *page 94*

eukaryotic cells have a nucleus and cell organelles, all of which are enclosed by membranes. *page 82*

evolution the way in which living things change genetically to produce new forms of life over long periods of time. *page 199*

excretion the removal of waste products of metabolism from the body. *page 12*

exocrine glands release their product into ducts or tubes. *page 358*

fertilisation the union of the male and female gametes to form a diploid zygote. *pages 174, 398, 426*

food chain (grazing food chain) a sequence of organisms in which each one is eaten by the next member in the chain. *page 30*

food web two or more interlinked food chains. *page 31*

gametes haploid cells capable of fusion or fertilisation. *pages 174, 393*

gene section of DNA that causes the production of a protein. *page 152*

gene expression the precise way in which the genetic information in a gene is decoded in the cell and used to make a protein. *page 152*

gene (or **point**) **mutations** changes in a single gene. *page 197*

general defence system acts as a barrier to all pathogens attempting to gain entry to the human body. *page 378*

genetic engineering the artificial manipulation or alteration of genes. *page 204*

genetic screening testing DNA for the presence or absence of a particular gene or an altered gene. *page 164*

genotype the genetic make-up of an organism, i.e. the genes that are present. *page 174*

genotype + environment = phenotype *page 175*

geotropism (or gravitropism) change in growth of a plant in response to gravity. *page 328*

germination the regrowth of the embryo, after a period of dormancy, if the environmental conditions are suitable. *page 403*

germ layers basic layers of cells in the blastocyst from which all adult tissues and organs will form. *page 430*

gestation the length of time spent in the uterus from fertilisation to birth. *page 431*

gonad organ that produces sex cells in animals. *page 420*

growth regulator a chemical that controls the growth of a plant. *page 329*

habitat place where a plant or animal lives. *page 27*

haploid cell one that has one set of chromosomes, i.e. it has only one of each type of chromosome in the nucleus. *page 140*

herbaceous (plants) those that do not contain wood (or lignin). **woody (plants)** those that contain wood (or lignin). *page 243*

herbivores animals that feed exclusively on plants, e.g. cattle, sheep, deer. *page 289*

heredity the passing on of features from parents to offspring by means of genes. *page 152*

heterotrophic (organism) one that takes in food made by other organisms. *page 221*

heterozygous means that the alleles are different. *page 175*

homeostasis the ability of an organism to maintain a constant internal environment. *page 302*

homologous pair two chromosomes that each have genes for the same features at the same positions. *page 141*

homozygous two alleles that are the same. *page 175*

hormone a chemical messenger produced by an endocrine gland and carried by the bloodstream to another part of the body where it has a specific effect. *page 358*

hydrotropism a change in growth of a plant in response to water. *page 328*

hypha a tube or filament in a fungus. *page 231*

hypothesis educated guess based on observations. *page 3*

immobilised enzymes are attached, or fixed, to each other, or to an inert material. *page 98*

immunity the ability to resist infection. *page 378*

implantation the embedding of the fertilised egg into the lining of the uterus. *page 428*

incomplete dominance neither allele is dominant or recessive with respect to the other. Both alleles work in the heterozygous genotype to produce an intermediate phenotype. *page 177*

induced immunity the ability to resist disease caused by specific pathogens by the production of antibodies. *page 381*

infertility the inability to produce offspring. *page 422*

insemination the relese of semen into the vagina, just outside the cervix. *page 426*

interphase the phase in the cell cycle when the cell is not dividing. *page 141*

inter-specific competition occurs between members of different species. *page 45*

intra-specific competition occurs between members of the same species. *page 45*

in-vitro fertilisation (IVF) removing eggs from an ovary and fertilising them outside the body. *page 428*

lactation the secretion of milk by the mammary glands (breasts) of the female. *page 433*

law arises from a theory that has been shown to be valid when fully tested over a long period of time. *page 4*

law of independent assortment states that:
■ when gametes are formed...
■ either of a pair of factors...
■ is equally likely...
■ to combine with either of another pair of factors. *page 181*

law of segregation (Mendel's first law) states that:
■ Inherited characteristics are controlled by pairs of factors.
■ These factors segregate (or separate) from each other at gamete formation, with only one member of the pair being found in each gamete. *page 180*

lenticels openings in the stems of plants that allow gas exchange. *page 260*

life the possession of all the following characteristics: organised, requiring nutrition and excretion, capable of responding and reproducing. *page 11*

ligaments strong, fibrous, slightly elastic tissues that connect bone to bone. *page 372*

linkage means that genes are located on the same chromosome. *page 184*

locus (of a gene) its position on a chromosome. *page 174*

meiosis form of nuclear division in which the four daughter nuclei contain half the chromosome number of the parent nucleus. *page 145*

menstrual cycle a series of events that occurs every 28 days on average in the female if fertilisation has not taken place. *page 423*

meristem plant tissue capable of mitosis. *page 243*

metabolism the sum of all the chemical reactions in an organism. *page 10*

mitosis form of nuclear division in which one nucleus divides to form two nuclei, each containing the same number of chromosomes with identical genes. *page 142*

morula solid ball of cells formed from a zygote by mitosis. *page 429*

mutagens agents that cause mutations. *page 197*

mutation change in the amount or structure of DNA. *page 196*

mycelium (usually) a visible mass of hyphae. *page 231*

natural active immunity occurs when a pathogen enters the body in the normal way. *page 381*

natural passive immunity occurs when a child gets antibodies from its mother. *page 382*

natural selection the process by which those organisms with genetically controlled characteristics that allow them to be well adapted to their environments will survive and reproduce to pass on their genes to following generations. *page 200*

neuron (or neurone) a nerve cell. *page 338*

nitrification the conversion of ammonia and ammonium (NH_4^+) compounds to nitrite and then to nitrate. *page 34*

nitrogen fixation the conversion of nitrogen gas into ammonia (NH_3), ammonium (NH_4^+) or nitrate (NO_3^-). *page 34*

non-endospermic seed has no endosperm when fully formed. *page 399*

nutrient recycling the way in which elements (such as carbon and nitrogen) are exchanged between the living and non-living components of an ecosystem. *page 32*

nutrition the way organisms obtain and use food. *page 11*

omnivores animals that feed on plants and animals, e.g. humans, bears, badgers. *page 289*

organ a structure composed of a number of tissues that work together to carry out one or more functions. *page 89*

organisation means that living things are composed of cells, tissues, organs and organ systems. *page 11*

organism a living thing. *page 2*

organ system a number of organs working together to carry out one or more functions. *page 90*

osmosis the movement of water molecules across a semi-permeable membrane from a region of high water concentration to a region of low water concentration. *page 133*

ovulation the release of an egg from the ovary. *page 422*

parasites organisms that take in food from a live host and usually cause harm. *page 221*

parasitism when two organisms of different species live in close association and one organism (the **parasite**) obtains its food from, and to the disadvantage of, the second organism (the **host**). *page 46*

passive immunity occurs when individuals are given antibodies that were formed by another organism. *page 382*

pathogen micro-organism that causes disease. *page 223, 378*

phenotype the physical make-up, or appearance, of an organism. *page 174*

phenotype = genotype + environment *page 175*

phospholipids fat-like substances where one of the fatty acids is replaced by a phosphate group or has a phosphate group added to it. *page 17*

photosynthesis is represented and defined by the balanced equation:

$$6CO_2 + 6H_2O + light \xrightarrow{chlorophyll} C_6H_{12}O_6 + 6O_2$$
(carbon dioxide) (water) (glucose) (oxygen)

phototropism the change in growth of a plant in response to light, usually from one direction (i.e. unidirectional light). *page 328*

pollination the transfer of pollen from an anther to a stigma of a flower from the same species. *page 396*

pollutants substances that cause pollution. *page 35*

pollution any harmful addition to the environment. *page 35*

population all the members of the same species living in an area. *page 27*

portal system a blood pathway that begins and ends in capillaries. *page 277*

predation the catching, killing and eating of another organism. *page 46*

predator an organism that catches, kills and eats another organisim. *page 46*

prey organism that is eaten by a predator. *page 46*

principle arises from a theory that has been shown to be valid when fully tested over a long period of time. *page 4*

producers organisms that carry out photosynthesis. *page 30*

product substance(s) formed by an enzyme. *page 94*

progeny offspring that are produced. *page 175*

prokaryotic cells do not have a nucleus or membrane-enclosed organelles. *page 82*

protoplasm all the living parts of a cell. *page 77*

pulse the alternate expansion and contraction of the arteries. *page 280*

pyramid of numbers representation of the number of organisms at each trophic level (or stage) in a food chain. *page 32*

qualitative study record of the presence or absence of something. *page 60*

quantitative study record of the numbers or amounts that are present. *page 60*

recessive means the allele is prevented from working by a dominant allele. *page 174*

reflex action an automatic, involuntary, unthinking response to a stimulus. *page 345*

refractory period short timespan after a neuron has carried an impulse during which a stimulus fails to cause a response. *page 341*

replicate a repeat of an experiment. *page 6*

reproduction the production of new individuals. *page 12*

respiration
- **aerobic respiration** the controlled release of energy from food using oxygen. *page 118*
- **anaerobic respiration** the controlled release of energy from food without the use of oxygen. *page 119*

response the activity of a cell or organism as a result of a stimulus. *page 327*

response the way in which all living things react to changes (called **stimuli**) in their environment or surroundings. *page 12*

root tuber a swollen, underground root that remains dormant during winter and from which new plants may grow. *page 414*

runners (e.g. on strawberries and buttercups) horizontal stems that run (or grow) above ground and from which new plants grow. *page 414*

saprophytes organisms that take in food from dead organic matter. *page 221*

scientific method a process of investigation in which problems are identified and their suggested explanations are tested by carrying out experiments. *page 2*

secondary sexual characteristics those features that distinguish males from females, apart from the sex organs themselves. *page 421*

selectively permeable membrane allows some but not all substances to pass through. *page 133*

self-pollination the transfer of pollen from an anther to a stigma on the same plant. *page 396*

sex linkage means that a characteristic is controlled by a gene on an X chromosome. *page 187*

sexual reproduction the union of two sex cells or gametes. *page 393*

species a group of similar organisms that are capable of naturally interbreeding with each other, but not with other such groups, to produce fertile offspring. *page 151*

specific defence system attacks particular (or specific) pathogens. *page 379*

sporulation the process of making spores. *page 232*

stamens the male parts of a flower. *page 393*

sterile means that all micro-organisms are destroyed, i.e. there is nothing living. *page 234*

stimulus (plural stimuli) anything that causes a reaction in an organism or in any of its parts. *page 327*

substrate the substance with which an enzyme reacts. *page 94*

symbiosis occurs when two organisms of different species live (and have to live) in close association and at least one of them benefits. *page 47*

synapse a region where two neurons come into close contact. *page 341*

synaptic cleft the tiny gap between the two neurons at a synapse. *page 341*

systole when the heart chambers contract. *page 279*

tendons strong, flexible, inelastic fibres that connect muscle to bone. *page 372*

theory a hypothesis that has been supported by many different experiments. *page 4*

thigmotropism change in growth of a plant in response to touch. *page 328*

threshold the minimum stimulus needed to cause an impulse to be carried. *page 340*

tissue culture the growth of cells in or on a sterile nutrient medium outside an organism. *page 87*

tissue group of similar cells that are modified (or adapted) to carry out the same function(s). *page 86*

transcription the copying of a sequence of genetic bases from DNA onto messenger RNA (mRNA). *page 166*

translation the conversion of a sequence of genetic bases on messenger RNA into a sequence of amino acids. *page 166*

transpiration the loss (by evaporation) of water vapour from the leaves and other aerial parts of a plant. *page 254*

trophic level feeding stage in a food chain. *page 31*

tropism a change in the growth of a plant in response to an external stimulus. *page 328*

turgor (or **turgor pressure**) the pressure of the cytoplasm and vacuole against the cell wall of a plant. *page 135*

ultrastructure the fine detail of a cell as seen with an electron microscope. *page 79*

vaccine a non disease-causing dose of a pathogen (or its toxin), which triggers the production of antibodies. *page 382*

valves control the direction of blood flow. *page 273*

variable a factor that may change in an experiment. *page 4*

variation (within a species) different characteristics shown by indiviudal members of a group of successfully interbreeding organisms. *page 151*

vegetative propagation (or **vegetative reproduction**) asexual reproduction in plants. *page 414*

woody (plants) those that contain wood (or lignin). *page 243*

Index

plasma membrane 133
plasmid 218
plasmolysis 136
platelets 268
pleura 306
pleural membranes 306
plumule 398
poisonous fungi 231
polar nuclei 396
pollen grains 380
pollen mother cells 394
pollen sacs 394
pollen tube 394
pollination 396
    cross-pollination 396
pollution 35
    domestic 35
    industrial 35
polynucleotide 166
polypeptide 18
polysaccharides 15
pooter 59
population 27
portal system 277
positive tropism 328
potassium dichromate 121
potassium iodide 121
potato tubers 257
predation 28
premolars 290
primary consumers 30
primary root 242
primary sewage treatment 38
prions 19
profile map 64
progametangia 232
progeny 175
progesterone 424
Prokaryotae 212
prokaryotic cells 82
prolactin 433
prophase 146
prostate gland 420
proteins 18
    test for (the biuret test) 19
protein synthesis 165, 168
Protista 240
Protoctista 213
protoplasm 77
proximal convoluted tubule 320
pseudopodia 240
ptyalin 291
puberty 421
pulmonary artery 275
pulmonary circuit 277
pulmonary veins 279
pulse 273
Punnett square 175
pupil 350
pure breeding 175
purines 167
pyloric sphincter 292
pyramid, ecological 44
pyrimidines 167
pyruvate 124
pyruvic acid 124

Q
quadrat 67
qualitative study (of habitat) 60
quantitative study (of habitat) 60
    frequency in 62

R
radicle 398
radius 368
reabsorption 317
receptacle 393
recessive 174
recognition site 205
recombinant DNA 204
red blood corpuscles 266
reducing sugar test for 16
reflex action 345
reflex arc 345
refractory period 346
renal arteries 317
renal vein 317
renal venules 318
renewal of bone 370
replication of DNA 159
respiration 118
    aerobic 118
    anaerobic 119
reproduction 12
    human 420
    plant, sexual vs. asexual 393
reproductive system
    female 422
    male 420
respiratory system 305
restriction enzymes 161
restriction fragments 161
reticulate venation 244
retina 350
retroviruses 389
rhesus factor 268
rheumatoid arthritis 372
rhizoids 232
rhizopus 232
rhodopsin 351
rhythm method 427
ribosomes 81
ribs 368
rickets 21
RNA (ribonucleic acid) 165
rocky seashore 52
rods 351
roots 242
root hairs 246
root pressure 254
rooting powders 330
round window (in ear) 353
runners 414

S
sacrum 368
saliva 291
sample size 8
saprophytes 289
scanning electron microscope 79
Schwann cells 339
sclera 350
scrapie 19

scrotum 420
scurvy 19
sebaceous glands 315
sebum 315
secondary consumers 30
secondary sexual characteristics 421
seed formation 398
seedless fruit 401
seedling growth stage 405
selectively permeable membranes 79
self-dispersal of seeds 402
self-pollination 396
semen 420
semicircular canals 354
semilunar valves 275
seminal vesicles 420
senses 349–54
sensory neurons 339
sepals 393
serial dilution 331–2
serum 266
sessile 244
sewage 38
sex determination 178
sex linkage 187
sexual reproduction
    flowers 393–405
    human 420–433
shoulder blade 368
sieve plates 246
sieve tubes 246
sight 350
sino-atrial node 278
skeleton 366–8
skeletal muscles 373
skimmed milk plates 407
skin 314–16
skull 366
small intestine 293
smell 350
smooth muscle 366, 373
snapdragons 177
sodium alginate 98–100
sodium hypochlorite 121
solar energy 93
solvent 22, 133
somatic 174
sparger 122
specific defence system 378
sperm 420
    low sperm count 422
sperm duct 420
spinal cord 338
spinal nerves 345, 367
spindle fibres 146
splash zone 53–3
spongy bone 369
spontaneous generation 10
spontaneous mutations 197
sporangium 232
stamens 393
starch 15
    test for 16
stem cells 8
stem 243–4
    in winter 244
sternum 368